LENNON

Also by Ray Coleman

McCARTNEY:
Yesterday and Today

THE CARPENTERS
The Authorized Biography

CLAPTON
The Authorized Biography

BRIAN EPSTEIN
The Man Who Made the Beatles

FRANK SINATRA
A Celebration

ROD STEWART
The Biography

STONE ALONE
Co-written with Bill Wyman

I'LL NEVER WALK ALONE
Co-written with Gerry Marsden

PHIL COLLINS
The Definitive Biography

LENNON

The Definitive Biography

RAY COLEMAN

PAN BOOKS

For Julian and Sean Lennon

First published 1984 in two volumes as *John Winston Lennon* Vol. 1 and
John Ono Lennon Vol. 2 by Sidgwick & Jackson

This edition with a new foreword, preface, discography and chronology
published 2000 by Pan Books
an imprint of Macmillan Publishers Ltd
25 Eccleston Place, London SW1W 9NF
Basingstoke and Oxford
Associated companies throughout the world
www.macmillan.com

ISBN 0 330 48330 7

A CIP catalogue record for this book is available from
the British Library.

Typeset by Intype London Ltd
Printed and bound in Great Britain by
Mackays of Chatham plc, Chatham, Kent

CONTENTS

FOREWORD

THE BEATLES have from their early days been fair game for writers of all kinds, and since his tragic murder twenty years ago the number of words written about John Lennon probably exceeds those in the Bible. This book by Ray Coleman is different, however. Ray always was a truthful and talented writer – he is sadly missed – and in this case he knew his subject well. While he lauds Lennon's greatness and genius he does not flinch from revealing some of the aspects of his darker side in his incredibly complex life.

John Lennon's existence was full of paradoxes. When I first met him in 1962 I found him to be charming and funny but perhaps a little quieter than the others. Paul came over as the more immediately attractive personality (he certainly had more to say), while George was the only one who dared to make fun of the boss of the record company whose approval they so desperately needed. As we know, later all that changed completely.

The early days seemed to be full of laughs. I remember looking at John's first book of nonsense stories and the warm laughter from all of us when he got Judy, my wife, to read them out in her crisp accent, a long way from viii   FOREWORD

Liverpool. There was always a hint of cruelty in his humour, but no more than that of the Goons and Spike Milligan; and our skiing holiday together was full of fun and joy. We loved him unreservedly. But John always wanted more. The ordinary became boring, and new experiences became a priority. What was in his mind seemed to be always better than reality, and his dreams were never fulfilled completely in his real life.

Like John Kennedy and Martin Luther King, also victims of assassination, John has become a figure larger than life, a true icon of our times. Ray Coleman has given us the most authentic testament of a truly extraordinary man.

SIR GEORGE MARTIN
June 2000

PREFACE

R AY COLEMAN often described the death of John Lennon as a watershed in his own life. It was a pivotal moment in his career when, after twenty years as a journalist with the music paper *Melody Maker*, he decided to become a biographer. John Lennon was to be the first subject of what proved to be a dozen books which took a serious, measured look at some of the icons of popular music.

Stunned by John's murder, which he compared in significance with the assassination of President Kennedy seventeen years earlier, Ray was determined that John's contribution to music and popular culture should be marked in a significant way. He proposed to write the definitive biography of Lennon's life: a book which would stand as a lasting tribute to the man whom he saw as a genius and who had shaped the lives of a generation.

Ray knew Lennon well. As a young reporter on *Melody Maker* he had been assigned to check out Brian Epstein's claim that the 'four ill-presented youths with untidy hair' he had discovered playing in Liverpool's Cavern Club would one day be as big as Elvis. He was the first music journalist to go to Liverpool to meet the group and recalled later that Lennon immediately struck him as the most fascinating of the four – and the most challenging. Typically, at that first meeting, John slipped in a dig about the paper only writing about jazz.

At that time *Melody Maker* did indeed concentrate on jazz, but it also covered popular music (rock had yet to be invented), including stories and record and concert reviews of artists of the calibre of Frank Sinatra and Bing Crosby. However, all this was soon to change.

Ray, who loved jazz and mainstream pop, was to witness and chart through the pages of *Melody Maker* the explosion of young musicians who soon knocked their revered musical forebears off the front page. He grew to know personally those performers who were to become renowned and lauded round the world in what became dubbed the 'Sixties Explosion': the Rolling Stones, the Who, the Animals, the Kinks and, most of all, the Beatles. And the Beatle to whom he became closest was John Lennon.

Ray and John gelled from the beginning. Apart from music, they seemed to have little in common: Ray the thoughtful, chess-playing journalist and John the irreverent, often vituperative, creative. But both men shared a sense of humour and a passion for music. Ray was instinctively drawn to the Beatle who was the toughest to interview but could be guaranteed to provide a good quote and who always had something newsworthy to say, whatever the topic. And John enjoyed talking to a journalist who took his views seriously, asked pertinent questions and sometimes challenged his interviewee's opinions. Ray was credited with coining the expression 'Beatlemania', which was to appear in banner headlines in newspapers all around the world.

On tour Ray and John would pass time playing 'winners and losers', a game popularized in *Melody Maker*'s gossip column, 'The Raver'. One would shout out a name and the other would categorize. Invariably, both would come to the same conclusion regarding the slot into which each character was peremptorily cast. Ray and John, of course, were both 'winners'! When John forgot the words of his own songs, as he often did, Ray, who had an amazingly accurate memory, would dictate them as John wrote them on his hand in Biro before going on stage.

John, whose relationship with the press could be unpredictable, was an avid reader of *Melody Maker* and periodically submitted letters to the paper's 'Mailbag' column. When he and Paul temporarily fell out when the Beatles split the two men verbally slogged it out through the paper's letters columns. Each week the writer of the best reader's letter would be awarded a prize of an LP voucher and John optimistically always ended his missives with the phrase 'LP winner'. Sometimes he signed his letters with his own name, sometimes he adopted a pseudonym: Dr Winston O'Boogie was a favourite. Jack Hutton, Ray's predecessor as *Melody Maker* editor, remembers Lennon being awarded a coveted voucher on at least one occasion.

After the shows John and Ray would talk at length way into the night and then Ray, the consummate professional, would go back to his typewriter and file his stories while the partying went on. Many years later Paul McCartney was to recall: 'We never could turn you on, could we Ray?' Perhaps because of his refusal to 'tune in and drop out' when all around were doing so, he was affectionately dubbed 'Uncle Ray'. It proved to be a wise gambit: he was one of a handful of those in the Beatles' inner circle who *could* remember the sixties . . . as this biography testifies.

Sometimes John, who was already married to Cynthia, would invite Ray back for a steak at their home in Weybridge in the Surrey stockbroker belt. The subsequent lifts home afterwards, with an inebriated, short-sighted Lennon at the wheel, stayed in his passenger's memory long afterwards.

As Ray charted the meteoric rise of the Fab Four and travelled around the world with them he became a trusted confidant because he knew where to draw the line. He didn't abuse their friendship. He could be a tough critic, but he was also discreet. He wasn't interested in peddling scurrilous gossip then or in later years. He scrupulously turned down all offers to try to persuade him to part with jealously guarded ex-directory telephone numbers and publicly condemned those who sought to besmirch John's name.

When a plethora of Lennon books came out after John's death Ray was frequently called upon to comment on radio and television and in press interviews. He was especially scathing about the book written by Albert Goldman. Goldman, like so many who purported to tell the Beatles' tale, never actually knew them.

Ray Coleman, however, knew all the Beatles well – and John Lennon in particular. He witnessed the changes in their personal circumstances as well as their growth as musicians. When Yoko appeared on the scene and John and Cynthia split up and John finally settled in New York, the two men stayed in touch. And whenever Ray went to the States to interview John, he would take him a packet of his favourite biscuits, chocolate Bath Olivers – the one British delicacy he said he couldn't get in New York. Ray had a packet of Bath Olivers waiting at home on the night of John's death, ready to take with him on his next trip to the States . . .

John Lennon's murder was the trigger that launched Ray Coleman's second career as the writer of respected and highly-praised definitive biographies. He had risen through the ranks at *Melody Maker* to become editor-in-chief, opened up a New York office, taken the paper's circulation to record-breaking heights and had launched new titles like *Black Music* and *Musicians Only*. But he became increasingly disillusioned with the calibre of the music which was currently topping the charts, and saddened by what he saw as a takeover by 'the suits' from the eccentric music-loving entrepreneurs with whom he had professionally grown up. He saw John's murder as signifying the end of an era. He wanted to mark it in his own way and to document for future generations what really happened in those hedonistic and hugely creative years. He wanted, above all, to tell Lennon's story like it really was. Plenty of writers were only too keen to dish the dirt, emphasizing the more sensational aspects of his life, rather than the man's music. Ray, noted for his scrupulous integrity, determined to set the record straight and tell the whole story.

His research was meticulous. Naturally, he drew on his own memories and he painstakingly transcribed the reams of notes in immaculate shorthand he had kept of his conversations with Lennon over the years – for these dated back to the days before reporters used tape recorders. And he also interviewed at length one hundred people who had played a part in John's story – relatives, friends, musicians, critics, associates.

He travelled extensively and spent two years gathering material in Liverpool, London, Germany and the USA. He persuaded people to talk who had never previously discussed their connection with John Lennon and were at first reluctant to speak publicly, like Astrid the girlfriend of John's best friend and former Beatle Stuart Sutcliffe. It was Astrid who cut the group's hair and invented their moptop look. In Hamburg he tracked down Rosa, the toilet attendant at the Top Ten club in the Reeperbahn where they played. In

Liverpool he talked to John's former school chums and to his long-suffering ex-headmaster, William Pobjoy. He coaxed John's Aunt Mimi to reminisce and bought her pot plants. He renewed his friendship with Cynthia Lennon, who was living in the remote countryside with a new man and making a new life for herself as an artist. In New York he waited several days until Yoko decided that the configuration of the planets indicated that the time was auspicious to talk. And then, at her insistence, interviewed her through the night.

It says much about Ray's style of working that he managed to maintain harmonious relationships with both Yoko and John's former wife Cynthia at the same time. They trusted him implicitly and his mild, reassuring manner and endless patience enabled him to draw fascinating nuggets of information from even the most hesitant interviewee.

He gathered so much material that the original hardback of the biography of John Lennon ran to two volumes. Diplomatic as always, Ray dedicated the first to Julian, John's son by Cynthia, and the second to Sean, his son by Yoko. The first editions came out in 1984 in England and a year later in the USA. Both have been reprinted many times and subsequently, as a single volume, the biography has been printed and reprinted in paperback, revised and updated, and translated into German, French, Italian and Japanese. Acknowledged as the ultimate Lennon treatise, it is used as an academic reference by universities around the world.

Tragically now neither Ray nor John is with us, and several of those who contributed to the Lennon story have also passed on. This present revised version of the biography contains a chronology and discography, which have been updated by Mark Lewisohn, who worked closely with Ray on all previous editions. The main text remains, in deference to Ray, exactly as he wrote it.

It is no exaggeration to say that Ray loved John Lennon. When he was desperately ill, the one topic guaranteed to make Ray smile was to recall his time with the Beatles, and with John in particular.

When Ray died in 1996 obituary notices appeared in leading publications around the world. He had written a dozen bestselling biographies, but it was his book on John Lennon which was most frequently cited.

Although in his lifetime he received accolades such as Writer of the Year and Editor of the Year, and was awarded the Gold Badge of Merit for services to music by the British Academy of Songwriters, Composers and Authors, Ray would have been astonished to know just how great was his influence and in what high regard he was held.

I was privileged to have been married for over thirty years to the nicest man in the music business and to share vicariously music history being made.

In the final paragraph of this book Ray writes of John's death: 'A light went out on 8 December, 1980. But his music and his spirit shine on.' When we lost Ray on 10 September, 1996 another light went out. But his words and his spirit shine on.

PAMELA COLEMAN
Cornwall
June 2000

The following extracts are taken from obituaries published on Ray's passing:

THE NEW YORK TIMES

'In a field where biographers often focus on lurid backstage gossip, Mr Coleman wrote with an evident admiration and sympathy for his subjects. Often he had their approval, or that of their families, yet he did not whitewash their problems . . . Mr Coleman's *Lennon*, published in 1984, four years after Lennon was killed, remains the most comprehensive biography of the former Beatle. Friendly with the Beatles since the early 1960s, when he covered several of their tours for *Melody Maker*, Mr Coleman published several books about them. In *McCartney: Yesterday and Today*, written with Paul McCartney's cooperation, he took the unusual approach of building a biography of Mr McCartney around an examination of a single song, 'Yesterday.' In *The Man who Made the Beatles: an Intimate Biography of Brian Epstein*, he conveyed a sense of the engaging and increasingly erratic personality of the Beatles' manager . . .

By adding investigative articles about the pop business to *Melody Maker*'s traditional mixture of artist profiles and reviews, he helped give rock journalism a harder edge . . . Mr Coleman was also quick to spot potential trends. Besides his enthusiastic coverage and cultivation of the Beatles during their rise, he gave both space and support to the early careers of Elton John, Bob Marley, David Bowie, Led Zeppelin and Genesis.'

THE TIMES

'Pop music has not merely achieved respectability, but has acquired its own "scholarship" and secondary literature. Coleman was, though not self publicizing or high profile, a significant figure in that area of the media which documented and, to a large extent, helped to influence that change . . . investigative reporting, rather than breathless reportage, was his style, and the paper [*Melody Maker*] acquired a new professionalism as a result.

When Beatlemania broke loose in 1963 . . . Coleman was dispatched on tour with the four Liverpudlians and his quiet professionalism quickly won their trust and respect, coming as a welcome antidote to the media mayhem unfolding all around them. His relationship with John Lennon proved particularly strong . . .

Always keen to promote new young talent, both journalistic and musical, he put the paper's considerable influence behind the fledgling careers of such pop acts as Elton John, Roxy Music and David Bowie, and was not fazed even when the first stirrings of the punk movement were noted in mid-1970s London.'

MELODY MAKER

'Ray Coleman . . . befriended the band [the Beatles], joined their first tours of America, and forged a symbiotic relationship with them as they conquered the world . . . People trusted him. He never misquoted people and never fantasized. He never used fancy phrases, but managed to convey the artists' feelings in an honest and straightforward way and in some depth.'

THE INDEPENDENT

'As the editor of *Melody Maker*, the world's best weekly music paper, Coleman was determined to exact Fleet Street standards from his staff. Through his own strong will and professionalism, he helped create a dynamic newspaper that prospered throughout the heyday of the Beatles and the Rolling Stones into the era of Pink Floyd and Led Zeppelin.

His own brand of hard-hitting popular journalism helped revitalize what could have remained a cosy trade journal. Banner headlines proclaiming 'BeatleMania!' and candid interviews with John Lennon and Paul McCartney brought a bold new realism to pop reporting. Tenacious and competitive, Coleman demanded and got the best interviews . . . He also delighted in controversy and confrontation.

Yet, behind the tough exterior of the 'foot in the door' reporter who became the copy-chasing editor was an essentially shy and nervously energetic man, who loved traditional jazz, chess, the songs of Bob Dylan and the music of Miles Davis.'

THE DAILY TELEGRAPH

'Ray Coleman . . . played a leading role in the growth of the music press in Britain during the 1960s and 1970s.

Under his editorship from 1970 to 1981 *Melody Maker* began to sell more than 200,000 copies a week – a figure never surpassed by a weekly music magazine.

After leaving *Melody Maker*, Coleman drew on the experience and contacts he had gained with the paper to write biographies of celebrated figures in the pop world.

These books were solid rather than sensational, but always respected for the thoroughness and accuracy of the author's research . . . Coleman was in the van of Beatlemania, travelling with the Beatles on tour and becoming particularly friendly with John Lennon. The Beatles, increasingly irritated by the crass questions hurled at them, welcomed Coleman's erudite, bespectacled figure into their dressing room.'

THE GUARDIAN

'The musicians he most admired included the troublesome ones whose self-appointed mission was to prick away at bland pomposity until it exploded. Above all he relished the fierce arrogance of Bob Dylan, John Lennon, Pete Townshend and Miles Davis, and their intransigence in the face of the showbiz expectations. The more awkward they became, the more he cherished them.'

BILLBOARD

'Ray Coleman . . . transformed British music journalism during his editorship of *Melody Maker* before becoming a leading biographer of some of the world's leading rock and pop stars . . '. Coleman developed his journalistic skills at UK regional newspapers in Leicester, Brighton and Manchester before joining *Melody Maker* as a reporter in the early sixties. He became a close friend and confidant of the Beatles, particularly John Lennon, at the outset of their spectacular success and kept *Melody Maker* amply supplied with exclusives as he toured the world with the band. Paul McCartney tells *Billboard*, 'Ray was a lovely man and very much admired by everyone in the business. He had a marvelous sense of humor and a good heart, and I was honored to have him write a book about my song, 'Yesterday.' I have fond memories of our early days together, and I feel privileged to have spent some happy moments with him during the last year of his life.'

AUTHOR'S NOTE

WHEN JOHN Lennon's dearest friend, Stuart Sutcliffe, died at the appallingly premature age of twenty-one, John told Stuart's distraught fiancée, Astrid Kirchherr: 'Make your decision. You either die with him or you go on living your life.' John would want *his* survivors to heed that same sentence: he loathed martyrdom or too much accent on history. He preferred to look ahead rather than over his shoulder.

Yet since the murder of John Lennon on 8 December 1980, millions of people have felt enriched by looking back on his life and his music. He continues to touch us with the power of his songs which will stand for ever, and with the continuing evidence of his searing honesty.

History will record him as one of the great pacemakers of the twentieth century. Teddy boy, pop star, rebel student, propagandist for peace, poet, artist, songwriter, musician, bandleader, sloganeer, philosopher, wit, loving husband, doting father — Lennon was all these things and more. The founder, the powerhouse, the engine room of the Beatles, he became a catalyst and a dream-weaver for a generation's ideals.

Without him, the Beatles would never have existed,

still less have become popular music's finest group; without him, they would have had no cutting edge, conscience, or originality. And without him, the 1960s and its people would have been very different, much colder, much poorer.

I knew John Lennon for eighteen years, but no one ever knew the complete person. He slipped through our fingers as a questing, restless spirit.

'He was a simple, complex man,' says his widow, Yoko Ono. As in any biography, the blemishes as well as the strength in the man's behaviour and character are reported here. He was brilliant, warm, tender, sensitive, generous. He was also infuriating, tough, aggressive, naive, and woundingly abrasive. He bruised many victims, often verbally, sometimes physically. But even to have been attacked, in any way, by John Lennon brought fame of a kind.

I saw him in Liverpool, a young man in a hurry before the Beatles achieved anything; and then in dressing-rooms, recording studios, hotel rooms, cars and planes and trains all over the world. I saw him at his home during his first marriage to Cynthia when he was wary of fatherhood and fame; and I saw him from 1966 with Yoko, indivisible, interdependent. John Lennon's music, a rich legacy, testifies to his enjoyment of the highest of highs and his introspection during the lowest of lows. He was both a butterfly and a bee. Yet it's an extraordinary fact that all the many women who passed through his life, whether rejected girlfriend or divorced wife, or grieving widow or aunt, still love him madly. The paradox of this achievement is that he remains very much a man's man.

There were many facets to his character, and although he enjoyed the Beatles, he quickly tired of the emptiness of life as a pop star. 'Here I am, rich and famous as I always wanted to be, and *nothing's happening*,' he said to me at his home in Weybridge, Surrey, England, in 1965. Hundreds of superficial pop idols have been satisfied with fame and fortune, but ephemeral success would never satisfy John Lennon. Part of his philosophy was, ironically, voiced on his penultimate album, *Double Fantasy*, when he sang: 'Life is what happens to you when you're busy making other plans.' John wrote these words for 'Beautiful Boy', the song to his son Sean. He wrote the song fifteen full years after talking about his disaffection with life as a Beatle, when as a pop star he had been gaining weight, gaining money, gaining the adulation of millions, but losing himself.

He did not have to wait long for his life, and particularly his art, to change dramatically. Within a year of his restlessness, the Beatles stopped touring and he met Yoko Ono. As man and woman, husband and wife, and artists who were both competitive and compatible, they began a journey unheard of for a pop star. Eventually, they captivated millions, but it was a long, hard road. At first reviled as 'the woman who broke up the Beatles', taking cuddly John from the world, Yoko Ono, with John's help, confounded the bigots with her patience, her grace, her imagination, and by propounding a message that everyone understood but few articulated so well: peace and love. John, understandably, was intensely angry at the hatred poured on his wife. It was, he said, an insult to him as well as to Yoko. John's first wife, Cynthia, graphically describing in this book the sequence of events leading up to their divorce, says of John and Yoko: 'It was a meeting of the minds . . . I knew immediately I saw them together that they were right for each other. I knew I'd lost him.'

Many of us who knew John Lennon in Liverpool, London, and New York, during three key phases of an exceptionally rich life, saw his extraordinary evolution from ambitious student, through the years of desperate, embryonic pop stardom, to millionaire, mature artist, and family man and philosopher. Few have achieved that sort of transformation with such distinction or with such heartfelt affection from the people. This book aims to capture the turbulence, the achievements, and the joy of John's forty years. The people who helped me shape it, John's relatives and friends, as well as detached observers, had a unique perspective of Lennon and have been a tremendous source of inspiration, observation, information, and illustrative material. Together with my own interviews with the man, these people have helped me portray John Lennon in his truest and most human light; their memories should allow readers to form their own views of an often misinterpreted artist.

My thanks to John's indomitable, ever-loving, late Aunt Mimi for hours of patient conversation and memories; to John's first wife, Cynthia, for her total, often painful honesty; and to Astrid Kirchherr for setting the scene in Hamburg.

I thank my wife, Pamela, and my sons, Miles and Mark, for their tolerance and for enduring and sustaining me in more than two years of research.

Yoko Ono Lennon's continual encouragement and unending patience have been an inspiration as well as a great practical help in recapturing the essence of their work, their marriage, and their extraordinary chemistry. In Los Angeles, Elliot Mintz, John's closest male friend in America since 1971, gave, unstintingly, hours of his time, contributing perceptive insights into John's moods and movements, particularly during his years of seclusion. In New York, Leon Wildes, John's lawyer during his four-year immigration battle, was an irreplaceable help in describing those harrowing years, and photographer Bob Gruen and café owner Vincent Urwand, who both had unique friendships with John, provided important recollections.

The chronology at the end of the book was compiled by Britain's most knowledgeable, indefatigable researcher on all things Beatle: Mark Lewisohn, who also undertook most of the picture research. Mark's suggestions, and his assurance of the accuracy of all the facts in this book, have been invaluable since its inception, and I thank him warmly.

My gratitude is due to many people, particularly in Liverpool, for their generous help: to Helen Anderson for great practical assistance and inspiration; John's half-sister, Julia Baird; Uncle Charles Lennon for remembering; Michael Isaacson for a memorable, informative night; Tony Barrow; Don Short; Brian Southall; Philip Norman; William Pobjoy, John's headmaster at Quarry Bank High School, Liverpool, and his housemaster, Eric Oldman; Dick and Stephen James in London; George Martin; George Melly; Victor Spinetti; Rod Davis; Ron King; Helen Shapiro; Arthur Howes; Johnny Beerling; Billy J. Kramer; Julian Lennon; Richard Lester; Clive Epstein; Kenny Lynch; Gerry Marsden; Cilla Black; Hilary Williams; Liz and Jim Hughes at the fondly remembered Cavern Mecca in Liverpool; Bob Wooler, the superb Cavern emcee with a fund of memories and a lifelong love of the 1960s; Bill Harry; Joe Flannery; Michael McCartney; Janet Webb; June Furlong; Ann Mason; Thelma Pickles; Phyllis McKenzie; Derek Taylor; and Neil Aspinall.

In a life that touched millions with its honesty and style, John Lennon became the victim of many myths. Chief among these was that he was an uncaring, rumbustious rock 'n' roller with little compassion. The reverse is true, as his music demonstrated from 'If I Fell', which he wrote in 1964, right through to 'Imagine' (1971), 'Woman' (1980), and 'Nobody Told Me', a record of extraordinary prescience released four years after his death. His anthems,

'Imagine', 'All You Need Is Love', 'Give Peace A Chance', and 'Jealous Guy', testify to his heart, his sincerity, and his lifelong search for his own truths.

RAY COLEMAN
Cornwall, England
June 1995

INTRODUCTION TO THE 1995
REVISED EDITION

LIFE AFTER DEATH

TWENTY-FIVE YEARS after the 'final' Beatles single, 'Let It Be', the work of John Lennon and the voices of all four Beatles still commanded the world of popular music. In 1995, fifteen years after his assassination, two hitherto unreleased Lennon compositions, 'Free As A Bird' and 'Real Love', were released as a new 1995 Beatles single. Originally recorded primitively by Lennon on cassette and never released by him, the songs were augmented by Paul McCartney, George Harrison and Ringo Starr with the aid of modern technology to present one of the most unexpected singles ever.

It came in a year when the Beatles consolidated their position as the mightiest group in the history of popular music. While many other acts from the 1960s continue to fill the stadiums – Eric Clapton, the Rolling Stones, Elton John, Rod Stewart and Pink Floyd, to name but a few – the mere name of the Beatles still conjures up a unique magic.

This new Beatles single followed the release in 1994 of *Live At The BBC*, a two-CD collection of the Beatles' radio music recordings, taped between 1963 and 1965. While that album was selling around the world, the three surviving

Beatles were at work on a visual anthology of their own story, for screening on television and later on video release.

It is thirty years since John Lennon was singing 'Help' and Paul McCartney was singing 'Yesterday', and Lennon, though he was killed as long ago as 1980, is very much alive in spirit as the Beatles story continues to grow. In death, as in life, his name continues to make the most resounding waves. Few deaths in the celebrity field have resulted in so much reflection, introspection and celebration of an artist's work. But then, John Lennon was never merely a pop star or solely the founder of the Beatles. He had grown beyond that, to become a poet, literate scribe, wit and philosopher.

He is remembered equally as a Beatle and as a solo artist, and though he tried hard to discard his Beatles past when he went to live in New York in 1971, he found it impossible. The legend of the Beatles will never fade, and towards the end of his life John had finally come to accept that. 'I'm a Beatle fan, too,' he told one friend.

With his death, the world felt diminished by the loss of an individualistic spirit, rather than of a pop star who epitomized his era. In the view of many who knew him, he was destined never to grow very old: he raced through life mentally and physically, continually establishing fresh horizons for himself. And he never sounded self-satisfied. He had a defiant view of his own image, and from the day I first met him, in 1962, until his death, he seemed to care little about what people thought of him. When he was dead, he forecast, people's opinions about him would matter even less than they had to him or to his family when he was alive.

Yet even the cynical John Lennon might have reacted with incredulity to the many events that have surrounded his life and death since he was gunned down outside his

New York home on 8 December 1980. Astronomical prices have been paid for his possessions and drawings at international auctions. Controversy has surrounded the exploitation of his life, his death, his work. The lawyers have been kept busy. Some forty books on Lennon have appeared, two of them devoted exclusively to his murder and to his politics. And there has been the general elevation of his memory to that of a deity. That, surely, would have made him smile, since he believed that all he was doing was 'leaving a few signposts' about the way he sped through life.

'Whatever gets you thru' the night, it's all right, it's all right,' he wrote and sang. That typified his manifesto for life. But surely, say students of Lennon, he would have been angered by the lies of the character assassination that has surrounded him in death; and surely he would have sneered at the maudlin praise by others. Perhaps. But second-guessing Lennon was always a dangerous pursuit, for there could be contradictory streaks in his reactions. He was both ruthlessly pragmatic and very sentimental.

After all the acrimony that had punctuated the break-up of the Beatles, with John and Paul battling in public, it is a fair bet that he would have welcomed the healing process that has happened since 1980. John would be fifty-five now had he lived; with the other three not far away from that age, an over-the-shoulder look at their roles has produced positive results. With rock now dead as a creatively evolving force, the Beatles, as leaders of its golden age, have recognized their need, even without John's presence, to keep their flame glowing as constructively as possible.

Hence the 'BBC' album, the new single, the anthology video and the resultant book from that operation, plus several independent books analysing their songs. And so it will continue. For as long as people listen to music, what

John Lennon created with Paul McCartney, George Harrison
and Ringo Starr will be celebrated and dissected. Emblems
of the 1960s though they were, it is for the originality of
their songs that they will be remembered, and Lennon was
more adamant about that fact than most. Once, asked in
New York if he had a message for fans gathering at a
Beatles convention, he said: 'Yes, tell them the music was
the thing.'

This re-emergence of the Beatles is perplexing news to
many commentators unable or unwilling to recognize their
pivotal importance. Faced with the impossible job of promoting new rock in the 1980s and 1990s as a valid successor
to acts they call sneeringly the 'wrinklies', British critics
have turned on the Beatles . . . and, by extension, on John
Lennon.

'Mop Top Flops Set for Shops,' jibed *The Times* on 24
November 1994. Beneath that headline, the paper's rock
writer, David Sinclair, wondered 'who could possibly be
interested in buying the imminent album of Beatles songs
now long past their listening-by date'.

In an arrogant 'review' of the record, Sinclair admitted
in his opening sentence: 'I have not heard the "new" Beatles
album, *Live At The BBC* . . . now resuscitated from the
archives. Nor am I particularly looking forward to doing
so. They are not the first rock act to have their old radio
sessions tarted up and put on commercial release . . . and
although these ancient recordings are perfectly good of their
kind, the idea that they will be of anything more than
curiosity value strikes me as a triumph of hope over
experience.'

Having thus dismissed fifty-six tracks without having
heard them, Sinclair went on to assert that 'there is usually
a good reason why certain recordings can still lay claim to
"previously unreleased" status a quarter of a century after

an act as successful as the Beatles ceased to exist. Basically, there has always been much better material on offer. But hang on to something for long enough and even a cornflakes packet will acquire some kind of value as a collectors' item. It is a measure of the enduring popularity of rock that so much time and energy is now routinely devoted to exploring its archives . . . but whatever the marketing men are saying, don't imagine the world is holding its breath to hear what the Beatles made of a Billy J. Kramer B-side thirty-one years ago.'

Such a shameful diminution of standards, coming from the same paper whose classical music critic William Mann, had broken new ground by famously praising the Beatles in 1964, told more of the prejudices of modern rock critics than of a public reaction to the early work of John, Paul, George and Ringo. Every other art form cherishes its historic glories. Why then cannot popular music, which is now forty years old, have an honourable history with icons such as Lennon and the Beatles considered seriously?

Within a week, David Sinclair had his reply – from a public vote. 'Fans old and new queue for new Beatles album,' his paper's news columns reported. Two hundred people waited outside London's Tower Records store in Piccadilly for its midnight opening, and 250 albums were sold in an hour and a half to people from all over the world. Kevin Howlett, the BBC producer who discovered the recordings in the BBC archives in 1982 while researching a documentary, said: 'It was like finding Tutankhamun's tomb.' George Martin, who compiled the album featuring much of John Lennon's early repartee with his Beatles friends, declared: 'These recordings show how good they were live, before we started doing the producing tricks.' 'I'm John and I play the guitar. Sometimes I play the fool' . . . that was fairly typical of innocent banter that abounded on the delightful album.

To *The Times* writer Joe Joseph fell the task of balancing the cynicism of his colleague. 'Still magic after all these years,' ran the headline over Joseph's description of the album. 'They remind us that music was once spontaneous rather than synthesized and conversation between DJs and guest stars was off-the-cuff rather than off-the-officially sanctioned press statement.'

But while some were quick to sneer at the 1960s in the hope that it was dead but would not lie down, the overwhelming majority could not wait to buy the record. Six million copies of the album sold within six months of its release. The sound of John Lennon and his mates was being heard afresh.

The intensive activity that was to mark the silver anniversary of the death of the Beatles actually began in New York on 19 January 1994. On that day, Paul McCartney inducted John Lennon posthumously into the Rock 'n' Roll Hall of Fame at a celebrity-packed event at the Waldorf-Astoria Hotel.

Paul made a moving speech, in the form of an open letter, to his old friend. He recalled the beautiful summer's day of 6 July 1957 when he had first met John, at a village fête where John was playing with his school skiffle group. He remembered them writing their first songs together at the McCartney family house, smoking tea in the pipe that Paul's father Jim McCartney kept in a drawer. 'We wanted to be famous,' Paul remembered. He described the earliest days of the Beatles, meeting George Harrison on the top deck of a bus and the recruitment of him and Ringo. There were anecdotes about the earliest days at the Cavern, their first tour, freezing journeys in the van, the trips to Hamburg to meet giants like Little Richard and Gene Vincent, and the creation there of the 'Beatle haircut'.

'And then came the USA, New York City,' said Paul, 'where we met up with Phil Spector, the Ronettes, the Supremes, our heroes, our heroines. And then, later, in Los Angeles, we met up with Elvis Presley for one great evening. We saw the boy on his home territory. He was the first person I ever saw with a remote control on a TV.'

The memories stirred by Paul went on to detail the symbiosis between him and Lennon and songwriting in the studio: 'I remember doing the vocal to Kansas City — well, I couldn't quite get it, because it's hard to do all that stuff, screaming out the top of your head. You came down from the control room and took me to one side and said: "You can do it. You've just got to scream. You can do it." So thank you for that. I did it.

'I remember writing "A Day In The Life" with you and the little look we gave each other as we wrote the line "I'd love to turn you on." We kinda knew what we were doing, you know. A sneaky little look.'

After that, Paul said in his open address to his old friend, 'There was this girl called Yoko. She showed up at my house one day. It was John Cage's birthday and she said she wanted to get hold of manuscripts of various composers to give to him, and she wanted one from me and one from you. So I said: "Well, it's OK by me but you'll have to go and see John." And she did . . .'

The years of bitterness and recriminatory messages to each other in the world's press seemed a lifetime ago when Paul referred to them and the healing process in their relationship: 'The joy for me, after all our business shit that we'd gone through, was that we were actually getting back together and communicating once again. And the joy as you told me about how you were baking bread now. And how you were playing with your little baby Sean. That was great for me because it gave me something to hold on to.'

Finally, emotionally, Paul stated: 'So now, years on, here we are. All these people, assembled to thank you for everything that you mean to all of us. John Lennon, you've made it. Tonight you are in the Rock 'n' Roll Hall of Fame. God Bless you'.

Yoko and nineteen-year-old Sean Lennon were at the ceremony, and the embrace between Paul and Yoko afterwards marked the end of one of the most fractious relationships in the world of entertainment. In the 1970s, John's war of words with Paul after the split of the Beatles had inevitably spilled over into 'bad vibes' between Paul and Yoko, John and Linda McCartney. The induction of John by Paul marked a mood of conciliation and friendship.

It also heralded the new single by the Beatles. Yoko handed Paul a cassette of John's raw, unfinished composition 'Free As A Bird' and, returning with it to England, Paul enlisted the help of George, Ringo, and long-time Beatles recording engineer Geoff Emerick to work alongside John's vocal to create the new Beatles single. Yoko felt that 'the world suffered from them [the Beatles] not being together . . . I wasn't going to be the element to say no,' as she told *New York* Magazine on 21 March 1994. 'Most people seem to think I should be the first person to object, in memory of John. I thought it was good karma for me to be able to help in any way I can.'

The B-side of 'Free As A Bird', John's poignant song 'Real Love', had first been heard in the biographical film *Imagine: John Lennon*, released in 1988. Although included on that film's soundtrack, the song was now strengthened by the work of the three surviving Beatles.

Again, voices of dissent were raised at the very idea of

a new Beatles record. 'Would John Lennon have approved?' asked the *Daily Telegraph*'s rock critic Tony Parsons. Writing under the second-guessing headline of 'Imagine What John Would Have Said', Parsons weighed in with: 'It is not difficult to imagine his acerbic response to the suggestion that one of his old demos should be dusted off to promote a new wave of Beatlemania. The Beatles are no more but Beatles Inc., an alliance of Paul, George, Ringo, Yoko and EMI, is very much with us. Beatles Inc. would not exist if John Lennon were still alive. Listen out for some background noise on "Free As A Bird": the sound of a deceased ex-Beatle revolving in his grave.'

This invective came, of course, long before Parsons or anyone else in the media had even heard 'Free As A Bird', and his hypothesis on Lennon's views was ill-judged. Having known Lennon and McCartney and watched their evolution since the Beatles, I would say that John would prefer that the custody of his music and the continuation of his integrity was safe in the hands of Yoko and Paul. We should trust their judgement rather than that of 1990s rock commentators like David Sinclair and Tony Parsons, who, having missed the party, imply that they know why the hosts threw it. And yes, Beatles Inc. would certainly have existed if John had lived; indeed, it always did in various forms. He had become proud of their heritage and he never saw anything wrong with making money.

Returning to the subject in the *Daily Telegraph* on 6 April 1995, Tony Parsons wrote, under the headline 'Just Let It Be, Boys': 'I find the prospect of new Beatles music an appalling prospect. The surviving Beatles are tampering with the most precious legacy in popular music. There has already been one Beatles reunion, at John Lennon's funeral. Now it is time to let it be . . . there were never mediocre Beatles, apart from Wings, of course.'

Since Lennon and the Beatles and McCartney at their most mediocre produced music far superior to most of the new sounds of the 1980s and 1990s, fashion-conscious rock writers resort to cheap denigration that would be laughable were it not a sad commentary on the sounds they promote. Beyond the enduring popularity of the Beatles, John Lennon's death has been marked and marred by fond memories, or spiteful acts, or vicious remarks made in the certain knowledge that the grave cannot answer back. Among those who knew him, respect for him grows amid the anecdotal evidence that he was a man with unrepeatable flair in every facet of his life and work.

When John was separated from Yoko during 1974, friends around the world became used to receiving his erratically typewritten letters. To receive John's spoken word could be an unnerving experience; the man's pen was invariably witty, but he knew little mercy when he was at his most acerbic. And 1974 was a year in which his emotions were frayed.

On 22 June 1974, John typed a letter in New York to his first wife, Cynthia, in Britain. They had divorced six years earlier but still communicated about their son, who lived with his mother in England. Julian was soon to visit John for a vacation, and John asked Cynthia when he 'should send May over for him'. John and May Pang, the secretary to John and Yoko who had become his partner during the separation, lived together at 434 East 52nd street in Manhattan – yet interestingly, at the top of his letter to his ex-wife, John gave as his address the Dakota apartment where Yoko remained.

The other surprise in John's letter, which carried a tone of conviviality and affection, was his interest in his Liverpool past. He asked to be remembered to 'Helen and the gang' – Helen Anderson, a mutual friend of his and Cynthia's when they were all at Liverpool Art College – and inquired about other student cronies of his youth, Jeff Mohammed and Tony Carricker. He signed the letter: 'Lots of love to you . . . your famous ex-husband John.'

Around that time, too, John phoned Cynthia's home in Hoylake, on the Wirral. When John's eleven-year-old son Julian picked up the phone, the boy said: 'Your old friend Helen's here.' Helen Anderson had remained friends with Cynthia, and she now enjoyed a telephone reunion with John, whom she had not seen since the Beatles years.

'I asked him if there was anything he missed about England, and he said that what he'd like most were black puddings and, if I could get one, his old college scarf,' Helen recalls. Such sentimentality for his past had always been buried deep behind John's façade of toughness, but in the years after the Beatles, and during visits to New York when I met John in the 1970s, I saw plenty of evidence that he cherished his memories. Once, when I phoned John from London to arrange an interview in New York, he requested that I took him a few tins of Chocolate Oliver biscuits, a British taste he missed. Nostalgia was clearly important to John during that period. He never knew that a quick conversational exchange with him – and all those scattily typed letters – would become so important a few years later.

What price, memories? Lennon, always accessible and communicative, left behind a treasure chest of memorabilia ranging from letters like Cynthia's to his artwork, which was prolific. In the years since his assassination, the selling of Beatles items has become a substantial industry. Because he left behind such a mystical legend, Lennon material is the most sought after and has become a multi-million-dollar territory.

Killed by a gun at the age of forty, Lennon made a profound impact on people of all generations, more as a philosopher than as a rock star. He was the moving spirit of the Beatles, and when that group ended, his adventurousness as an artist eventually triumphed over public scepticism. When he moved from London to New York in 1971, never to return, he began a decade of activity that, upon his death, provided a feast for two distinct camps: sincere students – and vultures.

Newspapers and magazines around the world perpetuate the legend, some creatively, some scandalously, in the certain knowledge that his name attracts sales. In March 1991, an American newspaper called *Sun* screamed across its front page: 'John Lennon Is Alive! He Is Brain Damaged and Living in An Italian Monastery.' With a picture of John, circa 1969, bearded, with granny glasses, behind a barred window, this amazing story said that monks and nuns were caring for him and that they had all taken vows of silence so that nobody would 'uncover the plot'.

The transparent nonsense of the story has been almost equalled by the exploitation of his name by those touched by his life. Aside from John's teenage hero Elvis Presley, no rock star has been so analysed in death, nor so tastelessly pillaged. Is it merely making money from his bones, or is it a natural extension of the legend? What would Lennon have said? And does 'The Selling of John Lennon' damage or cheapen his name?

Some vendors sell purely for profit; others say they want to expunge their memories. There was once put on sale John's telegram of apology after he had hit Liverpool disc jockey Bob Wooler. There was a biographical booklet on the Beatles, produced by Apple, which aroused John's ire and across which he had scrawled: 'Who made this shit without showing me – I want it withdrawn immediately. Lennon.' Inside, there were more vivid examples of his anger as he changed the wording.

Guitars, clothes, letters, boots, signed programmes – even John's credit agreement for a guitar in 1962 – have caused the market for memorabilia to spiral. It might have begun as harmless fun, but it is now big business. There's an uneasy feeling of money-grabbing exploitation, particularly when highly personal items are sold by the person they were sent to. But while there's a profitable market, supply will continue to meet the demand. Opinions differ sharply, but one positive result from these memorabilia auctions in incontestable: our knowledge, insight, and enjoyment of the complexities of Lennon's life have been enriched by the public view of so much of his work.

In December 1990, Helen Anderson 'went public' with a selection of drawings by John when he was a fifteen-year-old at Quarry Bank High School, Liverpool. (Some of John's drawings that he gave to Helen Anderson were first published in this biography.)

At Liverpool Art College, John took a fancy to a bright yellow cable-knit sweater Helen was wearing. 'John told me he wanted the jumper for a gig the following night,' Helen recalls. 'I said that would be fine, as long as he gave me some drawings in return.' John's highly personalized creations were interesting to his coterie of friends; in exchange for the sweater, he gave Helen a slim maroon exercise book packed with ink drawings and witty captions. There were hilarious impressions of teachers and boys at his previous school, Quarry Bank. The seventeen-year-old Lennon's fascination for the radio programme *The Goon Show*, the word-play of comedian Stanley Unwin, and the visual style of newspaper cartoonist Giles were evident.

Helen sold the exercise book for £16,000 at Sotheby's. Had she chosen not to, we might never have seen those inspirational sketches.

In August 1991, the 'Cynthia Lennon Collection' went on sale at Christie's in London. Included were the original loving hand-drawn Christmas card from John, and a moving letter from John in America expressing remorse about his absence from Julian. There were some true gems among this hefty collection. There was Cynthia's 18–carat gold bracelet watch, for example, given to her by John, and another item was John and Cynthia's telephone-address book from their Weybridge home, originally prepared by Brian Epstein with details of prominent artists such as Eric Clapton and Mick Jagger, and of restaurants. The directory also contained two Yoko addresses and phone numbers, both deleted, one by John and the other by Cynthia.

There were drawings by John in abundance in this collection, including one entitled 'Psychedelic Girls', said to have been done while he was under the influence of the drug LSD. A nineteenth-century Eastern robe of midnight blue velvet, which he wore around the house, was on sale – as well as his old chess set. John loved collecting clocks and boxes, and Brian Epstein enjoyed giving these to him on special occasions. Joining these in the sale were items from John and Cynthia's house: a Persian carpet, a mahogany writing table, ornate vases and jardinière stands, and assorted writings and notes by John.

Lennon's Ivor Novello Award, the most prestigious British award for songwriters, sold for £7,700. The address book fetched £3,850. John's passionately written Christmas card went for £8,000 – ironically the buyer was Japanese, as was the woman who followed Cynthia into John's life. Cynthia's profit from the whole sale was £56,843.

The London sale of Cynthia's possessions took place on

29 August 1991 – a quarter of a century to the day after the Beatles had played their final concert, in San Francisco. Her collection was a very personal one, and some viewed it as a distasteful selling off of 'the family silver', but Cynthia saw it as a valediction, as ridding herself of the ghost of a legacy. The memories, she averred, would always be with her, but the tangible items of her life with John should now be shared with others. She agreed that she wanted money, like all of us, but the chief aim of the sale was to achieve 'freedom'.

People ask of events like this: 'But what would John have thought of it?' Well, the Lennon I knew was exceptionally generous (once, when I visited his home, he gave me, on the day he had received it, his only proof copy of his first book); and yet he had a realistic attitude towards money which said: 'If you can make a few quid (or a few dollars), grab the chance!'

John was a curious fusion of freewheeling artist and enthusiastic monetarist. Referring to one of his songs during the Beatles years, he spoke of 'writing myself a swimming pool'. He relished the freedom money gave him, so that while he valued his millions and kept an eye on what came in and went out, he never allowed it to diminish his inventive spirit. As a rich man, he never carried money with him – but then, neither did he when he was an impoverished student. Money was a means to an end for him, and it's a fair bet that, above all other feelings, he might have laughed at the absurdity of the commercial value of the paraphernalia of his life.

As a schoolboy, as a teenage art college student, and later as a Beatle and solo performer, Lennon was driven by a unique talent that set him aside from traditional rock 'n' roll, traditional show business, or traditional artistry. Initially, John achieved fame and fortune by being a Beatle, but he gained notoriety and the status of a legend from ten years of iconoclastic solo work – and from being shot dead at the very moment he promised a fresh burst of creativity.

Since his death, his legacy as a philosopher has been constantly explored and explained – stage and screen studies of his life, recorded interviews, books and articles, as well as permanent tributes, have proliferated, and the spectrum of events during and after his life is set out in the chronology at the end of this book.

In the final year of his life, John spoke with disarming candour about his failings and about the aspirations that had driven him towards the early days of stardom and beyond, into adulthood and the fatherhood which he cherished. Partly, perhaps, because he was assassinated, some hoisted him to the status of a god, but that has proved as absurd as the determination to crush his memory with vituperation.

By his prodigious output of work over twenty years, John was able to go down to posterity with dignity. But like Marilyn Monroe, Elvis Presley, and John F. Kennedy before him, he could do nothing to prevent those looking for negativism in the dark corridors of his life from exploiting his memory. He always confronted the truth, and had he lived to see the international parade of distortion of his forty years, Lennon's waspish tongue would have dealt with it severely. But then, had he lived, the absurdities and untruths would never have been disseminated, and the sordid Lennon industry would never have begun.

The core of John Lennon's work was his collection of songs. And to many, his collaborative years with Paul McCartney represented the apogee of his achievements. In his last interviews John appeared proud of the Beatles years, and, like any successful songwriter, he was pleased to analyse finally the strengths, weaknesses, and motivations of the songs. As ever, he was lucid when talking about his former partner Paul McCartney. While there were many occasions on which he would orally plunge the knife into Paul, he was unstinting in his admiration for Paul's ability, as well as happy to point out that he chose two key partners in his life: Paul and Yoko. Not a bad record, as John said.

The man who gave peace a chance. The house-husband. The feminist. The father. The political activist. The drunk during a fifteen-month spree, separated from his wife. The philanderer. The arrogant swine with a heart of gold. Analysing the aspects of Lennon's character has never presented a simple solution. Part of the reason is that in his seventeen years in the public eye he was his own fiercest critic, making few claims except to rasp against those who ridiculed his efforts, his sincerity, his achievements inside the Beatles and beyond. He was particularly scarred by the general response to Yoko's arrival in his life, and this conditioned his defensiveness and assertiveness particularly after their marriage in 1969.

Since his death he has been worshipped and debunked, but neither sits comfortably around the memory of the man. In songs and in speech, he wrote his own commentary on his life, insisting that it was for others to make their own lives rather than elevate him to a spurious role of leader. Nevertheless, in the pantheon of dead rock stars immortalized in recent years (Jimi Hendrix, Buddy Holly, Jim Morrison, Bob Marley), Lennon towers as a colossus, and not because he was the victim of a gun. He was articulate, direct, sincere, and free of posturing. As the years roll past and the music and message of his life achieve more sonority, it's clear that while his assassin robbed him of the ultimate possession, he gave Lennon omnipotence in perpetuity as a seer and communicator. These were roles he never craved and often shunned; fate and history decreed otherwise.

In the wake of his death, a blurred picture of his complex character surfaced. The tributes, the grief, and the impact of his records eclipsed any attempt at a logical summary of John's life and work. Here was a dead rock star who attracted hundreds of thousands of people around the world to a silent vigil in his memory; who sold 2 million records in Britain alone within two months of his death; who attracted 2,000 people to a memorial service at Liverpool's Anglican Cathedral; who had a section of New York's Central Park set aside in his honour; whose memory began an astonishing trend in huge money transactions at auctions of rock 'n' roll memorabilia around the world – $2.2 million was paid in the USA for his psychedelically painted Rolls-Royce, and a tiny self-portrait fetched £10,000 at Sotheby's in London a year after his death.

These were controversial tips of the iceberg in 'The Selling of John Lennon'. Happily, they were quickly countered by acts of genuflection and sincerity. In Liverpool, two Beatles fans, Liz and Jim Hughes, sank their hearts and money into an ill-fated enterprise, the opening of Cavern Mecca, a meeting and sales point for the world's fans a few steps away from where it had all begun. This was succeeded on 1 May 1980 by a permanent exhibition called 'The Beatles Story', at Liverpool's Albert Dock which is a superbly executed testimonial to the city's famous sons. Part of it simulates the 'white room' of John and Yoko's Dakota home, with John singing 'Imagine'. In America, ubiquitous Beatles supporter Joel Glazier launched the John Lennon Peace Forest for Galilee, Israel, whereby for $30 fans could plant a tree as part of a living shrine in John's name.

The song tributes flowed quickly: George Harrison was first in May 1981, with 'All Those Years Ago', a jaunty yet oblique testimonial to his old friend in which he acknowledged to John that some people had 'treated you like a dog'. The song touched the public's heart as one ex-Beatle addressing his old buddy, and it gave George his biggest hit in eight years, reaching number two in the US and thirteen in Britain.

In 1983 Paul Simon offered the poignant 'The Late Great Johnny Ace' on his album *Hearts and Bones*. A year later, Elton John, godfather to John and Yoko's son Sean, offered 'Empty Garden (Hey Hey Johnny)', a song marked by Elton's emotional delivery, and he followed this in 1985 with an instrumental called 'The Man Who Never Died'. In April 1982, Paul McCartney's first album since John's murder, *Tug of War*, closed with 'Here Today', a moving and eloquent tribute to his irreplaceable collaborator. Describing it as a hard song to write, Paul explained it lengthily: 'I suppose John would have been the first one to laugh at that kind of stuff. I sat down one day and was just on those sort of minor type chords that open that song . . . if there had to be a thought in song about John, I suppose what's been going through my head is this idea – that if you were here today, what would you say about here's me writing a song about you? You know, which I'd never ever done of course. It takes finality of things like death to concentrate it and make you think, oh my God, that's the end, and it's such a horrifying thought really, that that was the kind of idea behind that. Well, you'd probably laugh and say that we're worlds apart anyway. Really, I'm saying, but we weren't. I know if we had you back here right now you'd say, oh, load of bollocks, he doesn't know what he's talking about . . . But it's not true, you know, that would be just bluff. We actually did know each other, we actually were very close, we actually had terrific ding dongs in the press, everywhere, especially after all that Apple stuff. But one of those things, you know, talking to Yoko since . . . She's a great lady, and I never really understood it because she and John just wanted to be off doing their own thing together and you felt intrusive to even suggest getting in on that scene. You thought, well they're just in love and what do they need with us, what do they need with me, or whatever? So I would tend to just see things in the press, where John would just be getting something off his chest or would be clearing away the cobwebs of the Beatles in order to give himself a bit of fresh air for his new life. At the time, obviously, it was not that easy to understand all of that. Now I can kind of see it. And talking to Yoko, she said that there was many a time where they just sat around and he would often be very complimentary about me, but just didn't want to be the cloying sycophantic sort of guy in public, saying, "Oh Paul's terrific, he's really great." He preferred to say, "Oh sod him, a load of cobblers," you know. And there was always the competitive thing with John, which I know was very good for me and I think he appreciated it as very good for him too.'

Dotted through the years, though, were tracks apparently intended as tributes but bizarre in their abstruseness: Mike (*Tubular Bells*) Oldfield with 'Moonlight Shadow', which reached number four in Britain in May 1983, Pink Floyd with 'Not Now John', included on their March 1983 album *The Final Cut*: Queen with 'Life Is Real (Song for Lennon)' on their album *Hot Space* in May 1982; Roxy Music with a grotesque and redundant reworking of John's

'Jealous Guy' masquerading as a 'tribute' in 1981. Lennon deserved better than these.

On the positive side, Mark Lapidos, an ardent Beatles supporter, has since 1974 seen his Beatlefest conventions grow to attract thousands to weekend events in New York, Chicago, and Los Angeles, for days and nights soaking up, studying, and celebrating the music and lives of the Beatles. Guest speakers, art exhibitions, Beatles soundalike contests, memorabilia auctions, and a giant sales arena have made Beatlefest an affirmation of faith for battalions of fans – and since 1981, Lapidos has dedicated the festivals 'with love to John Lennon'. That year, John's song title 'Come Together' assumed a real significance among many thousands of Beat-lefest fans who surged to these events to share their grief at his passing. The festivals have grown in size and stature every year, assuming a momentum that demonstrates the longevity of the Beatles' popularity; and whenever Lennon is debated, the affection and interest from people of all ages are remarkable. The average Beatlefest fan is in his or her mid-twenties, meaning they were not born when the Beatles were functioning; and when John Lennon was killed, thou-sands of these enthusiasts were around fifteen years old.

NEWS ITEM: 'Yoko Ono, the iron maiden of the rock world, is causing a lot of grief in Hollywood where a three-hour TV special based on her life with John Lennon is being planned. [This film was *John and Yoko: A Love Story.*] Producers think the film may never be made at the rate Yoko keeps rejecting scripts. She has scrapped three and is currently looking at a fourth. One harassed film executive said: "I can't put into polite English what's happening. I reckon she got upset when we told her she couldn't play herself in later scenes" ' (London *Daily Mail*, August 1985).

The above item was headlined, 'Why Yoko Is Saying
Oh! No' – a theme familiar to the world's media and to a
public which construed her as 'the woman who broke up
the Beatles', 'the woman who seized John Lennon's psyche',
and just plain eccentric Yoko, the self-styled conceptual
artist, a description her critics were pleased to abbreviate
to 'con artist'. And those sinister wraparound Porsche shades
hardened her image.

Scorned and hated, reviled and mocked, Yoko was the
target of two groups of people from the day in 1968 when
she and John first stepped out together. Beatles fans considered her outspoken, unorthodox, weird. Lennon's
unswerving post-Beatles followers believed simply that he
had lost his reason in surrendering his vital independence
to such a truculent feminist. Disregarding the validity of
either view, there was an anomaly here: how could Lennon
be universally lauded as a genius, the brain of the Beatles,
the brilliant mind, wit, original thinker, campaigner, artistic spirit, and trusted spokesman for his generation – while
when it came to choosing his partner, he was, by implication, inept, a cretin, a dupe?

The simple truth was unpalatable to many. When he
considered the Beatles story complete, John chose to
renounce the role of pop star and revert to art. Music was
the powerful medium with which to get his message across;
and when that period was over, his music became intensely
autobiographical.

That need to strike out, away from manufacturing
music as he did within the Beatles, was central to John's
growth. It might have been easier for him to stay a regular
rock star, churning out the hits. Instead, he travelled a
tougher route in his quest for personal truth, peace and
honesty. His murder was not that of an ordinary rock star
but of a man who was a symbol of considerable leadership

(however reluctant he was to admit it) and verve. For twelve years, Yoko and he had been soldiers together in a most extraordinary story; with his death, the focus shifted to her – and to John's family.

In 1978, Cynthia Lennon incurred the wrath of her former husband for publishing her autobiography and for having it serialized in the British Sunday paper the *News of the World*. Divorced ten years earlier, they had a son, Julian, born at the onset of Beatlemania in 1963. Since leaving London with Yoko to live in New York in 1971, John had paid scant attention to his past. As Julian entered his teenage years, there were phone calls, postcards, and gifts to his son, but from the age of eight, Julian had grown up with his father 3,000 miles away. Often, John's method of dealing with his past was to block it off, pretend it never happened, or speak against it vehemently – as he did for some five years about the Beatles when he moved to New York. His death, however, inevitably hurled his family and friends together in the eyes of the media: from Aunt Mimi who raised him, to college friends, through the people of the pop world, and, of course, to any woman who touched his life.

The relationship, if any, between a divorced wife and the widow of a murdered legend could never be simple. Speaking to me nine months after John's death, Yoko said of Julian: 'He is a very sensitive soul and we feel very close to each other and get on very well. He's going through difficult times, too, especially because he's seventeen. It's very delicate, Cynthia did a very fine job bringing him up and I don't want our closeness to interfere with his closeness to his mother. It's a very complex situation.' Cynthia's dignity and composure had thwarted the world's media, which, sensing that she and Yoko were polar opposites, had been baying for blood and hoping to 'get a good battle going' in the tradition of tabloid journalism. For some four years after the murder, neither Cynthia nor Yoko found it easy to keep a respectful distance.

And then, in 1984, twenty-one-year-old Julian Lennon decided to enter the music arena. During my preparation of this biography, I had spent some time with Julian when he moved to London to investigate his chances in music. We shared an admiration for the work of Billy Joel, whose abrasive lyrics reminded Julian of his father's; Joel's stance, in fact, attracted Julian to try his hand at songwriting at the piano with a combination of autobiographical notes and love songs.* Early in 1984 I was telephoned by a dear old friend, Tony Stratton Smith, founder of Charisma Records. A man with a long pedigree in the music business — he had launched the recording careers of Genesis and many other acts — as well as knowing the vagaries of the industry inside out, he was a sensitive catalyst for new artists. 'A friend of a friend,' Strat said to me, 'says I should meet Julian Lennon. You knew his dad. I believe young Julian's starting to write songs. Have you heard them? Are they any good?' I met Strat, alone and with Julian, several times for exploratory talks. Within a couple of weeks, Julian called me. Strat had offered him a contract and wanted him to record his first album — but he didn't have any songs completed.

Events moved quickly. Julian assembled a band. We went to France, and at a remote château near Nevers called Manoir de Valotte, Julian worked inspirationally and speed-

---

* Julian contacted all three ex-Beatles in these early days of his career, seeking guidance only. They were icily unhelpful. When he began making records, they became more convivial towards him.

ily under Strat's wing to write and record an excellent début album, affectionately named after the house where it was created.

Within three months, after a strong hit single tangentially referring to his father's death ('Too Late for Goodbyes'), Julian's first album *Valotte* had sold 1.5 million copies and was certified platinum in the US. His nasal voice sounded uncannily like John's, his physical characteristics were similar and the full tilt of media attention faced him around the world. He began a concert tour of America, but this was artistically premature. Naturally it brought him into close contact with Yoko and sealed his very special relationship with his half-brother Sean, then nine years old.*

Coincidentally, at that time, Cynthia was beginning a new career as a British television interviewer, and the first guest on her talk show was Julian, then at number six in the British charts. During the first show, in which she was interviewed, Cynthia was drawn into saying that Yoko was 'not my cup of tea . . . I think John and I were a great partnership. Yoko was the catalyst who created the break-up in the end.' She added that since John and Yoko had left for America, 'I haven't seen her.' Confrontation was never Cynthia's style. And yet, historically, those few words signalled the very first time that the first wife of John Lennon acknowledged that his first and second wives had nothing in common.

Julian now found himself in a difficult situation. Moving to America to consolidate his career, he walked into a physical proximity with his stepmother and half-brother while remaining close to his natural mother. Diffi-

* In one of the most inspired Beatles-related headlines, *Rolling Stone* magazine entitled its launch article on Julian's career 'Here Comes the Son'.

cult and delicate family relationships exist everywhere, but for the dignity of John's memory and for one of rock's first families, it was important that any tensions remained private.

In the first year after John's death, Yoko spent more than a million dollars on personal security. It was essential. The apartments she occupied at New York's Dakota buildings teemed with bodyguards. Sean was accompanied by one to and from school each day, and a walk by Yoko in Central Park or a visit to a restaurant needed tight security. After the trauma of seeing her husband shot dead, another nightmare unfolded. And it was to last for three years.

It was bad enough when Mark Chapman wrote to her from Attica jail to 'apologize' for murdering her husband. It was unreal when Chapman again wrote to ask Yoko's blessing for a book he wanted to write, adding that he would give the proceeds to charity (child relief organizations). Envelopes bearing a return address of Attica jail were not welcome at the Dakota. That particular chapter was closed, she and the civilized world hoped, with the picture of John's body in the mortuary which was front-paged by the *New York Post* and used in colour by (naturally) the *National Enquirer*. If Lennon was not going to be entitled to dignity in death, why should his rich widow not be a target for humiliation and torture?

'The Betrayal of John Lennon', a stunning piece of research journalism, was published by *Playboy* magazine in March 1984. Written by David and Victoria Sheff, the article evoked the cathartic tone of the watershed interview that John had given to David Sheff in September 1980, and which appeared on the news-stands the week he was killed. In a documentary-style survey of the high drama that closed in upon Yoko between December 1980 and October 1983, the 'Betrayal' article reported the pillaging of Lennon's 1975–80 diaries, clothes, pictures, manuscripts, tapes of songs – and even love letters. Yoko said: 'When John died, I thought it was the worst thing that could ever happen. But that was only the beginning. I cannot comprehend the meanness of it all'. The diaries (later to form the basis of John's posthumous autobiography, *Skywriting by Word of Mouth*, published in 1986) were finally returned after Yoko had paid out $40,000 to an intermediary.

The most tortuous aspect of that episode and others was that it involved action against employees whom Yoko (and John) had regarded as trusted friends as well as having been on their payroll. There seemed to be threats and problems everywhere she turned: blackmail, telephone tapping, illegal use of Lennon's artifacts and other properties owned by his estate, and a general air of hatred which young Sean found confusing after the trauma of December 1980 and the months that followed.

The harassment of Yoko Ono was based on two disparate prejudices. First, she was clearly rich, managing an estate estimated to be worth $150 million. Second, for as much as John was loved, cherished, and revered, many people had a problem with Yoko. And now she was alone and vulnerable. As Lennon had declared throughout his years with her, Yoko presented an easy target for chauvinists, cynics, and racists. Now, with John gone, smearing her character was never going to be enough for those who wanted her blood, either literally or metaphorically. They wanted her endorsement – and they wanted her money.

In 1983 I had personal experience of the bizarre, even creepy, events that surrounded Yoko. I received a phone call from her friend, confidante and general troubleshooter Elliot Mintz, who asked on her behalf whether I would do her a favour. Yoko had received a letter from a woman in London which was intriguing, had psychic connotations, and which appeared to have an insider's knowledge of what was going on surrounding Yoko. The woman gave no phone number, only an address, was not in the phone book, and asked that she be contacted personally before a certain date when she would be flying from London to South Africa. Her message included the tantalizing statement that she had some vital information for Yoko and wanted to give it to her personally. Elliot and Yoko were intuitive when it came to decoding letters from cranks, but this one attracted their interest. They asked me to try to make contact with the woman to 'check her out', and perhaps discover what 'information' she possessed.

On several evenings I drove to the letter-writer's address, a large house in residential west London. There was never any response to my ringing of the several door-bells, itself strange since this was clearly an apartment house. Finally, one night, a man opened a window and shouted down to ask what I wanted. When I named the lady I wanted to see, he briefly said she had gone away, but he asked my identity. When I refused to tell him, he became menacing and slammed the window shut. And that, I decided was that.

As I walked to my car, I became aware of someone writing down my registration number, then running away. As I drove the twelve-mile journey home, I gradually realized I was being followed by a car with two men in it. Such was the weirdness of the letter to Yoko, and so strong the aura of spookiness surrounding this and other situations I knew around her, that I was relieved when, several miles later and after some difficulty, I finally managed to 'lose' that car.

It could have been innocent, of course, but in those early 1980s, reality was irrelevant. I knew of the hostility, intrigue, and general air of danger that was enveloping Yoko in New York, and my perception of that experience was that it was courting difficulties at best, dangers at worst. Yoko and Elliot were immediate in their judgement: I should pull away from the inquiry and not enter potentially problematic situations. Perhaps it was just another of the cranky letters that were among the 250,000 received annually at the Dakota. Perhaps.

Just before the album *Milk and Honey* was released, Yoko sent friends a unique gift for Christmas 1983: a musical box that, when opened, played the tape of John's poignant vocal on his song 'Grow Old With Me'. It was an astute move by Yoko, who knows how best to blend art with commerce while also entering people's psyches. The box was accompanied by a note describing the handsome wooden box:

> 'Grow Old With Me' is a song John wrote in Bermuda in the summer of 1980. This box is made of Bermuda cedar, now in danger of extinction. John loved this wood because of its sweet scent.

The inscribed box was handsome enough. The message now made public from John did Yoko no harm, either. Here was her ex-husband imploring her, with a love poem, to move ahead through the years by his side. From any partner to another, it would be heart-rending. With the songwriter dead, this posthumous release had extra impact.

Yoko always had an ace up her sleeve which she had no need to play overtly: whenever the world set out to poison her, she would point to John's spoken devotion and admiration for her. No matter that she now stepped out with Sam Havadtoy, the interior designer who had begun to socialize with her and walk beside her in Central Park in the difficult aftermath of the murder. As Yoko succinctly put it: 'I will be another man's lover and share his bed but I won't wear his wedding ring. I couldn't marry again because I would feel I had betrayed John.'

Without doubt, Yoko was (and will remain) the legal custodian of John's affairs, with an important role in shaping his memory, but there are many others who feel they nurse significant parts of his life within them, and many of these unfold in this book. From his Liverpool Art College friends Helen Anderson and Thelma McGough, to the Beatles era when he encountered characters as diverse as Bob Wooler and Derek Taylor, through his period of self-discovery as a peace campaigner, across to America into the arms of such cohorts as Abbie Hoffman and Harry Nilsson, John was a travelling artist on a perpetual adventure, and no one person could claim to have much more than a period snapshot of him. Around the globe there are custodians of stories relevant to his life and work. It was part of John's devilish nature, however, to minimize his associations with some colleagues (he unkindly jabbed a finger at, for example, George Martin, Brian Epstein, Derek Taylor, Richard Lester, and, notably, Paul McCartney).

All these people marked Lennon's life. And though John was not comfortable at looking over his shoulder at difficult situations, his partnership with Cynthia, from art college into marriage and parenthood and the Beatles, was formative. When John died, the media blitz focused heavily on the woman who was his teenage fixation and who saw him change from loud teddy boy into poetic rock star.

In 1980, Cynthia and seventeen-year-old Julian were living in Ruthin, North Wales, where from the moment John was killed their home became a virtual fortress surrounded by journalists. Cynthia has a gentle, positive, and logical nature, and no attempt by Yoko and John to jettison her from the Lennon story would work, particularly now he was dead. She was part of it. And he was lucky to have such an ambassador from his past. She loved John, spoke of him with admiration and affection, and had no regrets. When this biography was first published in Britain in 1984 and in the USA a year later, Cynthia was interviewed extensively on both sides of the Atlantic and emphasized fairly her recognition of Yoko's importance to John, his need for change alongside Yoko, and her determination to describe his honesty, his towering importance, and how she would always remember him fondly.

'*But he dumped you!*' shouted a grizzled old radio interviewer in America's Midwest, trying to stir up a public display of hatred for Yoko. Cynthia faced taunts like this with aplomb. Ignoring the callous method John did in fact use to oust her from his life (see Chapter 16, 'Divorce'), Cynthia replied: 'Yes, but he'd found a new partner and he obviously needed one. Divorce is never easy, but I understood. He'd found his soul mate.' John was a genius, she would add later, and such a mind needed to be given plenty of space. Some found her attitude too passive and bloodless, but Cynthia would never be swayed. To have known John, seen him grow as an artist and as a Beatle, to have vivid memories, and to have had a son together was better than never to have met him, Cynthia declares. Such generosity of spirit has often been missing in others. John may have wanted his ex-wife treated like a leper for ever, but from

December 1980, this was impossible. She had a historic role, and moreover, she was able to describe it eloquently.

So certain events jarred among those of us who expected a balanced and rounded portrait of John to be a priority. In December 1985, in its *Everyman* series, BBC Television transmitted *John Lennon: A Journey in the Life*. The role of John was taken by Bernard Hill, to whom Lennon had sent a good luck telegram when Hill had starred in an excellent London stage production called *John, Paul, George, Ringo . . . and Bert*. Five years after Lennon's death, it was a unique opportunity to explain to millions in a ninety-five-minute TV documentary the rich panoply of Lennon's life. But this miserable, jaundiced and hopelessly unbalanced programme totally ignored the existence of Julian, relegated Cynthia to a bit part, portrayed John's mother as soft, and had dialogue that achieved the unthinkable: it made John Lennon appear a moronic puppet. The programme was immediately followed by a fifteen-minute interview with Yoko.

Predictably, some of Lennon's family (Cynthia, Julian, and John's half-sister, Julia) were appalled by the tone of the documentary, and by their own exclusion. It irritated Julia so much that she decided to write her own book to set matters straight on John's early years.

John's intellect, insightfulness, and impact deserved a sane perspective, but we had to wait for some years for that. In the mid-1980s, the sideshows took place on both sides of the Atlantic: John's Uncle Charlie in Liverpool, unveiling a luxury new British Rail engine called 'John Lennon', to serve the London-Merseyside route; John's psychedelically painted Rolls-Royce auctioned at Sotheby's in New York; Yoko and Sean officially opening, on 9 October 1985 (it would have been John's forty-fifth birthday), the three-and-a-half-acre garden at the Strawberry Fields site

in Central Park, New York; Cynthia launching an exhibition of her Beatles-impression drawings in the USA and
designing the frontage for Liverpool's new Cavern Walks
shopping complex. The world was hungry for anything that
enabled the legend of Lennon to be perpetuated, and as
long as succeeding generations discover the breadth of his
legacy, that hunger will continue.

Yet the invective persisted. Confident that he had begun
a strong career without help from any insiders, including
his stepmother, Julian threw a few broadsides towards Yoko.
By early 1985 he was saying that he didn't stay in touch
with her and had his own life to lead. He enjoyed playing
with Sean, regretted not having the freedom to walk him
in the park without minders in tow, and asserted: 'Yoko's
very paranoid about everyone and everything.' Julian said
he had played Yoko a couple of tracks from his demonstration tape, 'And she said she liked them but she's very
impatient, always fidgeting, doing things, moving on. She
hasn't followed my career in the last year . . . I don't know
what Yoko's up to. She's got so many little plans and ideas.
I want to get away from her and all the father bit. I don't
have to be involved with her in any way to do what I want
to do.'

Families usually bicker behind closed doors – so when
a member of the Lennon court generated internecine warfare
in this way, there was always an eager audience, part of
that huge body of people who, for reasons of envy or malice,
want to believe that millionaires or their relatives are
unhappy.

Paul McCartney fuelled the fire with an extraordinary
outpouring of emotion during a conversation with Hunter
Davies, author of a second, revised edition of *The Beatles*,
published in 1985. (Their conversation had been in May
1981 and Paul later declared that he had not intended his

remarks for publication.) Clearly stung by John's diatribes against him since the acrimonious break-up of the Beatles, Paul complained to Davies that John had hurt him by describing his work as Muzak, by comparing him with Engelbert Humperdinck, by failing to acknowledge that he and Linda had gone to Los Angeles to persuade John to return to Yoko from his 'lost weekend', by being selective in his memory of who wrote what, particularly the songs 'In My Life' and 'Eleanor Rigby'.

While Paul added more flattering remarks, saying he idolized John – 'the big guy in the chip shop . . . in the beginning he was a fairground hero, the big lad riding the dodgems and we thought he was great' – it was his anger that stuck. And Hunter Davies reported that it had all been triggered by an interview in which Yoko said that Paul had hurt Lennon more than any other person. That had truly upset McCartney.

What did all this add to our knowledge of Lennon? Little or nothing. Watching the fray – Paul criticizes John, Yoko offends Paul, Julian jibes at Yoko – was not a pretty sight. And there was much worse to come. Throughout his life, John had written songs with sentiments that were apposite in summarizing his situation. Unwittingly, he even managed it in death, with his 1984 release 'Nobody Told Me': 'Nobody told me there'd be days like these. Strange days indeed.'

Lawyers have been kept busy. Nine months after the murder, Jack Douglas, the co-producer of John's final studio album, *Double Fantasy* – which had sold 7 million copies by then – filed suit against Yoko and Geffen Records for alleged non-payment of his royalties. This was resolved at trial in April 1984, when Yoko was ordered to pay Douglas

$2.5 million in back royalties, plus more than $600,000 interest. Another legal battle involving that album came in June 1981, when Yoko Ono, Geffen Records, and distributor Warner Bros Records were jointly named in a copyright infringement lawsuit alleging that in her track 'I'm Your Angel', Yoko had plagiarized the 1928 standard 'Makin' Whoopee'. This was settled with an out-of-court payment.

Marshalling a colossal estate – no ordinary estate, but John Lennon's – is a formidable task. While performing that adroitly, Yoko has remained active in her old role as an artist and peace activist. By late 1985 she had completed a new album, *Starpeace*, and in the spring of the next year she began an ill-fated concert tour in Brussels. By the time she reached the US and went on stage in San Francisco, ticket sales pointed to commercial failure for the rest of the dates. After four shows the tour was cancelled, proving perhaps that while John and Yoko believed they were representing world opinion on the peace issue, the world did not want to pay to hear her sing about it. Undaunted, she went on stage for Amnesty International's tour called 'A Conspiracy of Hope' at Giants Stadium, East Rutherford, New Jersey, shortly after her own tour collapsed. And in February 1987 she attended a five-day Moscow anti-nuclear conference, returning to the US via England, where she supported anti-nuclear women protesters outside the Greenham Common airbase near London. Her critics would have to concede her persistence and consistency.

The dour moments of the decade were tempered by some moving positive tributes to John's memory, many spoken, many tangible. Fittingly, in February 1982, *Double Fantasy* was named Album Of The Year at the Grammy Awards in Los Angeles. Weeping as she received the award, Yoko said: 'I think John is with us today.' It might sound maudlin, but millions continue to empathize with those sentiments.

That same year, in London, the Performing Right Society (an association of composers, authors, and publishers of music, of which John was a member) launched an annual John Lennon Scholarship prize to give practical encouragement to young musicians. Yoko travelled to the London awards ceremony in 1988 and took particular delight in pointing out, when handing over an award to the joint winner, twenty-year-old Dominique le Vack, that 'John was a feminist.'

It was often difficult to comprehend the disharmony that marred his memory. When, in the year of John's death, George Harrison published his autobiography, *I Me Mine*, with scarcely a mention of John except in passing, Lennon did not miss the omission, especially as he claimed to be a mentor to George, bringing him into the Beatles. John registered his anger at George's book in some of his final interviews. Discord between the surviving three Beatles continued, and even in 1988, when they were inducted into the Rock and Roll Hall of Fame, George and Ringo were the only ones to attend the ceremony in New York. Yoko, Sean and Julian joined them on stage, but Paul stayed behind in London. He explained that he still had business differences with the others and, in a statement, added: 'I would feel like a complete hypocrite waving and smiling with George and Ringo at a fake reunion.'

It was a star-packed night, with Elton John, Bob Dylan, Mick Jagger, Bruce Springsteen, Billy Joel, the Beach Boys, and others joining George and Ringo on stage for 'I Saw Her Standing There' and 'Whole Lotta Shakin' Goin' On' – and George told the audience of one thousand at the Waldorf-Astoria: 'It's unfortunate that Paul's not here. It's hard to really stand here in what is supposed to represent the Beatles. But we all loved John very much and love Paul very much.' Yoko was much sharper when she took the microphone: 'John would have been here. He wouldn't have stayed at home.'

While Paul has fired a few criticisms to balance the interpretation of his association with John, he has been gracious about the stimulus he gained from his old partner. Since John's death, Paul has searched for a successor but without anything approaching the same degree of chemistry. He has co-written with Denny Laine, Stevie Wonder, Michael Jackson, Eric Stewart, Elvis Costello, and with his wife, Linda; he has said how much he misses the Lennon spark that helped ignite his work.

And yet there are often tinges of irritability mixed with his admiration and affection for John. The closest Paul has come to autobiography was in the handsome programme distributed free throughout his world tour of 1989–90. In it, he stated that he was interested in the avant-garde scene in London ahead of John – but he hardly implanted this seed into his work. He helped start the newspaper *International Times*, a totem of the counter-culture, and the Indica Bookshop and Gallery, where John met Yoko. It was John, however, who took the baton from Paul – and John was able and ready to absorb the avant-garde of the period into his life. McCartney points out that at that time he was living alone in London, while the other three Beatles, married and living in suburbia, 'were very square in my mind'. And when John went to McCartney's home, 'He was quite turned on by it all. When he made that album *Two Virgins* he was hopeless technically. I had to set up a couple of tape recorders and I showed him this whole system that I used and he, being John, the difference between him and me, he'd make the record of it. Whereas, being me, I'd do it and experiment with it and then bring it to our mainstream records. John always wanted to jump over the cliff. He once said that to me. "Have you ever thought of jumping?" I said, "Fuck off, you jump and tell me how it is." That's basically the difference in our personalities.'

Once John was united with Yoko, 'all the [avant-garde] shit he'd seen me doing for the last four or five years – he could do it now. He threw over his suburban life with Cynthia, got divorced. Then he went totally, unfortunately, too far. Went into heroin and stuff – well, crazy. He did masses of great stuff but then he could let it all out, be himself, and all these bizarre sides to his character that he'd never dared let out before, he suddenly let out.'

Paul had hinted at this before, but this was the first time he had boldly asserted that John's reinvention of himself was not wholly traceable to his meeting with Yoko. Once unleashed, this vital artistic flowering would dominate John's life, contribute to the break-up of the Beatles, and allow Lennon to cross the divide from entertainment into art. From 1969 on, while music would usually be his vehicle, he was able to divest himself of the past and assume the role of autobiographical philosopher. And then, at forty, when he was about to deliver yet another chapter of his story in words, music and lifestyle, he was shot dead, becoming a martyr and a hero. He was an impossible act to equal, because he was fiercely individualistic.

John Lennon left behind a life of blazing achievement, lapses of behaviour, artistic brilliance, and personal frailty. One of his gifts was in persuading us to examine ourselves. He did not believe in regrets, confronted his past head-on in a succession of cathartic interviews, and enjoyed combat, particularly when his own honesty or integrity was questioned. He revelled in a battle of words and wits with

McCartney, and between the bouts of blood-letting each acknowledged the other's contribution to ten golden years together. When John died, any criticism from Paul was at least soundly based: they grew together, enriched each other, and McCartney really had, and still has, a profound affection for John. Though they had different temperaments, Paul understood him. This could not be said for most of the armies of writers who debased his memory without mercy.

Few celebrities have come under such a penetrating biographical stare as Lennon in the decade since his death. Revelations about what John was really like were to spawn a plethora of books from almost every backroom girl and boy he ever knew or employed. One attracted particular fury from Lennon's admirers and even from his critics, who wanted fair play for a dead man. *The Lives of John Lennon*, a biography for which author Albert Goldman claimed to have conducted 1,200 interviews, was published in August 1988. The extended family and friends of Lennon and the Beatles had anticipated that the book would portray John savagely, not least because of the writer's track record with his previous diatribe on Elvis Presley. This was a coincidence John would not have missed, that he shared the ignominy of a biographer with his early idol. Even to his staunchest admirers, Lennon was no saint, hardly a person to be loved unequivocally. But even his critics gave him respect. When the Goldman book arrived, the outcry on both sides of the Atlantic was intense.

Goldman's version of Lennon was that of a crazed recluse: a schizophrenic bag of bones holed up in his Dakota apartment, totally under Yoko's spell, a manic-depressive junkie who kicked Yoko in the stomach while she was pregnant, 'knocked hell' out of her on a yacht, and once tried to set her hair alight. Yoko, alleged Goldman, carried on love affairs under John's nose; she procured him a mistress.

John was said to have mistreated Sean, even complaining to Yoko that he wasn't their real son because they looked so little like each other. Julian, too, is said by Goldman to have feared his father.

Goldman, who asserted that Yoko had a $5,000-a-week heroin habit, also theorized that pictures of John and Yoko in his last weeks did not reflect their happiness but were, instead, evidence of 'an impassive bitch and her blindly-sucking whelp'. The condemnation of John's artistry – he was castigated as a plagiarist who over-worked the chords to 'Three Blind Mice' – was matched by a suggestion that John so lacked physical coordination as to be virtually a spastic. (Yoko laughed this away, pointing out that John was, for example, excellent and natural when they did yoga together.)

Portraying Lennon as violent, Goldman cited the fracas at Paul McCartney's twenty-first birthday party in Liverpool in 1963. Bob Wooler, disc jockey at Liverpool's Cavern Club, had made a remark alluding to John's recent visit to Spain with Brian Epstein. Goldman wrote: 'Lennon doubled his fist and smashed the disc jockey in the nose. Then, seizing a shovel . . . Lennon began to beat Wooler to death . . . and ambulance was called for Wooler, who had suffered a broken nose, a cracked collar bone and three broken ribs.'

The facts are that no shovel was picked up by John. Wooler suffered no broken ribs, and Brian Epstein in his own car, not an ambulance, drove him to hospital. Wooler was not among Goldman's 1,200 interviewees.

According to Goldman, Lennon allegedly believed he might have helped kill his close friend Stuart Sutcliffe, the Fifth Beatle, by beating him a few months before Sutcliffe died suddenly from a brain haemorrhage. Curiously this alleged feeling by John was never conveyed by him to the

Beatles or to his wife Cynthia – and it was unknown to Sutcliffe's mother, sister, and German fiancée – none of whom were among Goldman's 1,200 interviewees.

In describing the interaction between Lennon and Epstein, who was homosexual, Goldman believes that Epstein was under Lennon's sexual dominance for years and that shortly before the Beatles manager's death in 1967, John was sexually manhandled by Brian at a party at the latter's house. Goldman says the event was interrupted by the arrival of Epstein's mother. Queenie Epstein told me she saw nothing of this nature, nor evidence to suggest it had happened. Others close to Epstein and Lennon never saw such an incident. Queenie Epstein was not among Goldman's 1,200 interviewees.

The book's notoriety lay not so much in its purported disclosures as in the misanthropic tone struck by its author. So many specific charges against John could be sifted and rejected by those who cared enough to check, and Lennon's self-examination laid himself bare with a great deal more articulacy than a highly slanted interpretation of his life – which Lennon could not answer.

At last, it seemed, the Lennon/Beatles family had a common cause for unity! How could this second assassination of Lennon be countered? Paul McCartney had no doubt: after reading excerpts from the book in a British newspaper, McCartney took time off from his summer holiday and, two weeks before the book's publication, issued a statement:

It's disgusting that someone like Goldman can make up any old bunch of lies he sees fit and can be allowed to publish them without fear of repudiation.

With the exception of his close relatives, I knew John longer than anyone. I would have thought that once in all that time, perhaps during a drunken or unguarded moment, there would have been a suggestion of the homosexuality referred to by Goldman. There was never even the slightest hint of this kind. In fact, quite the opposite – John was very attracted to women.

As for the claims about heroin, John had been through an unfortunate period with drugs but by the time his son Sean was born he was completely free of all drugs and urged other people to do the same.

I hope that I can give some words of comfort to Sean, Julian, Yoko, John's Aunt Mimi, his other relatives and the public at large, when I assure them that John was a great man, at times wild and whacky, but always deep down a wonderful human being. I urge people to boycott this book which in my opinion is nothing more than a piece of trash.

Cynthia Lennon told me: 'Albert Goldman approached me several times for an interview. I refused. I had several reasons, beginning with Mr Goldman's history. I had read his book on Elvis Presley and decided that his starting point was not one of love but of dissecting and pulling apart the memory of someone, rather than honestly writing about their lives and realizing that the subject had parallels with everybody's life. I expected Mr Goldman to annihilate the memory of John – and he did. Albert Goldman seems to accentuate the dark aspects of life, its miseries, its grotesque nightmares. I wanted no part in his book which does not depict the John Lennon I and so many others knew and loved. Understanding John Lennon was difficult enough, even for people like me and I knew him for ten years. No one will ever understand John's character without understanding his roots . . . For a New Yorker like Albert Goldman to believe he can get under the skin of a man like

John is truly a joke. He has not succeeded because he wasn't *there*. He will never understand the Northern English mentality of John, and the people he grew up with, the culture . . . to understand the man, listen to his music which is his poetry.'

George Martin said: 'I think it is iniquitous that people can libel the dead. If John was alive, that book would not have come out. It is largely untrue, but sadly, if mud is thrown it tends to stick.' He also described Goldman's book as 'codswallop'.

Support for the Goldman book came from May Pang, former personal assistant to the Lennons and John's companion during his 'lost weekend' separation from Yoko. On a visit to London, May, now married to record producer Tony Visconti, declared that Goldman's book was 99 per cent accurate; that John was skeletal; that he had been using cocaine. She blamed Yoko for turning John into a 'recluse'.

For Yoko, the vilification in the book presented a dilemma. To counter the many accusations against herself and John would inevitable stoke the publicity fire and, as well as making her appear worried and defensive, could have stimulated the book's sale. The best route would have been to starve the book of controversy, but with the battle raging outside she had to say something. In one interview, with Philip Norman for the London *Sunday Times*, she revealed that when portions of Goldman's book were first read to her over the phone, especially those concerning her alleged cruelty to John, a brief thought of suicide crossed her mind. 'I've been undergoing character assassination for the past twenty years so why does it still hurt? When this whole thing started I kept thinking of Picasso's wife and how she finally killed herself. Then I realized I could never do anything like that because I have Sean.'

Like Cynthia, she rejected the charge that John was violent: 'In all the time we were together, he never hit me.' On Brian Epstein: 'If there'd been any situation like the book says, John would have *bragged* about it.' There were so many allegations, she said, that she could not deal with them all. But, striking the most perceptive note of anyone in condemning the book, Yoko said: 'What I most detest about this book isn't so much the fact that it's all lies. It's that it robs John of all basic human dignity. The things said about me I hope I can prove wrong. But John isn't here to answer the things said about him. That's what chokes me up.'

For the sake of John Lennon's public, bemused by the huge publicity around the book, a public statement was needed. And so, in a one-hour radio programme that Westwood One (an American radio syndication company) broadcast on 14 September 1988, the Lennon camp, led by Elliot Mintz, delivered a rebuttal of the main statements in *The Lives of John Lennon*.

Dealing first with Goldman's sources, the author Jon Wiener declared that two of these were Fred Seaman and Marnie Hair. Seaman, a former employee of John and Yoko, had pleaded guilty in 1983 to grand larceny of John's files, papers, and personal journals, plus cash and stereo equipment. He had been sentenced to five years' probation. Could Seaman be considered a reliable source? asked Wiener. Similarly, Marnie Hair had been in legal conflict with Yoko. Could she, therefore, be considered an impartial source?

On Lennon's so-called 'bag of bones anorexia', Goldman wrote that this was caused by 'dieting, fasting and self-induced vomiting . . . he weighed only 130 pounds . . . a lack of purpose and exercise . . . he rarely left his bed . . . drugged all day . . . he spent his waking hours in a trance . . . he complains of the weight of his guitar . . . you can pour a cup of water into the hollows of his collar bones.' Responses pointing to John's good health came from Yoko, Sean and Julian – and from John himself, during his 1980 interview with David Sheff. Talking of his alleged years as a recluse, as a supposed Howard Hughes/Greta Garbo figure, John had laughed it away as 'Greta Hughes' and dismissed it: 'I just wasn't seeing the media or making records. I was not stuck in any room. I was all over the world – Hong Kong, Singapore.'

Yoko said: 'That year [1978] we travelled a lot and there is proof of that.' So many people had witnessed John leaving the Dakota, going for a walk, or to the coffee shop. 'He was very active. A lot of people saw him on a daily basis. And he was in good health.' Julian, declaring that his father 'never hit me, ever,' said of John's physique and alleged anorexia: 'The last time I saw him was on my birthday and we hugged a lot. If he was like Goldman says, I would have crushed Dad quite a few times.' He denied another allegation by Goldman, that he was 'frozen with fear in John's presence'.

On John's relationship with Sean, Goldman wrote: 'If in a rare example of affection he takes Sean on his knee, John Lennon will make sure to seat the child facing away from him so the boy will not have the opportunity to plant a wet, smacky kiss on his father's face.'

Yoko: '*Why*? He was a very kissy-kissy, lovey-dovey person – and with Sean.'

Sean: 'I doubt if anyone is going to believe that. It is so outlandish . . . blatant lies, just stupid. I have kissed him and I'd sit on his lap any way I want to.' Rejecting, also, a story that John 'pitched the cat down the hall', and 'kick[ed] his [Sean's] pampered ass', Sean stated: 'He never laid a hand on me. That is completely made up. He was a great person as a father and did enough fathering for twenty years in the five years I knew him.'

Mintz described as 'total fiction' an allegation that he had been involved in a plan by Yoko for John to go to a brothel; and Yoko denied the statement.

Speaking of Brian Epstein and their visit to Spain together, John said it was his first association with a homosexual, and though it was a 'pretty intense relationship', it was never consummated. Mintz asked Yoko if John was gay. 'No, he was not.' Had he had an affair with Epstein? 'He told me he hadn't and I believed him.' Paul McCartney spoke against the theory that John was homosexual (as reported elsewhere in this book) and said he suspected that the allegations had been raised in order to sell books by introducing a controversial issue.

These responses only scratched the surface of the book and could not deal systematically with its many other contestable statements. Yoko summed up her feelings by saying the book contained 'fiction on the most complex level, layers and layers of lies. It's exasperating.' In Liverpool, during a Beatles fan convention, there was an outdoor public bonfire of copies of *The Lives of John Lennon* . . . and it was never on sale at Beatlefest, the primary American annual gathering of fans in New York, Chicago and Los Angeles, where book sales are a central factor.

A month after the Goldman book's release, Yoko continued to respond by positive moves to reflect and celebrate Lennon's life. An exhibition of his art in London, called 'Imagine', was quickly followed by a film of the same title which had been three years in preparation and now seemed to have been immaculately timed to offset the hateful publicity surrounding John and Yoko in the previous month.

The movie traced John's childhood, the Beatles years, and his life and art alongside Yoko. It featured, also, face-to-camera interviews with key figures in John's life. Producer David L. Wolper, producer-director Andrew Solt, and writer Sam Egan decided on a narrative by Lennon himself throughout, leading us through his life. The result was a movie that moved many of the audience of celebrities to tears at the London première, which Yoko attended. (It was Julian who brought about the meeting of Cynthia with Yoko. When the *Imagine* film was being planned, he arranged for them to meet at the Russian Tea Room in New York. The atmosphere was a little strained, but at least contact was established between two women who were so often talking to the world about the same man. They met again at Manhattan's Hard Rock Café after one of Julian's concerts.)

Inevitably, the book of the film was entitled *Imagine: John Lennon*, and here Yoko again struck a note that echoed the views of millions rather than those of his detractors. 'John was a voice' she wrote. 'His voice was loved because it was the voice of truth . . . the world thought his voice was silenced by a gunshot. It wasn't. John is still singing. John is talking.'

There were other books, of course: biographies and memoirs, kiss-and-tells and investigative studies. They fell into categories best defined as the good, the bad, and the ugly. May Pang's *Loving John: The Untold Story* purported to describe her experiences when she worked as an aide for the Lennons, and later when she was his partner. May claimed that her relationship with John was essentially initiated, controlled, and then terminated by Yoko, themes pursued relentlessly in a book high on sexual and human drama. Disregarding its accuracy, disputed by Yoko, the talk of manipulation reflects badly on John's self-esteem and was in execrable taste. It deserves to be linked only with *Dakota Days: The True Story of John Lennon's Final Years*. Written by John Green, a tarot card reader, this painted a melodramatic portrait of a Lennon who had lost his muse, was haunted by his past, and for whom the 'last six years of his life were his darkest . . . he was unable to write music.' Green demonstrated a staggering recollection of precise conversations with Lennon, and, assuming he wrote these down or tape-recorded them, he could have been of enormous benefit to the American radio series *The Lost Lennon Tapes*, which desperately needed such archives. Alternatively, if Green's memory is all stored in his computered brain, he is undoubtedly one of the world's greatest reporters, with an award-winning future.

The most unexpected and welcome book on John's early years from an 'insider' came from Julia Baird, his half-sister. Entitled *John Lennon, My Brother*, this was surprising, because Julia had led a hitherto private life as a school-teacher and mother before deciding that John's memory needed some accuracy as well as her affectionate reflections. Published two weeks after the Goldman diatribe, Julia Baird's book attracted a lively, evocative foreword by Paul McCartney — 'Great days, great memories, let it all flood back,' he wrote.

Julia and John shared the same mother but not the same father. Almost seven years older than Julia, John did not speak about his father, she writes. 'If he had, we would not have known what he was talking about. We assumed we all shared the same Daddy.' Julia was eleven and John seventeen when their mother (also Julia) was killed, knocked down by a car. Her memories of this, the effect on John, and the intimate truth of their bumpy family life make it a compelling read, essential to any student of Lennon. His fractured childhood and the emotional trauma of his teenage years marked his life – and his work. Of his father, Alfred (known to friends as Freddy), John said: 'He pissed off and left me when I was a baby.' Of his mother, John wrote in his heart-searching song 'Mother': 'Mother, you had me, but I never had you.'

It was hardly surprising that John was confused about his early life and often preferred, during the Beatles years, to camouflage his innermost emotions under a veil of braggadocio. After a parental tug-of-war which John's mother 'won' when the child was five, John's father disappeared, returning to his life as a seaman – only to reappear in John's life at the peak of Beatlemania. There followed a fractious relationship between them. John's Aunt Mimi, who had brought John up, had portrayed Freddy as a born loser who had never been fit to marry her sister: Julia's unfortunate marriage to such a scoundrel had been a disastrous mistake, she declared.

John's attitude to the father he regarded as an absentee lurched from delight (at Freddy's return to him) to bitter resentment (John suspected his father was climbing aboard the Beatles wheel of fortune). Their relationship faltered. There were intermittent attempts at harmony for six years from 1964, but in 1970 John summoned his father to a meeting which quickly turned rancorous, John blaming Freddy for the pain he had suffered from childhood. During his vitriolic attack – coincidentally on his thirtieth birthday – John demanded that his father should never write an autobiography.

But Freddy Lennon, a rebel like his son, went ahead and wrote his life story in the firm belief that the stories Mimi had spread about his desertion and his character were grossly unfair. John, Freddy maintained, should hear *his* side of the story. He insisted that he had never wanted to leave John, that the real problem lay with Julia, who would not have him back in her life, and that the circumstances of his life as a seaman had inevitably made his attentiveness as a father haphazard. Freddy's manuscript never became a book in John's lifetime. In 1990, however, Freddy's widow, Pauline, adapted it into her own book, *Daddy Come Home: The True Story of John Lennon and His Father*. As an antidote to all the received stories of John's childhood, it added significant information and views as well as fascinating letters from John's hand.*

The first tense meeting between son and father, at Freddy's request, was after an eighteen-year gap and took place in John's dressing-room while he was working. 'What do you want then?' snapped John to the man he considered had deserted him. Freddy said he sought nothing. But John had good reason to suspect that his father was exploiting his surname, since he had 'gone public' with his identity in the media and had eventually made an excruciating record as a singer. This was no place for a real conversation, and they agreed to meet again; the bumpy relationship continued during meetings at John's home in the months and years that followed.

In 1967, six days after the death of Brian Epstein, John wrote to his father acknowledging a letter and anticipating a meeting; he said he was going to India for a couple of months but would try to arrange the meeting before he went. It was an optimistic, cheerful message. John knew

---

* Freddy Lennon met Pauline Jones when he was fifty-four and she was an eighteen-year-old university student. When they began living together, her mother sought to have Pauline named a ward of court. Pauline became John's stepmother when she married Freddy on her twentieth birthday in June 1968, a wedding to which John gave both his blessing and financial help. Pauline and Freddy had two sons, David Henry (born in February 1967) and Robin Francis (born in October 1973, after John had left for New York). So when John was killed in 1980, he had a seven-year-old half brother in Britain whom he had never met.

that relations between them might be awkward initially, but there was hope, he said. And there were dashes of that tart Lennon wit. He said he was glad his father had not produced a big family, since he had 'enough family to last me a few lifetimes'.

John eventually developed a convivial relationship with Freddy and Pauline – he gave his father a room at his home and later bought them a house. Work was found for Pauline as John's secretary at his Weybridge home; John wrote a letter of sympathy and support when Pauline suffered a miscarriage; and when they relocated to Brighton John wrote a letter wishing them well. John arranged their smooth passage to Scotland when they eloped to get married; and yet it seems that the conversation with John about his family background, which Freddy wanted so much, never happened. He wanted to emphasize that he had never planned to split permanently from Julia and that he would have preferred to have given John parental stability in his childhood.

What happened at their final meeting, according to Pauline Lennon, was a monumental fracas at Tittenhurst Park on 9 October 1970. Freddy had taken aftershave lotion for John's birthday but arrived to find his now bearded son fiercely confrontational. With Yoko at his side, he roared at his father: 'I'm cutting off your money and kicking you out of the house. Get out of my life – get off my back.' His voice raging, he continued: 'Have you any idea what I've been through because of you? Day after day in therapy, screaming for my daddy, sobbing for you to come home. What did you care, away at sea all those years?' (John had recently undergone primal scream therapy under Dr Arthur Janov at this time.) Pauline Lennon continues:

As his voice tailed off his rage seemed to change to

anguish and for one moment I thought he might even begin to cry. I felt genuine compassion for him and for the trauma I knew he had suffered as a child, but this was quickly replaced by a sense of indignation at the apparent unfairness of his attack on his father. 'You can't put all the blame on your Dad,' I protested. 'Your mother was just as much to blame for your problems.' Astonishingly, the mention of Julia now triggered a vicious verbal attack on his mother . . .

We were aghast . . . neither of us could believe it possible that John could talk about his beloved mother in this way and the horrifying thought struck us that Freddy's son was totally out of his mind; a suspicion seemingly confirmed by his following words: 'Look at me! I'm bloody insane. I'm due for an early death like Hendrix or Joplin and it's all your fault. Do you know what it does to a child to be asked to choose between his parents? Do you know how it tears him apart, blows his bloody mind?'

Pauline Lennon says that John threatened to have his father killed and his body dumped at sea if he revealed that day's events to anyone. Terrorized, Freddy left the house with Pauline, and they never met again.

Her book is unnervingly and surprisingly strong with verbatim reports of electrifying conversations, even the precise exchange when John in New York phoned Freddy on his deathbed in a Brighton hospital in 1976. 'I'm sorry to have treated you the way I did, Dad. I should never have gone to the head shrink. It was a big mistake.' Freddy: 'Forget it John. It's just bloody marvellous to talk to you again.' Freddy died on 1 April 1976 from cancer.

Flawed though it is, as the work of a doting, ultra-defensive widow, *Daddy Come Home* is an essential component in the Lennon jigsaw. The Freddy Lennon I met seemed an unattractive, dubious character, but given the unanswered attacks on him through the years, Pauline's book is a just and fair response. As for John — he had a wayward and absentee father, a frivolous mother who died at a critical point in his life, a domineering aunt, and two wives of utterly contrasting personalities. The edges, and perhaps the depths, of John's character could not but be marked by these factors.

Indispensable from an utterly different vantage point is *Come Together: John Lennon in His Time*, by Jon Wiener. An American university history professor, Wiener made a request to the federal government under the Freedom of Information Act, seeking the official files on Lennon. The result was a huge dossier, exposing the Nixon administration's harassment and intimidation of John, which contributed to his pressured life in New York in the early 1970s.

'In the spring of 1972, John Lennon knew that *they* were after him,' says Wiener. 'Too many people had come to fix the phone. Too often, cars that were parked outside his Greenwich Village apartment started up as he left the house and obviously shadowed him. He knew, too, why *they* were after him. He planned to do a concert tour in the summer of 1972 to arouse the youth of America to vote against the Vietnam war, against Nixon. *They* were scared that John Lennon, the ex-Beatle, the radical superstar with opinions and money, just might pull it off, just might interfere with Nixon's re-election plans. He had to be stopped.' Meticulously researched, the book is a fearless and crucial investigation into Lennon's difficult New York years, as well as a riveting historical record.

A much lighter volume — approaching John's psyche from a different angle — is *The Literary Lennon*. Written by another American professor, James Sauceda, this dissection of John's writings covers *A Spaniard in the Works*, *In His Own Write* and many other sources. John's writing talent, often overlooked, stands up well to light analysis and conjecture, and Sauceda's interest in this territory adds a worthy literary dimension to the millions of words written on John's utterances.

Such a study could not have predicted the publication, posthumously, of a further Lennon collection of prose and verse. With the manuscript rescued from the jaws of thieves soon after John's murder, Yoko published his *Skywriting by Word of Mouth* in the autumn of 1986. A valuable addition to his library, John wrote it 'at a time when the world was wondering whatever had happened to him', Yoko said in her afterword. 'Why wasn't he writing songs any more? Well, this is what he was busy doing.'

Yoko wrote that John 'wrote very quickly; he never had to stop to think'. That was indeed one of his characteristics – and in the autobiographical section of *Skywriting* which opens the book, his reproaches were often at full throttle. There were jibes at Brigitte Bardot, whom he had met when 'I was on acid and she was on her way out'; at Cynthia: 'Yoko ... picked up my spirits enough to give me the courage to get the hell out, just in time for me to avoid having to live with my ex-wife's new nose'; and at Britain, of which he was ashamed because of its xenophobic attitude to Yoko and his relationship with her: 'It was a horrifying experience ... the press led the howling mob and the foul-mouthed Silent Majority followed suit.'

Describing his life with the Beatles as 'a trap ... A tape loop', John delved into some fairly well-worn terrain; his infamous remark about the Beatles being more popular than Jesus Christ was now seen by him as a good episode for his life's journey. 'If I hadn't ... upset the very Christian Ku Klux Klan, well, Lord, I might still be up there with all the other performing fleas. God bless America. Thank you, Jesus.'

On the Beatles split: 'When I finally had the guts to tell the other three that I, quote, wanted a divorce, unquote, they knew it was for real, unlike Ringo and George's previous threats . . . I started the band. I disbanded it. It's as simple as that.'

In John's inimitable, direct style, this is pretty much a first-hand account of some of the major events that punctuated his forty frenetic years. His book segues into some of his delightful word-play, parodies-with-messages: 'Up Yours, A Closer Look at Feminism, by Deidre De Flowered, b.s.'; 'The Life of Reilly by Ella Scott Fitzgeraldine'; 'Never Underestimate the Power of Attorney'. And much more. It is reassuring to see that the man's wit and wisdom were as penetrating in the 1970s as they were in his delicious writings a decade earlier.

Two of the least expected events to mark John's life after his death cast us right back to that special day, 6 July 1957, when he performed with his skiffle group, the Quarry Men, at a church garden fête near his home in Woolton. On that day, when soon-to-be-seventeen Lennon met just-turned-fifteen McCartney, a local enthusiast Bob Molyneux switched on his Grundig tape recorder. The music he captured paid rich dividends thirty-seven years later. On 15 September 1994 at Sotheby's, the tape featuring two songs fetched £78,500.

That day also became the focus of one of the most inspirational books written about the entire Beatles phenomenon. *The Day John Met Paul*, the product of some eight years of research by American writer Jim O'Donnell, is written in the style of a dramatic novel, with immaculate attention to detail, from the temperature of the day, to the way the two youths woke up, got out of bed, dragged combs across their heads, to move forward inexorably to their first momentous meeting. O'Donnell's aim was vividly to recapture the spirit of Liverpool on that day, 'to get a sense of what it was like to be alive at that time. What I hope I've brought to the Beatles book party is the interplay of teenagers John and Paul with the whole process of living Liverpool.' This hour-by-hour account of how the Beatles began is an indispensable documentary of celebration and conscientious research. It will be published initially in the US by Penguin Books as a paperback in late 1995 or early 1996.

By the late 1980s, the assassination of John Lennon had become history. In Attica jail, prisoner number 81A3860, Mark David Chapman, was serving twenty years to life for the crime which he had admitted. The story of how he pumped five bullets into Lennon outside his home was consigned to history. The reality of that awful day, 8 December 1980, had been swept aside by people now absorbing John's life rather than dwelling on how he died. The Chapman case was closed. Or was it?

Since Chapman had, back in 1981, changed his plea from not guilty to guilty and so had not stood trial, the big question surrounding his assassination of Lennon – why? – had gone unanswered or had been the subject of speculation. The theories were simple: he was a 'lone nut', a 'crazed fanatic', a 'fan' of Lennon who saw himself as succeeding his 'idol' once John was dead; he was one of those disturbed individuals who seek fame of any kind for whatever reason. And yet . . . none of these reasons sounded plausible to anyone who chose to spend time looking for motivation. It took a prominent British barrister and journalist, Fenton Bresler, to undertake the most arduous, perhaps dangerous, task of investigating the strange story of Mark Chapman. Bresler came to the subject with no 'baggage' as a Lennon/Beatles fan, but with the eagle eye of an experienced barrister trained to ask questions. After six years of extraordinary research, Bresler published his book, entitled (in the USA) *Who Killed John Lennon?* and (in Britain) *The Murder of John Lennon*.

In 1974, when I met John in New York, he told me that he was being followed by people who suspected him of being too political, and that his phone was being tapped. He confirms this in his own posthumously published book, *Skywriting*. John's political affiliations and their consequences are laid bare in Jon Wiener's book. And yet, when Bresler emerged with a thoroughly researched, chilling, and cogent argument that Lennon's death could have been plotted and planned by the CIA for years, and that Chapman had been programmed to assassinate by 'undercover forces that controlled him', the theory was largely swept under the carpet. Eyebrows were raised, some people said Bresler had hit upon a strong possibility – but there it rested.

Chapman, Bresler argues in his book, was 'simply a cipher for the CIA who imagined that Lennon was a representative of dangerous political subversion'. Elsewhere, and in a conversation with me, Bresler maintains that he carried out his inquiries and wrote the book mainly to 'ask the questions that needed asking'. He regarded conspiracy theories, even his own, with some suspicion, 'but this wasn't a murder, it was an assassination, he was gunned down in the street. I was interested in it as a lawyer: I've never been a conspiracy buff. The only thought I had in my brain when I began was: *why kill John Lennon?* I was driven reluctantly to some kind of conspiracy theory because I

couldn't find any other explanation which would even begin
to fit the facts.'

Bresler writes:

> Perhaps in the end Chapman was only a 'lone nut', but
> as someone who has practised at the Bar in England for
> nearly forty years as well as journalistically investigated
> murder on both sides of the Atlantic for well over twenty
> years, I have never easily accepted the simplistic expla-
> nation for homicide. And in Lennon's case I have always
> thought it unlikely. Other international rock stars and
> entertainers from Elvis Presley onwards have received
> anonymous death threats from strangers and 'cranks' —
> but it is only Lennon who (without any prior threat)
> was gunned down. Why?

Bresler goes on to suggest that Lennon, 'the politically
most active rock star of his generation, and militantly left-
wing politically active at that, was shot dead outside his
own home by a killer who was merely a tool, a human gun
used and controlled by others to destroy a uniquely powerful
radical figure who was likely to prove a rallying point for
mass opposition to the policies soon to be implemented,
both at home and abroad, by the new United States government headed by Ronald Reagan'.

Among the many valid questions raised by Bresler is
this central one: precisely what *was* Chapman doing in
Chicago for three days before he flew to New York to kill
Lennon? The generally accepted story was that Chapman
took a plane from Honolulu to New York, changing planes
at Chicago. Bresler insists that Chapman in fact spent three
mysterious days in Chicago.

> . . . the baggage tag so conveniently left out in his hotel

room for the police to find has him flying on by direct connection on Flight 904 to New York. It simply cannot be. This whole ticket and tag affair does not hang together. To my mind, there can be no real doubt that Mark *was* in Chicago for three days before he flew on to New York . . . he *was* intending to use his return ticket for 18 December. But something happened to him in Chicago. Someone got hold of him. Someone got him back on course. Someone put murder yet again powerfully and dominatingly into his mind.

He had left Honolulu as Mark Chapman. He flew out of Chicago to New York as Holden Caulfield [the central character in *The Catcher in the Rye*, the book Chapman was reading when he killed John]. His special mission to assassinate John Lennon had entered its final stage.

On 29 April, Bresler reports of the period leading to the killer's change of plea from 'not guilty' to 'guilty'; science was brought in to aid the human factor in assessing Chapman's mental condition. 'It showed there was nothing organically wrong with him.' On 8 June, Chapman phoned his attorney to say that 'God had visited him in his cell and told him to plead guilty . . . He said I was to give up this trial for him. It would be a circus!' And, perhaps significantly, Bresler points out, Attica, where Chapman is held, is a jail for sane prisoners.

Bresler writes also:

None of Mark's nine mental health experts, whether for the prosecution or the defence, was ever asked to consider the question whether he might have been programmed or otherwise subjected to mind control to commit his crime. But would not someone with a supergrade 'narcissistic personality disorder' . . . be exactly the

sort of massively ego-centred person you would choose
if you wanted to programme someone into being a sort
of armed Superman gunning for a notorious enemy of
established society?

Bresler told me he believes his book could not have
been written by an American, since his status as a visiting
British barrister gave him an entrée to interviewers who
saw him as impartial. Reaction to his book has been mixed.
Interviewed on publication, Bresler found interest among
the forty- to fifty-year-olds who grew up with Lennon and
who thought there was maybe more to the killing than
met the eye. And there was scepticism. A condemnatory
review of the book in London's *Sunday Telegraph* was written
by Miles Copeland; in a polite letter to the paper after that
review, Fenton Bresler wrote: 'It would have perhaps been
more courteous to your readers and fairer to me for you to
have disclosed that Mr Copeland [Miles's father] was one
of the founders of the CIA.'
    On Yoko's attitude and reaction, Bresler says: 'When I
spoke to her on the phone she was interested. She actually
said: "I'm more interested in the living John than the
dead John." ' During Bresler's final stages of research, Sam
Havadtoy relayed a message from Yoko saying she could
not see him, since she was so busy and was working on her
own book at that time (*Imagine*); but Yoko wished Bresler
well in his project.
    For anyone continuing an interest in Lennon, the ulti-
mate sadness is that he was shot dead. To sweep aside the
assassination without a thorough examination is shameful,
and Bresler, in his book, points to too many disturbing
questions that have gone unanswered. 'I am very careful in
the book not to say whether I believe it or not,' he told me
of the conspiracy theory. 'I raise the question. What I am

prepared to say is that the official explanation is garbage. There are woeful inaccuracies in the official explanation and there were woeful inadequacies and failures in the police investigation. It wasn't what everyone thinks it was. Whether it was what I say it might have been, the reader can judge. As the years go by I'm more and more convinced it's . . . smelly.'

Did he think anything would happen as a result of his research? I asked. 'Sadly, no. A great sadness for me about my book is that nothing has happened and nothing will happen so far as the authorities are concerned. I have raised what I consider legitimate questions based upon my own years of experience in this field. Yet not one person has refuted any of my suggestions, not one person has answered any of my questions. It makes one think that perhaps I was right to ask the questions in the first place.'

At once provocative and unnerving, Fenton Bresler's book strikes a dissonant chord that should concern the millions who care for Lennon's memory. An essential dossier on the assassination and what surrounded and followed it, *Who Killed John Lennon?* is also important in assessing what went into John's life — because it poses the very question of why one or more people would want to end it.

Of all the millions of words about Lennon, the most surprising came eleven years after his assassination. Finally securing a publisher, John and Yoko's former assistant, whom they knew and we all knew as Fred Seaman, delivered his memories of his period in their employment. In America the book was entitled *The Last Days of John Lennon* and in Britain *Living on Borrowed Time*. On the cover, to add gravitas, he used his full name: Frederic Seaman.

Often, a reflection of experiences, true stories and anecdotes by a celebrity's ex-assistant might be informative, entertaining, and important as long as it didn't betray the confidence under which the author had been hired: quitting employment cannot automatically provide a moral freedom to disperse secrets. Seaman's decision to write such a memoir therefore took a top prize for chutzpah: on 14 July 1983 he had been sentenced to five years' probation after pleading guilty to grand larceny of John's diaries from the Dakota. So a felon's story of life with the Lennons, however authoritative, is tainted by its origins in a morally indefensible position. Add to that Seaman's opening paragraph, praising and thanking Albert Goldman, plus Goldman's endorsement of Seaman as a 'unique source', and you get a whiff of the stance of Fred Seaman's book, and his frame of reference.*

Seaman joined the Lennons in 1979 for a two-year span of fascinating activities with great contrasts. Though based at the Dakota, he saw them purchase their house at Cold Spring Harbor on Long Island, where he spent time driving them around; he went with John to Palm Beach for some heady experiences; and he witnessed the important change in John from years of silence to a creative renaissance in Bermuda, resulting in his return to music with *Double Fantasy*.

While his job seems to have been that of a high-class gofer, tending the Lennons' whims, including shopping for health food, cat food, and books, and sorting out John's wardrobe, Seaman emphasizes his comradeship with John. He clearly kept a diary, but while much of the book has a ring of truth it is spoiled by a grubby determination to scar Yoko at almost every turn: on her alleged lack of affection for John, on her music, on her character, on her

* Seaman filed a motion to vacate his plea, on the basis of 'ineffective assistance of counsel', in October 1984. This was denied, as was a request in 1985 for permission to appeal. In 1986, he was granted early termination of probation.

motherhood. Seaman thus puts himself in an impossible position. On the one hand, his clone-like adoration of John is enormous and sometimes suffocating; on the other, he casts his master as a moron in his choice of wife and partner. So John was a genius and a great guy, but an idiot to tolerate Yoko — presumably because Seaman does not care for her. Fred Seaman cannot have it both ways; to understand Lennon, it is essential to analyse just why Yoko became the essential adjunct to his life.

If the tenor of the book is negative, it's not all bad. John's Palm Beach sojourn is recalled with great colour and clarity. His lifelong kinship with Peter Sellers, and his reaction to Sellers's death, are put into perspective, as is John's rivalry with Paul McCartney. There are insights into John's mind, his ambivalence towards fame and success, and his over-reliance on Yoko: 'It made me sad, even a little angry sometimes,' writes Seaman, 'that the great John Lennon was in the humiliating position of having to call me, a virtual stranger, to ask if his wife was "available" for lunch or a chat on the phone.' Seaman insists that John was a prisoner 'of his wife, his staff, his fears, his superstitions'. But how is this to be reconciled with John's extrovert behaviour on trips to Bermuda, Hong Kong, Singapore, South Africa and Japan, testified by photographs? Or with his solo strolls, on so many mornings, for an espresso, a Gitanes, and a reading of the newspaper at the Café Fortuna around the corner from the Dakota? Seaman's depiction of Lennon as a hermit, when it suits the theme of the story, just doesn't sit comfortably.

The self-importance of Seaman reaches a peak when, alleging a marital problem between John and Yoko, he writes: 'I saw no point in alarming him [John] by telling him about the rumours that Yoko planned to divorce him . . . I worried that the shock might send him reeling back into seclusion and terminal depression.' How Seaman, a self-described 'virtual stranger', and a discredited employee, can ever imagine that he had any role or right to interfere in the rumoured marriage problems of his two bosses defies comprehension. And that's the nub of his problem: despite a multitude of interesting memories culled from a unique vantage point, Seaman never shakes off the major difficulty that arises in this book: he was an unhealthy acolyte of John Lennon who seems to have had an enmity towards Yoko from the start.

Overall, this is an unaffectionate book with more than a strand of bitterness throughout. And yet it makes one central point about the period of the murder that those who were close to John will have to live with. Writing about the security arrangements that might have saved or cost John's life, Seaman says of the Dakota staff: 'We were all here, working, getting paid. Yet no one had been guarding the king. We had all failed at the one thing we might actually have done for John.'

American loyalty to the Beatles, and by extension to Lennon, has no parallel in Britain. Some British Lennon-watchers insist that after a decade as a New York resident, John was mentally inching back towards his homeland, and, in addition to planning a world concert tour in 1981 on the heels of the album *Double Fantasy*, he was looking for a re-direction towards his roots. Such observers viewed his emigration to America as a mistake.

John knew that whatever the government view, the American people had adopted him with much more warmth and interest than Britons. There was startling evidence of this in the years following his death. In January 1988, the US radio syndication company Westwood One broadcast a three-hour special programme as a curtain-raiser to a new weekly series of one-hour shows, called *The Lost Lennon Tapes*. Narrated by Elliot Mintz, John's friend and aide to him and Yoko, the programme was planned for a year and promised to unveil all the lost treasures from John's personal tape archive, including alternate mixes of his songs and conversations. Amazingly and disgracefully, not one of Britain's radio stations came forward to broadcast the series, which ran for four years.

Only the staunch British fans who read the *Beatles Monthly Book* magazine could see reviews of the series highlights by Mark Lewisohn, and these were often tantalizingly insightful into aspects of John's multi-faceted character. Here was John parodying Bob Dylan with some wicked impersonations ('Serve Yourself'), evidence that by the early 1970s John had grown cynical towards the American who had once inspired him so strongly. John also revealed that he was embarrassed when Dylan visited him at his 'bourgeois' home in Weybridge, England – and that he and Dylan were nervous of each other. Here too was John's Aunt Mimi in typically searing style, explicit in her dislike of John's father. She dismissed Freddy Lennon's claims that his father (John's grandfather) had come over from Ireland with the Kentucky Minstrels, as had been passed into the history books. Saying she had asked Sid Lennon, John's uncle, about it she recounted that 'his mouth fell open' at the very idea. His and Freddy's father, mother, and grandfather had all been Liverpool-born. Mimi added, throwing in Sid's comment about John's father: 'That liar would say anything.'

In an astounding taunt that probably shook John, the outspoken Mimi confronted him in the tape she had sent to him at the Dakota: 'I hated it, what the Beatles did to you. I don't mean the boys themselves – I expect they were all right in their particular sphere – but I hated what ten years did for you. As soon as you started to make money, your character, your personality, everything, was altered. And it seemed as though you hated the sight of me. You couldn't bear the sight of me and you never missed an opportunity to cut me down dead, in front of other people as well, which was even worse. But it didn't do you any good, for people noticed. But you were very kind to Alfred Lennon, taking him around the West End and having him in your home. I don't suppose it ever crossed your mind that that would hurt me, especially when you couldn't stand the sight of me.'

John's riposte, had it been preserved, would have been worth hearing; part of the surprise of this blast was that it was broadcast on a radio programme authorized by Yoko.

Here also were some wonderful, irrepressible Lennonisms as he took listeners through the Beatles years as well as his own solo experiences. On the Beatles' famous 'butcher' album cover: 'I especially pushed for it to be an album cover, just to break the image.' He revealed how the album *Please Please Me* had been taped in one day, and how he had always been 'bitterly ashamed' of his 'Twist and Shout' vocal – by coincidence, this writer's favourite Lennon rock 'n' roll track.

The out-takes from legitimate sessions have often been hilarious. On a *Double Fantasy* session tape, John was caught improvising a version of the song ' "A" You're Adorable' – an alphabet-inspired composition popularized by Perry Como. After getting through 'A you're adorable' and 'B you're beautiful,' John lurched into 'C you're a cripple in disguise' – showing that even twenty years after leaving art college, here he was in a New York studio still nursing a truly manic fascination or obsession for cripples, a fact which emerges in the early portions of this book.

The Lennon quotes flew thick and fast: he said that Yoko 'didn't split the Beatles' and he never had any intention of playing 'She Loves You' when he was fifty and riddled with tuberculosis. How young Julian was like an unrecognizable child in the house when he'd returned from Beatles tours; Julian in turn said that he had never minded not having his father around and that, as a child, he was always occupied with someone else.

The music on *The Lost Lennon Tapes* has been a mouth-watering dip into the Lennon Estate's tape archive, with songs even the most diehard fans would find fresh: 'The Boat Song' and 'Help Me To Help Myself', for example. In one song, addressed to himself and called 'Dear John', John whistles, plays acoustic guitar, and sings: 'Don't be hard on yourself . . . the race is over, you've won.' Heartbreakingly, this was written in 1980 and recorded as a demonstration cassette at the Dakota a few weeks before he was killed.

The Lost Lennon Tapes ran for longer than its originally planned period, and the focus too often strayed from its subject, with precious little fresh material. But the master-pieces, oral and musical, made it important in extending our knowledge of the man's *oeuvre*; it should be edited and preserved on tape and compact disc for posterity.

In Prague, Czechoslovakia, police dispersed 400 fans gathered at a public memorial service on 8 December 1986 to mark the sixth anniversary of Lennon's death. In Hollywood, California, in September 1988, Yoko unveiled a pavement star bearing John's name outside Capitol Records' Tower, where John's reputation became immortalized along with those of the greats of the world of entertainment.

In Amsterdam on 25 March 1990, on the twenty-first anniversary of their 'Bed-In for Peace', the Hilton Hotel reopened Room 902, as the 'John and Yoko Honeymoon Suite', furnished with Lennon records, book, a guitar – and even a pair of 'granny glasses'. Liverpool named four streets after the Beatles; a range of John Lennon clothing went on sale in France in October, authorized by the Lennon Estate. In the USA, there were authorized drawings by John adorning T-shirts, mugs, posters, calendars, tote bags, watches, greeting cards, notepads, envelopes, telephone-address books, aprons, playing cards, and so on.

The Beatles' orbit of the earth continues. In 1990 the International Astronomical Union approved the naming of four asteroids (minor planets or stars) after the Beatles, at the request of two scientists at the Lowell Observatory in Arizona, which had discovered the tiny planets in 1982 and 1983. The asteroids, formerly known as 4147 (John), 4148 (Paul), 4149 (George), and 4150 (Ringo), are between five and ten miles in diameter and are too faint to be seen by the naked eye.

As we moved towards the fifteenth year since John's death, with millions of words written, spoken, and sung by him and for him, it became important that his memory should not be atrophied: 'dignity' was never a word that sounded quite right when applied to John, but it was a quality necessary among the keepers of the flame. It was in short supply. When, in the autumn of 1988, Cynthia Lennon fronted a new restaurant in London called 'Lennon's' (complete with Beatles and Lennon articles adorning the walls and granny glasses as part of the neon front), it presaged a year of intense activity around John's name. Cynthia withdrew from the restaurant venture after nine months. She marketed her own brand of perfume around this time, called 'Cynthia Lennon's Woman'.

In Cannes the following January, at the annual music business festival, MIDEM, Sid Bernstein, promoter of the

Beatles' first American concerts in 1964, distributed leaflets headlined: 'A Tribute to John Lennon'. Touchingly, Bernstein wrote: 'Lennon wrote "Beautiful Boy" and "Imagine". How many people have poured so much beauty out of their souls?' Bernstein went on to project a salute 'to this unforgettable artist' on 9 October 1989 in Milwaukee, in conjunction with that city's symphony orchestra and ballet. The concert-tribute idea was partly inspired by the hostile nature of Albert Goldman's biography, Bernstein explained. The proceeds would aid drug rehabilitation centres. The tribute, Bernstein added, would be a two-hour television special, 'honouring and remembering the good things he left us with'. Bernstein had often tried to reunite the Beatles in Lennon's lifetime, to no avail. When Bernstein placed a full-page advertisement in the *New York Times* asking them to do a fund-raising concert for the Vietnamese boat people, Lennon publicly scorned Bernstein with his rejection of any Beatles reunion.

Bernstein flew into London to try to attract support for what appeared to be a unique idea; he sought involvement from the ex-Beatles, a starring role with the Milwaukee orchestra for George Martin, and major rock stars of the calibre of Eric Clapton and Phil Collins. Cynthia Lennon was attracted into the project and endorsed it. The ninth anniversary date passed with no concert, but in December, Cynthia flew to Los Angeles to join Bernstein in a press conference announcing 'the show of the century' on 12 and 13 March 1990. Cynthia told the press conference: 'I've had a feeling for the past ten years that I wasn't able to pay my last respects to John. I wasn't there when he died. There was nothing I could do to say goodbye, so when this cropped up I thought this would be my way of saying goodbye to John.'

The line-up would include Paul, George, and Ringo,

Eric Clapton, Michael Jackson, Phil Collins, Elton John, Rudolf Nureyev, Liza Minnelli, and Russian singer-song-writer Mikhail Baryshnikov. When this failed to material-ise, Cynthia announced a memorial event (including a candlelit vigil) at Berlin's Brandenburg Gate on John's birthday, 9 October. This did not happen, either.

'Upcoming birthday bashes for John Lennon haven't yet caused a fight between Yoko Ono and Lennon's first wife Cynthia Lennon, but their camps are sparring,' reported *USA Today*. Cynthia was quoted: 'A fight between Yoko and me is a publicist's dream. If there's a cat fight, it will be manufactured.' In New York, Cynthia met the mayor to inspire civic interest in her project, and in Washington she met Coretta Scott King, widow of civil rights leader the Revd Martin Luther King, Jr; the two women attended ceremonies at the Soviet Embassy honouring Soviet leader Mikhail Gorbachev.

The irony of Cynthia's activities in America was accen-tuated by what happened next. As the Bernstein-Milwau-kee-Berlin plans fizzled out mysteriously, Yoko announced a huge concert for Liverpool on 5 May 1990: 'A Tribute to John Lennon'. This open-air televised concert at the Pier Head had altruistic motives, Yoko announcing her 'Green-ing of the World' theme, a programme 'to help raise global awareness for the need to stop the damage we are doing to our earth on various specific levels. And to set up a Lennon scholarship which will be given to the youth of the world for their education and to promote cultural exchange through it.' Spirit Foundation, a non-profit organization founded by John and Yoko, would be responsible for distri-buting monies raised for the programme – and all monies allocated to the United Kingdom would be channelled through the University of Liverpool, which would set up a John Lennon scholarship.

The concept of the concert was ambitious: a score of artists recasting some of John's compositions in a contemporary musical framework. Yoko and fourteen-year-old Sean flew into Liverpool and did a walkabout, with Sean enjoying his first wander down Mathew Street to see where his father's Beatles craft was honed; and into the Beatles Shop to see how the legend lives.

Liverpool, noted for its lack of pride or recognition of its unique artistic output, reacted to the Pier Head concert with predictable cynicism. A cab driver told me the £25 charge for tickets in a deprived city was 'disgusting' – a complaint echoed everywhere; a hotel receptionist moaned that the place had been taken over by noisy rock musicians – and what was the point of a tribute to Lennon when no ex-Beatles were present? Paul remarked on the concert: 'I can't help thinking: would John have liked it? Is this the kind of thing he liked?' Yoko disagreed: 'I just know John would have been very, very happy about their interpretations,' she said of the 'great artists who have come to Liverpool to sing John's songs'. Nevertheless, McCartney sent a video which appeared on a giant screen shown to the audience. This clip from a Tokyo concert showed him performing 'PS. I Love You' and 'Love Me Do' – neither of them Lennon compositions. Ringo's video was inspired, and he delivered the Lennon song 'I Call Your Name' with tremendous verve. From George Harrison there was only silence, and the non-appearance of Julian was interpreted as a 'snub'. A rival show two days earlier at Liverpool's Philharmonic Hall had featured Pete Best, billed sardonically as 'the only Beatle appearing in Liverpool this weekend', and other Mersey musicians of the 1960s. Their proceeds went to a local children's hospital.

Commercially, the Pier Head concert was unsuccessful, with 45,000 people expected but only about 15,000 there.

Musically, it was mixed, but there were some golden moments. Lou Reed sang controversial, but riveting, fiercely individualistic versions of 'Jealous Guy' and 'Mother'; country-and-western singer Randy Travis a wonderfully majestic 'Nowhere Man'; Joe Cocker a raw and tearful 'Isolation'; the Moody Blues' Justin Hayward and John Lodge a wistful, beautiful 'Across the Universe'; Natalie Cole an energetic 'Lucy In The Sky With Diamonds'. Some songs were massacred: Kylie Minogue bulldozed 'Help!'; Cyndi Lauper wrecked 'Hey Bulldog'; and Roberta Flack's 'In My Life', one of John's most significant songs, was messy. It wasn't easy, indeed it was brave, for any artist to be on stage in Liverpool adapting a Lennon composition, for he implanted each song with his own identity. Creatively, then, it was a patchy day, completed with a moving finale which drew Sean and Yoko on stage with the entire company for 'Give Peace A Chance' and 'Imagine'.

Yoko had told the audience: 'Hello, Liverpool. I love you. It's a great day, isn't it? I think John would be happy, too.' Yet there was a strand of thought that something was not quite right about the concert: that the cast of artists lacked a true British heavyweight of the calibre, say, of Elton John or Eric Clapton, both friends and admirers of John. There was a view that the show had been built for television rather than for a £25-a-ticket affair on the banks of the River Mersey. Another sentiment was that Lennon would have been appalled at the inappropriateness of the artists and wouldn't have gone near such a concert. That's probably true, but then John always preferred records, didn't like concerts, and attended very few.

I declare an interest in the Liverpool event: I wrote the script for the co-hosts, British disc jockey Mike Reid and actor Christopher Reeve, and I also wrote the official programme notes. Nobody can be blind to the event's imperfections: the memory of Lennon deserved something less ramshackle and more resonant in the tenth year after his death. Yet it was a statement, with a level of sincerity. Anodyne it was not – and Liverpool was the correct venue for such an event. On the day of the 'Tribute to John Lennon' concert, Paul McCartney commanded front-page news with his announcement of his show in Liverpool, at King's Dock, six weeks later, when 80,000 people would attend.

And so . . . on. In October 1990, in which would have been the month of his fiftieth birthday, seventy-three tracks of John's post-Beatles recording were issued in compact disc form. In Britain, BBC Radio One launched a ten-week documentary profile of John. On 9 October, Yoko delivered a four-minute speech from the United Nations building in New York to about 1,000 radio stations in fifty countries; the wife of the UN secretary-general, Madam Perez de Cuellar, read a short introduction, followed by an archive tape of John urging peace. In New York's Strawberry Fields, on what would have been John's birthday, fans took a cake with fifty candles.

The books and records continued to flow: *John Lennon: A Family Album*, by Nishi F. Saimaru, a collection of evocative photographs capturing John and Yoko's visit to Japan in 1976; Sean, Yoko, and singer Lenny Kravitz linking up in January 1991 for an updated version of 'Give Peace A Chance' as an antidote to the impending Gulf war. When John wrote that song, twenty years earlier, he was entering his political period; as the song was re-born with the world entering war, it seemed that nothing had changed. The BBC banned the new version; American radio stations hardly played it. In death, as in life, John Lennon was making waves, forcing a reaction. Wars rage, thousands die and starve, but the statements of Lennon refuse to be silenced.

And somewhere out there, his legend growing ever stronger, is the peripatetic voice of the man whom millions have come to consider a lifelong friend . . . and who said he would like to be remembered 'with a wink'.

This biography was first published in 1984. In Britain, it first appeared as two volumes, *John Winston Lennon* (1940–1966) and *John Ono Lennon* (1967–1980). In the USA it became one volume, entitled *Lennon*, published in 1985.

I began the story at Liverpool Art College because his period there shaped him – behaviourally, romantically, musically. To try to understand the real man, it's important to look not only at the last ten years of his life in New York, but at his Liverpool roots which unfold. Here is the restless rock 'n' roller who would go on to write, in the midst of the flower-power era, pop's most ambitious composition, 'Strawberry Fields Forever'; who in the midst of his drug-induced period of personal experimentation wrote a paean to his dead mother; and who, at forty, could transcend his old barriers of sentimentality to write for his son the song 'Beautiful Boy', a composition Paul McCartney considers one of John's finest.

Mary Elizabeth Smith, known to millions as John Lennon's Aunt Mimi, died on 6 December 1991, at the age of eighty-eight. She had been in poor health for years and died in her sleep at 126 Panorama Road, Poole, Dorset, the home John had bought for her in 1965. It was there that she would sit by the window, overlooking the harbour and the sight-seeing boats that pointed out, by loudspeakers, that they were passing the home of Lennon's famous aunt. And she would wince. For although Mimi was not bashful, she shunned the fame her nephew's notoriety had given her. With her husband, the passive Uncle George, Mimi had raised John from a young boy. 'I just did my job,' she would say so often. 'I wanted nothing to do with that Beatles business.'

While she and John were polar opposites in their make-up — she was authoritarian and strict with discipline; he was a free, poetic spirit — the bond between them was strong, loving, and mutually respectful. Irascible but kindly, Mimi was a woman of unshakeable opinions and principles. She was forthright in her condemnation of John's 'wasted' student years and his hedonistic life as a Beatle, but she gave shelter and breakfast to many fans who camped outside her Liverpool home awaiting a glimpse of him. She would give them train fares home and urged them to phone their worried parents. She was embarrassed by John's public rebelliousness, castigating him when he sent back his MBE medal to the Queen. She disapproved of John's relocation to New York, since she did not trust Americans, she told me. She frequently rejected his offer of a ticket to visit him and never visited John's adopted country.

John admired strong-willed women like Mimi, so it was not surprising that she established a good relationship with Yoko, who flew to Britain with Sean for the funeral at Poole on 12 December. Although Julian did not attend the crematorium ceremony, Cynthia was there to establish a rare moment when John's first and second wives were seen together. Paul McCartney sent a wreath with the message: 'Dear Mimi, it was great to know you in life. You were an exceptional woman and loved by many of us. God bless. Paul, Linda and the children.' There were also floral tributes from George Harrison and Ringo Starr.

With Mimi's passing went a vital link with John Lennon, for nobody knew him so well and so intuitively since his childhood. Although he lived 3,000 miles away for the last ten years of his life, his telephone contact with her remained. She could always stir his conscience with her blend of caustic wit and her irreverence for his fame and fortune. And towards the end of his life, the sentimentalist inside 'tough' John Lennon was often exposed by his admission that he truly hated to upset his aunt. So often, she said, she would wait for his midnight transatlantic phone calls and cherish his predictable farewell: 'Love you, Mimi.'

PROLOGUE

AUNT MIMI, who brought him up, never smacked him; but she long ago lost count of their arguments. They were usually about his studies or homework or the trouble he was getting into because of his terrible discipline at grammar school. Two or three days a week, at about ten o'clock, the phone would ring in her house, Mendips, 251 Menlove Avenue, Woolton, Liverpool.

'Oh Lord,' she'd say under her breath, knowing it was another call from the secretary at Quarry Bank High School. 'What's he done *now?*' John would have been disruptive, or involved in mocking teachers. He was often caned.

'And yet, you know,' said Mimi, 'the main reason he was such a worry to me while he was growing up was because I knew he had *something. He* knew he had it too. But he didn't know where exactly to put this talent he had, or where it might lead him.'

Day after day, Mimi would berate him. The reports coming from school told of his indolence, his trouble-making, and his potential expulsion unless he changed. And every time she scolded him, Lennon would say something like: 'I know what I want to do, and it's not coming from the teachers. It's in *here*.' And he would bang his chest.

'That's all right, dear,' said Mimi, 'but don't neglect your work.' She knew he was right, but she was worried that he would end his schooldays with no qualifications. She was right about that too.

But young Lennon, even from the age of ten, confronted authority. He was simply not interested in orthodox schooling. 'I'm not having people bending over my shoulder, rubbing my work out and telling me it's no good,' he would tell his aunt. But in Mimi Smith he met a dead end. She offered more resistance than any schoolteacher. She loved and cared for John Lennon with a passion and determination that he was not to understand until much later in his life. But she wasn't having her nephew playing a dangerous game with his future.

'The school reports are bad, John. I won't have it. How are you going to get yourself a job if you don't do well at school?'

'But the teachers are so boring, Mimi.' He was good at English, art, and French, awful at arithmetic, and made little effort at anything.

'Go to your room. Go on. Go, John. Do some homework.'

John stood for as long as he dared by the door of the morning-room at Mendips, a semi-detached house in a respectable suburb. Mimi kept it immaculately clean and well furnished. 'You wait,' he said. 'One of these days, I'm going to be famous and then you'll be sorry you were like this to me.'

'All right, then, John. Until that day when you are, get upstairs. Elvis Presley may be a very nice man but I don't want him for breakfast, dinner, and supper.'

Eight years later and after scores of similar scenes with

Mimi, John Lennon went back to Mendips, a successful Beatle, his face, his music, and his personality celebrated throughout the world. She cooked him his favourite: egg and chips and tea.

'He reminded me,' says Mimi, 'of what he'd said at the doorway when he was about sixteen.'

'Remember I said I'd be famous?' he said.

'Well,' said Mimi, thrilled but totally unimpressed. 'What always worried me, John, was that you wouldn't be so much famous as *notorious*. You were certainly *that* as a child. Think of the worries I had. If the Beatles hadn't come along, you could have ended up on the scrap heap without any school qualifications, and you'd soon have got through the bit of money I had.'

'Oh Mimi, if the Beatles hadn't happened I'd always have been able to write or paint or draw.'

She reminded him of her favourite phrase, when she would banish him to the front porch with the £17 guitar she had reluctantly bought him from Hessy's store in Liverpool. He had nagged her when he was sixteen to 'let me get the music bug out of my system.'

'The guitar's all right as a hobby, John, but you'll never make a living from it.'

John replied, 'Well, I can always be an illustrator.'

The castigation, so typical of Mimi in its opinionated certainty, reverberated around the world as the Beatles story gained speed and the legend of Lennon's tough but caring aunt grew stronger.

'He was a worry to educate at school, and he kept telling me he was bored at college. I'd have to lay down the law: "Get on that eight-thirty bus until your time as a student is up, John. *Then* you can mess about with the guitar."'

When he became a pop star and laughed at his aunt's reprimands, John said to her: 'Actually, Mimi, you were quite right. I'd never have made it as a single performer as a guitarist. I was never good enough. But, y'know, I always guessed something would happen. And I met Paul and we met George and — well, it turned out great, didn't it, Mimi?'

ONE

THE REBEL

'Oh God, Buddy Holly's dead'

SHE LOVED him, but the smell of scallops in his hair and on his body drove her crazy. Liverpool scallops were slices of potato surrounded by a greasy, thick batter, dipped into fat, and deep-fried. John Lennon was addicted to them. Most lunchtimes, as a student at Liverpool College of Art, he crossed the road to the chip shop in Falkner Street and piled himself up with a bag of chips and a bag of scallops. He would take them back to one of the classrooms, perhaps play the guitar while eating, and enthral a few students. The gentleness of his playing contrasted vividly with his hell-raising personality. To many students, this reprobate seventeen-year-old was absolutely magnetic.

But he stank. 'It permeated from his head, through his clothes, and his entire body reeked of greasy scallops,' recalls Helen Anderson, one of the students who adored the 'lovable swine' who dressed like a teddy boy. She nagged him to wash the grease out of his hair and get rid of the DA ('duck's arse') style at the back. 'Get lost,' Lennon would snap. The greased-back hair, DA at the rear, sideburns, drape jackets, crepe-soled shoes, tatty checked shirt, and drainpipe trousers, all based on Elvis Presley whom he regarded as the king, were central to Lennon's personality.

For they made him stand out from the rest of the students. Nothing was more important to him than individuality.

Helen Anderson had a unique, direct line to John Lennon's thoughts: he would confide in her about his love affairs. She was a patient listener and admirer of his wit, and since there was never any suggestion that they would become lovers she became a platonic friend and confidante.

She possessed a major attraction for John Lennon. At sixteen, she had actually *met* a pop star of the day, Lonnie Donegan, whom she had painted in oils for the astronomical fee of £50. There had been stories in the newspapers about her artistic talent. 'Hey, are you that bird who painted Lonnie Donegan?' John asked her on her first day at art school. He was impressed.

As John's undisciplined, hilarious behaviour made more of an impact on her, Helen would go home and tell her mother every day about John's crazy antics that had broken up the class. She demonstrated how John crept up behind people and suddenly boomed one of his favourite songs into their ear. It was Screaming Jay Hawkins's hit, 'I Put A Spell On You'. Helen and John's special friendship was sealed when he regularly gave her his trousers to narrow the legs into drainpipe style. 'Take these in for me, would you, Heloon, they're too bloody wide.' (Heloon was his nickname for her because she always laughed uproariously at his outrageous behaviour.) Dutifully, she often took John's black trousers home and returned them next morning tapered. The 'drainies' were worn *underneath* his 'regulation shape' trousers until he reached the bus stop on his way to college, where he slipped them off. That way, his Aunt Mimi would not see over breakfast that he was a latent 'ted'. He had to find many similar methods of fending off her wrath about his untidy appearance.

Those who were at art college with John Lennon are

unanimous: he was destined to be a great public figure, a triumphant star with unique gifts, or else he would be a layabout, a burden on society who achieved nothing. There would be no halfway for this extraordinary teenager who roared through Liverpool, making an impact on everybody who was willing to be touched by him.

'Even at sixteen I knew he was destined to some sort of grandeur and greatness,' says Helen Anderson. 'In his first six months at college, his paintings were very wild and aggressive. Every one he did incorporated the interior of a night club and they were very strongly drawn, very dark, and there was always a blonde girl sitting at the bar looking like Brigitte Bardot. There were always musicians in John's early drawings, a band on a bandstand, dim lights, something sleazy. I always liked them. But very few people noticed his work in his early days at college.'

To the teachers Lennon was a pest, a danger. His work, erratically presented, was the last thing they worried about. It was his behaviour as a catalyst for trouble in every classroom that they outlawed in unison. Eventually, Lennon and the masters became polarized, just as they had done at his previous school, Quarry Bank High School, Woolton. The more they bored him with their orthodox, predictable, unyielding methods of education which he abhorred, the more he would seek his own route. 'The masters were not interested in him,' says Helen Anderson. 'He was a nuisance to the entire college, distracting everybody else who wanted to learn.'

Lennon didn't care. He had his gang, camp followers like the laconically funny Geoff Mohammed, who was a perfect foil for John's pungent humour. There was Tony Carricker, who joined in the crowd who laughed almost non-stop at John's ribaldry. And there was even June Furlong, the twenty-seven-year-old model who was the subject of the life class in which they would all have to draw her body. Even she became convulsed with laughter on many days when she was supposed to be a serious art subject. Lennon discovered early in his teen years what was to be one of his most endearing characteristics when he was in deep trouble; he could always make people laugh with his very distinctive, cruel, exploitative sense of humour.

In the very warm life class of room 71 at the college, fifteen students were set their weekly task of drawing June. Some would doze off when the teacher left the room. Suddenly Lennon would give out a little giggle. Nobody would take much notice. Two or three minutes later, his giggle would be louder. That would disturb people, especially those trying to concentrate on drawing. A real laugh followed, and a few minutes later his loud, hyena-like cackle totally broke up the class. By then everyone was hysterical at John's calculated disruption. To top it off, Lennon then jumped out from behind his easel, ran into the middle of the room where June was sitting, naked, rocking with laughter and trying to stop her body from shaking for the benefit of the students who wanted to continue to draw it. Finally, for his *pièce de résistance*, Lennon brought laughter to the entire class by leaping around the room where silence and decorum were the rule.

During another life class session, the whole class produced proper drawings of the model which were soberly dissected by the teacher, Teddy Griffiths. When John came to hand in his effort, he had perversely drawn nothing of June. He produced a drawing of the only item on June's body – her wristwatch. Students were aghast at his nerve and originality.

While John's eccentric behaviour, non-conformist dress, and swearing in front of the teachers were enough to make him prominent, a less rational, disturbing side to his character emerged soon after he joined the art college. He quickly developed a bizarre obsession for cripples, spastics, any human deformities, and people on crutches. He had a particular fascination for warts. It was a subject that was to manifest itself through John Lennon's years of fame. It took root, firmly and with a gaggle of students embarrassed at their own sick sense of humour in laughing at him, here at art college.

Deformities cropped up in his drawings all the time. So did his dry wit, the quality that dominated his personality. For a seventeen-year-old he had a subtle sense of humour way ahead of his time. There was always life and movement in his drawings, to redeem that streak of cruelty. Every person he portrayed had a physical affliction, usually a wart sticking out of the side of the head. Asked why, John would shrug it off, with the implication that if you had to ask, you weren't on his wavelength, so there was no point in discussing it.

By 1958, in his eighteenth year, with all the guns blazing at the art college which bestowed upon him lots of freedom in dress and demeanour, but which was unsuccessfully grappling on all fronts with his wildness, John Lennon could not be missed. He was desperately short-sighted, which somehow added to his mystique among the girls. He wore teddy boy clothes, and his black horn-rimmed spectacles, worn only under the greatest pressure, for he had an ego, were held together at the joints by Elastoplast. He rarely had any money and borrowed it permanently from his gang. He scrounged cigarettes all the time, somehow managing to get through between ten and twenty Woodbines a day. He drank too many pints, usually black velvets, in Ye Cracke, the students' pub in Rice Street near the college, and since he could not take much beer without feeling its effects, he frequently behaved either obnoxiously or violently. He kept losing his artist's materials and would constantly ask his Aunt Mimi for more money on the pretext of needing a new pen or other equipment.

He was a startlingly talented, non-conforming artist, but so lazy that even his close college friend, the serious intellectual Stuart Sutcliffe, could not drag John's attributes into line and get him properly on course. Music, rock 'n' roll, Elvis Presley, Chuck Berry, Little Richard — it was all too much of a pull for Lennon, who would stalk the college with a guitar strapped to his back, ready for the lunchtime sessions over scallops and chips in Arthur Ballard's classroom with two other kids from the more academic Liverpool Institute next door. Their names were Paul McCartney and George Harrison.

On 4 February 1959 John walked solemnly into the classroom, visibly shaken. It was not often that students saw Lennon vulnerable, broken, unhappy. 'Oh God, Buddy Holly's dead,' he muttered. Holly, a vital pioneer of early rock 'n' roll, a singer of plaintive love songs wedded to jerky, haunting melodies, was one of John's idols. He had died in a plane crash in America. Unlike many of the students, John did not cry over the news, but went silent for the day and took some time to snap out of the shock. Lennon always buried his feelings deeply.

It was the third great emotional death to mark John's life, and he was still only eighteen. Seven months before Buddy Holly's death John's mother, Julia Lennon, had died instantly at the age of forty-four after being knocked down by a car when leaving the home of John's Aunt Mimi, with whom John was living. The death of Uncle George, Mimi's husband, who doted on John and had bathed him, protected him, and been a warm and loving father-figure during his childhood, had rocked John at the age of fourteen. And now, just as John was getting inspiration from Buddy Holly, and totally absorbing the wonderful, embryonic sounds of American rock 'n' roll music, it was like another death in the family.

For the teenager who had come from a broken home, despite all his natural inner orthodoxy, respect, and sentimentality, there seemed only one way to get through his early life after eighteen years punctuated by physical fights and emotional scars. That was to erect a cocoon of belligerence, aggression, sick or vicious wit, and castigation. The real John Lennon, from his birth until his death, was a vastly misunderstood man. His drawings and his spoken word may have injured or hurt, and he was capable of wounding with pertinent jibes that shot straight through the heart of the victim. But he always aimed his arrows at people he could not respect, and beneath that abrasive exterior beat a heart of pure gold. Eventually, it was to come out in his music as he mushroomed into one of popular music's most beloved, searingly honest artists who, more than anyone else in his field, wore his heart, as well as his art, on his sleeve. In 1959 the personality of John Lennon was changing quickly, but the world had not heard of him. A few were privileged to see the man shaped by his own grit as he rampaged through first Quarry Bank High School and then made an indelible mark on Liverpool College of Art before becoming an emblem for youth: artist, poet, and philosopher. The family, students, and friends who saw John Lennon as a schoolboy and teenager testify to one undeniable fact that marked him then as it marked his entire life: you could loathe him or like him. But you could never feel neutral about him. And you certainly could not ignore him.

Cynthia Powell knew that she had fallen helplessly in love
with John Lennon when, one day in the art college lecture
hall, she noticed one of her closest friends, Helen Anderson,
apparently stroking John's hair. Helen was sitting immediately behind John; Cynthia, a few seats away, began trem-
bling with jealousy at the sight of another girl touching
him.

To this day Cynthia believes that Helen and John were
romantically linked, at the very least. Helen denies it. She
was part of a coterie of Lennon college friends who formed
his essential audience. Helen says she was not fondling
John. Instead she was trying to straighten out his DA
hairstyle which she hated. But the fact that Helen cared
enough to make her presence known to John, and the banter
between them, was enough to arouse Cynthia's envy.

A year older than John, and a serious, formal art student, Cynthia Powell seemed theoretically, to other
students, the unlikeliest choice for a loud-mouthed, troublemaking teddy boy who was roaring through art college in
the days when words like beatnik and bohemian evoked
images of dangerous living. She lived her life, particularly
at college, 'by the book', as a conscientious, ambitious
student. But Cynthia had four key attractions that were to
attract John. First, she had the potential in his eyes to look
like Brigitte Bardot, his strongest fancy. Many of his previous girlfriends had to bow to his demand: 'Grow your
hair long, like Brigitte.' He would do drawings for them
of how they were expected to look. One student, Joni
Crosby, looked even more like Bardot, and Lennon drooled
over her in the canteen. During tea break he said to Helen
Anderson, day after day: 'Bloody hell – she's fantastic – just
like Brigitte Bardot.' Second, Cynthia came from snooty
Hoylake, 'over the water' on the Wirral, and 'spoke posh,
talked proper,' which he believed made her unattainable to

a lad from Woolton. Third, she was plainly besotted over him and would do anything to please him, even dye her brown hair blonde and grow it long. Fourth, and crucially, she was serene. As an eighteen-year-old art student, Cynthia had a composure that marked her out from the others in college. Lennon, the college performer who strove to make an impression by cackling in class, smoking when it was against the rules, and bucking the system at every twist and turn, was chemically attracted to Cynthia because she was supercool and different. *Vive la différence* was a character-istic that was to *drive* Lennon all his life. The orthodox and the predictable usually bored him, although he always clung strongly to traditional values in human relationships and family life.

Cynthia and John had two other important things in common. Cynthia was fatherless, her commercial traveller father having died when she was seventeen, so, like John, she knew the burdens of being a teenager with one parent; and Cynthia was, like John, hopelessly short-sighted and wore spectacles. But in his earliest days at college, he played her attractiveness to him very cool and hung around with other girl students on a platonic basis.

In the tradition of the freewheeling student, John and two college girls, Helen Anderson and Ann Sherwood, spent afternoons drifting across the ferry from Pier Head to Seac-ombe. This route was chosen because it was the cheapest boat; when they arrived they would walk the three miles down the promenade or along the sands to New Brighton, with John playing the role of entertainer. 'Be funny, John!' 'Sing us a song, John!' they asked him. And John, his guitar slung across his black jacket, would love being the clown, the star of the show, for Helen and Ann. The girls had dutifully done the work Arthur Ballard had set them, and the afternoons were free for them. John told them he could not be bothered to do his work, so needed no persuading to have a musical day at the seaside.

Musically, his repertoire was funny but thin. 'He only strummed his guitar. It was obvious he wasn't much of a player then,' says Helen Anderson. His songs included Buddy Holly and Little Richard with a little Elvis Presley thrown in. He'd ad lib with everyday phrases and extemporize on the songs that he was to be heard jokingly playing around with in classes: he'd wander around looking over people's shoulders at their work, mumbling 'Sugar In The Morning, Sugar In The Evening, Sugar At Suppertime', 'When You're Smiling', and the one everyone laughed at:

> I like New York in June, how about you?
> I like a Lennon tune, how about you?
> Holding Rabbis in the movie show, when all the
> Lights are low, may not be new, but I like it,
> How about you?

Says Helen Anderson: 'He definitely had a thing about Jews and loved taking the mickey out of them. The slightest chance to work them into a song and make it funny, he'd take it. But it wasn't nearly so cruel as his thing about cripples and afflicted people.'

In 1958, as John Lennon swept through art college, world events that were changing a post-war Britain from uncertainty into prosperity were making an enormous impact on young people. Khrushchev became Russia's premier, marking the start of a cold war; the first transatlantic commercial jet service began; and an aeroplane crashed on take-off in Munich, Germany, killing twenty-three passengers including eight Manchester United footballers. There were terrible race riots in London's Notting Hill, the first serious riots of their kind; General de Gaulle was forming his first French government; and magical, influential pop music names like Elvis Presley ('Jailhouse Rock'), Jerry Lee Lewis ('Great Balls Of Fire'), the Everly Brothers ('All I Have To Do Is Dream'), the Coasters ('Yakety Yak'), and the Teddy Bears ('To Know Him Is To Love Him') were forging a vital new impact for British pop music fans who listened to it in bed under their blankets on the barely audible, but adventurously hip, Radio Luxembourg.

The following year the M1 became Britain's first motorway, to presage a new era of speed and travel; the giant E.M.I. Records discontinued the use of 78 r.p.m. records in favour of 45 r.p.m. singles; and history was made by ten thousand members of the Campaign for Nuclear Disarmament marching from Aldermaston to London, the biggest demonstration of its kind until then. Musically, there was lots for Lennon and his friends to drool over, including Buddy Holly's 'It Doesn't Matter Any More', and Elvis Presley's 'I Got Stung'. Against all the good sounds that were grasped by Lennon, he developed an instinctive hatred for what he regarded as the bland, antiseptic music of new British stars like Cliff Richard, Adam Faith, and Craig Douglas.

The Lennon of these years, torn inside by a fractured family life, did not suffer fools. He was a young man in a hurry. But he did not know his destination. What he did recognize, immediately he felt it, was love. He had had torrid relationships with girls before he met Cynthia Powell. But with her, something else gelled to make her his automatic and serious partner. With the arrogance that characterized him, he accepted that she was, in the words of Helen Anderson, nutty about him and prepared to be used as a doormat, to please John's every whim and lend him her art materials. But no, to John that wasn't all: many girls were ready to be servile towards him, to laugh at his weakest jokes and physically titillate him in his quest to learn everything about sex during an era when it was taboo among teenagers. Cynthia offered much, much more than those attractions to which he had become accustomed. From Cynthia came also intelligence and the great, unspoken heatwave that was to make them inseparable for about eight years: love, understanding, care, and devotion. John returned it, for, with the death of his mother and the desertion of his father, the need for an anchor to his life was much more real than might have been apparent to the students who saw him as a court jester. All he needed was love, music, an escape route from the humdrum, routine, wage-earning future that many of his contemporaries seemed to regard as inevitable. To John Lennon, even at seventeen, nothing was inevitable. Deep down inside, he saw himself as special. His method of saying so was to project a rough and tough exterior, because he had no platform or power to do anything about it. Yet physically, mentally, and because her tranquillity offered a useful anti-dote to his excesses, Cynthia was his perfect partner.

Reflecting on those years, Cynthia is in love not merely with John – whom she will love to distraction until the day she dies – but with the sweet, innocent, yet passionate romance of the college years together. 'He had a strange fascination for many of the girls, like Helen Anderson and Thelma Pickles,' says Cynthia. 'He wasn't the sort of chap you'd swoon over. What concerned me, and drew me to him at first, was that he was so lazy about his work. He didn't give a damn and I got worried, being a conscientious type, that he would get into trouble and get kicked out of college. Everyone knew that he was in art college on suffer-ance. No teachers wanted him there, except Arthur Ballard, who was a similarly artistic type and saw some potential in

John. I cared more about his future and his work than he did. I saw in John so much talent, as an artist, but if he got chucked out of college, which was likely, where would he go? I was a lot older than him, mentally.'

The story of their first encounters sounds like fiction but is fact. Cynthia, in her second year at art college, was among a dozen students who had chosen to attend lettering class twice a week. Everyone there felt positive about the subject, except John Winston Lennon. He quickly became the talk of the class because he had been shoved there through a series of rejections by teachers who had grown tired of his disruptiveness in other classes. Lennon was not a candidate for the lettering class, either; his natural style was to draw cartoons of whatever his teachers had ordered.

Cynthia remembers that the two lettering class days, on which she would study John, became her 'fix'. For the rest of the week they were separated during studying hours, and she would roam the corridors of the college hoping for a glimpse of the boy who was the unruly focal point of the students but who had become her obsession. It was all too much for a conventional girl from Hoylake who already had a steady boyfriend who was saving for their future with a building society.

To be hooked on Lennon was also slightly dangerous because of his notoriety. 'On lettering days he always arrived late, anything up to half an hour,' says Cynthia. 'He looked a mess. He had scruffy black trousers, quiffed hair with a slight DA at the back, and it was an attempt to look like a teddy boy. But often, even though he was late, he'd have a screwed-up drawing under his arm to present to the teacher. And it would get him off the hook, in a way. Arthur Ballard would hold it up to the class and say: "Now look, this is the kind of original idea and inspiration we're looking for." ' The fact that it was unrelated to lettering didn't matter. Lennon had quickly found a way to buck the system.

'After I'd first experienced John in lettering,' says Cynthia, 'I couldn't get him out of my mind.' On lettering days she would arrive in the classroom earlier than anyone else to sit near where he had been sitting in the previous lesson. What finally drove them together was a playful test, among all the students one morning, of each other's eyesight. 'We had identical short-sightedness, and when we started talking about what we couldn't see – like when the bus was coming – we took off,' says Cynthia. Major romances have been built on stranger events, but for Cynthia Powell the moment of that discovery was magical. She blessed her disability, for her passion for the wild one was now all-consuming.

Still, she thought that she, with her short, permed brown hair, tweedy skirt, twinset, and Hoylake image, was too proper for Lennon. Cynthia could not see her attractiveness to him adding up to much. She loaned him materials during lettering; she had similarly bad eyesight; and he was always a fraction more polite to her than he was to the other students. But that was all. Her teenage crush seemed to offer no way out.

But fate smiled on her. As the college's vacation loomed for the summer of 1958, one of the students thought it would be fun to have a lunchtime end-of-term party. They got permission to use the smallest room in the college, and one of them brought a record player. That year's hits were the Everly Brothers' 'All I Have To Do Is Dream', Conway Twitty's 'It's Only Make Believe', and 'Tom Dooley' by the Kingston Trio. Cynthia's eyes rarely left Lennon at that party, but she had teenage blushes of embarrassment at herself, too. When John walked over and asked her to dance, slowly, to the song 'To Know Him Is To Love Him' by the Teddy Bears, she nearly collapsed with excitement. 'I think John was slightly embarrassed too, which was unusual for him,' she says. 'Perhaps he knew what was happening to us. It was painful and beautiful.' The other students looked on amazed at the unlikely combination.

As the party began to break up, John asked Cynthia if she was involved with another man. He said he'd like to meet her, out of college.

'I'm awfully sorry,' Cynthia said. 'I'm engaged to this fellow in Hoylake.'

John's retort to this was: 'I didn't ask you to marry me, did I?'

Cynthia, flustered, thought she had let him slip through her fingers, for the Lennon reply seemed cutting and final. But he wasn't as dismissive as she feared. He said to Cynthia and her best friend, Phyllis McKenzie: 'Let's go and have a drink.'

Cynthia and Phyllis had never before been to the college boozer, Ye Cracke. Here, black velvets were drunk and Woodbines smoked most lunchtimes by hard-up Lennon, surrounded by his cronies. To Cynthia and Phyllis, adjourning from college to anything other than the train and bus home wasn't done; but suddenly Cynthia understood what college life was supposed to be like. Lennon was, however, still far away in the crowd of men and made no attempt to chat her up in the bar, so she began to leave. She thought the dance with John, and the drink, probably marked the start and end of their relationship.

As she neared the door, Lennon's voice boomed out above the pub chat: 'Didn't you know Miss Powell was a nun, then?' It was a typically Lennonesque dig at her propriety. She spun round, their eyes met, and she walked over to his side. He persuaded her to stay. Both had had a few too many drinks and little to eat during the day when so much had happened. As the drinking session continued, it was obvious that John Lennon and Cynthia Powell were going to be together.

That night, they left the pub and spent all night together at the rented bedsitter in Gambier Terrace, a convenient two-minute walk from college, of John's best college friend, the serious-minded Stuart Sutcliffe, to whom Lennon turned when he tired of the audience of students who simply wanted him to act funny. Increasingly, John and Stuart became very close. There was never any discussion about what they had in common: it was intuitive. Sutcliffe and Lennon bounced off each other because they had the same speed of thought, restlessness, and a natural talent. In Stuart's case, though, it was a talent he marshalled and nursed.

Three months older than John, Stuart was a model student, a star pupil, and he wanted to become a famous painter. His drawings of skulls and skeletons, particularly, were outstanding and attracted Lennon's interest in the macabre. A year ahead of John in college, Stuart was concentrating on painting and sculpture and worked long, arduous hours. 'He was very spotty with horn-rimmed glasses and, just like John's, they were taped up at the edges,' recalls Cynthia. 'As a student, he was precisely the opposite of John, because he was working himself to death, totally dedicated. He wasn't eating properly and didn't have much to do with girls. His work was all-important to him.'

As Stuart and John became more friendly, Sutcliffe became more of a leveller to Lennon. 'John needed Stuart really badly,' says Cynthia. 'He was going down the wrong road with these two characters, Tony Carricker and Geoff Mohammed, and he probably realized it because John wasn't stupid. It was Stuart who persuaded John to concentrate more on his art and less on messing about. When John saw

Stuart's work, he was inspired by it. He started painting a lot more seriously himself, slapping great canvases around. Before, he had been working too tightly on little cartoons and on smaller areas. Suddenly, Stuart drew him into the painting rooms often and John at last had a mate to help show him the way. After college, Stuart would stay on and say to John: "Don't worry about it. Just slap it on, a bit here, a bit there," whereas John had always been very wary and careful and detailed. Stuart was great fun in art and their minds were right for each other. John obviously looked up to him, and he was bringing John out as an artist.'

But it was too late to hold John back from what was becoming his major interest: music.

Strong though Stuart was in trying to pull John towards serious work, Lennon had by now reached the point of no return. If a lesson or a day went by without his causing mirth in the classroom, he would have been diagnosed ill by those who were expecting him to perform.

'He was the biggest micky-taker I've met,' says Helen Anderson. 'He picked on all kinds of characters in school, whatever their backgrounds, and tried to find some way of laughing at them. There was one awfully nice, well brought-up fellow with frizzy red hair, whom John persisted in annoying by calling him Snodgrass and making everyone laugh. John wouldn't let go of something once it stuck with him: "Snoddy" this and "Snoddy" that, to the annoyance of this very straight student. Another poor student named Derek had the habit of picking his nose in front of everybody and didn't realize he was doing it. We'd be in the middle of a lesson, with everybody silent, and suddenly John would scream out at the top of his voice: "Dirty picky nosey, Derek!" Of course it broke up the class. We all fell about laughing.

'He used to make horrible jokes against the singer Alma Cogan, impersonating her singing "Sugar In The Morning, Sugar In The Evening, Sugar At Suppertime". He'd pull crazy expressions on his face to try to imitate her expressions. We all had hysterics. He was a real comedian.*

'We could always tell when he was about to come out with a gem of a joke or a phrase,' says Helen Anderson. 'His nostrils and cheeks would swell up. He was such a wit, he made an impression on everybody in the whole college. But contrary to what Cynthia believed, I loved him and adored him but never fancied him.' He was a natural comic, but in a style that wasn't expected. When students asked his name, when he first arrived at art college, he would say: 'Simply Simple Pimple. John Wimple Lennon.' He would preen a little when he gave his real middle name of Winston – not because he felt nationalistic about having been named after Britain's great wartime prime minister, Winston Churchill, but because it sounded posh and was different and unexpected.

Stories of his outlandish college behaviour abound. One panto day, the annual event for which the students dressed up and went around the city shaking collection boxes for charities, seven students got together to dress up. John roped in Paul McCartney and George Harrison from the Liverpool Institute next door, together with Ann Preece, Rod Murray, Helen Anderson, and Mona Harris. At John's instigation, he and Paul and George were to dress up as vicars. They found yellow sweatshirts which they wore upside-down with their legs inside the sleeves, and dog

* When the Beatles became famous, John was to become friendly with Alma Cogan and visit her home.

collars with black tailcoats. The Lennon plan was to 'raid'
every café in every department store in Liverpool. They
marched in shaking their tins and everybody would turn
round to look. Within a few minutes John would stand up
on a table and shout: 'My lords, ladies, and gentlemen. On
my right, in the red corner . . .' and Paul would jump up.
'And on my left, in the blue corner . . .' and George would
come out. The two would start fighting on restaurant tables,
in every chain store, to attract attention. And they were
ceremonially thrown out of every place they entered – but
not before raising a few pounds by the sheer noise and
audacity of their stunt.

Later that day the students went to the city's Adelphi
Hotel, where John persuaded the staff to lend him a bucket
and a mop. A crowd of several hundred gathered outside
the hotel to watch Lennon, still dressed as a vicar, singing
loudly and mopping the zebra crossing. He was the star
turn; the others were giving him moral support, loudly and
successfully, and shaking their tins.

The light, undisciplined atmosphere of college life
greatly appealed to John. After the formality of his previous
school, where he had trouble fighting the system and had
been an academic disaster, art college at least seemed to
give him the chance to behave as a young adult. There was
the array of pretty girls, many of whom looked on him as
a card as well as a rebel; there was encouragement from
Arthur Ballard, who, even though he didn't care for John's
refractory style, knew the boy had something and did his
utmost to encourage him; there was the security of the
gang of Geoff Mohammed and Tony Carricker and Jeff
Cane. There was, eventually, Cynthia with whom he had a
fast-moving love affair.

'Before me,' says Cynthia, 'there was another girl he
mentioned to me named Beth whom he was pretty serious

about. But her parents couldn't stand John. He kept saying to me: "Don't worry, they've banned me from seeing her anyway, they think I'm a ruffian. They won't have me round." ' Lennon had met her when he was fifteen and a pupil of Quarry Bank High School. The fact that he talked openly about her infuriated Cynthia during their early romance and reached breaking-point when, one night, he did not arrive for their nightly meeting. 'He quickly admitted he'd been to see Beth, to see if it was finished between them, and it was definitely all over and we were together.'

Unknown to Cynthia, there were other girls in John's life before their romance blossomed, and during their love match John would vanish from the college on some afternoons and go off with them. One of his gang would support him by spinning a story about where John had gone. Lennon frequently found himself arm in arm with a casual girlfriend walking back to college and suddenly went into a panic at the sight of Cynthia. He would flee round the corner in case she saw him. Outwardly sharp-tongued and tough though he was, even at that age Lennon did not want to hurt Cynthia, whom he quickly christened Cyn. She was on a pedestal, classier than any of the other girls with whom he had quickie affairs, and the last thing that could be risked was Cynthia discovering his unfaithfulness. Cynthia would remain blissfully unaware that there was any other heavy romance for John in his college days . . . which is exactly what John wanted her to believe.

With Stuart fast emerging as his bosom mate, and trying in vain to pull him solidly into art as a career; Cynthia having a powerful love affair with him and meeting him whenever she could; and the teachers throwing up their hands in dismay at the eighteen-year-old who wouldn't listen, John Lennon in 1958 was a complex, talented young man. His restless mood was partly summed up by the way he moved around. 'He gave off this feeling that he was already battling through life, even at eighteen,' says Cynthia. 'Whenever he was going anywhere or doing anything, he walked like lightning, as if he was being shot from an arrow. It was a kind of panic. He would look round as if someone was chasing him. He staggered, quickly, as though he believed that if he moved quickly, people might miss him.

'Those of us who loved him for his lunacy and his cutting remarks realized that inside John was a lot more than he was showing. It was trying to get out and hadn't found the right way. The teachers couldn't care less because they just judged his appearance and his track record, which wasn't very good. And they feared him because they didn't understand him. Stuart was intelligent enough to see something special in John. I did, and so did just a few of the girls at college. But the people who realized he was destined to be either a giant or a bum were few and far between in those days. Most people thought he was a dangerous, loud-mouthed, troublemaking layabout. He really needed his friends.'

The key to understanding the psyche of the errant teenager who arrived at Liverpool College of Art lies in his wounded childhood. Years later, he was to recapture the pain of those years with songs that spine-chillingly re-enacted the tensions of his early agonies. But the real pressure of nursing John Winston Lennon through his first twenty-two years of problems, while all the time believing that he had a special talent and ought eventually to 'go places', fell to one woman, Mary Elizabeth Smith, John's Aunt Mimi.

John's father, Alfred Lennon, was away from Liverpool at the time of his son's birth. He worked as a ship's steward, and his adventurous, romantic work, coupled with his care-free attitude to life which took him on passenger liners to otherwise unattainable places like New York, is what attracted John's mother to him. The son of a freight clerk, Alfred Lennon – Freddy to his friends – was born at 57 Copperfield Street, Toxteth Park, on 14 December 1912. He was one of five brothers and had one sister.

John's mother, Julia – known in her family as Juliet – was born on 12 March 1914, the youngest of five daughters of George Ernest Stanley, and Annie (née Millward). Julia was a cinema usherette before she married Freddy on 3 December 1938.

Named John after his paternal grandfather, he had a decidedly Irish heritage. Lennon is the anglicized version of O'Leannain, a clan strong in the Galway, Fermanagh, and Cork areas of southern Ireland. John's grandfather went to Liverpool from Ireland, as many did in the mid-nine-teenth century, to seek better prospects of work in an England that was becoming industrialized faster than their own country. Born in Dublin in the 1850s, grandfather John Lennon – nicknamed Jack – was an occasional singer who spent some years singing in a group in America. At the age of nine, in 1921, Freddy Lennon became an orphan when his father died of a diseased liver. Freddy went to the Bluecoat orphanage in Liverpool.

Julia and Mimi's father was an official with the Glasgow and Liverpool Salvage Company and often travelled on sal-vage work, retrieving submarines from the bottom of the Atlantic. His father had been a musician. Julia's mother, Annie, was the daughter of a solicitor's clerk; in the jobless Liverpool of the 1930s, a family like this was, for Julia and Mimi, something to be treasured, to be proud of, to mark out your values and aspirations. Compared with thousands of Merseyside people, they came from a privileged background.

Auburn-haired, slim, and vivacious, Julia was attracted to Freddy by one major characteristic their personalities had in common: they were both fun-loving and carefree. A year after their marriage at Mount Pleasant Register Office, Freddy was on the high seas as a head waiter, eventually berthing at New York. 'Freddy was a ship's steward on troop ships carrying soldiers between Liverpool and Southampton and France,' says Charles Lennon, his brother and John's uncle. 'They also went over to Canada to bring troops back.' He returned home for the Christmas of that year but was soon off again, and was jailed when one boat on which he sailed reached North Africa and he was accused of stealing a bottle of vodka. Erratically, he wrote home to Julia from his ships saying he was doing well, singing songs like 'Begin The Beguine' during crew concerts; but his absence during these dark war years was placing an impossible strain on their marriage. In one letter, he wrote to Julia saying his date of return was uncertain, and he suggested she should get out and enjoy herself and not sit around and mope.

Known throughout Julia's family as 'that Alf Lennon', he was considered 'not good enough' for her. And since Julia was having misgivings about the marriage, he should not have been surprised at the outcome of his message of 'freedom' to her. Julia's lively personality was matched by her attractiveness; she was a diminutive (five feet, two inches) but effervescent bundle of energy with beautiful hair at shoulder length.

Freddy's leave had become erratic anyway, and his work as a ship's steward often found him in tight scrapes when he went ashore; his letters home eventually became infrequent, and when payments to Julia from his shipping line ceased, the writing was on the wall for her.

In 1944, with Freddy still away, Julia met a young Army officer home on leave during a period when she worked as a waitress at a café in Penny Lane. She became pregnant by him; the father-to-be disappeared back into his Service, never to be heard from again. At this time, she and four-year-old John were living at her father's home. A daughter, whom she named Victoria Elizabeth, was born on 19 June 1945. The father's name is not listed on the birth certificate. At Julia's father's suggestion, the infant was adopted and is believed to have been taken by her guardians to Norway. No member of the Lennon family has heard from Victoria, who possibly does not realize that she is John Lennon's half-sister.

Shortly after Victoria's birth, Julia established a more serious and tangible love affair. John Dykins, a hotel waiter, was initially condemned alongside 'Alf' as unsuitable for Julia. Her sisters (Mimi, Elizabeth [nicknamed Mater], Anne, and Harriet) disapproved partly because Julia was not divorced, and they sceptically believed she was making yet another big error.

But Julia was as decisive as she was headstrong. Dykins, whom she nicknamed Bobby, moved with her and young John into a tiny, one-bedroomed flat in the Gateacre area of Liverpool. The family was stunned, and Mimi as the senior sister was their spokeswoman. She took the bus over to Julia and Bobby's home one weekend and demanded that the child be handed over to her, since Julia was not in a position to bring up a child. Mimi cited the birth of Victoria, plus Julia's financial position, as evidence of how John needed more stability. But neither Julia nor her lover accepted this, and Dykins was firm to Mimi: the boy was Julia's to decide on, he asserted.

But after a visit from a social worker (with Mimi) and another from Liverpool's social services department, Julia was told that her accommodation was inadequate: John did not have his own bedroom and was sleeping with her. He would have to go until she found a bigger flat. And so John was welcomed to the middle-class, very comfortable home of kind Uncle George and stern Aunt Mimi – Mendips, at 251 Menlove Avenue, Woolton.

Mimi treasured her nephew, and her husband 'thought John had been put here entirely for his pleasure,' she said. With no children of their own, they gave John a welcome fit for a king at the house around the corner from where George ran a dairy farm. John's pre-school years here were idyllic: his uncle would take him early in the morning on some days to see his cows being milked.

In July 1946, Freddy Lennon suddenly reappeared in an attempt to patch up his marriage and reclaim his son. He arrived at Mimi's house and persuaded her and John to let him take his son to Blackpool for the day. Walking John on the Blackpool sands, his father asked John what he wanted to be when he grew up. John answered: 'Prime minister, or on the stage.'

Freddy had a vague plan to take him to New Zealand and start a new life there, but it was a plan that went horribly wrong. When Freddy did not return to Mimi with John after several days, Julia found out where he was and arrived, unannounced, in Blackpool. She said bluntly that she wanted John back; she had set up a new home with a new man, and, she insisted, could offer John a better childhood than Freddy. The uncertainty of his father's life at sea was no substitute for what Mimi and she could offer.

The scene that followed in that Blackpool boarding house was traumatic for a five-year-old. By then he had got used to a comfortable family pattern: he lived with Mimi, but every day Julia would visit her son at Menlove Avenue. Gradually, he started to understand and come to terms with the situation, developing a rapport with his exuberant mother as well as a deep mutual affection with Mimi. 'Mimi' and 'Mummy' ran well together as the two women in his life; Uncle George was there as a benevolent, kindly man, an anchor, something of a substitute father.

One day, John said to his aunt: 'Why can't I call you Mummy?'

She answered: 'Well you couldn't very well have *two* Mummies, could you?'

Now, with his real parents arguing before his eyes over who was to have him, young John Winston Lennon was emotionally wracked. He had always hoped for the return of his father from seafaring, and Pater, as he called him, had given him a good time in Blackpool, romping in the sands every day. But his mother had been more constant than his father in his young life. Here, now, was a hideous tug-of-war.

It was Freddy who put John in the most hopeless situation. 'You have to decide if you want to stay with me or with Mummy.'

A tearful John replied: 'I'll stay with you.'

Julia intervened: 'Now John, are you sure about that? Do you want to go to another country with him, or will you stay here with me?'

'With Daddy,' sobbed John, tears pouring down his cheeks.

Freddy was triumphant and said to his wife: 'That's enough, Julia, you've had your answer. Leave him alone.' Freddy had already unsuccessfully tried to woo Julia back from the happiness she was enjoying with her new man.

Despite all her inner torment, and with the tears welling up inside her, Julia decided it was all over. She turned round and walked out of the door of the boarding house. She had lost her son.

When the door closed, the finality of his mother's departure and the uncertainty of a future with his father were too much for John. He ran after his mother, crying uncontrollably, and eventually found her in the street. 'Mummy, Mummy, don't go, don't go.'

They hugged each other in the Blackpool street, and Julia delivered him back to Liverpool, safe into the loving arms of her sister Mimi, who was to care for him with conscientiousness, strictness — and passion. Julia was so excited at having her son back that she forgot to get a train ticket at Blackpool and was apprehended by police when she arrived back at Lime Street Station. She explained her predicament and returned the next day with the money. Mimi's life, and much of Uncle George's, now centred totally on the little lad who had survived so much and who, soon after she had sent him at the age of five to Dovedale Road Primary School, had been described to her by the headmaster, Mr Evans, as 'sharp as a needle'.

Even at this age, John's character was shaping quickly. Part of his resilience, reaction against authority, aggression, and fierce independence may be traced to that anguished parting of his parents in Blackpool, when they threw an impossible decision into his young face. A second facet of his character was formed by the warm sanctuary of Mimi's home life. She brought him up with a rod of iron and a heart of gold, which he was never to forget.

Although John's half-sister Victoria was never to know him, Julia went on to give birth to two more daughters who figured largely in John's childhood. On 5 March 1947, Julia gave birth to a girl whom she named after herself; and on 26 October 1949 Jacqui Gertrude was born. They took the surname Dykins, although Julia and her partner

John Dykins were never married. Freddy Lennon's brother Charles says: 'Freddy worshipped Julia and told me he'd never give her the satisfaction of a divorce. He was broken-hearted when their marriage collapsed. He would have done anything to have her back but kept saying their future was ruined when she met Dykins.'

A larger family had given Julia and 'Bobby' Dykins the important benefit of state support with the provision of a bigger house not far from Mimi's home. Here, John began to be part of the lives of his new family; his return from Mimi was, however, considered unwise since it would have unsettled him still further.

'John didn't really want a stepfather – how many children do, given the choice?' says his half-sister Julia. 'But he got on very well with him and called him Bobby. John had a very strong family of women around to protect him; his relationship with Bobby may have been a bit strained along the way but not as far as we could see. John stayed in the house with him quite a lot and Bobby gave him his pocket money regularly and found him his first job, assisting him in the hotel.'

John never spoke to his younger sisters about his natural father. 'We assumed we all shared the same Daddy,' writes Julia in her book *John Lennon, My Brother*. 'We had never been told otherwise. It didn't strike us as odd that John called Daddy by his nickname, Bobby. Older brothers were allowed to do a variety of things which we weren't. We were well into our teens before we unravelled the complexities for ourselves.' Bobby suffered an occasional facial tic around his mouth, brought about by a nervous cough; the nickname John gave him because of this, Twitchy, was not used to his face, however.

With the war over and John's real father out of his young life, his mother tried to build a happy family unit.

John possibly took comfort from the bond between his
mother and Bobby. His regular visits to their home were
punctuated by knockabout fun with his young sisters, and
they remember his impish sense of humour.

And with his mother as keen as John about another
'infant' – this one a new form of music called rock 'n' roll
– John found a firm friend joining his baptism into the
new world of Elvis Presley. 'Mummy liked him to such an
extent,' recalls Julia, 'that when we got a kitten it was
christened Elvis.'

TWO

CHILDHOOD

'I was either a genius or a madman'

EVEN AS a toddler John was defiant, determined, and a leader. When he played cowboys and Indians, in the garden of Mimi's home, she recalled: 'He had to be in charge. Always. The other boys had to be the cowboys and he *had* to be the Indian. And when he said they were dead, they were dead. "Pretend properly," he would tell them.'

Nostalgia hardly suited Aunt Mimi, a tall, bold woman with a striking, no-nonsense, uncompromising personality, but she made an exception and enjoyed reminiscing on her favourite topic: John Lennon. She sat in the bungalow at Sandbanks, Dorset, which John bought for her in 1965. That year it became obvious that she could not survive, with sanity, the gathering hordes of fans rounding on John and Mimi's beloved home in Liverpool. 'The fans were not only sleeping in the driveway all night, without me knowing. They were phoning me from all over the world . . . America, Australia, everywhere. We kept changing the phone number but the fans found the new number every time. The Post Office said they'd run out of new numbers for me.'

John said one day: 'You're going from here, where do

you want to live?' Mimi was visiting him at his Beatle home in Weybridge, Surrey.

'Bournemouth would be nice,' said Mimi.

'Let's go,' said John.

He set off with her in his chauffeured Rolls-Royce, headed south, and made her choose the pretty bungalow overlooking Poole Harbour where, within months, the passing holiday launches would carry finger-pointing passengers on pleasure trips. And on the megaphone the guides would shout: 'Over there on the right, is where John Lennon's Aunt Mimi lives.'

Mimi, who went there seeking solitude and anonymity, groaned. 'Why can't they leave me alone?' In 1983, after an illness, Mimi moved back north temporarily to within a few miles of her former home: she wanted company and went to stay with her sister Anne.

In 1965, when he moved Mimi from north to south, John Lennon was considered to be generally at his most acid-tongued, and had a reputation as the 'hard man' of the Beatles. Yet Mimi had ample evidence that, underneath, he was unchanged. He disagreed with her on a major point of sentimentality; he wanted her to keep Mendips, even though she was leaving it.

'Mimi, I grew up there. Let's keep it,' he said, as they drove south.

'John, if I leave there, it has to be sold. Have you ever been back to an empty house? A gloom comes over it. Sell it.'

'Well,' said John, 'spend six months up in Mendips and six down here in Bournemouth. I don't want anyone else owning that house where I grew up.'

Mimi was adamant. She wanted a total break. Not for the first time, she won her point with John. He was never easily persuaded about anything, but Mimi was at least his equal at digging in. He loved and respected her for that, and even his 1965 status as a wealthy Beatle would not change either Mimi or him. Mendips was sold, initially to doctors. Today a sign outside the neat house reads: 'Official Notice, Private. No Admission, Merseyside County Council.'

The house is still a major focal point on Liverpool's tourist route. At dead of night, cars bearing people on pilgrimages from all over the world pull up outside, and dreamy passengers of all ages sit and stare. This, they reflect is where John and the Beatles were born. If the walls of that house could only talk . . .

Mimi remembered everything. From his birth, she was utterly enraptured by everything about the baby who would become world-famous. Because he was due to be born at the end of September, doctors planned a caesarean section on Julia Lennon. 'She was overdue and I was phoning the hospital every five minutes,' said Mimi. 'The same question they got tired of hearing: "Has Mrs Lennon had her baby yet?"

' "No, not yet."

'The caesarean became unnecessary. At six-thirty on 9 October I phoned and they said: "Mrs Lennon has just had a boy."

'Well, we were five girls as sisters in my family, and I nearly went off my nut. I said, "Mother, mother, a boy, a boy!" The air raids used to start at that time, so I ran to the maternity hospital to see her.'

That night, Hitler's Luftwaffe pounded Liverpool in one of its fiercest raids on a major city and port. 'I was dodging in doorways between running as fast as my legs would carry me,' said Mimi. 'I was literally terrified. Transport had stopped because the bombs always began at dusk. There was shrapnel falling and gunfire and when there was a little lull I ran into the hospital ward and there was this beautiful little baby. But they had this rough blanket around him and I said immediately: "Take this blanket off his face, it's too rough." Just as I lifted him up, the warning sirens went off again and visitors were told we could either go down into the cellars or go home but we couldn't stay. John, like the other babies, was put underneath the bed for safety. I ran every step of the way home.

'When I got home, I said: "Mother, he's beautiful."

'My father said: "Oh hell, they always say that. He'd *have* to be better than any other."

'I said: "He *is* better than all the others. You know, the others are all wrinkled and he isn't." '

Within a week, Julia and baby John had left hospital and went to live at 9 Newcastle Road, Wavertree. He was a model child, but there were early signs of determination: in his high chair with his feeding table in front of him, he would prefer to try to spoon feed himself rather than be fed. At ten months he was toddling, unsteadily, but trying hard.

When Julia and Mimi decided that John would be brought up by his aunt, Uncle George entered the picture very firmly. A gentle soul, George Smith came from three generations of farmers. 'They started in a very small way,' said Mimi. 'The great-grandfather had only one cow, and the next a bigger business, until George carried on as a big breeder, and the milk was supplied mostly to hospitals.'

At four and a half John was taught to read and write by George, who sat him on his knee and worked the lad through the *Liverpool Echo* every night. 'Syllable by syllable, George would work at him till he got it right. John couldn't spell at that age, of course, but he could get down what he wanted. My husband went through all the headlines in the newspaper with John every night.'

The habit may have accounted for John's avid newspaper-reading habit throughout his life. During the Beatles years, he told me he got many ideas for song lyrics from reading newspapers. He was always quick to identify the idiosyncrasies of each newspaper and was almost obsessively interested in the news of the day. It was a rare earthquake indeed that escaped his attention.

There were no toys in John's early life – the nearest was a plastic duck which swam in the bath with him. Books were his passion, particularly the *Just William* series by Richmal Crompton, which mirrored his own personality as a naughty but humorous boy. *Alice in Wonderland* was another favourite: he would re-read it until he could recite passages by memory. 'He never showed the slightest interest in games or toys,' said Mimi. 'I had twenty volumes of the world's best short stories and we had a love of books in common. John used to go back and read them over and over again, particularly Balzac. I thought there was a lot of Balzac in his song writing later on. Anyway, he'd read most of the classics by the time he was ten. He had such imagination and built up the stories himself when he and I talked them over.'

John had no illnesses when he was a child – just chicken pox (which he called chicken pots) when he was eight. 'He was never really ill for one day in his life, except for the occasional cold,' said Mimi. She ran her house, and disciplined him, the way she had been brought up: 'No picture-dromes. He never gave me any trouble when he was young, and he never asked for much. I don't believe in people giving children money to go to the cinema just to get rid of them. He had three interests: painting and drawing in bed, if he was down with a cold; having his friends of the same age round; and reading.'

In his bedroom haven above the porch, the studious

little Lennon was quiet for hours, aided by an extension speaker from the lounge radio, with long electrical wires stretching down the stairs from his room. With his pencils and crayons and drawing books, he would be totally happy apart from the occasional shouts like: 'Change the programme on the wireless, Mimi.'

Two special favourites were *Dick Barton, Special Agent*, the thriller serial that came on every night at 6:45 p.m., and *The Goon Show*. Said Mimi: 'When Dick Barton was in trouble, his face used to go deathly white. He couldn't sit down for worry. While it was on, George and I had to be absolutely silent. And with the Goons, he imitated their accents all the time. "I'm the Famous Eccles," John would say, and he would drive me crazy with non-stop mimicry of the various accents. He loved that play on words.'

Late at night, Mimi would get her instructions from above when her nephew was ready to go to sleep. She had tried to instill in him the value of money. 'We weren't short but we weren't rich and I couldn't bear waste, particularly of electricity. This little voice would shout down on so many nights. "Turn landing light out, Mimi."'

On his children's post office set, he would write letters to his Uncle George, saying: 'Dear George, will you wash me tonight, not Mimi?' Young John didn't take long to work out the benefits of living with his doting aunt and uncle: Mimi would forever be the staunch disciplinarian, and he was destined to spend his entire life persuading her that he wasn't all that bad; George was easily won over, and, especially when he was in trouble with Mimi, the kind uncle would bail him out with an encouraging word, a pat on the head.

'I had no time to go playing ducks in the bath with him,' said Mimi, 'but George would do anything John wanted when he was little. They adored each other. George would see him to bed with a smile, most nights.'

Bedtimes were happy, with George usually having to recite a nursery rhyme to John, traditional favourites like: 'Let Him Go, Let Him Tarry' or 'Wee Willie Winkie'. Mimi, ever practical, would be more concerned with scrubbing his knees.

Mimi would berate her husband, in the kindest fashion: 'George, you're ruining him. We can't have two fools in the house. One's enough.' No matter what he wanted, John could get it out of her husband. Whenever John was being rebuked or pulled into line by Mimi, George would give him the nod and a wink to go upstairs and look under his pillow. George, anticipating trouble, had put a sweet or a biscuit there for his surrogate son.

When John reached the age of five and it was time for primary school, Mimi applied her usual diligence to the task of choosing 'not just anywhere, but the best possible.' For a short period he went to Mosspits Lane, but after inspecting other state schools Mimi settled on Dovedale Primary, just down the road from Penny Lane. To get there, some three miles from Mendips, John would be taken by bus past the Salvation Army hostel in Strawberry Field, down to Penny Lane.

From his first visits to the school, John was considered bright. On his informal look around Dovedale, the school secretary asked the five-year-old to run an errand, to take a letter to a nearby classroom for her while she and Mimi talked. 'She remarked even then on his confidence and said: "What a smart little boy," ' said Mimi.

At the first parents' meeting to discuss their children's progress, the headmaster, Mr Bolt, told Mimi: 'There's no need to worry about him. He's as sharp as a needle. But he won't do anything he doesn't want to.'

In his first school, Lennon's individuality rose quickly. Doug Freeman, now a farmer in England's Lake District, went to Dovedale with John. 'To me, he was always stuck out as somebody different, even from the age of five or six. Whatever he did, he was going to be unusual. If there was anything out of the ordinary going on in the school it was centred on him. You definitely noticed him, even at that age. He was on a totally different wavelength from the others, and although he was sometimes causing trouble and disagreements, as kids do, no teachers could ever work out properly what it was about him that was different. It stuck out a mile. The teachers could never tie him down to anything. He was always the centre of attention; he was different from anyone else in the school.'

Sliding in the snow or ice in the school playground slopes and playing marbles were favourite hobbies among all the boys, but Lennon would not join in the communal games: he was off on his own, leading a pack. 'Always on the borders of getting into trouble, but never quite going over the edge,' recalls Doug Freeman. 'We were all a little bit frightened of him, too, and it stuck out to parents then that he was different. The mothers had their eyes on him as if to say: "Keep away from that one." ' Rather like the notices he puts up around some of the fields near his farm, Freeman makes this analogy: 'Chemically treated – beware.' John, he avers, had to be treated similarly – with great caution.

Art quickly became John's special subject at Dovedale. He was getting on well in all subjects, though with a notable weakness in mathematics, but in art he excelled. In an exhibition in the school hall, when he was just ten, John's drawing startled several pupils. He drew a picture of what several boys recognized as Jesus Christ, in itself an adventurous move. Twenty years later, John Lennon's bearded facial appearance, when he was not wearing the 'granny spectacles' which were to become his trademark for a time, exactly resembled that drawing of Jesus which he had done at Dovedale Primary School. 'It was certainly strange. The similarity of the drawing, and the John with very long hair we saw later, was uncanny,' says Doug Freeman.

Comedian Jimmy Tarbuck, who went to Dovedale with John, recalls: 'Even at the age of eight he stood out, and had his gang of admirers. He wasn't easily missed at school — he wasn't the sort of kid to stand in corners, studiously reading his books. Oh no, he had a load of energy even then. If there was a playground fight, he'd be involved in it. He could be quite aggressive and when I saw him out of the classroom he'd be making his opinions known, though he always talked very slowly.' Tarbuck remembers going on a school camping trip with John to the Isle of Man. 'It wasn't so much what he did that was special, but the way he spoke,' he reflects. 'You could register, even as a kid, that here was an oddball. Now I can see that he was a genius all along.' Tarbuck did not go to high school with John, but caught up with him when the Beatles emerged and the comedian was one of the regulars at Liverpool's Cavern. 'He was a bit of a teddy boy then, very sarcastic, but also very funny.' In later years, the two went around London together on club hops into the early hours. 'By then I was a comic, but John made *me* laugh. He would put down people with one crushing sentence. Some artists don't suffer fools gladly. John never suffered them at all.'

As an embryonic Beatle, Lennon said, looking back on his troubled childhood: 'I had a feeling I was either a genius or a madman. Now I know I wasn't a madman, so I must have been a genius.'

John was fourteen when Uncle George died from a haemorrhage. When he came home from holiday in Durness, Scotland, with Aunt Elizabeth, to be told by Mimi of George's sudden death, John went red-faced and ran to his room. After the separation of his parents, this was the second bitter blow to his young life. In the recurring arguments with Mimi about his lack of discipline, lovely Uncle George had been his mate. They had gone for walks together. He adored the man's gentleness. Mimi, heartbroken by the death of her husband who had not suffered a day's illness, put on a brave face but was quiet for days. Coincidentally, John was now seeing more of his mother. With her new man 'Bobby' Dykins, Julia lived a short bus ride away at 1 Blomfield Road, Spring Wood, Allerton. Apart from her maternal attraction, John found in her a total contrast with the authoritarian Mimi. Julia was effervescent, smiling, full of *joie de vivre*. And she enjoyed practical jokes. Most important to John, she tended to look down on authority.

Three years before Uncle George's death, John had sailed effortlessly through the 11–plus examination. He arrived home from Dovedale one afternoon and casually told Mimi: 'I've got it – I'm through.' His primary school days, though showing early signs of his individuality, had not caused Mimi any disturbance, so she was hardly surprised.

Uncle George had prepared for the great day, anyway. 'It's outside, what you were promised if you passed the exam,' he said. John immediately went out for a ride across the golf course opposite Mendips, on his new emerald green Raleigh Lenton bicycle. He used to show it proudly to the other boys who went to the garden fêtes in the grounds of the Salvation Army hostel at Strawberry Field in Woolton: Mimi took John to these often.

John was glad to be leaving Dovedale; even at eleven he felt he was outgrowing it, with its uniform of a black blazer, with a dove as the badge, and grey shorts. He had made his little stabs against school rules by often not wearing the blazer when he should have done, or by arriving at school assembly with his tie askew and top shirt button undone. Only a few boys were similarly careless in their dress. 'It was also a school where sport was encouraged, and John was totally uninterested in it,' says Michael Isaacson, today the boss of a highly successful London advertising agency. He had the unique experience of being a year older than John Lennon and seeing him arrive at all three schools: Dovedale Road Primary, Quarry Bank High, and Liverpool College of Art.

'He didn't do particularly well, academically, at Dovedale. Certainly nobody talked of his prowess at any subject although there were often drawings by him on display, just as there were by other boys. I do remember him at Dovedale as not making a lot of effort. But he had obvious talent, because getting through the 11–plus in those days wasn't an easy task. Only the minority passed. He was a bright, alert boy and you could see from his face that he was no fool. If he'd decided to be an academic, I imagine he'd have made a very good one.'

Even at primary school, John and a few others found a way of bucking the system and making a profit: he would take his dinner money, payable for school lunches, and not hand it in to the teacher. Instead of eating school lunch, he and three or four others would go down to Penny Lane on some days and buy sweets and their own 'lunch' — custard tarts. But he was shrewd enough not to get found out.

Quarry Bank High School was a different matter. When he went there, in September 1952, the sharp-eyed Lennon quickly realized he was going to be up against much sterner authority, more strictness, and rules. It was a state school with pretentions to being a public school (a fee-paying British system); the masters wore caps and gowns and the headmaster, E. R. Taylor, a tall, rangy-looking man and a devout Methodist, used the cane.

Lennon got the measure of the school very quickly and decided there was only one route for him: to confront it. He had done well in any fights at Dovedale, but here at Quarry Bank there were bigger boys. Combined with the aura of academic and disciplined heaviness about the school, it was intimidating, but on entering this formidable school John had a major asset: his two friends from Dovedale had also passed the 11–plus. While one of them, Ivan Vaughan, had gone to the more prestigious city school, the Liverpool Institute, another from the 'gang of three', Pete Shotton, was joining John at Quarry Bank. Mimi was pleased to see that John was not going to a city school but was continuing his education at a suburban high school. She would be able to keep an eye on him more easily if he didn't have long bus journeys. She scarcely knew what awaited her.

Quarry Bank High School's motto was *Ex Hoc Metallo Virtutem* (From This Rough Metal We Forge Virtue). In his black blazer, with red and gold stag's head badge, John cycled there each day, up the long Harthill Road and passing the old sandstone quarries on one of which the school was said to be built. Like most schools, it divided its pupils into houses. These were named according to the district in which the boys lived. It followed that boys from the middle-class homes would be together and boys from the rougher areas would be together. In pecking order of poshness and toughness, Childwall was the number one house, Allerton number two, and Woolton (John's house) was number three. The 'harder' houses were Wavertree and Aigburth. John, in a middle-class house, was thus expected to behave, like most of the others, with reasonable decorum and discipline.

But he didn't. 'From day one, he roared through the school,' says Michael Isaacson. 'He set out to be a noise, aided and abetted by Pete Shotton who had the face of an angel but was exactly the opposite.' John was, however, the leader in any partnership, and Shotton became his lieutenant in the hundreds of misdeeds that became legendary in a school that was to deliver brilliant students to universities.

John soon decided that he had no respect for most of the teachers, and academically he plummeted. A bright boy from Dovedale when he arrived, he failed to concentrate in lessons, did not do much homework, and dropped to the B stream by the third year. By the final term of the fourth year he was twentieth in the bottom class of the C stream. His school reports told Mimi more than she needed to know: 'Certainly on the road to failure . . . hopeless . . . rather a clown in class . . . wasting other pupils' time.' Mimi, worried by one report, took him to have his eyes tested. John read a figure 5 as an 8. Mimi's eyes watered with sadness as she realized that her young boy needed glasses. 'But he had said he wouldn't wear National Health glasses, so I had to buy him thick black-rimmed ones – even then on condition that when he grew up he could have contact lenses,' said Mimi. John hated wearing spectacles, and the fact that he couldn't see the blackboards properly without them may have contributed to his general despair about learning much at Quarry Bank.

Skipping lessons, swearing, and smoking became the three key activities in John's life at Quarry Bank. Every morning and night, Mimi would try to instill in him that it was his future at stake, as he dressed in the smart blazer that Mimi had had made specially at Uncle George's tailor in Woolton village. ('It lasted longer that way – and it looked nicer than the school outfitter's,' she said.) By the time he reached school, invariably late for assembly, John's uniform was liberally arranged around his body so that he looked as if he'd just tumbled out of bed in it.

'His uniform,' says Michael Isaacson, 'looked as if it had survived World War One. He rarely wore a tie until he was admonished for looking dishevelled.'

Lennon was particularly harsh on student teachers. 'He and Shotton could virtually send a new teacher who was standing in or studying at Quarry Bank for three weeks, to a mental home. They'd take no notice of anything he said, and do no work, and the teacher's only route would be to send them to the headmaster,' says Isaacson.

Lennon was caned literally scores of times, but the stick made no difference. He would receive it for rudeness to teachers, refusing or ignoring their instructions to do work to a set pattern, missing assembly, scoring a direct hit with a pea-shooter during a lesson, being late in class, looking slovenly, swearing, or causing a disruption in the school. The punishments mounted through the simple fact of schoolmasters' expediency: once a boy became notorious, like John, he was picked on, whether he was causing trouble or not. Caning had no effect: he got so used to it that he emerged from the headmaster's study with a smile afterwards. His view was: if *that* was the worst that could happen to you for leading such a liberal school life, it was worth suffering a raw hand. Pete Shotton, who often followed John Lennon into the caning session, saw John coming out with a smirk on his face, smiled back, and was admonished every more strongly for not treating the matter seriously.

In nearby Calderstones Park, Quarry Bank schoolboys

did cross-country runs. Michael Isaacson was captain of athletics, and head of the Woolton house which included Lennon. 'John and his bunch were the constant bane of my life. He would do anything to make the cross-country runs a total and utter mess. In sport Lennon was a total dropout. Not only did I not want him in any run, because my job was to get Woolton house as high as possible; I didn't want him anywhere *near* the run, because he'd do his best to screw up any effort we were making. Half of the lads were running their hearts out, the bulk of them did it because that's what they had to do, and half a dozen boys were so tubby that running was an effort. And of course, it was those fatties whom Lennon and Shotton would verbally torture if they were anywhere near. They'd stand there looking as if a dust cart had been dropped over them, smoking and swearing, mocking the fatties, and – if I'd let them – tripping them up as they ran. I saw they were dangerous to have around during any athletics and told them to get out of my way, very early on after a few experiences like that in Calderstones Park. Lennon and Shotton were as thick as thieves and they went out looking for trouble.'

Stealing became a habit too. In Woolton and Allerton sweet shops he would ask shopkeepers for a portion of sweets from a jar that was behind the counter and difficult to reach. The time needed to reach for the jar enabled Lennon to whip a bar of chocolate from the counter, unseen.

'Every situation I remember John in,' says Michael Isaacson, 'he led. The guys who were frightened of him, which was quite a lot, kept out of his way. He had a sharp tongue and didn't mind a fight. But those who adored him just followed.'

While the school curriculum was boring him increasingly, so that he plunged down in position in each form,

John continued the flicker of interest in art which he'd shown at Dovedale. He hung around the art room, recognized Michael Isaacson as the older boy from Dovedale, and admired Isaacson's prowess which was to win him the title of Young Cartoonist of the Year, at the age of nineteen, in a national contest in the *New Statesman* newspaper.

'I was never a mate of John Lennon's but we always got on OK. He knew I wasn't a pushover and he never tried anything on me,' says Isaacson. 'Despite having no real encouragement, I got a feeling he was good at art, early on at Quarry Bank. So he'd come in and have a chat when I was in the art room drawing cartoons, which were my forte. I had a sense of humour rather like his. My drawings were satirical.

'Despite his troublemaking, I quite liked him and he was very, very funny. I was having plenty of my own trouble with the school, which was very anti-Jewish, so we had this much in common at Quarry Bank; my attitude was to outrun them all and to be the top athlete and captain of athletics, to prove a point; John's attitude towards the school was "To hell with the whole lot of them." I'd say I was constructive, he was destructive. We had lots of laughs about this and the worse he got, the more I enjoyed it – as long as he didn't interfere with my hopes to win the athletics cup for Woolton house. I knew there was no way I could get him to jump three inches or run three yards. So he was happy to be told forcefully to clear off at game time.' Sport simply bored his restless mind. Even dear Uncle George's attempts to teach him to bowl met a dead end.

The more he dug a trench for himself, the more aggressive he became. The more appalling his school results, the more he would incur the unflagging persistence of Mimi. She was particularly upset about this in John as she was conscientious beyond reproach. Long before the phrase 'latchkey children' was invented, Mimi believed firmly that her duty was to be in the house whenever John arrived home from school. 'Wherever I was in the village, by early afternoon I'd watch the clock and make sure I was back home by about three to prepare his meal. He never came home to an empty house.'

But the decline in his school work coincided with his increased visits to see his mother, particularly at weekends. Julia could play the banjo a little and tried to teach him a few chords; even at the age of four, he had received from her a £4 guitar. Her playing was limited, but the fact that she chunked along and smiled was good enough for John. He was getting closer to his mother, and her casual approach to life, combined with a prankish sense of humour, was marvellous for a boy living with an aunt who was loving and caring but strict.

At Mendips, there were three cats in John's life. Tich, the marmalade-coloured half-Persian, died when John was at college. Tim, another half-Persian, was a stray found in the snowy street by John and became a specially pitied favourite. Sam was another cat he loved. And there was Sally, the mongrel dog who died when John was at art college. John often walked the dog around Woolton. As a young boy, John doted on the cats. Every day, he would cycle to Mr Smith the fishmonger in Woolton village to buy pieces of hake for his pets. Later, as a Beatle on tour, he would phone Mimi to ask how the cats were getting on without him.

'Nothing but the finest' was Mimi's motto for John during his growing years.

The solid middle-class values which Mimi Smith instilled into John were to earn her his love and respect when he grew up. As a Beatle, he would often phone her during his travels and say: 'Remember the old days, Mimi, when you told me off?'

And she would reply, 'There was always a reason, John. You had no job to go to. I was worried.'

John would laugh, secure in the knowledge that all was well in music.

'He only became obstreperous between the ages of fourteen and seventeen,' said Mimi. 'When he moved from Dovedale to Quarry Bank, the school reports became worrying to me. He'd bring them in, and throw them through the window before I could get to them. I knew something was wrong. "You've got a brain, be thankful and use it," I kept saying. He'd just look at me, even then, and in that tired way say: "Oh . . . Mimi." And then when he looked at me I couldn't go on any more. He'd give me a "squeaker" of a kiss on the side of my face and I'd say: "Don't soft soap me now," but he knew how to get round me.' Mimi, a great collector of books herself, remembered he could not get enough books to read; an encyclopaedia absorbed him at the age of twelve, particularly a section on magic.

Mimi's chief memory of the child is that he was not one to waste a minute. 'He was always looking for something to do or read, a very active child. And he loved to talk, about growing up and why I was so strong on discipline, and he listened.' He seemed interested especially in why she made a point of always being in the house when he came home from school around four o'clock.

'Because it's my duty John, to be here,' Mimi answered. John said, 'But you've no need to.'

'Ah,' said Mimi, 'but when you're older, you'll understand.' And he did, she said. 'He grew to appreciate that, and often mentioned that he never returned from Quarry Bank to an empty house.'

For all his general studiousness and interest in words, he was careless and casual about his possessions and constantly needed money to replace things. He always asked for it at the same time – just before the bus left. That way he knew Mimi had no time to argue. But Mimi confirmed that he was not mean; from early childhood he would buy her a bar of chocolate on her birthday, and his card to her would carry his own piece of poetry.

The first signs of John's enjoyment of being on stage came when he was about twelve. During an argument with her over discipline, he would pull funny faces and act out a part, recalled Mimi. 'He'd say, in a funny voice, "You know my name, doooon't you? Aim John *Winston* Lennon." ' Mimi's reaction was 'Save that for the music hall.' But she had a quiet laugh at John's talent.

St Peter's, the Woolton village church, had been the place of worship for Mimi's family for generations. John was sent to Sunday School there from the age of eight and sang in the choir. He was conscientious about ensuring that he had enough money from Mimi to give to the church collection each Sunday. And throughout his years of living with her, John said he was a believer. 'Somebody's listening up there,' he would say.

He was about eight or nine when he walked into Mimi's kitchen and informed her: 'I've just seen God.'

'Well,' said Mimi, 'what was he doing?'

'Oh, just sitting by the fire,' John replied.

'Oh,' Aunt Mimi said, nodding thoughtfully, 'I expect he was feeling a bit chilly.'

At that age, she recalled, he was 'really good looking with fair hair and beautiful brown eyes, but he was nobody's fool.' He was resolute in whatever he decided to do – such as sitting in puddles whenever he was wearing new trousers.

'He was a bohemian, even as a boy. He'd never work at anything he wasn't interested in.'

John marked the start of the Beatles years with his Aunt Mimi by inviting Brian Epstein to Mendips. Mimi was impressed with the 'charming, gentle man' who said that he had enormous hopes for the future of the group. He also assured her that John's talent was so special that, whatever the success level of the Beatles, her nephew would 'always do well.'

Brian stayed overnight at Mendips twice, talking of his grand plans to get a recording contract. 'It was his dream,' said Mimi. 'I said, "It's all very well for you, Mr Epstein, you have got your career. But these boys haven't. What happens if you can't get them on the road to a career? What happens then?"

'Epstein would allow no such dark thoughts. "Don't worry, Mrs Smith. They are so talented." ' He sent Mimi a potted plant after each visit to thank her for tea. Such politeness went down well with her.

But when John came home in 1962 with a demonstration of their debut single, 'Love Me Do', Mimi saw no reason to lose her scepticism. 'If you think you're going to make your fortune with that,' she said sharply, 'you've got another think coming.' She was proved right: it reached only seventeen in the bestseller lists. Next, John and Brian appeared with the demonstration of 'Please Please Me'. She was upstairs when they put it on. 'That's more like it,' she shouted down. 'That should do well.' She remembered clearly John's accurate prediction.

'Mimi,' he said, 'that is going to be number *one*.'

Mimi remembered John's Quarry Men friends visiting her home during their schooldays: 'When Paul first came to Mendips he had a buckle on his shoe. John had never seen anything like it. Then George Harrison came along, with his pink shirt and winklepicker shoes.' Mimi's disapproving stares spoke volumes. 'Mimi,' said John, 'can I have some clothes like Paul and George have – you know, shoes and shirts . . .?'

'Certainly not,' said Mimi, ending the conversation.

When he eventually had to move to London, Mimi missed him terribly. 'But I never said as much when he came to visit me. I was determined that there would be no clinging vine stuff.' The tough guy image which the public saw as a Beatle cut no ice with her: she remembered the little boy whom she had sent for a holiday to Scotland every year to his Aunt Elizabeth, nicknamed Mater by the family. When he had left the house with his Uncle George, he would always return to kiss Mimi and say, 'Don't be lonely or sad while I'm away. Read a good book.'

During early Beatlemania, Mimi kept a low profile. 'I didn't think it was any of my business to be seen and give interviews,' she said. And later, on a visit to Mendips, John said how grateful he was that she never pushed herself.

The old sparring between them returned one night at the height of the Beatles' fame. She was in their dressing-room at Glasgow. As the time neared for John to go on stage, he ushered her out, saying, 'You'll have to go Mimi, I've got to get changed.'

She rasped, 'Have you any idea how many times I've seen you naked in twenty-four years?'

He laughed. The reaction was typical of the woman who remained completely unintimidated by his fame, money, or egotism.

Mendips, during the Beatles years, was under siege from fans. 'I'd go out and tell them it was no use waiting, but they knew his movements and insisted he was going to turn up,' said Mimi. Some had hitch-hiked for hundreds of miles for a glimpse of John Lennon's childhood home, and stood taking pictures. Mimi, worried about some of them and their lack of cash, invited them in for tea and sandwiches. 'They'd beg me to give them John's cup. I'd tell them he'd used them all. They'd absolutely shriek with delight!'

If she went upstairs while playing 'open house' to the fans, she had to lock the kitchen door. 'Otherwise there wouldn't be a piece of crockery left in the kitchen by the time I came down.' She worried about the kids who stood outside in the pouring rain. She asked them in to dry out their clothes. 'Because I didn't have any girls' clothes in the house, I'd have to give them an old pullover of John's. They'd swoon on the spot.'

John's room above the porch was appallingly untidy. He left his clothes all over the place. Sometimes the girls would ask to see his room. She usually refused, but once, 'just to teach John a lesson,' she took them up to see the mess he'd left. Instead of being horrified, they made a grab for things.

That same year, 1964, the Beatles played thirty-two concerts in nineteen days throughout Australia and New Zealand, before 200,000 fans. John phoned Mimi two weeks before departure saying: 'You're coming on holiday with me. Get your jabs.'

The whirlwind struck her when she was whisked for the best trip of her life: 'one long party,' she recalled. On the flight through the Far East, John made sure particular attention was paid to her. 'I kept saying: "No special treatment, John." ' When they arrived in Wellington, New Zealand, Mimi made sure an exhausted John said hello, amid the pandemonium, to two second cousins he had never met. Mimi's mother's sister's children, John and Ann, did get to meet the hero of the family. 'He was quite interested in his family's history and finding out that they emigrated to become farmers,' said Mimi.

Memories of John's witticisms never left Mimi Smith. When American magazines asked her to write her memoirs, John said: 'Tell them! Take the money, Mimi! Tell them I was a juvenile delinquent who used to knock down old women!'

She recalled a press conference at which he was asked how, if he had never been any good at arithmetic, he managed to count his money. 'I just weigh it,' he answered.

And she saw him in her mind's eye, sitting in the lounge at Mendips writing poetry and lyrics. 'He never had a pencil out of his hand. He'd write something down, then screw up the bit of paper and throw it away and start again. And he'd say: "You ought to pick these up, Mimi, because I'm going to be famous one day and they'll be worth something."'

And she recalled, with heavy irony, a conversation with John at the start of the Beatles frenzy. 'I told him off about his accent. I said: "What's all this Scouse accent about, John? You weren't brought up as a little Scouser. You know how to speak properly."'

John just looked at her and rubbed his fingers together. 'It's about money,' he replied. 'The fans expect me to talk like that.'

THREE

SCHOOLDAYS

'Just let it roll'

FOR THE first four years of John's education at Quarry
Bank the headmaster was E. R. Taylor, whose memory
of John is of 'an under-achiever who made no really positive
contribution to the life of the school, either in sport or in
attempting to improve academic standards.' Says the ex-
head: 'He did not share in what we set out to do. When I
joined the school in 1947, I took over from an ageing
headmaster who had been ill, and most of the staff, like
me, had returned from the war. There was a major job to do,
in establishing *esprit de corps*, and building up the school's
standards. While there was never any question of expulsion
for John Lennon, I think he despised what we were trying
to do in our traditional manner.' He was not a 'grievous
troublemaker,' but the school punishment records showed
him to have been caned for offences which now seem minor,
such as, in the military jargon that lingered from the
teachers' army days, 'going AWOL' (absent without leave),
a euphemism for playing truant; he also gambled for money
on the sports field during a house cricket match – a travesty
in a school that took sport seriously.

'Liverpool,' in the immortal words of the playwright
Alun Owen, who wrote *A Hard Day's Night*, 'scars its

children for life.' One of the endearing characteristics of the Liverpudlian is to bounce back, never to take a verbal knock or a swipe without retorting with something at least as sharp. At Quarry Bank, part of the penal system entailed the distribution of marks whereby two bad marks resulted in an hour's detention. One teacher devised a way of alternating the marks system with one that had more effect.

'Do you want a bad mark or a very dirty look?' he would ask.

Lennon would lead the chorus replying: 'A dirty look.'

The master's leer would break up the class into laughter; and Lennon mocked the dirty look, for he always enjoyed mimicking. That kind of rapport, treating the pupils more as people than as inferiors, always pleased John, who spoke regularly about how he hated being 'talked down' to.

Rod Davis, who became a firm friend of John and the banjoist in Lennon's first musical group, found himself poles apart from John in attitudes towards school. 'I never saw any point in getting punished for anything, so I toed the line. I was probably a goody goody.' He became head boy, a fact that provoked Lennon's incredulity at a fellow musician managing to be so orthodox.

William Ernest Pobjoy was an energetic thirty-five-year-old when he became headmaster of Quarry Bank, taking over from the portentous, authoritarian E. R. Taylor. Mr Pobjoy's first year at the school was Lennon's fifth and final year, so that by the time he took up office the mould of John's irreverence and the troublemaking Lennon-Shotton axis was difficult to break. 'I went in there as a disciplinarian,' says Pobjoy. 'I was determined to stand no nonsense.' But he faced a major thorn in John Lennon. 'I inherited an extremely disruptive boy, the legend of the school. He was presented to me as my most urgent problem, he and his friend Shotton,' recalls Mr Pobjoy, a palpably kind but firm man who tried hard to get to grips with Lennon as a person rather than confront the problem with force.

'He didn't come my way until I'd been there a month. All the teachers tried again with him at the beginning of a new school year. Eventually he was brought to me as headmaster as a last resort. On that first and one occasion I gave three strokes of the cane, the ordinary thing to do in those days.' Shortly afterwards, Pobjoy abolished corporal punishment at Quarry Bank, and it has never been reinstated. 'Caning never stops misbehaving. I quickly realized that. And with or without the cane, John didn't stop misbehaving.

'Missing detention and all the other things John did might be regarded now as ordinary schoolboy pranks, but there was another side to it all. He did take advantage of anybody who was weak. He was extremely cruel.' There were incidents between John and some teachers which horrified them all in the staff room. Lennon was often brutally tough on teachers who did not know how to handle him. He raised his fists and flatly refused to obey instructions.

'When I did cane him on that one occasion,' said Pobjoy, 'apart from the usual "This is going to hurt me more than it hurts you," I reasoned with him. But it did not make a lot of difference with John. He was set in his ways by the time I arrived, and changing his attitude in favour of his school work was an uphill task.

'I saw his guardian, Mrs Smith, frequently. She saw him as not her problem but the school's. I recall her saying: "The school should do something about it." Well, with John's early history and parental background it's not easy in difficult family circumstances to get a boy to behave well — or even to work well.'

Mr Pobjoy's worst moment came when he was at an

afternoon football match at Goodison Park, home of Everton football club. An announced message called him to the telephone, and a distressed deputy headmaster told him of yet another Lennon problem. I said: "Oh, suspend him." John was suspended for a few days and I saw his aunt again, but he survived right through from that day in February until July, coming to the natural end of his five-year course at the school.

'I recall talking to him about his ability and saying he could achieve a great deal if he set his mind to it. But he was only a failure at school because he attached little importance to academic work. He failed each of his O-levels by a single grade, and could clearly have passed if he'd wanted to. It simply didn't matter to him. He was particularly fond of an English master, Philip Burnett, who was rather advanced in his approach, his ideas, and his own way of life. John was very interested in poetry and wrote it.

'Among the Quarry Bank staff, John was seen as a wayward talent. John had been a thorn in everyone's side at school. As headmaster, I had the difficulty of beginning with him by dealing out a punishment, and that wasn't the best way to begin an acquaintance. But he accepted his punishment as the natural consequence of something he had chosen to do.

'He resented any kind of constraint or discipline. He had no intention, even at Dovedale junior school, of being organized by others. He set out to cock a snook at authority and discipline from early childhood.'

Eric Oldman, John's housemaster and chemistry teacher, says: 'He was awkward but there was something *in* him. It wasn't sheer wickedness, but more spirit. He took up my time more than the others because he wouldn't conform so well. On football afternoons, he would slope off and we wouldn't be able to find him. He seemed determined not to conform to the rules.

'But he had a wit and a humour and ability. In chemistry and mathematics, which I taught a little, there was simple lack of any wish to get on. I remember writing, as his senior housemaster when he left Quarry Bank for art college: "Might make nothing of his life or something, if he brings out something *in his own way* to make a success of it." '

Gloom struck when the O-level results came. Mimi was distraught. 'What *was* I going to do? He'd been good enough at English and history, and when he began he picked up French quickly. I couldn't believe the results.'

John's artistic talent had been quite a talking point a Quarry Bank. But, an original even at that age, his drawings did not follow convention, and he did not respond to the art teacher's instructions about what he should draw. A regular method of disrupting the class would be for John to pass from desk to desk an exercise book in which he drew bizarre, outlandish caricatures of the teachers. The book was called the *Daily Howl*. Boys stifled their laughter during class as it was passed around, surreptitiously, under desks.

When the end of term neared, Mr Pobjoy discussed John's prospects with him. This was before his disastrous results in his O-level examinations, but the headmaster, with the knowledge that Lennon was a troublemaker, decided to try to plan his future. Pobjoy also had a long discussion with Mimi, whom he had come to regard, if not fear, as what he calls a 'determined, informed, and concerned guardian.'

The conversation with her was as electric as ever. 'Well, Mrs Smith, what are your thoughts about John's future? What do you think should be considered?'

'Well,' rasped Mimi, 'what are *you* going to do? You've had him for five years. You should have his future all ready.'

Mr Pobjoy said his standards in English, literature, and poetry were well above average, but in art he seemed to have a particular talent which should be encouraged. If he tried to get him admitted into art college, would Mimi finance his first year there, after which he would qualify for a grant?

'Yes,' said Mimi. 'Any port in a storm.'

'It wasn't very unusual in those days to get into art college without any GCE passes,' says Pobjoy. (The General Certificate of Education was the basic British high school exam.) 'He produced a portfolio of samples of his work and I had to say that he was suitable, without doing too much violence to my conscience. I did believe that he had talent and should be encouraged as a lively intelligent boy. The question was: Would he behave any better at college? He didn't, of course.'

His talent for line drawing, his attention to detail, and, above all, his grotesque sense of humour were obvious in all these drawings. The targets, the teachers, were sitting ducks for his blistering satire when he was fifteen. Lennon had little respect for any of them. And as subjects for his drawings, they were appropriately bizarre in their daily behaviour. One master sewed a golf ball into the hem of his gown: he was literally a cracking shot. His walks around the school corridors and classrooms were punctuated by his taking aim and hitting troublesome boys on the backs of their heads with the golf ball. Another teacher was the talk of the school because he stank all day, every day, and the boys would openly put two fingers to their nose whenever he came near them. Yet another had a fifteen-foot-long pole which he held throughout lessons and which he swept through the air when a boy wasn't listening. He had perfect aim so that the pole smacked the offending boy across the back of his neck.

So John did not need to use much of his fertile imagination to satirize the schoolteachers. But the pungency of his wit, and the devastating captions to his drawings, were uproarious. In one red-covered exercise book which he gave as a gift to a friend, he gave the teachers names: Psyche, complete with the school badge of a stag but with a face bearing warts and a caption 'Spare Us, Oh Psyche', a commentary on the teacher with the deadly aim with the ball in his gown. A fascination with deformities was rife throughout John's drawings. Psyche's mate, with bulging eyes and warts, was balding, while another drawing of the Psinging Psychies featured six men with deformities in their faces. 'The Wife' was captioned 'My Little Glad', and the woman had a deformed eye. There were wart-ridden features all over a character nicknamed Rigo. 'Typical Hairy Hairless Smell-Type Smith', a dig at the teacher who was notorious for his odour, had a teddy boy hairstyle and a desperate caption: 'Ooh, Mate, HELP! Phew, Mate'.

There was even a drawing of himself headed: 'Simply a Simple Pimple: Short-sighted John Wimple Lennon'. He drew himself as learned, studious, and wearing his horn-rimmed spectacles, with thick bushy hair and holding a dripping candle. But the clincher of the drawing was that he had claws, not human hands, and drainpipe trousers. Nick O'Teen, described as an Irish madman, was drawn smoking with both hands and a cigarette in his mouth. A man and a woman were depicted in bed and in church, saying, 'I do,' while another couple were wheeling a pram with seven deformed children.

John's grasp of word-play was imaginative even at fifteen. He was shaping his sense of the absurd, his lampooning of hapless victims, his keen awareness of the ridiculous,

and – always – a tilt at authority. This would become the
hallmark of his character later, with his two books *In His
Own Write* and *A Spaniard In The Works*, which were
acclaimed by critics as signalling a great new literary wit.
But at fifteen, students and teachers at Quarry Bank had
to assess poems like this:

> Owl George ee be a farmer's lad
> With mucklekak and cow
> Ee be the son of 'is owl Dad
> But why I don't know how
>
> Ee tak a fork and bale the hay
> And stacking-stook he stock
> And lived his loif from day to day
> Dressed in a sweaty sock
>
> One day maybe he marry be
> To Nellie Nack the Lass
> And we shall see what we shall see
> A-fucking in the grass
>
> Our Nellie be a gal so fine
> All dimpled wart and blue
> She herds the pigs, the rotten swine
> It mak me wanna spew!
>
> Sometimes perchance ee'll be a man
> But now I will unfurl
> Owl George is out of the frying pan
> 'Cos ee's a little girl.

Even the teachers, hard-pressed to smile at Lennon,
laughed. They passed John's *Daily Howl* around the staff

room and enjoyed being lampooned. They admired John's spoof on the weather forecast: 'Tomorrow will be Muggy, followed by Tuggy, Wuggy and Thuggy,' and his send-up of Davy Crockett, entitled 'The Story of Davy Crutch-Head'.

While John clearly defied high school, there was ample evidence later in life that he reflected on those years at Quarry Bank with a hint of affection. In 1967 a Quarry Bank pupil, Stephen Bayley, wrote to John. This was at the height of the controversy surrounding the Beatles and drug-taking and when their milestone-making new album, *Sgt. Pepper's Lonely Hearts Club Band*, was released. Scarcely expecting a reply, the boy asked a few questions about the songs and added a postscript about John's old school and its innovations, like the addition of Russian to the curriculum.

John's handwritten reply demonstrated his interest in the school no matter what he said; his patience for anyone who genuinely was inquisitive about his work and opinions; and his waspish wit:

Dear Stephen,

As Quarry Bank was never a very *high* school, the changes (?) sound OK. How about sending me a copy of that magazine? All my writing has always been for laughs or fun or whatever you call it. I do it for that first. Whatever people make of it afterwards is valid but it doesn't necessarily have to correspond to my thoughts about it. OK? This goes for any books, creations, art, poetry, songs, etc. The mystery and shit that is built around all forms of art needs smashing, anyway. It must be obvious by today's trends. Enough said.

The song of Mr Kite is taken almost word for word from an old theatrical poster including the Hendersons.

Is Mr Burton* (English) [sic] still there? If so say hello. He was one of the only teachers who dug me and vice versa.

Russian, eh? Not in my day. How we've progressed. Don't tell me they let you into Calder† as well for experience and lessons. I think they asked me years ago rather vaguely if I would like to go back and look but I saw enough of it when I was there. I have fond memories, not too fond though. I have the same trouble as you in writing, but the answer is: just let it roll.

Love,
John Lennon

P.S. I don't want to start a rush of letters from little Quarrymen so play it a bit cool as they say in Swinging London. But do say hello to any of those teachers – not quite the right word. Even Pobjoy who got me into art school so I could fail there as well. I can never thank him enough.

Quarry Bank produced many eminent public figures, among them William Rodgers and Peter Shore, who went on to become British government ministers; trade union leader David Basnett; actor Derek Nimmo; and prominent industrialists. William Pobjoy looks back on Lennon's days at Quarry Bank with a smile, but he was irritated by one aspect of John's perverse attitude to schooling. 'I think he was against school, not Quarry Bank, because he said during the Beatles period: "Look at me now, I've travelled all over the world and done these interesting things. I'm so well off and there are people who taught me at Quarry

---

* John meant Philip Burnett, the progressive English teacher with whom he had a good relationship.
† Calder (Calderstones Park) is the girls' school next door to Quarry Bank where Lennon often trespassed.

Bank who are *still there!*" He seemed to think that to still be here in one place was a sign of failure. At that time it obviously didn't enter his head that there might be such a thing as vocation, where material matters were of little account. But I think he probably changed later on.'

The sentimentalist inside Lennon did change his over-the-shoulder look back at his old school. One day in 1965 Aunt Mimi, out walking in Woolton, met Mr Pobjoy, who asked how he was. The answer to the question was obvious, for Beatlemania was at its height: John was a world-famous star. But she astonished the former headmaster by saying: 'John's scared to come back to the school, but he sleeps with a picture of it over his bed.'

At Quarry Bank John travelled quickly from his earlier desire merely to emulate the cheeky Just William: he was titillating girls with obscenities when he went to hang out in Calderstones Park. Rose Lane School nearby had a fair proportion of belligerent pupils, and John would enjoy a confrontation with a few of them in a café, or on Allerton Road, where both he and his mob and the Rose Lane crowd skipped lessons. He was rarely involved in actual fights, mostly backing off when fisticuffs were near. 'He regarded fighting itself as a waste of time, but if anyone set on him he could take care of himself,' says Michael Isaacson, who left the school a year ahead of John to go to art college.

One day, Isaacson returned to Quarry Bank from art college to collect some of his old drawings. Bumping into John in the art room, Michael asked how he had fared in his O-levels, and John told him the bad news.

'You should try to get into art school — I'm having a marvellous time drawing nudes,' said Isaacson.

'Cor, that sounds good,' said Lennon.

FOUR

ELVIS!

'Let me get it out of my system, Mimi'

IT CANNOT have been a coincidence: John's hell-raising final two years at Quarry Bank coincided with the arrival in his life of a force that was to be his *cause célèbre*, his saviour, his lifeline. To John Lennon at fifteen, the arrival of two films was virtually a mirror-image of his own outlook on life.

Rebel Without a Cause, starring the mumbling, sharp, resentful hero James Dean, was youth's first stab at the establishment, its first statement against such cosy pictures as *Oklahoma* and *A Star Is Born*. And *Blackboard Jungle* was even more important, for it reflected schoolboy aggression and catapulted a new music into the world. The music was electrifyingly urgent; the message of the film might have been written for Lennon and his cronies at Quarry Bank. But the star, Bill Haley, wouldn't do. He had no real charisma, and his personality totally lacked the tough directness of his driving songs like 'Rock Around The Clock'. Still, the die was cast; the old guard of what was then called the hit parade, including ballad singers Jimmy Young, Tony Bennett, Dickie Valentine, and Tennessee Ernie Ford, now had a deadly rival. The infant was called rock 'n' roll.

In 1956 when John Lennon was sixteen, the film that was dramatically to re-route pop music was shown in Britain. *Rock Around The Clock*, starring Bill Haley and the Comets, disc jockey Alan Freed, the Platters, and Freddie Bell and the Bellboys, was not a strong movie, even by those days' standards. It had no story line and was merely a vehicle for the bands to play this new music called rock 'n' roll. In America, the film went unnoticed. In Britain, it began what is still called the generation gap.

This new music, loud, irreverent rock 'n' roll, thundered through the cinema halls of Britain. Parents looked on in horror as their sons and daughters – but mostly sons – identified with this clarion call to confrontation. The best news of all, for young people, was that adults thought it wasn't 'music'. It wasn't, indeed, mere music: it signalled a new approach to growing up. Rock 'n' roll was the new international anthem of youth.

American teenagers emulated their big heroes of the screen, the mumbling Marlon Brando and the gaunt, haunted James Dean, by adopting jeans and T-shirts. In Britain, a much more definite uniform was adopted. It was called the teddy boy outfit, so described because of its vague similarity to Edwardian fashions.

Greasy hair was one of the major requirements of a ted. It had to be shaped like an elephant's trunk at the front, coming down on the forehead and – crucially – a DA (duck's arse) at the back, with side whiskers extending well down the face. Very tight trousers, called drainpipes, bright socks, perhaps luminous, thick crepe-soled shoes (called 'brothel creepers'), and a long drape jacket were *de rigueur*.

Pop music may have been fey until this point, but it was at least a little escape from the drudgery of school work. And in a house with no television, the nightly listen to Radio Luxembourg, broadcast at the time on the difficult-to-tune 208 metres from deep inside Europe, was mandatory for schoolchildren. The BBC broadcast light music. Luxembourg was well ahead of the game, playing non-stop pop. Its poor reception somehow added to its clandestine magic.

Lennon did not have to wait long for his Pied Piper. It was from this station one night that he heard Elvis Presley's earth-shaking new anthem for rock 'n' roll, 'Heartbreak Hotel'. 'After that,' John told me in 1962, 'nothing was the same for me. He did it for me, him and Lonnie Donegan.'

Elvis's weapon was a triple ace. His robust voice was powerful, virtually beyond plagiarism; his songs, with the worldwide chart topper 'Heartbreak Hotel' quickly followed by 'Don't Be Cruel' and 'Hound Dog', were revolutionary. They grabbed every listener by the ears as well as the hips. And then there was the way he looked.

Elvis was an Americanized version of the teddy boy. For him, the uniform was not necessary, but he was quickly christened King of Rock 'n' Roll because of his look, his leer, his loudness, and his rudeness: his hip swivelling was the talk of the critics who branded him as a danger to morality. Sexuality oozed from him. For anyone remotely concerned with teenagers at that time, Presley was the partisan demarcation line: make up your mind, whose side are you on? It was them and us, the kids and the adults. The more adults bemoaned Presley's arrival, the more the newspapers screeched about the new music of youth, the more Lennon and thousands of sixteen-year-olds like him loved it.

Aunt Mimi remembered the period well. 'It was Elvis Presley all day long. I got very tired of him talking about this new singer. I was particularly upset because suddenly he wouldn't let me into his bedroom. If I opened the door, he'd say: "Leave it, I'll tidy it up." He became a mess, almost overnight, and all because of Elvis Presley, I say. He had a poster of him in his bedroom. There was a pyjama top in the bathroom, the trousers in the bedroom, socks somewhere else, shirts flung on the floor.'

Mimi's voice would boom up the stairs: 'There's going to be a change in this house. We're going to have law and order.' Throughout his life John would use the same sentence to tease Mimi about the 'Elvis period' as he reflected on it. 'And of course,' said Mimi, 'when John said it, later on, we would just both burst out laughing about the past. He was lucky to get away with what he did. It was because I'm a book lover and a bit of an artist myself, so I understood his attitude. What he wouldn't come to terms with was that I had a house to run. Oh, he *was* a mess and a problem in those years. Elvis Presley! If John's Uncle George had been alive even he certainly wouldn't have understood the bohemian bit.'

The anchor of Elvis, his music and what he represented, marked John's life as significantly as Lennon was to mark millions of young lives only ten years later. There was to be one vast difference between Presley and Lennon: the American rock giant was a physical phenomenon who rarely spoke, and when he did it was an unimportant mumble. Elvis called nearly all strangers 'sir' as a mark of polite nervousness. John was to combine an intuitive grasp of fundamental rock 'n' roll ethics with highly cerebral leadership. He probably never called anyone 'sir' in his life.

But in the mid-1950s the personal pull of Presley, quickly followed by Little Richard, Jerry Lee Lewis, Buddy Holly, the Coasters, Carl Perkins, and the Everly Brothers, meant liberation for the academic flop that John Lennon had become. It also perfectly fuelled his inherent resentment of authority.

If Presley was John's clarion call to stand up and stand

out, Lonnie Donegan was, in 1956 when John was sixteen, just as great a catalyst for his life. This time the hero was not just a distant, masculine figure propelling rock 'n' roll into millions of teenagers' brains. Donegan, clean-cut and formal, in suit and tie as befitted his jazzy background, was nobody's idea of high fashion. He was nasal-voiced, played guitar and banjo, but mesmerized a nation with a curiously British interpretation of the songs of the great American folk singers Woody Guthrie and Huddie 'Leadbelly' Ledbetter. Donegan, who emerged from the traditional jazz ranks of the Chris Barber band, galvanized British youth into his music, named skiffle, with a record called 'Rock Island Line'.

Donegan's influence on British pop music has been incalculable. He had a basic three-chord style, easy to copy, and the line-up of his group at the time (one other guitarist, upright double bass, and washboard player) inspired hundreds of thousands of young people to make do-it-yourself music. The sound was unimportant. What was crucial was that it wasn't difficult; the guitars were props, allowing the singers to be actors. Here was do-it-yourself rock 'n' roll for thousands of young people. Donegan's cute little songs, like 'Putting On The Style', 'Does Your Chewing Gum Lose Its Flavour (On The Bedpost Overnight)', and 'Cumberland Gap', became the anthems of sixteen-year-olds everywhere. Skiffle groups, formed in schools and clubs, played as much for fun as for money.

Lennon, then a bellicose schoolboy, went for skiffle like a homing pigeon. Jazz audiences already knew of skiffle, because splinter groups formed from the bands led by Chris Barber and Ken Colyer played mostly in London clubs and a few knowledgeable provincial clubs like Liverpool's Cavern and Iron Door. All Lennon knew initially was 'Rock Island Line', which even the BBC was playing. He thought its acceptance by *that* bastion of respectability, which even Aunt Mimi acknowledged as tolerable listening, was the key to his breakthrough. 'All the boys of my age are getting guitars,' he told Mimi. 'Could you lend me the money to get one?'

John was seeing more of his mother and asked both Julia and Mimi to buy him a guitar. Every afternoon, on her daily visits to Mendips, Julia would be asked, but she did not want to override Mimi's authority by installing John with a guitar under her roof. John alone was enough of a responsibility for her sister. Julia could see, anyway, from his interest in her banjo playing, that with a guitar in his hand his studies at school, already a cause for concern, would plunge into irretrievable disaster.

But he needed a better instrument and so he decided to send away for his first model himself. From a mail order advertisement in the *Daily Mail* he ordered a £5 10s model, 'guaranteed not to split', and was canny enough, at this stage, to have the guitar posted to Julia's address where he would run less risk of a scolding. His musically minded mother was less of a risk than Mimi. He took it to Mendips eventually, telling Mimi that Julia had got it for him.

Armed with the cheap guitar, which he would occasionally leave at Julia's in order not to push his luck with Mimi, John concentrated heavily on all the pop music sounds he could hear on Radio Luxembourg. Buying records was generally out of the question: they cost six shillings. But he did invest in a 78 rpm record of Donegan's 'Rock Island Line'.

The person to whom Lennon quickly sold that record, for two shillings and sixpence, once he had played it to death on Julia's old record player, was to be one of the players in the group that John formed at school. Rod Davis, a studious, successful, A-stream student at Quarry Bank, met Lennon only because he too lived in Woolton. At the forty-five-minute prep sessions after each day's classes, students got together in classrooms according to the house they were in. As Davis and Lennon and his inseparable partner Pete Shotton were in Woolton, they met on most days. The record Lennon persuaded Rod Davis to buy had a damaged centre hole: Davis felt conned when he realized why John wanted to sell it.

Inspired by the Donegan craze, Rod Davis had bought a Windsor banjo for £5 from his uncle. Excited about his purchase, he said to a classmate, Eric Griffiths, 'I went and bought a banjo yesterday.' Davis was surprised to be told that Lennon and Griffiths already had guitars, and that Shotton was learning to play the washboard, an integral part of any skiffle band's line-up. 'Why don't we have a practice on Thursday?' said Griffiths. 'We're going to start a skiffle group.'

Davis had known Lennon and Shotton since they were all about six. He remembered Lennon as the scourge of St Peter's Sunday School classes. 'He arrived looking resentful at having to come on Sunday mornings,' says Davis, 'and he chewed gum throughout the lessons. It just wasn't done to chew gum at the Sunday School.' Eventually John and Shotton were invited to leave, although Mimi said that he was confirmed, at his own request, at the same church. 'Religion was never rammed down his throat, but he certainly believed in God, all through his childhood, and he asked to be confirmed,' she said.

But the only religion that seriously grabbed Lennon at the age of sixteen was music. Even William Pobjoy, headmaster of Quarry Bank, noticed the passion with which young Lennon, the terror of the school, was interesting himself in skiffle. It was, he reflects, good to see him feeling positive about *something*.

Mr Pobjoy was also surprised, and pleased, that making music seemed to be encouraging a generous side to John's nature; some schoolboy entertainers, however amateur, would ask for money to play at school dances and other functions. 'But John would always be most polite, and certainly not ask for money, when he offered the services of his group,' says the ex-headmaster, who retired in 1982. 'Some boys asked outrageous fees but John was really grateful for the chance to play free.' Pobjoy pointed out this attribute to those teachers who were despairing of him.

Inevitably Lennon and Shotton were the pilots of the skiffle group. After a few weeks of practice, with John hammering out 'Rock Island Line' and 'Cumberland Gap' as his *tour de force* songs and Shotton playing the washboard with thimbles – the accepted percussion for all skiffle groups of that period – Lennon felt in full swing.

Now that this 'new music' of Lonnie Donegan and Elvis Presley was the talk of the school, particularly in the C stream into which Lennon had plunged, the official formation of a school skiffle group was the next move. When John told his mother of his group, she suggested holding practices at her house after school. The first line-up was John (guitar), Rod Davis (banjo), Eric Griffiths (guitar), and Colin Hanton (drums). The first rehearsal was in Griffiths's house in Woolton. Later they would play in Julia's bathroom, one player standing in the bath to get the tinny echoey sound of amplification. 'John's mother really enjoyed us playing and encouraged us a lot,' says Davis. 'She obviously preferred the banjo to the guitar so I got on well with her. I was always impressed with the fact that she played banjo with the back of her nails.

'John was the undisputed leader for two reasons. First, he knew one more chord than the rest of us. His mother's banjo playing had given him the edge – she used to teach

John some banjo chords, and they used to tune the top four strings of his guitar to banjo intervals, forget about the bottom two strings, and play banjo chords on the guitars! It was all right for me – Julia would help me tune my banjo properly. So I'd probably be the only one in tune. I think everything was in C – I remember having terrible trouble playing F chords on the banjo.

'Secondly John was keen on singing and the rest of us were never particularly good at vocals. We joined in choruses but he sang lead.' The earliest songs were 'Don't You Rock Me, Daddy-O', 'Love Is Strange', 'Rock Island Line', Cumberland Gap', 'Freight Train', the big hit made famous by Chas McDevitt and Nancy Whiskey, Johnny Duncan's 'Last Train To San Fernando', and 'Maggie May'.

'John used to belt the daylights out of his guitar and was forever breaking strings,' says Davis. 'When this happened, he'd hand me his guitar and I'd have to change the string for him because I was better at it than him. While I was changing it, he'd borrow my banjo, so he's actually played my banjo quite a few times.' Today he guards the instrument as a priceless memento.

The first name for the group was the Blackjacks. They hit upon the uniform for their much-hoped-for public performances: black jeans, with green stitching, and plain white shirts. Two new recruits to the band alternated on playing tea-chest bass; Ivan Vaughan, who had gone to Dovedale Primary School with John but went on to the posh Liverpool institute when John joined Quarry Bank; and Nigel Whalley, who went to Bluecoat Grammar School, but who knew John from his Sunday School days. In a rare show of allegiance to his school, John quickly changed the name to the Quarry Men, the line-up of which was erratic, and at one time included a bass player, Bill Smith, who was in John's class. But he did not arrive regularly for rehearsals and soon left. Eventually, the bass-playing role fell to Len Garry.

The fact that Nigel Whalley and Ivan Vaughan were not at Quarry Bank made their regular inclusion in the line-up difficult to arrange, anyway; but Nigel, highly organized and ambitious for the group, said he would try to get them some bookings. He persuaded shopkeepers in Woolton to put notices, free, in their windows: 'Country, Western, Rock 'n' Roll, Skiffle, The Quarry Men, Open for Engagements.'

John named the group the Quarry Men partly as a tongue-in-cheek dig at the school in which they had been born, and partly because the name had a ring of skiffle about it, anyway. 'Quarry Men Strong Before Our Birth' was the school song, sung lustily by most boys at the end of term. Lennon and Shotton, when they were not smiling or making up rude words to the school song under their breath, quietly admired its sentiments. John saw the adoption of the school song within the name of the group as a means to an end; it gave them a stamp of credibility. And he was to foster the 'means to an end' rule throughout his life. It was Lennon who thought of the name, and he told the others. That was that.

Slowly but encouragingly, occasional engagements were secured for the Quarry Men by Nigel Whalley. Childwall Golf Club, St Barnabas Church Hall at Penny Lane, and St Peter's Youth Club were among the earliest. The group had made its public debut playing on the back of a lorry at a carnival in Rosebery Street, Liverpool 8.

John's beer drinking had its beginnings during these days. Payments for Quarry Men concerts at Conservative dances and youth club parties were only a few pounds, but of equal attraction to John was the liberation of an evening out, the chance to chat up girls outside his normal Woolton beat, and drink, often 'on the house' as he was a performer.

The teddy boy movement was gaining ground by the time the Quarry Men secured some bookings. At dances, teds would ask the group to play some rock 'n' roll instead of the comparatively mild skiffle. The request hit a chord inside the ever-restless Lennon, who had adopted a bit of a teddy boy look with the beginnings of 'sidies' down his face and tight jeans which were as near as he could get to the obligatory drainpipe trousers. The Quarry Men entered several skiffle contests, failed to win or get a position at any one, and John was particulary taken aback by a group from Rhyl which won the Carroll Levis Discoveries night at the Liverpool Empire. 'They were really putting their act over, the guitarist was all over the stage and really full of a show,' recalls Rod Davis. 'We were really purist by comparison. John learned a lesson from that night. He said: "You've got to put it over a bit to do rock 'n' roll." ' In his mind, if not in the minds of the others, that was going to be the route to success. If Lonnie Donegan had provided the *will* to play, Elvis Presley was still the foundation upon which his musical attitude was based.

'None of us thought of it going any further than a good school lark that earned a few bob,' says Rod Davis. But Lennon thought differently and swung the songs towards rock 'n' roll. 'Jailhouse Rock' and 'Blue Suede Shoes', Lennon favourites, took him way beyond the purism of the early skiffle sounds and gave full rein to his increasing stage personality. His mother taught him, in one week of solid tuition after school, the chords to a hot Lennon favourite, Buddy Holly's 'That'll Be The Day'. It was the first song John learned to play and sing accurately. There was growing dissent in the group about the increasing rock element from John. Nigel Whalley secured the Quarry Men a coveted booking at a jazz stronghold in Liverpool city centre, the Cavern in Mathew Street. Lennon disliked jazz fans because they were, he thought, elitist. Here, in a club which tolerated skiffle because it was a jazz offshoot but which banished rock 'n' roll as the trashy sound of youth, Lennon bit off more than he could chew.

Davis argued on stage with him that the idea of doing rock songs would be unacceptable to the audience, and anyway that wasn't the original idea behind the Quarry Men. John maintained that as he was the only singer in the group, he had a right to decide what would be sung; anyway, the skiffle repertoire was restricting and boring. It was time to move on. And so the jazz crowd, dressed, as Lennon later sneeringly described them, in their 'GCE sweaters', jeered and booed as Lennon went through his rockers. Davis said to him: 'We shouldn't be playing rock 'n' roll on stage at the Cavern of all places, John. It's a jazz place.' He was also concerned that John didn't know the words to many other rockers he was putting forward. He was making up any words as he sang along. But Lennon totally ignored Davis's opinions and announced the songs as he wanted them: Presley's 'Jailhouse Rock', 'Don't Be Cruel', and 'Heartbreak Hotel' were more exciting than the restricting skiffle repeats.

The £5 guitar was not standing up to the strain of all these public performances. 'He kept bothering me for what he called a real one,' said Mimi. 'I wasn't too ready to provide it because I thought he should be getting on with his school work a little more seriously. But he kept on and on: "Let me get it out of my system, Mimi."

'I said: "All right, get it out of your system."'

And so, one Saturday morning she took him along to the famous musical instrument shop, Hessy's, off White-chapel in Liverpool. 'There were guitars hanging all around the room and John didn't know which one to choose for the best. Finally, he pointed to one and the man took it down and he played it and said, "I'll have that one." What I do remember is John nodding his head to me and me paying the £17 there and then for it. He was as happy as could be on the bus home.' The Spanish-styled guitar had steel strings which quickly made John's fingers sore from his many hours of strumming in his bedroom, to the exclusion of homework and to the continuing irritation of Mimi.

Finally, when she could no longer stand his foot tappings on the ceiling, Mimi ordered him into the porch at Mendips. It was to become his refuge, and coincidentally, he preferred the acoustics, with the echo. On one occasion when he was bandished there by an impatient Mimi, she boomed the words: 'The guitar's all very well, John, but you'll never make a *living* out of it.'

At sixteen, John Lennon stood out as no ordinary schoolboy or teenager. Within the Quarry Men, the only disagreements were about skiffle versus rock 'n' roll. He was getting used to using his fists in a fight: being in the C stream, the going was rougher than in the academically higher streams, and he would not hesitate to punch when there was a verbal battle that couldn't be solved. At home, the tension between him and Mimi increased as she tired of the regular morning phone calls from the headmaster's secretary, relaying John's latest misdemeanour. He was getting used to the prospect that he would have to battle his way through life, a fact confirmed by the punch-ups he saw in boozy audiences when the Quarry Men played at dances, particularly in the rough area of Garston.

Strangely, the most crucial decision in his professional life was to happen as a result of one of the most genteel events the Quarry Men played. It was there that he first met Paul McCartney.

The group was drifting between engagements and had fared poorly in talent contests when they secured a booking for the afternoon of 6 July 1957, as the music attraction at St Peter's, Woolton, garden fête. The weather was sunny and perfect for the Quarry Men – on this occasion John Lennon, Pete Shotton, Eric Griffiths, Colin Hanton, and Len Garry on tea-chest bass – to perform their limited repertoire on a raised platform in the furthest field from the church. John, seizing Woolton's big day as an occasion when he could 'come out' and make an impression, dressed in full teddy boy regalia for the first time: tight drainpipe trousers which left nothing to the imagination; a jacket with heavy padding at the shoulders; blue and white checked shirt, and – vitally – greased-back hair.

The Elvis Presley imitation fell stonily on Mimi, who began his day with a scolding. She reminded him that his school reports were appalling and for a high school boy to be adopting such a personality was a repudiation of all the standards she had been trying to instill into him. Lennon, never rude to his aunt but intransigent and defiant when it came to asserting himself, simply walked out in mid-morning and teamed up with Pete Shotton, ready for the afternoon's big appearance. John, who realized that the big garden fête audience could mean an important day for the group, steeled himself by buying bottles of light ale from the Woolton off-licence and getting mildly inebriated, but not drunk. All his life, drink was to be a recurring problem. He enjoyed it to relax, or celebrate, but he could never take much before feeling the effects. And when John got merry, he became aggressive.

That fateful sunny Saturday Aunt Mimi did not know John was taking his Quarry Men to the Woolton fête,

and John did not realize she would be going to the fête with
her sister. 'It was a gorgeous day, with all the young women
in their backless dresses and summer frocks,' said Mimi.
The chief attraction was the band of the Cheshire Yeomanry;
the Quarry Men had to walk the gauntlet of stalls selling
home-made cakes and fruit and vegetables, past the
children's sideshows, before they could take the stand. The
vicar, the Revd Maurice Pryce-Jones, was doing the rounds
and welcomed the band that was to provide the afternoon's
skiffle, a particularly trendy attraction for a church event.

'Well, when I got there and stood talking to young
people over a cup of tea, there was suddenly this loud beat
– bang, bang, coming from the bottom field. It shook
everybody up,' said Mimi. 'All the young people left their
stalls and proceeded down to the field. I said: "Where are
they going?" and my sister said: "There must be a band,
let's go." '

The sight that greeted Mimi as she neared the band
platform transfixed her. 'I couldn't take my eyes off him,'
she said. It was the first time she had seen, and heard, John
in full cry with the Quarry Men. 'There was this grin all
over John's face and then he spotted me walking towards
him and his expression changed a bit. I don't know why –
I was pleased as punch to see him up there.' But Lennon,
in his mildly alcoholic haze remembering the row that
morning about his teddy boy attire, feared the renewed
wrath of Mimi. He began to re-phrase the words to the
song he was singing: 'And Mimi's coming down the path,
oh oh.' The songs played that day included 'Cumberland
Gap', 'Railroad Bill', 'Maggie May', and 'Come Go With
Me'. On that song, John characteristically – and irrever-
ently, for a church affair – changed into the more suggestive:
'Come little darling, come and go with me.' It was a lyrical

tactic he was to employ to devastating, often hilarious, effect later in his life as a writer.

John's shock at seeing Mimi was softened when she led the applause as the group finished its set. But that was not to be the only significant part of the day. Among the audience, unknown to John, casting a keen fifteen-year-old's eye on the music which he regarded as very primitive, was a boy from neighbouring Allerton: Paul McCartney. He and John had a mutual friend, Ivan Vaughan, who lived in a house immediately behind Mendips and had attended Dovedale Primary School with him. When John went to Quarry Bank and Ivan to Liverpool Institute, the posh high school alongside the art college, Ivan became friendly with McCartney, another Institute student. Realizing Paul's interest in rock, Ivan thought it would be good if he heard the Quarry Men and met John. 'You've got to come and meet this guy John Lennon,' Ivan said to Paul. 'You'll get on well with him.'

Paul stood with Ivan watching and listening as John stood on the stage, even at the age of not quite seventeen a commanding figure, undeniably the leader. Musically, John and the Quarry Men exuded more energy and enthusiasm than talent, but it was infectious enough. What impressed McCartney as much as anything was that these schoolboys, only a little older than him, had actually got a group together. His talent as a guitarist, coming from a musical family, was prodigious compared with John's; still, it had no outlet.

Ivan Vaughan led Paul across to the church hall after the Quarry Men finished playing. There, introductions were made. As Paul recalled later in a warm and amusing foreword to John's first book, *In His Own Write*: 'At Woolton village fête I met him. I was a fat schoolboy and, as he leaned an arm on my shoulder, I realized that he was drunk.

We were twelve then [sic] but in spite of his sideboards we went on to become teenage pals. Aunt Mimi, who had looked after him since he was so high, used to tell me he was much cleverer than he pretended.'

But that day at Woolton fête it was the clever young McCartney who held the aces. First, John was floored by the fact that Paul could actually tune his guitar, thus correcting the banjo tuning that John had inherited from his mother. Second, McCartney was able to demonstrate a stunning knowledge of the words to a favourite of John's beloved rock 'n' roll: Paul wrote down the words to Eddie Cochran's 'Twenty Flight Rock' from the film *The Girl Can't Help It*. Next, he ran through other rockers and shocked John with what, to the skiffler trying to become more adept in musicianship, was the performance of a virtuoso.

Lennon had never had an inferiority complex. A sixteen-year-old schoolboy hell-raiser, a defiant challenge for his caring Aunt Mimi, he had so far not needed to project himself beyond a punch-up, always backing off when the going got really tough or dangerous. But that day in July 1957 was to prove a watershed for John. The meeting with Paul McCartney had come just before he left Quarry Bank School, sadly failing all his O-levels. John didn't show signs of worrying much about that. He had a chip on his shoulder about formal education and 'pieces of paper that say you're bright'.

But the Quarry Men, for all their amateurism, were important to John. With school success slipping away, he desperately wanted to stamp his personality on something, anything that would mark him out as a success. The skiffle group was obviously going to have to grow or go. That night, as he sobered up after the evening performance at the village fête, long after McCartney had gone home to

20 Forthlin Road, Allerton, the leader of the Quarry Men was tortured by a question. Should he invite McCartney to join the group? A stronger guitarist than John, and with a better knowledge of rock 'n' roll songs, he was going to be a formidable performer. Lennon's leadership might be threatened. The alternative was to shun competition and plod on with the Quarry Men, going the same aimless way as thousands of skiffle groups all around Britain.

At first the decision was tough, but eventually it proved logical that he should offer Paul the chance to join. First, he would have a powerful, talented ally in the swing to break away from skiffle and make it a rock 'n' roll band. Second, he had enough confidence in his own dominance to believe that he would have the edge over a boy two years younger. Third, the group needed new blood.

It was Pete Shotton who passed the news to McCartney. 'John wants you in the group,' he said to Paul as they cycled one day over Allerton golf course. McCartney was pleased but cool. It would be two months before he could get into the Quarry Men, he said; he was going to scout camp.

FIVE

THE ART STUDENT

'I want to be rich and famous'

FOR THE art college's vital day of judgment on him, John's carefully groomed appearance and his sober demeanour complemented the kind recommendation of William Pobjoy. He was accepted as a student at Liverpool College of Art. The soot-blackened building was just around the corner from Liverpool Institute where Paul McCartney, his brother Michael, George Harrison, and John's old friend Ivan Vaughan were studying.

When he went for an interview, John took an impressive portfolio of his Quarry Bank work which included his satirical drawings of his teachers. This corroborated Mr Pobjoy's generous description of Lennon to the college principal, Mr Stevenson, that the boy deserved a chance. Mimi went to the college with him for the interview; as on all bus journeys with her, he travelled alone upstairs on the bus while she sat downstairs – a typical teenage embarrassment at being seen out 'in the care' of a relation. 'He'd hardly been into town before that, certainly not on his own,' said Mimi. John dressed soberly for the big day, wearing Uncle George's old brown jacket, plus a shirt and tie. 'He was himself, not nervous, quite confident,' said Mimi; 'he was never one to *show* his feelings, even then.'

The interview went successfully. John was told that he would be expected to work hard on his own initiative, and he started college in September 1957.

As John entered college the Quarry Men continued, but with less momentum. The pace of things was reduced because Pete Shotton had left Quarry Bank to become a police cadet, with Nigel Whalley holding things together with regular bookings. But all of them were preoccupied with getting used to new daily environments; John had the additional distraction of girls at college. No more did he have to climb the walls of Calderstones Park Girls' School, near Quarry Bank, to eye the schoolgirls, chat them up, and make rude signs to them. At Liverpool College of Art, in the autumn of 1957, there were pretty girls in every room. The beatnik period was under way: it meant teenage assertiveness and individuality in tandem with the recent youth explosion that had come with Elvis Presley, Lonnie Donegan and skiffle, James Dean, and the surly style of a great new young film actor, Marlon Brando, in *The Wild One*. It was a perfect period for the individualism in John Lennon to grow.

One student who got to know John from his first days at college was Phyllis McKenzie. They travelled on the number 72 bus together every morning from Woolton to Canning Street, near the college in Liverpool 8. Although John didn't care much about it in the early days of these journeys, Phyllis was the closest friend of another student, Cynthia Powell, whom she had known since they went to the Secondary School of Art together at the age of twelve.

Lennon could not be ignored on that bus, recalls Phyllis. He was scruffy, often in a black leather jacket, and always travelled upstairs so that he could smoke. John held his Woodbine between his first two fingers, with all four fingers curling around it, using the thumb as a support. It struck Phyllis as strange.

'He might have been scruffy but he was always clean,' says Phyllis. 'And he was not mean – he'd usually offer to pay my fare, eight old pence, just because he knew I was, like him, a hard-up student at the college.' As the months went by and he realized Phyllis was Cynthia's best pal, he became wary of talking to her, lest whatever he said should be repeated. 'He used to say I was his rival for Cynthia's attention.'

Art college was legendary to any young person in Liverpool. 'You just knew you were in for a good time,' says Michael Isaacson, who left Quarry Bank a year before John and was installed at art college when Lennon arrived. 'But it was tricky establishing yourself because a lot of people there were a lot older than high school boys like John and me. The Korean War was on at the time and there were a lot of older men who had returned from Korea and got a grant.' The procedure was for all new entrants to go into the painting school for their first year and then go into specialist areas like illustration, sculpture, graphic design, or lettering.

'John had a tremendous amount of confidence, even then,' says Isaacson. 'Most of us spent the first few months, or maybe the first year, wondering what we should do and trying to be industrious in our work. Not John – he went straight in, played his part to the limit, and gathered people around him, and looking at him, from almost day one.'

There was an unlikely rapport between Lennon and Isaacson, just as they found at Quarry Bank. 'I wasn't a pushover and he knew that and probably liked it,' says Isaacson. 'He knew I was good at art, and I drew cartoons not unlike the doodles which he did whenever he had a spare moment. Also, I decided not to join his teddy boy or beatnik element but to stand apart. My trick was to be the cleanest guy there. I found a shop in London Road where they made incredible silk brocade waistcoats. I didn't have much money but I bought lots of these in different colours, and I looked like something out of Wyatt Earp. John looked totally the opposite. We used to eye one another and size each other up. He admired my individuality.' John respected people who were different.

'When John was on his way to join art college, I knew things would happen when he got up to his tricks and I looked forward to the years ahead with Lennon. He was a terrible guy, actually, but I liked him.' Other students say Isaacson despised John and they clashed, but he denies that: 'Of course I frowned on everything he did, his work and his attitude, but his responses were always beautiful, so we did get along fine. When you look down on someone, you can do it with total disrespect, or with respect.'

Lennon's recognition of Isaacson rose when he realized Michael's prowess. A year older and demonstrably more ambitious, Isaacson quickly became the art college artist who 'got printed', extensively at first by the Liverpool University students' union magazine and later, at the age of eighteen, by the *Liverpool Daily Post*. 'John was certainly aware of me. He commented on my success and said, "You're successful because you bloody well want to be, aren't you?".'

Isaacson's most animated clash with Lennon came, not unexpectedly, on the subject of music. Isaacson, who coveted leadership whenever it was available, took it upon himself to run the art college music club and provided a staple diet of jazz, notably the trendy sounds of Miles Davis and the Modern Jazz Quartet.

Lennon, who by the time he entered college was deeply into all things Elvis, confronted Isaacson one day in the music room. Eyeing the records by artists whose names he had never heard of, John said: 'What a lot of fucking shit you play. Why don't you play something proper – like Little Richard, Chuck Berry, Elvis Presley?'

Isaacson's retort was a challenge: 'What do *you* know about it? Most of the people here like this. If you really want to do something, bring your group to the art school dance and prove yourselves. I'll put you on and give you a break.' The group did play, and Isaacson says they were a shambles, with a poor sound, and deservedly got a thin reception.

The dominating characteristic at college inside everyone with ambition was a burning desire to get out of Liverpool. 'Lennon told me quite candidly even at that age, that he wanted to be rich and famous. That was the drive inside all of us at that time and that's why Liverpool in the late 1950s and early 1960s was such an exciting place.' Isaacson went to London, became a successful political cartoonist for the national media, and eventually formed his own advertising agency.

Reflecting on Lennon, he says: 'I think if he had not become successful he may well have become more than just a wayward bum. He might well have become a really nasty piece of work. It's all hypothetical, but I fear the worst could have happened. If he hadn't become famous his anger could have been vented in another direction. Where his energy was channelled into creative music, it would have gone into something destructive instead of creative. He was strictly an all-or-nothing kind of guy.'

None of the students who attended college with John recalls him as a profound person. He was more physical than cerebral. He had little time for lengthy discourse on anything beyond music and girls, notably Cynthia Powell, who had the most electrifying effect on him once she had become as besotted with him as he was with her. Once John had secured her love, his possessiveness about her was over-powering. Although he followed his own roving eye, the slightest move towards another man by Cyn brought forth John's fury and cross-examination. 'She was very pretty, Bardot-like, and I enjoyed looking across the canteen at her,' says Michael Isaacson. Another student, Ann Mason, says Cynthia was attractive enough to have been the girl-friend of many others at the college, but her passion for Lennon was incredible. 'It was certainly surprising that a girl like Cynthia had been caught by this shit called Lennon,' says Isaacson. 'They looked at each other adoringly. They were totally fixated.'

Ann Mason's link with John was not romantic, but she was unique in having, as her boyfriend for one afternoon, another student named Stuart Sutcliffe, who came from Prescot Grammar School and was John's closest friend. John recognized in Stuart's gentleness the reality of his own personality. The difference was that John's quiet studious nature was submerged beneath an outward veneer of rug-gedness, which often manifested itself in raw aggression. Stuart was the opposite; quiet outside, tough inside. This tension was to lead to Stuart's blinding headaches which would later prove fatal. But when they were together, Lennon and Sutcliffe found a rapport which neither, in their teenage simplicity, needed to explain.

John also developed a good non-musical friendship with another student who found it hard to concentrate on his work.

Geoff Mohammed was five years older than John, of much bigger build, and came from Manchester. His father was Indian, his mother French-Italian. Geoff was dark-skinned, good-looking, and for most of the time clowned his way through the classes. It was his irreverence for orderly work, and failure to complete his work, together with his great sense of humour, that drew John to him.

'I never had much time for John,' says Ann Mason, Geoff's one-time girlfriend. 'I despised him because he didn't work hard. He was a terrific tearaway but he had this strange thing about him: he was either going to land up as a great, or in the gutter. It wasn't because of anything he actually did, because his art work was rather poor. But there was this strange destiny about him. Geoff Mohammed had the same quality.' Geoff died a few years before Lennon, having left college to become a security man at the Whitworth Art Gallery back in his home city of Manchester.

Ann remembers her ex-boyfriend as 'intelligent, philosophical, and far more sensitive than John.' He also had a neat line in self-deprecating fun. Aunt Mimi remembered that John went home one day roaring with laughter at a story about himself and Geoff who had been in a café where there were a lot of black people. The dark-skinned Geoff had them all laughing uproariously as he opened the café door and shouted: 'Right, all foreigners OUT!' This sense of the ridiculous appealed to John: in 1959, on the day they both received some money from their college grant, they went out together into the city and returned dressed in identical clothing – dark green suede shoes, dark grey trousers, and fawn donkey jackets. They were also boasting about having been to the barber's for a shave, an unnecessary extravagance for hard-up students. It was an innocent example of doing anything to make an impact.

'I was afraid of John because he could be so caustic,' says Ann Mason. 'I was never on the receiving end of his sarcasm. Maybe I was protected by being Geoff's girlfriend. People found John very amusing at times, but there was always this underlying fear that he might turn his wit around and use it against them. What made the partnership interesting between Geoff and John was that John respected Geoff, but Geoff in turn wasn't afraid of John as some were.' He was keen on palmistry, which also fascinated Lennon.

When Geoff had a row with Ann Mason, he and John went out for the night and got drunk. Everyone at college knew by the sight that greeted them all in the college canteen next morning; the two of them had returned late at night and filled the canteen with stuff they had stolen from the trendy Bold Street area of the city – street nameplates, signposts, posters, and even parts of cars and bicycles. They were admonished by the college principal, but both quietly laughed. The prank – and the emotional release it had given Geoff during a heavy row with his girlfriend – was well worth the rebuke, and the hangover.

At the art college some students were serious about their work, others there mostly for the enjoyment of it all, letting their career take its own direction. John enjoyed art and was talented in an unorthodox way, particularly as a caricaturist, but he was not prepared to let art get in the way of his determination to press on with his rock 'n' roll.

Most lunchtimes, in Arthur Ballard's room 21, guitarist Len Garry from the Quarry Men would join Paul McCartney and George Harrison from the Liverpool Institute next door. About twenty students would finish their canteen lunch and form the audience as the musicians spent an hour playing Buddy Holly and Everly Brothers songs, finishing off every day with Lennon singing the old British variety favourite, 'When You're Smiling'. He would inject the names of college teachers into several of the songs, in a song satire that amused all the students.

John eased himself into college life with a central characteristic that was to mark his life. He *used* every moment. He manipulated every minute he was given to make it work to his advantage. Even the teachers who riled him, like the strong, colourful Welshman Charles Burton, who regularly picked on Lennon for his artistic inadequacies, had their value to John. They would crop up in his songs, used as target practice.

'He was an original, and being one myself, I could single him out as a true individual,' says June Furlong, who enjoyed a strangely intuitive relationship with Lennon from his first weeks in the art college. 'I'd see him sitting in life class, or outside the pub Ye Cracke, and I can remember saying to myself about this seventeen-year-old teenager: "Where will your original talent take you? This is no ordinary boy student . . . he's going to do something unusual . . ."'

June Furlong was the art college model whose class in room 71 John attended twice weekly during the day, and occasionally in the evenings if he wanted to return with any of his friends like Stuart Sutcliffe, Geoff Mohammed, Tony Carricker, or Dave Davies. To some, drawing a model while still only a teenager might have been the source of much nudging and winking. Occasionally, John would say to his friends when drawing June: 'Christ, I wonder what Mimi would have to say about *this*.' But that light joke was merely to emphasize the stern background from which he came. Most of the time, John was an earnest and conscientious member of June's drawing class. 'He was a completely charming and one hundred per cent decent person. Nobody alive could pull a fast one over him, but if he realized you were genuine and interested in talking intelligently to him, about art or anything else, he would talk to you for hours. And we did,' says June Furlong. 'He had no time for flippancy in conversation.'

He fascinated her. Their friendship was purely platonic, but during the sessions when he would be drawing her, their conversation would strike the most personal chords. 'He hadn't got it all together, mentally, when I first met him, but there was this . . . well, originality is the word, there was this total originality about him. I could see some potential in his mind, although his drawings were just average. John could just hold his own in art, and that was that. He wasn't anywhere near his closest friend, Stuart Sutcliffe. Stuart was not just good, he was great, but he had a streak in him which appealed to John. He lived every day as if it was going to be his last. The teachers all knew he had a rare talent, but they had to hold him back and try to channel him. "Yes, OK, Stuart. It's excellent work, but take it easy. Less output and more plan of thought," Charles Burton told him.'

But it was precisely that non-stop drive that endeared Stuart to John. And they both had this in common; they were determined to capitalize on what they were good at – for Stuart art, for John music.

'I could see from the first few times I met him that here was a bloke who wasn't prepared to play life from the sidelines,' says June Furlong. She sits in her house in Liverpool, just five minutes' walk from the college, where she was born, where John Lennon visited her, and remembers the college's most famous student with fondness. 'Always, he either wanted to be in the scrum half, or he wasn't going to be involved in the game. I'd say that when he entered a room, or started a class like the life class, his attitude to everyone was: "What's going on here, what's this, who's that?" And that's how he quickly got to know all the people around him, in his groups, their strengths and their weaknesses, their hang-ups, their difficulties, and the obstacles. His sarcasm with the weak was very cutting.'

Lennon wanted his own way in most things and didn't relax his pressure until he got it. After the evening life class sessions he went through a phase of insisting that some students join him in going to the Liverpool Empire to see comedy acts like Robb Wilton; Wilson, Keppel, and Betty; Morecambe and Wise; and the famous drunk comic Jimmy James. The more traditional the comedian, like Robb Wilton, the more John enjoyed mimicking him. He would roam about college next day repeating Wilton's famous phrase: 'The day war broke out, my missus, she says to me: "What are you going to do about it?" ' Despite his outlandish behaviour, and assertiveness as a rock 'n' roll trailblazer, John was quite normal in his taste for traditional British humour.

Stuart Sutcliffe was not among those who went to the variety shows with John and the other students. He was not particularly interested in the stage, a fact that might at first have ensured that John and Stuart would be able to sustain only a casual, art college friendship. 'But I've never seen two teenagers so close as those two,' says June Furlong. 'John, as an extrovert personality, used to attract a lot of blokes who were not extroverts. He didn't have to have a lot in common with his best friend to consider him his best friend.' He expected a vast amount of loyalty from his friends but gave a lot in return. Underneath an exhibitionist exterior, Lennon had a fermenting brain. Sutcliffe was a quiet, intellectual thinker. With his spiky hair and lithe physique, he didn't have to make any effort to be vulnerably attractive to women, whereas John kept working on his looks. Stuart, a runaway artistic talent whom all the teachers reckoned would be a star student in the years

ahead, possessed the brooding authenticity that John
secretly yearned for. In John, Stuart saw a speedy mind and
a demonstrative style that he could never summon. The
pair were inseparable, and whatever other male friendships
John forged, nothing compared with Stuart. 'That was his
only friend,' said Aunt Mimi. 'He was the only other boy
he really enjoyed being with for long periods of time.'

Stuart's drawings of June were stunning. 'I wonder what
happened to them,' muses June Furlong today. 'He liked
me in one particular pose, and he did several.' Normally,
she did not bother to inspect students' interpretations of
her poses, but Stuart's were so good that she took a particular interest in all his work.

Lennon's twice-weekly sessions in the life class during
the week were augmented by his wandering over to Stuart's
nearby flat at Gambier Terrace in the evenings from seven
o'clock until nine. 'I was his foil for a while,' says June. 'I
was attracted to him, not in a physical way but in a
Liverpool way. He was a positive Liverpudlian, and there
was this streak of iron and steel in his character, every
moment. Look at anybody who's made it, and if they came
from Liverpool, it's partly *because* they came from Liverpool.
John hadn't the artistic talent, but to speak to, whether he
was joking about the strictness of his Aunt Mimi, or
whether he was on about last night's show at Liverpool
Pavilion, he had this *edge*.'

Lennon always reacted firmly to the person he faced or
the treatment he was given. Confronted by a fool asking
cretinous questions, as he often was during Beatlemania,
John was the most scathing, often vitriolic, adversary. But
treated sensibly, engaged in serious conversation by anyone
who was genuine and an enthusiast about his own craft –
which didn't necessarily mean enthusing over music – John
was a powerful, discerning conversationalist. 'He was a great

sender-upper of other students,' says June Furlong. 'If he came across one who was crude or stupid or a bit of an upstart, he'd play on that. But I've never met anyone who could move so fast in detecting what made people tick.'

SIX

ROCK 'N' ROLL

'Be careful of that John Lennon'

ALWAYS SPEEDY at analysing situations, John realized that while art college might not be crucial to him as a place to learn art, it offered other tremendous benefits, such as his deep attachment to Cynthia and his friendship with Stuart; and the infectious atmosphere in the college's Liverpool 8 district, which made it equivalent to Paris's Left Bank, was a perfect escape route for John from the genteel middle-class environs of Aunt Mimi's Woolton. The pubs of the college area, Ye Cracke, and the Philharmonic, and the Jacaranda coffee bar at 23 Slater Street, were places to hang out and become an adult. Mentally, Lennon was always ahead of his years and sought out people who would travel with him as speedily as possible. And a fourth benefit was the 'fix' he was to get at lunchtime from sessions with Paul in Arthur Ballard's room.

Pop music was steadily taking over his life. In the months that followed their first meeting at the Woolton church fête, a teenage empathy had developed between John and Paul. The reluctant art college student and the more studiously rounded, conscientious academic from the posher Liverpool Institute (the 'Inny') next door had a friendship based solely on music. Lennon was increasingly nervous

about letting Paul into the Quarry Men, but it became a
fait accompli in the light of Paul's runaway talent.

George Harrison was a different matter. Another Liverpool Institute scholar, he was three years younger than John
but a gifted and accurate guitarist. Paul would bring him
occasionally to the lunchtime sessions at the art college,
and John was impressed with his skill. George quickly
decided that the older, irreverent, and altogether adult John
Lennon was great. Lennon and Cynthia became irritated by
George's constant presence as he waited for them to come
out of college together at lunchtime. With the insensitivity
of youth, George did not realize that a passionate love affair
needed privacy.

'Hi John, hi Cyn,' George would say.

'Oh hi,' John would say, coolly turning right quickly
and increasing his and Cynthia's pace towards Gambier
Terrace.

The loving couple regarded George as a bit of a hanger-
on but tolerated his youthful lack of understanding. Harrison hero-worshipped Lennon at this stage. John, who eventually invited him to Menlove Avenue when Mimi was in,
eventually had good reason partly to reciprocate and respect
the teddy boy taste of young George, the son of a bus
driver. When George had left her house, Mimi told John
she disapproved of his mode of dress. 'He had a *pink* shirt
on! And *winklepicker* shoes!' recalled Mimi. 'I wasn't having
any of *that*.' That rejection was enough to clinch the acceptance by John of George as a fully-fledged Quarry Man.

Paul's mother, Mary, a nurse, had died from breast
cancer on 31 October 1956, nine months before he first
met John Lennon; Paul was fourteen then. Paul's father,
Jim, had two sisters, Auntie Jinny and Auntie Millie, who
went into the McCartney family house at 20 Forthlin Road,
Allerton, every Monday to cook the 'Sunday' roast dinner.

Paul's background was similar to John's in that he was living without a mother, but his father was a major influence on his life. A cotton industry salesman, Jim McCartney was a kindly man of firm British values. He was also an accomplished pianist who once ran his own jazz band, so that the McCartney home was full of the most fashionable sounds of the period. Jim's favourite song was 'Stairway to Paradise', and young Paul was weaned on a diversity of sounds ranging from musicals to hot jazz.

The major difference in Paul's and John's attitude to making music lay in McCartney's background. While Lennon had to fight every inch of the way to get Mimi to see he was serious about playing, eventually persuading her to buy him a guitar, McCartney was actively encouraged. Family parties became singalongs with Jim at the piano, and he also played trumpet in various bands. Paul warmed to the sounds of pop on hearing the Everly Brothers, Lonnie Donegan, and Buddy Holly, and his Dad bought him a trumpet which Paul traded for a Zenith guitar. Michael says: 'Dad made it look hard because he had to pay for it, and that was his way of making Paul appreciate what he was doing. But really, he was knocked out that his eldest son was getting into music. The only thing that bothered him was Paul's partner, John the ted!'

Paul's background was much more working-class than John's; his father, a widower at fifty-three, had a tough time raising two young sons. In fact, of all of the Beatles who eventually emerged, John was the one from the most affluently middle-class home. But McCartney – whose surname John perversely mis-spelled as McArtrey for several years – was such an asset to John's confidence in learning music that any differences in background quickly became submerged by the joy of musical togetherness. 'Paul was very serious about his guitar,' said his brother. 'He demanded to know every facet of it, every conceivable variation. Chords he hadn't heard of, or couldn't learn from a book, he'd make up. He was heavily into rock 'n' roll, of course, but not to the exclusion of other music. He never turned away from a thing just because it wasn't Elvis Presley or Little Richard, much as he liked them.' That catholic taste was to be both the strength of the Beatles and the cauldron of the songwriting partnership of John and Paul, as well as an artistic contrast and melting pot for them in the years ahead.

John always conceded Paul's instrumental superiority and never made any claim for his own ability as a guitarist. Paul had his own pressures at home; his father regarded Lennon as an undesirable influence on the life of his son, who, far from needing encouragement down the teddy boy road, 'ought to have his sights on a decent career, like entry into a teacher's training college, or accountancy.'

But to Paul, a kindred rock 'n' roll spirit like John was the catalyst he needed. To John, Paul deserved respect not just for his prowess but because he had also actually started writing his own songs. A few months after meeting, John and Paul had engineered a way to meet secretly together, with no interruptions from other students; when Jim McCartney was out at work, they would safely install themselves in the living room at Paul's house and start playing and writing songs together, often daring to smoke tea from a pipe, and indulging in what became known as 'afternoon sagging off school'.

It was an electric partnership at the time between two personalities that at first sight looked destined to clash. John was, at seventeen, caustic, cynical, assertive, and brash. Paul was, even then, more quietly diplomatic and certainly more attractive to girls. He was an academic grind who lived an orderly life. He wanted to please his widower father. Theoretically, Lennon should have loathed him, but both realized that, at that moment in life, they needed each other for a mutual passion: making music.

Michael McCartney, two years younger than Paul, enjoyed observing the afternoons which were to give rise to the most significant songwriting partnership in modern popular music. Sitting in the McCartneys' home in Forthlin Road, he 'saw this extraordinary-looking ted coming down the road, with long sideburns and wearing skin-tight dark blue jeans with a polo neck sweater and winklepicker shoes.' The McCartneys, Michael avers, had such a conservative upbringing that within days of being introduced by Paul to John their father warned both his sons: 'Be careful of that John Lennon. He could get you into trouble.' For Paul and Mike, the warning had the effect that parents everywhere risk: 'Paul and I were immediately drawn to John like moths to a flame because of what Dad said.' It was a remarkable parallel with John's bond with George Harrison, fired by Mimi's condemnation.

Brotherly love was one thing, but the braggadocio of Lennon was quite another: Michael grew to hero-worship John, for all his outward spunk and all his inner softness. 'Young as I was, and certainly later during the Beatle years, I decided he was a "pretend hard" man. He was a performer, all his life, and from his toughness right through to his teddy boy looks, he wasn't really either. It was just that, whatever he adopted, John did it with more reality than anybody else.' The smouldering fire inside John's mind did not allow him to go the whole way in any direction for very long. Teddy boy, beatnik, peacenik, poet – all were mantles to be adopted for periods and then discarded, victims of his chameleon-like personality at various points in his life. But when he was an eighteen-year-old playing truant from college, his intuition and desperation to convert the hobby of music into something worthwhile made him work feverishly on his partnership with Paul.

It was a matter of expediency. By the skin of his teeth he'd got into art college with no credentials from school, and now he was pretty sure that art would not offer him a career. With Mimi bearing down on him, and a bleak future pretty well assured, Lennon clung to music, and McCartney, like a life raft.

He had plenty to offer Paul, though. McCartney had a wider grasp of music, and particularly its variety of styles from ballads to jazz, but John compensated for his technical inferiority with an almost indefinable, animal quality that screamed rock 'n' roll. If music had not pulled them together, there would have been no reason for John Lennon and McCartney to have developed any bond of friendship. But both realized, even as teenagers, that they needed each other if their music was to flourish.

'I saw it, but our Dad didn't want to know,' says Michael McCartney. 'When John came round to the house, as far as Dad was concerned it might just as well have been the Devil. Yet there would be a double-edge, because Dad would realize that, musically, there must be something there in John.' Sometimes he would verbally condemn John's appearance. 'John didn't dare reply, because he respected my Dad as a good bloke who was looking after Paul and me. But once, Paul said something in defence of John and my father said: "Bloody hell, you will *not* have your trousers as tight as his. They're teddy boy trousers and not only will you not wear them in this house, you won't wear them, full stop. It's a bad thing." ' A diplomat, Paul knew when a boat should not be rocked. He took far fewer chances with his father than John took with Mimi. The afternoon meetings and the chance to sing and practise a few tunes and write a few lyrics, as well as hone hits made famous by Eddie Cochran and the Everly Brothers, were too precious to fritter away by alienating his father completely. George Harrison's council house at 25 Upton Green, Speke, was to prove an alternative refuge for the three of them, but Paul's Forthlin Road home was their favourite, partly because it was closer to Woolton and meant travelling a shorter distance with their guitars.

Mimi approved of Paul as a 'nice polite boy', but John knew that even asking permission to play rock 'n' roll there would be regarded as a heinous crime. The tactic adopted to arrange meetings was that Paul would coolly enquire of his father what time he would be home, most days, and strategically inform John that it was safe for him to arrive at a prescribed time for their two-hour 'sagging off school' sessions.

On some afternoons when plans had been laid by John and Paul, young Michael would be paid two shillings as the incentive to 'go to the pictures, see what's on at the Gaumont.' This was Paul's ploy to guarantee privacy for the songwriters, but not only to make music.

'Hold on,' said Michael, 'you never give me anything for nothing. What's happening?'

'Well,' said Paul, 'John's coming round and . . . girls, well, you know what girls are, don't you, Mike? But you're a bit young. You do things with them that you don't understand. It's big boys' stuff, this.'

'Oh,' said Michael, 'I think I'd better stay. I can't take the money off you!' Michael faced a dilemma: whether to stay and wait for the girls to arrive, or take the money from Paul and head for the cinema in Allerton. Paul always ended such a discussion by threatening to go elsewhere with John, which would have denied his young brother both the money *and* the chance to see the action. Michael took the money and vanished. On the whole,

Michael was happy enough just to be allowed to take photographs, a burgeoning hobby, when the two musicians got together.

One of the first songs written by John at these songwriting sessions was 'One After 909', and another was the unrecorded 'Winston's Walk'. Sometimes when he entered Forthlin Road he would wear the black horn-rimmed spectacles which he had managed to persuade Mimi to buy him, rather than be saddled with wire National Health-style glasses which ironically, later in his life, he was to make fashionable. 'He'd never be seen with specs on if he could avoid it,' says Michael McCartney. 'But without them he was blind as a bat. He'd walk down the path to our house, squinting, and whenever I saw him walking outside art college he'd hardly be able to see you. People used to think he was being off-hand or rude, not saying, "Hi", but it wasn't rudeness. He just couldn't see.' Glasses were too 'sissy', John would tell me years later when the Beatles story was at its height. He wore contact lenses, and we would hunt for lost lenses together on bedroom carpets and in dressing-rooms from Cheltenham to Munich and New York.

Just as his friendship with Paul blossomed and bore creative fruit, with tentative songwriting and a style taking shape that merged ballads and music with a beat, another powerful relationship was fast developing in John's life. He was getting to see more of his mother. She lived only a short bus ride from Woolton, in Spring Wood, with 'Bobby' Dykins. Julia, often called Julie by neighbours and friends in the street, had a twinkle in her eye and a style and vivacity that were at odds with the seriousness of these post-war years. Her handing over to her sister Mimi of the raising of her son had been a painful but rational decision, based on her uncertain home life with John's father Fred away at sea. Vitally, Aunt Mimi and Uncle George were not short of money but were not ostentatious with what George had earned through his hard work as the Woolton dairyman. Paul McCartney's exaggerated claim that John's family 'almost owned Woolton at one time' can be seen as a comparative judgment. Certainly Mimi and George were better off than any other Beatle's parents. 'John wanted for nothing,' said Mimi proudly. 'But he was never spoiled. I wanted him to learn the value of money.' She would make him mow the lawn at Mendips for five shillings. 'He'd do it when he came home from school or college, and do it quickly and not well. As soon as he'd finished a bit of lawn and he thought he could get away with it, he'd come in with his hand out,' said Mimi.

John's reunion meetings with his mother were becoming more and more frequent, but he spied a weak streak in 'Bobby' because he gave him too much pocket money for no reason. John viewed this as courting popularity with Julia's son. But he took the money: it came in useful to upgrade the cigarettes he normally bought – when 'Bobby' gave him a windfall, he would buy Senior Service instead of the lower-priced Park Drive or Woodbines.

Because she missed his company so much, Julia over-compensated John whenever they were together, at teatime after school *en route* to Mimi, and at weekends when he would spend whole days with her. She was more of a friend than a mother-figure and had an infectious sense of fun. She dressed colourfully and was the first and only woman in her street to wear trousers – which in the early 1950s was rare for women. Julia loved music and wanted to know every move John and the Quarry Men were making.

When John was waiting at her house in Spring Wood

one warm July evening in 1958, Julia was paying a visit
to Mimi for the traditional cup of tea and chat. The sisters
had totally different temperaments, but Julia loved Mimi
for her bookish intelligence and worldliness, while Julia's
sense of humour and warm personality were adored by
Mimi. Julia went to Mimi's on most days, and nodded
knowingly at the catalogue of problems in bringing up
John with which Mimi would regale her.

On some nights Mimi would walk Julia to the bus stop
two hundred yards away. But that night Mimi said, 'I won't
walk with you tonight, Julia – I'll see you tomorrow.'

Julia's words were to be prophetic: 'Don't worry.'

Julia crossed one side of the two-lane road, stepped
through the hedge to cross the second half towards her bus
stop, and was sent spinning into the air by a car. She died
instantly, at age forty-four.

A policeman broke the news of the accident to John
and 'Bobby' at the house in Spring Wood. They went
together to Sefton General Hospital which, ironically, five
years later, John would joyfully re-visit to see his wife
Cynthia with their son, Julian, who was born there. It
wasn't until they reached the hospital that the horrifying
truth was given to John by a doctor: 'I'm sorry, but your
Mummy's dead.'

John was appalled: the woman he was coming to discover as his best friend had been cruelly snatched from him
when he was seventeen, and just as his life was becoming
structured by the routine of college, its camaraderie, and
the growing importance of the Quarry Men, Paul McCartney, and Stuart Sutcliffe. His father's absence had been
capped by his mother's death. His early tears were replaced
by silence on the subject.

Mimi was distraught. 'It was a terrible, terrible shock
to me. One minute she was sitting here, having a cup of

tea with me, the next' – Mimi snapped her fingers – 'she'd gone. I never told any of the family where she was knocked down, to save them the pain. They drove past the spot every day. It wasn't just a case of my sister dying in a car accident, either – I'd got her little boy, so our relationship was very special. We'd never quarrelled about John and who should have him. She found a new man and I wasn't interfering with her life. After all, she'd had a rotten deal with that other thing [John's father]. When she went with the new man, I said that to think of another man providing for him shoes, clothes, and food and perhaps grudging it later on – it's not fair. Nobody was going to have the chance to look sideways at one of ours. And Julia agreed. So as John got older, he naturally got to know his mother better and everything was happy. He was brokenhearted for weeks. He just went to his room, into a shell. First his Uncle George, now his mother. I was in a state.' Julia was buried in Allerton Cemetery as Mrs Lennon.

The agony was prolonged by a court case. The car that knocked down Julia had been driven by an off-duty policeman who stood trial but was acquitted. The scars in John's young life were beginning to mount: the Blackpool tug-of-war between his parents; the death of lovable Uncle George; the self-inflicted abysmal failure of his schooldays; and now, at the emotionally crucial age of seventeen, the loss of his mother so suddenly was crushing.

John's hurt ran deep, but he did not allow it to be seen. He bottled up his sadness at Mimi's house, and at college there were only a few occasions when, sitting alone in class, students would notice him becoming uncharacteristically quiet or, shortly after Julia's death, the tears welling up. Ann Mason, girlfriend of John's friend Geoff Mohammed, says: 'Most of us knew his mother had died, but he shied away from talking about it. We knew it wasn't a subject to be discussed.' Twelve years later, John was to articulate the pain of his mother's loss with poignant songs called 'My Mummy's Dead', 'Mother', and 'Julia'. But the immediacy of the tragedy was too much for a teenager who had already absorbed enough traumas.

Lennon sought early refuge in drink. The atmosphere of Liverpool 8 district dominated by the art college and the Institute was conducive to behaving like an artist, poet, or writer. Lennon found comfort in the pubs of the area and on many afternoons returned to Arthur Ballard's classroom drunk, accompanied by Mohammed. Most students and teachers, knowing the reason behind John's behaviour, turned a blind eye to his wildness.

Only one person fully understood John's suffering. Paul McCartney had been similarly hit by the loss of his mother two years earlier. Few words were spoken between John and Paul about Julia's death. 'We didn't say anything about our mothers' deaths, but I did notice a quieter, more serious John for a while afterwards when he came round to our house,' says Michael McCartney. 'Suddenly, though, Paul and John had a bond that went beyond even the music.'

The Quarry Men – later briefly called Johnny and the Moondogs – continued throughout 1958 with a succession of line-ups, notably adding George Harrison on guitar. The rounds of youth club dances and social club events, particularly in the Woolton area where they had a name, kept them active. It was a useful diversion from college for John, still feeling desolate as the impact of his mother's death lingered. Later, during the Beatle years, John would muse on these uncomplicated years as a Quarry Man playing for a pint of light ale and a pie: 'We were doing it for fun then. Now it's a job.'

John's attitude to his college work was not endearing him to the teachers. Only Arthur Ballard, who supervised painting, saw him as having much potential and developed a rapport with John partly through drinking with him in Ye Cracke at lunchtimes; this was the kind of language John understood, trading light ale for black velvet (a unique British cocktail). John's poor punctuality in the morning, leaving for lunch with his eye more on making music with Paul and George in Ballard's room, or the canteen, than on college lectures, and erratic attendance in the afternoons, made him stand apart from most students and teachers. Dressed as a teddy boy, albeit a mild version, he was a marked man.

He added up to a dangerous ally for all but the brave, like the wild-eyed Geoff Mohammed, with his manic sense of humour and lightweight ability in art, and Stuart Sutcliffe, who could read John like a book. Indeed, Stuart was to write of John later, in a deadly accurate portrayal of the college Lennon:

> Sometimes a girl or boy would ask him about his sudden changes of mood, why he could be charming one minute and distasteful the next. His reply was always the same, if he bothered to reply. Usually when he did he felt no sympathy with his interrogator and would say: 'I hate you. Why should you like me, charm is only superficial and is easily exposed as having no concrete value.' Underneath the reserve that he piled upon himself at times like this, we knew there beat a human heart. A heart as kind and gentle as could be. He really hated hurting people and hated himself for doing so. He regarded people as conniving scoundrels, endeavouring to have a private view of his behaviour.

This was the cynicism of John Lennon stripped bare and placed in perspective by one who knew and loved him.

Since the death of his mother there had been a few girl students with whom Lennon had a relationship — Annette and Thelma and Barbara and Beth. But now his character was firmly shaped. He would be a loner.

SEVEN

ROMANCE

'Don't blame me just because your mother's dead'

'Hey, John, I believe your mother got killed by a police car.' The cold, clinical way in which a girl student greeted John in art college on their return from a long summer holiday in 1958 stunned the crowd of students gathering to sign on in the foyer for the start of a new term.

John was sitting across the 'signing in' table, his legs dangling, his expression introspective. His reaction to the girl's greeting was as impassive as the remark itself was tactlessly stark. 'Yeah, that's right.' He remained insouciant.

Thelma Pickles was stunned. She was introduced to John by another student, Helen Anderson. And Thelma did not know how to react to the embarrassment that the girl had caused her by speaking so brusquely about such a sensitive subject.

But Thelma need not have worried. 'I couldn't believe John's reaction. He didn't register anything. He didn't choke on it. It was as if someone had said, "You had your hair cut yesterday," or something like that.'

In the next six months Thelma came to understand a little more about the mind and emotions of John Lennon, to whom she was immediately drawn that day. Tony

Carricker, one of John's pals, was sitting with him on the table in the college foyer. 'But my eyes definitely set on John. Tony was prettier, more handsome, with dark hair and dark eyes, but John was so powerful. When he was in a group like that, the focus of attention went to him. He had a presence. I found him very striking from that moment on.'

A year younger than John, Thelma was to figure in one of his most torrid teenage love affairs before he met Cynthia. Their friendship blossomed in a spectacular conversation one day as they walked after college to the bus terminus on Castle Street. In no hurry to get home, they sat on the steps of the Queen Victoria monument for a talk. 'I knew his mother had been killed and asked if his father was alive,' says Thelma. 'Again, he said in this very impassive and objective way: "No, he pissed off and left me when I was a baby." I suddenly felt very nervous and strange. My father had left me when I was ten. Because of that, I had a huge chip on my shoulder. In those days, you never admitted you came from a broken home. You could never discuss it with anybody and people like me, who kept the shame of it secret, developed terrific anxieties. It was such a relief to me when he said that. For the first time, I could say to someone: "Well, so did mine."'

At first Thelma registered that he didn't care about his fatherless childhood. 'As I got to know him, he obviously cared. But what I realized quickly was that he and I had an aggression towards life that stemmed entirely from our messy home lives.'

Their friendship developed, not as a cosy love match but as teenage kids with chips on their shoulders. 'It was more a case of him carrying my things to the bus stop for me, or going to the cinema together, before we became physically involved.' John, when she knew him, would have laughed at people who were seen arm in arm. 'It wasn't love's young dream. We had a strong affinity through our backgrounds and we resented the strictures that were placed upon us. We were fighting against the rules of the day. If you were a girl of sixteen like me, you had to wear your beret to school, be home at a certain time, and you couldn't wear make-up. A bloke like John would have trouble wearing skin-tight trousers and generally pleasing himself, especially with his strict aunt. We were always being told what we couldn't do. He and I had a rebellious streak, so it was awful. We couldn't wait to grow up and tell everyone to get lost. Mimi hated his tight trousers and my mother hated my black stockings. It was a horrible time to be young!' Lennon's language was ripe and fruity for the 1950s, and so was his wounding tongue. In Ye Cracke, one night after college, John rounded on Thelma in front of several students and was crushingly rude to her. She forgets exactly what he said but remembers her blistering retort to him: 'Don't blame me,' said Thelma, 'just because your mother's dead.'

It was something of a turning point. John went quiet, but now he had respect for the girl who would return his own viciousness with a sentence that was equally offensive. 'Most people stopped short,' says Thelma. 'They were probably frightened of him, and on occasions there were certainly fights. But with me, he met someone with almost the same background and edge. We got on well, but I wasn't taking any of his verbal cruelty.'

When they were together, though, the affinity was special, with a particular emphasis on sick humour. Thelma says categorically that John and she laughed at afflicted or elderly people 'as something to mock, a joke.' It was not anything deeply psychological like fear of them, or sympathy, she says. 'Not to be charitable to ourselves, we both actually disliked these people rather than sympathized,' says Thelma. 'Maybe it was related to being artistic and liking things to be aesthetic all the time. But it just wasn't sympathy. I really admired his directness, his ability to verbalize all the things I felt amusing.' He developed an instinctive ability to mock the weak, for whom he had no patience.

In the early 1950s Britain had National Service conscription for men aged eighteen and over who were medically fit. John seized on this as his way of ridiculing many people who were physically afflicted. 'Ah, you're just trying to get out of the army,' he jeered at men in wheelchairs being guided down Liverpool's fashionable Bold Street, or 'How did you lose your legs? Chasing the wife?' He ran up behind frail old women and made them jump with fright, screaming 'Boo' into their ears. 'Anyone limping, or crippled or hunchbacked, or deformed in any way, John laughed and ran up to them to make horrible faces. I laughed with him while feeling awful about it,' says Thelma. 'If a doddery old person had nearly fallen over because John had screamed at her, we'd be laughing. We knew it shouldn't be done. I was a good audience, but he didn't do it just for my benefit.' When a gang of art college students went to the cinema, John would shout out, to their horror, 'Bring on the dancing cripples.' 'Children often find that kind of sick humour amusing,' says Thelma. 'Perhaps we just hadn't grown out of it. He would pull the most grotesque faces and try to imitate his victims.'

Often, when he was with her, he would pass Thelma his latest drawings of grotesquely afflicted children with misshapen limbs. The satirical *Daily Howl* that he had ghoulishly passed around at Quarry Bank School was taken several stages beyond the gentle, prodding humour he doled out against his former school teachers. 'He was merciless,' says Thelma Pickles. 'He had no remorse or sadness for these people. He just thought it was funny.' He told her he felt bitter about people who had an easy life. 'I found him magnetic,' says Thelma, 'because he mirrored so much of what was inside me, but I was never bold enough to voice.'

Thel, as John called her, became well aware of John's short-sightedness on their regular trips to the cinema. They would 'sag off' college in the afternoons to go to the Odeon in London Road or the Palais de Luxe, to see films like Elvis Presley's *Jailhouse Rock* and *Kid Creole*. 'He'd never pay,' says Thelma. 'He never had any money.'

Whether he had his horn-rimmed spectacles with him or not, John would not wear them in the cinema. He told her he didn't like them for the same reason that he hated deformity in people: wearing specs was a sign of weakness. Just as he did not want to see crutches or wheelchairs without laughing, John wouldn't want to be laughed at. So he very rarely wore his specs, even though the black horn-rimmed style was a copy of his beloved Buddy Holly.

'So in the cinema we sat near the front and it would be: "What's happening now, Thel?" "Who's that, Thel?" He couldn't follow the film but he wouldn't put his specs on, even if he had them.'

Even then she was attracted to his 'very straight, lovely, Romanesque nose' which was accentuated by his habit of tilting his head back. The stance became a crucial hallmark of John's stage posture as a Beatle; it was generally thought to be part of his arrogance, a defiant declaration of his domain. In fact, the stance was caused by his short-sightedness. 'He'd take ages to see things in a room,' recalls Thelma. 'He'd say: "Who's that in that corner?" when it was someone he should have recognized immediately.'

It was not a big step from cinema visits and mutual

mocking of people for John and Thelma to go beyond the drinking sessions in Ye Cracke. 'It wasn't love's young dream, but I had no other boyfriends while I was going out with John and as far as I knew he was seeing nobody except me.'

On the nights that John's Aunt Mimi was due to go out for the evening to play bridge, Thelma and John met on a seat in a brick-built shelter on the golf course opposite the house in Menlove Avenue. When the coast was clear and they saw Mimi leaving, they would go into the house.

'He certainly didn't have a romantic attitude to sex,' says Thelma. 'He used to say that sex was equivalent to a five-mile run, which I'd never heard before. He had a very disparaging attitude to girls who wanted to be involved with him but wouldn't have sex with him.

' "They're edge-of-the-bed virgins," he said.

'I said: "What does that mean?"

'He said: "They get you to the edge of the bed and they'll not complete the act."

'He hated that. So if you weren't going to go to bed with him, you had to make damned sure you weren't going to go to the edge of the bed, either. If you did, he'd get very angry.

'If you were prepared to go to his bedroom, which was above the front porch, and start embarking on necking and holding hands, and you weren't prepared to sleep with him, then he didn't want to know you. You didn't do it. It wasn't worth losing his friendship. So if you said, "No", that was OK. He'd then play his guitar or an Everly Brothers record. Or we'd go to the pictures. He *would* try to persuade you to sleep with him, though.

'He was no different from any young bloke except that if you led him on and gave him the impression you would embark on any kind of sexual activity and then didn't, he'd be very abusive. It was entirely lust.'

The art college in the late 1950s was a hotbed of promiscuity. 'There was much weeping in the loo,' says Thelma. 'At sixteen we were very ignorant; it was very much hit and miss. Suddenly there was a pregnancy explosion, and five students were pregnant in one year. They had to leave college. It was a social stigma, no matter what circle you came from – working-class, middle-class, or whatever.'

John never talked about the dangers of pregnancy. 'He wouldn't care. It wouldn't enter his mind to think about it.'

Thelma was John's girlfriend for six months. 'It just petered out,' she says. 'I certainly didn't end it. He didn't either. We still stayed part of the same crowd of students. When we were no longer close, he was more vicious to me in company than before. I was equally offensive back. That way you got John's respect.'

Her memory of her former boyfriend is of a teenager 'very warm and thoughtful inside. Part of him was gentle and caring. He was softer and gentler when we were alone than when we were in a crowd. He was never physically violent with me – just verbally aggressive, and he knew how to hurt. There was a fight with him involved once, in the canteen, but he'd been drinking. He wasn't one to pick a fight. He often enraged someone with his tongue and he'd been on the edge of it, but he loathed physical violence really. He'd be scared. John avoided real trouble.'

One day in the lettering class at college the uncouth rebel who looked unkempt, who delighted in disruptive behaviour and acting the fool in class, and who needed

nursing with loaned ruler or paintbrush, became a source
of fascination for another girl – Cynthia Powell. The story of
their unlikely mutual attraction has already been told. At
home, over tea one day, John said of Cynthia: 'Do you know
what, Mimi, there's a girl sending me chocolate biscuits
and coffee in the canteen at college.'

Mimi said, 'You don't accept them, do you?'

'If she's fool enough to send them,' replied John, 'I'll
eat them.'

The girl from the posh side of the Mersey seemed at
first sight the least likely partner for the college troublemaker. She spoke very softly, neither drank nor smoked,
and behaved decorously. She had had a strict upbringing
with her two older brothers. Like John, she lived with one
parent, her strongminded mother, Lilian. Her father had
died of cancer two years before she met Lennon; also like
John, she was seventeen when she lost a parent.

It would be easy to analyse their mutual attraction as
Cynthia the mother substitute and John the swaggering
teenage tough guy, Cynthia's concession to dangerous
living. But from the time they got together, it was more
than just another fling for them both. It wasn't long before
John and Cynthia were spending afternoons and nights at
Stuart Sutcliffe's flat. This was a dangerous affair, demanding lies of both John and Cynthia: she would tell her
mother she had stayed at a girlfriend's flat for the night,
and John would concoct a story for Mimi about playing
with the Quarry Men too far away to get home. Neither
Lilian Powell nor Aunt Mimi were to know of the affair,
still less the intensity of it, for many months.

Cynthia's memory of John during their earliest days
together is of a 'rough diamond with a heart of gold'.
There were only two problems about him, in her view: his
ferocious temper and his incredible jealousy if any other

man should go near her. In true chauvinistic style, he
considered it all right for him to dabble with other girls,
as long as Cynthia did not discover it. Today, she smiles at
the fact that she was kept under strict surveillance by him
while he had other girlfriends. 'But it didn't matter. What
mattered, in my eyes at that time, was that while John was
with me, I was blind to anything else. He gave me his
everything when he was with me, and I didn't need any
other assurance.' In a small community such as Liverpool 8
at that time, secrets were hard to keep, but Lennon did
pretty well. His absence from college lectures and the lack
of interest by the tutors in disciplining him gave him *carte
blanche* to vanish at all sorts of odd hours to consolidate his
trysts.

Just as he scorned the physically afflicted, John mocked
people who were conventional, toed the line, and didn't join
in his flouting of authority. Cynthia Powell, the epitome of
middle-class Hoylake, was in that category. She was among
the smartest dressed of the girl students, with pale pink
twinsets and fancy embroidered collars. She was as polite
as John was aggressive, and was not among the girls who
joined Lennon's table during lunch in the canteen. There
were different camps. 'I was in his camp of boys,' says
Thelma Pickles, 'because I was a bit of an arty beatnik.
Cynthia was dainty and sweet. We used to take the mickey
out of her, but John always said he fancied her. He called
her Miss Prim, and he said to me: "It's a pity she's a bit
posh," implying there was a gulf he would never be able
to overcome. He was certainly always attracted to her from
the first time he saw her in the canteen.

'It wasn't that John thought *she* had any feelings of
superiority. He just recognized her different background,
because she was from over the water. It was *our* inverted
snobbery. When she walked into the room, he'd say: "Don't

talk like that, 'cos Cynthia's here." He meant we had to be on our best behaviour.'

John was acutely aware of one other girl at college who was besotted with him. 'She sat weeping over him,' says Thelma, 'but instead of feeling sorry for her and giving her a kind word, he'd put her down verbally.' John could not tolerate such a public display of emotion. He despised the girl for *showing* what he considered a weakness. What weaknesses *he* had he either kept well hidden or exploited, as in the case of cripples.

Thelma Pickles heard when she was temporarily away from college that John and Cynthia had become close. 'I was startled but pleased. I thought she'd be good for him, temper his aggression. I knew she'd have to tailor herself into looking like Brigitte Bardot for him, and I remember reflecting on the fact that he'd teased her so much about being so proper. I remember thinking: "He's got what he wanted – again." '

Cynthia believes that most of the staff and tutors were frightened of John. This led to mutual disrespect, as John could not stand weakness. 'He was constantly being told off for coming in late. If it hadn't been for Arthur Ballard, who acted as his guardian, I think some terrible things might have happened between John and the teachers. I heard Arthur Ballard saying to the others: "Look, he's not a bad lad, he's going through a bad patch. He's talented." '

But his greasy, quiffed hair, with the DA at the back, contrasted with most of the other students' long hair. His scruffy black trousers, with tight 'drainies' altered by Helen Anderson, and his shiny black jacket, made him look utterly different from the traditional bohemian student look of casual jacket, with leather elbow pads, or duffle coat. Even- tually John demurred and, in another change which sur-

prised students, came to school regularly in his Uncle
George's brown tweed jacket and grey trousers.

'All the changes in dress, and particularly that teddy
boy period, were a throwback to his younger days,' says
Cynthia. 'At Dovedale and Quarry Bank, he told me he felt
he had to look tough and hard. It was his wall against the
world, in case somebody picked a fight. So he dressed in a
tough way. When he first went to college, he felt as if he
had to be on guard. Most of the students weren't tough or
aggressive, but he'd come from a tougher school background. Woolton was a genteel area but he didn't want to
be regarded as a genteel lad, so he played a hard role. It
was his friendship with Stuart and then with me that
changed him and made him realize there was no need for
that acting at all.'

Nothing could deter Cynthia. Her work suffered as she
spent every minute at college thinking of him or seeking
him out. She had plenty of conventional reasons for saying
'enough is enough' and dumping John. He could not take
his drink, and once, when a fellow student was rude to him
at a party at a tutor's house, Lennon dragged him out to
the street and pinned him to the ground within seconds,
thumping him. 'I was dancing with Stuart Sutcliffe upstairs
when the row began. We wondered where John had gone
but were soon told there was a fight,' says Cynthia. 'It was
the drink again – he had a very small capacity before he
became aggressive. The slightest thing would have him in
a terrible temper.' To a prim girl from the Wirral, he was
quite a visual spectacle as he slouched into lettering class
twice weekly, battered guitar slung nonchalantly across his
shoulders. His fingers were permanently stained by nicotine
from the twenty cigarettes he got through most days, most
of them scrounged tersely ('Gimme a fag?') from the nearest
student. The profile of John as an undesirable was com-

pleted by big ugly callouses on his fingers, the effect of his
guitar picking.

The effect Cynthia and John had on each other was
immediate. Within about a year, John had dropped even
his teddy boy posturing. He took to an 'arty' look, wearing
scarves, ordinary black jackets and trousers, and combing
his hair more traditionally. That was his concession to
Cynthia's conventional appearance and also an indication
that their love affair was giving him fewer reasons to make
a dramatic visual impression. He was growing up. Cynthia's
change, for John, was much more radical. Aware of his
fanatical enthusiasm for Brigitte Bardot and Juliette Greco,
and a more pouting expression than she naturally showed,
'Cyn' took to wearing black fishnet stockings with seams,
tighter skirts, and suspender belts. All three features were
requested by John. Crucially Cyn, who had arrived at art
college with reddish brown hair, gradually lightened it
until she was dyed a beautiful golden blonde. The transformation was complete: John had secured his Brigitte
Bardot look-alike. For Cynthia, it was not just a pleasure
but a political move, too: no more would John be able to
drool to others in the canteen at lunchtime. Cynthia, infatu-
ated or in love, was acutely aware of what she perceived as
competition.

During these teenage pre-Beatle years, Cynthia was the
only person in whom John would confide his deepest feelings. Three people figured in his conversations with her
about his home life, besides the omnipresent discipline of
Aunt Mimi. There was Uncle George, whom John missed
terribly and said so. He would proudly tell Cynthia when
he was wearing one of George's old jackets. They did not
fit, but he did not care. His father was a taboo subject:
John had this vision, which he gave to Cynthia, of a great
seafaring man, with a wonderful singing voice, 'a hero in

the distance' whom he could not see because he had to go away for important work at sea. It clearly troubled John, but he had closed his mind to his father's existence. Third, of course, there was his mother and the pain of her recent accidental death.

'He didn't talk about his Mum to anybody but me,' says Cynthia. 'It shattered his life. He often said how terrible it was that he'd lost her just at the time she was becoming his best friend. I could see the feeling welling up deep inside him, then he would say something like that, and close down. I'd say: "Come on, John, I want to know all about you." And he'd shake his head as if to say no. It was obviously too painful for him to open up very much. I'm sure that's why he went completely crazy at college and why the combination of drink and anger made him so aggressive. It was a bitter rage. When he became successful as a Beatle he was a different person altogether. The aggravation was restrained. He became gentle. He still drank but he didn't get so aggressive.'

John's jealousy and possessiveness about Cynthia were almost overpowering. When she could not stay the night with him, he insisted she stay in Liverpool until the last train left Central Station at 11:20 for Hoylake, getting her home just before the critical midnight hour. 'He always made me get that last train home to make sure he was the only man I was seeing that night.' After college, they would adjourn either to Stuart's flat or the cinema, or go for drinks. 'He wanted total commitment and I was pleased to give it,' says Cynthia. 'If I as much as looked at another man, he would go mad and say: "Who's *he*?" in a moody voice.' With her daily allowance of eight shillings, Cynthia plied John with cigarettes – the cheapest varieties, Woodbines or Embassy – because he was usually broke. 'He wasn't mean, just always broke from spending his cash on black velvet, the mixture of Guinness and cider which was the students' cheap way of getting drunk quickly: four pints most lunchtimes. But he was very moral – he pooled his money.'

Cynthia is philosophical about affairs that John had before and during his college days. 'When John was with me, it was total commitment. Whatever he did outside our relationship didn't seem very important. We were together such a lot of the time that whatever other affairs he had once we met couldn't have amounted to much because I was with him most of the time. He kept me in Liverpool as late as I dared stay. It wasn't as if he wanted to get rid of me. Later on, during the Beatles' very busy period and when he was away a lot, it was a different matter. But love is blind.'

Once their betrothal was clinched, and they couldn't bear to be apart, John and Cynthia decided it was time they met each other's families. 'After a few months, I went up to Mendips and got on fine with Mimi. The only thing that was kept secret from her was that John and I spent some nights together in Stuart Sutcliffe's flat. She must have thought I was a nice young girl. Little did she know.' After tea of eggs and chips and bread and butter, John and Cynthia and Mimi would sit talking before, eventually, Cynthia would go and stay with her best friend, Phyllis McKenzie, who also lived in Woolton.

The trips by John to Trinity Road, Hoylake, were less frequent: he clashed with Cynthia's mother on their first meeting. 'He ran out of the house after he and Mum hadn't got on well. It was all very tense, that first meeting. I ran after him and found him halfway between the house and the station. He wanted to get back to Liverpool quickly. But I persuaded him to return and patch up the argument for my sake. Mum wasn't mad about his appearance and made it clear to him. She'd much rather I'd chosen a clean-cut office type.' John only went across to the Wirral three times. He was destined never to get on well with Cynthia's mother, not even during the most joyful days of Beatlemania. When she lived at his Weybridge mansion, he regarded her as an intruder.

The year 1959 was a significant one for John. First, he made a tentative move from Mimi and Woolton, and went to live with Stuart in Gambier Terrace, in a house with an impressive view of the Anglican Cathedral which was then being built. To describe Stuart's home as a flat would be an exaggeration; it was a room with a shared toilet in a large Georgian house. There were mattresses on the floor as beds, paints and kettles and all the trappings of student living spread chaotically around the floor. Its appeal to John was its very disorderliness, and also the fact that it was a haven for him and Cynthia to sleep together. 'Even though both our families knew we were seeing a lot of each other,' says Cynthia, 'in those days kids were not as open about their lives together. John and I took the view that with Mimi and my Mum, what the eye didn't see the heart couldn't grieve over.' She made no move to leave her Hoylake home, but her mother noticed an increased number of nights when Cynthia said she was staying at Phyllis's home in Woolton. Cynthia's alibi was perfect. But Mimi was furious about John's departure to 'dirty' Gambier Terrace.

'Please Cynthia, try to get him to move out of that place. It's filthy and it's unhealthy.'

'There's not a lot I can do, Mimi,' said Cynthia. 'He wants to be with Stuart.'

John rubbed salt in Mimi's wounds by technically not leaving Mendips: he would return there every few days to collect and deliver dirty and clean shirts, underpants, and socks. Mimi consoled herself that at least she saw him regularly and made sure he got a square meal.

Living with Stuart had another stabilizing effect on John; there was his company, and conversations long into the night with the male friend he admired more than anyone, plus Stuart's encouragement to John to try his hand with painting. In return for the casual art lessons, John tried to teach Stuart bass guitar. He was never a good player, but John loyally brought his mate into the Quarry Men and later into the early Beatles. Even if he couldn't play well, and disguised the fact by turning his back on the audience so they couldn't see his inadequacies on the guitar, Stuart had a major redeeming quality which John liked: he looked mean and moody, and the girls liked him, complete with his adolescent spots. Stuart's quiet vulnerability made him something of a heart-throb. Visually, if not musically, he was an asset to the group at a time when they needed all the fans they could get. To Stuart, the music was light relief from his intensive work as a painter: at college he was known as a workaholic.

Cynthia remembers that, at this stage, John was totally consumed with music. 'It was his complete conversation outside college and a lot of the time in college, too. He couldn't get enough rehearsal time in and he seemed genuinely keen on the partnership that was developing with Paul McCartney.' Locations for rehearsing the hits of the day, particularly the prophetically titled Buddy Holly hit 'It Doesn't Matter Anymore', were getting better. Despite his mother's death, John remained in touch with 'Bobby' Dykins, and he, Paul, and Cynthia would use Bobby's house in Spring Wood for jam sessions and songwriting when they wanted a change from Paul's home. 'If Twitchy [Bobby] was in, he'd let us in. If he wasn't, we'd break in through a window, raid the larder, and leave after a jam session lasting two or three hours in the afternoons and early evenings,' says Cynthia. 'John suffered Twitchy all right. They were polite to each other, that's all. But his house came in useful. That's the way John would have seen it.'

Paul – then, as now, highly organized with fine attention to detail – carried an exercise book in which he wrote down the words to the songs he and John were working on. This year, too, they formally shook hands on an agreement that was to inscribe their names together in the history books. They agreed that, from then on, whether a song was written individually or together, they would have both their names stuck on them as songwriters, thus: 'Lennon-McCartney'. It was a touching manifestation of togetherness at a time when neither knew how significant the partnership would become, or how much rancour would result ten years later.

'It was a beautiful period,' reflects Cynthia, looking back. 'It wasn't just a musical convenience that put them together. By the time I saw them playing at the college, they were friends, at one with each other. They seemed to have been friends for many years. It was intuitive. George, being younger and not writing songs, didn't have the communication with them, but John and Paul couldn't stop playing together, practising the chords of the latest Elvis Presley song, the Everly Brothers, and getting the confidence to try writing their own words. I sat there, on these "away days" of rehearsals, absolutely mesmerized. Their harmonies were so beautiful. John had this image of being the toughest boy in college but his music showed what all of us knew was underneath. He had a gentleness that needed to come out, and it did in those songs.'

Cynthia saw music come to be Lennon's salvation. Mimi might have thought she was punishing him by banishing

him to the porch when she tired of his guitar strumming;
but John relished it, because the acoustics were better than
inside the house. The college lunchtime sessions with Paul
and George only once attracted a crowd of any size. In the
canteen, students who saw him during lectures as the wild
one were astonished at the music that came from him. A
typical programme would be 'Peggy Sue', 'Good Golly Miss
Molly', 'Rip It Up,' 'All I Have To Do Is Dream', and
always, as a finale, 'When You're Smiling', sung by John
in a cackling, Goon-like voice.

'He didn't like an audience for these sessions with Paul,'
says Cynthia. 'But luckily for the big audience he didn't
have his glasses on so he couldn't see how many people had
gathered round. I remember several of the students saying:
"My goodness, this is a different John Lennon." They'd see
him walking round with a battered guitar and thought he
was trouble. Suddenly, at the sight of him playing soft
melodic music, they realized that inside him was so much
more.'

Money, fame, and ambition for the Quarry Men were still
secondary to John's love and lust for Cynthia and a rarely
admitted desire to please Mimi. 'I don't think that at
nineteen John had the faintest idea he would be rich or
successful, or even hoped for it in the same way that some
people hope to win the football pools,' says Cynthia. 'Paul
was a keen schoolboy but John wasn't like that. He was
just happy doing what he wanted. He was carefree.' Underneath that indifference, though, was a conventional wish.
As the Quarry Men earned a few pounds from their engagements, John would love the pleasure of giving Mimi a
bundle of notes, erratically. 'He'd give her £10 or so from
time to time. I saw the expression on his face that almost

said: "Look, we've *made* it!" Even though they hadn't made it at all, he wanted Mimi to think he was doing something well. "There's the money for my keep," he'd say to his Auntie.'

Every student who was with Lennon at art college has a different anecdote about him. But they all agree on one central point: if John had not emerged successfully with the Beatles, he could easily have gone seriously off the rails. Cynthia says that if he had not had Paul McCartney to cajole him, and their son, Julian, to motivate him to make some money, and still later Brian Epstein as Beatles manager to push him, 'he would have ended up a bum. . . . It's hard to say that now, after what happened, but he wouldn't have cared that much. I'd have gone out to work, he wouldn't have any qualifications whatsoever because he was falling foul of the art college, and Mimi would have pushed him in all sorts of directions. He would have needed to learn a trade, or go back to school again, and I can't see him concentrating. He'd have gone downhill.'

EIGHT

HAMBURG

'Have a coffee. We've been chucked out of college'

PREDICTABLY LENNON failed his lettering examinations. Even the combined faked papers from Cynthia and Thelma could not save him. His disorderliness at college, his swearing and contempt for the teaching system had all but resulted in his being expelled. Arthur Ballard came to the rescue and gained a stay of execution for Lennon, partly because of John's association with the brilliant Stuart Sutcliffe: this, it was claimed, redeemed Lennon as far as his ambition was concerned. Geoff Mohammed was thrown out of college, and John and he were to be seen celebrating in a city coffee bar. Michael McCartney walked in to find the pair in jubilant mood: 'Hey, Mike, come on in and have a coffee. We've been chucked out of college!' It was not technically true in John's case, but it might well have been. Lennon was not the sort of nineteen-year-old who returned confidences or even the compliments of Arthur Ballard. His attendance at college became more and more erratic. He regarded himself as a 'visitor' rather than a permanent student.

Luck came to John's rescue; within a few weeks of facing expulsion, he would visit Germany as a musician, an event which was to mark his entire life.

Days were now spent mostly drinking coffee in the Jacaranda, a club not far from the college on Slater Street. The *Sunday People* newspaper focused on Stuart and John's shambles of a room — with its stolen Belisha beacon and macabre, empty coffin as part of the furniture — in an exposé entitled 'This is the Beatnik Horror'. John, free of the shackles of Mimi's home, felt physically and mentally liberated. He could now enact all the fantasies of the world to combine rock 'n' roll with all that being an art student meant, without producing much art.

The 'Jac' was a coffee bar run by Allan Williams, a Welsh-born hustler with a keen eye on the pop scene. He proved to be an important stepping stone in the Beatles' success story. Through his affinity with Stuart Sutcliffe, whom he admired, Williams found himself constantly harangued by Lennon for a few sessions for the Quarry Men in the basement of the 'Jac' when regular groups like Cass and the Casanovas, Derry and the Seniors, and Rory Storm and the Hurricanes (featuring Ringo Starr on drums) failed to show up or were not available.

Williams relented. John dragged Stuart into the group on bass guitar (he had bought the instrument with the money he had won in an art competition). Within days, Stuart's delicate artist's fingers were in shreds. Lennon now believed that rock 'n' roll was the only avenue open to him, for he started to look moderately tidy for the sessions that Williams fixed. The band wore black polo-necked Marks and Spencer's sweaters, dark blue jeans, and white plimsoll shoes.

It was against this background of a fading interest in art and increasingly bohemian living, accompanied by life with Stuart in a flat of their own, that John slowly became more aggressively ambitious for his group. He pestered Allan Williams for dates and eventually landed one at the

Grosvenor Ballroom in Seacombe. It was a notorious local bloodbath where gangs went not for music or dancing, nor to find women partners, so much as 'have a scene' with rival groups: 'a scene' meant a punch-up. The band playing rock 'n' roll from the stage would have a tough job making itself heard and not getting involved in the trouble. Although he would be one of the first to run at the sight of real danger to himself, John enjoyed being on the precipice overlooking a battle. The rock 'n' roll music he loved was anyway full of assertiveness, and a spot of bother seemed appropriate to the combative stance and sound of Elvis Presley. In his mind, John was moving well away from skiffle and such soft music as the Everly Brothers' 'Cathy's Clown' and mellow ballads like Cliff Richard's 'Travelling Light'. (John was later to describe Cliff Richard to me as the epitome of all he hated in British pop. 'He's so bloody Christian I can't stand him and his lot.') Rock 'n' roll was a clarion call for John, an act of such defiance that a change of name for his group was now on the horizon.

The momentum of the group was now quickening. Paul might have been the better musician, singing the more acceptable, poppier melodies ('You Are My Sunshine', 'Home', and 'You Were Meant For Me') while John went for the slightly more abrasive, beatier stuff like 'Ain't She Sweet'. But Lennon remained firmly the leader. When name changes were discussed, to try to steer them away from Quarry Men which was 'too skiffly and restricting,' said John, his own name would invariably be mentioned as an alternative. Long John Silver, a parody on his name and a character in a favourite childhood story, *Treasure Island*, was quickly rejected. It was almost as corny as the pop music of Cliff Richard and Frankie Vaughan and Craig Douglas which John was now trying to debunk.

Stylistically, no pop act came near Buddy Holly in John

and Paul's affection at that time. The light beat of Buddy Holly's distinctive songs was a perfect progression from skiffle. John was attracted by the name of Holly's backing group, the Crickets, and played around with names to emulate that. It was Stuart who first came up with the Beetles, as a 'play' on Crickets. It appealed to John who, in a masterly example of his skill in word-play which was to stay with him throughout his life, later modified the spelling to Beatles, to incorporate the word 'beat' which was fast becoming conversational currency in Liverpool, with its proliferation of pop groups that no other city could match.

John continued to pester Allan Williams for more work. They secured a drummer who, even though he was thirty-six, was very competent on the instrument which all groups regarded as vital. Tommy Moore, a fork-lift truck driver, was a fine player and technically the best John, Paul, and George had in those years. What he lacked in youthful exuberance he compensated for by improving the tightness of their sound. John had little patience with the slow-moving personality of Moore but saw him as a means to an end, of raising the group to a higher musical level than the other groups on Merseyside.

The Quarry Men's last performances under that name were at a club in the Liverpool suburb of West Derby run by Mona Best, mother of the Beatles' future drummer, Peter. In August 1959 they played at the opening of the club, and over the next three years were to play there about a hundred and twenty times, going through various name changes along the way until they finally reached the Beatles. The problem in filling the drum chair was not easily solved by John, Paul, George, and short-lived guitarist Ken Brown. So difficult was it that, when they entered a Carroll Levis talent contest in Manchester towards the end of 1959 under the skiffle-like name of Johnny and the Moondogs, John, Paul, and George were without a drummer at all. Their appearance was a failure.

The Allan Williams and Jacaranda connection, as well as Williams's control of another club where the Beatles played, the Wyvern Social Club, later called the Blue Angel, at 108 Seel Street, was to be important in the Beatles' next phase. Larry Parnes, a famous name from London, had a reputation for creating top British pop stars and giving them names that evoked a positive image in a pop scene that was mostly spineless. After discovering Tommy Steele in the 2 I's coffee bar in Soho, Parnes had gone on to launch such luminaries as Marty Wilde, Vince Eager, Duffy Power, Johnny Gentle, and Dickie Pride. It was a pop stable with Elvis Presley stereotypes, painfully British in its imitative stance, and people laughed. But in the late 1950s Parnes was a name to be noted by anyone with an eye on making headway in the pop music world.

Through Allan Williams, John's group, then known as the Silver Beetles, secured an audition with Larry Parnes in Liverpool. The winning group would accompany another Liverpool singer from the Parnes stable, Billy Fury, on a nationwide concert tour. The Silver Beetles failed that audition but were offered something equally attractive — the grand sum of £18 a week to accompany one of his lesser-known singers, Johnny Gentle, on a tour of the far north of Scotland. John and Stuart were ecstatic. They would find it simple to skip college for one week. Paul was equally determined to make the break from his studies for school exams. He had an uphill job persuading his father that the break would rest his brain and be beneficial, but with the aid of his brother Michael he clinched it. With Tommy Moore, George, and Stuart, the Silver Beetles set off from Liverpool's Lime Street Station, and for a week enjoyed for the first time the life of hotels, autograph hunters, and importantly, non-Liverpool audiences. The money proved barely adequate, but the freedom from home and school was wonderful, particularly for the wanderlust in John, who did not have parental security as a backdrop to his life.

Two people were to be the butt of John's cruel streak on that Scottish tour. Curiously, neither was prepared to join in his verbal jousting or retaliate, and since John preferred fighters to pacifists, they were easy targets. He got a special delight out of taunting Stuart, whose attempts to keep up with the music were simply beyond his capabilities. It didn't seem to occur to John that it was he who had dragged a reluctant Stuart into playing bass in the first place. Now, Stuart was verbally pummelled by his best mate for not coming up to scratch. More cold-bloodedly, Lennon had no patience whatsoever for Tommy Moore. When the group van, which singer Johnny Gentle was driving, had a bump with a car, and Moore was taken to hospital, it was Lennon who went to his bedside and insisted that he get up in time for that night's show.

Scotland had a more profound effect on John than on the other four. Tommy Moore left the Silver Beetles immediately on their return, feeling the age gap too much and the prospects not too rosy. Paul and George went back to the Liverpool Institute, while John's art college days were sliding into disarray. While he was away in Scotland, Cynthia had heard of his failure in lettering. Nothing could redeem his all-round lack of art college application. It was at this time that he hit his worst patch with Mimi, too. 'What was I going to do with someone who had no certificates from school and who appeared to be going the same way at college? I didn't stop worrying,' said Mimi. 'I'd say:

"You must think about getting a job instead of messing about with the guitar, John. Concentrate on your studies. You know you're good at drawing."

'And he always replied along the same lines. "I'll be OK, I don't need the bits of paper to tell me where I'm going." '

Rock 'n' roll as a livelihood was clearly established in his mind by now, though he was less sure about how he would manage it. He increased the pressure on Allan Williams to get them work. Weekly sessions at Mona Best's Casbah Club, and the support work at the Jac, as well as the occasional accompaniment of a stripper in the New Cabaret Artistes Club, were not enough. Fresh from the taste of a proper concert tour in Scotland, John was fired with a hunger for engagements almost nightly. Allan Williams was now more convinced of their potential. They were even rivalling Derry and the Seniors and Gerry and the Pacemakers as local favourites. Before long, Allan Williams was getting the Silver Beetles engagements at the Grosvenor Ballroom in Seacombe and at the Neston Institute. The teddy boy movement plummeted to its nadir at some of these halls. Boozed-up teds were infuriated that the band on stage was highly fancied by the 'birds' they had brought along, and they took it out on the musicians. The aggression usually stopped short of fist fights, but not always. John, faster with his reflexes than anyone in the group, had come to the rescue of the physically slighter Stuart one night. A group of teds set on Stu and kicked him in the head after a dance. Lennon set about Sutcliffe's assailant with a ferocity rarely seen. It was as if John needed a good excuse, like the battering of his best friend, to show even himself the strength he now had at twenty. Though there was a lot of blood, and Stuart went home with a

Eight-year-old John with his vivacious mother Julia in her sister
Anne's garden in July, 1949 (Tom Hanley)

Above left: John aged seven, a pupil of Dovedale Primary School,
Allerton, Liverpool (Dezo Hoffman/Rex Features)

Above right: Outside the front porch of 'Mendips', the house where he
lived with Aunt Mimi. She would banish him there with his guitar
when the noise became too much for her (Tom Hanley)

Left: Ten-year-old John outside the house at 251 Menlove Avenue, Woolton, Liverpool, where he was raised (Tom Hanley)

Below: John's rebellious spirit began at Liverpool's Quarry Bank High School. He is at the centre of the third row, with his best friend Pete Shotton to his right (Ron Jones)

Right: John's familiar hunched frame was captured by fellow Art College student Ann Mason when he sat for more than two hours for this painting in March 1958 (Ann Mason)

Left: Thelma Pickles, who speaks in this book about her intense relationship with John when they were both students at Liverpool College of Art (Thelma Pickles)

Right: One of the first photographs of John with his future wife Cynthia Powell, before she dyed her hair blonde at his request. In October 1958 they are in the alleyway of the Art College pub, Ye Cracke, in Rice Street. Seated in the front, from left, are students June Harry, Pat Jordon, Jim Reynolds and Hazel Dorothy (Thelma Pickles)

Above: In this college photograph, taken in September 1958 by Thelma Pickles, one of his girlfriends, John's greased-back hair shows his identification with Elvis Presley. Students in the picture, taken near Liverpool College of Art, are (from left, on the back row) John Lennon, Carol Balfour, John Wild, Jeff Cane, Gill Taylor, Peter Williams; (seated, from left) Marcia Coleman, Ann Preece, Violet Upton, Helen Anderson, Diane Molyneux; (front from left) Ann Curtis, Sheila Jones

Opposite page: Aunt Mimi, who raised John with firm discipline. This picture, taken in March 1971, shows her with a cat John took home as a stray (Tom Hanley)

A youthful-looking John and Cynthia at the beach at Ostsee, near Hamburg, in July 1961. The snapshot unfortunately shows the effects of having been carried around for years in Cynthia's handbag (Astrid Kirchherr/Cynthia Lennon)

With Cynthia on a skiing holiday in St. Moritz, Switzerland, in 1965 (Cynthia Lennon)

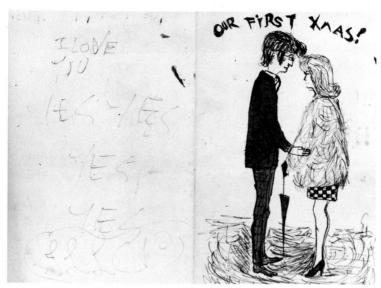

Above: Early days of romance, drawn by John's talented pen. He drew
this Christmas card for Cynthia in 1958 (Cynthia Lennon)

Below: John's well-documented obsession with deformities is evident
in this drawing, done when he was aged sixteen at art college
(Helen Anderson)

At the time of John's twentieth birthday, in October 1960, George
Harrison, Stuart Sutcliffe and John are pictured at a funfair in a
Hamburg park where they often played to boost their income
(Astrid Kirchherr)

gashed forehead, it could have been much worse without John's retaliation.

Most of John's energy was not used for punch-ups, however: it was going into his passionate love affair with Cynthia; his songwriting sessions with Paul; the night-time shows whenever they came up; perfecting his mean, Elvis-like looks; and into trying to get more work for the group, which he now feared was probably going to be his only real hope of making money. Not surprisingly, he pestered Allan Williams more than anyone. 'Al, get us some work.' 'Al, what's next for us?' John would say when they played the Jacaranda. 'What have you got lined up for us next?' Williams was as enthusiastic as they were, but he had a roster of other bands to protect. Williams was to relinquish his link with the group, and Brian Epstein eventually became manager of the Beatles. Fourteen years later Allan Williams wrote a book about his experiences with the Beatles, entitled *The Man Who Gave the Beatles Away*. After reading it, Lennon, in a classic example of his rapier-like wit, referred to Allan as 'The Man Who Couldn't Give the Beatles Away'.

A strange quirk of fate led John, Paul, George, and Stuart from struggling through £10–a-night dances in Liverpool to kicking their act into blistering, world-breaking energy in Hamburg. Allan Williams was again the man who caused that trip to happen.

The Royal Caribbean Steel Band, his regular act at the Jacaranda, went to Hamburg and wrote to him saying there were great opportunities for British pop groups there. About the same time, the Silver Beetles had dropped the 'Silver' because John felt it was too insipid and reminded him of the absurd suggestion that he should call himself

Long John Silver. From a show in June 1960 they were styled as the Beatles. Other groups in Liverpool, who traded under more thrusting imagery (the Seniors, the Pacemakers, the Hurricanes, the Searchers), laughed at the corniness of merging the still-new word 'beat' with something else. It had no precedent, but then neither had John Lennon. He was as perverse about the decision to change the name permanently to Beatles as he was in many other directions.

It was the Beatles, then, that Allan Williams sold, during a visit to Hamburg to follow up the attractive-sounding letter he had received from his beloved steel band. His first call was to a club on the Reeperbahn, then as now a neon-flashing street teeming with sex shows, clubs, bars, and prostitutes. The manager of the Kaiserkeller club, one Bruno Koschmider, hired the Beatles, and they were booked for their first shows there in August 1960.

It was just as well for John: college was a write-off. He was never formally expelled like his best mate Geoff Mohammed, because Arthur Ballard, his faithful mentor, was lobbying for him to be moved on to a new section called the Faculty of Design. But Ballard's pleas were falling on obstinate, more conservative ears. Other tutors now regarded Lennon as definitely more trouble than he was worth. During this period of debate about whether John was to remain an art student, the Hamburg offer came in and clinched it: he was off, and told everyone so. Even Mimi had no argument against John's proud claim that they would be earning £100 a week each. 'I feared the worst,' said Mimi. 'But of course, he was getting older by then, not a child, so it was not so much a question of telling him what I thought as advising him. I couldn't see any future in going to Germany but he told me the money would be good.'

Before they went, they needed a drummer. At the Casbah, Mona Best's son, a handsome, mean, moody-looking boy named Peter, had often sat in with John, Paul, George, and Stuart. He was rather more introverted than John and Paul, and they had little in common beyond the music, but that was enough: he was a good, lusty drummer. Other forces were causing ripples in the group. Paul and Stuart were starting to clash. The perfectionist inside McCartney had no patience with Stuart's thinly veiled attempts to play bass guitar properly, and Paul was constantly criticizing his playing. With George improving all the time and functioning strongly as the lead guitarist, individual roles needed defining more clearly. John was a competent rhythm guitarist, but there was no need for two. McCartney took the bass-playing role. There was also jealousy for Lennon's attention. McCartney could not understand why John, as hard a man as one could wish to meet, could be so stupidly loyal as to have his incompetent best friend in the group against his better judgment. Stuart was also competition for the attention of girls.

But for the Hamburg trip, expediency was essential. Peter Best lacked a sense of humour but had been hugely popular with the girls at his mother's coffee bar. He was in.

There was a problem finding John's birth certificate, which was essential to get a passport for the German trip. The problem in getting documentation for Paul, George, Stuart, and Pete was worrying enough for Allan Williams. In the case of Lennon, with no parents to sign the papers, and the vital birth certificate only found at the last moment, it was touch and go. He also won the difficult battle of persuading the parents of every member of the group that they would be safe and that a profitable trip lay ahead in

Germany for the band, which was, he assured everyone, full of potential.

And so on 16 August 1960 the Beatles' first journey to Hamburg began. This was the trip that was to convert John Lennon, aged nineteen, Paul McCartney, aged eighteen, and George Harrison, aged nearly seventeen into world beaters. The Hamburg Experience, as they later called it, was to teach them not only to hurl themselves full-bloodedly into making a great show; it was to teach them survival and introduce them to stimulants in the form of pep pills.

Parting from Cynthia was painful. For two years John and Cyn had hardly been out of each other's company – and even then only a twenty-minute train journey away – and the thought of separation for an unknown time in a foreign country was worrying for Cynthia. As four months elapsed, Cynthia's feelings for John increased. He kept a single promise, and hardly a day went by without a letter from Hamburg arriving at Hoylake. Envelopes were emblazoned with all the messages of teenage love: kisses and hearts, codes like SWALK (sealed with a loving kiss), 'Postman, postman, don't be slow, I'm in love with Cyn so go, man, go.' John's loving verse would almost obliterate the address. Inside, John would tell her of how much he wanted her – particularly sexually – needed her, and missed her, but also how well the Beatles were doing in Hamburg, despite the fact that Bruno Koschmider was exploiting them, working them hard, and giving them living quarters consisting of three filthy rooms containing only camp beds and blankets. He also said the washing and toilet facilities were appalling and that their rooms were situated behind a cinema screen, the cinema having been converted from an old theatre. Cynthia still worried about the girls available to John in promiscuous, dangerous Hamburg – 'the love and warmth of his letters made me feel wonderful and miserable at the same time,' she says candidly.

Immediately after John went abroad, Cynthia realized that she and John did not have photographs of each other. So she took to going to a Woolworth's photo booth every week. Carefully combing her hair, she dressed in her finest and turned on her most seductive pout for John to receive a picture of her. That, she hoped, would dissuade him from the German blondes.

With one of these photographs, Cynthia asked John to send in return pictures of himself from a coin-in-the-slot machine. The result was an unmistakable stroke of Lennon. He mailed Cynthia pictures of himself in grotesque poses: his face would contort, he would pretend to be a hunchback, his eyes would leer maniacally, and he would try to make each picture more sick than the last. Despite this, from the scores of letters she received from Germany Cynthia decided that John's aggression was waning. He was more ambitious for the Beatles, more enthusiastic about their success, than anything else, she says. 'I could sense his feeling that it was all starting to happen for him. It was just as well, as there was nothing much for him to come back to in England, as far as work was concerned.'

The Indra club, which they played almost immediately on their arrival, was a small and seedy basement. The audience was only about half a dozen strong, but the opportunistic promoter who had booked them, Bruno Koschmider, was scarcely a man with whom Liverpool teenagers would argue. He had a limp, a crooked nose, and all the authority that came with having fought in the war with the German Panzer Divisions. His idea in booking the Beatles was to inject some life into the place, and to try to get them to do for the Indra what their Liverpool rivals,

Derry and the Seniors, had done for the Kaiserkeller: swell audiences and thereby raise the bar takings.

The Indra had previously been used as a strip club and had a tiny, cramped stage. The Beatles' performance was stifled, and when a woman in the flat above the club complained to the police about the noise, Koschmider decided that the energy of the group would be better used in his much larger Kaiserkeller club. Derry and the Seniors had played there to packed houses; in Germany there was no admission charge, but patrons had to buy drink, and plenty of it, which had a boisterous effect on many of them, resulting in fights. Here was born the full-blooded, almost animal-like rock 'n' roll in John Lennon.

Koschmider had heard Allan Williams trying to instil a touch of show business razzmatazz into the Beatles' act. Allan had often told them 'to make a show,' to attract customers. Soon, the forceful Koschmider was using the phrase 'Mak show, mak show' to the boys all the time. Lennon, more than the other four, realized the *carte blanche* he was being given to perfect a wild stage personality. Besides, the demands Koschmider was making on them were physically punishing, so something more than music was essential. The contract called for the Beatles to perform from eight in the evening until two in the morning, with the occasional fifteen-minute break. What this amounted to was about six sets of forty-five minutes each. The schedule taxed the group's repertoire to its limit, and the chance of varying from set to set was minimal. It was little wonder that they tired of 'Roll Over Beethoven', 'Be-Bop-A-Lula', and 'Long Tall Sally'.

Survival was everything to John and the others. From the tough audiences, beer would arrive on stage together with an occasional request for a song. In Hamburg, John, often drunk but never incapable of delivering a power-crazed blast of rock 'n' roll to 'the bloody Krauts' as he called them, revelled in the challenge of it all. For a group of teenagers fresh from Liverpool, the violence as the waiters jostled with drunken customers, gangsters, and prostitutes in the audience, and the hilarious language barrier, made it all larger than life. Customers who got out of hand were often threatened by the bouncers with truncheons and flick knives. John said later: 'I grew up in Hamburg, not Liverpool.' But the key to the Beatles' endurance lay in their first serious use of stimulants, in the form of pep pills.

Preludin was a mild stimulant which John and the others acquired mostly from the waiters, and in John's case, not surprisingly, from a barmaid girlfriend. Basically they were slimming pills which had to be taken with beer to have the right effect: they stirred the brain and the body into such activity that, until the effects of the pills wore off after twelve hours, the pill-taker could not bear to be still. Adrenalin poured from the system. Conveniently, the pills killed the appetite for food.

One effect of Prellys, as John and the Beatles christened them, was to give them a false confidence. After a few weeks John had grown to dislike the innate aggressiveness of the Germans. His waspish wit, born on Merseyside, was to be sharpened to perfection in Hamburg as the easy targets of nationalism and inhumanity during the war dawned on the super-sensitive John that hid beneath the loudmouth. 'What did you do during the fucking war? Bloody Krauts, Heil Hitler, back to your tank,' he would shout from the stand to nobody in particular, when he knew that amid the din nothing could be heard. John totally refused to learn German, though Paul and George and Stuart managed a few words and Pete Best had an O-level in the language. For John the Hamburg Experience, like hundreds of other very important periods in his life, was to be absorbed, used, then disposed of.

Hamburg was a hard baptism, but there were side benefits. The young teenage girls who went to the clubs and the Reeperbahn cafés looking for men were attracted by the five good-looking, comparatively innocent young British lads. The girls warmed to John, Paul, George, Stuart, and Pete as a refreshing change from the tired businessmen and sex-starved sailors. There was not a lot of time for much besides working, sleeping, and playing cards – usually 'brag', a variation on poker. John, like the others, had the occasional relationship with girls during his first four-month visit to Hamburg. But to paint a picture of five teenagers wallowing in scenes of orgies and depravity – which has regrettably become part of the Beatles mythology during those years – is to fall victim to rumour and exaggeration. They dabbled with girls from time to time, but work, music, Prellys, and sheer exhaustion were by far the most important factors in their lives.

One girl, particularly, was to make an indelible impression on the Beatles, especially on Stuart and John. Astrid Kirchherr, born in 1938, the daughter of a sales director of Ford Motors in West Germany, was at first sight the least likely fan to visit the tacky Kaiserkeller club in which the Beatles played seven nights a week. Her visit there, and her subsequent closeness, particularly to Stuart and John, came through her boyfriend, Klaus Voormann. From childhood, and particularly during her teenage years, Astrid had taken a keen interest in art and had designed and made all her own clothes. Her friendship with the Berlin-born doctor's son had blossomed at a private art academy, Hamburg's Meisterschule. Klaus was crazy on rock 'n' roll and, as an illustrator, kept saying how much he wanted to design pop album covers. Astrid's emergent talent lay in photography, and she switched to studying that after first entering the college for dress design.

Klaus lived in a room in the house occupied by Astrid and her mother in the middle-class Hamburg suburb of Altona. Astrid's father had died when she was seventeen. When the Beatles arrived in Hamburg, she was twenty-two, with an air of cool, independent assertiveness that perfectly matched her riveting good looks. Her cropped blond hair, pure white skin, and big expressive eyes put John once again in mind of his goddess, Brigitte Bardot.

It was a row with Klaus that took Astrid to the Reeper-bahn one summer evening in 1960. A few days earlier Klaus had walked out after their first argument, gone to the cinema, and then drifted into the seedy St Pauli district of Hamburg. Nice people never went there, still less inside the Reeperbahn clubs. But Klaus, hungry for the sounds of rock 'n' roll, was drawn to a noise coming from a street called the Grosse Freiheit. He went downstairs in search of the sound and, once inside, unknowingly sat next to the Beatles who were watching the group on stage. They hap-pened to be another Liverpool group, Rory Storm and the Hurricanes, featuring Ringo Starr on drums.

Klaus's first memory of that night is vivid, 'I couldn't believe the look of the boys whom I sat next to, and there wasn't much conversation as they couldn't speak German. But the sound when the Beatles eventually went on stage was amazing.' When John tore into rockers like 'Sweet Little Sixteen' and 'Roll Over Beethoven', the combination of teddy boy hairstyles and their music bowled over the enthusiastic Klaus. He wanted to talk to the group, judged Lennon to be the leader, and, when the session ended, asked John about designing album covers, which was his ambition. Lennon beckoned Klaus in the direction of Stuart, saying: 'Show it to him, he's the artist in the group.'

The next evening Klaus Voormann returned to the club to see the Beatles' full session. As an artist, as much as a rock 'n' roll fan, he was particularly fascinated by Stuart's appearance, for despite his lack of musical prominence he looked like the artist he was: scrawny, fragile, James Dean-like, with moody dark glasses, winklepicker shoes, and an air of shyness.

Klaus did not consider for a moment that in persuading Astrid to visit the club, three nights after his discovery of it, he would be marking the end of his own love affair. But immediately the leather-jacketed Astrid entered the Kaiserkeller with the Beatles on stage, her eyes fell on Stuart. The magnetism she radiated, all elfin-chic with a detached beauty that lifted her a million miles from the Reeperbahn scrubbers they had been used to, attracted Stuart.

Astrid's effect on the Beatles was enormous. On their four further visits to Hamburg in the two years that followed, she was to offer them much more than the warmth, eggs and steaks and chips which they desperately missed, and total commitment as their closest German friend. She was to invest them with style and point them in a direction that would stir the world.

Her own firm leanings were towards the 'exis', who formed most of her friends at the Meisterschule. Derived from the existentialists, they were in the foreground of the avant-garde. They believed firmly in rejecting universal values and stamped their own imprimatur on everything from appearance to opinions: in art, fashion, music, and in personal behaviour the 'exis' were fiercely independent. Most of all, they wanted to define youthful freedom.

Stuart and Astrid were together, surprisingly without any resentment from Klaus, within a few nights, and both Astrid and Klaus and another friend, photographer Jürgen

Vollmer, were to become part of the Beatles' coterie, inseparable from them when they played the club, and during
the day too. Astrid persuaded them to let her and Jürgen
take their photographs, and within a few weeks Stuart had
moved into the Kirchherr home. Astrid's mother worried
about his thin frame and decided he needed food and care.

Astrid and Klaus were the first intellectual Beatles fans.
Before they arrived John and Stuart had enjoyed a long-
standing special relationship, and Paul and John both felt
passionately about music, but as a unit they came together
only for blazing rock 'n' roll. Now Astrid and Klaus introduced them all to her home, to her friendly mother who
spoke not a word of English but loved cooking them eggs
and chips. And Astrid gave them a glimpse of her style,
mirrored in her all-black bedroom with its floor-to-ceiling
silk sheets and huge mirrors which screamed individualism.

Today Astrid remains in the Hamburg she loves, her
memories of Stuart and John indelibly etched in her mind.
She carries her attachments to them both, for both John
and Stuart gave her their guitar plectrums which she wears
in her pierced right ear, as earrings. Her reflections on John
and Stuart as twenty-year-olds, and the interaction of the
Beatles before their meteoric rise to fame, are tempered
with her visible love for the two.

'When I first met him,' she says, 'John had this knowledge of everything that surrounded him, because he had
particularly high intelligence. But he didn't have much
experience, and he was so *nosey*. He wanted to keep finding
out everything. He had an innocence and didn't stop investigating, asking questions – about art, about clothes, about
the German people, who fascinated him. Of course, he
would take the mickey out of us: "Bloody Krauts", and all
that. But I thought of him as a gentle, sentimental boy
who was in such a hurry to find out about everything.

Stuart was the same, but really he had a deeper natural intelligence than John. When they were together, it was very powerful for them both.'

No serious photographer had been near the Beatles. When Astrid took them to pose for her in the parks and fairgrounds they were 'incredibly excited,' she says, at the results. 'I did big prints showing their expressions naturally, not asking them to pose, and they went crazy. They'd never seen anything like these in their lives. Jürgen Vollmer came down to take pictures of them too. He was fascinated by their appearance.' Indeed, one picture of Lennon standing in a Hamburg doorway was chosen by John fourteen years later as the cover for his 1975 album, *Rock 'n' Roll*.

Astrid says her clique dressed mostly in suede or velvet clothes, always black with white collars, and she often wore a short leather skirt. 'They'd never seen anything like the way we looked.' Still less had they witnessed a hairstyle like Klaus's. Tired of the fast-scissored traditional formula of Hamburg hairdressers, and looking for something that would emulate her own sense of the eccentric, Astrid had cut Klaus's hair herself for years. She *never* combed his hair backwards, always out from the side, and it was always longer than the accepted length. 'The Beatles were dressed like teddy boys, with these very, very pointed shoes which we in Hamburg had never seen before. We were fascinated with those, just like they were with our things,' says Astrid. 'And their very tight trousers and little tiny grey jackets. They didn't have many clothes, of course. And their hair was combed back with sideboards, like teddy boys.'

Stuart, the first to have his hair cut and styled by Astrid, faced John's scorn when, one night, he arrived at the club for work with what later became known as the Beatle haircut. 'John collapsed laughing,' Astrid says. 'He didn't have the guts to say, "Hey, that looks great," which is what he really thought. John was a complicated person when it came to showing his feelings like that: he hid his emotions. Because he could not bring himself to say what he really thought, he would cover it up and in doing that he would hurt people.' Shy Stuart was an easy target. The situation was not helped by the obviously strong love affair that had bloomed between him and Astrid.

'Stu at that time was really mad on her,' remembers Paul McCartney. 'We all fancied her a bit but it was, kind of, you know—"Hands off, I'm serious." I know you lot, you just like her, OK, but I mean this one, for me. . . . And anyway, she liked Stu. They hit it off very well and we used to chat with her friends. There was Klaus and Jürgen and Astrid, who were like the gang, and they used to have a couple of other mates of theirs who were from art school. They used to hang around the club, and got to like our band particularly because we were sort of different, too, from all the other groups. We were a bit more into the black leather and black polo sweaters. It was a different look at that time, like new wave or punk later. Astrid and her friends were great. They were like a different race of people because they dressed very differently. They dressed in all the black leather and black polo necks, and she had blonde, short-cut hair. She looked really great. I think all of us thought she looked great. But Stu . . .'

Paul, always more conscious than the others about his appearance, was the next to ask Astrid to style his hair. 'He asked me what started me in cutting Klaus's hair. I told him I couldn't stand my boyfriend having greasy hair swept back, and the same with all my friends at art school. The boys did the girls' hair, and the girls did the boys'.'

John was the last Beatle to succumb to the Beatle cut. Only Pete Best declined, retaining his quiff and teddy boy aura that attracted the girls. 'John was the same with the collarless jackets which I designed and Stuart was the first to wear,' recalls Astrid. 'They all laughed when Stuart went in wearing one, and John always said he fancied my leather pants and jacket. But it took all of them to adopt the jacket before John could be bothered. He was defiant about clothes and appearances. He didn't like to be led, you know – for someone else to have thought of something before him.'

Astrid and Klaus had been together for two years, but she and Stuart became serious after two weeks. 'It was very hard for all of us. Klaus liked Stuart a lot, and Stuart had a conscious hurt about falling in love with me and hurting Klaus. John and Stuart had no problem about our love – we were in a sense all together, laughing at the same jokes, and John and Stuart had the same sense of humour, very black, very sick.'

It was Astrid, then, who injected a sense of style, in hair and clothes, into the Beatles. It wasn't just a question of how they looked, and what they wore, she would tell them at the club and at her home: it was their general presence, the way they moved, off stage as well as on it. The message got home years later when, as international stars, they acknowledged their debt to their Hamburg days and to Astrid.

If John and Paul got together as opposites, then Stuart was John's foil in an utterly different way. 'They had similar outlooks on life, and attitudes,' says Astrid. 'John really loved Stuart, in the best sense, but Stuart was never made aware of that love and worried about it. John always had to be the hard man, teasing Stuart about his looks, his bass playing, his singing, anything. Stuart took it all, and, being highly intelligent and sensitive, never replied much. John would know how far he could go. But something deep inside John stopped him from putting his hand on Stuart's shoulder and saying: "Hey, I love you." Which he did. I think John regarded Stuart as a mental rival.'

Stuart was less reticent about his friendship with John. Most of the time, when they were not working, John and Stuart were together. 'At first Stuart was very tight about talking because he was together with four boys who acted very rough. But when Stuart became loose, he talked to me about his love for John, how John was the only one in the group he could relate to. Stuart knew he was not a musician and only came into the group for John. Stuart was a genius and would have been a very, very great writer and painter.'

While John was heavy on Stuart from a paternal standpoint, Paul waded in with the impatience of a long-suffering perfectionist who was exerting his ambition and ability. Paul was playing the piano frequently between belting out 'Long Tall Sally' and other Little Richard rockers. When Stuart stepped forward with his tiny physique to take a singing solo with the Elvis Presley ballad 'Love Me Tender', McCartney would berate him. Paul didn't like the slowness of the song after the rockers, says Astrid.

But while Stuart would take John's knocks for his weak singing, Paul's digs cut more deeply. Stuart felt very inferior, with reason. 'He knew he couldn't play, and criticism coming from Paul was more than he could take,' says Astrid. 'John had persuaded Stuart to play bass guitar but he knew in his heart it was ridiculous. He was simply not a good player. Paul played bass better than Stuart, Paul played piano better than Stuart and John, and Paul played guitar as good as John, and Paul played drums. His heart and soul were in music. Paul used to have a lot of arguments with Stuart. He didn't like his singing much. But Paul was in a difficult situation. John was the leader, up there on stage. However good a musician Paul was, John just gave off this feeling of being the leader. And John wanted Stuart in the group. It was bound to lead to tension.'

Paul remembers Stuart as 'a great fellow, a very good painter who used to get picked on by us generally.' On the clashes, Paul says: 'One of the main problems was: he wasn't that good on bass. So what you had to do, if you were having a photo taken, was tell Stu to turn away, do a mean moody thing looking over his shoulder, 'cos you didn't want anyone to see what he was actually playing. 'Cos anyone who knew would realize he couldn't play it. He just used to turn his amp down and sort of make a bass noise. It was quite good. But he didn't know what key we were in half the time. He just put a lot of bass on it and sort of bluffed and stamped a lot, you know.'

An insight into the twenty-year-old Lennon comes from Astrid's memories of her drug experiences with him. 'I was always close to John,' she says, 'but he never allowed anyone to get inside him. Only when we took the pills did he open up about himself.' And to set the record straight about the pills, she says: 'Drugs? It was just a big laugh. The stories that the Beatles were all doped up during their visits to Hamburg is so much rubbish. We were young kids. George, particularly, was a baby of seventeen. We could only afford to drink beer, which was the cheapest, and then one of us discovered these little pills called Preludin. They were pep pills so that when you took them you felt no hunger. We called them slimming pills. We discovered that when you took them and drank beer, you felt great. You didn't get drunk but you got all speedy and talked away like mad. They were fifty pfennigs each and my Mummy used to get them for us from the chemist – you had to have a prescription for them, but my Mummy knew somebody at the chemist.

'We had maybe one and a half for the whole night. They'd last for seven or eight hours. And it was from those pep pills that I had my best talks with John. He and I would take them and then go out of the club for a long talk. The pills would make a person feel more relaxed. When John took one, he lost all his inhibitions.

'He would talk about his feelings and the things he liked. He'd say: "Oh, I want to tell you so much how I feel. I love you and I love Stu." Without the pills, he could never have given me this honesty. He would have choked up at telling the truth. And so most nights John would say: "Come on, Astrid, let's take some beans and talk." But to say he was kept going by pills in Hamburg is really rubbish. He was kept going by something deep within himself,' says Astrid forcefully.

Beatles mythology says that the five young men on their Hamburg trip wallowed in a sea of orgies and carried on as depraved sex maniacs, drug addicts, and alcoholics. John, Paul, George, Stuart and Pete have been painted as five Liverpool louts rampaging through the Reeperbahn red light district, high on pep pills, using prostitutes. Astrid, who was closer to the group than anyone, says adamantly that the stories are inaccurate and have grown over the years into sheer fantasy. 'Prostitutes!' she laughs. 'First, they were too frightened to go anywhere near them, and secondly, they didn't have the money. Thirdly, and most importantly, they didn't need them. There were girls in the club sitting around waiting for John or Paul or George to go and sleep with them. But there were no sexual orgies. They all had their little affairs in Hamburg, but in 1960 even teenagers had a totally different sexual attitude towards one another. The girls were not prostitutes, they were seventeen or eighteen years old, and officially couldn't get into the club until they were eighteen. They were salesgirls or workers or students like me.

'The Beatles were five sweet, innocent young men, and they couldn't believe girls were falling in love with them. Yes, they had the occasional affairs, but definitely there was nothing wild about their behaviour.' In the popularity stakes, Paul was the most popular with the girls in the audience. 'He was always so neat and clean and the girls loved that,' says Astrid. But among the student friends whom she brought along, John and Stuart carried the honours. 'We all thought they had more style,' says Astrid. It was John who christened Astrid and her friends the 'exis'.

On their relationship, the subject of much speculation by Beatles watchers, she says, 'He was attracted to me, and me to him, but it was more mental than sexual. We would hold hands occasionally but he would find it hard even to do that, because he would never, never have done anything to hurt his best friend Stuart. John always called me the German Brigitte Bardot and he admired my blonde hair and small waist. I used to dress in the style he found fantastic – he went on and on about my black leather gear.

'I loved his mentality, not because I thought he was a sexy boy. That was reserved by me for Stuart, whom I adored and fancied right from the start. John was pleased for Stuart. Also, John told me he had left his girlfriend at home in Liverpool, so that was that.'

Alone among the Beatles, John would trudge to the Hamburg post office every week to send back to Cynthia the £35 he eventually earned at the Star-Club. 'I couldn't believe what he was doing,' says Henry Henroid, one of the club's booking agents who often walked with John to the post office. 'I said, "If you do this every week, what do you live on?"

'He said, "Oh I can earn a few marks by playing for this stripper round the back street in the afternoons.' It was incredible – very responsible behaviour for a boy of that age. All the musicians seemed to booze their money away. John had to get it back to Liverpool quickly.'

John's obsessive 'noseyness', as Astrid describes it, was especially evident at her home. He raided her book collection, taking a particular interest in works by the Marquis de Sade, and looking for any connection with sadism. 'You read books like *that*?' he said to Astrid once. 'It's dirty!' She reminded him of his own tendency to learn the rudest words in the German language, to augment what she describes as 'John's most basic version of Hitler Deutsch'. 'He loved poking fun at the Krauts, shouting "Where's your tank?" at audiences. I told him about Jean Cocteau and books I'd read, whenever I met him, and he wanted to know everything. I'd end up buying them for him, in English, which was not easy to find.' Classical records formed most of Astrid's collection, with the odd Nat King Cole thrown in. Paul often went straight for her Stravinsky records, but John would shout: 'Take that off.'

Routine for the Beatles during their first Hamburg visit was totally bound up with work. They would collapse into bed around dawn after all-night sessions, sleep until midday, and often be collected by Astrid in the early afternoon for the ten-minute drive to her home. Nostalgic for British breakfasts, which Astrid or her mother cooked, they tucked into bacon, eggs, beans, and toast at their whim. John struck up a particular affection for Astrid's mother: 'George and Paul just shook her hand and said hello, that was all. But never John. He always kissed her and put his

arms around her. My Mummy admired John most after
Stuart.'

Astrid smiles at aspects of the John Lennon she knew
so closely. He choked up at the mention of the death of his
mother two years before he went to Hamburg. 'John was
rough and sweet and gentle all together, I often used to
wonder if this was a mixture of his emotions at losing his
mother and the fact that his father wasn't there during
his childhood. If you asked him a question he would answer,
but without being asked he wouldn't tell you anything
about himself, unless he had taken a pill. You had to work
very, very hard to get deep thoughts from inside him. But
if you asked and you were sincere, as I was, he'd pour them
out. "Yeah, most of my friends grew up with a Dad and a
Mum," he'd say. "I missed all that." '

Because music and success meant more to him than to
Stuart, John adopted a fiercer, more penetrating character
in Hamburg. Realizing that it was a heaven-sent make-or-
break city for them to knock their act into shape, his
humour was blacker even than during his Liverpool Art
College years. 'Stuart shared the sick sense of humour,' says
Astrid, 'but his was much happier than John's, which was
always mean and cruel. I never knew why.' Postcards and
letters to Mimi would be conventional and tell nothing of
the exhausting test that was Hamburg. He told her nothing
of the money problems, either; the £100 a week they
expected fizzled into more like £15 a week each, says Paul
McCartney. 'They were always broke, always,' says Astrid.

'John used to have his dreams about being as famous
as Elvis Presley. George would say it would be OK to be as
popular as Cliff Richard, that would be a start! Stuart said:
"When I'm a famous painter, I'll buy you a Rolls-Royce."
I said, "When I sell my first picture of you all to *Life*
magazine I'll buy you a new leather jacket." '

John did indeed grow up in Hamburg, but the experience was to be more valuable to him than profitable. Word about the lively British teenagers' energetic appearances at the Kaiserkeller, and their indefatigable improvement in the face of the demon promoter Koschmider, soon spread around the tough city. Peter Eckhorn, a reputable promoter who ran the rival, bigger Top Ten club, invited the band over to watch another British act, Tony Sheridan, who worked as a solo singer. Unknown to John and the other Beatles, Koschmider had a friend who told him the fateful truth: the Beatles had appeared on stage with Tony Sheridan in a jam session, which was strictly forbidden under the terms of Koschmider's iron-fisted contract. He also feared that, like Tony Sheridan before them, the Beatles intended to leave the Kaiserkeller for the more sophisticated surroundings of the Top Ten club. In Hamburg, inter-club warfare was almost as intense as the fights that broke out inside them.

Koschmider struck back at the Beatles for their truancy in a devastating way. He called the police. George Harrison, aged seventeen, was arrested and jailed for a day for being under-age while working in a foreign country, and deported home. Paul and Pete Best were ordered by Koschmider to leave, after allegedly causing a small fire to some sacks by using candles in their tacky digs behind the cinema screen in the club. Lennon, unscathed but broken by the anticlimax of it all, wended his way home alone, leaving Stuart to the comfort of Astrid's home. They had become engaged, and Stu wanted to pursue painting in Hamburg.

John was penniless. The dreams of riches had been illusory. They had not made nearly so much money as expected, and what Deutschmarks they had earned had gone on clothes, beer, fags, and food. Dejectedly, he drifted across the ferry from the Hook of Holland to Harwich and

by train to Lime Street Station, then took a taxi home to
Menlove Avenue.

Cynthia was at once pleased and sad at his return.
Mimi, once more vindicated by the unlucky turn of events,
had the additional irritation of having to pay his cab fare.
'What happened to the £100 a week you mentioned?' she
asked John.

John's reply was to typify his sharp retorts as the Beatles
story got into its stride later, 'Spent it all, Mimi.'

He was contrite, recalled Mimi, but with all her spirit
she respected the streak in him that was to strike terror
into the hearts of those who asked him 'damned stupid
questions'.

'Once his mind was set on something,' said Mimi,
'nobody and nothing could shake him. He was down but
not out.'

NINE

LIVERPOOL

'Right then, Brian, manage us'

RETURNING TO Liverpool ignominiously from Hamburg, penniless and with an uncertain future, was bad enough. Going back to Aunt Mimi after experiencing the liberation of Gambier Terrace, the illicit nights with Cynthia, and Hamburg's wildness, was stultifying for John. With his best friend left behind, in love with Astrid, Lennon was at one of his lowest psychological ebbs during December 1960.

There were two consolations to add to the physical improvements of being back in a comfortable house, with Mimi's cooking and Cynthia's faithful knock on the front door, which came within a day of his return.

Both were musical. First, he was now equipped with a Rickenbacker guitar, a much sought-after Club 40 model which was his pride and joy. Second, less tangibly, the reputation of the Beatles' huge impact on Hamburg audiences had spread back to Liverpool's burgeoning beat scene. Derry and the Seniors had put the word about that the Beatles had taken the Kaiserkeller by storm and had only been ejected from Germany by an act of spite.

They had improved their act beyond all recognition in Hamburg, developing an almost manic energy and a

repertoire twice as big as when they left Liverpool. Yet
John knew that while he was a dominant leader on stage,
he was not pushy or organized enough to give the group
its thrust. His own ambition, to be bigger than Elvis, was
unshaken. He had a new aggression after Hamburg. What
he needed now, for his band so curiously called the Beatles,
was a stroke of luck.

The twist of events throughout early 1961 and the rest
of that year was to put the Beatles on the fastest-moving
escalator to fame and fortune in the history of entertainment. Throughout his school and college years, and in the
fights at the ballrooms and clubs of Liverpool and Hamburg,
John had relied intuitively on fate smiling on him. It was
as if someone was watching over him, bailing him out of
disasters in every step of his twenty years. Now, having
flounced out of college, blown it in Hamburg where their
name was being sullied by Koschmider as unreliable, and
having to persuade Mimi that all would come right, John
was irritable.

The biggest problem was, as ever, getting work for the
Beatles in an increasingly competitive Liverpool beat scene.
They sought refuge back at the Casbah in West Derby,
where Mona Best welcomed her son's group with a triumphant poster on the door of the cellar in which they
played: 'The Fabulous Beatles Are Back!' The coffee, snacks,
and Cokes were a far cry from the beer and Prellys of
the Kaiserkeller, but in Liverpool, in December 1960, the
Casbah was a haven for four young men facing the spectre
of failure. Nor was there much joy at the Jacaranda, where
Allan Williams was licking his own Hamburg wounds. But
it was then, in that coffee bar, that the Beatles met the
man who was to mark their career so forcefully.

Bob Wooler was a twenty-eight-year-old ex-railway
clerk turned disc jockey whose knowledge of the mush-

rooming Liverpool beat group scene was encyclopaedic. John and Paul found a receptive ear in the man who was to be a vital link in the chain that ensured they got work. Wooler, with his unequalled grapevine knowledge of which group was coming up, sensed that the Beatles' Hamburg experience had made them special. He got them a date for £6 at Litherland Town Hall where promoter Brian Kelly was amazed by their fiery energy. 'On their first appearance I was completely knocked out by them. They had a pounding, pulsating beat which I knew would be big box office. When they had finished playing I posted some bouncers on the door of their dressing-room to prevent some other promoters, who were in the hall, entering. I went inside and booked them solidly for months ahead.'

More Litherland dates became important for the Beatles, but Wooler was yet to deal his ace to them. He urged Ray McFall, owner of the Cavern club, a dingy, dank cellar and stronghold of traditional jazz at 10 Mathew Street in Liverpool's city centre, to give them a try. Lennon was ecstatic at the chain of events that was slowly but surely unfolding through Wooler.

Cynthia was still at art college. As far as Mimi was concerned, so was John. But in his mind he had quit college the day he set out for Hamburg, and had returned hell-bent on music as a career. Until he was successful, he decided, it was best not to rock any boats with Mimi.

Wooler's memory of John in that desperate year of 1961 is of a hungry, difficult young man. He knew, says Wooler, that the Beatles were on the precipice of something, but worried that, instead of becoming successful, the scales might tip against them for want of both work and luck.

The Cavern, however, was to be the turning point for John and the Beatles. From their first appearance there the Beatles attracted not only their regular fans from West

Derby, the area of the Casbah, but from Aintree and Litherland. Girls with beehive hairstyles from the typing pools nearby, on North John Street and Whitechapel, formed a new, quickly growing army of Beatles fans.

The Cavern, with little ventilation, appalling acoustics, walls dripping with dampness, stale air, and cramped stage conditions, would tax even the most enthusiastic of young musicians. Its history was similar to that of dozens of cellar clubs in Britain in the late 1950s. It was a hotbed of traditional jazz featuring Liverpool's favourites, the Mersey-sippi Jazz Band and Manchester's Saints, with regular visits from top London names such as Acker Bilk and Kenny Ball. The audiences were, in John Lennon's opinion, snobs against rock 'n' roll. He hated them for their superior attitude as trained musicians, their anti-pop attitude, and most of all because they always seemed to be so well educated!

Over the next two and a half years the Beatles played the Cavern 292 times – lunchtime and evening sessions, for a payment of around twenty-five shillings a session. The Cavern was to represent, to John, something much more than success for the Beatles. He saw it as a crusade against jazz and all it stood for, 'with all those bloody musicians and their GCEs.'

John told jazz singer George Melly, who had played the club with the Mick Mulligan Band: 'You lot kept us from getting into the Cavern and other places much earlier. All that jazz crap held us back.' Melly conceded this point to Lennon; once the steamroller of rock 'n' roll had gathered speed, the death knell of traditional jazz's boom years was sounded. Through Acker Bilk, Chris Barber, and Kenny Ball, 'trad' had enjoyed a brief flirtation with pop success. But with rock 'n' roll groups, led by the Beatles, pulling in students, previously the jazz fans' natural audience, 'the

game was up' as Melly succinctly puts it. Lennon relished
the kill. The tiny Cavern stage bulged with Pete Best's
drum kit and cheap amplification, part of which had been
'permanently borrowed' from the Liverpool Art College
music room. Lennon's demeanour on that stage could be
likened to that of a caged tiger: this was his domain. Here,
he honed his short-sighted, head-tilted, legs-astride stance
into a statement of defiance, much more than mere music.
By the time that Lennon reached the Cavern, the Hamburg
experience had galvanized his lithe, tallish frame into
demonic energy.

Even now, the creative tension between John and Paul
was rearing itself as they vied for the choice of songs. John
made most of the announcements, taking the mickey out
of the 'men in suits' who came. 'Shurrup, you with the
suits on' became a regular Lennon message, especially to
young teenagers who came during their lunch breaks from
the insurance offices nearby. He mocked them for taking
'regular jobs'.

Among the regulars at the Cavern lunchtime sessions
(admission one shilling) was Liz Hughes. She was a fourteen-year-old schoolgirl from Rock Ferry, across the Mersey,
who saved the five shillings dinner money her parents gave
her every week to spend on ferries and buses across to the
city centre. Cavern sessions began at noon. At 11:45 precisely, dozens of Liverpool schoolgirls like Liz would eye
the clock and get their belongings together to make a dash
for it when the bell sounded. 'It was twelve-forty or even
one o'clock before we reached the Cavern if we missed the
first ferry,' says Liz. 'But it was worth it. Going to
the Cavern and seeing the Beatles, the Big Three, and
later the Clayton Squares was almost like religion to certain
kids of my age in those years.'

Few women in Liverpool, outside the Beatles' family,

can feel the warm nostalgia of that period with Liz Hughes's passion and intensity. She studied the style of John Lennon during the year that was the turning point of his life, the switch from potential bum to success beyond his wildest dreams.

'John always had this air about him,' says Liz. 'It give all us kids the impression that if the audience dropped dead, it would have gone right over his head. His attitude was as if he was saying: "I can take yer or leave yer. I'm here because this is something I wanna do, and I'm doing you lot a favour, not for the money."

'He looked as if he'd just stepped off the back of a motor bike. He usually wore dark clothes, crumpled trousers or jeans, and a polo neck, but it was always unironed. They weren't in uniforms. It seemed that whatever caught their eye, or was on the back of the bedroom chair when they got out of bed, went on their backs. Except for Paul. He was the gentleman, the neat and tidy one who all the girls thought would be lovely to take home to their Mum. Paul played the part of the nice guy. But that John – he was the *animal*. The girls stood a bit back from him, a bit frightened. You never really knew which way he'd jump.

'I think John fed off Paul, but it was John who made most of the announcements. Paul would add to what John had said, but John made most of the first moves. They were obviously having a lot of fun. George was very quiet. A lot of the girls said he shouldn't be up there, he looked so embarrassed.' In the tiny dressing-room from which Bob Wooler would make his introductions of the Beatles, so much more majestically than for any other group, a few lucky teenage girls would huddle with the sweating Beatles after the session. They giggled at George's admission that he stuffed cardboard in the toes of his precious winklepicker shoes to ensure they remained pointed.

'Paul was safe and pretty, neat and tidy. George was so vulnerable. John looked like the sort of lad who would whip you up an entry, say thank you very much after he'd pleased himself, and ta-ra. All the girls were wary of him. He gave the impression of being so hard.'

What separated John, particularly, from all the other musicians who got on that three-feet-high Cavern stage, was his complete lack of professionalism. He would just stop singing or playing a song – dead – in the middle and start talking to Paul, for no apparent reason. He would light a cigarette, announce a new song, and carry on, with no explanation to the audience. 'It was like a permanent rehearsal. But he was someone you couldn't take your eyes from,' says Liz Hughes. 'My friend Deidre was absolutely crazy about him, but if he'd spoken to her, she'd have run a mile. That was a typical reaction. Her admiration was mixed with a fear of John. He was dangerous to all the girls, and that's what made him so attractive.

'The men in the audience took to him. He was a real man's man.' Jim Hughes agrees. 'Some of the lads modelled themselves on him. They'd lounge around the walls of the Cavern trying to imitate his stance, the way he held a fag, the legs astride, the lot.'

The music was like nothing else heard in Britain at that time. John's favourite songs, giving full rein to his leathery vocal work which had been hardened by the Kaiser-keller, were included in a set which usually featured this repertoire, refined in Hamburg: 'What'd I Say', 'Boys', 'Will You Love Me Tomorrow', 'Wooden Heart', 'C'mon Everybody', 'Twenty Flight Rock', 'Hallelujah I Love Her So', 'Mailman', 'Red Sails In The Sunset', 'Crying, Waiting, Hoping', 'Over The Rainbow', 'Mean Woman Blues', 'Lucille', 'Hey Good Looking', 'Blue Moon Of Kentucky', 'Love Me Tender', 'Corinna Corinna'.

But it was John's magnetism, and his merciless mickey-taking of anyone in the audience who proved an easy target, that gave them that edge. There was no alcohol in the Cavern, and the Coca-Cola the Beatles always had by their side was in bottles, for these were the days before cans. It was just as well, for one day, early in their residency at the lunchtime sessions, Aunt Mimi decided to visit the Cavern. John had still not told her that he had left college. His days were spent hanging round the record shops, playing at the Cavern, or meeting Paul wherever they could manage it, to develop their songwriting. Mimi, uncharacteristically lost for words at the sight of Lennon in full flight amid the sweat in such unsalubrious surroundings, could manage just eight sardonic words when he came off stage to take a break. She awaited him in the dressing-room.

'This is nice, John. This is *very* nice.'

John put his arm around her, but she stomped off.

The longer the Beatles dug in as the resident band at the Cavern, the more confident and more aggressively ambitious he became. Soon they were so popular that they played on Monday, Wednesday, and Friday lunchtimes as well as on Wednesday and Sunday nights. It was a claustrophobic hell-hole but a massive breakthrough to Lennon; apart from Cynthia, this was the greatest anchor of his life so far. Even Mimi, who now knew by mid-1961 that he was channelling everything into a life in music, had to concede that at least he had a goal, however errant. He was also earning a little money.

The fans, who hung on their every song, soon developed unswerving loyalties. The roles were cast. John, the tough, abrasive, fiercely masculine leader whose quick mouth could wound in a flash, carried the male vote. Paul wooed the girls with his flashing big eyes, comparatively immaculate dress, and romanticism set to music. George, enigmatic, shy, getting the music right, the apprentice electrician at Blackler's department store opposite Lime Street Station, was by far the best guitarist. And Pete Best at the back, on drums, had those sharply defined features but slightly sulky detached air that made him very popular with the girls. The contrasts, together with the electricity within the group, meshed perfectly.

Even in 1971, when the Beatles had split amid acrimony, Paul was admitting that his 'best playing days were at the Cavern lunchtime sessions.'

'We'd go on stage with a cheese roll and a cigarette and we felt we had really something going in that place. The amps used to fuse and we'd stop and sing a Sunblest bread commercial while they were being repaired. We used to do skits. . . . I'd do a Jet Harris impersonation because he'd played there. He fell off the stage once and I'd fall off it, too. You couldn't beat it.'

There was no contest between Lennon and McCartney for attention. They knew they attracted different people. Paul developed a warm friendship with the fans, while John tended to keep at a distance, retaining his slightly sinister mystique compounded by his increasing short-sightedness and refusal to wear glasses.

Before long, Lennon had nicknamed the crowd of schoolgirls who surrounded the stage most lunchtimes the Beatlettes. Between the ages of fourteen and seventeen, the eight members of this elite clan shouted song requests, fetched the boys Cokes, and were the group's earliest known entourage. After evening sessions, the Beatles' blue Commer van, driven by Pete Best's friend Neil Aspinall, would even drop the girls at their homes to demonstrate to their parents that everything was 'above board' and that nothing was happening to their daughters, whatever the hour.

Hilary Williams, then a confirmed Beatlette of sixteen

and now a Liverpool nurse, says that for all John's toughness he showed her and her schoolgirl friends a different side to his character at lunchtime or evening sessions. 'It was he who realized we were too young to have much money. The Beatles were each allowed one guest free in the club and John said we should be given that free ticket because we had been with them from the start. And one day he bought me a cup of tea for threepence. I couldn't believe it. Neither could my friends. "*What?*" they said. "Lennon the big he-man, bought you a cup of tea? Why?" It was because he asked me how I could afford to keep coming, and I said I couldn't and I was broke that lunchtime. He just came up and put the cup by my side.'

John was palpably sexual, even to sixteen-year-old girls in 1961. But Hilary Williams remembers that he had a code of honour with her and her innocent friends. 'John would swear more than anyone else from that stage. If a string broke on his guitar, or if he was angry with the way a show was going, he'd curse all right! But in the 1960s, there were either decent, well-brought up girls, or there were tarts. He knew the Beatlettes were not tarts and treated us kindly and carefully.' Hilary Williams still has a rare memento of those years, a leather jacket she dared to wear on her Cavern outings. It still reeks of the unmistakable Cavern dampness, which I experienced too.

When the Beatles adjourned for beer to the Grapes, the pub just along Mathew Street from the Cavern, the Beatlettes and other supporters who were under drinking age would mournfully leave them and go into the Kardomah coffee bar in nearby Whitechapel. John and Paul would follow them later and buy them tea. Lennon's staple lunch would be a cheese sandwich followed by his own special weakness, red jelly. Hilary Williams said to her two brothers, who admonished her for bothering with the ruffians at the Cavern: 'They'll be famous one day, just you wait and see.'

For the schoolgirls who went to the Cavern and lived and breathed Beatles as a hobby, there was one major problem: Cynthia Powell. She was known to be John's art student girlfriend, and the very sight of her entering the Cavern made the possessive Beatlettes go schoolgirl crimson with a combination of jealousy and embarrassment. Outwardly, they were friendly to the twenty-two-year-old, but as they huddled together beneath the stage and in the Kardomah they could not contain their resentment. 'We called her Cindy to try to appear friendly, but it was no use,' says Hilary Williams. 'We couldn't compete. She had long blonde hair, and black leather, a real arty look, whereas we were dressed in denim. Looking back now, it's obvious she was a lovely girl, but at the time feelings were very strong against her. She'd got our John!'

When Cynthia went to the Cavern, John's behaviour changed. 'He swore less from the stage and was more gentle. There was even a rumour that Cindy was not his steady girlfriend but that he'd been out with another girl named Iris. Well, a few of us decided that was a cover-up to put us off knowing that he was serious with Cindy.' Hilary and other Beatlettes saw their defeat at the hands of Cynthia avenged one night. After a Cavern session, Paul McCartney conscientiously drove the girls to their homes in the Allerton area. First to be dropped off, in Menlove Avenue, was John. 'It was two o'clock in the morning, very late. We'd all just been talking after a session,' recalls Hilary Williams. 'Cynthia came out of his Auntie's house and hit him over the head with a bread board. We all collapsed with laughter in the van.'

The Beatles' popularity in Liverpool spread like an epidemic throughout 1961. 'It was horrible when that happened,' says Hilary Williams. 'They weren't ours any more. Girls used to come in at lunchtime and in the evenings from Widnes, St. Helens, and Aintree. They were the ones who started the screaming for John or Paul. The earliest fans never screamed. But the new ones took sides with whichever Beatle they fancied.'

Competition was intense among the groups. Although they had different sets of fans, there was a special rivalry between the Beatles and Gerry and the Pacemakers. 'There was this contest for who was the best band in Liverpool,' says Gerry Marsden. 'But the nice thing was, we never nicked songs from each other. For a start, the Beatles didn't have a pianist as we did, so that gave us more room for Jerry Lee Lewis-type songs. We watched the Beats, as I called them, and they watched us, but there was this unbreakable rule that we never nicked songs. It was all done very politely, as a swap: John would say: "Ere, can we have 'Jambalaya' if we give you 'Some Other Guy' or something like that?" '

Gerry remembers Lennon as more outgoing than the other Beatles. 'He was always more involved in more things than the others were. It wasn't just the group to him during the Cavern and ballroom dates. He was interested in seeing whatever else was happening around him. I spent more time with John because he was always up and ready.'

The Beatles and Gerry and the Pacemakers shared the bill on scores of Merseyside dates, even combining forces, at one memorable, crazy night at Litherland Town Hall, to become the Beatmakers. 'After a show, it would always be John who'd be the first one to say, "Yeah", if I said, "Coming for a pint, then?" Paul or the others would more often say: "No, I'm just going to run through this song." '

Marsden, the former British Railways van driver, and Lennon, whose caustic wit was more than a match for Gerry's sharpness, became firm friends. That closeness developed in Hamburg, where Gerry's group played the Top Ten Club while the Beatles played the Kaiserkeller. 'So we never had a chance to see them on stage in Hamburg. We played the sets and met for drinks or meals afterwards.' Gerry went to the Cavern to see them immediately after they returned from Germany. 'And I said to my brother Fred, who played drums with my band: "John and Paul are going to be big, big, big. Never mind what happens to the Beatles, there's nothing can stop those two." I couldn't believe how good they were. The energy, the way they shaped up to the microphone together, you know – Paul, the left-handed bass player, John standing there, couldn't give a shit, the *attitude* of the man. I thought: "They'll be the first band out of Liverpool to make it." '

Lennon was not even a great guitarist, says Gerry. 'John never claimed to be a great player: "I'm a cinema-verité player," he once said. Nor was he a good pianist, although he dabbled on it when there was no one around. But I could always tell a Lennon guitar touch, even when he was just strumming. It came at you from an angle. It wasn't like anyone else. And that voice! In the Cavern, on the stage at Litherland, he'd belt out "Memphis Tennessee" or any Chuck Berry songs and I'd say to myself immediately: "*That's* John Lennon!" Much more important than anything is to have a distinctive voice. It's more important than any other quality. It doesn't have to be fantastic in any way, or never sound flat, or never raunchy. It's got to be a voice on its own for rock 'n' roll, and John had that like nobody else I know. His vibration on stage was special, because he simply stood there, with this attitude: "I'm going to have a bloody good time, hope you'll join me." '

Gerry shared John's sick humour. 'He'd sit in a pub doing a drawing, which appeared quite straight, a doodle. Then suddenly at the back would be a pair of crutches. I'd fall about laughing, because he had this black macabre sense of sick humour. He was always taking the mickey out of cripples, or walking down the street around Liverpool he'd pretend to be one. I went along with it because I found it funny, too.' Once, in a Paris jazz club, a drunken John and Gerry did a crushingly accurate imitation of cripples. As the two men lurched uproariously around the club, the mostly sober audience sat back, flabbergasted at the sight.

Another who was at the Cavern one lunchtime was a girl named Priscilla Maria Veronica White. She was never the official hat check girl at the cellar but occasionally, when she was broke, Priscilla asked the doorman if she could be allowed in free if she volunteered to help with the cloaks.

It was Lennon who remarked, 'Pretty girl, Brian,' to Epstein one lunchtime, when Epstein had become their manager. And the girl went on to become, under the name Cilla Black, a singing star and comedienne in the Gracie Fields tradition.

Cilla recalls: 'I played truant from Anfield Commercial College to see the Beatles at lunchtime sessions. At that time I was singing with some of the local bands, billed as "Swingin' Cilla", on a semi-professional basis. But this was the first time I had my chance to sing with the Beatles.

' "What's your name, girl?" asked John.

'When I told him he yelled: "Do you hear that, lads? She's got a boy's name. This is Cyril who is going to have a bash at singing something with us."

'John went on: "What key do you sing in, Cyril?"

'When I said I had no idea – because I'd never had a lesson in my life! – he shouted: "Let's try a Yale!"'

'The group had just come back from Germany and wore gear they'd bought in Hamburg. John's hair was much longer then than Brian Epstein ever let him wear it later on. It was brushed forward instead of back and he had an enormous pink leather hat over it. He had black leather pants on, lined with red satin, black T-shirt, black leather jacket, and high black boots with Cuban heels. I took one look and thought: "Oh, my God!"'

'At the end of 1961 I was appearing with Kingsize Taylor and the Dominoes at the Tower Ballroom in New Brighton. The Beatles were on the same bill. I noticed a very smart man deep in conversation with John. John told me it was their new manager, but I just laughed because I thought this was another of John's jokes. Then he took me over and introduced me. It was Brian Epstein and he'd just signed the Beatles. Even then John was still doing his "Cyril" thing with me: "Come over here, Cyril, I want you to meet Brian Epstein."'

'It was John who persuaded Brian to listen to me. He told Brian that he should sign me up. I did an audition at a club in Birkenhead with the Beatles backing me. I must have been dreadful because I was very nervous. Brian didn't say anything at all and I didn't like to ask him what he thought. Eight months later he signed me. I remember I used to be dead scared of John, although he was the one who had helped me most. He had this aura of super-intelligence. I hated being left alone to speak to him. Once he said: "What's wrong with you, girl? Don't you like me?"'

'I confessed, "I'm frightened of you, John."'

'He roared with laughter: "And I thought you were a snob!"'

'After that we often talked. John loved coloured singers

– many of my own American favourites. He talked about his songs, but the memory which stands out is the way he admitted he longed to become a famous actor one day.'

John loathed crowds. He told me, in the midst of the Beatles fans' wildest scenes, when he was waving at thousands of them from a hotel balcony in Munich: 'I'd hate to be in the middle of that. I couldn't stand being hemmed in.' The seething Cavern crowds made him feel claustrophobic, too.

If Liverpool rock 'n' roll was a religion in the early 1960s, then the parish priest was Bob Wooler. Until the old Cavern was closed on 27 May 1973 to make way for an excavation shaft for an underground railway link, Wooler was able to take people down there and affectionately recreate those halcyon days. Today, the great Cavern master of ceremonies is an institution among Beatles fans who marvel at his place in history, having survived the stifling, sweaty cubby hole they called a dressing-room which he shared with the Beatles. His memories of Lennon, tempered by a historic punch-up with him, are warm and respectful. When the Beatles returned to Liverpool for the northern première of their film *A Hard Day's Night* in 1964, Wooler went to Speke airport and was greeted by a typical Lennon remark: 'Hi, Bob. Has anyone given you a black eye lately?'

McCartney was his perfect foil, says Wooler; both John and Paul realized that the group needed John's edge, but Paul was there to apologize when John offended people. 'I have rarely seen any one person embody youth so much as Lennon did in those years,' says Bob Wooler. 'He had aggressiveness, but not aggression. He would stand straddling the far left of the stage and look, unseeingly, into the audience because he was *so* short-sighted. It was obvious the applause was washing over him, but he loved it. He managed to give off this attitude of not caring two hoots, but deep down I know he did. He loved every minute. I told him he reminded me of the actor Kirk Douglas and he said that was rather high-sounding. He did have a cleft chin like Kirk Douglas and that was part of his appeal to the girls. But he was adored by both sexes.'

Wooler remembers John as a 'very black and white character who couldn't be bothered with people'. The identification of Lennon in black and white is significant: the Cavern was totally black and white in appearance and in atmosphere, and John often told his friends that he preferred the earthy simplicity of mono films and art to colour: it was partly because the film *Help!* was in unreal colour that he felt it ended up looking tawdry. 'In the Cavern,' says Bob Wooler, 'the shadows and the starkness helped the Beatles create a great drama from their music. It was love us or loathe us, but that's how we are, straight ahead, black and white.'

From his close encounters with Lennon, Bob Wooler's overall view is that there was so much loneliness in his life that the thing he most feared was showing his tears. As an example of John's vulnerability, Wooler recalls the day Aunt Mimi went to the Cavern lunchtime session. 'It was the custom, if a father like Jim McCartney or any close relative came to see the group, to dedicate a record to him or her,' says Wooler. 'But John insisted that no record should ever be played for Mimi or any of his mates. I think she would have loved it, but it might have given people in the crowd the feeling that John was a softie, and that image was never allowed to register.'

The problem for John, when the Beatles became famous, was that, never having believed in himself, he could not fully absorb what was happening. 'Paul's horizon had already been in focus, so he was ready. But John was really thrown by it all,' says Bob Wooler. Lennon, he says, had a love/hate relationship with the Cavern but often admitted that, because it was so difficult to play on account of its acoustics, it had played a big part in forcing the Beatles to 'play hard'.

Coincidentally, Liverpool Art College canteen, where they first played, was also a basement with arches. But, in a totally different sense, the ambition to climb out of the damp, sweaty, unlicensed catacomb that had no acoustics became John's greatest incentive for the Beatles. 'We couldn't get out of the place fast enough,' he said. He wasn't ungrateful for what the Cavern had done for them, but to John any form of regularity very quickly became monotony. This was the restlessness that was to mark his life and make him so utterly different from his partner, Paul McCartney. Once a thing was rolling along, Lennon wanted to move on: a new kick, a fresh challenge, something a little dangerous. Thus the Cavern had to be escaped from.

Many people who were in Liverpool during 1961 could claim to have played a big role in giving the Beatles the thrust that enabled them to break out of the confines of the city into a London recording studio, with all that led to. Bill Harry, who saw most of their Cavern shows and had been at art college with John, encouraged John in his early writings, diverted Brian Epstein to the Cavern, which was to lead to a great partnership, and can claim to have been the first to publish John's words.

Harry saw the rumblings of a big beat group scene on Merseyside in 1960. With Stuart Sutcliffe, he was on the students' union committee, so it was inevitable that Sutcliffe would lobby for his best friend's band to get work. As a friend of Stuart's, Bill had been to the Gambier Terrace flat which Lennon shared with him. There he first became aware of John's weird sense of humour, his special way with words, and his ability to draw. 'We'd drink at Ye Cracke and then spend entire evenings at the flat in Gambier Terrace or at another student's flat in Huskisson Street,' says Bill. They played games, many of them invented by John. They sat in a circle, including Rod Murray and his girlfriend Dizzy who occupied the flat next to Stuart's. 'John suggested we create stories by saying whatever came into our heads. One person would reel off a few sentences, and the following person would continue unfolding the story. We laughed till the tears ran down our cheeks at some of the tales, particularly John's, which were often cruelly suggestive with references to spastics, cripples, and crutches.

'When Margaret Duxbury fell asleep on the bed, John suggested we get potatoes and use matchstick legs to make them look like spiders. We suspended them from the ceiling so that she'd get a shock when she woke up. All this made me realize that John had a macabre sense of humour and a creative turn of mind.'

It was that electricity from Lennon that connected with Bill Harry when he was about to launch, with great foresight, a newspaper called *Mersey Beat*. Bill had talked about poetry with John in Ye Cracke. Lennon said he wrote it occasionally and grudgingly showed some of his rough work to Bill. 'I liked it, particularly since it wasn't a pastiche of Beat Generation poetry which was all the rage with other students,' says Bill. 'It once again indicated his individuality. In fact, the group actually backed a beat poet named Royston Ellis. He'd been booked by Liverpool University to read his poetry there, and he later talked the Beatles into providing backing for his readings at the Jacaranda.

'In 1961, when I was preparing *Mersey Beat*, I remem-

bered John's poetry and decided to ask him to write for the
paper, beginning with a biography of the Beatles.' Bill was
a fan of the group and saw them perform several hundred
times.

'I met him at the Jacaranda for the copy and he shoved
two pieces of paper torn from an exercise book into my
hands. He seemed embarrassed by the piece. It was like no
other biography of a band and I told him I'd be pleased to
print it, which cheered him up no end.' In the piece, John
spelled Paul's surname wrong, calling him McArtrey, as he
had done in letters to Cynthia from Hamburg. The humour
and light touch of John's first printed work was a talking
point among the local beat population; it read like this:

BEING A SHORT DIVERSION
ON THE DUBIOUS ORIGINS OF BEATLES
Translated from the John Lennon.

Once upon a time there were three little boys called
John, George and Paul, by name christened. They
decided to get together because they were the getting
together type. When they were together they wondered
what for after all, what for? So all of a sudden they all
grew guitars and fashioned a noise. Funnily enough, no
one was interested, least of all the three little men. So-
o-o on discovering a fourth little even littler man called
Stuart Sutcliffe running about them they said, quote
'Sonny get a bass guitar and you will be alright' and he
did – but he wasn't alright because he couldn't play it.
So they sat on him with comfort 'til he could play. Still,
there was no beat, and a kindly old man said, quote
'Thou hast not drums!' We had no drums! they coffed.
So a series of drums came and went and came.

Suddenly, in Scotland, touring with Johnny Gentle,

the group (called the Beatles called) discovered they had not a very nice sound, — because they had no amplifiers. They got some. Many people ask what are the Beatles? Why Beatles? Ugh, Beatles how did the name arrive? So we will tell you. It came in a vision — a man appeared on a flaming pie and said unto them 'From this day on you are Beatles with an A.' Thank you, Mister Man, they said, thanking him.

But before we could go we had to grow a drummer, so we grew one in West Derby in a club called Some Casbah and his trouble was Pete Best. We called 'Hello Pete, come off to Germany!' 'Yes!' Zooooom. After a few months, Peter and Paul (who is called McArtrey, son of Jim McArtrey, his father) lit a Kino (cinema) and the German police said, 'Bad Beatles, you must go home and light your English cinemas.' Zooooom, half a group. But even before this, the Gestapo had taken my friend little George Harrison (of Speke) away because he was only twelve and too young to vote in Germany: but after two months in England he grew eighteen, and the Gestapoes said 'you can come.' So suddenly back in Liverpool Village were many groups playing in grey suits and Jim said 'Why have you no grey suits?' 'We don't like them, Jim' we said speaking to Jim. After playing in the clubs a bit, everyone said 'Go to Germany!' So we are. Zooooom. Stuart gone. Zoom zoom, John (of Woolton) George (of Speke) Peter and Paul zoom zoom. All of them gone.

Thank you club members, from John and George (what are friends).

Readers told Bill Harry they liked the piece, so he asked John to contribute a regular column. 'He turned up at the office with an untidy bundle of papers and I leafed through

them, completely enchanted by the strange stories, drawings, short tales, and political satires.' As a fan of the *Daily
Express* column Beachcomber, Bill Harry decided to call
John's column Beatcomber because John's work seemed to
have 'inspired lunacy'.

His first piece under the name Beatcomber was headlined SMALL SAM, and read:

> Once upon a Tom there was a small little Stan, who was
> very small. 'You are very small, Stan,' they said. 'I am
> only little,' replied Stan answering, feeling very small.
> Who could blame him, for Stan was only small. 'You
> must be small, Stan,' people were oft heard to cry, notic-
> ing how extremely small Stan was in fact. But being
> small (Stan was small) had its condensations. Who else
> but Stan (the small) could wear all those small clothes?
>
> Stan was highly regarded by everyone (for Stan was
> small and little). However, one day Stan saw an adverse
> in the Mersey Bean for 'Club you quickly grow your
> boots.' So on that very day Small Stan (by name called)
> purchased a pair of the very same. So now when Stan
> passes by, folks say, 'Is that not small Stan wearing a
> pair of those clubs you quickly grow you boots?' And
> it is.

In a satire on the hit record 'The Lion Sleeps Tonight',
by the Tokens, John's Beatcomber column one week had a
safari theme:

ON SAFAIRY WITH WHIDE HUNTER

> In the jumble . . . the mighty jumble . . . Whide Hunter
> sleeps tonight. At the foot of the bed, Otumba kept

wogs for poisonous snacks such as the deadly Cobbler and Apple Python.

Otumba awoke him with a cup of teeth, and they lit up towards the jumble.

'Ain't dat Elepoon Pill?' said Wipe Hudnose, 'wearing his new Basuti?'

'Could be the flying Docker on a case.'

'No he's walking,' said Otumba in swahily which is not arf from here as the crowbarks. All too soon they reached a cleaner in the jumble and set up cramp.' Jumble Jim, whom shall remain nameless, was slowly, but slowly asking his way through the underpants (underware he was being washed by Whide Hunter).

'Beat the bus Otumbath!' commanded Whide Hunter.

'No, but maybe next week it will be my turn to beat the bus now standing at platofrbe nine.'

Jumping Gym, who shall remain Norman, spotted Whit Monday and the Barking Doctrine shooting some rhinostrills and hipposthumous and Otumbark.

'Stop shouting those animoles!' But it hab no influence upod them. They carried on shotting, alligarters, wild boats, garriffes, lepers and Uncle Tom Cobra and all . . . Old Buncle Ron Gabble and all . . . Bold Rumple Bom Dobby and all . . . Bad Runcorn Sad Toddy and all.

Walking into the *Mersey Beat* office at 81A Renshaw Street one day, John forked out his own cash to place these five classified advertisements in the paper, asking that they should definitely not be printed in sequence, but should be scattered among other adverts:

HOT LIPS, missed you Friday, RED NOSE
RED NOSE, missed you Friday, HOT LIPS
ACCRINGTON welcomes HOT LIPS and RED NOSE.
Whistling Jock Lennon wishes to contact HOT NOSE.
RED SCUNTHORPE wishes to jock HOT ACCRINGTON

Clearly, John's early poems, together with his famous exercise book of lampooning called the *Daily Howl* which he had invented at Quarry Bank, were an indication of the literary style for which he was to be lavishly praised only a few years later. *In His Own Write* and *A Spaniard in the Works* were more sophisticated continuations of these early stabs at poetry and satire. There was an Englishness to his work that ran in sharp contrast to the stream-of-consciousness poetry of the American beat poets of the day, like Allen Ginsberg. John's work was to presage the rise of Liverpool beat poets and can now be seen as an indicator of the assertiveness of Liverpool people in various arts, away from the American influence of the time.

Mersey Beat acquired another occasional contributor: Brian Epstein. Aged twenty-seven, he ran the record department of the local NEMS store in Whitechapel. Fascinated by the activity of local beat groups, he had read the newspaper from cover to cover after first stocking it at Bill Harry's request. The first issue sold a dozen copies in Epstein's department; the second sold two hundred and forty copies. 'It was a musical wonderland on his own doorstep which he hadn't been aware of, and he asked if he could contribute a regular record review column,' says Bill Harry. 'He'd call me each week and I'd visit him in his office for chats about the local scene.' About this time, the expanding *Mersey Beat* needed new offices, and during the paper's move many of

John's poems were lost. When he was told, Lennon wept on the shoulder of Bill Harry's wife, Virginia.

Theoretically, Epstein was the least likely mentor of the Beatles, particularly after the rumbustious Allan Williams. He spoke articulately, or, as the Beatles would describe it, 'posh'. He dressed immaculately, in suit and tie, and carried a briefcase. He was painfully shy and would wilt at the slightest dig against his personality. And he was from a middle-class, respectable, Jewish family.

Pride and punctiliousness, rather than a love for pop music, led Epstein to the Beatles. He was more interested in Sibelius than any other sounds. As a businessman, though, he wanted all his teenage customers to be satisfied. One of his biggest boasts was that if he did not have a record in stock when it was asked for, he would get it.

So when Raymond Jones, a regular NEMS record buyer, walked into the shop on 28 October 1961, and asked for 'My Bonnie', by the Beatles, Brian Epstein was flummoxed. He had heard of neither the group, whose weird name he could not spell, nor the record. Jones explained that it was a Liverpool group and the record had been made in Hamburg. Epstein promised to investigate and wrote down on his familiar pad: 'My Bonnie, The Beatles. Check on Monday.'

A few phone calls on Monday elicited some facts. The Beatles had made the record in Hamburg as a backing group, and copies of it were available on the Polydor label. And not only did the group still exist — they played regularly, unknown to Brian, a little more than two hundred yards away in a cellar club he had never heard of, called the Cavern. He suddenly clicked with the familiarity of the names from the pages of *Mersey Beat*, and he asked Bill Harry to arrange for him to go to the club.

The man who was to become the Beatles' manager was a complex character. His background, although more

genteel and conservative, shared one striking characteristic
with the Beatles. He had been expelled from Liverpool
College at the age of ten 'for inattention and for being
below standard.' The crunch that caused his expulsion came
when, during a maths lesson, he designed beneath his desk
a programme featuring dancing girls. 'My parents despaired
many times over the years, and I don't blame them, for
throughout my schooldays I was one of those out-of-sorts
boys who never quite fit,' Epstein wrote later. 'I was ragged,
nagged and bullied and beloved of neither boys nor masters.' By ten, he had been to three schools and settled in
none of them. He was top of his class at art, poor at
mathematics and the sciences, and, after failing many
entrance examinations for public schools, was accepted at
Wrekin College in Shropshire. He went to RADA before
deciding that actors were too narcissistic, and subsequently
returned to Liverpool and the family business after an
apprenticeship in salesmanship at Times Furnishing in Lord
Street, Liverpool.

By the time he reached the Cavern, Epstein had seen
the Beatles without realizing it. They had visited his record
department in the afternoons, and he had dismissed them
in his mind as scruffy layabouts whom he hoped would go
away. 'I had been bothered a little with the frequent visits
of a group of scruffy lads in leather and jeans . . . chatting
to the girls and lounging on the counters listening to
records. They were pleasant enough boys, untidy and a
little wild, and they needed haircuts,' said Brian.

'I mentioned to the girls in the shop that I thought
the youth of Liverpool might while their afternoons away
somewhere else but they assured me that the boys were
well behaved and they occasionally bought records. Also,
said the girls, they seemed to know good discs from bad.
Though I didn't know it, the four lads were the Beatles,

filling in part of the long afternoons between the lunchtime and evening shows in the beat cellars.'

Epstein's first visit to the Cavern embarrassed him for two reasons. First, he felt conspicuous as the well-dressed adult amid a surging crowd of schoolgirls with beehive hairstyles who spoke a language all their own between Cokes and ham rolls. Second, Bob Wooler, the Cavern disc jockey, marked Brian's arrival with a magisterial announcement that 'Mr Epstein of NEMS' was in the audience and would the crowd please give him a big hand. Brian blushed.

'I had never seen anything like the Beatles on any stage,' Epstein recalled later. 'They smoked as they played and they ate and talked and pretended to hit each other. They turned their backs on the audience and shouted at them and laughed at private jokes.' Epstein was both irritated and mesmerized at the unruly group that radiated raw talent. Whatever it was coming from that stage in a dungeon, he could not take his eyes from it.

Although he had several girlfriends, Epstein was a homosexual. It has been said that he had a fixation for John Lennon in particular, from that first sight of him on the Cavern stage. Brian had a deep fascination for John, but Lennon was an extremely active heterosexual with the traditional contempt of those years for the people who, in 1961, were called 'queers' and who kept their preferences secret. Homosexuality was a taboo then. To say, as some commentators have, that Brian Epstein's ambition for the Beatles was based mostly on his initial love of Lennon, is speculative nonsense.

I knew Brian Epstein well enough to know that he was in love with the Beatles as an entity. He was fiercely protective of them all, ambitious for all four of them individually, and totally committed to make them the world's best-known pop act. It was something that went way beyond any sexual preferences.

'Sitting right here today,' Epstein told me in a Liverpool restaurant one night in 1962, 'I can't think why I didn't walk out of the Cavern within a few minutes. I can still remember these four ill-presented youths and their untidy hair.' Brian had invited me, as a writer with the weekly music paper *Melody Maker*, to Liverpool; I was the first London music journalist to go to the city to hear about the Beatles. He told me of his great hopes for the group, how they would be world-beaters, and how lucky I was to be in at the birth of such an explosion. I was interested, but cynically apprehensive. The British pop scene, dominated for so long by America, was slowly developing its own identity. With it came a new breed of swaggering managers who phoned me and many other writers every day to tout the new sensation. Elvis Presley and Cliff Richard had been joined by Acker Bilk's 'Stranger On The Shore', Frank Ifield's yodelling 'I Remember You', and the Tornados' number one hit 'Telstar', to mark America's first communications satellite, launched that year. John Lennon was getting heavily influenced by a raunchy American single, 'Hey Baby', by Bruce Channel which was to inspire John's harmonica playing. Against the general background of gimmicks and ballads and the trickle of good records, and the omnipresent Elvis Presley, a group of Liverpool boys with the unlikely name of the Beatles sounded doubtful starters. Epstein, who exuded charm, impeccable manners, and persistence, was insistent. 'Stay and meet them in my office tomorrow,' he said to me.

Brian told me how, a few months previously, he had invited the Beatles to his shop one afternoon. Although he had no firm plan of what they should do together, 'the idea of management occurred on both sides.' They had arrived at the NEMS store in Whitechapel, taking along Bob Wooler as if to mark the seriousness of the occasion. It was Lennon who broke the ice, saying 'This is me Dad,' when introducing Wooler to Epstein.

Wooler, who had seen the group's popularity soar, had confided in Epstein earlier that the Beatles were enormously popular but lacked regular work. Brian confirmed this with the group, had a general vague talk about contracts and their future, and invited them to return a week later. This time he got to the point briskly. 'Quite simply, you need a manager. Would you like me to do it?'

No one spoke for a moment or two, and then John, in a low, husky voice, blurted: 'Yes.'

The others nodded. Paul, ever wary, asked: 'Will it make much difference to us? I mean, it won't make any difference to the way we play.'

Assured that it would not and assured of Epstein's enthusiasm, the five men sat looking at each other for a few minutes, not knowing what to say next.

Lennon again broke the silence. 'Right, then, Brian, manage us, now. Where's the contract? I'll sign it.'

I did meet the Beatles the day after the dinner with Brian Epstein. It was a brief encounter in Brian's office. John and George bounded in and asked for cigarettes. 'Love Me Do' had just been released. They were cheerful, optimistic, and not at all unkempt. John got in a quick dig that the *Melody Maker* 'only ever writes about jazz,' but he said it with the cynical smile that was to become endearing even when he was at his most cutting. I remember thinking it was difficult to reconcile the tidy men with the uncouth image which Brian had described from the Cavern.

Even in those days, Epstein's impact was considerable. Before he began the long, frustrating search for a record contract, he informally laid down certain rules for them. First, he was a stickler for punctuality. Bob Wooler had trouble getting them on stage on time, and also in getting them off it. They needed tightening up, Epstein told John. Next, Brian suggested they stop drinking Cokes and eating sandwiches on stage, and they were not to shout abuse to people in the audience. He insisted on a tighter act of a maximum of an hour, and that they build a fairly rigid repertoire. The Hamburg experience of playing everything by ear and lambasting the audience was to be dropped. Their music on stage was, under Epstein, never to be as free and easy, but it was the sure route to directing their talent into mass popularity.

With slight reluctance, John accepted Epstein's theory. In a coffee bar Lennon bumped into the art college model June Furlong, who asked him how the group was progressing. He said they had met a posh man named Brian Epstein who had definite ideas for them but it would mean a radical change. 'He seemed unsure of whether it was a good thing,' says June Furlong. 'I said: "Go with it, John. What have you got to lose?" And he roared with laughter.

' "Yeah, June, how true. What have we got to *lose*?" '

He went also to the Renshaw Street offices of *Mersey Beat* and demanded back some of his ruder poems from Bill Harry, lest they should be published. They would, he thought, clash with the new, cleaner image that Epstein intended for the project. On two visits to Mendips, Epstein secured Aunt Mimi's seal of approval. 'A charming gentleman, a restless soul just like John,' she said. 'Always so polite.'

But the next part of Epstein's master plan was to shock John to the bone. As a successful salesman, Brian believed that the great British public would never go for an act that looked scruffy, however primitive their music was to remain. He insisted that the Beatles should wear suits, shirts, and ties. Brian pointed to the Shadows as an example of success. Cliff Richard's backing group were the epitome of that antiseptic pop which John loathed. But secretly, however much Lennon resented Epstein's grooming, he was prepared to give it a whirl. Brian's salesmanship law said that, once a brand name had set a pattern, if it was successful then it should be followed. The Beatles would retain control over their music, of which he knew nothing but that it was spine-tingling with earthy excitement. But when it came to packaging, he told John, he knew what he was talking about: the Shadows were successful, and they wore suits.

It was a major decision and a successful one. But John was going against his instincts in letting Brian mould the group in this direction. It might have been the first moment the group polarized, with John and George rebelling against the 'super packaging' idea which was propounded by Epstein and strongly supported by Paul McCartney.

Clive Epstein, Brian's brother, told me that John was a frequent visitor to the Epstein family home long before the first single was made. 'Brian and John had long, serious discussions about how to project the group,' says Clive. Lennon was keen on learning about Brian's marketing techniques, something utterly foreign to him. 'He had a lot to say and they became very animated. Brian told me privately he believed John was a genius, and of course he assured my parents and me that they would be bigger than Elvis Presley, even before the first single was a small hit. Brian was definitely closer to John than the others; there was a mental contact between them that was perfect and really vital for the group's future.'

Long after the euphoria of Beatlemania, John said in

the *Melody Maker*, 'In the beginning it was a constant fight between Brian and Paul on one side, and me and George on the other. Brian put us in neat suits and shirts and Paul was right behind him. I didn't dig that and I tried to get George to rebel with me. I'd say to George: "Look, we don't need these suits. Let's chuck them out of the window." My little rebellion was to have my tie loose with the top button of my shirt undone, but Paul'd always come up to me and put it straight.

'On the first television film we ever did, the Granada people came down to film us, and there we were in suits and everything. It just wasn't us, and watching that film I knew that that was where we started to sell out.' In most pictures of John he is seen with his tie at least a little askew and, often, with his top shirt button undone.

He said all that with the benefit of hindsight. But in 1962, even for John, the end justified the means. Epstein's logic was unarguable: the devoted fans who thronged the Cavern and the ballrooms for the Beatles would have to be augmented by much wider appeal if they were to be a successful concert, television, and recording group. And the route to real pop success in Britain in 1962 was through the hit parade charts. While Brian tidied them up and slowly improved their fees and number of engagements, he set about the major task of getting them a record contract. It was to prove a heartbreaking hurdle.

Meanwhile, the virtual emigration of his best friend to Germany had left Lennon feeling isolated. John missed Stuart. 'The only real friend John ever had' is how Aunt Mimi described him. 'The bond was beautiful, whenever they met. You could see it immediately,' says Cynthia. Astrid, Stuart's fiancée, would work away in her photographic studio in Hamburg while Stuart worked in an attic in her Hamburg home, alternately painting or writing long letters to John in Liverpool.

Equally, Lennon wrote letters to Stuart with an open-hearted intensity he usually reserved for Cynthia. His twenty-page letters to Stuart were different. Each bemoaned the state of the world, and little was said of the Beatles' progress. What came through, from John to Stuart, and then from Stuart to John, was a restlessness about life, and from John the freedom at last to feel he could unleash his innermost emotions, perhaps about his own venomous tongue which had hurt so many people. Once he wrote to Stuart:

I can't remember anything without a sadness
So deep that it hardly becomes known to me
So deep that its tears leave me a spectator of my own
    stupidity.

As the Epstein plan gathered momentum, the Beatles were to fulfil, on 13 April 1962, an engagement to open Hamburg's Star-Club, their most prestigious appearance so far in a city that they had grown to adopt as their second home. With a new manager behind them, a fresh confidence surged within the group as they travelled. This time, Epstein's style insisted on the Beatles flying to Germany rather than going by train and boat. He wanted to impress them with his largesse and give them confidence that he was serious about making them gigantically successful.

John had been aware of Stuart's very bad headaches through his letters, but only Astrid and her mother knew how really serious they were becoming. 'There were days when poor Stu was convulsed with pain,' says Astrid. 'When I went back to Liverpool with him at Christmas in 1961, everybody said how ill he looked. He fainted at art college once and we all decided that as he was in such agony, and it was impossible to know when a severe headache was caused, he had better stay at home in bed or in the attic, and at least my mother and I could be near him when he needed help.' It also gave Stuart the attention of the Kirchherr family doctor. He sent him for X-rays, but nothing untoward showed itself.

On 10 April, as the plane carrying the Beatles took off from Manchester to Hamburg, Astrid received a phone call from her mother saying that Stuart was in such pain from headaches that she could not even contemplate calling the family doctor. 'He has to go to the hospital right now,' said Frau Kirchherr. Astrid sped home and insisted on accompanying her fiancé in the ambulance. 'He died in my arms on that journey,' says Astrid. 'I cannot say it was unexpected but the suddenness was . . .' Her voice trails off. Cause of death was given as cerebral paralysis.

Astrid went from the hospital to Hamburg airport to meet John, Paul and Pete Best. (George did not arrive until the next day.) They knew nothing of the drama of the day, still less of twenty-one-year-old Stuart's death. 'I don't know how I got through that moment, after what happened,' says Astrid. 'I can see John walking into the airport hall and he got sight of me and came over, waving his arms, "Hello, I'm *here*, how are you . . . oh, what's the matter?" ' He could see darkness in Astrid's doleful, expressive eyes.

'Stuart died, John. He's gone.'

Lennon's reaction was to burst into laughter. He said nothing at all to anyone. 'He never cried,' says Astrid. 'Not once. He went into this hysterical laughter, and couldn't stop. It was his way of not wanting to face the truth. John went deep into himself for just a little while after the news. But he and I didn't speak much about Stuart. I knew that he and Stuart genuinely loved each other. They told me so, when they got loose. I know Stu would have preferred to have died rather than go on in the pain he was suffering. But the loss to me was great, and to anyone who knew him, because he was a genius, with a great mind and an original talent as an artist. He would have been outstanding, if he'd lived. How John got over that period I'll never know.'

Lennon's method of recovery was the same that he had adopted when first he had that awful choice between his mother and father, then the death of Uncle George, then the death of his mother. His period of mourning was quiet, totally personal, and not shared with anyone else. He believed in getting on with living immediately.

Astrid suffered a deep depression for months afterwards, and it was mostly John who pulled her out of it. 'He saved me,' she said. Paul and George particularly were sweet to her, she says, but John knew the onus was on him to look after her because of his relationship with Stu. 'In his rough way, he was so beautiful, and he imposed his own method of recovery on me without me knowing it,' says Astrid. 'Come on, make up your mind, live or die,' he would say. 'You're coming to the Star-Club with us tonight. Stop sitting at home – it won't bring Stu back.' John showed many times his demonstrativeness towards Astrid's mother, who had borne the brunt of Stuart's illness when Astrid was away in her photographic studio so often during the days. 'My mother would say: "John, you are supposed to be a rough rocker." He would put his arms around her and carry on as if he lived in the house, which she loved.' Astrid says John kept her from becoming morose, and she did, indeed, go to the Star-Club when the Beatles opened there on 13 April for seven weeks.

They were in a mood of despondency at Stuart's death, and optimism at their career prospects; the Star-Club was a step up, and they had, after all, been chosen to open it. One of the men who helped run the club, Horst Fascher, recalls John as being the one with the most bizarre behaviour during the seven weeks they were at the Star-Club. 'On that opening night, we had the Beatles and other groups and Brian Epstein also came. There was lots to drink. The next morning we all went to a club and Brian was a bit drunk and John Lennon poured beer all over him. There was a slight argument.'

Fascher knew the Beatles from 1960 when he had worked in the Kaiserkeller, the second Hamburg club they had played. He was also the manager of Tony Sheridan, with whom the Beatles had made their first record in Hamburg, called 'My Bonnie', which had been the subject of that first request to Brian Epstein. Fascher recalls: 'They were different from the start. There was something I liked about them, and their clothes and special sound impressed me.' He was also amused by their eccentricity: 'One day,' he says, 'they all went to the fish market in Hamburg and bought a pig. They walked it, on a lead, up and down the Reeperbahn. Some people who saw it were annoyed and called the police, who took it away to be slaughtered. It was typical of their outlandish behaviour.'

As the kings of the Cavern back home, and now knowing Hamburg where their reputation was soaring, John, Paul, George, and Pete Best were in a lively mood. They stayed in a flat above the Star-Club. John's often outrageous behaviour, during that month, may have been traceable to his submerging of Stuart's death. The Star-Club owner, Manfred Weissleder, sometimes travelled to Africa and bought animal skins which he suggested the Beatles wore onstage. So on one occasion John appeared on the Star-Club stage as a monkey. When the show ended, he walked outside, up and down the Grosse Freiheit and the Reeperbahn, in the same outfit. Then he and the others went into a club, and Horst Fascher had a call from the police, saying the Beatles had gone into a club and 'scared people to death.' People had run away and not paid their bills, so the owner insisted the Beatles should pay the bills. 'They had no money, so I had to pay.'

One Saturday night, after the Beatles had been playing at the Star-Club until nearly dawn, thirty people attended a party at their flat in the Grosse Freiheit. The toilet facilities were inadequate, with just one lavatory shared among the flats, up five flights of stairs: John urinated over the edge of the balcony. 'We were all just normal human beings,' says Paul McCartney, confirming the event. 'I seem to remember John had a pee over the edge. But what happens is that all these stories grow into great legends.' McCartney says that the story that John urinated on nuns who were going to St. Joseph's Catholic Church, next door to the flats, was untrue. 'On a separate occasion, there were some nuns and we shouted at them, not crazily, but like "Oy oy, sister" and generally like young people do. The two stories got together, so we get this really outrageous story where John's peeing on nuns. It never really was like that. It all just grew into really crazy stories out of what most people would agree is boyish craziness.'

A drunken John did take the stage of the club with a toilet seat around his neck at the end of the show when most of the audience wanted a bit of a cabaret. During that trip in Hamburg John was certainly wild. Says Gerry Marsden, who was playing at the Top Ten club and who saw the Beatles socially: 'Remember we were all kids who had basically never been anywhere apart from Liverpool. You're suddenly free of parents, friends, anybody who knows you, and getting paid decent money. So John did his own thing more freely because his Auntie wasn't there to say: "Stop it." Like all of us, John went a little bit mad.

'As for booze, yes, we all drank too much, including John. He started work around seven in the evening and played half a dozen sets or so, ending at around two in the morning. Rum and Coke was sixpence a big glass, and we couldn't afford that stuff in England. So by the early hours of the next morning, we'd all had quite a lot of bevvies. And you'll still be high because the adrenalin was pumping away from performing your heart out. So then you'd go out to eat, until four or five in the morning, maybe with the Horst Fascher family, and of course sleep in till about three o'clock next afternoon. Then it was down to the Seamen's Mission on the dockside for a fry-up breakfast. That was the pattern for all the groups in Hamburg. It was like a rehearsal every night, and John told me many times after-wards that it was an experience he could never have got anywhere else. If you can survive Hamburg, with all its audiences giving you hell, and the demands of the nights, you can survive even Beatlemania! It trained John to have the really hard voice that became famous as part of the Beatles. It wrecked everybody's vocal cords singing for such long periods, but when you keep on singing every night like that, and shouting back the first thing that comes into your head at the crowds, your voice's power increases. John used to enjoy the hurly burly of it all.'

Gerry saw Lennon in many punch-ups in Liverpool and Hamburg. 'But I'd not describe him as a hard lad. He'd lose his temper and hit people, but more often than not he'd get a smack right back in the mouth. In Liverpool, John was lucky that he had a strong reputation and the name of the Beatles behind him, otherwise he'd have got beaten up even more than he did. He behaved like a typical Scouse teddy boy, a ruffian, but he was no harder than lots of other people of those days. But when he hit, he got smashed back. You don't walk away often, on Merseyside, when you give a mouthful of abuse to someone. I saw him get many a pasting.'

The worst scene Marsden saw involving John happened in Hamburg. Playing cards in the flat above the Star-Club, John was drunk. There was an argument. 'John got up and hit the fellow over the head with a bottle. I thought: "That's really out of order." Within seconds the fellow had got up and knocked hell out of John, pasting him all over the flat. And all of us stood there and let him do it, because we agreed that you just don't go round hitting people over the head with bottles and expect to get away with it. I saw John bashed about many times, but never so hard. He really took it that night. But he asked for it, and he said later it was fair because he shouldn't have done what he did. Put it like this: I'd never have employed John as a bodyguard. He wasn't that hard.'

Twenty years after the Beatles were in Hamburg, there were still people closely connected with that period who warmed to the memories. Rosa, for example: two decades later, at eighty-six years old, she was still the toilet attendant in the Top Ten club in the Reeperbahn, extolling to me, through a translator, her love of the boys whom she cooked, laundered, and made beds for. 'John's reputation as the wild one was true,' says Rosa. 'He was like the devil on that stage. I remember John as the ambitious one. He said that one day they would be very famous. "Mama," he would say. "*Mutti!* We go to America, be very big, very famous, make LOTS of money." '

She says that he often drank too much and would lie on the dance floor and cry. 'He was really angry sometimes,

but the public thought it was a show. What he was angry
about was the group sound, when it was not as he liked.
Then he would drink as a kind of consolation. I heard them
quarrelling a lot. I would worry about the amount John
was going to drink when they argued.'

Hamburg, with its punishing physical demands onstage, the absurd time-keeping and irregular sleep and food,
and the combativeness of the audience, was John's gruelling
training ground. With the sadness evoked by the city's
constant reminder of his best friend's death, it provided
him with a steely exterior. As the years went on, that
characteristic became confused with toughness. The curious
fact is that the older he became, the less tough and abrasive
and the more human Lennon emerged.

He was given to odd streaks of sentimentality. In Hamburg that bleak spring, trying to console Astrid and Stuart's
heart-broken mother, Millie Sutcliffe, John asked particularly for Stuart's long, woollen college scarf, striped in navy
and pale blue and yellow and cream. It was to remain his
most prized souvenir of their bond. It reminded John of
their days together, huddled in Gambier Terrace and the
alleyways of Liverpool 8.

TEN

MARRIAGE

'Don't worry, Cyn. We'll get married'

O N O N E of his first drawings, which he gave to a student
as a gift, John captioned a particularly gruesome-look-
ing figure 'The Wife', almost as a commentary about what
he feared the role of a woman in his life could be: overbear-
ing and domineering, hideously ugly.

But the first serious woman in his life, who was inseparable from him when they met at college in 1957 and
became his wife during Beatlemania as well as the mother
of his first child, was the opposite of that fearsome drawing.
Cynthia scarcely realized how John's macabre sense of the
absurd would manifest itself into a tender moment in their
lives, a year after their marriage. On 8 April 1963 their only
son, John Charles Julian Lennon, was born at Sefton General
Hospital, Liverpool.

It was not an easy birth. Cynthia says, 'I was something
like three days in hospital before Julian arrived and then
he had jaundice, the umbilical cord was around his neck,
and he had a very large mole on his head. He had to be
left alone for twenty-four hours; I couldn't touch him. I
was petrified about all these things. But I was scared more
than anything about the birth mark, the mole. Knowing
John's horror of deformities, I was absolutely panic-stricken

about what John's reaction would be.' When Julian was born, John and the Beatles were busy criss-crossing Britain on a hectic schedule of ballroom appearances to consolidate their new fame. John phoned the hospital, excitedly enquiring about his wife and baby, and was triumphant at the news that it was a boy.

After three days Cynthia welcomed John to the hospital – and made sure that the baby's head was resting against a pillow so that the prominent mole could not be seen by the sensitive, eagle-eyed father. 'When John came in, I decided not to hide it. I said: "Oh he's beautiful, wonderful, John, but he has this birth mark on his head."

'John replied: "Oh, it doesn't matter. His hair will grow over that."

'I was still bothered because I wanted the perfect child for John, but he couldn't have cared less. He was just thrilled, the typical father.'

In the weeks that followed, Cynthia carefully covered the baby's head with a hat at every possible moment – so that John would not have his attention drawn to the mole. The prospect of a baby Lennon that was anything less than physically perfect haunted her.

Julian Lennon was conceived at Cynthia's £3-a-week bedsitter at 93 Garmoyle Road, off Smithdown Road, a stone's throw from Penny Lane. It was also very close to Sefton General Hospital, where Julian was born. They had never taken birth control precautions, from their first experience together in Stuart's flat.

'There was no planning. There was no pill in those days. We considered nothing except ourselves and didn't consider the consequences. As far as I was concerned, ignorance was bliss. Neither John nor I gave pregnancy a thought. My parents didn't advise me and I didn't ask them, and I'm sure John wouldn't dream of asking Mimi.

We weren't thinking about anything like prevention, just enjoying each other naturally as two kids.

'But when the reality dawned first on me, I was full of absolute shock. "My God, what am I going to tell my Mum?"'

'And he had the same reaction: "What am I going to tell Mimi?"'

'It was guilt. Even though we didn't have the pill, we did have respect for our elders. Aged twenty in 1962 was rather like being aged sixteen by today's standards,' Cynthia observes. 'We were both kids basically.'

But John's reaction, on being told, was that if a girl became pregnant, the man must 'do the right thing' and marry her.

'I don't think we'd have been married if I hadn't become pregnant,' she says. 'He wasn't the sort at the age of twenty-one to say: "Will you marry me?" It was all so immediate we hardly realized the seriousness of it all: making love, getting pregnant, getting married.

'If we had carried on seeing each other without a child arriving, I had it in mind to obtain my qualification as an art teacher. That would have enabled me to support John whatever happened, because his life at that time was music and I couldn't see his future in it. He was messing around at college and within music and I thought: "Well, I love him. Whatever happens, if he can't make money, I'll be there and I'll have my art teacher's diploma and I'll be able to teach." That was at the back of my mind.'

But her attention to her studies suffered when she got involved with John. Cynthia failed her art teacher's diploma exam. And John went on to do rather well with his music.

'One thing's for sure,' says Cynthia. 'I didn't marry John for his money. He didn't have any, I didn't appreciate it, and it's never done me any good. I had more money

than he did in the early days of our love affair and I was
funding him every day at college. So if money was important to me I'd have chosen a rich boyfriend.'

John's attitude to being a father was similar to his
approach to everything else, from the launching of the
Beatles to pursuing art, to getting married and divorced,
and buying houses. The same principle applied throughout
his life: first decide, then do it, then move on to the next
situation – a new challenge. Although whatever he became
involved in was done wholeheartedly, the restless spirit
inside him was always powerful. Lennon had many varied
and brilliant assets within his character, but stability was
never among them.

'I don't think he was ready for a child any more than I
was,' says Cynthia. 'He wasn't ready to settle down.' When
they married he was twenty-one and she was twenty-two.
'Whatever happened with John was always a compromise.
He had to get everything over with quickly. He was committed to it while it had to be done, but he'd want to be
moving on to the next thing fast.'

Cynthia's cramped flat in Garmoyle Road was not far
from Woolworth's in Penny Lane where she worked as a
counter assistant during summer vacations from college.
When Cynthia's father died – uncannily about the same
time that John was hit by the death of his mother – her
mother went to Canada to act as nanny to Cynthia's cousin.
The family house at Hoylake was rented out, and Cynthia
fancied a flat of her own.

In August 1962 John was visiting Cynthia at her flat
when he found her particularly quiet.

'Is everything OK?' he asked.

Cynthia was in the kitchen, washing up. 'No, it's not
OK.'

'What's the matter?'

'I'm pregnant, that's what's the matter.'

'Oh Christ, what are we going to do?' said John, moving over to put his arm around her. Panic seized him, then a quick flash of practicality: 'Look, I'll go and tell Mimi. Don't worry, Cyn. We'll get married.'

John's instinctive decision to 'do the right thing' and marry a girl who was pregnant in 1962 was very much a reflection of the times. They had been having an affair, but nobody knew and the first time John's Aunt Mimi knew that they had slept together was when he went home that night and said, 'Cyn's pregnant.'

Mimi erupted. 'John told me there had been the most tremendous scene, one of the worst things he'd ever had to go through,' Cynthia says. 'Mimi threw everything at him – "You stupid children, getting yourselves into this situation! The whole family will have nothing to do with you. You've got yourself into this mess, now get yourselves out of it." '

Lennon certainly did not *want* marriage at this stage. He told several people close to him that he had to get married to protect Cynthia and the child, and Cynthia will always doubt that he would ever have married her if she had not become pregnant. But Cynthia's closest friend throughout and after college years, Phyllis McKenzie, disagrees. 'They were totally opposite but right for each other and, although they came from different backgrounds, they were a perfect match,' she says. 'I think they would obviously have taken longer to get married, but it *would* have happened. They loved each other very much. There was no separating them.'

Once the decision was made, John panicked about the ceremony. 'Christ,' he said to Brian Epstein. 'What am I going to do? How can I fix it all up and get on with it quickly?'

If ever John needed evidence that he had the right manager, this was that moment. The smooth, organized skill of Epstein rose to the occasion. 'Don't worry, John. I'll fix it.'

An early sign of her acceptance of the situation came when Aunt Mimi gave John the money to buy the wedding ring. He went with Cynthia to a jeweller just a few doors from Epstein's NEMS store in Whitechapel. She chose a simple £10 gold wedding ring and there was no sentimentality attached to buying it.

For all his bravery when he was with Cynthia, John broke down with his Aunt Mimi the night before his wedding. 'I don't want to get married,' he said, wandering restlessly around Mendips. He was choking back the tears at the seriousness of the situation.

'I told you before, John. You're too young. But what's done's done.' She regarded Cynthia as not bright enough for her brilliant nephew. 'Now, John, I've said it. Once the ring's on the finger, I shall hold my peace.' She pointedly refused to attend the wedding.

Brian Epstein arranged a special licence for the marriage at Mount Pleasant Register Office. He arranged for a car to collect Cynthia from her flat, where, shaking with nerves, she had dressed in a well-worn purple and black check two-piece suit. John was dressed formally, almost funereally, in black suit and tie, with a white shirt, and his friends Paul McCartney and George Harrison were dressed exactly the same. The other guests were Cynthia's brother Tony and his wife, Margery, who shared the honour of signing their names as witnesses on the marriage certificate with 'James Paul McCartney.'

The mood at the wedding was one of controlled panic. In the register office waiting-room John fidgeted nervously with his tie and his hair. During the three-minute ceremony a pneumatic drill outside started up bang on cue, just as the registrar began his short speech. The noise virtually drowned the event: that broke the ice.

Giggling nervously, they walked out into torrential rain, down the hill past Liverpool's grand old Adelphi Hotel. At Brian's suggestion, the wedding celebration was a lunch in the unlicenced Reece's restaurant. John did not realize that the same register office and Reece's had been his parents' wedding day rendezvous. It was just noon, and the Beatles party had to queue up for a table before sitting down to the set lunch of soup, chicken, and trifle. They toasted the bride and groom with glasses of water. The bill came to fifteen shillings a head, and Epstein paid.

'It was hysterical. We were like nervous children going to the dentist, from start to finish. We were laughing uncontrollably at anything in sight,' says Cynthia. 'People's hats, the women who go into Reece's – we were laughing all the time at anything to make sure we didn't take it seriously. I was the only one thinking about the future, I think, because I knew what I was in for.'

At Reece's Epstein told John and Cynthia of his special gift to them – free, unlimited use of his flat at 36 Falkner Street, a street almost opposite the art college. Cynthia believes that the shrewd Epstein did not relish the thought of the leader of the Beatles living in her spartan bed-sitter in Garmoyle Road – 'it might have been bad for the image.' Brian's flat was, anyway, comparatively luxurious and in what was at that time a fashionable area of the city. They even had use of a small, walled garden.

On the wedding night, John and the Beatles had a show at Chester. The new Mrs Lennon, relieved that one of the most testing days of her life was over, moved her meagre possessions from Garmoyle Road to Brian's flat and relaxed.

For John, though, the speed of events in his musical career was a perfect diversion from what had just happened. Brian Epstein's industrious efforts to obtain a recording contract had achieved success three months before John's wedding. Twelve days after his marriage to Cynthia, John was excitedly in London recording the McCartney song that was to start the most astonishing, influential event in entertainment, and rocket John and the Beatles into a prominence previously known only to film stars and statesmen.

On the van journey to London for that recording session, they would all wait for the signal from John to recite the short poem that he had concocted. It was a little rhyme that in a year became even truer than he ever dared hope:

> *John:* Where are we going, fellas?
> *Chorus:* To the top, Johnny to the TOP!
> *John:* And where *is* the top, fellas?
> *Chorus:* To the toppermost of the poppermost!

With the Beatles' career moving ahead decisively, Epstein was adding to Lennon's arrogance a remarkable new factor: confidence that he had a spectacular future. Repeatedly, Eppy told anyone who would listen that 'the boys' would one day be bigger than Elvis Presley. Events proved Epstein absolutely accurate, but at that time most people were convulsed with laughter at Brian's promise that Liverpool lads could achieve anything like Presley status. Elvis was an untouchable god. Moreover he was American, and America always led in pop. British artists were consigned to plagiarism at best, weedy pap like Cliff Richard or Frankie Vaughan at worst. Four Liverpool scruffs to dominate the world? Forget it, Brian!

But the Beatles thrust happened so quickly under

Brian's devotion and the prescience of George Martin that it needed John's total attention. Their roots at St Peter's church fête, Woolton, may have been a dim, distant memory, but John and Paul were able to draw on a formidable reserve of experience – particularly of live shows, and tough audiences in ballrooms and clubs – by the time they were pitchforked by Epstein into the big time. Lennon, more than the other three, loved the hoop that Brian was putting them through. When George Martin told Epstein that Pete Best needed replacing as the Beatles' drummer before he would offer a record contract, John's reaction to an anguished Brian at Mendips one night was immediate: 'OK, but you tell Pete he's out and I'll get Ringo in.' John and Paul had always admired Ringo Starr's work with another local band, Rory Storm and the Hurricanes. Next night, John phoned Ringo, who was playing at Butlin's holiday camp in Skegness. 'You're in, Ringo – the sidies will have to go, though.' John's remark recognized that Ringo's cheek-length sideburns would clash with Epstein's master plan to tidy the Beatles up.

Mentally high on the Hamburg experiences, and having a faster instinct than any of the other Beatles, John knew that once they had recorded a song and marshalled their image and their fans properly, they would be unstoppable. From childhood he had never lacked confidence in his ability; the only difference was that now it was not a wayward, artistic talent. It had direction. It was blazing enthusiasm for music to the exclusion of everything else. When John got hold of something – anything – he became blinkered to the world beyond it.

The qualities John admired in McCartney were exactly those that John lacked: Paul was artistic, creative, and a wonderful foil to offset John. But he had a valuable extra ingredient: determination to see a job through. He insisted on every detail being completed. His appearance reflected the inner man: he looked casual, but he was always tidy.

When John talked to Cynthia about Paul, it was in terms of incredulity at Paul's self-discipline. John, who had stalked his way through grammar school and college, and lurched into a rock band, was thrilled at the prospect of moving ahead in music with McCartney's methodical touches at his elbow. He would not have said so at the time.

There was another quality in the immensely heterosexual Lennon that he admired in Paul: an ability to attract a woman, and have a fling with her, and then move on very quickly. John did not master that art until later, in his mid-twenties. Adventurousness, and the appetite for moving on, applied to John in everything except his associations with women. It could not have been related to the death of his mother, for long before she died he was having an affair with a girl in Woolton named Barbara whom he had dated for two years before her parents warned her to drop him. The length of that affair, and his intense relationship with Cynthia, demonstrated that he never did things by halves.

Now, as a married twenty-two-year-old, John was pulled in two directions. His wife and baby were in Epstein's flat just as the Beatles caravan began to look as if it would roll. After the row with Aunt Mimi about Cynthia's pregnancy, and her boycott of the wedding, John now felt he had to crack on with music to the exclusion of everything else.

In what must rank as one of the world's most bizarre honeymoons, John – after going to Chester on their wedding night – continued to travel, first to London, then to Manchester and other cities as the Beatles' success gained momentum in the north-west. After the Beatles' first entry into the hit parade, preparations for their first proper concert tour around Britain, with Helen Shapiro, took John away from Cynthia at the very time that they should have been consolidating their relationship.

'We were both sort of bowled over by the fact that we were married,' says Cynthia. 'It wasn't a question of "What's happened to us, have we done the right thing?" It was all perfectly natural that we should be together. But John didn't get a chance to be first a real husband or later a real father. He was too busy, and put himself under a lot of pressure to make sure that, once the Beatles ball was rolling, he kept pushing it.'

After three months of pregnancy, Cynthia had a threatened miscarriage. 'I was alone, John was away, and I started panicking.' Her brother, Tony, rushed over to be with her, but the doctor's orders were straightforward: stay in bed for three days. John phoned her at the flat, but she didn't tell him, in case he should be diverted from what she knew was vital to him at this time: success with the Beatles.

'When John came home I told him about it, and said I was particularly frightened while I was pregnant, because if I had lost Julian there was nobody there to help me at all. I suddenly said, "Why don't we go and see Mimi, ask her advice." ' He had often said to her, 'I wonder how Mimi and Mendips is.' He was nervous about seeing her after the terrible scenes that took place before the wedding. He hadn't seen her for three months – the first time in his life they had been separated since childhood.

Cynthia said, 'Come on John, she's your Auntie, I'm sure she'll be OK now.'

He said, 'Are you sure?'

Cynthia reflects now: 'I knew in my heart of hearts that she was missing John like mad, that she was upset about the whole business, and wanted peace. Knowing Mimi and John, I also knew it was always a quickfire temper, soon over with. She was obviously going to be missing her "son" and John was, I think, missing her.' He felt isolated from his family.

On a sunny day they got the bus and with some trepidation walked down the drive at Mendips. John knocked at the door, Mimi opened it with outstretched arms, and the three of them went in for a warmer welcome than John and Cynthia had dared hope for. Mimi made eggs and chips and tea and asked the now visibly pregnant Cynthia how she was feeling. Cynthia told her of the threatened miscarriage.

'I'm very worried about you,' said Mimi. 'You can't stay in that flat on your own. Come and live with me. I'll move upstairs and you and John can live downstairs. It will be cheaper, and better for you because you need someone with you while you're pregnant.' The garden outside would soon be essential for the pram, Mimi added.

The move to Mimi's house was speedy and practical, but disastrous for Cynthia, who felt Mimi resented the intrusion on her home, despite her invitation. There was another torment for Cynthia: at a meeting before she became pregnant, at Cynthia's home in Hoylake, Mimi and Cynthia's mother had clashed. Their temperaments were totally opposite: Mimi was artistic, bookish, and utterly possessive of John whom she regarded as very special; Lilian Powell was the archetypal protector of her daughter's virtues. At the frosty encounter, which had been suggested by John and Cynthia, the two women sought refuge in picking faults in John and Cynthia. John and Cynthia left the room in red-faced embarrassment as the two women carried on grumbling about them and poured scorn on their relationship. Eventually John took Mimi home, silently, on the bus; but he was never to forgive his future mother-in-law for hosting such a destructive meeting.

'John and I were very upset. We were both in love with each other,' says Cynthia, 'and for the two dearest people in our lives to stand in front of us saying what terrible people we were, and how they hated us for getting together, was awful. I think they did it because they didn't get on and they didn't want us to get on either. But the experience was horrible.'

As soon as Cynthia moved into Mendips John was off on the road again. Cynthia now felt terribly exposed: she felt uneasy because Mimi was ill with bronchitis and Cynthia's arrival had meant she had to move upstairs; and to increase her tension, John had told her that Brian Epstein insisted she keep her pregnancy secret because a married Beatle would be bad for the group's image.

In those years, pop stars were expected to be 'available' in the eyes of girl fans. A chief Beatle with a wife, heaven forbid a pregnant one, might have turned away the teenage girls who were now rallying round the Beatles as they travelled the country. At stage doors, in dressing-rooms, and as their van drove them away to their digs or cheap hotel for the night, sixties girls with beehive hairstyles, hopelessly high heels, and heavy mascara would queue in wait for a glimpse of their favourite Beatle. A chatting-up would be even better, and if it led to a night together – great. Paul McCartney's handsome, brown-eyed stare made him the early favourite among the girls, but John's tough guy stance and leer, plus his raw aggression on stage, made him a very close second. Cynthia was to be kept firmly and privately at home.

Epstein's rule suited Lennon perfectly. It tied in with his maxim that, whatever the job in hand, it must be concentrated upon 100 per cent. The job was the Beatles, and the pace of events was speeding up.

During Cynthia's pregnancy John travelled all over

England as the Beatles set about consolidating their record success with 'Love Me Do'. On tour with Helen Shapiro, he phoned Cynthia at Mendips regularly. He sounded tremendously excited that things were taking off for them, and relieved that she had had no recurrences of the threatened miscarriage. 'His music was coming together well, the crowds were gathering for them, and it was a terribly exciting time,' says Cynthia.

The pressure on her was considerable. Mimi took in students who knew that John Lennon of the Beatles was her nephew; the same students, or their friends, had lodged with her year after year. Mimi took pride now in the fact that the Beatles were having a little success, but Cynthia had to play out a charade. 'I said to these students, and people nearby, that I was John's girlfriend, but I was also a student and that's the reason I gave them for wearing smocks. "I'm an artist and I do some work here at home," I'd say. What they didn't realize, I hope, was that the smocks were getting bigger and bigger to hide the baby.'

John, on the phone, was sounding excited at the prospect of being a father. He never minded whether it was a boy or a girl as long as it was healthy. Mimi, however, repeatedly told Cynthia: 'It's got to be a boy, just like John.'

The choice of names came quickly and easily: John after the father, Julian because it was close to John's mother's name, and Charles in memory of Cynthia's father. One thing worried John in the maternity ward when he and Cynthia discussed it: 'Hey,' he said, 'someone said Julian sounds a bit poofy.' But they laughed it away and decided that the closeness to his mother was what really mattered.

Three factors had always made Cynthia's relationship with Mimi difficult and tense. Mimi was constantly worried that John's poor school results would mean that he would end up unemployed; she felt incredibly possessive about her surrogate son; and her dislike of Cynthia's mother was reflected in her attitude towards Cynthia.

'When John first took me home,' says Cynthia. 'I suppose Mimi looked on it as a childhood romance, nothing serious. We were about eighteen and no aunt would expect her nephew to be seriously involved at that age. The more it drifted on for months, the greater I could see Mimi worrying and looking concerned. It wasn't anything she said, just her general attitude towards me at that stage, after a few months of John and me together and me visiting Mendips. I don't think she went overboard.'

Mimi's full wrath had come one afternoon. For the very first time John had earned some money from some of their Cavern dates, and other work, in 1961. He proudly asked Cynthia what she would like as a celebration present. She asked for a brown suede coat. John went with her to C & A's store and spent £17 on the three-quarter-length coat. 'It wasn't very high quality, it was rough suede, but for me at the time it was the most wonderful gift,' says Cynthia.

They went straight from Liverpool city centre to show it off to Mimi. Cynthia said they shouldn't go empty-handed, so they took her a cooked chicken for their tea. Neither John nor Cynthia could believe the fury that greeted them.

'Do you like Cyn's new coat?' John said as they entered the hall.

Mimi flew into an immediate rage. How could John go buying things like that when he didn't have a proper job. 'But we've brought you a cooked chicken, Mimi.'

'Take your chicken and your gangster's moll and get out,' Mimi roared. 'You get a bit of money in your pocket and go and blow it on *her*.' Finally Mimi sat down in tears, and Cynthia tried to calm her down.

292   LENNON

'I'm sorry if you're upset, but we'll be all right,' said
Cynthia. 'Take it easy, Mimi.'

'Go away. Don't talk to me,' sobbed Mimi, inconsolable.

And that's just what John and Cynthia did. When John
returned later, after taking Cynthia home to Garmoyle
Road, Mimi was silent. John crept up to bed, and the next
morning the row had been forgotten.

But it had been a sharp example to John and Cynthia
of Mimi's touchiness. John knew she was not a woman to
cross lightly. Now he had proof. 'All over a bloody coat,'
he mused to Cyn.

Mimi's fury at John's display of largesse was, of course,
justified by the facts. With no O-levels at school, and now
apparently having left art college, on which she had pinned
all her hopes, John was drifting into full-time pop music.
That future was not secure enough for Mimi. The Beatles'
success was a mere pipe dream to her.

One day she called his bluff and put the fear of God
inside him. 'I said: "All right, so you don't want college
and you don't want any more education. But what are you
earning? Five shillings, which you're spending on your way
out of that Cavern. You're just not earning enough at this
music game, John, so I've found a proper job for you." '

'What are you talking about?' John said, shaken.

'It's no good, John,' Mimi went on. 'I can't go on like
this. The worry's too much. I've got a job for you on the
buses – as a conductor. They can't get staff anywhere. I've
signed you on.'

'Me, me!!! I'm not a *working man*. If you think I'm
going to go out at nine o'clock in the morning and come
home at five, well I won't.'

Mimi retorted: 'What do you think you've been study-

ing for if it isn't to be a working man? Think about it,
John. It's either that or brushing the snow. I've had it with
you.'

John's face went scarlet, and he ran up to his room.
Here was his privacy. Mimi was never allowed there. A
picture of Brigitte Bardot was stuck to the ceiling above
his bed.

Half an hour elapsed before John slowly walked downstairs. He said nothing but sidled up behind Mimi who
was sitting in his favourite armchair. 'Make up your mind,
John,' she said. But she could not keep it up any longer,
and her face cracked into a smile. 'I wasn't serious, but I
was just trying to stir him up and worry him into work,'
said Mimi.

The scene ended when John said, 'I knew you were
joking, Mimi.'

'Oh, no, I'm not, John.'

'Yes you are. I can't add two and two together – how
can I be a bus conductor?'

ELEVEN

FAME

'I battered his bloody ribs in'

SATIRE AND comedy that leaned towards innuendo, rather than knockabout humour of the custard pie variety, had always attracted John. He grew up listening carefully to two radio programmes, *Up The Pole*, starring Jimmy Jewel and Ben Warris, a double act who lampooned each other, and, more significantly, *The Goon Show*. Spike Milligan and Harry Secombe's voices were clever, but John particularly loved the droll Peter Sellers, whose dry satire was captured on one of Lennon's favourite records of the period, *The Best Of Sellers*. Another favourite was Stanley Unwin, who specialized in converting the English language into gibberish. He was a major influence on John's word-play in his own books.

John's saltiness gave the Beatles their edge, on and off stage, in the recording studio and when they were travelling. It was a characteristic felt early on in the desperate attempt by Brian Epstein to secure them a recording contract.

Returning one night from London to Lime Street Station, Epstein had grim news for the Beatles: he was not getting any interest from the record companies. Their future was in jeopardy, although his hopes and determination were undimmed. He called Paul McCartney and asked the Beatles to meet him in Joe's Café in Duke Street, a haunt of night workers, lorry drivers, and anyone else needing a cup of tea until 4:00 a.m.

'I'm afraid it's no use, I've had a flat "No",' Epstein began. Decca had turned them down, in what was to become one of the legendary rejections in the history of music. Pye had also said no.

John broke the spell and the gloom. As they all sat drinking tea and smoking, he flicked a teaspoon high into the air and said, 'Right. Try Embassy.' Embassy was something of a joke record label, run by Woolworth's and featuring pale copies of the hits of the day.

John's remark was worthy of *The Goon Show*. He did not realize then that the Beatles' eventual recording contract was to be secured by Brian with the man who had been the Goons' recording manager, and who had been with them in the studios during the recording of phrases immortal to John's ears, such as 'Ying Tong'. It was a neat irony.

George Martin, trained as a classical pianist at the Guildhall School of Music, also played the oboe, and was artists and recording manager in charge of the Parlophone label at EMI. Although he got on immediately with Epstein, whose refined accent he shared, the odds were that four young rock 'n' rollers from Liverpool would be at odds with his attitudes and his musical preferences. He was steeped in light orchestral music but had a penchant for comedy. Lennon relished the prospect of making records with a man who had rubbed shoulders with such wonderful mimics.

It was during that fateful visit to Hamburg, with news of the death of Stuart so fresh in their minds, that Epstein's telegram arrived: 'EMI CONTRACT SIGNED, SEALED. TREMENDOUS IMPORTANCE TO US ALL. WON-

DERFUL.' They returned their delight in crisp messages on postcards. Paul wrote: 'Please wire £10,000 advance royalties.' George wrote: 'Please order four new guitars.' John wrote: 'When are we going to be millionaires?'

Their recording career took off like lightning, with 'Love Me Do' as their debut hit, helped by John's catchy harmonica playing. When they moved to London, and met the Rolling Stones, John was teased about that solo by the late Brian Jones, who played the harmonica on the Stones' first records.

On a visit to the Crawdaddy Club in Richmond, John was asked by Brian during the Stones' set: 'Are you playing harmonica or a blues harp on "Love Me Do"?'

Lennon replied: 'A harmonica, y'know, with a button.'

John recalled later that Brian wondered how he got such a deep bottom note during the record. John told Brian that it was 'impossible to get "Hey Baby" licks from a blues harp.' A top favourite of the Beatles at the time was Bruce Channel's harmonica-based hit, 'Hey Baby'. John did his utmost to copy that style when he played the harmonica.

One of John's most adamant statements, during the years I knew him, was that there was nothing original in rock 'n' roll, or in what he and the Beatles were doing. 'It's all rip-off,' he would say repeatedly. Reading the music papers, particularly the outlandish and pompous claims of some musicians, John would blurt out: 'This is a load of crap' at singers' or musicians' claims of originality. Rock 'n' roll to him was totally derivative. Elvis Presley, Buddy Holly, and the newer sounds of the Miracles and Tamla Motown were the *real* music, he kept saying. 'We're the receivers, we're just interpreting it as English kids. Don't let anybody ever kid you it's original. It's all a RIP OFF!'

*

The momentum of the Beatles' that began in that autumn of 1962 with 'Love Me Do' gathered with a speed that is often forgotten. Epstein summed up the astounding pace of events after George Martin's offer of a recording session. 'Two years later,' wrote Epstein, 'the Beatles were the greatest entertainers in the world; they had met the Queen Mother and the Duke of Edinburgh and their pictures were on the walls of the noble bedrooms of the young aristocracy. Prince Charles had all their records and San Francisco had the ticker-tape ready. They played the Hollywood Bowl, had the freedom of Liverpool. Ringo was asked to be President of London University and Lennon was the world's bestselling writer.'

In a single turbulent year for John, the Beatles had acquired an active and ambitious manager; they had an audition in the big city, London, resulting in a record contract with EMI; his best friend had died in Hamburg; Pete Best had been fired as drummer, to be replaced by Ringo; his girlfriend had broken the news that she was pregnant, and they had hurriedly married; and the Beatles had made their television debut before going to Hamburg for their fifth and final club trip.

The Beatles began 1963 in a remarkable frenzy. They were booked for their first major British concert tour by package tour promoter Arthur Howes, who specialized in putting artists of the calibre of Cliff Richard and the Shadows around the cinema halls of Britain. John was particularly elated, especially as the tour coincided with the release of 'Please Please Me', their second single which shot to number one in the bestselling record charts. Top-of-the-bill singer on their tour was the most popular girl singer in Britain that year – Helen Shapiro, aged sixteen. A teenage prodigy,

Helen had burst on the pop scene two years earlier as a schoolgirl, with her EMI records 'Don't Treat Me Like A Child', 'You Don't Know', and 'Walkin' Back To Happiness'. Because of her youth, she became a national phenomenon.

Helen Shapiro was beside herself with excitement that the Beatles would be touring with her and that she would top the bill, because she had a colossal crush on John Lennon. On the coach that carried her with the Beatles across a Britain gripped by arctic weather conditions, on that one-night-stand tour, she contrived to sit next to him and hoped he would not guess that her blushing hid a teenage fancy for the Beatle who was six years older than she was.

'I had a special feeling for John,' says Helen. 'He probably realized I had a crush on him. He called me "Helly" and was incredibly protective. I was mad on him, really mad. I had the biggest crush on him any sixteen-year-old could have on a guy.

'On the coach once between cities, I picked up a copy of the *Melody Maker* and opened it up to a headline: "Is Helen a has-been at sixteen?" John was sitting right behind me then, reading over my shoulder. I was really upset, but it was he who comforted me. "Don't let the swines get you down," he said to me.'

Helen had met the Beatles on stage where they were setting up their equipment. John told her that he and Paul had written a song for her, called 'Misery', but it had been rejected by her management.

In a Sheffield hotel room, Helen sat with John watching the Beatles on television. 'He was fascinated but rather put off by the way he looked, because he used to have this stance with the guitar across his chest and the legs rather bowed, going up and down. He was quite horrified. But he was excited at seeing himself on the screen. Then Gerry and the Pacemakers came on and John said: "Hey, this is our mate." We were leaning out of hotel windows, throwing photographs of ourselves at fans, and it was an incredible period, looking back.'

The protectiveness of John towards 'Helly' contrasted sharply with the 'hard man' image which built up even in the early days of the Beatles. She saw, so early in his successful career, the tender, caring side of the man. 'He would always look after me. I looked up to him not in a fatherlike way, but as a teenage girl with a wild crush. He never took advantage of me. He was always such a soft, warm, attentive fellow.

'He'd make sure I ate properly when we were travelling. He'd put his arm round me and make sure I crossed the road properly. Of all the Beatles he was by far the most polite.' At the Abbey Road recording studios the Beatles were occupying studio two, which Helen normally used, and she had to make do with studio three. 'It was John who came in with a cup of tea and kind of apologized because he'd heard I had been moved to make way for them,' says Helen. 'He came in with a cup of tea for me and a big hug.'

At Great Yarmouth in 1963, however, Helen was doing a summer season, and the Beatles came in to do a Sunday concert. 'Then I realized how big they were. Everybody was all over them and I could hardly reach John. There were girls everywhere. I was incredibly jealous, for no reason, in my sweet innocence. I remember thinking: "Oh, they go with *girls!* And they drink *Scotch* and Coke." '

On the band coach, Lennon would both embarrass and amuse Helen and the rest of the cast: singers Kenny Lynch, Danny Williams, the Kestrels (featuring Roger Greenaway, later to become a major British songwriter and chairman of the Performing Right Society), and master of ceremonies Dave Allen. There were jam sessions, John with guitar breaking into Beach Boys' and Shirelles' songs, and Helen joining in. A strong favourite of John's was Little Eva's hit, 'Keep Your Hands Off My Baby'. Then, suddenly, Lennon would take on the role of the court jester. He would launch into his manic impersonation of cripples and spastics. He'd pull faces out of the window. Passers-by in busy High Streets would look on aghast at the absurd facial contortions of the leather-jacketed man with uncommonly long hair. 'He was very sick,' says Helen Shapiro. 'Especially if he saw a couple of nuns walking by. He'd pull the crudest faces at them.' One night in Sunderland, the practical joker in John petrified Helen when she awoke in her bedroom in the middle of the night, in virtual darkness, to see him standing there with a hat and a raincoat on.

For a cynic, Lennon was acutely aware of his responsibility to fans. Autograph signing was a chore he undertook, if not enthusiastically, then fairly conscientiously. (Tragically, John's openness with fans who cared and waited was to be one reason for his ultimate murder in New York in December 1980. His assassin had lain in wait for him after getting his autograph earlier in the day and waited for him to return home to the Dakota building the same night.) In 1963, before demands for autographs and Beatles' photographs had become so big that their road managers would forge their signatures, John was as diligent a signatory as any Beatle. 'He was portrayed, partly by himself, as the hard man of the group. But I recall him as a softie,' says Helen Shapiro. 'He certainly did care about the fans, in hotel foyers and stage doors. More than the other three, I think he valued the fans.'

Her memories of the man she fell for crystallize into quick images. 'I loved his very raw, bluesy voice, and told him so. He was surprised. He said I obviously didn't realize that it was him singing the high falsetto voice on "From Me To You". He said: "I can do the high stuff better than Paul." I do remember that.'

He moaned to Helen about his rotten teeth after seeing a picture of himself smiling. He told her to sing more songs by his favourite, Mary Wells, then Tamla Motown's undiscovered star, whom the Beatles eventually brought to their British tour when she had a huge hit with 'My Guy'. He used to mock Helen at the Ad Lib club in London's Soho, every time she went to the toilet. 'Ha, Helly, been for a secret ciggie, have we?' Helen used to smoke secretly at that time, as she was below the smoking age. 'Helly's a secret smoker,' he'd shout.

Although Beatlemania had not gripped Britain like the fever it became by autumn of that year, there were early signs as the Helen Shapiro package tour criss-crossed the country's cinemas. Despite Helen's popularity, John, Paul, George, and Ringo were getting more cheers. The promoter, Arthur Howes, had to keep changing the concert running order around so the Beatles would get more than their allotted twenty minutes. Nobody wanted to go on just before the Beatles. It was a 'dead spot', with the girls in the audience getting too excited about the next act. Most of the bill resented the attention being focussed on four relatively unknown lads from Liverpool. 'One day,' recalls singer Kenny Lynch, 'Arthur Howes came to me and said, "Look, you'd better go on just before the Beatles. You're the only one who doesn't care how badly you go down." ' Lynch became the man who introduced the Beatles every night. 'I'd only got to mention "the lads" and a cheer went up. I'd say: "I'm not bringing *them* on until you're quiet."

There was bedlam. I knew it was a bloodless revolution the music business was experiencing. I'd say: "Ladies and gentlemen, *the lads*," and the kids would rush the stage. For a virtually unknown group, it was incredible. The game was up.'

Kenny, a warm-hearted, tough East End Londoner, struck up a strong friendship with Lennon. Both shared an abrasiveness, a dislike for humbug and convention. Lynch's first meeting with the Beatles had been at the Liverpool Empire, before that tour, when Brian Epstein had presented them in concert. 'I'd been asked by Brian who I'd like backing me and I said: "Who's on the bill with me?"

'He said he had his own group, the Beatles.

'I said, "Oh, they'll do, then, but I've brought my own group."

'When I arrived, the Beatles said, "Do you want us to back you?"

'I said, "No thanks, I have my own musicians who always back me."

'They said, "Well, we'd like to back you."

'I couldn't let my people down, but John never let me forget the moment later on. He reckoned that I was one of the first guys to turn the Beatles down.'

A clear view of John's ambition during that first tour comes from Kenny Lynch's memory of a conversation, across a grand piano on the stage of the ABC cinema, Carlisle.

'I said to John: "Well, what do you expect to get out of this game then?"

'He replied quickly: "All we want to do is earn a million quid each and piss off."'

Lynch guffawed. 'Listen, you've got some chance! I've been at it for years and I haven't got two halfpennies to rub together.'

In those days, before the British motorway system

expanded, the coach journeys took longer. The pop package tours forced creative people together for four or five hours at a stretch. Apart from sleeping and jam sessions, songwriting was often done on the coach, and stage acts were debated.

'I remember John and Paul saying they were thinking of running up to the microphone together and shaking their heads and singing, "Whooooooooooooo". It later became a very important, terrifically popular part of their act when they sang "She Loves You". But at the time they were planning it, even before the song was written, I remember everybody on the coach fell about laughing. I said, "You can't do that. They'll think you're a bunch of poofs." I remember John saying to me he thought it sounded great and they were having it in their act.'

But Lennon was less pleased when Kenny Lynch played him his version of the song 'Misery', which was mostly John's own composition. The song had been intended for Helen Shapiro, but Kenny remembers her saying she disliked it because it sounded dreary. 'I'll have it,' said the eager Lynch.

But when he played his record to John and Paul, in the offices of their music publisher, Dick James, off Charing Cross Road, Lennon said, 'Your singing's OK, but who's that playing the telephone?'

It was John's way of blasting the guitarist.

Lynch replied: 'Don't blame me, I don't pick the musicians. Anyway, he's OK. It's Bert Weedon.'

Weedon, a solidly established player from the old school, played with great technical efficiency but little individuality. He epitomized the stylistic barrier between the Beatles' new vibrancy and the Old Guard of British musicianship. 'I said I thought Bert was OK, and that made things worse,' says Kenny Lynch. 'Lennon didn't stop bollocking me for days and weeks about Bert Weedon being on the first recording by somebody else of his song. "Bert WEEDON – he's fookin' LAST!" John kept saying.' The word became popular among the Beatles in denigrating what they mocked or regarded as unhip.

As the Beatles' popularity increased, and they made their first album in one eleven-hour recording session, John and Paul emerged as incredibly prolific songwriters, and John's aspirations to improve his writing became more and more evident. On the road, he would always be writing down phrases that occurred on the coach, in conversation. 'There was no booze and certainly no drugs on the road,' says Lynch. 'It was transport cafés, eggs and chips, Cokes and milk. John always smoked a lot but, whatever they'd done in Hamburg, they were getting their kicks from just performing and making such a quick impact on audiences all over England. They didn't need any false effects from drugs.'

Slowly, the contrasting personalities of Lennon and McCartney were becoming obvious. Although the Beatles as a group attracted girl fans by the million, Britain's fans, and later the world's, were dividing and uniting behind their own favourite within the group. 'Paul was more of the spokesman, but John had the veto,' says Lynch. 'John stood there in the dressing-room, for example, listening to Paul saying: "We're going to do this and we're going to do that," and John would suddenly stop him by saying: "Fuck it, we're NOT." And that would be it. John's word was law. It was like an offer nobody in the Beatles could refuse. There was very often this sudden interjection by John after Paul had tried to lead everything his way.' At later press conferences, Paul did most of the talking. He seemed to be taking the role of the most articulate of them. But John was the 'heavy'.

John's creativity was evident as much during that first tour as during the prolific songwriting years that were to follow. In hotels and theatre dressing-rooms and on the band coach, three Beatles went through a passion for movie cameras. John would film horses and cattle in the fields as they travelled around; but, significantly, he was the first to drop the hobby.

What separated John from the others in the eyes of Ron King, the highly efficient coach driver who took them everywhere on that first tour, was his interest in the written word. He remembers John burying himself in the news-papers more than anyone else on the coach. 'And I remem-ber him telling me he could get ideas for his songs from reading. He'd be watching television in his hotel, or in a dressing-room, and suddenly he'd jump for his cigarette packet on which he'd write a phrase or something he'd heard. Later, I'd hear it crop up in a song, like "I Wanna Be Your Man". I thought how clever he was. He always had books or magazines or newspapers when he was on the coach for hours on end. We'd forget he was there, or some-body would doze off, and suddenly John's voice would come up from the back: "Anyone got a ciggy?" ' In the dressing-rooms, Lennon was addicted to tea.

If 1962 had been a turbulent year for John, with Stuart's death, his own marriage, and the Beatles' breakthrough, 1963 was his year of tumult. As well as the birth of his son, John experienced four long, major tours of Britain including the one with Helen Shapiro. The other three found the Beatles sharing the bill with both Tommy Roe and Chris Montez, and then topping the bill over their old friends Gerry and the Pacemakers and Roy Orbison, the American singer who had influenced their work, and over Peter Jay and the Jaywalkers. They had such a close physical resemblance to the Beatles that they were used as decoys to fool the crowd into believing John, Paul, George, and Ringo had arrived at the theatre. Then, half an hour later, the real Beatles could coast in quietly after the stage door siege had dispersed.

Although Beatlemania did not properly grip Britain until the autumn, they were still making news and causing more adulation than any other British group. It was a year of sociological, political, and musical ferment. A British government minister, John Profumo, figured in a sex scandal with names that have since passed into history: Christine Keeler and Mandy Rice-Davies. A telephone 'hot line' was established that year between the White House and the Kremlin. Pope John XXIII died, at the age of eighty-one. President Kennedy visited the Berlin Wall. One thousand people died in an earthquake in Yugoslavia. Back in Britain, £2 million was stolen in the legendary Great Train Robbery. The Revd Martin Luther King, Jr, made a vital speech that united black Americans. And on 22 November, the night the Beatles played the Globe Cinema, Stockton, to mounting scenes of fanmania, President Kennedy was assassinated in Dallas, Texas.

I saw a lot of the Beatles that year. *Melody Maker*, on which I was then assistant editor, had its roots in jazz. Started in 1926, the paper had a tradition for upholding 'good musicianship'. Pop singers who 'sang in tune', like Frank Sinatra, were often allowed to cross the line into the paper, but teenage pop had been treated with contempt, as if it had nothing to do with music. It was regarded as the preserve of teenagers who were tone-deaf. The events of that year, and the infectious change in emphasis of the bestselling record charts towards new 'beat music', forced the paper to switch its policy and report the new sounds. The Beatles were front-page news every week, and I went in and out of their tours, nagging Brian Epstein for exclusive access and for news stories.

One major reason the Beatles were so acceptable to the Old Guard, even to jazz snobs, was the outspoken style of John Lennon. Quite apart from their records that were pounding up the charts ('She Loves You' was at the top for seven weeks, and 'I Want To Hold Your Hand' for four weeks), Lennon's acrid interviews became the group's unexpected strength. The music could take care of itself, but the electricity generated by John, more than any of the Fab Four, was so alive that he quickly became the most sought-after Beatle.

Most pop stars before John had had a problem sustaining a conversation beyond the bland talk of their latest record and their narcissism. Lennon single-handedly stood that credo on its head. In his speech alone, pop music grew up. The worlds of jazz and adult music, which had grown too holy and insular, found themselves threatened not merely by great, energetic, self-made music led by the Beatles; in Lennon, above all, they faced an articulacy unheard of in popular music. He would talk about anything and everything; he would criticize himself and claim nothing whatsoever for his group, unlike the established singers who placed themselves on a pedestal. And to clinch it all, he didn't care if the Beatles were denigrated.

The rapport I built up with John Lennon in 1963 was, curiously, based partly on the musical snobbery of the old *Melody Maker*. Because the paper had a slightly older readership than other pop papers, we tended to ask more adult questions of everyone we interviewed. Glossy fan magazines pestered the Beatles for the names of their dogs and their aunts, and asked whether they preferred marmalade or honey for breakfast, as well as their height and weight. *Melody Maker* treated the beat group players as the new musicians, and they would be invited to weigh in on any interesting subject, even old taboos like politics and religion. Lennon loved this. He hated jazz, anyway, but enjoyed talking to a paper that at least gave him credit for being intelligent – and fallible.

What made John stand apart, to me, was the interest he took in everything. He was always inquisitive, rarely pleased with a stage show, and generated intelligence as well as almost belligerent energy. It was obvious to me that, while the Beatles caravan was gaining speed, he was not satisfied merely with being rich and famous. There was always 'but . . .' in his armoury. Millionaire status and all that went with it as success came so quickly was lovely, he would imply. 'But then what?' Clearly, this was no moronic idol.

It was not a matter of self-improvement: that was not in his plan. Paul McCartney, with his keen eye on being the Beatles' diplomat and self-appointed publicist, was the social climber. He desperately needed self-improvement and worked towards it. John once said to me: 'I've got a built-in shit detector.' He was talking specifically about music, but he might as well have been referring to his entire outlook.

Our interviews would be in dressing-rooms and hotel rooms, in the back of the Beatles' Austin Princess, on the phone, on a plane or train, or at his home in Weybridge, Surrey. There, John and Cynthia spent £19,000 on a Tudor-style mansion, Kenwood, in St George's Hill in the stock-broker belt. He told me he never liked it: he felt hemmed in, he said, by its 'bourgeois' atmosphere. Possibly, because he spent so little time there, it didn't have a chance. His moods at Kenwood ranged from restless, creative, and talk-ative to monosyllabic and depressed.

At the height of Beatlemania I caught up with John

on the road: I was with them on 1 November 1963 for the opening of their big autumn tour at Cheltenham Gaumont. Before the show, in the dressing-room, he had just washed his hair. 'I get such terrible dandruff, I think it'd be better if we cut it all off, nice and short. Think what that would do for the Beatles!' He relished the thought of rocking the boat.

He signed autographs, as he often did, while watching television or having a conversation. He rarely looked at the paper or book or programme as he signed his name on it. That night, John was at his most acerbic. In conversation with someone else, Paul McCartney had joked: 'Two things I hate in life, y'know: racial discrimination and coloured people.'

John weighed in instantly and uncomfortably at Paul: 'People who talk like that really don't like coloured people, otherwise they wouldn't think that way at all. I've heard it all before.' Adopting a broad Lancashire accent, he went on: 'Aye, theer all reet but they're so dirty and they bring down the value of property.'

Even at the age of twenty-three, John was contemplating his future from a position of pop supremacy. The Beatles were en route to big things, and when the Rolling Stones became friends of the Beatles he had discussed with Mick Jagger how long they would all last at the top. 'I said during a conversation with Mick Jagger that I didn't want to be fiddling round the world singing "Please Please Me" when I'm thirty. If we move into films, and they work out OK, I'll like that. People say that's where the Beatles are heading and I suppose that makes sense. But I also like A & R-ing records. Haven't done much of it but I've enjoyed watching it being done, like by Uncle George Martin. I'd like to see more of it. Recording interests me more than anything.

'I'd like to continue writing for other people and I hope we still carry on making records for a long time. I still enjoy playing live. I get slightly less kick out of things now compared with a few years ago before we had any hits. But that's natural.'

As the tours continued, and John and the others became trapped by Beatlemania, John became furious at the enormous demands made on him as a celebrity. The standing joke between them was the requests for autographs and signed photographs from mayors and mayoresses and police chiefs throughout Britain. These would usually be accompanied by the civic leaders saying: 'It's not for me, it's for my daughter.'

Lennon exploded once to me: 'I don't mind the *fans*. They've paid for a good show and they can go potty. That's OK. But I'm sick of meeting people I don't want to meet. Boring lord mayors and all that. It spoils things for me because I suppose I'm a bit intolerant. But is it any wonder I get fed up? They keep sending in autograph books and we sign them only to find they belong to officials, promoters, police, and all that lot. Real fans, who'd wait for hours and days, get treated by the same cops as half-wits because they want our signatures. But the cops make sure they get theirs. I bet every bloody policeman's daughter in Britain's got an autograph. Half of them aren't our fans. it's unfair on the kids who really want them.'

Paul McCartney, sitting opposite and listening to John's anger, shouted: 'Hey, I've had enough of you blasting off, John.'

Lennon retorted: 'You say what you want to say and I'll say what I want to say, OK?'

The sharp division between John and Paul was getting easier to define. John didn't care much for coating what he said with a veneer of acceptability: he spoke as he felt.

Paul not only adopted the role of diplomat, but sometimes
trespassed into John's independence. The banter between
them, joking but with serious undertones, continued during
that evening.

Paul said, 'You're bad for my image!'

John retorted, 'You're soft. Shurrup and watch the telly
like a good boy.'

John's waspish wit was at its most crushing when the
adrenalin of travelling on concert tours gave him a special,
edgy thrust. In October 1964 I was travelling with him in
the Beatles' limousine when word came that the Duke of
Edinburgh was reported as having said that the Beatles
were 'on the wane'. Lennon's trenchant retort was immediate: 'The bloke's getting no money for his playing fields
from me.'

Later, the Duke said he had been misreported or mis-
heard: he had actually said the Beatles were 'away', meaning
out of the country. John's dig at his playing fields referred
to the Duke's involvement with the National Playing Fields
Association.

John dealt savagely with journalists who asked absurd
questions. In 1964 you'd have had to have been a monk,
at least, not to know where the Beatles had come from.

One reporter asked him: 'Where's your home town,
John?'

Lennon answered: 'Huddersfield.' That ended the
interview.

A Leicester policeman, thrusting his autograph book
into the limousine and into John's hand, fancied himself as
a comedian. 'I see you have the same limousine that you
came in last year. Money getting tight then, boys?'

John weighed in: 'Yeah, and you've got the same bloody
uniform on that you wore last year. I recognize it.'

The perennial questions about the Beatles' trend-setting

long hair were met with some classic Lennon one-liners:
'Our popularity will never decline. It will *recede* . . . No, we
don't have our hair cut, we have it *diminished* every now
and then.' He often wore a trilby hat when entering restaurants or hotels in a vain attempt to pass unnoticed. But
the stealth and intuition of Beatles fans in seeking them
out always impressed him. When a fan broke through the
security net, John was always fascinated to ask how he or
she had achieved it.

John rebelled against anything that he regarded as a compromise with the truth. In the early 1960s, pop stars were
theoretically supposed to be unmarried. As the Beatles' fans
were now being counted in millions, Brian Epstein regarded
John's marriage and fatherhood as dangerous. When John
and Cynthia moved to London and the news trickled out,
Epstein was furious. John scarcely cared what was said
about him by the press and revelled in being quoted and
photographed, as long as he was interestingly presented as
someone other than a brainless 'moptop', as papers called
the Beatles. John's wife and child became public knowledge
early in 1964 when the couple moved into a flat found for
them by their friend, photographer Robert Freeman, at 13
Emperor's Gate, West Kensington. Within weeks the flat
became known as the Beatles residence and the fans began
to lay siege outside. Cynthia became exhausted, too, with
carrying the baby and her shopping up five flights of stairs,
so they started househunting and headed for the suburbs.
    Lennon fought with Epstein about maintaining secrecy.
'Brian had an obsession about not letting the marriage
become public,' says Tony Barrow, who was the Beatles'
press officer at the time. 'At a very early stage of my
involvement, John mentioned the fact that he was married

and Brian went berserk about it to me. He said: "I don't know why he's told you that. Yes, of course it's true, but he's told awfully few people and I want you to make quite sure you don't tell anybody else." '

Barrow believes that Epstein's determination to hold back the truth about John was directly linked to his own homosexuality. 'He feared that some of his own private life could be made public. He was particularly touchy about conceding any part of his artists' private lives, simply because he had so much of a scandalous nature to conceal in his own.' Lennon regarded Eppy's edict as wrong for two reasons: it was going to come out later, anyway, so why not get it over with; and it would make no difference to the Beatles' popularity. He was proved right, for when Cynthia 'went public' the Beatles' popularity continued to rise. She, meanwhile, knew nothing of John's battle with Epstein about their marriage. 'He kept so many things from me, bad and good,' says Cynthia. 'I only heard much later that Brian wanted me kept quiet,' John knew, however, when to draw the line. Shortly after they moved to London, I asked him if I could interview Cynthia to prepare an unusual profile of him. 'I'd like to ask her what it's like being married to you, and what it's like being the envy of millions of girls,' I said, when John asked me why.

He fixed me with a withering look. 'No bloody fear,' he said. 'I'm the bloody star around here.'

Fielding the press, radio, and television became an art and a full-time job. Tony Barrow, Liverpool-born and the record reviewer of the *Liverpool Echo* under the pseudonym of Disker, had been pestered by Epstein from the early days to write about 'the boys'. When eventually he was lured to London to take on the job of press officer for Epstein's fast-growing NEMS organization, Barrow was invited by Brian to meet them for the first time in a pub, the Devonshire Arms, near EMI's Manchester Square headquarters.

'John was relatively quiet that night,' says Tony Barrow. 'Paul seemed to dominate the proceedings. He came round asking everybody what they wanted to drink and I was very impressed by this, until I realized that he relayed the whole order to Brian Epstein, who picked up the bill.'

Lennon did not speak for a while to the man who would handle his press work. When he eventually was introduced to him, John said: 'Well, Tony, if you're not queer and you're not Jewish, why are you joining NEMS?' Brian overheard the remark but ignored it. It was among the many taunts which John was to toss at Brian. When Eppy was writing his autobiography in 1964, he asked John if he had a suggestion for a title. 'Why don't you call it *Queer Jew?*' said John. The book was called *A Cellarful of Noise*. John parodied that as *A Cellarful of Boys*. The crushing remarks made by John simply increased Epstein's admiration and respect for him.

Brian's fascination with John was obvious, and Lennon interpreted it as a kind of weakness. It was John's clear masculinity, fearlessness, abrasiveness, and aggression, which Epstein could not match, that proved such a powerful attraction. Nor did Lennon shrink from cruelly putting Brian down in public. At Abbey Road recording studios one day, Epstein ventured an opinion about the sound they were making. Across the studio, with everyone listening, John said: 'You stick to your percentages, Brian. We'll make the music.' When he put the verbal knife in like that, his voice would have a toughness that invited no reply.

John's resentment of Epstein's involvement with their music went back a long way. He maintained that they had been turned down by Decca mostly because Brian had insisted that at their audition they sing mostly standards like 'September In The Rain' and not 'ravers which we went down well with at the Cavern.' John never forgot or forgave Brian for inflicting his own, wrong choice of material on the Beatles which resulted in that rejection, and he decided that never again would he let Brian near a decision about their music. Epstein kept his peace – reluctantly, because he considered he had a good ear for music.

Three weeks after the birth of Julian, and between the vital British tours with Chris Montez/Tommy Roe and Roy Orbison/Gerry and the Pacemakers, the Beatles were officially on holiday. John went to Spain for twelve days with Brian Epstein. 'I didn't think anything about it,' said Cynthia. 'John said he'd been working very hard, with the concert tours and the album. He needed a break.' She was frantically busy, anyway, with a new baby and setting up temporary home in Mendips.

Lennon knew, of course, about Brian's fixation on him, but he could not have anticipated the campaign of whispering that holiday would give rise to. As one who was close to him during the Beatles' rise to fame, I saw a solidly heterosexual man. He did not boast of his exploits, but he made it abundantly clear that he enjoyed women. John would hardly have taunted Brian so mercilessly about his sexual preferences if he felt any empathy with him as a homosexual.

When John returned, he was livid at the rumours. The girls in the NEMS office, naïve about homosexuality, which was illegal, giggled nervously and were told by John, patiently, and for the first time in their lives, what homosexuality meant. He told them in general conversation and 'from a distance'.

But his Spanish trip with Epstein erupted into a scandal. John and Cynthia, along with many Liverpool musicians, like Gerry and the Pacemakers, Billy J. Kramer, and the Shadows from London, went to Paul McCartney's twenty-first birthday party on 18 June 1963, a party held mostly in the garden, and in a marquee, at the house of Paul's Auntie Jin, in Dinas Lane, Huyton.

John had little to eat and too much to drink at the party. Bob Wooler, the old friend who had introduced the Beatles on stage at the Cavern nearly three hundred times, said something to John about his visit to Spain with Epstein. John laid into Wooler with a ferocity that landed the disc jockey in hospital with a black eye, bruised ribs, and torn knuckles. Epstein drove Wooler to hospital.

The party broke up in disarray. Cynthia, who left with John, recalls: 'John said: "He called me a queer so I battered his bloody ribs in."'

Billy J. Kramer was at that party. (John had injected the 'J.' into his name during a chat in Epstein's office. 'He thought it had more flow. I said: "What's the J. for, if anyone asks me?" John said it was for Julian.') Billy J., as John called him, was in the marquee at Paul's party with several show business personalities. 'I remember asking Bruce Welch of the Shadows what he thought of the Beatles, and his reply: "They've written a few catchy songs, nothing special. Once they dry up that'll be the end of them."' Kramer recalls the conversation because John had said it was one of his greatest ambitions to 'blow the Shadows out – he couldn't stand their clean music.' Kramer recalls that after he had laid into Bob Wooler, John grabbed the body of a girl who was standing next to him. 'I said: "Lay off, John." But he lashed into her. He'd had too much booze. I was semi-professional at the time, and he was winding me up as I left before him, shouting: "You're nothing,

Kramer, and we're the top." ' Lennon was at his most withering when the demon drink fuelled his insecurities.

Kramer was furious. Epstein apologized for John to him next day, but Billy said: 'I refuse to take a second-hand apology.' A few days later, Lennon met Kramer in a Liverpool street and immediately put out his hand to shake: 'I'm really sorry about what happened that night,' said John.

News of John's fisticuffs with Bob Wooler filtered through to the northern newsdesks of Britain's national papers. Tony Barrow received several phone calls next day. 'What's your lad John Lennon been up to? Been a naughty boy, has he?' Barrow's first thoughts were that news of John's marriage to Cynthia had leaked and he would face trouble from Epstein. 'Although Julian was two months old by then,' says Barrow, 'the news that John was married, let alone a father, was still a secret. Some fans in Liverpool knew, but nationally it was still unknown.' When the press confronted Barrow with the news of the Lennon-Wooler punch-up, Tony phoned John to find out what his reply should be. 'He was completely unrepentant. He said: "The bastard was saying I was bloody queer so I smacked him one, I punched him one, he deserved it, he went a bit too far, and I don't care what the press make of that, sod it." '

But by the time the *Daily Mirror*, through its show business reporter Don Short, had got to Lennon, his story had become either more apologetic or more diplomatic, on Epstein's advice. In the first national newspaper recognition of the Beatles' importance, Don Short wrote in the *Mirror* under the headline: 'Beatle in Brawl – Sorry I Socked You':

Guitarist John Lennon, twenty-two-year-old leader of the Beatles pop group, said last night: 'Why did I have to go and punch my best friend? I was so high I didn't realize what I was doing.' Then he sent off a telegram apologizing to twenty-nine-year-old [*sic*] Liverpool rock show compère and disc jockey Bob Wooler . . . who said: 'I don't know why he did it. I have been a friend of the Beatles for a long time. I have often compèred shows where they have appeared. I am terribly upset about this, physically as well as mentally.'

John Lennon said: 'Bob is the last person in the world I would want to have a fight with. I can only hope he realizes that I was too far gone to know what I was doing.'*

John badly damaged his forefinger. Back at Mendips, he walked around hiding his right hand from Mimi for several days in case she should see his injuries and ask him how it happened.

Years later, the homosexual leader of a rock band, Tom Robinson, maintained that the first gay rock song was written by Lennon in 1965. Millions heard the song, 'You've Got To Hide Your Love Away', as a sentimental ballad written in John's period of great influence by the songwriting style of Bob Dylan. But Robinson believes the words were a message to Brian Epstein.

A few years later, John wrote a message to an American publication called the *Gay Liberation Book*. The editors had solicited contributions from prominent people, and John's read as follows:

> Why make it sad to be gay?
> Doing your thing is okay.

---

* Two days after that incident, Lennon sent a telegram of apology to Bob Wooler which read: 'REALLY SORRY BOB STOP TERRIBLY WORRIED TO REALIZE WHAT I HAD DONE STOP WHAT MORE CAN I SAY STOP JOHN LENNON.' The telegram was auctioned in a rock 'n' roll memorabilia sale at Sotheby's, London, on 30 August 1984 and fetched £550.

Our body's our own, so leave us alone
And play with yourself today.

Anyone who knew John Lennon would dismiss the suggestion that he was a homosexual. On tour, he was an aggressive woman hunter, something he was to confess to Cynthia when their marriage foundered. He had a massive sexual appetite for women, and particularly for new conquests. Women who had been with him spoke of John as an enthusiastic lover but 'rough and ready, never kind and considerate.' All through his life, he was a woman chaser.

'I slept in a million hotel rooms, as we all did, with John and there was never any hint that he was gay,' says Paul McCartney. The rumour that caused Lennon to punch Bob Wooler for a suggestive remark was explained by Paul in an interview on London's Capital Radio with Roger Scott:

> When the group was formed John was a smart cookie. Brian Epstein was going on holiday to Spain and Brian was gay. He invited John along. John, not being stupid, saw his opportunity to impress upon Mr Epstein who was the boss of this group. And I think that's why John went on holiday. And good luck to him, too – he was that kind of guy, he wanted Brian to know who he should listen to in this group, and that was the relationship.
>
> John was very much the leader in that kind of sense; although it was never actually said, we were all sort of leaders. But in truth . . . John was probably the deciding vote. He was into that.
>
> So they say he went on holiday with someone who was known to be gay and therefore he is gay.

Paul recalls someone asking John once if he had ever tried homosexuality, and Lennon's crunching reply, 'No. I haven't met a fellow I fancy enough!'

And the girls at college with him echo Cynthia's statement on the subject: 'You'd have to look a long way to find a more heterosexual man. The suggestion that he was anything else is too ridiculous for words.'

For people inside the Beatles circle, John needed to be treated with kid gloves. Paul, ever charming, polite, informative, was never a media problem. Ringo assumed the air of a cuddly, amiable guy, lucky to be hoisted aboard the Beatles just before the group shot to fame. George, who hated invasions of his privacy, was not comfortable with the press, but he was tolerant and spoke intelligently. John was different. 'I was sometimes nervous of what impression he would make upon third parties, rather in the same way one sent home sensitive aunts and uncles if John Lennon was due to drop in,' recalls Tony Barrow. 'I wasn't wary of asking him to do interviews. He was co-operative, although he'd grumble and curse if it wasn't convenient. But I was selective about the journalists I sent to him. It had to be someone sufficiently worldly, or sophisticated, with a decent and preferably way-out sense of humour, to accept John as he was. The journalist didn't have to be offended by the guy. John was always asked for someone who shared his outrageous sense of humour, who would come back at him with something as nasty and cynical as he gave them. Otherwise he might just turn a bit nasty on an ill-informed or inexperienced journalist. Or he'd particularly turn on one who thought he knew too much or knew all about the Beatles.'

Billy J. Kramer later had good reason to appreciate their healed relationship. The first song given to him by Epstein was a tape of Lennon playing acoustic guitar and singing the demonstration of a song he'd written called 'Do You Want To Know A Secret'. 'John later apologized for the tape quality but said he'd done the demo in the toilet, as it was the quietest place he could find.' The sound of the loo flushing at the end confirmed John's story. 'God,' says Kramer, 'if I had that tape now it would be worth a fortune.' John and Paul went on to give him several hits that boosted his career: a number one with 'Bad To Me' plus 'From A Window' and 'I'll Keep You Satisfied'.

John's intake of alcohol rose a lot during the heady Beatles years. As undisputed kings of the Swinging London decade, the Beatles held court at the Ad Lib club, above the Prince Charles cinema in Leicester Street, Soho. It vied with two other clubs as the focal point for pop and cinema stars, photographers, and fashion people. The other night spots were the Scotch of St James in Masons Yard near Piccadilly, and the Bag o' Nails in Cromwell Road, West Kensington. The night began around one o'clock after a concert. Often, Lennon, getting steadily more drunk on Scotch and Coke, and smoking incessantly his favourite brand, Peter Stuyvesant, would become more and more emotional as the drink took hold.

A favourite habit when he was lubricated was to seize one person for a verbal hammering and not let go until that person was utterly exhausted by the sheer persistence of John's argument. There was a streak in John that could not bear to lose a battle. With Mick Jagger or Alan Price, both intelligent men with plenty of opinions, John would rant all night about music or a city or who was winning the popularity race between the Beatles, the Rolling Stones, the Animals, and the Hollies. He particularly hated Manchester's Hollies. He regarded them as syrupy copyists of the Beatles' vocal style.

It could be argued that John Lennon was always worldly, even as a Quarry Bank pupil lampooning the teachers and as a perverse Liverpool Art College student. Those qualities grew within the fast-moving Beatles story. Music aside, and there were some catatonic moments in which he and Paul touched the heights, John was intuitive enough to understand that it was an unstoppable bandwagon. If it wasn't exactly out of control, it was moving too fast for him to have a lot of impact on it, so he might as well get stuck in and enjoy it, particularly the money, while Beatlemania gripped Britain, and quickly, the impossible dream happened: they conquered America.

Just before that happened, Britain had its first national glimpse of the subtle difference in personalities within the Beatles whom they had previously regarded as four lovable Liverpool lads with perhaps equal brightness. At the Royal Variety Show in London, it was John who entered the history books with the irreverent, hilarious line: 'Will the people in the cheaper seats clap your hands? All the rest of you, if you'll just rattle your jewellery.' John was determined to have a dig of some kind at royalty. He learned, very early, the art of manipulating an event, a situation, and also a person. Cynical about the royal patronage, he told Epstein of the joke he planned backstage. Brian used every ounce of his persuasion in stopping John from saying: 'the rest of you just rattle your fucking jewellery.'

No group, before or since, could have 'closed ranks' more forcefully than the Beatles. However close to the band anyone felt, when the hotel suite, or limousine, or dressing-room door was shut, the four men insisted on privacy and group unity when they needed it. The only man who could remotely be described as the fifth Beatle was Neil Aspinall, who went to Liverpool Institute with Paul and George. He was the man who drove their Commer van for them back in the Cavern days, and who gave up a solid career in accountancy to become their utterly trusted friend, confidant, and world-travelling tour manager. 'Nell', as he was to the Beatles, is still today the managing director in London of Apple, the company still run by the Beatles after they split.

Brian Epstein liked to regard himself as the fifth Beatle, yet for all their affection for his loyalty and what he achieved for them, the Beatles did not consider him a true insider. Precision, style, presentation, and urbanity were his strengths. The more the media screamed that the Rolling Stones were unkempt and a danger to daughters, the more Epstein concentrated on projecting his 'boys', as he insisted on calling them, as intelligent and clean. It worked perfectly. As hair everywhere got longer and skirts were shorter, Beatlemania became the acceptable face of Swinging Britain.

Epstein's admiration of John directly affected what the Beatles did. Eppy clashed with Paul about many things, from the timing of tours to the lists of people in the Beatles' entourage who should accompany them. There was an unwritten rule that the Beatles and the Rolling Stones would never have a single record out at the same time because a 'same day' release might split and confuse the fans – and one of the two supergroups would be kept from the coveted number one spot. It was Paul who did the arranging of the timing, usually with Mick Jagger. Epstein did not like Paul's intrusion, but just how adept McCartney was at managing his career became obvious when the Beatles split and he became the world's most successful popular musician and songwriter.

'Paul can be temperamental and moody and difficult to deal with,' said Epstein. 'This means that we compromise on our clash of personalities. He is a great one for not wishing to hear about things and if he doesn't want to know he switches himself off, settles down in a chair, puts one booted foot across his knee, and pretends to read a newspaper, having consciously made his face an impassive mask.'

Epstein's interpretation of John was, predictably, more convoluted. Writing in his autobiography, Epstein said:

> John Lennon, his [Paul's] friend from boyhood, his co-writer of so many songs, the dominant figure in a group which is virtually without a leader, is in my opinion a most exceptional man. Had there been no Beatles and no Epstein participation, John would have emerged from the mass of the population as a man to reckon with. He may not have been a singer or a guitarist, a writer or a painter, but he would most certainly have been a Something. You cannot contain a talent like this. There is in the set of his head a controlled aggression which demands respect.

Brian went on to say how John had sometimes been abominably rude to him.

But because he loved him so much, Brian would take it. As the speed of Beatlemania demanded decisions faster than subtlety, McCartney realized that Lennon was able to influence Epstein very strongly on any matter involving the group. So when he thought there might be a clash with Epstein, Paul would feed his demands through John, who could get his own way every time. Because he was such a smoothie, Epstein was intrigued by John's cruel tongue. Though it hurt him, he would take it.

Yet for all his foibles, and for all the warts, business and personal, attached to his discovery and management of the Beatles, Brian Epstein was a superb manager for them.

His devotion was unyielding, his belief in their originality infectious, his sense of fairness a byword. When he died in 1967, the Beatles began to fall apart as a group. Epstein was a man of strong principles, right for his time as the mentor of the world's greatest pop group. He succeeded in helping them become 'bigger than Elvis'. Those of us who knew him well remember his warmth, his passion, and his precision which was more important to the success story than we knew at the time. 'Paul has the glamour, John the command,' said Epstein. It was an astute observation in 1964, which will always hold true.

Listening to John on stage, it was difficult to believe he was the master of the sharp jibe. On the British and European tours, the screams were so loud that the Beatles' performance became more of a ritual than a show. The music was unimportant. 'It's like we're four freaks being wheeled out to be seen, shake our hair about, and get back in our cage afterwards,' he said to me. He became irritable about it but grew reconciled to Beatlemania. He expected the Beatles to last about five years, and in terms of live performances he was not far wrong. His stage personality was electrifying in 1963 and 1964. Legs arrogantly apart, head tilted back slightly to emphasize his prominent nose, guitar across his chest, John excluded an air of detached uninterest. By then he wore contact lenses, recommended to John by Bobby Goldsboro during the British tour by Roy Orbison and the Beatles. (Goldsboro, then Orbison's guitarist, later emerged as a successful solo singer, with records like 'Honey' and 'Summer (The First Time)'.) John told me that Goldsboro's recommendation was a great idea and a drag as well. 'I mean, I couldn't be seen in horn-rimmed specs on stage, that would never do for a Beatle, folks! But the contacts are not easy to control.' They were regularly falling out either on stage, causing him visual chaos, or in dressing-rooms or hotels where I, like many others who were with him, spent many an hour fumbling in thick pile carpet looking for a missing lens. 'Can you imagine what it's like,' he once said, 'hearing all that noise and playing, and not seeing a *thing?* It's frightening.'

John's reputation for repartee was certainly not born from his communications on stage. 'We'd like to sing a number from our new LP' was typical of the inanity that he managed above the roar. But the difference between John and Paul was as easy to define in a concert as millions have found on records.

John would be at his blistering best on his cherished favourites, rockers like 'Twist and Shout' and 'Money', while Paul would woo the girls in the crowd with his romantic specialities, 'All My Loving' and 'Till There Was You', the unlikely song from the show *The Music Man* which the Beatles used on stage to break up their rock 'n' roll diet. John would roar into his own songs 'I Feel Fine', which he claimed was the first-ever record to feature the feedback technique, and would lead on the autobiographical 'Help!' Paul dominated on 'Can't Buy Me Love' and, as if to reclaim his rock 'n' roll roots, often hammered out a powerful 'Long Tall Sally'.

Lennon's lack of interest in live performing struck me forcefully one night in Exeter. He had forgotten the words to 'I Want To Hold Your Hand' and asked me to write down what I could remember of them on the back of his hand. They were ingrained into my consciousness at the time, so I did, in Biro.

'It wouldn't matter if I never sang,' he said cynically. 'Often I don't anyway. I just stand there and make mouth movements. Nobody knows. I reckon we could send out four wax-work dummies of ourselves and that would satisfy the crowds. Beatles concerts are nothing to do with music any more. They're just bloody tribal rites.'

Just as he got no thrill from performing, John took no interest whatsoever, in the 1960s, in seeing other artists on stage. 'I'm a record man,' he said. 'I just like records. It always spoils it for me when I see someone whose records I like – they're never as good live.'

The squeals of Beatlemania seemed insane to John. The debasement of the music, the pandemonium, the hurling on stage of dolls and teddy bears, and jelly babies once they had said they liked to eat them, was all too juvenile for his speedy mind. He went along for the ride, but, as always in his life, there was a 'get-out' clause. He devised his own method of coping with the lunacy. 'Nice endings to songs don't work in that situation,' said John. 'The kids are all getting worked up about something that's not music.' He let out that pent-up shriek of resentment at what he had to do to get to the top and stay there. At the end of a song, as a wave of screaming cascaded around the hall, John would screech out an obscenity to complete the song. It was his own release.

'The others didn't have John's resentment of having to do what he was doing to be a Beatle,' says Mike McCartney. 'They thought they were just bloody lucky they were getting away with it for so long. But John always had that drive, something ticking over, the need to do something else. It was: "Ah, so *this* is what we have to do to be bigger than Elvis? OK, let's go, but I'm not going to give it one hundred per cent of me." ' That individuality stayed and marked him out as the most original of the four.

'On the road, in dressing-rooms, and hotels. John usually had an aggressive attitude,' says British tour promoter Arthur Howes, who presented most of their concerts right from the start of their nationwide popularity. 'But I could see it was defensive, a cover-up for the real John who was a nice, soft-hearted man. At dinner after concerts he would launch into Stanley Unwin-type double-talk. I'd never met anyone with such a fast style in one-liners. At Dublin airport once, a reporter asked the Beatles where Brian Epstein was, and, quick as a flash, John replied: "Oh, he's in America signing up a new rhythm-and-Jews group." On aggression alone, John was the leader of the Beatles.'

'When he wasn't bullying or bellowing, he could be very kind and considerate,' says Tony Barrow. 'He was very friendly and very popular with the NEMS office staff in Liverpool. And once, when Brian Epstein fired a girl typist in a fit of temper, merely for messing up a Dictaphone tape, John was there and turned the whole episode into a joke. He laughed a lot about it. And if Lennon laughed, Epstein laughed. So the girl got her job back.'

His sense of the absurd and obsession with deformity in people gave him both laughter and tears on the road. This was another escape route. He once autographed a programme: 'Sodoffy from John Leper.' And when he spoke of things he did not like, he would sometimes say: 'It was horrible – really spastic.' I challenged him about it one night over one of Cynthia's chicken dinners at Weybridge. He had made a strong little speech about success. It was in 1965.

'I want no more from being a record star. I'm not uninterested but there is more, now, than making good records and selling them. I'd like to see us making better and better films. That's very difficult. Unlike pop music, it allows you to grow up as a person. I'm not craving for any more gold discs even though they're a nice boost. That's all over. I just want to be an all-round spastic – think how awful it would be to be an old Beatle, or a grey-haired Beatle, or a spastic Beatle.'

Cynthia gave him a crushing look.

'Enjoying your dinner?' said John. 'Look, I mean nothing *nasty* about these spastics. I don't think I'd know a real spastic from a Polaroid lens. I'm not hung up about them. When I use the word "spastic" in general conversation, I don't mean it literally. I feel terrible sympathy for these people. It seems to be like the end of the world when you see deformed spastics, and we've had quite a lot of them on our travels.

'In the States, they were bringing hundreds of 'em along backstage and it was fantastic. I can't stand looking at 'em. I have to turn away. I have to laugh or I'd collapse from hate *of the situation*. Listen, in the States, they lined 'em up and you got the impression the Beatles were being treated as bloody faith healers. It was sickening.'

Tough, cantankerous, and iconoclastic John was, but there were also signs of enormous wit and compassion. That night, after dinner, we all went out to a private showing of the Michael Caine film *The Ipcress File*. On the twenty-mile journey from Surrey back into London, John's Rolls-Royce was smeared with lipstick and dented by fans as they waited at traffic lights and they spotted a Beatle in the back. Girls banged on the doors and wings and blocked the road. 'John, John,' they screamed. He carried on reading and locked himself in. The chauffeur became irritable and was about to get out and push them away. 'Leave them,' snapped John. 'They bought the car. They've got the right to smash it up.'

TWELVE

DRUGS

'But Cyn, It's Fantastic, It's Wonderful'

IT WAS not a normal marriage, and he could never be a normal father. When Cynthia was heavily pregnant in February and March 1963, John was touring Britain; he was also appearing with the Beatles when Julian was born on 8 April in Liverpool; and by 18 May he was off again for another three-week tour, this time with Gerry and the Pacemakers and Roy Orbison.

The Beatles did four major tours that year, and went on to become one of the busiest travelling groups in pop before they finally ended live work in 1966. John was the only Beatle who had embarked on that long and winding road with a wife and son.

The first clash in John and Cynthia's marriage occurred when Julian was nine months old. John was appearing in the Beatles' Christmas Show in London and had not been in touch for several days. Cynthia decided the time was right for the baby to be christened and went ahead with organizing it in Hoylake Parish Church, opposite her home in Trinity Road. She had gone to Sunday School there as a child.

The christening passed off quietly one Sunday morning, except for Julian's show-stopping habit of knocking the vicar's glasses off his face. But when Cynthia carried him outside the church, there were photographers. Next day, newspapers featured pictures of a Beatle's baby being carried away from his christening.

John phoned Cynthia when he read about it in the newspaper during his tour. He was livid. 'What's all *this?* He didn't need baptizing or christening.'

Cynthia argued that he did, to give him a seal of religious belief in his life. 'It's simple, it doesn't harm anybody, and it's over and done with.'

John's anger continued: 'Well I didn't want it done, and you should have told me.'

Cynthia said she was sorry, but with John away on tour she had to get things done and she did not expect him to react so strongly.

There were, says Cynthia, four major changes in John's personality during their marriage: the student, the father, the meeting with Brian Epstein that shaped his future, and the rich, famous Beatle. But the one over which John agonized the most was his fatherhood.

'As far as our marriage was concerned,' says Cynthia, 'we got on great. It wasn't the greatest whizzo-active relationship and once he became a Beatle we didn't go out much and see the sights, as husband and wife. But we had holidays with the other Beatles and we were strong as a unit in that home.'

Apart from the christening eruption, Cynthia recalls one other major blow-up by John. Returning from another tour to family life at Weybridge, John was having breakfast with Cynthia and Julian one morning. While eating, Julian made a typical three-year-old's mess of the food and everything else on the table. 'John stood up and blew his top, screaming at this little boy who couldn't understand this man who he very rarely saw!' says Cynthia. 'Julian wasn't

the tidiest of eaters as a child and needed coaxing and he
was a crying baby too.

   'When John screamed at Julian, I flew off the handle.
I disappeared upstairs in a fit of tears. I said: "If you were
here more often, you'd understand your child. You can't
just come home, blow your top, and take it out on a little
boy who doesn't understand." John was sweet then, very
apologetic and understanding. It was the only real row we
ever had. He'd just come home from a tour, all hyped up
and nervous, and somebody was going to get it. It was
unfair that Julian and I were the people he chose.'

   The stress of life with this agitated, extraordinary pop
star who darted in and out of their home took a heavy toll
on their marriage. 'It was very hard for him to adjust to
home after two or three weeks of all the adrenalin of screams
and being hyped up after concerts here or in America or
Europe,' she says. 'We were on different wavelengths. The
patterns of our thoughts were obviously different. I decided
to offer him security. I tried to stay the same person for
him. It was probably the worst thing I could have done. I
should have gone out and got on with other things,
developed my own activities. But I didn't. I thought: "Well,
at least if I'm here and Julian's fine and he has me, he has
these roots." But there were too many people pulling on
these roots in those Beatle days. I couldn't get them into
the ground quickly enough.'

   The magic moments for Cynthia were when they took
off on holidays, at the height of Beatlemania. There was
Tahiti with George and Pattie Boyd, St Vincent in the
Caribbean with Ringo and Maureen Starr, St Moritz with
George and Judy Martin, swimming in the sea, playing
Monopoly and drinking Scotch and Coke and eating well.
'John became quite hefty and was really enjoying the
pleasure of being rich. I could see he felt under pressure,

but I didn't know how much. But he enjoyed the holidays, there were no drugs, and he reverted to being a Liverpool lad.' They managed to stay anonymously in hotels: the machinery of Brian Epstein's organization ensured that manager and staff did not blurt out the news of their presence to anyone.

Indulgence, in fact, was John's pleasure for a time. On buying Kenwood in Weybridge, the value of the house was quickly doubled by the building of a swimming pool. John wanted the pool bottom to be a full-sized mirror, but ended up accepting a gigantic eye painted on the bottom. The pool and its adaptations cost £20,000. John didn't blink an eye at the cost.

Despite his absence from home, Lennon enjoyed the fact that he was a father. The tears of joy that welled up in him when he first visited Cynthia in hospital and held his son for the first time stayed during the boy's years as a toddler. 'He often said it was a shame his family had to be pushed into the background,' said Cynthia. 'He regretted it, but once the Beatles wagon was rolling, he could not get off it if he wanted to. He became exhausted and irritable when he was at home, and angry at his own absence when he wasn't there.' In 1966, when he was heavily into smoking marijuana and sleeping until two or three in the afternoon when he was at Weybridge, John let out his thoughts in his song 'I'm Only Sleeping':

> When I wake up early in the morning
> Lift my head, I'm still yawning
> When I'm in the middle of a dream
> Stay in bed, float upstream
> Please don't wake me, no, don't shake me
> Leave me where I am, I'm only sleeping.
> Everybody seems to think I'm lazy

I don't mind, I think they're crazy
Running everywhere at such a speed
Till they find there's no such need
Please don't spoil my day, I'm miles away
And after all, I'm only sleeping.

'One big change I noticed in his habits, once the Beatles got going, was in his sleeping,' says Cynthia. 'He would collapse into a dead sleep and be immovable until afternoon unless there was an appointment to be kept earlier. We were both book fanatics and read until the early hours. I'd usually fall asleep before he did.' An avid collector as well as reader, John would stop his chauffeur and make weekly swoops on bookshops throughout London and Surrey. Tennyson, Swift, Tolstoy, Oscar Wilde, Aldous Huxley, and all the *Just William* books from his childhood ranged across the huge bookcase in the lounge. When Cynthia's mother lived at the house, John asked her, 'Lil, go and fill the bookshelves.' He could not stand the sight of empty bookshelves. He chauvinistically told Cynthia she could not have a full-time nanny for Julian; he wanted his son to have the mother he had been deprived of when he was a child.

John enjoyed spending money. He would make unscheduled stops with his chauffeur and return with expensive clocks, a huge leather-bound Bible, or a compendium of toys, and one day a suit of armour which he had ordered was delivered. 'This is Sidney,' John announced: the armour occupied pride of place in the hall. Nearby reposed a more quixotic, priceless gift from George Harrison; a pair of crutches.

When they closed Harrods for the Beatles to do their Christmas shopping, John arrived home and presented Cynthia with several fur coats and 'naughty nighties'. But he always forgot birthdays. 'It wasn't important to me,' says

Cynthia. 'John was soft, generous, and gave when it was least expected. He never was tight, going right back to college. If he had a cigarette he would always offer you one, and light it.' But she always gazed jealously at something Ringo did when he and Maureen joined John and Cynthia at either one of their houses. 'Ringo had this habit of lighting up two cigarettes, one for Maureen at the same time as he lit his own. I remember thinking it was a loving thing to do, and wishing John did it for me. But that would have been too obviously demonstrative, maybe, for John.'

Her pocket money was £50 in cash a week, and a similar amount was arranged by John to go to Aunt Mimi. 'It was quite a lot, considering I didn't have any bills to pay,' says Cynthia. 'All the food and nearly everything else was on accounts, so there was nothing to spend it on.' Like royalty, John rarely carried any cash or a cheque book. 'Send the bill in,' he would say, whenever he was in a club or restaurant or bookshop.

John, as always, was in a hurry. Beatlemania was great, but it left him feeling strangely unfulfilled, for all the tangible benefits it brought. What Beatlemania brought John, above all, was freedom. Or so he thought.

Drugs entered their marriage, and contributed to its eventual collapse, quite innocently. 'John was always seeking interesting ways to get rid of the mundane and close a chapter. The Beatles were so big, the pressure on him and Paul so much, that he kept looking for new things to occupy his mind. We all went to a party at Brian Epstein's flat in Williams Mews, Knightsbridge, and that was the first time John and I smoked marijuana.' Paul was the only Beatle not there.

After several puffs, John said: 'The only thing this is doing to me is giving me the giggles.' Cynthia's reaction after smoking the joint was to be violently sick. She rejected offers of more marijuana at the round of dinners to which she and John were invited; but John got steadily more engrossed in smoking during 1965.

When a dentist spiked their coffee with LSD, the first effects were again horrific but John thought it was potentially enlightening and worth investigation.

'I warned him against it,' says Cynthia. 'At times I felt like a mother, shouting at him for being a naughty boy but he'd say: "But Cyn, it's FANTASTIC, it's WONDER-FUL. Why don't you do it?"

'I said, "No, because I know what it does, it makes me ill, sick."

' "But it's great, Cyn," John continued, "you've got to be with me, you've *got* to do it." '

Says Cynthia, 'He was so enthusiastic and so happy about the whole thing, and I just couldn't be. We couldn't meet on that level, and although I did try I didn't see what he saw. He obviously saw his escape from whatever he was running away from. I wasn't running away from it. So I didn't really need it.

'What I think John wanted was a kind of mental freedom. He was trying to shed responsibility. I don't think John was a very responsible person. He didn't want to account all the time to anybody but himself. He didn't want to account to Mimi all the time when he was living with her, and now he didn't want to account to me. He's a man who should have been unencumbered until he was about thirty. He wasn't prepared for the two big things running side by side: one or the other, marriage or the pop scene, and certainly not marriage with a growing son. It was a bit too hard to take, and he was wide open when all the pushers kept offering him more and more of what he thought were interesting drugs. He was a sitting target.'

Although she does not feel drugs themselves ended their marriage, Cynthia says, 'They had an important effect in that they separated us. We were on different mental planes. John's thoughts would always be much more expansive than mine. I'd seen the effects of drugs and I didn't want to be there. He did. He kept saying that on his trips he was seeing beautiful things.'

One heavy drug-taking weekend occurred when John went, alone, to the Ascot house of Derek Taylor, the former *Daily Express* writer who had been lured into the Beatles' coterie by Brian Epstein, to whom he became personal assistant. Taylor, an early convert to marijuana and LSD, had a particularly strong intellectual rapport with John.

Derek and Joan Taylor also had five children. Returning from their home, John was aglow at the LSD-tripping he had enjoyed during the weekend. Derek had done wonders for John's ego, 'telling me what a good person I am,' he explained to Cynthia. Normally, during drug experiences John was the more experienced one, guiding less frequent users; this time Derek had assumed the dominant role.

Derek had just returned from a lengthy stay in California, where the blossoming of flower power had made drug-taking almost mandatory. Taylor strongly advocated its use at the time, and to John he was virtually a guru. Mentally, John was going through a period of uncertainty about his marriage, his fatherhood, the Beatles, and himself. During several LSD trips that weekend away from Cynthia, John had his ego massaged by Taylor: it was just the kind of pampering John needed. 'You're OK, you're clever, and you have no real problems,' Taylor told Lennon in many different ways. John returned to Kenwood smiling through the haze.

'Oh, Cyn,' he said when they reunited at Weybridge. 'It was wonderful. Why don't we have lots of children, a big, big family, and everything will be wonderful? That's what we should do.'

Cynthia nodded. She knew he was tripping but felt her hands tied behind her back. She remembered the last time John was so clearly high on dope. He had talked gibberish then, about 'buying an island in the sun, switching the sun on and off and totally controlling the weather.'

'I couldn't switch John's brain off, could I?' asks Cynthia. 'One normal person couldn't compete against that barrage of experiences. Unless they were extraordinary, dominant, and in a position of power, which I wasn't. I was just Mum.'

Reading about the new drug culture, and the Beatles' endorsement of it, Aunt Mimi was on the phone immediately to John in Weybridge.

'By jove, I had a lot to say very quickly,' she remembered. 'John said: "Mimi, I'm *old enough* now. You don't understand the kind of lives we lead. The tension. I've had lots of tensions. And anyway, I used to see you taking aspirins."

'I said: "Yes, John, but only when I had a very bad headache. Look, the worry of it is nearly killing me. I don't approve of it any more than your Scouse accent. I still can't understand a word you're saying in all these interviews, and now there's this worry over drugs. What do you need drugs for and a Scouse accent?"

'And he answered: "Don't worry, Mimi. The accent's put on for money. They love it in Brooklyn. And I can handle the drugs."'

Mimi was equally strong with her final words: "Well, don't have me to come over to your house while all this is happening.'

*

Julian Lennon has two prized possessions: one is a big brown floppy hat on which is embroidered 'Dr Winston O'Boogie', John's nickname for himself; the other is an electric guitar, a Les Paul copy, which Julian received as a Christmas present in 1974. Featuring a plaque with the inscription 'To Julian, Happy Christmas', the guitar is adorned with mirrors. Both were unique gifts from John to his son.

What John could not give Julian during his growing years was time. From his birth at the onslaught of Beatlemania through the turbulent years at Weybridge, Julian was a toddler and a growing boy with an absent dad.

When John was at his most frenetic as a Beatle, from 1964 to 1966, Julian registered very little of his father's fame. 'All I knew was that he was away a lot. When he came home, and we were together, I recall most of all the fun like flying a kite in the garden, or the riding on the back of Dad's motorbike down to Ringo's home. The rest of my childhood with Dad is a fog.' He says he has picked up the full story of his father's old group from news clips and films. 'More than anything, I can remember Dad's way with words, his humour and sense of fun. I know he used to say something about enjoying a good laugh.'

Julian has grown into a great admirer of his father's work – more his non-Beatle songwriting and efforts for peace than his straight Beatles hits. But he finds life today, as Lennon's first son, hazardous. He has regrets about the lack of father-son relationship which he says he desperately needed. 'But if Dad was going to be a musician, then he obviously had to be away from home a lot. Nobody's blaming him. I just missed him and wished he was around more.'

Educated at private schools, Julian went first to Heath House, Weybridge, then to Kingsmead in Hoylake,

Cheshire, going to a variety of preparatory schools and finally settling at Ruthin School in North Wales. There, he followed the family tradition of John and his mother, leaning heavily towards art and hoping for an A-level in the subject. He lacked interest in most other subjects and planned a career in engineering. But he failed all his O-levels, just like his father, and set his sights firmly on music. At school in Hoylake he had a year's tuition on guitar, and with his close friend Justin Clayton played rock 'n' roll classics like 'Roll Over Beethoven', 'Rock Around The Clock', and 'Kansas City'.

As he grew up and listened to his father's work, particularly his lyrics, Julian decided to carry on his tradition. 'But in my own way, and playing mostly piano,' says Julian. 'I prefer ballads to hard-driving rock 'n' roll. I don't want to face any comparison with my father for the songs I'm writing, although I'd have to agree that his work has been a big influence.' His favourite song is 'Isolation', with tracks like 'Dear Prudence', 'Sexy Sadie', and 'A Day In The Life' among the ones he particularly loves.

Growing up as John Lennon's son brought its hurdles for Julian as a schoolboy. 'The other kids thought I was a rich brat, and make jokes like: "He's got ten pound notes as wallpaper", but there were only a couple of times the kids in North Wales tried to beat me up just because of jealousy over who I am. The kids at Ruthin School really thought I had a fortune, and it was never like that.'

Julian recalls very few conversations with his father about his life as a musician, songwriter, or pop star. 'He didn't like to talk to me about it much when I was growing up,' says Julian. 'He'd had enough of talking about the Beatles by the time he got home. He just talked about normal things — like my school work, my games, my clothes. I remember asking him once if he regretted anything about the Beatles and he answered: "No, it was great fun, but I'd hate to have to go through it again." '

Living life as the son of John Lennon, despite its problems, fills him with pride. 'I know everything my Dad did, good and bad,' says Julian. 'He said I was born out of a whisky bottle on a Saturday night. Makes no difference. I love him and respect him and I'm really proud of him.'

In 1984, as Julian prepared for his own entry into a musical career, as a songwriter, pianist, and bandleader, his father's words echoed in his mind. Julian wants to keep the Lennon tradition of songwriting aflame. 'My father's name and reputation has made me even more keen to follow on. I see my work as a continuation, though I'm aware of the dangers of comparison. I'll do it my way, and don't want to be compared with him. I'm just glad I had a father with so much talent.' And what would John say to him if he saw his son launching himself into a career in music? Julian thought for a long time. 'I think my father would say: "Do it – but don't blame me." '

THIRTEEN

MONEY

'A room and a car and a car and a room'

Fame was hemming him in, but there was one massive compensation – money. By mid-1964, with American success assured, and record sales and song-writing royalties pouring in, John was a millionaire. Only four years after leaving art college, and only two years after signing with EMI, the material world was at his feet. In America, merchandising of Beatle-related paraphernalia (wigs, pillows, scarves) swelled their income beyond John's wildest dreams. Only George, who nursed a grievance bigger than John's at the craziness of Beatlemania, shared John's understanding of the mayhem that was surrounding them.

Yet for all the status and all his money, which he enjoyed, John kept his feet firmly on the ground. He told me on tour once that he still had Mimi buy his combs from Woolworth's in Penny Lane because they were the best and he'd grown up with them. He was a great experimenter with fads: he tried vegetarianism but quickly rejected it. 'Nut cutlets! Ugh! I chucked them away and asked Cyn for a fry up of bacon and eggs.' Mentally he was on a fame planet, but deep down his roots were unshaken.

George was absorbed by the money. He prodded Brian Epstein as much as he dared about how much this record had made, how much their royalties were, what concerts would yield. Quickly, Harrison was dubbed the 'money Beatle'. He fought a vain battle for recognition by John and Paul of his own songs but was mostly held off by the sheer weight of Lennon and McCartney's output. In their sense of humour, the more time the Beatles spent together the closer John and George became. The friendship was strengthened when, cost being of little consideration, John bought his Surrey house, Kenwood, in St George's Hill, Weybridge, while George bought Kinfauns, Claremont Estate, Esher, four miles away. His girlfriend and wife-to-be, Pattie Boyd, soon moved in with him. She got on well with Cynthia. Ringo was a neighbour of John's at Sunny Heights, on the same estate. Paul stayed in London, initially at Jane Asher's flat in the West End, but he eventually bought his own home in St. John's Wood, West London.

George was a regular visitor to John's home, which was a pop star mansion, a symbol of success. It was bought hurriedly by John and Cynthia as a refuge from the fan-besieged flat in West Kensington. Within a month of buying it, John was off to America on tour. When John returned, the home and possessions began to interest him more. There was his art nouveau Rolls-Royce eventually painted in a rainbow of swirling floral patterns on a bright yellow background, with smoked one-way glass in the side and rear windows to keep the curious at bay. It had a television and drinks-packed refrigerator inside. He bought a Ferrari and a black Mini Cooper, and took driving lessons, successfully passing his test in February 1965. 'He was a terrible driver,' says Neil Aspinall. He had no sense of direction, often getting lost on the way home. The décor of the house was both spectacular and bizarre, a distinct contrast to the conformity of the sedate estate on which the house stood: purple velvet lined the dining-room walls –

'It sets off the old scrubbed table we eat off,' said John. Most rooms had a television set, which John liked to have permanently switched on with the sound off. He was a self-confessed TV addict: 'I get lots of ideas from it,' he explained to me. 'I think with it on.'

'Then there's the funny room upstairs. I painted that pink and green, changing from one can to another as I emptied each can of paint.' A conducted tour of the house by John gave me an insight into the Beatle insisting on his individuality when he felt it was threatened by Beatlemania. Shortly after he moved in and took me on a tour of Kenwood, I asked him for a list of prized possessions, and he came up with this list:

My first Rickenbacker guitar: it's a bit hammered now, I just keep it for kicks. I bought it in Germany on the hire purchase – whatever it cost, it was a hell of a lot of money to me at the time.

Three cars: a Rolls, Mini Cooper and Ferrari. The Mini for pottering about in, the Rolls for relaxing in and the Ferrari for zoom. I do very little driving. I'm not a good driver.

Swimming pool: I enjoy a swim at home. It's a luxury. All rich people have to have a pool.

Two pictures drawn by Stuart Sutcliffe, our old bass player. I'll always keep those, for sentimental reasons.

A lump of stone: we found it on the doorstep and somebody said it was prehistoric. I've since been enlightened and I believe it's a load of crap.

A stone frog: I like to see this in the fireplace, near the TV set, looking at us all.

About twenty suits; but I only wear about two, both black. I've got an evening dress but I only wear it when

I have to because it's so uncomfortable. I get my clothes from Dougie Millings.

The Singing Postman's record: just part of my huge record collection, but I particularly like this 'cos it's stupid. I've got everything, electronic, Indian, classical and modern jazz.

Pin table: football game machine and fruit machine: in my 'den' here at home, just for a laugh.

Juke box: it's got forty-eight records on it, but I keep it mainly for rock 'n' roll standards like Gene Vincent's 'Be Bop A Lula', and the Big Three's 'Some Other Guy'.

A studio which has two very good tape recorders from which I can make my own records. And twelve guitars, some of which are wrecked.

Aldous Huxley books. I've just started reading him, because he's the new guvnor, it seems to me.

There were several tape recorders on which John would write his songs. He claimed to be the first British owner of the Mellotron, which occupied pride of place in the middle of the lounge. And on the mantelpiece was the winking 'nothing box' which begged the question: 'What's it do?' John enjoyed replying: 'It does nothing. It's a nothing box. It just winks all day and all night, but you can't tell where it's going to wink next.' The red flashing lights on his cherished nothing box had a hypnotic effect on all visitors. Its useless absurdity made John smile every time he looked at it.

John was always determined to move forward creatively, particularly in the Beatles' use of instruments. When he adopted the harmonica on 'Love Me Do', their debut single, he hoped it would mark a breakthrough for the instrument, but he was just beaten to the bestsellers by Frank Ifield with his harmonica-accompanied number one, 'I Remember

You'. In 1963, John became interested in the first 'organ-guitar' being developed in Britain by the entrepreneurial instrument manufacturer Jim Burns. John became deeply involved in all stages of the instrument's development. 'I played a Hammond organ on our second LP,' said John, 'and I fancy a guitar that plays like an organ as well as a guitar. It'd be gear.'

By the time the Beatles went on tour and into the recording studios as a successful group, John's pride and joy was the guitar he had hankered after during his lean, struggling years. It was a Rickenbacker model number 1996, slimline. It cost an astronomical 159 guineas at the beginning of 1964. John cherished it like a child with a new toy and asked the Beatles' road manager, 'Big Mal' Evans, to take great care of it. It can be heard making the particularly pretty guitar figures during one of John's most under-rated solos, 'You Can't Do That'.

John enjoyed indulging himself. 'I do get fits worrying about money,' he told me about this time. 'I worry about being one of those idiots who spend, spend, spend and do it all by the time I'm thirty. I thought I'd been a bit extravagant and bought too many cars, so I put the Mini and the Ferrari up for sale. Then one of the accountants said I was all right, so I got the cars back from the showroom.'

The problem was that he did not know how much money he had. 'I've tried to find out, but with income tax to be deducted and royalties coming in from all over the place, the sums get too complicated for me. I can't even do my times table. Every now and again the accountant clears some money of tax and puts it in my account and says: "That's yours but don't spend it all at once." But I have learned this much: to spend £10,000 I have to earn £30,000 before tax to get it.' His generosity often overtook him: on the rare occasions when he carried money he would give £5 or £10 tips to astonished waiters in restaurants.

He would leave messages on the answering machine of Wendy Hanson, Brian Epstein's personal assistant. One said: 'Wendy, send Aunt Mimi one of those maps of the world that has bottles in it.' She had several similarly enigmatic instructions from him. 'I knew he'd have seen it in Asprey's,' said Wendy. 'He was always rushing through there making mental notes. It was a globe. He was very impetuous, rather than acquisitive. Asprey's [the exclusive and expensive store in Bond Street, London] was a favourite. I once had John Asprey keep the place open late just for the Beatles to tour the shop, like they did at Harrods one Christmas. John thought it was a joke. He simply bought some jam.'

Wendy, who as Epstein's chief lieutenant was on the receiving end of John during what she feels was 'one of the most extraordinary phenomena of modern times', describes him as 'like a crab, a tough shell outside, a softie inside . . . He wasn't tough at all. In France a fourteen-year-old girl fan hid in Lennon's bedroom to await his arrival at the Negresco Hotel, Nice. Her mother phoned Wendy to say: "A Beatle has raped my daughter."

'John was distraught for this girl,' Wendy continues. 'He said: "Wendy, call this woman up and tell her that her child hasn't been touched. She's hiding under my bed and won't come out. She's absolutely fine but worried because she says her mother's going to beat her up when she gets home." It was extraordinary. We got the girl out, but I remember how much John cared and was very gentle about it. He made sure long after the chaos of the event that we checked to make sure the girl got home safely. I remember saying to someone: "So much for the tough guy." '

*

The change in status, from a college student who had had
to scrounge cigarettes and cinema money only four years
previously, to being one of the most sought-after personalities in the world, amused John. His telephone answering
machine at Weybridge reflected his frivolity. A favourite
game would be to play the messages over and over again,
laughing maniacally at people's accents, mimicking them,
and rarely returning phone calls. It was John's Goon-like
sense of humour surfacing. Guests at the house, like singer
P. J. Proby, whose audacity Lennon admired, Liverpool
schoolfriends like Ivan and Jean Vaughan and Pete Shotton,
were bemused by the new Lennon.

As Beatlemania mounted, John became irritable at the
lack of privacy. Kenwood was invaded on Saturdays and
Sundays by fans who regarded the sighting of a Beatle at
home as a pilgrimage to the Promised Land. 'I'm fed up
with it,' he told me during one particularly exasperating
night. 'Some weekends it gets so bad we go away, anywhere,
to get away from the fans who come to gawk. No, stop
that word, they're not *fans*! They treat my house like a
bloody holiday camp, sitting in the grounds with flasks of
tea and sandwiches. What do they think this is, a Beatle
National Park? They're adults too, not all kids. I went out
and told them all to sod off once, and they said they
wouldn't buy any more of my records! I said they should
find something better to do with their spare time.'

The fans collected anything as mementoes of their visits.
They took photographs of the strange brass doorknocker in
the shape of a naked woman. They took blades of grass
from the lawn as souvenirs of a Beatle mansion. John wanted
it to be a haven for himself, Cynthia and Julian, their two
tabby cats, called Mimi and Babaghi, and their brown
labrador dog, Nigel. But it was an uphill fight. He never

knew what was going to await him when he returned home.

John's own spare time, when he had not been writing songs or travelling or in the recording studio, had been spent writing and doodling. On the backs of envelopes, in cars and trains and planes and hotel rooms, John scribbled away and drew caricatures of the characters he invented. It was his private diversion from the mayhem of Beatlemania. The stories were continuations of the theme he had begun, seven years earlier, at Quarry Bank school, in the *Daily Howl* exercise book. Brian Epstein, seeing John's verse and doodles one day, offered to get them published. It had not occurred to Lennon, but the result was the debut, in 1964, of John as an author.

In His Own Write, published by Jonathan Cape in 1964, was lionized by the literary establishment. 'Worth the attention of anyone who fears for the impoverishment of the English language and the British imagination,' said *The Times Literary Supplement*.

The obvious influences at work in the book were Lewis Carroll, Spike Milligan and *The Goon Show*, and the gobbledegook linguistic comedian Stanley Unwin. The 'Alice' books had exerted a strong influence on John since childhood and were later to percolate into his writing, notably 'I Am The Walrus' which derived from Carroll's 'The Walrus And The Carpenter'. The first verse of 'Lucy In The Sky With Diamonds' recalls Alice's gentle voyage with the sheep in *Through The Looking Glass*. Lennon was familiar with Carroll's lengthier, surrealistic poems like 'Jabberwocky' and 'The Hunting of the Snark', and loved his verbal word-play and jumbling of images. The titles of John's hilarious essays told their own story of the satirical slants. 'On Safairy with Whide Hunter' (written, as John put it, 'in conjugal with Paul') and 'No Flies on Frank', 'The Fat Growth on Eric Hearble', and 'At the Denis' demonstrated a grasp of humour that had the critics showering praise. One Conservative MP Charles Curran, seemed to miss the point. He stated in Parliament that John's book highlighted the poor education in Liverpool, and claimed Lennon was illiterate.

John's first book topped the British bestseller list. It sold more than one hundred thousand copies in its first printing, and he was fêted at a prestigious Foyle's literary luncheon at London's Dorchester Hotel. Immediately, John was recognized as the intelligent Beatle. Demand for tickets at the lunch exceeded the requests when George Bernard Shaw was the guest. The lunch itself was animated enough, with a high attendance of the literary establishment, but John was not to be drawn into making the customary speech for a guest of honour. He rose and said: 'Thank you very much, God bless you.' Many were disappointed, but he explained later that he did not feel up to it. 'Give me another fifteen years, and I may make a speech. Anyway I daren't today. I was scared stiff.'

John's speechlessness did nothing to dent his mystique among the expensively dressed debutantes, bejewelled dowagers, waiters, and aristocrats who jostled outside the Dorchester Hotel like teenage fans, demanding John's autograph. 'For my daughter', of course.

One woman clutched ten copies of his book and thrust them into his hand, saying: 'Put your name clearly here.'

John looked at her, astonished, as she said to her friend: 'I never thought I would stoop to asking for such an autograph.'

John cut her with: 'And I never thought I would be forced to sign my name for someone like *you*.'

John's second book, *A Spaniard in the Works*, was more disciplined than the first. 'It was starting from scratch,' explained John. 'The publisher said you've got so many months to write a book in. With the first book, I'd written a lot of it at odd times during my life.'

John had nearly a year to produce *A Spaniard in the Works*, during which he observed, as always, the passing scene and was able to develop his thoughts into prose and satire. There was a tilt at the *Daily Mirror* columnist Cassandra (whom John called Cassandle), which John said was because the writer had been knocking the Beatles. There was a send-up of newspaper letter columns called Readers Lettuce. There was John's glorious irreverence captured in Last Will and Testicle:

> I, Barrold Reginald Bunker-Harquart being of sound mind you, limp and bodie, do on this day the 18 of September 1924th, leave all my belongings estate and brown suits to my nice niece Elsie. The above afforementioned hereafter to be kept in a large box until she is 21 of age.

'The National Health Cow', 'Snore Wife and some Several Dwarts', and 'The Singularge Experience of Miss Anne Duffield' – with which John had some help in writing from George while they were on holiday in Tahiti – were more examples of John's acute sense of the ridiculous.

A keen insight into the literary Lennon came with his broadcast in July 1965 on BBC radio's *World of Books* programme. Interviewed by Wilfred De'Ath, John said his books were mostly spontaneous and undisciplined productions.

'I'm selfish about what I write, or big-headed about it. Once I've written it I like it and the publishers sometimes say, "Should we leave this out or change that?" And I fight like mad because once I've done it, I like to keep it. But I always write it straight off. I might add things when I go over it, before it's published, but I seldom take anything out, so it's spontaneous.'

That desire reflected John's recording preferences. He hates songs to linger for long, to be refined in the studio. He liked to work, in records as apparently in books and all his art, rather like a daily newspaperman: write it, see it released very quickly, then move on. He wanted his records out overnight, and when his life as a Beatle was replaced by the Plastic Ono Band, John did have records out within days of completion. It mirrored, also, his philosophy of life as a fast run.

On that radio interview John admitted only two influences in his literary work: Arthur Conan Doyle, who had marked his work in the Sherlock Holmes-inspired tale, 'The Singularge Experience of Miss Anne Duffield', and Lewis Carroll. 'I always admit to that because I love *Alice in Wonderland* and *Through the Looking Glass*, but I didn't even know he'd written anything else, I was that ignorant. I just had it as a birthday present as a child and liked them.'

'A lot of people say your pieces are sick. What do you say to that?' asked the interviewer.

'If it makes people sick. But I can read it and it doesn't appear sick to me,' replied John.

Denying other influences tossed around by literary reviewers, who quoted Edward Lear, James Thurber, and others as his evident inspirations, John said: 'I deny it because I'm ignorant of it. Lear I'd never heard of. Well, I'd heard the name obviously somewhere but we didn't do him at school. The only classic or very highbrow anything I read at school or knew of is Chaucer. I might have read a bit of Chaucer at school because I think they do that. And so I bought all the books they said it was like. I bought one book on Edward Lear, I bought *Finnegans Wake*, Chaucer, and I couldn't see any resemblance to any of them.'

He only read what he stumbled across, he said, not what it was 'right' or accepted to read. He had never read anything by Jonathan Swift. 'Charles Dickens I don't like too much. I've got to be in a certain mood. It's too *school*. I'm too near school to read Dickens or Shakespeare. I hate Shakespeare. I don't care whether you should like him or not. It doesn't mean anything to me.' He had just discovered Winnie the Pooh, 'which I'd never read as a child. I just discovered him about a year ago.'

By far the longest essay in *Spaniard in the Works*, 'The Singularge Experience', spread over nine pages. When Wilfred De'Ath described his written works as 'mini pieces', John said: 'To you they're mini pieces, to me they're *marathons*. With Sherlock Holmes, I was seeing how far I could go. I forget which characters have come in and I just get lost and fed up and bored. That's why I usually either kill them off – well, I killed the lot off in the first book.'

On his Cassandra lampoon, he said, 'I did it mainly because he knocked us. We get a lot of knocking which we don't mind. We don't want everybody to love us, if somebody doesn't like us they're entitled to, but we have no defence against people like that writing about us in newspapers, because we can't say anything back. And this is just my way of having a go back. It was just a sort of personal joke amongst ourselves. I'm definitely planning on Bernard Levin for the next one.'

Singer George Melly met John at a party to launch John's first book. Melly had written a glowing review of the book in the *Observer*. 'I approached him,' says George, 'in what I thought was a friendly manner, with perhaps an element of patronization. He was quite drunk and so was I.

'He started on me about the fact that I came from trad jazz which he hated because it blocked him and his friends from the Cavern. So he called me one of the blockers. He was quite aggressive.

'I said, "Did you like the review?"

'He said he hadn't read it.

'I said how much I enjoyed it, and referred to his James Joyce influence.

'He said: "I don't know who you're talking about. I've never heard of him. Who the hell's Joyce?" '

This was not true, because he *had* heard of James Joyce.

Finally, Lennon and Melly nearly came to blows when Melly brought up the subject of black singers. George said: 'Of course, you must feel as I feel in my sphere, that one's real debt is to black singers like Muddy Waters and Chuck Berry, who invented the idiom in which we both sing.'

John became furious. He said he accepted nothing of the sort. He refuted all influences. 'I could eat 'em for breakfast . . . they don't make anything like I make,' he roared, the drink talking. The shout-up continued, with Melly insisting that Lennon's music was as derivative as his own. 'It nearly came to a fight,' says Melly. 'I'm glad it didn't because he would certainly have won.'

Yet once he had achieved success, John felt ambivalent about singing on the same concert bill as black acts. With the other Beatles, notably George Harrison, he had invited cult Tamla Motown singer Mary Wells ('My Guy') to tour with them in Britain in 1964; but when she came, superb though she was, John felt uncomfortable. 'I hate singing "Twist and Shout" when there's a coloured artist on the bill,' he told me. 'It doesn't seem right, you know. It seems to be their music and I feel sort of embarrassed. Makes me curl up . . . they can do these songs much better than us.'

He had no patience with other beat groups, who, he declared, 'are pinching our musical arrangements down to the last note.' He said to me: 'Look, we copied nobody. I am not a Negro so I can't copy a Negro singer. We've got our own style based on the music we grew up with, and it annoys me a lot to find groups getting on the wagon by copying sounds we were playing two years ago. Why can't these copyists make their own styles like we did? It happens in hairstyles as well. I see players in some groups have even the same length of hair as us. It's no good them saying they're students and they just happen to have long hair. *We* were students, as well, before we came to London, and we didn't have these hairstyles then. The difference between the Beatles and some of these others is that we didn't sit around in the 'Pool saying: "We're going to be big stars." Music was part of our lives. We played it because we loved doing it, not just for the loot. Unlike some groups, we don't go around even now saying: "Look, we're stars." I just consider myself a lucky layabout from Liverpool who has had some success. My Auntie used to say (and here he would brilliantly mimic Mimi's authoritarian voice): "You're not seriously thinking of making a career in *that* line! The guitar's all right as a hobby, John, but you'll never make a living from it."

'And I'd say: "No, it's just a passing thing." '

When he was speaking fast and furious and wanting it reported, John would urge a journalist: 'Get it *down*, get it down in that book.'

Asked by a radio interviewer whether he would prefer to be remembered as a writer or as a Beatle, John replied: 'I don't care whether I'm remembered or not. After I'm gone, I don't care what happens.'

John adapted to the lifestyle of a millionaire star with ease. He drank too much, but some kind of release from the pressures of being in what he later called a 'goldfish bowl' was essential. He had a few formal dinner guests at his Weybridge home, and those who did stay, like the pianist-singer Alan Price, would find themselves driven there nearer breakfast-time after all-night drinking at the Ad Lib club, exchanging hilarious tales of fights in their mad youth – John regaling people with stories of Hamburg, Price with ones of his Geordie childhood.

Spectators who did not participate in debates, like American singers Dionne Warwick and Mary Wells, would look on in disbelief at Lennon's Scotch-and-Coke-soaked antics. This was not the cozy Beatle whose moptop image had been pumped across the Atlantic as something clean and pure. Here was a drunk!

John's realization of just how enormous his group had become occurred when the Beatles returned home for a civic reception at Liverpool Town Hall. More than one hundred thousand people turned out for the day, and John, on a secret visit to Mendips, found his old home had become a shrine. Fans and journalists from all over the world were besieging his house, and Aunt Mimi was too exposed for comfort. She lived there alone, since John's move to London, save for Tim, the fat ginger cat.

'I kept changing the phone number,' said Mimi, 'but the fans would keep discovering the new one within a few days.' Rich and successful with the world at his feet, John's welcome was tempered by Mimi with her traditional reserve. 'He knew better than to tell me how well they were doing,' said Mimi.

'I simply said: "I'm glad it's working out well, John."

'He said: "I told you it would."

'And that was that.'

A year later, John persuaded Mimi to stay with him at Weybridge. 'I'm going to buy you a new house, Mimi,' he said to her over his usual breakfast of two or three bowls of cornflakes topped with bananas. 'Where's it to be?'

Mimi, stumped for a reply, said the first seaside place that came into her head: 'Bournemouth.' That morning, John and Mimi set off in his Rolls-Royce, chauffeured by the faithful Les Anthony, armed with maps of Hampshire. John never just sat in his Rolls. He lay down in it. He operated the electrically controlled windows with his feet, playing ups and downs with them all the time. He smoked a lot, often passing a cigarette to his chauffeur. At traffic lights, people glanced inside in disbelief at sighting a Beatle. He gave them the world's most freezing stare.

The estate agents in Bournemouth provided them with some suitable houses for sale, and Mimi took a fancy to a white-painted bungalow overlooking Poole Harbour. She particularly loved the view, with its lounge window facing the terrace which led down to the water. Mimi pictured herself here, watching the pleasure launches and seeing the seagulls. 'Like it, Mimi?' said John. Within hours of starting the search, he was on the phone to his accountant and had bought the house in Panorama Road, Sandbanks.

Mimi sold Mendips, finally persuading John, who wanted the backdrop to his childhood years preserved, that there could be no turning back the clock. For the next eight years, John rang her phone several times a week on his world travels as he developed increasing love and respect for the daunting woman who had brought him up. He visited her regularly too, slumping in the armchair with its sea view and over cups of tea confiding his innermost thoughts about the Beatles, his marriage, and his restlessness. 'The older he got, the better we got to know each other,' reflected his aunt.

When the time came for Mimi to leave Liverpool, John asked her to take special care of his childhood books and the huge grandfather clock on which Uncle George had taught him to tell the time. 'I'll need it some day,' said John.

During an interview I had in 1964 with Bob Dylan, he referred to a song whose title he could not remember: the Beatles' 'I Want To Hold Your Hand'. It held the number one position for seven weeks in America. 'You know,' he said, 'that song about dope?' I must have looked even more baffled than I felt.

It transpired that Bob believed the real words, 'I can hide, I can hide,' at the end of one chorus, were 'I get high, I get high.' Dylan was astonished that it was not a drugs song, and by his discovery, on meeting them in America, that they were not into marijuana. British pop stars were several years behind their American counterparts in adopting drugs as part of their lifestyle.

Dylan is popularly regarded as having switched the Beatles on to marijuana during their visit to America. But his significance to John, during the mid-1960s, was his spectacular command of words and ability to combine intelligent imagery with electric folk music. Lennon was quickly hypnotized by Dylan's album *Bringing It All Back Home*, a brave adventure by a former folk singer-guitarist into the world of rock. John played the album a lot at home but would not be drawn much on it. It was as if he felt the presence of a genuine literary rival.

His inquisitiveness, though, triumphed over his apprehension. There followed a distinct 'Dylan period' as John called it, when he wrote songs in Bob's style and even invited the singer to his home. But there was an edginess, a nervousness of each other, in the air, and the Weybridge meeting did not form the basis of a long and lasting friendship. Spiritually, as totally original artists, Lennon and

Dylan were too alike to become close. Recognition of each other was enough, and John, who before Dylan turned him on to marijuana had only got high on booze or 'Prelly's' in Hamburg, acknowledged the maestro with songs like 'I'm A Loser' and 'Norwegian Wood', both introspective. One of his favourite 1965 singles was Dylan's 'Subterranean Homesick Blues', which John described as 'very Chuck Berry-ish'. He and I spent a lot of time at his Weybridge home trying to work out the words.

Dylan, and Lennon's fresh songwriting phase of looking inwards, had arrived at an important juncture in John's life. It was natural, thought Brian Epstein, for the boys' personalities to be captured in films. Their first tentative move was in *A Hard Day's Night*, followed the next year by *Help!* and subsequently by John's solo role in *How I Won the War*, alongside Michael Crawford. The director of all three films was Richard Lester. John struck up an immediate rapport with the laconic American, partly because, like George Martin, Lester had been involved with John's cherished Goons, having filmed Spike Milligan and Peter Sellers in *The Running, Jumping and Standing Still Film*. Zany comedy was still John's favourite brand, and he envisaged a desperately needed switch from the rigours of Beatle-mania. The scriptwriter was Alun Owen, a Liverpudlian who went with Lester to meet the Beatles during their Paris trip in January 1964.

A Hard Day's Night was devised, simply, as a black and white fictionalized documentary of the Beatles' crazy life as pop stars, covering their experiences as musicians, in the recording studios, their television appearances, their pressures in concerts. 'The film was based on their life living in small boxes, as prisoners of their own success,' says Richard Lester. 'The concept came from John's reply to a question I asked him about a trip they'd made to Sweden.

' "How did you like it?" I said.

'John said: "Oh, it was a room and a car and a car and a room and a room and a car."

'That became our signal of how to do *A Hard Day's Night*.'

The film was shot on location at Marylebone Station in London and on trains.

'We tried very hard to make sure that nobody had more than one sentence to learn at any given time,' says Richard Lester, 'and John fell into line with the rest of them. It was eight o'clock every morning make-up and eight-thirty on the set, no arguments. I think that came as a great shock to them, but their road managers, Neil Aspinall and Mal Evans, made sure that they were all there on time.'

Wherever the Beatles went in the public eye in the mid-1960s, fans gathered in the hundreds or thousands very quickly. 'The biggest problem in making *A Hard Day's Night* on location was that we could, at best, get two takes on anything when we were on a street,' says Richard Lester. 'The streets would get so blocked with fans we'd have to change locations and start again. We had to get the Beatles on and off the set very quickly!' This meant the Beatles tearing quickly into a shop, doing their scene, and making a rapid exit at the other side of the shop to fool the crowds. All this had to be done in minutes and led to one of the most expensive days in Lennon's life.

Darting in and out of Asprey's, John managed to spend about £80,000 within minutes. 'God knows how he managed it. I think even John was amazed at how much he ordered from the place,' says Lester. He ordered furniture, jewellery, and bric-à-brac.

The song title became the title for the film after Ringo had come up with the phrase to recall a heavy night. John's

composition, and his searing vocal, make it one of the most
enduring Beatles songs.

   Help! was a more adventurous enterprise. Filmed over
a nine-week period, it had a weak story similar to the James
Bond themes. A crazy scientist joined a search for a valuable
ring that ended up on Ringo's hand. The movie began life
as *Eight Arms to Hold You*, but when John wrote the title
track it was such a powerful song that it was adopted as
the film's title.

   Shooting began over two weeks in the Bahamas, where
John quickly showed that, even as a multi-millionaire pop
and film star, he was not likely to be conned into high
society. 'One didn't want to have a tongue lashing from
John, but it did come out in Nassau,' recalls Lester. 'We
were all guests at dinner of the Governor, and we had
been filming in a mental hospital where conditions were
outrageous.'

   Actor Victor Spinetti, who was there and who developed
a strong friendship with John, says, 'We all went looking
around what appeared to be an army barracks. We thought
it was deserted. In fact there were a lot of spastics and
cripples and old people in there and John was shocked that
they had been shoved away under this terrible corrugated-
iron army hut.'

   'It was a black-tie affair,' says Lester, 'with the equivalent of all the hoorays of the Bahamas. John let loose. It
was a perfectly justifiable sense of outrage for anyone with
a sense of social conscience.'

   Victor Spinetti says Lennon was especially appalled by
the contrast between the champagne and caviar they were
offered at dinner, and the living conditions of the afflicted.
John said to the minister of finance: 'I saw this place today
which was meant to be a hospital. People were in there
under the most terrible conditions.'

'The minister replied: "I do my best, you know. I'm not being paid for being the minister of finance."

'To which John answered: "Oh, in that case you're doing better than I thought you were doing." '

The press turned on the Beatles because of John's sharpness, but he was unrepentant and told everyone he loathed the Bahamas.

'He made the very strong point,' says Richard Lester, 'that these people were hypocrites and condescending to the Beatles because they *were* the Beatles, and that he couldn't stand. He was very, very tough on the authorities after that. The power of John's attack on that government figure makes me remember him very strongly from the weeks in the Bahamas, much more than the others at that time.'

After the Bahamas, the location work moved to the ski slopes of Austria, in a small town called Obertauren, two hours' drive from Salzburg. By now John and the others were smoking marijuana heavily, but not so much that they could not work. They would hardly have been able to work so vigorously, or write the songs, or drink until the early hours in the hotel, if they had been stoned non-stop. But John's euphoria after going to his room for a smoke, and his enlarged pupils, made it obvious when he was high.

Perhaps it was a release from the Bahamas, but John was in a particularly buoyant mood when I visited Austria for a week during location work. He was agile at skiing, which he enjoyed. He thought the film story was ludicrous but was able to laugh at the fact that it was unstoppable, expensive, and a waste of such a lot of time and money; he struck up a warm friendship with actress Eleanor Bron and was often to be heard in conversation with her, talking politics and philosophy, over drinks in the hotel bar. In political beliefs John thought like a socialist but said he would have to vote Conservative because they knew how to manage the country. Money came into it quite strongly, he used to tell me. 'Deep down,' he said, 'I'm Labour. Politics is a state of mind but you've got to protect your money, haven't you?'

It was in Austria that John and Paul and I concocted an amusing, childish, but absorbing word-game one night in the hotel bar. The game was called Winners and Losers, and appealed immensely to John. One person called out the name of a person, country, drink, or anything tangible, and the others would pronounce it a winner or a loser. There were no hard rules for this daft, arbitrary game. It relied purely on intuition rather than definition. Thus, John pronounced EMI a winner, Decca a loser; France (where the Beatles had just appeared, with only moderate success) a loser country, America a winner; Coca-Cola was a winner, Pepsi-Cola a loser; New York was a winner, Los Angeles a loser; tea a winner, coffee a loser; the whole of Fleet Street a loser because the journalists were so very late realizing the Beatles were a force. And so it went on, becoming highly personalized, argumentative, often cruel, and great fun.

In a chance remark to a British musician he greatly admired, Tony Sheridan, John said, as the Beatles' success grew: 'I've sold my soul to the devil.' Sheridan, who had recorded with the Beatles in Hamburg, had been particularly friendly with John and knew immediately what John meant, for fame of this kind was never what Lennon expected.

The *Help!* film coincided with what John later called his 'fat Elvis' period. It was difficult to realize it until later, but John was slightly overweight, eating and drinking too much, materialistically collecting possessions, but too much of an artist to be swept along by show business. He was more dissatisfied even than he realized: he thought he had lost his art. Cynthia, however, maintains that 1965 was his finest songwriting year.

When he wrote 'Help!' something from deep within him gave vent to his insecurity, his feeling that all was not well, despite the millions of record sales, the adoration, the frustrating mansion in Weybridge which he described as 'like a bus stop, you wait until something comes along.'

John's *cri de coeur* emerged with painfully honesty, although nobody was listening carefully to his title song as the autobiography it was . . .

When I was younger, so much younger than today,
I never needed anybody's help in any way.
But now these days are gone, I'm not so self-assured
Now I find I've changed my mind, I've opened up the doors.

Help me if you can, I'm feeling down
And I do appreciate you being 'round
Help me get my feet back on the ground, won't you please,
please help me?

And now my life has changed in oh so many ways
My independence seems to vanish in the haze,
But every now and then I feel so insecure
I know that I just need you like I've never done before . . .
Help, I need somebody, help, not just anybody, help . . . help!

Characteristically, John was the first Beatle to debunk the Beatles. He could not stand the inflated descriptions of what the Beatles were, or being constantly paraded, or the dukes and lords who regarded it as a social cachet to be photographed with a Beatle. To John, what had begun as rock 'n' roll had become an industry. He did not see himself as a profound performer, and while he admired Paul McCartney's musical strengths, the two men were not reacting in the same way to fame. Paul loved it.

One rainy afternoon in 1965, in an interview with me at Weybridge, John was in a morose mood. His restlessness was evident as he took me up to the music room where, amid countless tapes, recorders, and amplifiers, and a mess of paper, he was strumming his guitar and writing a song which turned out later as 'Nowhere Man'. With hindsight, it was a prophetic title: a moment, a day, when the change in John Winston Lennon was more evident than at any time since they first scored a hit record.

He was both defensive and confused about fame as he ate his afternoon breakfast of cornflakes, a dish he was likely to eat at any time of the day. He smoked incessantly and started talking about how he felt old at the age of twenty-five. 'According to the rules of the pop world, we're old,' he said. 'But we don't look any older than the Stones, do we? We certainly don't act any older. I've seen Jagger looking a hundred and The Who looking at least thirty some nights. Christ, we felt old when we started, when Brian Epstein found us. We thought we'd left it too late to make it. Years don't affect your mind. They can give your face wrinkles, but it's your attitude and outlook that counts. I've met people of thirty who aren't thirty in their mentality. The calendar alone says they've lived thirty years, and although age can give you experience, some people aren't capable of using that experience. I'm twenty-six next year. The rules say that I'm a fully grown man, settled down and all that. I'm not – I've still got a young outlook!'

What nagged away at him was the fear that the Beatles were no longer a rock 'n' roll group but were generally appealing to mothers and fathers and adults. 'There was a time back there when we seemed to be doing everything at once – getting older people interested in what we're doing as well as the young. But I don't like that.' He said he had not enjoyed their Christmas concerts in London for that reason. 'It doesn't seem natural to see old people out there looking at us. They should be at home doing the knitting.'

Asked if he regretted the size of the Beatles' popularity, John said, 'No, I'm glad things got as big as they did. Because when we got *nearly* big, people started saying to us: "You're the biggest thing since . . ." And I hated that. I wanted the Beatles to be just *the* biggest thing. It's like gold. The more you get the more you want.'

John said British fan mail for the Beatles was declining from the peak it had reached a year or so earlier. 'I'm talking about the stuff I get myself now. Paul gets a lot every day. Mine fluctuates – goes up when we've got a new record out. Since our European tour we've been getting plenty of mail from Yugoslavia, Italy, and for some reason, Japan.'

The attitude of the fans still bothered him, he told me. 'It's annoying when people turn round and say: "But we MADE you, you ungrateful swines." They did, in a way, but there's a limit to what we're bound to do, as if it's a duty. When I had black windows put in my Rolls-Royce, a fan wrote to me: "You're hiding, turning your back, and running away from the people who made you."

'Rubbish! If I go to a shop down the road and buy a bunch of roses I don't expect the bloke to be so grateful that he spends his life bowing and scraping. I like the roses, so I buy them, and that's that.

'I don't want to sound as if we don't like being liked. We appreciate it,' said John, his Aunt Mimi's training conspicuously keeping him balanced. 'But we can't spend our lives being dictated to.

'Think about these Kellogg's cornflakes. If you buy cornflakes, do you expect Mr Kellogg to spend his life being told how to do everything, how to behave? No. And if you buy a loaf of bread and it's lousy, you just don't buy it again.

'It's not all that different with us. We make a record and if you like it you buy it. If you don't, don't buy it. It's up to the public to decide.

'The Beatles can't win at the moment. If we try to please everybody, right across the age groups, it's impossible. We'd end up in the middle with nobody liking us. People think of us as a machine. They pay six shillings and eight pence for a record and we have to do what they say, like Jack-in-the-box. I don't like that side of being a pop star.'

Cynthia came into the room, with Julian and John's cup of tea. Julian stayed a while, and I casually asked John how old the boy was. 'He's two, I think,' said John. And then, in a rare flash of correction, 'That's awful. I'm away so much I've forgotten how old he is. Yeah, two it must be.'

When Cynthia left the room, John said how glad he was that his, and Ringo's, marriage had been accepted by fans. 'I don't think the two of us being married has had any bad effects on our popularity. Remember, when it got out that both Ringo and I were married, there hadn't been anybody in such a position as we were in, who had got married. It was Silver Disc, as opposed to Gold Disc, people who'd got married before us! People who relied on the fact that they wiggled, sexily, in their stage acts. We didn't rely on wiggling, we still don't, and we won't. We were never dependent on fans being in love with us so much as others are. Not like Jagger. He's the Charlie Chaplin of rock 'n' roll. Now *he* can't afford to get married! The Stones would be all over.'

Although John and Mick got on well superficially, there was a distinct impression that Lennon thought Jagger was trying, through the Stones, to overtake the Beatles, and John regarded that as pathetic. Later, John slammed the Stones' *Satanic Majesties Request* album as an imitation of *Sgt. Pepper*, and loathed the Stones' record 'We Love You' which John said was 'She Loves You' backwards. Coincidentally, both John and Paul had sung on the record which Lennon blasted so forcefully. John had very little artistic respect for the Rolling Stones. When he was drinking, he tore into them for merely copying black music.

The trappings and status of fame seemed strangely, suddenly shallow. The fine wines in the cellar at Weybridge were ordered by John or Cynthia or the housekeeper, Dorothy Jarlett, at random. Expensive restaurant dinners were nice but were making him mentally, as well as physically, bloated. He and Cynthia dined with good friends, like Victor Spinetti, who introduced him to light escapism in the theatre and shows like *The Student Prince* and *The Desert Song*. Afterwards, they would adjourn to La Cappannina, an Italian restaurant in Romilly Street, Soho, and talk the night away. John enjoyed visiting the home of Peter Cook, whose sense of humour was endearing, and he was a regular, often alone, at the trendy discotheque called the Scotch of St. James, where he traded stories with visiting American musicians. 'Before going out for a night on the booze,' he said, 'I drink a pint of milk and take two Aspro. Stops you getting a hangover.' John was funny when inebriated, but could be aggressive if he didn't win an argument. And in that period, he was subconsciously seeking new routes. He would vent his tension in odd ways.

In Paris, at the posh Hôtel Georges V, John stubbed a cigarette out in the middle of a giant extravagant cake which reposed in the Beatles' suite. It was John's way of

commenting on the sickliness of the cake and the stupidity
of its appearance and extravagance. Next to the Queen,
nothing in Britain was a better-known institution than the
Beatles, and privately that was precisely what bothered
John. At Kenwood, he had spent nearly £50,000 on decorat-
ing and furnishing a house which had cost only £19,000
to buy. Now, nourished by his success as the author of two
books, he started looking around outside the Beatles for
activities.

Touring was a drag. The film *Help!* had been a disaster
to John, whatever anyone else said, 'I was only an extra in
my own film,' he told Richard Lester. He was encouraged
to make another film, away from the Beatles, the following
year, but by then John had a built-in distrust of acting. 'Of
the four, he would have been the best actor, an unexpected
actor,' says Lester.

'I told him: "You're obviously a good actor if you want
to be."

'He replied: "Acting's silly and daft." '

Concert tours were a wider issue. Live work was what
the Beatles had been born from, yet now, mounting a tour
was more like a military operation than ever. The 'car and
a room and a room and a car' syndrome had gone beyond
anyone's comprehension and was no longer a joke. On the
road, particularly in America, the compensations were
the women and the speedy American way of life. But to the
Beatles on stage the shows were charades. They could hear
only deafening screams, and the music counted for nothing.
They were like a circus act. 'Just dummies,' John said. 'They
can't even see us from that distance. We're specks on the
horizon. Why they pay money to come and see us, like
fifty-five thousand at Shea Stadium in New York, I'll never
know.'

And then there was flying. John had always hated it.

Next to George, who had a pathological fear of getting on a plane, John was the worst flier. He joked his way nervously through most flights, and shored himself up with alcohol. Yet the jokes flowed when he was aboard. Flying Lufthansa from London to Munich, he said to me in a voice that thankfully none of the German crew heard as we climbed the steps: 'It's good to fly Lufthansa to London – all the pilots know the way.'

John's tongue was at once his most endearing characteristic and his worst enemy. On stage in Hamburg during the Beatles' emotional return there in 1966 for a triumphant German concert tour, John told the crowd, 'Don't listen to our music. We're terrible these days.' He meant that their stage work had lost its bite. It was the truth, but he hurt a lot of people with the remark. And he could not understand why all those millions of screams came from people who simply wanted to attend an *event*.

Lennon had a macabre sense of humour about dying in a plane crash. 'We'll either go in a plane crash or we'll be popped off by some loony,' he said to me on a plane in America. The remark was to echo with devastating, appalling irony in New York fourteen years later.

Once, as the Beatles' plane was coming in to land at Portland, Oregon, the group were joking with the *Daily Mirror's* Don Short that they were so famous, there could be no more big stories. They had cracked America wide open, and they would soon no longer be newsworthy. John and Don sat together drawing up a list of what could be concocted to spin out the Beatles' news value.

John said, 'I know. I'll run off with Ringo's wife on Howard Hughes's plane.' Just then, one of the plane's engines caught fire and the plane started billowing black smoke.

Short said: 'Well, John, this is one story we haven't accounted for yet.'

And John answered: 'Oh Christ, how are we going to tell this?'

John then wrote his own obituary, got a film spool from a travelling photographer, wound the paper round the spool, and sealed it down, so that when the plane crashed his own 'black box' would be there to tell the story of his death in his own words.

The plane landed safely, amid ambulances and fire engines and general pandemonium. John roared above the madness: 'Beatles and children off first!' In Paris, before that tour, John had studied a list of American cities they might visit. They had escaped from the Hôtel Georges V at four in the morning for a stroll and wandered into one of the cafés on the Champs-Elysées, just like they used to on the Reeperbahn in Hamburg after their club work. Someone reflected on that forthcoming American tour and pondered how Beatlemania, which was so enormous, could possibly end. 'It will all end in an air crash,' John said, throatily through his Gauloise. 'It's got to be Cincinnati. Just as the plane is landing. Cincinnati sounds a great place to die.'

Meeting Elvis Presley was something that John Lennon could never have comprehended when he was a devoted fan as an art student five years earlier. But in the summer of 1965 he was to come face to face with the idol who had changed his life. It happened during the Beatles' stay in Los Angeles when they rented a house on Mulholland Drive, and the meeting was arranged by journalist Chris Hutchins of London's *New Musical Express*. He persuaded Colonel Tom Parker, Presley's manager, and Brian Epstein to get them all together. Hutchins had no trouble persuading the Beatles, but for days there was tension over who should be the host: the Beatles were undoubtedly hotter than Elvis, but Presley was the more senior act and it was his town. 'In the end,' says Hutchins, 'the Colonel's wisdom and experience won over Brian Epstein's lack of determination and basic politeness.' An evening was set for the Beatles to glide in their limousines to Elvis's gigantic mansion in Bel Air.

John was full of genuine anticipation as Elvis entered the room dressed casually in red shirt and grey trousers. But the first few minutes seemed like hours: both Elvis and the four Beatles were struck dumb at the size of the occasion. Finally, John and Paul wandered off to corner Elvis and talk about songwriting.

Presley asked how many hits they had written, and it was Lennon who confronted the King with the question all self-respecting rock 'n' roll fans throughout the world were asking: 'Why don't you go back to making rock 'n' roll records?' Presley had been pummelled by all his old fans, like John, for slumping into a tiring routine of making trashy Hollywood movies, and his records were soundtracks.

'It's my movie schedule,' Elvis said. 'It's so tight! I might just do one soon, though.'

John retorted: 'Then we'll buy that!'

They jammed a while on Elvis's guitars, only riffs and no complete song tunes, and adjoined to the games room to play the pinball machines. But the atmosphere was stilted, and, although he enjoyed the occasion, John was disillusioned by his idol. 'It was like meeting Engelbert Humperdinck,' he later said scathingly. The Beatles' mementoes of the uneventful meeting, handed to them by Colonel Parker, were a complete set of Presley albums each, a table lamp shaped like a wagon, and holsters with gold leather belts. 'It was obvious Elvis was high and the Beatles knew very little about dope then,' says Chris Hutchins. 'Neither side desired the meeting that much and the politics of it made it so heavy.'

FOURTEEN

MUSIC

'DO something with my voice'

THE COMBINATION of John Lennon and Paul McCartney, as friends as well as songwriters, must rank as one
of the great examples of opposites being drawn to each
other like magnets. McCartney's background, with a father
as a jazz pianist and a mother determined that her academic
son stay on course to a 'proper job' in one of the professions,
was traditional and musically conventional.

John carried the scars of a lost father and a mother
killed in a road accident at the time he and Paul set off on
their musical collaboration. Lennon had been a teddy boy
who had virtually roared through Liverpool, leaving broken
hearts and many scars among the hundreds who knew that
either he would end up a catastrophic loser, or his streak
of artistic genius and prescience might carry him through
the heights. McCartney was simply an orthodox teenager.

By the time they reached London and became immersed
in recording, the general opinion was that it was easy –
despite the songwriting credit line of Lennon-McCartney
which appeared everywhere – to detect who wrote what.

Whoever sang the lead vocal had usually written the
song. If it haunted you, it was a McCartney. If it baffled
you, made you think, it was a Lennon. If it grabbed you

by the heart ('Yesterday', 'All My Loving'), it was one of
Paul's. If it was autobiographical, and made a pungent
personal statement ('In My Life', 'Norwegian Wood'), it
was John's.

It was certainly music, rather than their contrasting
personalities, that drew John and Paul together. Although
John had established that he, as a Libran, was theoretically
supposed to get on well with Paul, a Gemini, they were
poles apart in personality and temperament. That difference
extended deeply into their musical collaboration, with great
mutual benefits.

Or so it seemed. In reality, both men were utter contra-
dictions. Lennon's apparent toughness was always a complete cover-up. He was a complex man who seemed afraid
to let his inner self be seen. The hard front was without a
shred of doubt a screen for the real, tender man of which
there were hundreds of examples, particularly when the
Beatles split.

McCartney, conversely, came across during the Beatles
years as the Beatle who melted most girls' hearts, with his
big brown eyes and his songs of unashamed love. On the
surface, he was the suave, smooth, debonair romantic. This
misconception paralleled the inaccurate theory that John
was tough. In fact, McCartney was always the tougher of
the two. He totally outstripped John when it came to
business acumen, planning his life with a fine eye for detail
that later made him popular music's richest man.

From the moment the Beatles went to London and
marshalled their raw talent as musicians and songwriters
into tunes the world could whistle, one man stood beside
them in what at first seemed an incongruous partnership.
John, in particular, had always made blistering remarks
about 'the men in suits'. Yet when it came to associating
the Beatles with them, he would always say that the end

would justify the means. John always said he wanted to be rich and famous – particularly rich. Brian Epstein was attractive because his respectability seemed a good bet to get them a record contract, John and Paul's most cherished ambition.

The man who eventually came to be linked with the Beatles as their record producer, and forge a unique bond with them at a critically formative peak in their lives, was George Martin. He wore a suit and a tie. He was a staff producer at the giant EMI Records and recorded classical music, jazz, pop, and particularly comedy by such artists as Peter Sellers, Bernard Cribbins, Spike Milligan, and Flanders and Swann.

Heard today, 'Love Me Do' is simple, catchy, earthy – a natural debut sound from the Beatles as we grew to love and understand their music. But at the time George Martin was unimpressed. 'To begin with, they gave me very few songs,' says Martin. 'Love Me Do' had been written by Paul when he was sixteen, with John contributing to the middle. 'That was the best of the stuff they had, and I thought it pretty poor,' says Martin. 'I offered them "How Do You Do It" as their first song (later this became a number one hit for Gerry and the Pacemakers) although this was not written by them. They didn't fancy it and we pressed on with "Love Me Do". But they learned very quickly after that and when they got the success of "Please Please Me" under their belt they were fired by it, and from then on everything they brought me was pure gold.' 'Please Please Me' was written totally by John; he later told me that he was imitating the falsetto sound of American singer Roy Orbison. The haunting harmonica sound by John on 'Love Me Do' was inspired by the record 'Hey Baby' by US singer Bruce Channel. The harmonica player on the disc whose style Lennon admired was Delbert McClinton.

Success came so rapidly to John and Paul, and their creativity flowered so speedily as a result, that George Martin's role as a catalyst became a joy to him. George believes that rivalry, rather than competitiveness, was the key to their mutual respect. A spark of tension, each songwriter wondering what the other would do or say next, gave them both a thrusting edge. 'It was like a tug of war,' says Martin.

'In the studio, their rivalry was based purely on friendship. They had a very close relationship because in many ways they were incredibly similar. Some people accentuated the differences between them — John being the acrid, bitter one and Paul the soft one. That was basically an image built up by the press.

'The truth is that deep down they were very, very similar indeed. Each had a soft underbelly, each was very much hurt by certain things. John had a very soft side to him. But you see, each had a bitter turn of phrase and could be quite nasty to the other, which each one expected at certain times.

'They did love each other very much throughout the time I knew them in the studio. But the tension was there mostly because they never really collaborated. They were never Rodgers and Hart. They were always songwriters who helped each other out with little bits and pieces. One would have most of a song finished, play it to the other, and he'd say: "Well, why don't you do this?" That was just about the way their collaboration worked.' Gradually, as they were always individual songwriters, they became positively solo operators as success led them on.

'Imagine two people pulling on a rope, smiling at each other and pulling all the time with all their might. The tension between the two of them made for the bond.

'John was such a creative thinker, one notch higher than most,' says Dick James, the man whom Epstein turned to on his arrival in London, and who became the publisher of the Beatles' songs. 'He had more sensitivity. John *had* to be cynical, because he was very vulnerable and could hurt very easily, and so he surrounded himself with this cynical crust. He was very difficult, particularly later in his career.'

Dick James had the unique position of hearing all the Beatles' early work before it went on record. 'To this day,' he says, 'my office receives tapes from groups who are trying to sound uncannily like Paul or John, as lead singer, with the same kind of appeal. But the original model was so special. I could hardly believe my ears when Brain Epstein would come into my office and play me the next song.

' "What do you think, Jamesy?" John would say.

'And right after "Please Please Me", I'd have to say: "Dare I say it, John and Paul? Another number one." '

In 1963 James borrowed £10,000 and handed it to Brian Epstein as an 'advance' on their royalties. 'It's usually six to eight months before the initial income comes in from world sales. The boys were in debt to Brian, who had given them eating money. They couldn't believe the figures we were talking about. They'd been in poverty street. I hadn't known them then, but I did know the song publishing world and knew they would be earning a lot of money. I had to borrow the money for them against that first number one, "Please Please Me". I had no trouble getting the cash. I knew it was a winning investment'.

As a veteran of the old school of songwriters, Dick James looked on the new school of beat musicians led by the Beatles with a critical ear. 'If the songs came around today, brand new, they'd still be world-wide smashes. The quality was amazing. I could not believe what I was hearing. It was the perfect entertainment machine: John, Paul, marvellous songwriters, George a splendid musician, Ringo a wonderful drummer for them, and a foil.'

His outstanding memory of John was of 'a great stub-bornness which was essential to them in their early days. His contribution to the Beatles' success was definitely equal to Paul's, not one iota less.' Lennon looked on James as an amiable benevolent uncle. It was a view that was to change in 1969 when a business clash divided John and Dick. 'But when we went public with Northern Songs in 1965, I said to John: "The songs will go on earning money well into the next century."

'He smiled. "Good on yer, Jamesy." '

Visitors to London's Abbey Road number two studio during Beatles recording sessions could not be aware that pop music history was being made. A Liverpool group, bucking the trends of the time (Cliff Richard, traditional jazz, and Chubby Checker's big Twist craze), did not represent an overnight phenomenon at the recording studios. Martin, tall, angular, punctilious, was an easy target for the Beatles' quicksilver raw sense of humour. And so because of that they would rarely tease him. They respected him and enjoyed his straightforwardness and particularly his expertise.

As the linchpins for the group, writing hit after hit, John and Paul had a special relationship with George Martin. It began as record producer and young pop stars and then developed into that of a wise uncle, and eventually to friendship. But when their popularity began moving swiftly upwards, a marked difference became apparent in John and Paul's make-up.

Typically John would want to move from song to song in a hurry. He would be involved in a song for only as long as it took to get it recorded satisfactorily. Then he was on to the next. McCartney took a different, more thorough attitude. Later, Paul's persistence in worrying a session to death, until one of his songs had been drained dry of every possibility and permutation, irritated John.

John nursed an inner grievance that McCartney's songs got more studio attention and finishing touches than his. 'That's probably true,' Martin reflects, 'but that's because Paul was more interested. John's irritation was a little unfair. John's songs got a great deal of attention, but possibly what he meant was that they never got the attention to detail that he thought they needed. So they didn't quite work out the way he wanted them. But they worked out the way I wanted them.

'Maybe I thought my communication was pretty good in getting inside his brain and finding out what he wanted. He would always say: "Yes great, lovely, OK, fine," at the playbacks. But only later did he tell people he'd never been really happy with anything he'd written.

'Some of John's works we recorded in the Beatles days were some of the best stuff I've ever heard, so it's a matter of opinion.' As he outgrew the early Beatles, John asserted that Martin was 'always more like a Paul McCartney producer than for my music.'

John's reputation as the most intelligent Beatle with literary aspirations was firmly established by 1964. Each one of the four was quick-witted, but none of the other three matched Lennon's perception and lucidity. Only in the recording studios, with Paul's melodic strengths and eagerness to discover every twitch of every switch, was there any contest. That was because John's restlessness to move on to the next song differed from Paul's need to get the current work meticulously right. That year, George Martin released his own orchestral album of Beatles hits. Despite Martin's natural affinity with McCartney, his album featured a commercially powerful sleeve note written by John which allowed Lennon to hark back in dry literary style to his satirical *Mersey Beat* newspaper ramblings. He wrote:

George Martin is a tall man. He is also a musician with short hair. In spite of this he records rock groups such as (Beatles, Billy J. Kramer, Gerry and the Pacemakers) to name four, and has earned the respect of everyone in the business (what business you might well ask). We all owe a great deal of our success to George, especially for his patient guidance of our enthusiasm in the right directions (it was a patient George Martin who, on one of our early sessions, explained to a puzzled Ringo that it was a bit much playing a full drum kit, tambourine and maracas at the same time).

Us Beatles are genuinely flattered that a 'real musician' as we call him should turn his talents to arranging an LP of our songs, considering that he has previously worked with such great artists as Peter Sellers, Shirley Bassey, Jimmy Shand and a machine that sings 'Daisy Daisy'. Some of the sounds on the album may be new to you (and me), that's 'cause George has a great habit of matching unlikely instruments together (like a Jew's harp and a twelve-stringed finger) but the results are great and I think he should get a raise. So plug yourselves in and listen.

P.S. Please tell all your friends to buy it too, so George can be rich and famous – after all why not?

> Good George Martin is our friend
> Buddy Pal and Mate
> Buy this record and he'll send
> A dog for your front gate

> Chorus: With an arf arf here
> And an arf arf there, etc.

Sung to the tune of Old Macdonald Had An Arm by
the Beatles a band.

Martin felt the sharp end of Lennon's tongue when John
went to New York and publicly attacked old friends like
Derek Taylor and George Martin, for, as he implied, having
too big an idea of their own importance. Lennon snapped
his frequent jibe that nobody made the Beatles, the Beatles
made themselves. It was always true . . . but this time he
chose old pals like Martin and Taylor as his targets. They
were deeply hurt.

When the Beatles split, John adopted a fiercely defensive stance on behalf of his old group. It seemed that
only he, or the other three, were allowed to damn the
achievements, particularly, of the Beatles. John's comment
about George was: 'Who does he think he is, anyway?
What songs has he ever written?' But Martin remembers
going for dinner with John in Los Angeles in 1973 and,
typically, John apologized for his outburst which had
embarrassed Martin. 'I'm sorry George,' John said. 'I didn't
really mean those things about you and all the others. I
was smashed out of my mind when I was speaking.'

The difference inside the studios between John and Paul
was obvious to George from the start. 'Paul would sit down
and ask what I planned to do with his songs, every note
virtually. "What do you think the cellos should be doing
here, George?" and I'd have to describe to him on the piano
what it would be. He'd say: "Yeah. OK, but what about
changing that note?" Lots of the arrangements to his songs
were very much his ideas which I would have to implement.

'John would be more vague in what he wanted. He

would talk in metaphors about his ideas. I'd have to get inside his brain to find out what he wanted. It would be more of a psychological approach. He'd say – for example, on "Being For The Benefit Of Mr Kite!" – "This song's about a fairground. A little bit mystified. I want to get the feeling of the sawdust and the feel of the ring. Can you do something about it?" I'd then have to think how that imagery could be transformed into sound. The difference between John and Paul, fundamentally, was that Paul would want to know *how* I was going to go about achieving what he wanted. John couldn't care less. He just wanted the result.

'On "Strawberry Fields Forever", we did one track and he said: "Well, I like it but it's worked out much harder than I thought it would be. I'd like you to do a score and maybe use a few cellos and a bit of brass." That was it.'

Another odd clash of opinion between Lennon and Martin occurred from the start of the Beatles' success. John's singing voice – leathery, raw, lung-bursting on their anthems like 'Twist And Shout' and 'Money' – was a stark contrast with Paul's melodic qualities. But John had that distinctive, lived-in, untrained hardness in his voice. It made him stand out; it was the voice of a new breed of rock 'n' roll guitarist who couldn't give a damn. There was nothing crude about it, but it was the voice of someone who had lived, despite his youth. John was genuinely bashful about his voice. I remember telling him how much I liked it on one particular track. 'You Can't Do That', and he was astonished that anyone should single out his vocal work for any praise. 'You really mean it?' he asked incredulously. 'I can't say I ever liked hearing myself.'

The nagging self-doubts about his vocal abilities were to manifest themselves into a considerable issue with George Martin. 'John was a great admirer of Elvis Presley's early records, particularly the "Heartbreak Hotel" kind of sound.

He also had an inborn dislike of his own voice which I could never understand, as it was one of the best voices I've heard,' recalls Martin.

'He was always saying to me: "*DO* something with my voice! You know, put something on it. Smother it with tomato ketchup or something. Make it *different.*" And he was obsessed with tape delay. In technical terms, it's only a delay of about thirty milliseconds which gives you that kind of effect John sought, a sort of very near-echo which he used a lot when he made his own records. I used to do other things to him, and as long as it wasn't his natural voice coming through, he was reasonably happy. But he'd always want his vocals to get special treatment.

'On "Tomorrow Never Knows", he wanted to sound like a Dalai Lama singing on a hilltop. He actually said to me: "That's the kind of sound I need." So I put his voice through a loudspeaker and rotated it. It actually did come out as that strangled sort of cry from the hillside.

'He simply always wanted to distort his voice. But I wanted to hear it in its own natural quality. So after he left me, he did all his own distortion to his heart's content. And I didn't like that — after all, the raw material was so good.'

Martin looks on John's work after the Beatles split with mixed feelings: 'There were lots of things I didn't like about them and that I would have done differently. My favourite song of all was "Imagine" and that was a great album – I loved that. Some of the stuff he did on that was pure magic. I'd like to have produced that.'

Conversely, Martin was disappointed with John's final album, *Double Fantasy.* 'He hadn't been in the studios for a long time, and it shows. It's not vintage Lennon, not the greatest stuff he ever did.'

And to the question that concerns Beatles students

throughout the world – who was the more important to the group, Lennon or McCartney? – Martin reflects: 'I'm a melody man rather than a lyric man, being a musician and not a lyric writer. My brain accommodates music much more easily than it does words. Paul's melodies and his harmonic structures appealed to me more than John's because John's melodies and his music were tailor-made to fit his words rather than the other way round. The lyrics would lead and develop John's songs. He would write one verse and the music was already there once the words told him the way the line would go.

'As for comparing their value to the Beatles, it's impossible. It's like asking what's the most important constituent in a sauce vinaigrette, the oil or the vinegar. Both were fundamentally important: one without the other would have been unthinkable in terms of the Beatles' success.

'It's quite likely that, in terms of success, Paul's songs will last longer than John's because they get more to the average man, to the heart strings, than John's did. That's being really commercial about it. But I couldn't put a cigarette paper between them.'

On a British concert tour in 1964, I interviewed John specifically about his attitude to his guitar. Asked if he ever practised, he laughed and took another drag on his cigarette, 'I never *did* practice! I only ever wanted to learn to play to back myself. In the early days, we all used to sing. Originally, I'd do one, then Paul'd do one, then George and so on. So you didn't need to be a genius of a guitarist to back yourself.'

Did he find it a handicap, not being able to read music? 'It's not essential for what I'm doing. No, I've never found it a handicap. These dance bands that play pop on the BBC radio programmes – they sound all right at *that* because they can read it off music sheets. But have you heard some of them trying to play rock? It's rotten!

'If I wanted to read music I'd have to pack all this in and start from scratch. Sometimes I think I'd like to, but I'm a cheat. I can't play finger style. I just manage to do something that makes it sound like I can. I started with a banjo when I was fifteen, when my mother taught me some banjo chords. She could play it pretty good. When I was young, I played the guitar like a banjo, with the sixth string hanging loose! I always thought Lonnie and Elvis were the greatest and all I ever wanted to do was vamp. I got some banjo things off OK, then George and Paul came along and taught me other things.'

Asked why he took to the guitar, he told me: 'Oh, the usual kid's desire to get up on stage, I suppose. And my mother was a big encouragement. She said she could play any stringed instrument and was able to give me the first ideas.'

Of his musical role within the Beatles, John, who was officially described as rhythm guitarist, said: 'The job of the normal group rhythm guitarist is to back the solo guitarist like the left hand does on a piano. Unless the lead guitarist is very good and can back himself like the finger-style guitarists can, he needs someone else to help fill out. Most of our stuff in the early days was twelve-bar stuff. I'd play boogie and George and would play lead. I'd vamp like Bruce Welch [of the Shadows] does, in that style of rhythm.

'We always have someone playing rhythm in the set style all the time, although it's too thin for records so we just both go full-out.

'I'd find it a drag to play rhythm all the time so I always work myself out something interesting to play. The best example I can think of is like I did on "You Can't Do

That". There wasn't really a lead guitarist and a rhythm guitarist on that because I feel that the rhythm guitarist role sounds too thin for records. Anyway, it'd drive me potty to play chunk-chunk rhythm all the time. I never play anything as lead guitarist that George couldn't do better. But I like playing lead sometimes, so I do it.'

Of his songwriting tactics, he said: 'When Paul and I started writing stuff, we did it in the key of A because we thought that was the key Buddy Holly did all his songs in. Holly was a big thing then, an inspiration, sort of. Anyway, later on I found out he played in C and other keys but it was too late and it didn't worry us anyway. It all sounded OK in A so that's the way we played our stuff. Oh yeah, we keep up with all the keys – C, D, G, F (joking) but we keep out of B flat and that. It doesn't give you an artistic sound. Heh Heh!'

John Lennon was an addicted rock 'n' roll *fan*, just like the teenage Paul Simon or Bruce Springsteen and thousands of other musicians for whom it was a force as tribal as it was musical. All were mesmerized by Elvis Presley, who brought colour and meaning into their lives. Rock 'n' roll was the foundation for Lennon. The ensuing years may have seen him stray into strange unconnected territories; may have seen him put his head on the chopping block of public scorn and ridicule, but right to the end Lennon stayed true to the *idea* of rock 'n' roll. On record and in print, Lennon was moved to the core, and that music still had ability and power throughout his life, even when it was obvious that the music he was making far transcended in impact and quality the music that inspired him. 'There is nothing conceptually better than rock 'n' roll,' he said. 'No group, Beatles, Dylan, or Stones, have ever improved on "Whole

Lotta Shakin" ' for my money, or maybe I'm like our parents: that's my period and I dig it, and I'll never leave it.'

When 'Heartbreak Hotel' floated across the Radio Luxembourg airwaves into Mendips, John Lennon succumbed and was forever lost. 'When I heard it, I dropped everything!' Elvis across the ether was followed by dozens more, each as glamorous, raucous, and liberating – Buddy Holly, Jerry Lee Lewis, Gene Vincent, Little Richard, Lloyd Price, Chuck Berry, Eddie Cochran, Larry Williams. That music, those performances, made real the world that had been glimpsed in the movies. Part of the appeal of rock 'n' roll was its remoteness, which helped created a code amongst the young English audience. The terms used were alien, but the emotions were direct. In a whole generation of English teenagers, those raw emotions touched a chord.

Lennon's first group, the Quarry Men, was formed with school mates and everybody mucking in for fun. The gigs were standard for the time – working men's clubs, club dates, ballrooms, and fortuitously, village fêtes. Rock 'n' roll was for (and by) the young. Rock 'n' roll was for NOW! Lennon remembered the time: 'As kids we were all opposed to folk songs, because they were so middle-class. It was all college students with big scarves and a pint of beer in their hands, singing folk songs in what we called la-di-da voices. When I started, rock 'n' roll was the basic revolution of people of my age and situation.' That revolutionary aspect obviously appealed to the rebellious Lennon. Before – so the cliché ran – the only way out was through crime or boxing. Now there was a third, more glamorous, alternative – music. It meant you could get girls, get drunk, and get somewhere. That early, classic rock 'n' roll was raw and primitive; it could be learned, if you practised, which was

boring, or if someone taught you. That was the sound that
John Lennon wanted George Martin to record.

Years later, Lennon could remember with great accuracy
and affection the music that so moved him as a restless
teenager: ' "Long Tall Sally" – when I first heard it, it was
so great, I couldn't speak! "Bony Moronie" – I remember
singing it the only time my mother saw me perform before
she died. "Ain't That A Shame" – the first rock 'n' roll
song I ever learned. My mother taught it to me on the
banjo before I learned the guitar. "Whole Lotta Shakin" ' –
I like the take he did in 1956, on the record. I'm not
interested in the variation of the theme . . . I'm a record
fan . . . Those are the records I dug then, I dig them now,
and I'm still trying to reproduce "Some Other Guy" or
"Be-Bop-A-Lula".'

Thrown together in Liverpool and Hamburg, Lennon
and McCartney collaborated, bolstering each other, goading
each other to reach new heights. Such was their diversity,
they could assimilate virtually any style into their songwriting; the lyrical dexterity of Leiber and Stoller, the touching
teen pains of Goffin and King, the hiccuping sensitivity of
Buddy Holly. The evidence of the earliest Beatles recordings
demonstrates Lennon tearing into such rock classics as 'Ain't
She Sweet', 'Memphis', 'Money', and 'Sweet Little Sixteen'.
Even early on in their career, the Beatles were typecast –
Paul was cute and John was hard. Like all clichés, there
was an element of truth in it, but Paul was also capable of
whipping up a storm on rock standards, and John proved
he could be a sensitive performer handling ballads.

For fans tired of the saccharine sweetness of British and
American pop, tired of the manufactured idols, they found
something raw and refreshing in the Beatles' performances.
There was a healthy irreverence in Lennon's crashing about
the stage, cajoling and insulting the audiences. They poured

their hearts into the music, sweating it out night after night, playing from dawn to dusk, with an astonishing turnover of music. The music came from diverse sources – show tunes like 'Besame Mucho', 'Falling In Love Again', 'Till There Was You', the first tentative performances of their own songs, 'I Saw Her Standing There', and 'Ask Me Why', classic rockers like 'Twist And Shout', 'Honey, Don't', and contemporary hits like Joe Brown's 'A Picture Of You'. These marathon sessions proved invaluable in shaping the Beatles' music. It gave them an edge and a variety their contemporaries never matched. While the pop world sank in the quicksand of mediocrity, and Elvis went missing in trashy Hollywood films like *Blue Hawaii*, the Beatles kept a flame burning for the music that had so moved them as teenagers.

The earliest known live recordings of the Beatles available on disc was recorded by Ted 'Kingsize' Taylor, at the Star-Club in Hamburg at the end of 1962. Despite the dreadful sound quality, they make great listening and provide a fascinating insight into the roots of the Beatles' music. Recorded during one of those marathon sessions, the group are ragged and committed, tearing into their songs, young and full of fervour, determined to rattle the walls. It was that musical baptism, forged in Hamburg and honed in Liverpool, that gave the Beatles their musical edge. But, tellingly, one of the reasons the Beatles came out ahead of Faron's Flamingoes, Rory Storm, and Gerry and the Pacemakers – all of whom paid their musical dues in Hamburg – was that they had their own two songwriters, and didn't have to go on endlessly pillaging the familiar pool of material which all the Mersey beat groups used.

The evidence contained on the album of the Beatles' Decca audition displays just how Brian Epstein had cleaned the group up (and how he was thinking of 'the end of the

pier show' as the ultimate ambition). The Beatles sound
stilted and uncomfortable as they meander through 'The
Sheik Of Araby' and 'To Know Her Is To Love Her'. Their
collective studio knowledge was minimal. Aside from some
Quarry Men demonstration recordings of the late 1950s,
the Beatles' inauguration in recording took place in Hamburg. John, Paul, and George cut 'Fever', 'September Song',
and 'Summertime', in a Record-Your-Voice booth at the
back of Hamburg Railway Station in 1960. They were
backing a singer called Wally – Lou Walters – from Rory
Storm's group, the Hurricanes. Rory's drummer, Ringo
Starr, also sat in on the impromptu session, two years before
he joined the Beatles.

The best-known pre-Parlophone recordings were with
the Hamburg-based singer Tony Sheridan in May 1961. The
subsequent album (issued long after their initial success) is
of historic interest, featuring a raucous Lennon vocal on
'Ain't She Sweet', and the only known Harrison-Lennon
collaboration on the instrumental 'Cry For A Shadow'. But
it took those sessions to bring the Beatles to Brian Epstein's
attention. The Sheridan/Beatles version of 'My Bonnie' was
a moderate chart success in Germany.

By the time the Beatles arrived at Parlophone in 1962,
they were pretty near the bottom of the pile. Decca turned
them down in favour of Brian Poole and the Tremeloes,
because they were more accessibly based in Dagenham. It
took the intuitive sympathy and knowledge of house producer George Martin to realize the Beatles' sound fully and
coalesce it on record.

Those early Parlophone sessions harnessed the Beatles'
enthusiasm and Martin's studio mastery – a combination
which was to prove unbeatable over the next seven years.
Parlophone was always regarded as a joke by EMI, its parent
company. But by working closely together, Martin and the

Beatles came together. They respected his innate musical pedigree, and he saw their strengths as lying in their harmonies, and the fact that they wrote their own material – with strong views on how it should be recorded – rather than accepting their manager's hand-me-downs. The fruits of that collaboration were first seen on 5 October 1962, when the Beatles' first single, 'Love Me Do', was released.

It eventually reached a healthy number seventeen on the British charts (in competition with the perennial Cliff Richard and 'Bachelor Boy' and Little Eva's 'The Loco-Motion').

It was the release of the second single, 'Please Please Me', in early 1963, that really established the group. It's hard to imagine the effect it had on the record-buying public. Initially Lennon's harmonica was the novelty that drew the casual listener in. The prominent guitars and driving rhythm were emphasized by the rudimentary harmonies. Hearing it again now, what still strikes the listener is the Englishness of the vocals. Until then, English pop stars adopted mid-Atlantic accents, or went for stage Cockney like Anthony Newley. The Beatles made no effort to disguise their Liverpudlian origins, even if the vocal mannerisms were American. 'Please Please Me' was a Lennon original: 'I remember the pink eyelet down over the bed, sitting in one of the bedrooms in my aunt's house on Menlove Avenue. I heard Roy Orbison doing "Only The Lonely" on the radio. I was intrigued by the double use of the word "please" in a Bing Crosby song. So it was a combination of Bing Crosby and Roy Orbison.'

As a writer, Lennon was a great one for plucking individual lines or phrases from other songs and expanding them into his own material. 'Run For Your Life' came from Elvis's 'Baby Let's Play House'; 'Do You Want To Know A Secret?' was a line from *Snow White And The Seven Dwarfs*;

'I'll Be Back' was based on a chord variation from a Del Shannon song.

The infectious 'From Me To You' repeated the Beatles' hit formula and went to number one in May 1963. But by then the Beatles had proved their merit on album. *Please Please Me* was released in March and proved remarkable in a number of ways – there were eight Lennon-McCartney originals, a remarkable achievement in those days of manufactured product. Either hit songs came from established shows, or writers were chosen by a manager, or, more likely, British pop songs were innocuous covers of American hits. To write and perform your own material was revolutionary and threatened the Tin Pan Alley stranglehold.

The bulk of material on the Beatles' debut album encapsulated their influences to date. Much of the original material was jointly written while touring Britain, on the long coach journeys up and down the newly opened motorways. 'I Saw Her Standing There', though, was a composition John and Paul knocked off in Paul's front room, playing truant from school. Of equal interest, though, were the cover versions. Instead of going for the obvious versions of Elvis or Pat Boone hits, the Beatles chose obscure songs that they admired – the Shirelles and the Cookies were not names English audiences were too familiar with. 'Twist and Shout' had been a hit in America for the Isley Brothers and was written by Bert Russell and Phil Medley.

It is to George Martin's credit that, in an eleven-hour spurt, he managed to capture the verve and enthusiasm of the Beatles on record. But the vigour sprang from *them*. As writers and performers, the Beatles obviously had something fresh to offer a jaded public. Lennon is seen and heard as a sensitive interpreter on that first album, notably on 'Ask Me Why' and 'Anna' (written by Arthur Alexander, who also wrote the Stones' 'You Better Move On' and Ry

Cooder's 'Go Home Girl'). Lennon also sounds plaintive on 'There's A Place', a place where he can go, when he feels low. Conversely, his manic version of 'Twist And Shout', which closes the album, recalls the ardent rocker from the Cavern. Nothing that demented had been heard on record since 'Hound Dog'.

It was that hard side which the world saw in Lennon – the hard rocker, embittered by his mother's early death and his father's desertion, his own belief in himself, his inability to display a softer side. Lennon was painted the hard man of the Beatles.

Despite the typecasting – the 'hard' Lennon and the 'soft' McCartney – it helped give their partnership a balance which was crucial. Their individual writing efforts were born out of a desire to prove themselves, out of individual insecurity. Once they gained confidence in themselves, they grew apart, but there was still that question of balance. They sparked each other off, and even if it was only altering a word, suggesting a title, Lennon and McCartney could, and did, inspire each other. That balance saw them through the hysteria. They couldn't go out, so they stayed in, and – among other things – wrote songs. That partnership lasted a long time and only grew irrevocably apart when they found other partners.

With their second album, Lennon and McCartney were already being called 'the outstanding English composers of 1963' and William Mann of *The Times* singled out 'the Aeolian cadence at the end of "Not A Second Time" ' (the chord progression that ends Mahler's *Song Of The Earth*). Lennon said he thought 'Aeolian cadences were some sort of exotic birds!' William Mann's eulogy, which finally set the seal on the Beatles as being more than 'just another pop group', is of interest for his comments on the group's early impact. Leaving aside the 'pandiatonic clusters' and 'melismas with altered vowels', he does make a number of interesting points: 'For several decades in fact, since the decline of the music hall, England has taken her popular songs from the United States, either directly, or by mimicry. But the songs of Lennon and McCartney are distinctly indigenous in character.' Mann went on to cite 'the exhilarating and often quasi-instrumental dueting' and the 'discreet, and sometimes subtle, varieties of instrumentation', which led him to conclude: 'These are some of the qualities that make one wonder with interest what the Beatles and particularly Lennon and McCartney, will do next, and if America will spoil them or hold on to them, and if their next record will wear as well as the others.' If only he had known; if only *they* had known.

With the Beatles had been preceded by the fourth Beatles single, 'She Loves You', which established them as *the* British showbiz phenomenon. The song became an anthem, which helped a nation 'yeah, yeah, yeah' its way into 'the swinging sixties'. Lennon remembered that crucial song thus: ' "She Loves You" was written by the two of us together. I remember it was Paul's idea. Instead of singing I love you, again, Paul decided we would have a third party passing by and latch on to something else . . . the woo-woo was taken from the Isley Brothers' "Twist And Shout". We stuck it in everything – thinking when Elvis did "All Shook Up", that was the first time I heard "uh huh", "oh yeah", and "yeah yeah" all in the same song.'

By the end of 1963 it was apparent to everyone in Britain that the Beatles were more than just a pop group about to be usurped by the Dave Clark Five. There were invitations to perform before royalty, eulogies in the press, and hysteria at their every appearance. But they were still judged by their music. *With the Beatles* (released on the day of President Kennedy's assassination) again dipped back to the Hamburg days ('Roll Over Beethoven', 'Till There Was You'), and, despite the prolific Lennon-McCartney partnership, the album contained six cover versions. But this time, drawing heavily on the contemporary music sound of black America – 'Please Mister Postman', 'Money', and 'You Really Got A Hold On Me', all emanated from the burgeoning Tamla Motown. Here was the 'hard side' of Lennon, screaming 'Money', and 'It Won't Be Long', while Paul opted for the softer 'All My Loving' and 'Till There Was You'. With George Martin drafted in as ancillary pianist, the Beatles made their first tentative steps to expanding their group sound in the studio.

From *With the Beatles* on, things started getting crazy: 'I Want To Hold Your Hand' sold twelve million copies. There was the first American tour, their first film, endless concerts. Brian Epstein still saw touring as the logical step to ensure that the cash came in, and that the Beatles' name was kept in the public eye. Who could blame him? There had never been any precedent on how to handle a phenomenon such as the Beatles. Touring kept John and Paul together, and in the interminable gaps between shows and venues they stared out of their cocooned existence and wrote. Fragments, images, and catch-phrases cropped up in their songs. Hermetically sealed, they poured their energies into their songs. Creatively, those rigorous years of touring paid off.

A Hard Day's Night was the first album consisting solely of Lennon-McCartney originals. Composed during their visits to France and America, and when filming in England, the finished album reflected a remarkable variety and assurance. Remarkable too was the intensity of the partnership. Consider the pressure they were under from the moment Beatlemania broke at the end of 1963, and indeed the pressures which lasted until the end of touring in 1966 –

the Beatles were expected to undertake at least two major tours and come up with three original singles, two albums of original material, plus TV and film work. It is an itinerary that would make many of today's pampered groups blink with disbelief. What makes the Beatles' achievements so astounding is not only the quantity, but more important, the *quality*, of their music those years inside the bubble.

Once the hysteria began, the Beatles' performances became little more than a charade. They *were* a fine live band, as evidenced by *The Beatles Live at the Hollywood Bowl*. The album of those 1964–65 concerts was only released, finally, in 1977, at the height of the punk explosion. What comes across from those recordings is how good they still sounded. Given that there were no feedback monitors, so they couldn't hear themselves play, nothing could beat the persistent, cacophonous screaming. The Beatles still sounded hungry, angry! It is a testament to their musical inventiveness and ability. The studio recordings are the ultimate proof, but contained on *The Beatles Live at the Hollywood Bowl* is the proof that there was a certain chemistry, or *magic*, which sustained them.

Concerts by then offered fans little more than an opportunity to see the gods made mortal. There were the constant problems of security, isolation, and safety. Then there was the music. Within a year, the Beatles had found themselves elevated from a 'beat group phenomenon' to an international showbiz institution. It was a double-edged sword, and one which Lennon particularly resented. He told *Rolling Stone* magazine editor Jann Wenner, in 1970: 'Brian put us in suits and all that, and we made it very, very big. But we sold out, you know, the music was dead before we even went to the first theatre tour of Britain. We were feeling shit already, because we had to reduce an hour or two hours' playing, which we were glad about in one way, to twenty minutes, and we would go on and repeat the same twenty minutes every night. The Beatles died then as musicians . . . because in spite of all the things, the Beatles could really play music together.' The Beatles had, after all, only set out to make it 'bigger than Elvis'. Within months, they had already achieved that. And after that, where else was there to go?

Lennon found the whole thing developing into a macabre charade, which was, inevitably, reflected in his music, the only place where he could relax, create, and be himself. Listening to the album of *A Hard Day's Night*, one is struck by the aching cries for help and the feelings of isolation. Here he was, the idol of millions, one of the world's most eligible men, an acclaimed author and composer; but in his songs you find introverted sentiments, and feelings of great sadness and lost innocence. That innate sadness was, of course, buried beneath the ebullient high quality of the Beatles' music. By the time of *A Hard Day's Night*, Beatles fans, like Lennon himself, only listened to the *sound* of the record. The lyrics, if they made any impact at all, were simply the choruses the fans could memorize and sing along with.

'Tell Me Why' is full of tears, lies, moans, apologies, pleas: 'I'll Cry Instead' has tears and loss, 'a chip on my shoulder that's bigger than my feet'; 'Any Time At All' cries for a response, begs a friendly response. 'I've got no time for trivialities,' sang Lennon on 'When I Get Home'. The public and the private Lennon merged on *A Hard Day's Night*.

Lennon's musical experiments were encouraged by George Martin and the other three Beatles, notably the first recorded use of feedback on 1964's 'I Feel Fine'. Lennon had a small studio at Kenwood, where he tinkered with tape recorders and fragments of songs, the results of which would manifest themselves the following year. But the greatest impact on Lennon's music during those crazy Beatlemania years was made from the only man who could be said to have rivalled the group in terms of influence – Bob Dylan.

During the early and mid-1960s, Bob Dylan gave pop music a voice. His songs had lyrics of personal and political relevance – even his early love songs were bitter and aching, hardly the fodder for unthinking pop fans. But Dylan swiftly found an audience and articulated their dissatisfaction and compassion in striking, vivid images. Dylan was now tiring of his typecasting as 'spokesman for a generation'. From adolescence he'd been a fervent rock 'n' roller. His high school ambition, he said, had been 'to join Little Richard.' When Dylan heard the Animals' electric reworking of the traditional 'House Of The Rising Sun', and the Beatles' 'I Want To Hold Your Hand' in 1964, it helped him decide which direction his music was to take. The British invasion was a prime force in making Dylan switch to 'folk-rock', with his devastating *Bringing It All Back Home* and *Highway 61 Revisited* albums of 1965.

Dylan first met the Beatles on their first American tour in 1964 and turned them on to marijuana, but made a more permanent impact in shaping their musical direction. Latterly, Lennon denied Dylan's influence on the group, saying he never listened to anything after the seminal 1965 albums, and was quoted as saying: 'I remember the early meetings with Dylan, he was always saying "Listen to the words, man" and I said "I can't be bothered. I listen to the sound of it, the overall sound." ' Lennon did admit, though, that, like so many others, Dylan helped him think for himself and inject more honesty into his own lyrics. The two did enjoy a sporadic friendship. Lennon appears in the rarely seen *Eat the Document*, a surreal account of Dylan's controversial 1966 British tour.

Dylan's achievements then became Lennon's goal, an attempt to marry the power of rock 'n' roll to lyrics of some substantiality. The Dylan influence first manifested itself on the Beatles' fourth album, *Beatles For Sale*. Derek Taylor's sleeve notes announced that the album was 'straightforward 1964 disc-making . . . there is little or nothing on the album which cannot be reproduced on stage!' Such jolliness disguised the intensity with which Lennon approached the album. *Beatles For Sale* displayed the bleaker side of the Lennon persona. 'No Reply', 'I'm A Loser', and 'Baby's In Black' formed a pretty bleak trilogy to open an album by the Fabs at the height of their power.

'No Reply' opens with the jaundiced 'This happened once before'; it is a song that bitterly sifts through the embers of a dying relationship, symbolized by the failure to communicate. The song is conveyed by a particularly lugubrious Lennon vocal, a dispirited opening to an album that was meant to celebrate *triumph*. On 'I'm A Loser', the title says it all, and Lennon's singing is suitably atmospheric as the song traces the disintegration of a love affair. It may not match Dylan's searing sense of loneliness or loss evoked by his contemporary 'Boots Of Spanish Leather' or 'Ballad In Plain D', but it was an attempt to inject some honesty and genuine emotion into the fairytale world of the Beatles.

Similarly, while never reaching Dylan's heights of absurdity or depths of despair, Lennon's couplet 'Although I laugh and act like a clown/Beneath this mask I am wearing a frown' seemed an ironic comment coming from a man with the world at his feet. 'Baby's In Black' continues in the Dylan vein, another splint to help bolster up a shattered soul: 'Baby's in black and I'm feeling blue.' He was juggling with dark colours, but questioning, probing, pleading, rather than celebrating.

Hindsight reveals the internal friction in the group by then, which subsequently led to open antipathy. Lennon's character was always the rebel, the cynic, and he was the one to express his dissatisfaction most forcefully. As he admitted in a *Playboy* magazine interview: 'I was always like that, you know. I was like that before the Beatles, I always asked why people did things and why society was like it was. I didn't just accept it for what it was apparently doing. I always looked below the surface.' The overt politic- izing didn't come till much later, but Lennon was keen to avoid the showbiz stereotypes: 'We don't want to learn to tap dance or take elocution lessons,' he told Michael Braun in his 1964 book, *Love Me Do*.

Critics have pointed out that *Beatles For Sale* was cut at the height of Beatlemania, which accounted for the number of cover versions. In many ways, though, the Beatles' fourth album is perhaps their most revealing in terms of musical influences. The six covers take them right back to those manic all-night rave-ups in Hamburg – Carl Perkins's 'Everybody's Trying To Be My Baby' and 'Honey, Don't'; Buddy Holly's 'Words Of Love'; Leiber and Stoller's classic 'Kansas City', sung by Little Richard; and Chuck Berry's anthemic 'Rock And Roll Music'. Such was the Beatles' enthusiasm that they disinterred 'Mr Moonlight' from the B-side of a single by the original Dr Feelgood, Willie Perryman (Piano Red). It took the Beatles' championing for these (by now) forgotten rockers to re-acquaint American audiences with their own rock 'n' roll history. It was only by studying the songwriter credits that thousands of Ameri- can fans realized that 'Words Of Love' wasn't a Lennon- McCartney original, and the dedicated pursued it back to its source, thereby discovering the joys of Buddy Holly.

The Beatles' pioneering work in helping Americans trace their rock heritage did not go unrecognized by musicians. Bob Dylan's 'Bringing It All Back Home', his first wholesale rock 'n' roll work, was a title that acknowledged the group's efforts.

The Beatles' fifth album, *Help!*, was also the soundtrack of their second film. Although removed from the documentary pressures of *A Hard Day's Night*, the Beatles were, by their own admission, constantly high on marijuana during filming. Lennon was also obsessed about his obesity, concerned about the state of his marriage, and worried that his role as a 'pop singer' was too insubstantial for someone of his abilities. ('If there is such a thing as genius, I am one! If there isn't, I don't care.') On the surface 'Help!' was another catchy Beatles single which went automatically to number one. It contained all their hallmarks – an unforgettable chorus, infectious harmonies, and quaintly memorable lyrics. But, as Lennon admitted, it really *was* a cry for help.

The finished album is riddled with insecurities, lack of assurance, and self-doubt. Lennon gratefully accepted the instant obliteration offered by drugs, barely disguising his distaste for the parody he felt the Beatles had become. That distaste is nowhere more evident than in 'You've Got To Hide Your Love Away'. The Dylan influence is particularly strong, vocally, musically, and lyrically. ('That's me in my Dylan period. I am like a chameleon, influenced by whatever is going on. If Elvis can do it, I can do it. If the Everly Brothers can do it, me and Paul can. Same with Dylan.') The song finds Lennon as the poet alone, head buried deep in hands, surrounded by clowns. The paranoia is obvious; twitchy at what people will think, he is told to hide his love away, fearful that any open display of emotion will be ridiculed.

The growing distance between Lennon and McCartney

musically was demonstrated by the sequence of two of their tracks on the finished album – Paul's rather smug 'Another Girl' ('She's sweeter than all the girls, and I've met quite a few'), and John's jaundiced 'You're Going To Lose That Girl'.

Help! is probably remembered for the Haunting McCartney ballad, 'Yesterday'. Lennon was not complimentary about Paul's ballad which would go on to become the most recorded song in history. As if emphasizing his rocker credibility, John finished the album with a blistering version of Larry William's 'Dizzy Miss Lizzy'. Williams was one of Lennon's early musical heroes. The Beatles recorded his 'Bad Boy' in 1965; 'Slow Down' appeared on their 1964 'Long Tall Sally' EP, and Lennon included Williams's classic 'Bony Moronie' on his 1975 *Rock 'n' Roll* album. 'It's Only Love' displayed Lennon's softer side on *Help!* but even that is tainted by druggy imagery and a reliance on Dylanesque word-play.

The use of a string quartet on 'Yesterday' and the flutes on 'You've Got To Hide Your Love Away' marked the first inclusion of musicians outside the Beatles' immediate orbit on their material. With such an intuitive and astute interpreter as George Martin, the group could experiment in the studio and feel genuinely creative. Live, it was impossible – the screams obliterated everything. Even with the intolerable pressure of touring and filming, the Beatles could relax in the studio and were receptive to Martin's ideas and suggestions on how to expand their sound. Lennon and McCartney's compelling musical codes found swift acceptance with George Martin's classically trained musical mind. By the middle of 1965 they were setting themselves dauntingly high standards. Creatively, George Martin was certainly the fifth Beatle but he could only work with what was presented to him *by* them. In a 1983 interview, Martin said: 'I've always held that the role of the producer is the person who can look back on the picture, and not just at the detail. When you have your picture taken in a school form, the first thing you look for is "Where am I?" You don't look at the picture, you look at yourself. And this is true of most instrumentalists, of most people who make records, they tend to listen to the bit they were doing.

'I also believe that the producer's role is a minor one compared to the performer's. There's been a tendency in recent years for that to be reversed. I think that the fellow who creates it is the important thing, and the producer is the guy who helps him shape it. I don't see the producer as a Svengali mastermind. The role of the producer has become slightly inflated, and it's strange for me to say that, because maybe I've had something to do with that. But it's something I haven't been comfortable with.'

The high standards the Beatles had attained can be seen simply by looking at their two film soundtracks. The normal thing for soundtracks (particularly 'pop' film soundtracks) was to stretch one theme song over an album, patched up with 'mood' instrumentals. The Beatles changed all that – *A Hard Day's Night* and *Help!* were crammed full of potential hit singles, and there wasn't an ounce of surplus flesh on either. By *Help!*, the sound of the Beatles on record was a lot deeper, deferring to Martin's orthodox musical knowledge; the group were keen to enrich the standard two guitars, bass, and drums sound. The percussive effects on 'Tell Me What You See', John's harmonium on 'We Can Work It Out', and the pianos and organs, strings, and woodwinds dotted around their records of the period all point towards a flexing of the Beatles' musical muscles, which would culminate with the majestic *Sgt Pepper* only two years later.

Running parallel to the album, of course, were the

astonishingly assured and varied singles. Again, the Beatles set new standards, even down to the packaging of their material. Prior to them, LP's were simply regarded as vehicles for collected singles, B-sides, and cover versions, which the record company duly issued to extract the final penny from diehard fans of these short-lived phenomena – pop groups! The Beatles changed all that.

By the middle of 1965, Beatles songs like 'She Loves You', 'I Want To Hold Your Hand', and 'Can't Buy Me Love' had entered the public consciousness. The experimentation started with 'I Feel Fine' (with its use of feedback and jagged rhythms); the Motown feel of 'Day Tripper' and the fairground atmosphere of 'We Can Work It Out'; the fluid 'Ticket to Ride'. The quality of those singles is reflected by the variety of artists who covered them, an astonishing cross-section – Ella Fitzgerald, Otis Redding, the Carpenters, Dollar, and Stevie Wonder.

From early on, the Beatles were determined that their albums should be regarded as separate entities. It helped, of course, having what press agent Tony Barrow called 'their own built-in tunesmith team of Lennon and McCartney'. Even at the time it was apparent that the compositions were no way split fifty-fifty. If John sang a 'Lennon and McCartney' song, you could bet that the majority of the work had been his, and vice versa. There were arguments in the studio about whose songs should get priority as A-sides.

Even as they grew apart as writers, there was still that balance to the Lennon and McCartney partnership. The individual contributions to joint compositions may have been minimal, but they mattered, and helped shape the songs. Such was their intuitive reading of each other that they played off against each other, goading each other into making the song perfect. It may only have been a change

of tense, a switch in direction, but this joint honing strengthened the song.

Lennon defined the partnership around this time when
he told *Playboy*: 'In "We Can Work It Out", Paul did the
first half, I did the middle eight. But you've got Paul
writing "We can work it out", real optimistic, y'know, and
me, impatient: "Life is very short and there's no time for
fussing and fighting, my friend." ' The full flowering of
that creativity was to come with the Beatles' sixth album,
the punningly titled *Rubber Soul*. Newly honoured by Queen
and Country, despite the unremitting pressures (the album
was recorded in under a fortnight) the Beatles showed they
were well ahead of the field. In these days of high-tech-
nology recording, where months and sometimes years are
spent preparing an album, it is remarkable to look back on
the pressure under which the Beatles recorded, and see how
confident and progressive, in the best possible sense, their
music sounded. By the end of 1965, rock 'n' roll had grown
up. Dylan's electric experiments had spawned a clutch of
imitators who gradually grew into their own style (Simon
and Garfunkel, the Byrds), and the Beatles were under
pressure from their contemporaries (Who, Stones, Animals,
Yardbirds) to stay one step ahead. They were no longer the
cocky rockers of only three years earlier, but they hadn't
forgotten their roots. And they proved they could still whip
up a storm on a song like 'Dizzy Miss Lizzy'. But with
their growing confidence as writers, and their growing
understanding of the studio, the Beatles' material grew in
stature.

Lyrically, at the end of 1965, they found themselves
commenting on the craziness of their situation, occasionally
distorted by drugs. 'Norwegian Wood' was John's veiled
admission of an affair; 'Nowhere Man', his observations on
the unreality of it all; there was also the wistful nostalgia

Two Liverpool lads, in the front room of a Liverpool council house, writing music that would enshrine them in history. At Paul's home, 20 Forthlin Road, Allerton, in September 1962, a bespectacled Lennon and left-handed guitarist McCartney grapple with the words and chords, written in Paul's exercise book, to 'I Saw Her Standing There' (Michael McCartney)

Above: Visiting London from Liverpool in January 1963, the Beatles drop in to the Austin Reed store in Regent Street to buy the Cuban-heeled boots that would start a fashion style (Pictorial Press)

Below: A scruffily-dressed John with Paul and drummer Pete Best prepare for a 'Riverboat Shuffle' down the Mersey on the ship *Royal Iris* in July 1962. Top of the bill was Acker Bilk's traditional jazzband (Michael McCartney)

Above: John launches into one of his imitations of deformity in a jokey backstage scene at the Cavern. Paul gives a helping hand; Cavern owner Ray McFall joins in; and Cynthia watches the camera (Michael McCartney)

Below: George, John and Paul: an early rehearsal picture (Michael McCartney)

John and Paul with legendary rock 'n' roller Gene Vincent at the
Cavern Club (Michael McCartney)

Above: At EMI's Abbey Road Studio, John casts an eye towards producer George Martin in the control box during the recording of the album *With The Beatles* (Times Newspapers)

Right: Tie askew, shirt button undone, John as he appeared with the Beatles on the coast-to-coast American TV programme *The Ed Sullivan Show*. An estimated 73 million people saw them in what was their big breakthrough to the US audience (Dezo Hoffman/Apple Corps)

Waiting for the action during the filming of *A Hard Day's Night* on a platform at Marylebone railway station, London (David Hurn/The John Hillelson Agency)

John with Brian Epstein relaxing in Miami, Florida, where the Beatles performed on two TV shows during their triumphant first American tour in 1964 (Dezo Hoffmann/Rex Features)

At the height of 'The Twist' dance craze, John and Cynthia went in February 1964 to the club that was its birthplace, New York's Peppermint Lounge, where a soundalike group called The Beetles were playing (Camera Press)

of 'In My Life'. Paul's 'You Won't See Me' and 'I'm Looking Through You' were remarkably bitter comments on the price of fame and the superficiality of the Beatles' status.

Musically, too, *Rubber Soul* was a progression. The public noticed the introduction to pop of the sitar on 'Norwegian Wood'. But there was also a greater reliance on keyboards than before. *Rubber Soul* catches them between the hysteria of Beatlemania and the acid excesses of *Sgt Pepper*. They finally sound comfortable in the studio, willing to experiment, but never straying too far away from the three-minute pop song, a form they had perfected. *Rubber Soul* will always stand superbly on its own merits.

For Lennon, particularly, the album marked a personal progression in his craft. Personal honesty and confession, which were to characterize his later work, were inherent. His songs are marked by a more poetic approach, and he was beginning to find his own voice, rather than copy Dylan's. 'Girl' opens with the plaintive 'Is there anybody going to listen to my story?' before moving on to what would become a familiar Lennon preoccupation. Was she told when she was young that pain would lead to pleasure? He later remarked that the song was a personal favourite, a move away from the Tin Pan Alley style of songwriting.

'Nowhere Man' is a curiously nihilistic 'pop' song, casting Lennon as a monarch of nothingness, without opinion, power, or desire. The Nowhere Man is an impotent, hollow symbol of the swinging sixties – 'Nowhere Man, don't worry/Take your time, don't hurry/Leave it all till somebody else/Lends you a hand.' It was his view of life from the emptiness of the mansion he called a 'bus stop, awaiting action'. 'Norwegian Wood' is the vacuous swinging sixties again. Druggy, floating, random ('She told me she worked in the morning, and started to laugh'). Lennon's vocal is weary, dispassionate, that of an outsider viewing something intensely personal.

'In My Life' is the curtain-raiser for a trip down to Strawberry Fields. Although nothing is mentioned by name, there is that overriding impression of nostalgia and yearning for home. Lennon said: 'It was the first song I wrote that was consciously about my life . . . "In My Life" started out as a bus journey from my house at 251 Menlove Avenue to town, mentioning all the places I could recall. I wrote it all down, and it was so *boring*. So I forgot about it and laid back, and these lyrics started coming to me about friends and lovers of the past.' It was an extraordinary position to be in. Only five years before he had been 'Lennon', a scruffy Liverpudlian rocker, with prospects as bleak as the view across the Mersey. Half a decade later, he was J. W. Lennon MBE, millionaire, surveying his world from the stockbroker security of Weybridge. 'In My Life' echoes the theory that 'you can never go home again', 'Though I know I'll never lose affection/For people and things that went before/I know I'll often stop and think about them.' The song marked a rare moment of retrospection and sentimentality for Lennon; the lyrics are tinged with a resignation that all is gone, that the only security lies ahead.

As 1965 drew to a close the Beatles stood untouched, at the height of their influence and powers. The extent of the Beatles' popularity at that time is hard to imagine today, when every group that manages two consecutive number ones is cited as 'the new Beatles'. No cracks had appeared in their facade; they could still be *seen*, screamed at, touched. But the drive to the 'toppermost of the poppermost' had ended. They had reached their summit. Like kings, they viewed the world at their feet.

By the Beatles' gruelling standards, 1966 was a relatively quiet year which saw them pour their creative energies into recording, rather than squeezing in sessions between tours. The earliest fruit of those labours came with the 'Paperback Writer' single in June; a bubbly, clever Beatles single, just like the old days. But the B-side, 'Rain', was of particular interest. 'Rain' was written at John's home studio, where he was experimenting with tape loops, which explains the weird, distorted atmosphere on the song. The dreamy feel was accentuated by the druggy lyrics ('I can show you, when it starts to rain/Everything's the same'). There are echoes in the song of future Lennon classics: 'Can you hear me that when it rains and shines/It's just a state of mind.' It precedes 'Strawberry Fields Forever' and 'Lucy In The Sky With Diamonds' with its remote and ethereal feel. Spiked on acid, Lennon was seeing the world through hazy shades. The drugs added a translucent element to his music, and aided and abetted the desire to drift into the dream world of Lewis Carroll, where nothing was real, and 'the slithy toves/Did gyre and gimble in the wabe.' To be a Beatle meant that reality was distorted anyway. Their cocooned existence saw them grow more and more remote. By mid-1966 touring had become a physical and mental strain, particularly after the American reaction to Lennon's 'We're bigger then Jesus' quote and their hostile reception in Manila.

The spring of that year was spent in the studio, recording what turned out to be the *Revolver* album. The first track they recorded was the last to appear on the album – Lennon's mysterious 'Tomorrow Never Knows'. It marked the zenith of the Beatles and George Martin's studio ingenuity at the time – backward tapes, loops, chanting choirs, oddball lyrics, all underpinned by some relentless Ringo drumming.

Still ahead of its time, 'Tomorrow Never Knows' has John hurling himself into the psychedelic maelstrom, with lyrics drawn from the Tibetan Book of the Dead, although the actual title was a Ringoism Lennon used to diffuse the lyrical obtuseness. It was one of the earliest attempts by Lennon actually to make music that, until then, had been confined to his mind. For the first time, it let us 'see the meaning of within.' It had been a long, crazy journey from 'Be-Bop-A-Lula'!

All sorts of other wondrous potions can be found inside the jar which is the *Revolver* album – 'I'm Only Sleeping' carried on the theme of floating, of dreaming of being at the centre of something, and letting others glimpse in through layers of sound and mystery, of being a reluctant idol, at the centre of attention, but needing to look inward, and find out exactly what makes him/them tick ('Please don't spoil my day, I'm only sleeping').

'She Said, She Said' evoked images of his druggy dreams in Laurel Canyon, California, where the song was written. It played out John's private agony in public: 'I know what it's like to be dead! Who always knows what it's like to never have been born/sad/mad.' It was a trippy odyssey from birth to death, with Lennon returning to the precious world of his childhood, to the home he never had: 'I said no, no, you're wrong, when I was a boy/Everything was right.' It never had been, but by then, he could convince himself that it was.

In 'And Your Bird Can Sing' John issued his early message of independence from the Beatles' cocoon: 'Tell them that you've got everything you want . . . But you won't get me!' For they had seen the Seven Wonders, they had heard 'every sound there is,' and it still wasn't enough.

Isolated and immunized, John called, more and more, on 'Dr Robert', a euphemism for drugs, and took 'a drink from his special cup.' He had all the answers. The more the Beatles dipped into that special cup, the more reliant they became. With distorted perspective and lost time, they knew that there was always one constant: 'Day or night, he'll be there, anytime at all.' Any time at all grew into the void of 'Tomorrow Never Knows', and they were gone! They disappeared on 29 August 1966. It was actually in Candlestick Park, San Francisco. It could have been anywhere. To all intents and purposes, outside of the comfortable insularity of the recording studio, the Beatles ceased to exist.

After leaving the stage at Candlestick Park, the Beatles became their own bosses. For the first time in three years, Parlophone didn't have the obligatory Beatles album for Christmas. Without that, for many people Christmas was not complete. *A Collection of Beatles' Oldies* did appear, with its cover that epitomized the Swinging London which the Beatles had helped so much to shape. There they were, all their best songs. Created in the fiery furnace of a three-year burst, here was the vinyl proof of rock's maturing. With touring definitely vetoed, with no film projects to occupy them seriously, for the first time in a decade, the Beatles were suddenly no longer a group. From now on there would be no more 'songs', no more product manufactured to meet a particular schedule. The balloon had come down to earth. They tasted freedom. It was the end of 1966. Ahead lay the unknown.

FIFTEEN

PRESSURES

'We're more popular than Jesus now'

A FANTASTIC scene awaited John one day in 1965 on his return to Weybridge from London in his chauffeured Rolls. Sitting in his lounge, drinking a cup of tea, was his father, whom he had not seen since he was five years old in Blackpool.

Dishevelled, with long greasy grey hair and a shabby suit, totally unkempt, fifty-two-year-old Fred Lennon was working as a kitchen hand, washing up dishes in the Greyhound Hotel, Hampton Court, a few miles from John's home. Drinking in a pub one day, he had got chatting to a man who drove the Beatles occasionally for a car hire firm.

'If you're Fred Lennon,' said the man, 'I drive your son.'

Fred said: 'Oh, well give me a lift to his house. I haven't seen him for years and I'd like to see him.'

When Fred arrived, Cynthia answered the knock on the door. 'Hello, Cyn, I'm John's Dad and you haven't seen me before.' He had his foot in the hall before she could react.

'He was a charmer in his own way,' says Cynthia. 'There was no way I could have shut the door on him. He looked like a tramp but he was John's Dad. I had no alternative but to ask him to wait for John to return.'

John was staggered. After the initial shock of seeing his father sitting there, and Cynthia's obvious discomfort, John said, in the scathing voice that people feared: 'Where have *you* been for the last twenty years?' John was dumb-founded not only at his father's appearance, but at his demeanour. As a child, he had built up a totally different image of his dad as a swashbuckling, seafaring Errol Flynn-type character romantically sailing around the world.

'Discovering him to be a pretty foul-mouthed washer-up of dishes, with a real Scouse accent which John, with his upbringing, never had, was not a pretty sight,' says Cynthia.

Freddy Lennon, an inveterate beer drinker, made good money as a ship's steward, and when he worked as a hotel porter. But he was always broke and scrounging cash from friends and relatives.

The atmosphere grew steadily worse. 'He kept on about what a hard life he'd had, how he was having to work as a skivvy to earn a few bob, and John and I never had it so good,' recalls Cynthia. 'Within an hour or so of coming in the door, he was saying how he didn't want to take anything from his son. But it was obvious he was coming for a handout.'

John felt uncomfortable for his father almost as much as he felt irritable with himself. He remembered how his relatives, his aunts and cousins, older than him, felt suddenly different in *his* company now that he was a famous Beatle. But try though he did, he could not take the arrival of his lost father with a hard luck story.

'He was so embarrassed,' says Cynthia. 'He was in and out of the room like a cat on a hot tin roof. He was nervous and said he suddenly felt ill at ease in his own home.' John's feelings were not helped by the obvious fact that his father had come primarily for money. 'I suppose Fred was proud of what John had achieved,' says Cynthia, 'but his main object was to rip off some cash from John.'

Out of sympathy and to relieve the tension, Cynthia asked Fred if he would like to stay at Kenwood for the night, hoping that it would help the atmosphere. John fixed Cynthia with a stare that asked: 'Do you realize what you're doing?' Fred stayed for three nights, and the pressures on John mounted so much that he was out more often than he was at home, leaving Cynthia with the unpleasant job of talking to his father.

When he was with his father, John's insatiable quest for the truth about his childhood and his father's reported desertion of his mother forced several confrontations. 'Why did you leave Julia – she would have had you back, y'know,' said John.

'How could I, John? Julia left *me*. I didn't leave Julia, she decided she would leave me.'

And so the conversation went on, with John insisting that his mother would have welcomed Fred back to rebuild their marriage, and giving him a happy parental background, while Fred argued that Julia had found another man while he was at sea, and didn't want him back.

It was a fruitless discussion which only confused John even more about his childhood and reminded him of his mother's death.

To Mimi, who had a low opinion of Fred, John said on the phone: 'Oh Mimi, how could my mother marry a man like that? Why didn't you tell me what kind of father I had?'

Mimi answered: 'Dear boy, how would I know what kind of father you had? I didn't know him well myself. Did you want me to bring you up telling you he was a bad man who left you? Would that have made you any happier? You've been happy, haven't you?'

Mimi said John replied: 'Yes, I'm the happiest person in the whole family.'

In 1968 Fred presented John and Cynthia with a further problem. He had met a girl and wanted to marry her, but she was only nineteen and had been made a ward of court.

John groaned to his father: 'Oh, no, isn't one failed marriage enough?'

'Fred said he was madly in love with her but didn't have enough money to set himself and her up in a home,' says Cynthia.

The girl was Pauline Jones, a former Exeter University student. Fred persuaded John and Cynthia that his life with her would be easier if she had some work to do, and as she would make a great secretary, she could help John and Cynthia typing their letters.

'John and I talked about it for a while and although he didn't like the idea much, he said he'd like to help his Dad if he could,' says Cynthia.

'I said: "Let's give it a try." '

John dealt brusquely with his father, saying, 'I think it's time for you to leave,' when it became obvious that he would have stayed there for ever, given half a chance. Pauline worked as a live-in secretary for about five months, but her sobbing and wailing kept John and Cynthia up nights. She was tearful about her difficult relationship with Fred.

And there was not enough work for her. 'She was at as much of a loss about knowing what to do as we were,' says Cynthia. 'We'd never had a permanent secretary and she was going through a bad emotional patch in her life.' Eventually Pauline was asked to leave, but John eased the way for Fred by paying for his court cases and eventually for Fred and Pauline's wedding in Scotland.

'I want you to be happy,' he told his father, finally. He bought him a £15,000 house near Kew Gardens, Surrey, and gave him *carte blanche* to order furniture. He arranged for him to receive £30 a week from the Beatles' company and established a reasonable, if distant, relationship with him.

Fred Lennon became an embarrassment to John. When Fred arrived one day after that first meeting John was under particular Beatles' pressure. He could not face another conversation with the father who had ingratiated himself into his life. John simply slammed the door in his face. Later Fred delivered his ultimate insult to his brilliant son by condemning the decorations at his Weybridge house, criticizing Beatles music as unlike the ballads he sang, 'not as good as the old stuff, say "Begin The Beguine",' and by hawking himself to national newspapers and magazines as the father of a Beatle. He arrived at the *Melody Maker* office to promote his unspeakable record, 'That's My Life (My Love And My Home)', and told me his record company wanted him to make more. They were even paying for him to get his teeth capped, he said. John Lennon kept up a remarkably dignified silence throughout all this. But not for nothing did he christen his father 'The Ignoble Alf'.

John had proved his generosity, and in spite of provocation had done the right thing for his father. There were other examples of his big heart. He did a special drawing for charity Christmas cards to help famine relief. He was an easy touch for many worthwhile causes like orphans. And to divert his own interest a little from the Beatles and songwriting he became, with George Harrison, a founding director of Hayling Supermarkets Ltd on the Hampshire coast. The other director, and active in running the supermarket towards which John gave £20,000 was his old Quarry Bank school mate and Quarry Men washboard

player, Pete Shotton. John and George resigned their direc-
torships in September 1969, leaving Pete in control of the
supermarket.

It was impossible to compute John's fortune by 1965.
Albums and singles were selling by the million all around
the world. Concerts, films, and assorted tie-ins with Beatles
merchandise made all four of them millionaires as well as
Brian Epstein, who received a percentage of their income
on a sliding scale of up to 25 per cent. The key to John
and Paul's equal money lay in that handshake at the
McCartney home at Forthlin Road, Allerton, only eight
years earlier; they would write as Lennon-McCartney,
whether one wrote a song alone or not. The link resulted
in Maclen, their own company within Northern Songs,
the company that raised eyebrows when it went public in
February 1965. There was astonishment in the City at
pop stars, even the Beatles, considering themselves mighty
enough to go public on the London Stock Exchange, but
shares were snapped up quickly. John and Paul's income
from songwriting alone made them millionaires, and the
royalties soared as hundreds of artists around the world
clamoured to 'cover' their work, notably Paul's romantic
ballads like 'Yesterday' and 'And I Love Her'.

It was said during that year that, at any single moment
in any twenty-four hours around the world, a Beatles song
was being played on the radio somewhere, just as their
records were selling as fast as EMI in London and Capitol
in America could press them. America's *Time* magazine said
the 'most conservative estimate' put the net worth of George
Harrison and Ringo Starr at $3 million each, with John
and Paul at $4 million each because of their extra earnings
as songwriters. 'The figures could easily be twice as high,'
said *Time*. They were out of date before the magazine was
published.

The Beatles were not merely bigger than Elvis, as Brian Epstein had vowed they would be. In three bewildering years they had become virtually a royal family of youth. The world hung on their every word, particularly John's, and he retained the title of the 'most outspoken Beatle'.

Ever since the Beatles had triumphed at the Royal Variety Show in 1963, they had been courted by the Establishment. It was this very fact that got under John's skin. Rock 'n' roll, he said, was the antithesis of comfortable upper-class values. He had parodied Sir Alec Douglas-Home, the British prime minister, as Sir Alec Doubtless Whom, and had a generally healthy disregard for the aristocracy.

One day at Weybridge, among his usual batch of letters from Brian Epstein's office and American fans who simply addressed their envelopes: 'John Lennon, England', there was an official letter saying that he had been selected as a potential recipient of the MBE. He was asked if he would accept it publicly. Offering the Beatles the medal of Member of the British Empire, an award bestowed by the Queen, was staggering for pop musicians. It had been building up, surely, but the reality of it was front-page news in all Britain's newspapers that June in 1965.

John's first reaction was to say no. He had already had quite enough of the canonization of the Beatles. The knowledge that lords and ladies and debutantes were fawning over them, and the colossal distance they had travelled from enjoying the beer and sweat of Hamburg and the Cavern, was all too much. 'The money's nice,' he said to me, 'but *this*,' pointing to the sweeping lawns of his Weybridge mansion, 'is not necessary. It's all too much. What I'd have liked would have been the money and the hit records without the fame.'

John threw the letter from Buckingham Palace into a
pile of fan mail. 'I thought when I saw a brown envelope
saying "On Her Majesty's Service" that I was being called
up,' said John. A few days later, Epstein asked him on the
phone if he had received it. John said yes, but his instinct
was to turn it down. What were the others doing? Epstein
pointed out that they would all have to accept the honour,
and that was that. John reluctantly agreed that to refuse an
award from the Queen would do colossal damage to the
Beatles. Paul, George, and Ringo felt honoured. So John
grunted and agreed. He was always a terrible compromiser.
'Taking the MBE was a sell-out for me,' John said later.
'We did manage to refuse all sorts of things that people
don't know about. For instance, we did the Royal Variety
Show [in 1963] and we were asked discreetly to do it every
year after that, but we always said: "Stuff it." So every year
there was always a story in the newspapers saying, "Why
no Beatles for the Queen?" Which was pretty funny, because
they didn't know we refused it. That show's a bad gig
anyway. Everybody's very nervous and uptight and nobody
performs well. The time we did do it, I cracked a joke
on stage. I was fantastically nervous but I wanted to say
something, just to rebel a bit, and that was the best I could
do.'

John's witticisms, usually laced with a slice of irony or
invective, were aroused when the Beatles' MBE award
became known. He said: 'I thought people got these things
for driving tanks, winning wars.' Retired colonels erupted
in fury at a pop group like the long-haired Beatles receiving
such an award. And some people returned their awards to
Buckingham Palace in protest. John rounded on them with
blistering attacks. Army officers received their medals for
killing people, he said. 'We got ours for entertaining. On
balance, I'd say we deserve ours more.' In any case, he

pointed out, the Beatles had received their medals for exports, bringing into Britain millions of pounds' worth of trade.

'Beatles MBE' stayed as national news in Britain for weeks, confirming John's private theory that they should never have accepted it.

Lord Wilson, then Harold Wilson, British prime minister, had recommended the awarding of the MBE by the Queen. He was criticized by many for jumping on the bandwagon of youth, but Lord Wilson told me of his decision: 'Some of the heavyweights in the press had probably never heard of the Beatles, and if they had, they wouldn't have understood the role the Beatles had come to play in young people's lives. I saw the Beatles as having a transforming effect on the minds of youth, mostly for the good. It kept a lot of kids off the streets. They introduced many, many young people to music, which in itself was a good thing. A lot of old stagers might have regarded it as idiosyncratic music, but the Mersey sound was a new, important thing. That's why they deserved such recognition,' Lord Wilson told me in 1982.

Lord Wilson recalled a chat with John Lennon at the Variety Club luncheon in 1964, when the Beatles were named Show Business Personalities of the Year. As a Merseyside Member of Parliament, Lord Wilson talked to him about his background. 'John recalled they had started their learning as a group in the Labour clubs and trade union clubs near his home in Woolton. I recall that Penny Lane is a mile or so outside my constituency, so a lot of young people from my constituency would do their courting there. I thought John Lennon had an irrepressible sense of humour.'

John's wit struck Lord Wilson at the Variety Club lunch. The Beatle had risen to accept the award for the group. He was sitting between the then Leader of the Opposition and Prince Philip. Addressing the Variety Club chief, John said: 'Mr Chief Barker . . . and [turning to the Opposition Leader] . . . Mr Dobson.' The confectionery firm of Barker and Dobson was known mostly to Merseysiders: it was a beautifully timed line. Said Lord Wilson: 'It got very few laughs because they were all ignorant southerners on our table. But *we* enjoyed it.'

There was a typically Lennonesque twist to the MBE affair. On the day of the investiture at Buckingham Palace, with thousands of fans crowding the gates outside, the Beatles' limousine drew up and the immaculately suited moptops stepped out. John's secret was that inside one of his black boots were several marijuana joints. Just as the investiture was about to start, the Beatles adjourned together to a small toilet inside Buckingham Palace where they passed around one joint among them.

The MBE presentation passed uneventfully through their good cheer. That Christmas, John took his medal down to Aunt Mimi's new seaside bungalow. 'Keep it, Mimi,' he said. It occupied pride of place on the sideboard, underneath her favourite picture of John, a huge print taken by Astrid.

John very rarely, if ever, apologized. He believed it to be a sign of weakness, and that to refuse to capitulate was an example of strength. Only Aunt Mimi could elicit a 'sorry' from him, and that was when he knew that, if he didn't say it, the after-effects would last for months.

Still less had John been known to cry. The 'tough guy' bravado approach, a complete veneer for the soft, humanitarian inside, meant that he could never be seen to shed a tear. 'I never once saw John cry,' says Cynthia, 'in the ten years we were together.'

The spring of 1966 became a debacle for John Lennon. In London's *Evening Standard* he had been profiled, as always, as an iconoclastic, deep-thinking, restless man, way ahead of Beatledom and the perimeters of pop stardom. The writer, Maureen Cleave, was a friend and confidante of John's. He admired her intellect, trusted her, and was always at his frankest when journalists of her calibre treated him as a person with thoughts, outside the confines of pop music. Most stars of the 1960s projected themselves as vacuous. John set out to impress informed writers like Maureen Cleave that he had a sharp mind and wanted to learn. Talking to her was, for John, cathartic. As always, Maureen Cleave portrayed Lennon as a thinker; she coolly reported him as saying: 'Christianity will go. It will vanish and shrink. I needn't argue with that; I'm right and I will be proved right. We're more popular than Jesus now; I don't know which will go first – rock 'n' roll or Christianity. Jesus was all right but his disciples were thick and ordinary. It's them twisting it that ruins it for me.' He was, she reported, reading extensively about religion. And that was the end of the sermon.

Britain, numbed by four years of some pretty outrageous Lennonisms, did not react to the remarks. The comments had appeared, unsensationally, midway through an erudite article. The Beatles family applauded their leader for again projecting himself intelligently.

Four whole months after Cleave's article appeared, and had been forgotten, it reappeared under a syndication arrangement with an American magazine, *Datebook*. This time it was not submerged within the context of a general article but was front-paged: Lennon was claiming that the Beatles were bigger than Jesus Christ!

American reaction, two weeks before the Beatles were due to begin a long concert tour, was instantaneous and devastating. The Beatles, and particularly John, were denounced as sacrilegious, and a wave of anti-Beatle demonstrations fanned out across the American South, the Bible Belt. The Ku Klux Klan marched; there were bonfires of Beatles records; and an estimated thirty-five radio stations across America banned Beatles records. The country that had adopted the Beatles as the 1960s' biggest single social phenomenon was rejecting them. Love and hate, those two closely related emotions, had met. The Beatles were bad news, and Lennon's tongue had caused it.

Promoters who had planned the Beatles' concerts of America were worried about guaranteeing the safety of the group on stage. The Vatican commented that 'some subjects must not be dealt with profanely, even in the world of beatniks.' One minister threatened to excommunicate any member of his congregation who attended a Beatles concert.

Responding to alarming phone calls from America, Brian Epstein immediately flew to New York. His first instinct was to cancel the tour, to protect the Beatles' safety. But he was told that if John made an apology at a press conference in the United States, then things might cool down sufficiently for the tour to proceed. Brian telephoned John at his home in Weybridge. John's immediate reaction was: 'Tell them to get stuffed. I've got nothing to apologize for.' He asked Brian to cancel the tour. 'I'd rather that than have to get up and lie. What I said stands.'

The seriousness of the anti-Beatles campaign was more evident to Brian, in America, than to John in the seclusion of his home in Surrey. There were hundreds of letters arriving daily, addressed simply: 'John Lennon, England' or, searingly, 'Jesus Lennon'. John took a dispassionate interest in reading some. 'How many for and against today?' he would ask Cynthia. Epstein cajoled and pleaded with John, insisting that, unless he made an exception of his golden rule never to apologize, the Beatles' future in America looked bleak, not just for the forthcoming tour but forever. Next day, South African radio banned all records composed or played by the Beatles. Faced with mounting pressure, John had little choice; he called Epstein and said he would deal with the matter at the Beatles' press conference in Chicago three days later.

Brian, meanwhile, had tried his best to damp down the flames. He said at his own press conference in New York: 'The quote which John Lennon made to a London columnist nearly three months ago [sic] has been quoted and misrepresented entirely out of the context of the article, which was in fact highly complimentary to Lennon as a person and was understood by him to be exclusive to the *Evening Standard*. It was not anticipated that it would be displayed out of context and in such a manner as it was in an American teenage magazine.'

In London, Maureen Cleave did her utmost to place John's remarks in their true perspective. 'John was certainly not comparing the Beatles with Christ,' she said. 'He was simply observing that so weak was the state of Christianity that the Beatles were, to many people, better known. He was deploring, rather than approving, this.' The irony of the American uproar was, to many British clergymen, the uncomfortable truth that John was right — witness the number of people who attended the Beatles' concerts and brought their records, compared with church attendance figures.

When John arrived, distraught, in Chicago, he was met by Brian Epstein and Tony Barrow. They took him to a hotel room to brief him on what to expect from the hostile journalists and disc jockeys who were waiting to eat him at the press conference.

'We discussed very, very seriously what should be said by John,' says Barrow. 'It was most unusual for John because for the first and only time in his life that I knew him, he was very willing and ready to apologize.' But under pressure, John broke down and cried: Epstein was explaining what was involved in cancelling the whole Beatles American tour, and Barrow was telling John what the line of questioning would be from the baying journalists. 'I said to John he should try to *explain*.' Brian feared the Beatles might be assassinated during the tour.

John was immediately worried for the safety of the others. He threw his head down into his lap and sobbed loudly, holding his head in his hands. 'I'll do anything,' he said. 'Anything, whatever you say I should do, I'll have to say. How on earth am I going to face the others if this whole tour is called off? Just because of me, just because of something I've said. I didn't mean to cause all of this.'

Epstein's mention of death threats made no impact on John personally. This was odd, because to be 'level' with a Beatle on such major problems and fears when there was an element of potential trouble was most unusual. All four of them were always protected from grim truths and left alone with the job of being Beatles. For Epstein to tell Lennon of his real worries was a big break with tradition. For John not to react puzzled Brian. He asked John if he realized the seriousness of what he'd said. But it was more what Paul, George, and Ringo would think of him, if a remark by him had caused the danger of cancellation, that bothered John. Here was John's conscience, exposed for perhaps the first time in his life. He was definitely ready to do whatever was necessary to quell the pandemonium that was gripping America on the subject of the Beatles.

When John took the microphone at the press conference in Chicago that night, he looked shaken and apprehensive as he faced a crowd of newsmen on the scent of a cowering Beatle. 'If I had said television is more popular than Jesus, I might have got away with it,' he began, 'but I just happened to be talking to a friend and I used the word "Beatles" as a remote thing, not as what I think – as Beatles, as those other Beatles like other people see us. I just said "they" are having more influence on kids and things than anything else, including Jesus. But I said it in that way which is the wrong way.'

Some journalists were dissatisfied. They thought John had made a stumbling apology and was virtually restating his original folly.

Said one reporter to him: 'Some teenagers have repeated your statements – "I like the Beatles more than Jesus Christ." What do you think about that?'

John replied: 'Well, originally I pointed out that fact in reference to England. That we meant more to kids than Jesus did, or religion at that time. I wasn't knocking it or putting it down. I was just saying it as a fact and it is true more for England than here. I'm not saying that we're better or greater, or comparing us with Jesus Christ as a person or God as a thing or whatever it is. I just said what I said and it was wrong. Or it was taken wrong. And now it's all this.'

The apology that John had conceded would be forthcoming when he had spoken earlier to Brian Epstein and Tony Barrow was not coming out clearly. A radio interviewer brought the matter to a head: 'But are you prepared to apologize?'

John thought he had done so. His face reddened with anguish, and his voice became firmer. 'I'm not anti-God, anti-Christ, or anti-religion. I was not saying we're greater or better. I believe in God but not as an old man in the sky. I believe what people call God is something in all of us. I wasn't saying the Beatles are better than God or Jesus. I used "Beatles" because it was easy for me to talk about the Beatles.'

But would he apologize?

'I wasn't saying whatever they're saying I was saying. I'm sorry I said it really. I never meant it to be a lousy anti-religious thing. I apologize if that will make you happy. I still don't know quite what I've done. I've tried to tell you what I did do but if you want me to apologize, if that will make you happy, then OK, I'm sorry.'

The press conference broke up amid the usual clatter of microphones and newspapermen fighting for the tele-phones. In the more traditional line of questioning that followed, few people took much notice of the resurfacing of the old Lennon venom. He condemned American involve-ment in the Vietnam war. Two months before that day, American planes had bombed Hanoi. John said he thought American action was unnecessarily warlike. It was his way of reasserting the real John Lennon. Public opinion on the Beatles being what it was in America at that time, he was lucky that his remark on the Vietnam controversy was not picked up and exploited. Fortunately, the general news line was that Lennon had apologized. Behind all that furore America wanted its Beatles back, cuddly, tuneful, joyful. The apology did not reach Alabama, deep in the Bible Belt, in time to prevent two thousand screaming teenagers tossing records and pictures of the Unfab Four on to a bonfire in a ceremony organized by a radio station, WAAX. But across the street, a smaller group of fans chanted: 'Yeah Beatles, Boo WAAX.' And a disc jockey, announcing the cancellation of another bonfire arranged for later that week, said he accepted the Lennon apology in the same spirit in which it had been made. The Beatles, he suggested, were now aware that they must use 'some degree of judgement and wisdom.'

Against that uncomfortable backdrop, the Beatles' 1966 tour of America could hardly lack tension. They were off the hook, but psychologically weakened and defensive. The 'Jesus' eruption had followed some riotous scenes in the Philippines. After a concert in Manila, the Beatles were alleged to have snubbed the president's wife by not attending a party. Paul said they were never invited, but the word got out that they had been rude, and they were jeered by many and jostled at the airport by thirty thugs, some with guns.

As always, the party invitation was simply a matter of confusion. But on their way out to the airport, thousands cheered while a few booed. 'All along the route there were people waving,' said John back at Heathrow, 'but I could see a few old men booing us. When they started on us at the airport, I was petrified.

'I thought I was going to get hurt so I headed for three nuns and two monks, thinking that if I was close to these people that might stop them. I was just pushed around. But that's the Philippines finished for me. No plane's going through the Philippines with me on it. I wouldn't even fly over it.'

America, in the aftermath of the 'Jesus' affair, threatened worse. With the real danger of assassination by the 'loony' John had so often joked about, it had little chance of being a coast-to-coast celebration. Fifteen concerts, two in the 55,000-capacity Shea Stadium in New York, one before a similar crowd at the Los Angeles Dodger Stadium, testified to the power of America's love of the Beatles. But something had happened deep inside; as far as John was concerned, a chapter had closed. It was turning sour and a drag. The Beatles road show was over. It had been a bore for long enough. Now it was also dangerous.

That tour was the finale of the Beatles' live work. Their last appearance, at Candlestick Park, San Francisco, on 29 August 1966, was a firm decision they made early on during that tour. When they told Brian Epstein, he was dejected. He realized his paternal role with the Beatles whom he loved would be virtually over, except for business relationships. For in the recording studio, as he had found to his cost, he was only welcome if he played no artistic role.

George Harrison had been instrumental in forcing an end to touring. Fed up with the poor sound and never enthralled by Beatlemania, he wanted to spend more time in the studios perfecting their finished recordings. There, there could be no duff notes going unchecked, unlike at the concerts where nobody cared. Now they'd proved they were enormous, they didn't need the hassle, he argued. He was able to win over John because Lennon disliked the discomfort of touring. He was shouting more obscenities at the screaming crowds who knew nothing of this curious 'release' when he was on stage. He was second only to George in his nervousness of flying. The restrictions and lack of freedom, and scarcely knowing which town they were in, had finally become too much. The nail in the coffin was the bitter taste in the mouth from the Philippines and America from things that had happened *off* stage.

Paul McCartney enjoyed touring. He strongly resisted the Harrison-Lennon partnership and argued that that was what a rock 'n' roll band was all about. A showman in the grand tradition, Paul needed an audience's approval and applause. He said that it was a vital part of the act. But

while George laid out the unarguable facts about the quality
of their music in the huge stadiums, John weighed in with:
'It's got too far from the Cavern.' Even though Ringo
enjoyed touring, there could be no road show with John
and George so reluctant. The only bright aspects were the
women and drugs and parties which customarily marked
the end of the American tours: the camaraderie between the
Beatles and other musicians which became a ritual in
the rented house high in the Hollywood Hills. But now,
that too had lost its appeal.

    Britain was hopeless, anyway. The halls were too small
to contain their millions of fans. A tour would disappoint
more people than it would please. So on the road, at least,
it was all over. On the plane back from San Francisco,
George breathed a sigh of relief: 'Now I don't have to
pretend to be a Beatle any more.' Epstein, who had not
been able to bring himself to attend the final concert, got
drunk on champagne. In London, weeks later, when Brian
told John of the concern of promoter Arthur Howes that
they would never tour Britain again, Lennon snorted down
the phone: 'Tell him to send out four wax dummies of the
Beatles that shake their heads at the right time. The kids
won't know the difference.'

Returning from the tumult of touring to Weybridge proved
hard for John. Cynthia was there to welcome him, with
Julian and a big batch of post from religious zealots, particularly from America, seeking to educate John about
Jesus. For a few days John enjoyed domesticity, putting
Julian to bed, reading him a story, making his tea occasionally. There was, though, a fear inside him: though the
Beatles had not disbanded, 'What the hell am I going to
do?' All his working life the Beatles had been a travelling

band. Now they were not. Of all the Beatles, he was the
most individualistic, and the least reliant on the group.
But he felt suddenly alone. The rungs on the ladder from
the Cavern had been quickly climbed until he had
reached the very pinnacle: hit songs, no money worries,
films, wife, child, fame, power of a frightening nature, and
two bestselling books.

The restlessness that had driven him since childhood
now gnawed away at him. 'Doing more of the same was
never my solution to a problem,' he said. The Beatles,
although they still had years of good music to make, was
no longer a challenge. John was now an insatiable newspaper reader, particularly of the *Daily Mirror* and *Daily
Mail*.

Cynthia noticed a softening in John in the aftermath
of the American tour. The tongue was not so quick. The
battle for the Beatles had been won, an era closed, and John
seemed more like his old self than the cocky Beatle-on-the-
road. He told her that he was pleased touring was all over.

His ego remained strong. Offers for him to build up
his literary and artistic career poured in. Would he design
another charity Christmas card? Would he open this, give
his blessing to that, donate some money here, there, and
everywhere? John sought refuge by accepting his first solo
acting role in the film *How I Won the War*. He would take
the role of Private Gripweed in a story that tilted against
war, a favourite theme for John, and, importantly, the producer and director was Richard Lester. 'I was flattered at
being asked,' said John. 'The ego needed feeding, with the
Beatles at a kind of crossroads.'

This first major move by a Beatle outside the Beatles
involved not merely an acting role, but a significant change
in his looks. First he was shorn of all his long Beatles hair,
and next he needed to look like a soldier, so he adopted

wire-framed National Health spectacles – 'granny glasses' as they became known. The specs, a bizarre flashback to the ones he had rejected when Aunt Mimi took him to an optician in Liverpool as a schoolboy, started a craze as surely as the Beatles' haircuts had seen to it that any self-respecting man of 1966 in the Western world had a hairstyle resembling that of the mop-tops.

Shooting for *How I Won the War* was in Germany, where John's locks were cut, and Almeria, Spain. Ringo and Maureen went out to socialize with John, who broke with his own tradition and invited Cynthia to visit him. Conditions were primitive in the rented house, but there was glorious solitude. After four years of relying to some degree on Paul, George, and Ringo, John was now alone in a creative situation. He played cricket with Richard Lester, enjoyed the company of actor Michael Crawford, and practised music making for much of the time. 'The harmonica was with him throughout the filming,' says Lester.

Lennon identified completely with what the film projected: 'It represented a genuine, heartfelt emotional attitude in response to its time,' says Lester. 'It will live on because it doesn't lead, it doesn't change society, but it does reflect a desperately sincere attitude towards the glorification of war by show business that was prevalent in the mid-sixties.'

In the wake of the Vietnam conflict John was vocal about war, even though he felt like a novice as an actor. 'I was an apprentice in the middle of professionals,' he said of his colleagues in the picture. When the film was completed, he took to wearing a badge with the initials CND, supporting the Campaign for Nuclear Disarmament.

What had attracted Lennon to the film was Lester's theory at the time: 'One of the gross obscenities about war is the war film itself. War on the screen is treated like a great big adventure with extras being killed in the way of a Western.'

John said: 'I hate war. The Vietnam War and all that is being done there made me feel like that. If there is another war I won't fight – and although the youngsters may be asked to fight I'll stand up there and try to tell them not to. I hate all the sham about war.'

John liked the experience of that solo film, but it was not enough to propel him into a serious acting career. He loathed the endless waiting in the desert, or on film sets in Germany and Spain, and learning lines, however short, drained his patience. No matter how often Lester told him sincerely that he had the ability to develop a role as a fine actor, John would have none of it. He reverted to his lifelong theory about the stage and the cinema: 'people up there trying to pretend they're somewhere else.'

On his return home, it was obvious to Lennon that he had already lived at a pace, and absorbed enough, that matched three times his age. Doors had opened and closed during his twenty-six years with fantastic speed: art, music, books, dramatic acting, recording, concerts, success on a scale undreamed of. Yet they all left him feeling empty, and without much sense of achievement. His scepticism about politics remained: in a British General Election year, he said to me during an interview on his political beliefs: 'The motto seems to be: "Keep the people happy with a few fags and beer and they won't ask any questions." I'm not an anarchist, but it would be good if people started realizing the difference between political propaganda and truth.'

His own search for the truth manifested itself that autumn in two diversions that were dramatically and tangibly to affect the next two years of his life, and his years beyond them. Those diversions were drugs and his desire to get back in some way to the world of art from which he sprang. Combined, drugs and artistic visions would produce the psychedelic sounds, the next year, of *Sgt Pepper's Lonely Hearts Club Band*. But in 1966, desperate for a new route that nourished his own psyche, John Lennon believed he had found spiritual and physical uplift in the drug LSD (lysergic acid) and a constant round of London art galleries.

Lysergic acid was slipped quietly into John and Cynthia's coffee one night when they were out with George and his wife, Pattie, the model whom he had met on the set of *A Hard Day's Night*. For John, the mind expansion, the discovery of oneself within, the check on one's ego, the release, the heightening of his perceptions, were not just the perfect backdrop for the new vibrancy of Swinging London. The drug's ability to detach him from the mundane and transport his mind into a kind of nirvana was, he told me, an answer to his prayer. Attending a round of parties in London connected with the art world, John found out how to get what he described to me as 'the best stuff it's possible to get in the world.' He took large amounts of LSD in the autumn of 1966, mixing up potions at home. He became a vegetarian, ate infrequently, and looked dangerously wasted within a few short months.

John tried unsuccessfully to lure Cynthia into his never-ending use of marijuana or LSD. 'It seemed to be all right for him, although I was totally against it,' she recalls. 'It opened the floodgates of his mind and he seemed to escape from the imprisonment of fame. Tensions, and bad tempers, were replaced by understanding and love as his message.' Pressured by John's constant pleading, Cynthia did relent and tried an LSD trip, during which John carefully guided her. But she was not mentally receptive.

When she 'came back' from her horrifying experience of a bad trip, she decided categorically that she would never dabble again. 'This upset John, but I could not handle it,' she says. 'Suddenly there was this new mental barrier between us.' Her rejection erected an even bigger wall between them than already existed. For weeks she had become increasingly worried about the retinue of drug pushers and the undesirable caravan of hangers-on who were arriving back home with John, pouring out of his Rolls-Royce at dawn, after a night of clubbing and hard drinking in London. A drunken John was something Cynthia had learned to cope with for years, but a combination of drink and drugs and a coterie of odd unknown people who squatted in the sumptuous lounge of their home drove her to despair. She told John she was worried about the environment in which Julian was having to grow up and go to school from each morning. But John was deep within himself, and when he did not want to reply he would pretend not to have heard. 'I knew then that our marriage was in trouble,' says Cynthia. 'We had lost communication. John was on another planet.'

John was looking for something way beyond the Beatles, and even he did not know what it was. Slowly, his songwriting as well as his life was infiltrated by the hallucinatory effects of soft and hard drugs, though the world did not know it. He hid his marijuana and LSD in the garden at Kenwood, fearing a police raid. The evidence was there in two songs in particular: 'Day Tripper' alluded to anyone who was not properly into drugs, but was what John called a weekend hippie; and in 'We Can Work It Out', written mostly by Paul, John composed the middle part. McCartney was still optimistically looking at life with the sunny outlook that inspired the title, while the suspicious John interjected the words in the middle: 'Life is very short and there's no time . . . for fussing and fighting, my friend.' Love and peace, man, was now his chief passion. The man who had told me at Weybridge at the height of Beatlemania that he was 'waiting for something to happen' set about *making* it happen.

As the seeds of flower power and psychedelia were planted in Swinging London, two of the most thriving industries were boutiques and art galleries, which opened by the score. The Chelsea set, and the tourists, gravitated to the King's Road. Art people headed for Mayfair, Piccadilly, or South Kensington

Through Mick Jagger and singer Marianne Faithfull, one of the least durable partnerships of the swinging scene, Lennon was introduced to John Dunbar, Marianne's former husband and owner of a small art gallery, the Indica, in Mason's Yard, off St James's, Piccadilly. One of its investors was Peter Asher, whose sister Jane was Paul McCartney's girlfriend at the time. Peter had also, as half of the vocal duo Peter and Gordon, recorded a McCartney song, 'A World Without Love', whose lyrical corniness sent Lennon into fits of derisive laughter. 'Please lock me away' was, to John, hilarious.

Dunbar told John that an interesting and unusual exhibition would be opening on 10 November 1966 and that, to ensure that he wasn't harassed as part of a crowd, John might consider popping in to a private preview.

John and Cynthia often did different things in the evenings; she would draw or paint, or do needlework, happy to play the role of contented mother and wife in Weybridge. Besides, drugs had started to rock their partnership. John often went out alone.

On 9 November John's chauffeur-driven Mini Cooper with its tinted windows drew up outside the Indica, and he stepped inside for what Dunbar had told him by telephone would be a 'happening'. John was intrigued. Anything that was off-beat, that fed his druggy inspirations, was going to attract him. This sounded an extraordinary exhibition. He thought a 'happening' might mean an orgy, he said. He was mentally geared up for an *event*.

The exhibition was called *Unfinished Paintings and Objects*. As he leafed through the catalogue, John thought it was very freaky but fascinating, off-beat and weird enough for him to take his time walking round. The catalogue featured pictures of objects like wall cabinets, glassware, a big black bag captioned 'with a member of the audience inside', an apple (apparently meaningless to John), a 'mirror to see your behind', a 'sky TV' described more fully as closed-circuit TV set up in the gallery for looking at the sky, an 'eternal time clock'. Accompanying the pictures were words describing the exhibits: 'I would like to see the sky machine on every corner of the street instead of the Coke machine. We need more skies than Coke.' And: 'The mind is omnipresent. Events in life never happen alone and the history is forever increasing its volume. The natural state of life and mind is complexity. At this point, what art can offer is an absence of complexity, a vacuum through which you are led to a state of complete relaxation of mind. After that, you may return to the complexity of life again. It may not be the same, or it may be, or you may never return, but that is your problem.' And: 'Man is born, educates himself, builds a house and a life and then all that vanishes when he dies. What is real? Is anything real? A thing becomes real to us when it is functional and necessary to us. As long as we strive for truth we live in self-induced misery, expecting in life something that is not an illusion. If we recognize that nothing is true nor illusory . . . then we can proceed from there on to be optimistic and swallow life as it comes.'

The catalogue offered John the most bizarre introduction to the 'happening'. There was a 'Painting to Shake Hands – a painting for cowards: drill a hole in a canvas and put your hand out from behind. Receive your guests in that position. Shake hands and converse with hands.'

The carefully designed, handsomely printed catalogue had pictures on stickers for tearing out and placing over captions to feed the imagination: 'Painting to Hammer a Nail'; 'Painting to Let the Evening Light Go Through'; 'Bag Wear'.

A commercial sales list in the catalogue increased the smile on John's face. On offer, through mail order, were items like this: 'Soundtape of the snow falling at dawn, twenty-five cents per inch (types: snow of India, snow of Kyo, snow of Aos).

'Crying machine: machine drops tears and cries for you when coin is deposited: 3,000 dollars.

'Word machine: machine produces a word when coin is deposited: 1,500 dollars.

'Disappearing machine: machine that allows an object to disappear when button is pressed: 1,600 dollars.

'Danger box: machine that you will never come back the same from (we cannot guarantee your safety in its use): 1,100 dollars.

'Sky machine: machine produces nothing when coin is deposited: 1,500 dollars.'

The list went on: a transparent house, intended so that the people inside cannot see out and the people outside can see in; special defects underwear for men; underwear to make you high, for women, description upon request; imaginary music; books called *Grapefruit*.

'What's all this *about?*' an incredulous Lennon asked John Dunbar.

'Bringing you here,' replied Dunbar, 'is my conceptual work of art.'

As John finished reading and moved round the gallery to look at the startling exhibits, the artist herself, a slight woman, under five feet tall, dressed all in black, her head framed by thick, long black hair, handed him a card on which was printed one word: BREATHE.

Her name was Yoko Ono.

SIXTEEN

DIVORCE

'When I met her, I had to drop everything'

I THINK,' SAYS Yoko Ono, 'that I was probably the successor to Aunt Mimi in John's life.' Her comparison of herself with the formidable but intensely caring woman who raised John Lennon through his entire childhood is both brave and astute. The qualities in his stern Aunt Mimi, which John grew to admire and respect, were to be re-created in a much more bizarre fashion by Yoko Ono. And she too had a profound, devastating effect on him.

Their first meeting set the pattern of their loving, creative, and often tempestuous relationship. At London's Indica Gallery in late 1966 one of the exhibits in Yoko's show as an avant-garde artist was an apple which she had on sale for £200. John was taken aback by the absurdity of it. 'Look, I don't have to pay all that money for an apple,' he said, smiling cynically with that familiar curled bottom lip. He appreciated the dry humour in her work immediately. Yoko Ono had won her point: she had elicited a firm response. For the artist in her, contact had been made.

Next she asked John to climb a stepladder and hammer an imaginary nail into the wall. This, she said, would cost him five shillings. John's retort was as swift as one might have expected from a no-nonsense Liverpudlian: 'I'll give you an imaginary five shillings,' he said, 'if you'll let me hammer the imaginary nail.' The joke was that there were no nails left. Yoko permitted herself a rare smile. John said later that he regarded the event as 'nutty'. But Yoko remembers that they both felt a certain electricity in the air as they 'connected'. Lennon was a sucker for experimentation. Yoko says she recognized in him that evening an artistic sense of humour that placed him apart from his professional role as 'millionaire Beatle'. She was anyway totally unimpressed by the fact that he was rich and famous: 'I was a conceptual artist and had no interest in pop music. The Beatles' thing, rock 'n' roll, had passed me by.' Lennon, conversely, was drawn to the art world like a magnet. The restlessness that simmered underneath the pop star at the end of 1966 had resulted from his deep involvement with drugs.

On the evening he first met Yoko his demeanour virtually reflected his inner self: confused and dissatisfied with the mad whirl of Beatlemania. Crucially, at the time of his meeting with Yoko, he was looking for a new force in his life. With the uncanny sixth sense of communication that was to manifest itself between them as the years unfolded, Yoko realized after that odd encounter at the Indica Gallery that something had happened to her too. 'He played exactly the same mind game as me,' she says.

John's account of that first meeting is somewhat longer but just as immediate. 'Imagine two cars of the same make heading towards each other and they're gonna crash, head-on. Well, it's like one of those scenes from a film – they're doing a hundred miles an hour, they both slam their brakes on and there's smoke everywhere on the floor and they stop just in the nick of time with their bumpers almost touching but not quite. That's what it was like from the first time I got to know her.' The analogy was perfect.

There was a problem, however. Both John Winston Lennon and Yoko Ono were married.

Back at home in Weybridge, Surrey, John's wife, Cynthia, firmly believed her role was to continue as before Beatlemania: as the rock-solid, unquestioning, loving, home-building wife and devoted mother to their three-year-old son, Julian. John's absence as a travelling Beatle had forced her to shoulder all the domestic chores. Passive, maternal, at all times understanding, except on the subject of drugs, Cynthia was still the contented, tasteful, resilient Hoylake girl who had first won John's heart at art college. Being the wife of a millionaire star whose face was in the newspapers and on television every week had not changed her one scrap. The problem was that John *had* changed. And he regretted that Cyn had not changed with him. He was looking for new action. And he wanted it quickly, like everything else.

'There was nothing basically wrong with my marriage to Cyn,' John told me. 'It was just like an amber light. It wasn't on go and it wasn't on stop. I suppose that me being away so much during the early years of our marriage, I never did feel like the average married man.'

His artistic flirtation with Yoko took months, and a determined pursuit by her, before it developed; in the beginning he was sceptical of her strange world but intrigued too. Soon after their meeting Yoko sent John a copy of her small book, *Grapefruit*. Its simplicity infuriated him, but it played on his imagination just as Yoko had intended. Effectively it was a continuation of the odd images conjured up in the catalogue which he had smiled over at the Indica Gallery. *Grapefruit* featured Yoko's instructions to: 'Cut a hole in a bag filled with seeds and place the bag where there is wind.' One entry read: 'Hide until everybody goes home. Hide until everybody forgets about you. Hide until everybody dies.'

John read *Grapefruit* in bed at night. Beside him lay Cynthia, who once asked what he was reading. 'Oh, something that weird artist woman sent me,' he replied. Neither husband nor wife realized that within two years that same 'weird artist woman' would radically re-shape both their lives and that John would write as his introduction to the reprinted version of *Grapefruit:* 'Hi, my name is John Lennon. I'd like you to meet Yoko Ono.' Alongside the terse message would be his drawing of the woman who by then had won his heart as well as his head.

John was no saint, and Cynthia knew it. The temptations for a Beatle, who was one of the most famous people in the world in 1966, adored, mentally and physically, by thousands of women, would have been almost impossible for a full-blooded male to resist.

'But I had blind faith,' says Cynthia. 'I couldn't imagine John being involved with another woman. And even if he had, I would have ignored it because he always came back. Whatever John did outside our marriage, he didn't flaunt anything. So when I learned later about the temptations he had succumbed to, I had the satisfaction of knowing he had protected me at the time, just like he had since we first met.'

Cynthia says she had more fears about his desirability when he was a student than when he was a Beatle. 'Once he became famous, he was like a national institution, not easy to be picked off for flings – well, easy maybe, but he had to be careful about it, be careful who knew.'

Honesty, one of John's most endearing characteristics, forced him to confess to Cynthia one day early in 1967. Cynthia was washing the dishes when John came behind her, put his arms around her waist and said: 'I want to get it off my chest, Cyn. There have been hundreds of other women.'

It could have been an explosive moment. But such was Cynthia's love and devotion to John that his honesty and his tender way of breaking the news of his affairs developed into one of the frankest moments in their marriage since the turbulence of Beatlemania and drugs had pulled them apart. 'Strangely,' says Cynthia, 'it was a very loving moment. I was in tears, not of anger or shock, but tears of happiness that he could tell me, that we'd once again got close enough for him to get rid of it, talk it through and put it on a different level. Perhaps it would have been better if I'd been able to be a bit more aggressive. But I was so happy that at last he felt he could open his heart and tell me what was on his mind.'

Their marriage had been 'rolling along nicely with no fireworks,' she recalls. Although she had suspected that John had been involved with other women, she had shut herself away from the possibility, preoccupied with running a house, bringing up Julian, and cosseting John when he returned from work. His extra-marital affairs did not concern her.

Mentally the rift between them had begun more than a year before with John's increased interest in drugs and Cynthia's steadfast refusal to join him on his trips. Now, in 1967, the full flowering of John's personality was to take shape; his own confrontation with his marriage was a central part of this.

'When John told me he'd had all these affairs, I felt as though we were being brought together again,' says Cynthia. 'He'd been leading his life as a musician and pop star and I'd led mine as a wife and mother. Conversation had become very thin on the ground. He was doing so many things I wasn't involved in.'

John's confession had a strange irony. A few weeks earlier he and Cynthia had been watching television when a programme mentioned the number of times a week an average married couple would make love. They fell far short of it, says Cynthia, because John was away so much. He said to her: 'God, we're just like brother and sister, aren't we?' But their marriage had ticked over until that crucial session of owning up. And that was the major problem. John's mind was expanding so fast by then that he did not want anything in his life to 'tick over'.

'Our relationship was one of friendship — we were always mates and we'd gone through a lot together,' says Cynthia. 'But I did know we couldn't pretend it was like the student days once he'd made it to the top. Once Julian was born, we were parents, responsible people and John was a big star. If any of John's agony, self-torment, or torture was worrying him, then he kept it hidden from me. I wasn't aware of it.'

John's admission of other women in his life might have been therapeutic for both him and Cynthia, but the physical flings were only a surface indication of something that ran much deeper. What he would not say to her, because he did not want to hurt her, was that he was desperately looking for some new milestone in his life. He did not feel comfortable in his Weybridge mansion in the stockbroker belt. The house was merely a status symbol, bought hurriedly to hide from fans thronging their central London flat. The roller-coaster of Beatlemania had lost its attraction for him. Drugs were increasing their hold over him, and the continuing clash with Cynthia over his use of LSD rocked their marriage still further. He became increasingly irritable when, as he took LSD at home, Cynthia said:

'Please, John, it would be wise for you not to do it. You will go mental if you're not careful. Think about Julian, think about everything.'

Cynthia comments: 'But his reasoning power over what was important had gone. Whatever anyone said when he was taking LSD was not to be treated seriously. Me, I didn't get involved because I saw my role as his wife, and Julian's Mum, as running the house and being the mainstay of his life when he was there.' She regrets not having been more positive, perhaps even slightly more aggressive, to counter John's excesses. 'I couldn't change my character, though, could I?' But Cynthia had miscalculated the degree of intellectual stimulus John was now seeking.

In midsummer 1967 the Beatles' manager, Brian Epstein, threw a small party at his house at 24 Chapel Street, Belgravia, to mark a very special event in the career of the four men to whom he still paternally referred as 'the boys'. Few of the guests, including me, expected the new album from the Beatles to be so revolutionary. The record that blared out from behind tables groaning with exquisitely chosen gourmet food was *Sgt Pepper's Lonely Hearts Club Band*. The music perfectly captured the mood of that psychedelic, flower-power summer when Swinging London, mini skirts, Carnaby Street's fashion liberation, and love and peace were precursors of a generation's change. It became a soundtrack for psychedelia.

There had been little indication to the public that the Beatles had gone so far down the road with drugs. A few months earlier John's song 'Strawberry Fields Forever' – one of his finest – evoked nothing more spiky than his childhood memories of ice-creams in a Salvation Army children's fête, while Paul's 'Penny Lane', on the reverse side, completed the Liverpool connection with flashbacks to the bus shelter where John and Paul, as fiendish schoolboys, would meet and eye the girls. But *Sgt Pepper* was different, a triumphant leap forward in songwriting ideas by John and Paul. Two Lennon songs in particular – 'A Day In The Life' and 'Lucy In The Sky With Diamonds' – were revolutionary even for the ever-questing John, the first being banned by the BBC for its implied condoning of drugs, the second being a haunting stream-of-consciousness song which John had written after Julian had come home from school (Heath House, Weybridge) one afternoon and shown him a picture he had drawn, inspired by his friend Lucy.

At Epstein's party John looked haggard, old, ill, hopelessly addicted to drugs. His eyes were glazed, his speech slow and slurred. I had a brief chat with him about music, and he said he was worried that they had gone too far for public taste with the new album. 'Will they buy it? I like it, we all feel it's another step up, but will it sell?' I was astonished at his coherence while he was clearly under the influence of drugs. We spoke a little about the state of the music scene, and he said there was one 'dope' record which he couldn't get off his mind. He couldn't remember the title. All other pop music of the period was 'crap', one of his favourite words at the time. John said he wasn't eating much and was on a vegetarian diet.

He smoked and drank wine incessantly. Talking later to Brian Epstein, I said how horrifying and worrying John's physical state seemed. 'Don't worry. He's a survivor,' said Brian.

Next day John phoned me. 'I remembered after I'd gone what the record is that I can't stop playing,' he said. 'It's that dope song, Procol Harum's "Whiter Shade Of Pale". It's the best song I've heard for a while. You play it when you take some acid and . . . whooooooooooooo.' What was most surprising about the phone call was that he'd actually remembered our conversation the previous evening. As he was later to prove, his eye and ear for detail and his memory, even when on drugs, would surprise anyone who thought him inattentive.

Talking of the making of *Sgt Pepper*, producer George Martin says: 'That was an incredible thing because it took on its own character, it grew despite us. It was a complete change of life, a very long and arduous series of recordings and I suppose that looking back on it, *Pepper* would never have been formed in exactly that way if the boys hadn't got into the drug scene, and if I hadn't been a normal person. I don't think it would have been as coherent . . . I just had to be patient. You can't do much with a guy when he's giggling all the time. If they hadn't been on drugs, it's possible something like *Pepper* would have happened but not quite so flowery, maybe.'

Drugs, *Sgt Pepper*, his psychedelically painted Rolls-Royce, the gipsy caravan in his garden at Weybridge, and his total embrace of a more freewheeling way of life hardened John's attitude to his home environment. Yoko both fascinated and annoyed him. A steady stream of letters arrived at Weybridge from her, and for a period, postcards arrived daily, saying: 'Dance' or 'Breathe' or 'Watch all the lights until dawn.' John alternately found them intriguing or simply dismissed them.

At this point in his life John was at his most vulnerable. The Beatles had stopped touring and had just produced an album which was critically acclaimed as setting new standards for popular music, lifting Lennon and McCartney into a new echelon of composers. This crossroads in the Beatles' position, coupled with his foundering marriage and his enthusiasm for drugs, made him easy prey to anything that offered new kicks.

As for the other Beatles, George Harrison had succumbed to Eastern mysticism, entranced by the sitar-playing of his tutor and new friend, Ravi Shankar. Paul McCartney, with actress Jane Asher at his side, moved ever upwards in the social whirl of London hip society, which held no appeal for John. Ringo, living a few minutes away on the same estate at Weybridge, enjoyed dispensing drinks from his private bar, the Flying Cow, and was useful to John when he wanted to lock into light-heartedly playing the Beatle role. But when Pattie Harrison, George's wife, said she had heard from a friend about transcendental meditation, which encouraged a deeper, cooler form of consciousness and awareness, John was hooked. Together with Cynthia, George and Pattie, and Paul and Jane, he attended a lecture on meditation by the Maharishi Mahesh Yogi at London's Hilton Hotel.

By now the phone calls from Yoko had increased; she sought his support for her artistic ventures and even visited his home when neither he nor Cynthia was there. The housekeeper, Dorothy Jarlett, allowed her in one day to make a phone call, and next day Yoko phoned John to say she must return because she had left her 'very precious' ring by the phone. John was getting used to her unpredictable behaviour, and her spacey conversation attracted him, especially when he was high on drugs. Cynthia was blissfully ignorant that their relationship had any potential until that night after their baptism into transcendental meditation. Yoko was also at the meeting – alone.

As John and Cynthia climbed into their chauffeur-driven Rolls-Royce afterwards, Yoko followed them into the car. 'John and I both looked at each other as though we'd gone crazy,' says Cynthia. 'I said to him: "What's going on?" He said: "I dunno." Neither of us had the courage to say: "Excuse me, madam, but where are you going?" She got in the car and asked to be dropped off down the road, which we duly did. For all I knew, there could have been something going on between John and Yoko even then but I don't think so judging from the look on his face. It was pure shock. It couldn't have been put on.' Yoko was dressed all in black. With her long hair and tiny figure even Cynthia admits she was fascinating. 'We thought it was quite amusing afterwards,' she recalls. 'We joked about it.' When John introduced Yoko to Cynthia, Yoko almost immediately propelled herself into talking about *Grapefruit*. Cynthia drew long and hard on her ever-present cigarette and pondered the weird woman in black who, according to John's reports, 'kept popping up all over the place' in his life.

At home later that evening Cynthia confronted John about Yoko and her strange behaviour.

'What is it with Yoko then?'

John replied: 'Oh nothing, she's crackers, she's just a weirdo artist. Don't worry about it.'

Cynthia persisted: 'Well what's all the phoning about, all these letters and leaving rings behind and knocking at the door?'

'Oh don't worry about it,' John insisted, 'it's not important. Crazy crazy crazy, Cyn! She's another nutter wanting money for all that avant-garde bullshit.'

Cynthia recalls: 'There was, though, something coming across constantly. It was worrying me but I had no tangible evidence. . . . Although he and I didn't properly argue about it, the fact that he was smoking and taking LSD made it hard to communicate. He kept pleading with me to join him and take it, but I wanted to keep my sanity. . . . During one of these scenes, I said to him: "Perhaps Yoko's the one

for you, John." I remember he said: "Don't be stupid. That
weird artist!" '

The day after that bizarre encounter John went with
the other Beatles to Bangor, North Wales, to be properly
taught transcendental meditation during a Bank Holiday
weekend seminar. After a frantic dash to London's Euston
Station, Cynthia arrived to see the train leaving and John,
hanging from the window, a face in the distance. The
moment flashed before both John and Cynthia's eyes as
strangely underlining the split in their marriage. When she
eventually arrived alone, John sarcastically berated her for
'always being late' and brought Cynthia to the brink of tears
during what was supposed to be a weekend of tranquillity.
The weekend, as well as widening the rift in John's marriage, proved to be a turning point for the Beatles.

On 27 August 1967, a day before he was due to travel
north to join the Beatles for the meditation course, Brian
Epstein died, a victim of an accidental drug overdose at his
London home. Amid his beads and robes and peace in the
North Wales countryside, John reacted to the news with
the same pent-up emotion which he had felt at the deaths
of his mother, his Uncle George, and his best friend, Stuart
Sutcliffe. Lennon did not believe in prolonged grief. The
Beatles returned to London to face the press and try to
marshal their thoughts about the millionaire, thirty-two-
year-old manager who had steered them to the dizziest
heights of world fame.

His death, so unexpected in the context of his success,
was a puzzle. Brian was a complex, narcissistic man, very
much a loner, and yet in a mere six years he had converted
four scruffy rock 'n' rollers from Liverpool to legendary
status and international social phenomena. It was a stupen-

dous achievement. John had a love-hate feeling about Brian's triumph. He wanted the riches and fame which Brian's zeal had made possible, but he resented the fact that Epstein had cleaned them up and robbed them of their raw roots. Even so, John often demonstrated his big heart, sending Brian flowers or little gifts when Eppy was low.

That Bank Holiday Monday afternoon John invited me over to Weybridge to talk about the impact of Brian's death. Robed in white and lazing with Ringo by the pool, he seemed dazed as the words came together slowly.

'We all feel very sad but it's controlled grief, controlled emotion. As soon as I find myself feeling depressed, I think of something nice about him. But you can't hide the hurt – you know, I went to the phone book and saw his name and it hit me a few minutes ago. The memory must be kept nice but of course there's something inside us that tells us that Brian's death is sad.

'It hurts when someone close dies and Brian was very close. You know, we've all been through that feeling of wanting a good cry. But that wouldn't get us anywhere, would it?

'We all feel it, but these talks on transcendental meditation have helped us to stand up to it so much better. You don't get upset, do you, when a young kid becomes a teenager or a teenager becomes an adult or when an adult gets old? Well, Brian is just passing into the next phase.

'His spirit is still around and always will be. It's a physical memory we have of him and as men we will build on that memory. It's a loss of genius, but other genius's bodies have died as well, and the world gains from their spirits.

'It's up to us now to sort out the way we, and Brian, wanted things to go. He might be dead physically but that's a negative way of thinking. He helped to give us the strength to do what we did and the same urge is still alive. It's a drag he didn't come up to the meditation course with the Maharishi.'

I asked John for his evaluation of Epstein's role in the Beatles' success and whether they would still have broken through without him. 'Not the same as we know it, no. But if he hadn't come along, we would all – the four of us and Brian – have been working towards the same thing, even though it might have been with different aims. We all knew what we wanted to get over; he helped us and we helped him.

'We're all going to India soon for a couple of months to study transcendental meditation properly. The only plans we had, before Brian died, were to make a record, do a TV show, and make a film. But meeting the Maharishi changed our thoughts a bit and Brian's death has changed it a lot. It makes it more worthwhile, now, somehow, to go to India.

'We want to learn the meditation thing properly so we can propagate it and sell the whole idea to everyone. This is how we plan to use our power now – they've always called us leaders of youth and we believe this is a good way to give a lead. We want to set up an academy in London and use all the power we've got to get it moving. And all the people who are worried about youth and drugs and that scene – all these people with the short back and sides, they can come along and dig it, too.

'It's no gospel, Bible-thumping, singalong thing and it needn't be religion if people don't want to connect it with religion. It's all in the mind.

'It strengthens understanding, makes people relaxed. The whole world wants to relax more and the people who get to know a bit about meditation will see it's not just a fad or a gimmick but the way to calm down tensions. You learn about thoughts, the meaning of thoughts, how to trace your thoughts – and it's much better than acid.

'We have no idea of whether we'll get a new manager. We have always been in control of what we're doing and we'll have to do what we have to, now. We know what we should do and what we shouldn't do. Brian was a natural guide and we'll certainly miss him.

'If Brian had been in on the lectures on meditation he would have understood. This is the biggest thing in my life now and it's come at the time when I need it most. It's nothing to do with mysticism. It's about *understanding*.

'Brian has died only in body and his spirit will always be working with us. His power and force were everything, and that will linger on. When we were on the right track he knew it, and when we were on the wrong track he told us so and he was usually right. But anyway, he isn't really dead.'

Just before he died Epstein had tried, unsuccessfully, to persuade the Beatles to re-consider their decision to stop touring. But John and George were resolute in their determination that the 1966 American trail had been the last. Brian died a dispirited man, empty at the realization that 'the boys' no longer needed him and that they did not respond to his requests. If they were to be a group that existed mostly for recording, John's whiplash tongue would see to it that, like any other visitor to their sessions, Brian kept silent when the music was being rehearsed or completed. Epstein had simply been left with an untenable role – a manager with no power and little control. His 'boys' had become men: rich, independent individuals with positive plans, widening horizons, and the talent to move on.

Or so it seemed that heady midsummer in 1967. That year, as the message of love and peace wafted from California to London on a tidal wave of good vibrations, as Scott

McKenzie sang 'If you go to San Francisco be sure to wear some flowers in your hair' and John Lennon chewed gum before 400 million people on world television singing 'All You Need Is Love', John stayed cool. But later he would be forced to admit, 'The Beatles were finished when Eppy died. I knew, deep inside me, that that was it. Without him, we'd had it.'

As John and Cynthia left Heathrow Airport for the concrete chalets of Rishikesh, India, early in 1968 to accompany George and Pattie Harrison at the Maharishi's meditation academy, he looked, felt, and spoke like a man with problems gnawing away inside him. He was no longer the lovable mop-top Beatle whose steely wit had won the admiration of millions.

In Rishikesh the meditation was a healing influence and the changed environment was good for John, but Cynthia noticed his jittery behaviour. 'Every morning he would be up and out of our room before me, at seven o'clock, saying he was off to meditate alone,' she says. 'He cut me dead in the mornings. The first week we were in India he was fine, but after that, he cut me off from himself. We'd always done things together. . . . "Hang on wait for me John," I said.

' "No, no, I'm off," was his answer. I couldn't understand why at the time; I put it down to being away and his changed attitudes to meditation and the beauty that there were now no drugs. Meditation had killed the pushers stone dead, which I was thrilled about because it was getting to a very dangerous state. I thought heroin had to be the next stage. But now he was on edge. I realized later that he was going to collect the morning mail with letters from Yoko, but at the time I had no idea.

'It got to the stage when we were in the same room together that we would get on each other's nerves. Meditation has different patterns and I would sometimes go into deep meditation when John wasn't in the mood, and when we shared the same room, it was bad for both of us. . . . He seemed very isolated and would spend days on end with the Maharishi, emerging bleary-eyed and not wanting to communicate with me or anyone. So I believe he underwent a big change in Rishikesh. He went so deeply within himself through meditation that he separated himself from everything.'

John took meditation very seriously. He and George believed in its calming powers far more than the others in the party. For eight hours a day John would meditate, and for the rest of the time during the eight weeks spent at the academy he wrote fifteen songs.

Yoko's flow of letters, some handwritten, others which she had typed immaculately, struck just the right mood for John's relaxed frame of mind. 'I'm a cloud. Watch for me in the sky,' she wrote. John, who quickly moved to a separate bedroom from Cynthia, reflected on her hypnotic words back in Weybridge: 'Perhaps Yoko's the one for you.' Perhaps, he decided, she was dead right. He could hardly wait to see her again.

Coupled with this was a growing disaffection with the Maharishi's behaviour and personality (although not with his methods). John and Cynthia announced they were leaving two weeks ahead of their original plan. Paul and Jane Asher, and Ringo and his wife Maureen had already returned home. There were too many Indian flies in the air for Maureen, and Ringo commented with his dry humour that the academy resembled a Butlin's holiday camp. Lennon, asked by the Maharishi, whom he had grown to

distrust, why he was leaving early, replied tersely: 'If you're
so bloody cosmic, you'll know why.'

With his interest in Yoko growing rapidly, John was
eager to get back to England. On his return, however, he
was bedevilled by problems which even he found hard to
face.

With no manager, he and the other three Beatles decided
to launch their own company, Apple, and a new album was
also in the offing. By far the biggest issue in his mind,
however, was his relationship with Cynthia. It wasn't that
they were quarrelling much. It was more of a communication barrier. The mental rift caused by drugs was now
increased by the meditation scene. 'We went through some
bad times,' Cynthia says. 'It was very confusing, coming
back to reality after meditating in India.'

John said to her that as he had an album to prepare
and business to attend to he would be in the studios a lot.
'Cyn, why don't you get away for a couple of weeks on that
holiday in Greece that Jenny and Alex are going on?' he
said. Jenny Boyd was the sister of Pattie Harrison; Alex
was 'Magic Alex' (his real name was John Alexis Mardas),
a Greek-born electronics wizard who had inveigled himself
into John's life and was a constant visitor to the Lennon
home.

Cynthia agreed. 'We both needed space to breathe,' she
says. 'I don't think he was intentionally getting rid of me.
He just wanted to sort himself out, after India, just as I
did. He was unsure of himself and the way his life was
going. He felt he'd been let down by the Maharishi, the
Beatles were obviously going to have to reconsider everything now Brian Epstein was dead, and then there were the

uncertainties between us. It seemed a good thing for me to get away and let him concentrate on work.'

John's first major sign to Cynthia that he was going through agonizing decisions came the day she was packing for her Greek holiday. 'He was upstairs lying, fully clothed, on our bed, staring into space, not saying a word. It was as though he had so much on his mind he couldn't speak. Normally he'd have come down and waved me off in the taxi, but he was on a different planet that day I left. There was no getting through to him. He'd obviously got to the brink of planning what he wanted from his life and what was going to happen a week later with me on holiday. And what John wanted, he usually got.'

Cynthia left Weybridge under a cloud. John had decided that it was now or never with Yoko Ono. It was time to resolve their clandestine relationship and follow up the stream of curious, intriguing letters.

The only other person living at Weybridge during Cynthia's absence was his old schoolfriend from Quarry Bank, Liverpool. Pete Shotton was a little surprised when John said he thought he would invite Yoko Ono over for an evening the night before Cynthia's return. Shotton said he was going to bed anyway. John phoned Yoko in her London flat, and his chauffeur-driven Rolls-Royce was sent to bring her, clad in her customary black, up the gravel drive into Kenwood by mid-evening.

John was apprehensive; he realized this might not be another of his fast affairs. He and Yoko sat talking nervously downstairs in the lounge for several hours: he about the pressures of being a famous millionaire Beatle and how he now no longer felt the same sense of challenge as before; she about the frustrations of being an artist. 'Yoko and I were on the same wavelength right from the start, from that first night,' John told me years later. 'That first night convinced me I'd have to end my marriage to Cyn.'

John took Yoko to his upstairs den with its two tape recorders on which he had first practised some of his songwriting gems like 'Nowhere Man', 'I'm A Loser', and the classic 'Norwegian Wood' which told of his affair with a prominent woman journalist. John and Yoko introduced each other to their different worlds. Lennon had always experimented with sounds and was interested in electronic effects and comedy; Yoko's interest was the human voice and extending its potential beyond the realms of orthodox singing. 'We improvised for many hours,' she recalls. 'He used the two tape recorders and put through them any sounds that came into his hands, you know: old recorded sounds. I sat down and did the voice. We were both involved and enjoying the uncertainty of how it would all turn out. And that was it. We called it *Unfinished Music*. The idea is that the listener can take from it, or add to it in his mind, or her mind.' Challenging her public was a central theme in Yoko's work. John was mesmerized by her sense of artistic adventure. From his guitar and pen, everything had been channelled into straightforward commercial songs. Yoko's world, he suddenly decided, was not 'avant-garde crap' as he had earlier feared. It opened up real possibilities. They went to bed together at dawn as the birds were waking. 'It was very beautiful,' John recalled. 'I had no doubt I'd met The One.'

Next morning Pete Shotton became the first person to know. John told him that he was going to look for a new house in which he and Yoko could live. A flabbergasted Shotton asked him what he was talking about. John replied that he had met the person he'd been looking for and was prepared to cash in everything, whatever the cost, to be with her. Beatles, houses, money, fame – nothing counted

except his future with Yoko Ono. The chemistry between
them was unbelievable; her physical attraction was strengthened by her intuitive knowledge of what fired John's
thoughts. If there was one moment when John Lennon
ceased to be a committed Beatle and chose, instead, to
become an artist, it was that spring night and dawn in May
1968. And, as always when John decided on something, it
was irrevocable.

When, one afternoon, a joyful, refreshed Cynthia returned
from her holiday she was bubbling and optimistic that the
short separation might now improve her life with John.
Mysteriously, the outside porch light was on, and all the
curtains were drawn. 'It was eerily silent,' she recalls. 'Normally there would be a gardener around, or Dot the housekeeper, or Julian playing, but it was deserted, as if there
had been an all-night party. I had no idea what would
confront me when I got in. I knocked on the door like mad
at first but there was no reply. The whole of the front of
the house was in darkness but looking through to the big
lounge there was a light coming through, rather eerily.'
   Once inside Cynthia, followed by Jenny Boyd and
Magic Alex, walked slowly around shouting: 'Is anybody
there? John? Julian? Dot?' Still there was no sound. Cynthia
ran round all the rooms on the ground floor, until finally
reaching the dining room and kitchen. Off this, in the sun-
room, the sight that faced her left her 'dumbstruck'. John,
in his green-and-white-striped towelling robe, hair dishevelled, mug of tea in his hand, sat on the small settee, facing
Cynthia as she walked in. Yoko, her mass of black hair
cascading down the back of a chair, making her instantly
recognizable, sat on a chair facing John. She was motionless,
her back to Cynthia who had stopped dead at the doorway.

'It was like walking into a brick wall, as if I didn't belong any more. I felt absolutely shut out from communication,' says Cynthia. Within seconds Jenny and Alex were standing behind her, open-mouthed.

John broke the silence of what seemed hours and was probably a minute. 'Oh hi,' he said coolly, taking a drag from his cigarette. He might have been addressing the gardener or a waiter.

Cynthia, feeling the unreality of the situation, was shattered and lost for words. She attempted to pacify the ugliness of the experience. 'Oh hi,' she said to John. 'I had this great idea,' she went on quietly. 'We had breakfast in Greece, lunch in Rome and Jenny and Alex and I thought it would be great if we all went out to dinner in London to carry on the whole holiday.'

With no expression in his voice, John answered bluntly: 'No thanks.'

At this point Yoko turned round and gave Cynthia 'a very positive, confident look'. She was dressed in a black silk kimono. 'I suppose I should have been prepared for it but I wasn't,' says Cynthia. 'It took my breath away. I wasn't angry. I was just absolutely shattered at the vision. John wasn't talking to anybody – not just me, but to nobody. He was just staring, expressionless. So instead of starting a battle and asking questions about what was going on, I felt I had to get out of that house immediately.' She went upstairs and, in the panic, re-packed the kind of things she had just returned with from her holiday in the sun: toothbrush, shoes, make-up, coat, toilet bag. Passing the guest bedroom, Cynthia saw a pair of Japanese slippers outside the door: the final, crushing evidence, if she needed it, that Yoko had spent a night there.

Seized by a need to get out of the house as soon as she could, Cynthia was ready to leave within fifteen minutes of her arrival and confrontation. 'I decided John had been almost willing me to go. I took his silence as saying, "Don't interrupt this fantastic situation. Get lost. You're spoiling things." I got the message immediately without any more words.' She says she travelled faster than the speed of sound.

Cynthia went to stay with Jenny Boyd and Alex Mardas at their mews house in central London. 'I knew Julian would be safe with Dot, the housekeeper. He often went there,' she says. Three days later, having collected her thoughts, Cynthia warily phoned Kenwood. Dorothy Jarlett, the loyal housekeeper, now in an impossible situation, answered. No, she said, John was not in. Cynthia enquired if Julian was all right and said she was returning home that day.

To her amazement, John greeted her as if nothing had happened. 'I can't understand why you went off,' he said. 'What have you been up to?' Cynthia apologized and said she couldn't cope with seeing him and Yoko looking so together. John insisted that their liaison was purely intellectual, Yoko and he had 'messed around with tapes all night' and it was quite wrong for Cynthia to misconstrue the situation. He would not talk about his association with Yoko. Cynthia says: 'It was strange that he would talk about the other women he'd been involved with, but with Yoko he stopped the conversation flat.'

Superficially, a warm, welcoming John gave Cynthia the impression all was well with their marriage. 'But I noticed his unease when I said, several times: "I see a great similarity between you and Yoko. John, there's something about her that's just like you. Look, you may say these things about Yoko, that she's crazy, just a weird artist, but there's an aura about her that's going to click with you."' Cynthia succeeded only in irritating John when she said: 'I can see more into your situation with her than you can.' As she says: 'I knew immediately I saw them together that they were right for each other. I knew I'd lost him.'

Despite John's assurances, Cynthia knew in her heart that their relationship was now threatened. Superficially, however, life seemed to return to normal, and she had no reason to fear an immediate marriage crisis. For several weeks during their reunion she asked if she should cancel the family holiday in Italy she had planned for herself, Julian and her mother. 'No, no, you go ahead and have a lovely time,' said John. But he became increasingly distant as the time neared for them to go to Pesaro. There was no chance of his going with them: he had work to do, and besides, the prospect of John going on holiday with his mother-in-law was unthinkable. They had always kept their distance, and he told several people how much he resented the intrusion of Lilian Powell into his domain.

Cynthia felt that she should press on with the holiday 'for Julian's sake.' If she had feared that her absence would crucially affect their marriage, she would never have gone. 'But I didn't. We were back together again and everything seemed fine.' Until, that was, her day of packing and flying. John was in a panic-stricken mood. 'He obviously knew something was going to happen while I was away and he was upset and frightened because he didn't know how it would turn out. Also he was probably worried about losing his son and he was already concerned that he'd spent a lot of time away from Julian when he was growing up.' John was very distant as Les Anthony, their chauffeur, packed the Rolls-Royce that took them to Heathrow. 'We left with a cloud over the holiday,' says Cynthia. 'John was in a trance. He didn't even come to the door to say goodbye.'

John had decided to end his marriage to Cynthia, but he didn't want to be the one to pass her the painful news. She thought it odd that, just before she left, he asked her if she had any affairs outside their marriage. 'No way. I've been totally faithful to you,' she answered. 'There have been mild flirtations but nothing serious that would jeopardize our marriage.' John seemed pleased, she says. His feeling for Yoko was now an obsession. As soon as Cynthia left, John saw as much of her as he could, despite a very busy work period.

An Italian newspaper brought home to Cynthia for the first time the fact that John and Yoko were now inseparable and her marriage irretrievable. Resting in bed with a sore throat, Cynthia was brought a newspaper by the hotel owner, Roberto Bassanini. It contained pictures of 'John Lennon, the Beatle, hand in hand with Japanese artist Yoko Ono,' attending the opening night of a play, *In His Own Write*.

'I knew when I saw the picture that that was *it*,' says Cynthia. 'He'd obviously waited for me to go away to appear in the open with Yoko. He probably thought it would be easier for both of us. I knew it was the end because he would never flaunt something like an involvement with another woman if it were not very serious. It had been building up, I suppose, and was obvious to outsiders but not to me because John had kept up his same attitude, not hurting me.'

Next day John sent an unlikely emissary to give Cynthia a message – Magic Alex Mardas. Alex was to pass on his message to Cynthia and also to hire a private detective to monitor every move she made in Italy. After a tense breakfast with Cynthia, hotelier Roberto Bassanini, Julian, and Cynthia's mother, he insisted on speaking to Cynthia alone. His message could not have been blunter: 'Well, John says he's going to divorce you. He's going to take Julian away from you and he's going to send you back to Hoylake.' His job done, he left immediately for London.

Cynthia's immediate reaction had been that John could

not possibly do as he threatened and ignore her rights in this way. Her mother, vowing she would 'get to the bottom of this', also left immediately and headed for 34 Montagu Square, in London's West End, a flat which had been used alternately by rock star Jimi Hendrix and Ringo Starr, and to which she had moved after Cynthia's first encounter with John and Yoko. On her arrival, she found a bouquet of flowers from John at the door with the cryptic message: 'Beat you to it, Lil.' It was his caustic way of telling Cynthia's mother he knew she had got home quickly to try to play the role of amateur detective, to try to rock the boat between him and Yoko.

Back in London with Julian, Cynthia also went to Montagu Square. She had been shadowed by John's private detective, for within five minutes of her arrival there was a knock at the door and a solicitor handed her a writ for divorce on the grounds of her alleged adultery.

In the five months that followed before John and Cynthia's eventual divorce, rancour and mistrust ran alongside John's frenzied involvement with Yoko which he never sought to hide. His image with the Beatles' public changed dramatically as he openly courted the woman who was to change his life. The last six months of 1968 were electrifying for him: Yoko became pregnant; they began their artistic activities together; Apple was launched; he met Brigitte Bardot, his teenage idol, in a formally set-up meeting in London's Mayfair Hotel; he was arrested for possessing drugs; and he was divorced. John always loved fast action, but this rapid turn of events, combined with the tensions surfacing within the Beatles, pushed him to the limits of his endurance. He leaned increasingly on LSD and drink, usually Scotch.

The run-up to the divorce was complex and often ugly. Cynthia was angry at the speed with which her contact

with John was severed. 'One minute I was with him at
Weybridge, the next the whole fabric of my life and Julian's
was destroyed.' After appointing her own solicitor, she
phoned the Beatles' office and said she needed to talk to
John.

She arrived at Weybridge with Julian and her mother
in tow, probably a psychological blunder considering John's
dislike of Mrs Powell. Yoko and John met her looking as
one: both all in black, John extremely tense. Cynthia's
mother waded in instantly by saying to Yoko: 'I think you
should go in the other room and leave these two together.'

John interjected: 'No, Yoko, you stay here.'

Eventually Yoko left of her own volition: she could not
stand the tension any longer as John and Cynthia lumbered
into a battle neither could win. For fifteen minutes they
argued about who had committed adultery. John insisted
that Cynthia had done so; Cynthia denied this: 'You're
totally unjust in putting me on the spot when you're the
one breaking up the marriage.'

John said: 'We'd better get it in the hands of solicitors
and get it all sorted out.' Cynthia said *she* was suing for
divorce. Cynthia's mother fussed in and out saying her
daughter should not be left on her own.

Finally John could stand her no longer: 'This is my
house – you get out,' he roared.

In the end John and Cynthia agreed to disagree and to
hand the divorce arrangements to their solicitors. Practicality was then re-established amid the thick cigarette
smoke that filled the library. John said that as Cynthia was
caring for Julian, it would be best if he and Yoko moved
out to Montagu Square, and Cynthia, her mother, and Julian
moved back into Kenwood. The house swap happened next
day.

The lawyers began their work, and there followed some

attempts by Cynthia, by telephone, to arrange the terms of the separation. Her personal savings amounted to a mere £2,500 and she clearly needed provision for her immediate future if she was to maintain Julian. She told John on the phone that it might be better if they fixed all the details privately because lawyers wanted her to 'screw him for hundreds of thousands of pounds'. An irate John roared: 'Look, my last offer to you is seventy-five thousand. What have you done to deserve it? Christ, it's like winning the bloody pools!'

A disastrous attempt at harmonious separation took place next on neutral territory: Paul McCartney's house in St John's Wood, London. Against her solicitor's advice Cynthia went along to try to arrange things with John. But Yoko was there, apologizing for not being able to make English tea, and John's demeanour was still aggressive. Cynthia left in tears, frustrated at her failure to break any ground in talking things over with him.

The lawyers set to work. In August Cynthia filed a counter petition against John, alleging his adultery with Yoko, which their solicitors said they denied. But by 25 October John and Yoko announced that they were expecting a baby the next February. That decided the legalities of the case: Cynthia was granted a decree nisi on 8 November 1968, and a settlement payment to her of £100,000 was agreed. She was granted custody of Julian, and John was said in court to have made 'generous and proper provision for Julian.' Additionally she received £2,400 a year for Julian's school fees from a separate trust.

This trust was set up by John for Julian, providing him with £100,000 at the age of twenty-five. He would be the sole beneficiary unless any further children were born to John. When Yoko gave birth to Sean, Julian's entitlement from the trust became £50,000 plus the accrued interest, and Sean's the same.

Emotionally battered, Cynthia withdrew from John's life. Inevitably their paths would cross many times in the future, for John had said he wanted proper access to Julian who was five at the time of the divorce. Cynthia went on to marry Roberto Bassanini, the Italian hotelier from Pesaro. That marriage, and another to Liverpool electrical engineer John Twist, ended in divorce. 'I'll always be in love with John Lennon,' says Cynthia. 'We went through some great times and bad times together, but whatever happened he made such an impression on everyone he touched.' The relationship between Cynthia and Yoko was tense. Cynthia was heart-broken in the early days of their break-up. Eventually, however, she accepted that John had met his match. 'It was a meeting of two minds and nobody could fight that,' Cynthia says candidly.

John had changed. Yoko, he said, took him back partly to how he was as a Liverpool rebel: fiercely independent, opinionated, an activist, a champion of causes. 'The Beatles had got rid of all that in me. The Beatles had turned me into a puppet. It was OK, but once we'd made it so big, the fun had gone and so had my own strength. The Beatles, if you must know, sapped me.'

In Yoko Ono he faced a formidable counterpart. 'But when I met her,' he told me later, 'I had to drop everything.' It was 'Goodbye to the boys in the band!' Jealous of her previous lovers, John questioned her closely and repeatedly about the men she had been with in addition to her husbands. And he wanted to know everything, quickly, about the art world from which she sprang into his life.

Her world was populated with dilettantes, artists with

great inspiration but little notion of how to communicate. In the parlance of the art world, so few of them 'got it together'. Yoko was not among them. A shrewd communicator whose outlandish conceptual art exhibitions had gained her underground notoriety for originality, she believed firmly that if an artist produced a piece of work and then failed to get it through to the public, 'Then what's the point?' One of her greatest strengths lay in that simple truth: she was, and is, a gifted and thrusting sales person. She never believed that being described as avant-garde or underground meant she should lie fallow and hope the people would discover her. She believed implicitly in packaging an original product and marketing it with a degree of humour. By 1968 the stage was set for the launch of a partnership that was a perfect foil for her sometimes fanciful ideas and a magic carpet ride for John's submerged personality. Amid the dying embers of the Beatles, the public had to understand just what Lennon meant when he repeatedly wrote of his new world as *JohnandYoko*.

SEVENTEEN

BEATLES

'I'm breaking the group up'

YOKO ONO – her first name means Ocean Child – was born on 18 February 1933 in Tokyo. Her father, Eisuke, left Tokyo University with degrees in mathematics and economics. He was a pianist before taking up a banking career and quickly rising to head a Japanese bank in San Francisco. Because of his move from the East in pursuit of his career, he did not meet Yoko until she was two; she had stayed in Japan with her mother.

Yoko's aristocratic mother, Isoko, came from one of Japan's richest business families, specializing in property investment, insurance, and banking. Yoko grew up in an environment with maids and tutors and a strikingly attractive, slightly aloof, though caring, mother who enjoyed the material things of life like jewellery and good clothes. That may, Yoko believes, account partly for her own eventual adoption of art as her way of life: 'Inside me I could feel a certain rejection of my mother's show of her possessions but I got over that as I grew older,' she says. She coolly points out, however, that she was never the pauper seeking the millionaire pop star: in her life money had never been a problem. Yoko has a brother, Keisuke, three years younger, and a sister, Setsuko, eight years younger.

By the time Yoko was eighteen, her father had been appointed president of the Bank of Tokyo in New York, and the Ono family had moved from Japan to the high-class suburb of Scarsdale. Yoko attended the prestigious Sarah Lawrence College in New York but dropped out to elope with her first husband, Japanese-born Toshi Ichiyanagi. He proved to be her early partner in the discovery of the world of avant-garde artists. In her loft apartment at 112 Chambers Street, Greenwich Village, Yoko began her lifelong association with art, staging informal events, writing poetry, and developing the conceptual theories that marked her out as an artistic radical. For years her work met either derision or a dull local response. 'I *do* know what it is like to be a frustrated artist,' she says with irony. One of her early liaisons was with American jazz musician-film producer Anthony Cox; he linked up with her to encourage her to stage exhibitions of art objects that demanded a response and some input from the observer rather than answering all the questions. Cox became Yoko's second husband, and their only child, a daughter, Kyoko, was born on 8 August 1963, four months after John and Cynthia Lennon's son, Julian.

As an ambitious and highly organized partnership, Yoko and Tony Cox had a reputation in Europe in the underground art world for staging uncanny exhibitions. There was, as London art people recall, some kudos to be gained from staging a show planned by a talked-about Japanese woman who lived in New York; thus they arrived for their first trip to London in 1962 if not to rapturous acclaim, then certainly amid considerable curiosity. They came back frequently during the next four years.

London artist Adrian Morris, in whose flat Yoko stayed in 1967 soon after going to London from New York, recalls his first meeting with her at a party off the King's Road.

He asked her what kind of artist she was, and she answered: 'I deal with music of the mind.' She had been heavily influenced by the 'extended and repeated image' work of Andy Warhol in New York. As their conversation flowed and Adrian Morris warmed to her, she said she was waiting to move into a flat but there was a complication. Adrian Morris said she and Tony Cox could stay the weekend with him and his wife, Audrey, at their home at 57 Tedworth Square, Chelsea. Yoko accepted with enthusiasm: the weekend lasted three months. The couples became friends, and Adrian Morris attended several of her artistic events.

Yoko had arrived in London with a reputation for having made a film in New York about famous people's bottoms. She decided to repeat and extend the movie, called *Four Square*, in London, this time using 365 people's bottoms.

'I enjoyed their company and I was broadly sympathetic to what they were doing,' says Morris. He saw Yoko at London's Roundhouse, then a base for embryonic artists. She was performing a 'Word Piece', throwing a word into the audience and asking them to respond. Morris was intrigued by her determination and surrealist humour.

A day at London Zoo with the two couples joined by four-year-old Kyoko, who was staying elsewhere with friends, turned into humour when Yoko asked someone to take her photograph alongside the bottoms of the baboons. 'Yoko,' Morris says tellingly, 'was always aware of what she was doing, observing and always profound. Once I came home to my house and, walking towards the kitchen from the back garden, I saw her listening to a clock with a stethoscope. She was running an exhibition at the time called *Time Piece*. Photographers were taking pictures of her and I then realized she was unique.' The kitchen was the scene of a favourite Yoko activity: cooking steamed mackerel on a bed of beanshoots, a dish that impressed everyone.

Yoko's marriage to Tony Cox was fraught with tension. Adrian and Audrey Morris were not surprised when Yoko told them privately that she was 'hung up on this guy' who later turned out to be Lennon. Soon after Yoko had told her friends she was 'miserable out of this guy's company', the newspapers were full of their liaison and her split from Tony was inevitable.

Although the Morrises recognized her talent as an artist working in a difficult field, they were equally impressed by her business acumen. 'She was clearly an entrepreneur and absolutely brilliant at working things out,' says Adrian. 'One day in the kitchen, I playfully patted her on the head during a conversation and called her Little Yoko. I vividly remember her response: "You say *little* Yoko," she said. "But I have a *universe* in my head." '

While John's relationship with Yoko deepened, leading eventually to the break-up of his marriage, the Beatles loomed as a parallel crisis. With Brian Epstein dead and the meditation honeymoon over, the Beatles decided to grasp the business nettle. They launched the Apple organization, first as a boutique and then as a record label and management company. John was never quite as confident as Paul or George in the utopian hope that Apple would be a freewheeling 'umbrella for new talent'. But he accepted that there was an urgent and immediate need to do something about the management of their affairs. With Epstein gone, John felt that not even a tenuous link remained with NEMS Enterprises, now run by Brian's affable brother Clive. Apple, set up in London at 95 Wigmore Street, with a boutique at 94 Baker Street and later with offices at 3

Savile Row, was intended to be both philanthropic and efficient in handling the Beatles' business affairs. It was originally conceived to invest in new talent in music, electronics, films, publishing, retailing, and records. 'Those were the days, my friend, I thought they'd never end,' sang sweet-voiced Mary Hopkin on her number one hit for Apple Records, produced by Paul McCartney. But they *did* end and quickly. Apple was doomed. And with John feverishly reshaping his life and his attitude around Yoko and art, so were the Beatles.

Lifestyles and aspirations were at the root of the quarrel that erupted between John and Paul, eventually causing John, who had never been content with his achievements with the group, to inform the Beatles he was leaving. Despite the fact that he was high on drugs in 1967 and 1968, he characteristically remained, throughout his life, exceptionally clear-headed whenever business was called for and hard decisions were needed.

The rift with Paul dated back to McCartney's assumption of the leadership of the Beatles when Epstein died. It was Paul who concocted the ill-fated *Magical Mystery Tour* TV film. The Beatles' first real failure, it was never screened in America. It had a threadbare plot which consisted of a busload of Beatles and others travelling around the West Country as a kind of circus act. The songs were weak and decidedly McCartney-ish. John loathed the whole affair. He was angry at the cost – £75,000 for what he derisively called 'the most expensive home movie ever'. It came, also, right at the time when John was becoming intrigued with Yoko. The *Magical Mystery Tour* was McCartney's attempt to have the Beatles continue just as before.

John, however, was not prepared to sit back and be ordered about. McCartney also underestimated John's dedication to Yoko and his boredom with the Beatles. The two

of them had launched Apple in America, at a press conference at New York's Americana Hotel and on nationwide
television on the *Tonight Show*. John had fainted on the
plane *en route* to New York, a victim of too many late
nights, too much dope, and not enough food. He arrived
in New York with a plaster on his cut chin, but he was in
fine form, taking the chance to scorn the Maharishi publicly
as well as to boost the Apple idea and prop up the Beatles'
declining popularity in America.

It had taken a beating when they went to India, and
Sgt Pepper, released the previous summer, had made little
impact with the millions of screaming fans in America: it
was too far from 'She Loves You' and the Beatles most
Americans loved. It was, however, a giant hit with the
more discerning listeners, staying at number one for fifteen
consecutive weeks and half a year in the top three.

When the job of publicizing Apple had to be done,
John was semi-serious. 'We've decided to sell India and buy
the Garden of Eden,' he said. As for the Maharishi, 'We
thought he was God,' said John. 'I told him not to go on
tour with the Beach Boys,' he jibed at the Maharishi's
pretence to showmanship.

The entire American trip was an anathema to John. He
was a lousy hypocrite. Privately he knew the Beatles were
doomed. His polarization from Paul was accelerated by
McCartney's acceptance of the show business embrace.
However talented he was as a songwriter, Paul was, in
John's view, content to continue churning out more of the
same. The massive acclaim for 'Yesterday', the all-McCart-
ney classic, had gone to Paul's head, John decided. The
Beatles, Paul's bossiness, Apple – the whole package was
stultifying to John, more than even he would admit. For
the sake of unity, he kept the peace for a few months to
give himself time to develop his relationship with Yoko.

But soon that too became a vital issue. The other Beatles treated her shabbily and provocatively. In the Abbey Road studios during the summer of 1968, the Beatles were recording the 'White Album'. (The album was officially titled *The Beatles* but because of its all-white cover, and for easier identification, it became known colloquially around the world as the 'White Album'.) It consisted mainly of songs they had written in India including 'Yer Blues', 'Sexy Sadie', and 'The Continuing Story Of Bungalow Bill'. John broke a rigid, unwritten rule of the group: that their women would never be allowed in the studios. Getting inside a Beatles recording session was hard even for the accredited inner circle – Brian Epstein and song publisher Dick James were often invited to stay away and judge the *results* rather than see the group fiddling for hours with an embryonic song. John perversely attended every session for the 'White Album' with Yoko at his side. His message, unspoken, was obvious to all: they were inseparable. She sat on the speakers, offering suggestions and, incredibly, criticisms.

Their chauvinist pique apart, George, Paul, and Ringo were in a sticky situation in their resentment of Yoko's arrival. John Lennon was by now obviously changing even more tangibly than they had realized if he brought this peculiar Japanese artist so deeply into his life that she was even allowed to sing on one of his compositions ('Bungalow Bill') and help on another song, 'Revolution 9'. What flabbergasted them was John allowing Yoko to comment on the Beatles' work. Only the four of them, plus George Martin, had ever been allowed that privilege. But they might have guessed his seriousness when he sang on 'Julia', the song about his mother: 'Ocean child calls me,' his first recorded reference to Yoko's letters to him in India.

George Martin was unconvinced of the merits of enough of the songs to justify putting it out as a double album, but John loved the record's individualism and persuaded him. The album remained John's favourite Beatles work because it demonstrated the development of personalities rather than the Beatles as an entity, of which by 1968 he had become tired.

With her thick, cascading black hair and unsmiling demeanour, Yoko was also destined for a difficult time at the Apple offices, where she and John held court in their own ground-floor office overlooking Savile Row. At Apple, where she usually dressed in white and exchanged ideas with a beleaguered staff coping with a daily invasion of artists, wayfarers, and good causes wanting money and the Beatles' seal of approval, Yoko was treated with disdain. George, Paul, and Ringo, particularly, did not give her the warmth and fair reception she deserved, both as their leader's new woman and as an artist. 'I'll never forgive them,' John said later. 'They were bastards to Yoko and they knew it mattered to me.'

John naturally regarded the coolness towards Yoko as an insult to himself. How, he reasoned, could people applaud him as a force for good and as a fine artist while condemning his choice of woman? He could not be great and dumb at the same time. When Yoko's increased melodicism on *Double Fantasy* was noted by reviewers in 1980, John was thrilled that at last she appeared to be getting recognition. She had always been ahead of her time. 'I've had two partners in my life, Paul McCartney and Yoko. That's not a bad record, is it?' he once said to me.

In 1968 and 1969, the most important years of his life, John had few friends, inside or outside the Beatles family. 'Yes, it was hard,' recalls Yoko, 'but he and I had no doubt we would get through. John's excitement at doing things together with me as an artist was so obvious that he didn't have that much time to get upset about what people were thinking, you know.'

The relationship was too important for both of them for any opposition to dissuade them: 'We both think alike,' said John. 'We've both been alone. And we seem to have had the same kind of dreams when we *were* alone. I can see now that I always dreamed of a woman like this one coming into my life. You can't go out *looking* for this kind of relationship. It's like somebody was planning it from above.'

While relationships with George, Paul, and Ringo simmered, with George as always the one with the best rapport with John in his new life, John and Yoko boldly stepped out in public to emphasize their togetherness, artistically and as man and woman. By now he was parting his hair in the centre to match Yoko's style, and they both invariably dressed in all-white suits.

Their first 'event' in June 1968 fuelled the cynics' view that John had gone crazy. As part of the National Sculpture Exhibition John and Yoko decided to plant two acorns, one facing east, the other facing west, in the grounds of Coventry Cathedral. The idea, which was John's, was to symbolize the meeting of John and Yoko as the combination of two different cultures, and the phrase 'Plant an acorn for peace', coined by John, was to accompany the event.

The couple were driven from London in John's Rolls-Royce for the one-hundred-mile trip to Coventry, where the event attracted only minor interest, considering it was an activity by a Beatle. The acorns were duly planted; the media scoffed; and Beatles fans everywhere knew that whatever John Lennon was now up to, he meant it. The planting of acorns in the cathedral precincts – disallowed on consecrated ground lest the Church should be seen to condone the couple's liaison – was of great significance to John, more so than to Yoko. It marked his concentration on art and his first conscious proclamation of peace.

In contrast, John and Yoko's second public outing in the same month faced the full glare of national publicity. Word spread to a gleeful newspaper world that John's marriage was on the rocks and he was living with Yoko at 34 Montagu Square, London W1. The couple were pursued by photographers twenty-four hours a day: a married Beatle escorting an unknown Japanese artist/actress had strong news value. But the couple faced the music, going hand in hand to the opening of the play *In His Own Write*. Photographers shouted: 'Where's your wife then, John?'

Angrily but firmly he retorted: 'I don't know.'

The play was directed by John's old friend from the films *A Hard Day's Night* and *Help!*, actor Victor Spinetti. When Victor phoned John with an idea from the noted American writer Adrian Kennedy, that Lennon books be converted into a play, John burst into laughter. 'They must be fucking mad!' he screamed into the phone. But then he quickly added that he always thought that *he* was mad until he came across a word called surrealism and had thought: 'Oh, that's what I am, I'm a *surrealist*.' When Spinetti brought the conversation back to earth, John readily agreed to grant him the theatrical rights.

They began working on the adaptation, and John and Yoko attended a meeting with Sir Laurence Olivier, who ran the Old Vic, then the home of the National Theatre where the play was to be staged. During the meeting Sir Laurence told John that when the play went ahead, they might be faced with other business decisions, such as film and record rights. Lennon, sitting next to the white-hatted Yoko and looking like a bored hippie, suddenly stunned the assembled company. In a mildly peremptory manner he said slowly to Sir Laurence: 'Don't you have people that

you pay to talk about these kinds of things who can talk
to the people that I pay to talk about these kind of things?'
    Spinetti had immediate proof of the speed of Lennon's
thought. He had asked John for a Queen's speech for one
sequence in his adaptation. 'Without thinking,' says Victor,
'and instantly, he took hold of a piece of cardboard used to
keep a new shirt firmly in place, and started writing:

> One second's pause . . .
>   'My housebound and eyeball take pressure
>   in denouncing his ship . . .'

Spinetti points out that although John often said he had
no knowledge of Chaucer, his instinct was distinctly Chau-
cerian, and the word 'housebound' was a variant of 'husband'
in Middle English. John, however, was adamant that the
expression was his own.

John and Yoko's child was expected in February 1969, but
in November 1968 Yoko was rushed to Queen Charlotte's
Hospital, Hammersmith, where she suffered a painful miscarriage. She was thirty-five, and the nursing staff said she
might have expected problems. John insisted on staying in
a spare bed alongside her, and when that was no longer
acceptable to the hospital he slept on the floor.
    Although he had officially given up smoking during
that period, Lennon persuaded Victor Spinetti to pop in at
eight-thirty each morning 'before the crowds arrive' and
sneak him a packet of twenty Players Gold Leaf. 'He looked
truly awful,' recalls Spinetti. 'I said to him: "Which one of
you had the miscarriage?"' The loss of the child had a
traumatic effect on John, and, coming on top of all the
other dilemmas that clouded his love of Yoko, he became

nervous, edgy, and less happy than ever with his role as a public Beatle.

That autumn developed into a harrowing period for John. The one problem he did not expect to face was a drugs charge. For some five years various pop stars had been closely associated with the use of cannabis, but so far the 'Holy Beatles' had escaped the law. Anyone talking to them was aware that they smoked pot, and in the pop world it was commonplace. But now the public view of the Beatles, and particularly Lennon, was not so cosy. To be ensconced with a crazy Japanese actress who made a film about bottoms was bad enough. To be *en route* to the divorce court, having planted acorns for peace, and having embraced and subsequently rejected the Maharishi and meditation, condemned John to public scorn.

John and Yoko were in bed at the Montagu Square flat when police with Alsatian sniffer dogs hammered on the door. John, shocked and confused by this rough awakening, did not open the door immediately. He phoned solicitor Nicholas Cowan, the partner of David Jacobs, who was representing Epstein's estate and doing other work for the Beatles. 'John said there were a number of people outside the flat who said they had a search warrant and were threatening to break the door down,' says Cowan. By the time Cowan arrived, half a dozen police and a dog were inside the flat. The police made a quick and thorough search of the premises. 'The basement was full of recording equipment,' says Cowan, 'all of which appeared to have been on for some time and the temperature was extremely high. In one room there was a large trunk full of clothes in which a dog was showing interest. A search of the trunk revealed a small piece of hash. John and Yoko were asked to go to Marylebone police station where they were formally charged and fingerprinted in my presence.'

A cuddly Beatle no more, Lennon's anguish showed on his face in the days that followed. A Beatle being busted for dope was big news; journalists besieged the police station, and John and Yoko were given permission to leave by the police headquarters' back door. They lay low for the night at Nicholas Cowan's home in Redcliffe Road, Fulham. Next day their case was adjourned for six weeks.

When the court case finally came up, John pleaded guilty to a charge of unauthorized possession of 219 grains of cannabis. He was fined £150 with twenty guineas costs. John and Yoko were found not guilty of obstructing the police in execution of a search warrant. It was a terrifying episode, John confessed later. He was always convinced that the bust was a 'set-up'. Don Short of the *Daily Mirror* had warned him three weeks previously that the police were on their way, so John said he had 'cleaned the place up, especially as I knew Jimi Hendrix had this flat before Ringo and me.' He maintained that the dope had been planted in the trunk, a spot in which he would never have tried to hide it. 'It was a frame-up. I guess they didn't like the way the image was looking. The Beatles thing was over. No reason to protect us for being soft and cuddly any more – so bust us! That's what happened.'

The drugs conviction in itself did not concern him, but he was well aware of the problems it might cause if he wanted to visit America. Musicians lived in dread of being busted because American immigration authorities were so hot about it. But even John did not realize, during that heady period, that the straight conviction for possession of pot would so painfully affect his future. At the time, however, there were enough pressures to divert him. He could handle his own change of identity perfectly well: his metamorphosis from hit-making pop star to thinking artist, and his publicly declared love for a ridiculed avant-garde artist, were things he revelled in. He loved taking on the public at the game of 'Who is Lennon?' What he found exhausting was the continuing problem of Apple and the Beatles.

By the summer of 1968 Apple Music, the Apple Boutique, Apple Films, and Apple Electronics had not made a film, sold a single invention, or opened shops outside London. When the Baker Street boutique closed, thousands of pounds' worth of clothes were given away to the public in an astonishing – and unbusinesslike – gesture of largesse. What Apple *had* done was spend £1 million of Beatles money, which had been frittered away on overstaffing, extravagant salaries, and an endless supply of alcohol for visitors.

Apple, beautifully described as 'the longest cocktail party' by one of its employees, Richard DiLello, in a hilarious book on the episode, was great fun. It was also cripplingly expensive and not functioning well. In its earliest days, with visitors like Peter Sellers, Harry Nilsson, Twiggy, and Kenny Everett, John enjoyed the fantasy of playing host to the world's artists. He also grew to believe more in Apple's philanthropy. But it surprised some who believed him to be the dopey Beatle, the druggy one, the one hopelessly diverted by Yokoism, that he became the first to say, effectively, 'enough is enough.' At the time John decided to sound the warning shots, Apple was costing the Beatles £50,000 a week.

During an interview with me in January 1969 for the pop weekly *Disc and Music Echo*, I asked John if he was happy with the way Apple was shaping. He answered: 'No, not really. I think it's a bit messy and it wants tightening up. We haven't got half the money people think we have. We have enough to live on but we can't let Apple go on like it is. We started off with loads of ideas of what we wanted to do – an umbrella for different activities. But like one or two Beatle things, it didn't work because we aren't practical and we weren't quick enough to realize that we need a businessman's brain to run the whole thing.

'You can't offer facilities to poets and charities and film makers unless you have money definitely coming in. It's been pie-in-the-sky from the start . . . We did it all wrong – you know, Paul and me running to New York saying we'll do this and encourage this and that. It's got to be a business first; we realize that now.

'It needs a new broom and a lot of people there will have to go . . . It doesn't need to make vast profits but if it carries on like this all of us will be broke in the next six months.' (Typically Lennon did show the accounts to someone right at the top – Lord Beeching. After studying the books he gave Lennon terse but sound advice: 'Go back to music!')

I asked whether he and the Beatles missed Brian Epstein's guidance. 'Sure we miss him,' John replied. 'His death was a loss. That's probably what's the matter with Apple or the Beatles at the moment – Brian's death left us on our own. He handled the business and we find it hard to.'

Lennon's outburst rocked Savile Row and reverberated around the world as international newspapers, television, and radio picked up on the confession by a Beatle that they had made a colossal mistake and might go broke. The Beatles had no more desire to be shopkeepers, John told me, than to become rock 'n' roll museum pieces and part of the showbiz Establishment. It was time for them to own up. The interview confirmed the unpleasant truth that nobody had wanted to face since the disastrous *Magical Mystery Tour* and optimistic founding of Apple: the Beatles, as an operating company, was in an appalling mess. While the fans were shocked, the media had a field day. It also

brought the uneasy relationship between John and Paul to
the breaking-point.

A week after my interview with John, I visited Apple
to see him again. Coming out of John's office, I met the
heavily bearded McCartney. He was furious with my
decision to publish John's comments. 'What did you want
to go and use all that for?' he snapped. 'You know this is
a small and young company, just trying to get along. And
you know John always shoots his mouth off. It's not that
bad. We've got a few problems but they'll be sorted out.
I'm surprised it was you – we thought we had a few friends
in the press we could trust.'

Paul was suggesting that John's remarks should have
been considered as 'off the record'. Like many writers who
had been close to the Beatles from the start, I had used
discretion when secrets were either unimportant to the
public or impolitic to reveal for the sake of the Beatles or
their families. But on this occasion Lennon talking about
Apple's looming disaster for the first time was manifestly
an on-the-record interview. John knew it would be used
and that it would be big news: he was an avid media freak,
he knew the value of a quote and always said what he
wanted, on reflection, to be left out of any interview. The
day he spoke he was as clear-minded as he had ever been.
Thus began the long, bitter battle between John and Paul.
A few weeks later I saw John again, and he did not mention
his explosive comments on Apple. Had he regretted them
or their ramifications, he would certainly have told me. For
Apple, and the Beatles, the end was in sight.

The musical rapport between them – as well as the
accord – had long gone. But before the end they had a
commitment to fulfil: to complete their third film, *Let It
Be*, which was to show their album being made. The four,
with Yoko, shuffled desultorily into Twickenham Film

Studios in early January 1969 to undertake the multi-media
project. The internal bickering and antipathy can be seen
in the finished film. Ironically it also shows them performing much of their early Hamburg/Liverpool repertoire, joy-
ously together, and revelling in the therapeutic qualities of
the music. It was a painful, if evocative affair, in particular the twenty-minute session on the roof at Apple. John's
words to the crowd spoke the Beatles' epitaph as poetically
as we had come to expect from him: 'I'd like to say thank
you on behalf of the group and ourselves . . . and I hope we
passed the audition.' It had been a long journey from
Liverpool Cavern, but for John, life was just beginning.

By now the Beatles were virtually dead as far as he was
concerned. Paul, who had steadfastly been arriving at Apple
each morning at ten o'clock (often travelling in from his
home in St John's Wood by bus), did not realize how serious
John was about quitting the Beatles. It wasn't simply a
question of his utter absorption with Yoko. It was the
growing mental distance between him and Paul. Apple
Records' first number one hit, and one of the Beatles'
greatest single successes, had been 'Hey Jude', a song which
Paul wrote during John's separation from Cynthia and composed partly on his way to Weybridge to comfort Cynthia
on the breakdown of the marriage. Paul later admitted that
John had helped him decide on some lyrics for the song,
particularly Paul's line which John loved best, 'The movement you need is on your shoulder.' John had reluctantly
agreed to it being the major side of the record, rather than
his own song, 'Revolution', which became the B-side.

Commercially there was no choice. But it emphasized
finally to him the different directions he and Paul were
taking. While Paul was still composing beautiful melodies
and writing of love, John's words tilted at the student
revolutions in Europe during 1968.

But if you want money for people with minds that hate
All I can tell you is brother, you have to wait . . .
But if you go carrying pictures of Chairman Mao
You ain't gonna make it with anyone, anyhow.

John simply believed that his new rock 'n' roll should have
his mind and his message in the music. The old Chuck
Berry and Little Richard rave-ups would always be his
roots, but mentally he was moving quickly and his profound
new music had to accommodate the change in him. Paul,
intimidated by Yoko's presence, felt that every time he was
in John's company and making music, he ought to be
producing something avant-garde. It was not in his nature.
The split was inevitable and acrimonious.

John broke the news of the break-up of the Beatles in
his usual rapier-like style. Paul remembers a meeting at
Savile Row in which all the Beatles sat stonily discussing
business. 'The group was getting very tense,' says Paul. 'It
was looking like we were breaking up.

'One day we came in, had a meeting, all Apple business,
and it was getting very hairy and nobody was really enjoying themselves. We had forgotten the music bit; it was just
business. I said: "I think we should get back on the road,
small band, go and do the clubs, sod it. Let's get back to
square one and remember what we're all about." ' McCartney suggested several other projects which he thought
would be the only thing to occupy the group's creativity
to the full and hold them together: a concert – no ordinary
show but the Beatles playing a Roman amphitheatre in
North Africa; or the Beatles as a house band on a round-
the-world cruise. John would have none of it.

'John's actual words were: "I think you're daft. I wasn't
going to tell you but I'm breaking the group up. It feels
good. It feels like a divorce." And he just sat there. And

our jaws dropped. And that was it. No one quite knew
what to say. Then after that we thought we should give it
a couple of months. It was a big act to break up just like
that. We talked for a couple of months but it was never
going to be on. Looking back, it was largely that John
needed a new direction that he went into headlong, helter
skelter. He went right in there and did all sorts of stuff he
had never done before – with Yoko. And you can't blame
him because he was that kind of guy. He wanted to live
life, do stuff and there was no holding back with John.
And it was what we all admired him for. So we couldn't
really say: "Oh we don't want you to do that, John. Stay
with us." You'd feel so wimpy. It *had* to happen.'

What was remarkable about John and Yoko's frenzied
activities together is that they managed to do so much
despite the business problems of 1968, 1969, and 1970.
Between John's divorce, Yoko's miscarriage, the drugs bust,
and the bickering between the Beatles and worry over
Apple, John and Yoko released their first album and continued their assault on a now punch-drunk public by
appearing in a large white bag on stage at the Royal Albert
Hall, London. This was an event called the Alchemical
Wedding, the underground art movement's Christmas
party.

The move that was to shake the foundations of John's
most ardent supporters was the release of their debut album.
Unfinished Music No.1: Two Virgins, a collection of bizarre
sounds and effects, the result of their first collaboration that
night in Weybridge when Cynthia was away, was neither
surprising nor important musically. It was their decision to
have themselves photographed nude on the front and back
of the album sleeve, however, that convinced Lennon's
detractors – and many of his supporters – that he had now
indeed gone insane.

The pictures were taken by John with an automatic camera. The *Two Virgins* concept was his: Yoko was 'terribly embarrassed' by it. Any theory that it was a continuation of her film theme of people's bottoms was absurd, she says. 'We were both very shy about it, really,' she recalls. 'But John had the original idea. He thought it suited what we were doing at the time.' In those days nudity on the London theatre stage in the show *Hair* was making front-page news. John, who told me eventually that he was 'testing people's reactions, and it was mostly bad,' enjoyed extending his and Yoko's audacity as far as he dared.

The nude pictures caused an immediate censorship problem. Apple Records were distributed through the Beatles' original record company, EMI, whose chairman at the time was Sir Joseph Lockwood. He remembers the Beatles arriving for lunch at his official dining-room in Manchester Square, a few weeks before the problem with the nude pictures arose. 'When the four boys came they had with them this person all in white, surrounded by hair, and I couldn't see anything. I wasn't sure if it was a human being or an animal. John Lennon introduced her to me: "This is my secretary," he said. After the lunch, he told me she had tape-recorded everything we had said. It was a business meeting. John was pretty clued up on everything that was going on.'

Sir Joseph's meeting with John and Yoko a few weeks later was more pointed. They arrived at his office with the nude pictures which they wanted released by EMI/Apple for their *Two Virgins* sleeve. Paul McCartney went with them to act as diplomat. 'He didn't want any row,' says Sir Joseph. 'At that time he was very anxious to prevent a falling-out with EMI.'

As he looked at the picture Sir Joseph was asked by John: 'Well, aren't you shocked?'

The EMI chief said: 'No, I've seen worse than this.'

John weighed in quickly: 'So it's all right then, is it?'

'No, it's not all right,' said Sir Joseph. 'I'm not worried about the rich people, the duchesses and those people who follow you. But your mums and dads and girl fans will object strongly. You will be damaged and what will you gain? What's the purpose of it?'

Yoko said: 'It's art.'

Sir Joseph answered sharply: 'Well, I should find some better bodies to put on the cover than your two. They're not very attractive. Paul McCartney would look better naked than you.'

Sir Joseph recalls: 'It didn't go down too badly, except that poor old Paul McCartney blushed. We went on and on for a long time. They wouldn't give way. They were pressing and pressing.

'Paul McCartney was not in favour of it, I'm sure. He just wanted to prevent me from blowing up with them, which I had no intention of doing.'

Finally Sir Joseph established a perfect British compromise. EMI would press the album, but Apple would have to distribute it themselves. EMI would have nothing to do with the actual sale of *Two Virgins*. John reluctantly agreed, and Paul, whose great commercial future was bound up with EMI, breathed a sigh of relief. Sir Joseph, who regarded John as the most controversial Beatle, with Paul the most commercial, felt vindicated when thousands of exported copies of *Two Virgins* were impounded by customs men and eventually confiscated. The record was a critical and commercial failure both in Britain and America, but John felt it was 'a statement'.

*

On 12 March 1969 Paul McCartney married New York photographer Linda Eastman in London. No other Beatle was invited to the wedding.

Paul's choice of bride had a marked effect on the cauldron that was by then the Beatles' business empire. John and Yoko, on the advice of Mick Jagger, had decided that a fast-talking American show business lawyer, Allen Klein, should be hired to weed out the chaos at Apple. George and Ringo went along with the Lennon line, eventually signing a business management contract with Klein, who convinced John that he could streamline Apple and negotiate better record deals for the Beatles. Paul flatly refused to become involved but was outvoted at a board meeting by three to one. Klein was in. Paul had wanted his new father-in-law, widely respected American entertainment lawyer Lee Eastman, to handle his affairs, and he went ahead and appointed him to manage his personal business concerns. The stage was set for the rift to become even wider.

Klein, whose openly stated ambition was to manage the Beatles, had flown to London immediately he heard of John's interview with me in which he laid bare the Apple financial quandary. All his life, Klein, the New Jersey orphan who had clawed his way through the pop jungle, wanted the 'fabulous Beedles'. Once in Britain, through Jagger, he quickly met John Lennon who told him that he did not 'want to end up broke like Mickey Rooney.'

The American went about his work with savage determination, alienating Sir Joseph Lockwood at EMI with his foul-mouthed demands – on one occasion Sir Joseph ordered him out of the building – and encountering stubborn resistance from McCartney. Paul's tactic was simply to stay away from the Apple he had so conscientiously nurtured. Len Wood, managing director of EMI, noticed that John had confidence in Klein during their meetings together; even when letters with major proposals for an Apple takeover came in and Klein wanted John's views, Lennon waved him away saying it was his job to deal with them. Allen was visibly thrilled at such a vote of confidence.

By mid-1969 the only question unanswered about the Beatles' future was how the group could split formally. John simply didn't care. He was off and running with Yoko. As far as he was concerned, he'd served notice on Paul, George, and Ringo, and Klein could hammer out the details with Lee Eastman.

The Plastic Ono Band had utterly eclipsed the Beatles in John's affections. Its appeal lay in its spontaneity: in September 1969 John and Yoko had been asked to appear at a rock concert in Toronto, and Lennon actually did what McCartney had urged the Beatles to do – get back on the road as a small band. Instead of talking about it, John got a band together, literally overnight. Eric Clapton recalls a phone call from John twenty-four hours before the show: 'He said: "We're doing this concert in Toronto. Why don't you come over with us?" ' Eric, thinking it would be fun, agreed, and bass player Klaus Voormann, John's old friend from Hamburg, joined in. They rehearsed old rock 'n' roll songs on the plane on the way over. The music on stage, though scrappy, had a raw quality John liked. On the plane he had told Clapton and Voormann that the Beatles were finished.

On his return, I asked John about the Plastic Ono Band, the Beatles, and his current attitude to Paul. Was the Plastic Ono Band more crucial to him than the Beatles? 'Neither more important nor less,' he said. 'Sometimes the Plastic Ono Band sessions are a drag, sometimes great. Sessions with the Beatles likewise. Just meself and a tape recorder can be good, sometimes it's boring. I like *change*.' Were the Beatles split? I asked. 'We're going through

changes, sure. The thing is — we change in public. It's a
menopause or something like that.'

When had he last seen Paul? 'About two months ago.
I keep meaning to go and see him. We write a lot —
postcards to each other. I see Ringo and George every other
day because they're here at Apple but Paul hasn't been here
for ages. I want to ask him why.' It was an astonishing
turnaround in the pair's behaviour: Paul had until this
period been the determined executive, always keen on discovering and nurturing new talent like Mary Hopkin. John
was not so keen on talent-hunting; he was too busy discovering himself.

Drastic change was affecting John, privately and professionally. With Allen Klein at the helm in Apple, he was
back in a buoyant mood, despite the rift with Paul. 'It's
going to be great here at Apple,' he said as their record
successes increased. He was trying to boost his confidence
in Klein. But yet another business crisis hit him badly.

Dick James, the friendly, enthusiastic song publisher
who was managing director of Northern Songs, which
owned the copyright to nearly all the Lennon-McCartney
songs, had been wooed for several months by Sir Lew Grade,
then chairman of ATV, who wanted to take over the valuable
Beatles song catalogue. With a vision that the songs would
earn money for the copyright holders well into the twenty-
first century and probably until the end of time, Grade
repeatedly offered James a great deal of money, but one
man alone could not decide to sell about two hundred songs
that dated back to their earliest hits such as 'From Me To
You', 'She Loves You', and 'I Want To Hold Your Hand'
and went through to their now huge-selling album titles.
'When Brian Epstein died and the Beatles were visibly torn
asunder, Grade began romancing me,' recalled Dick James.
'In old money the shares for Northern were marketing at

seven shillings and ninepence at the start and fourteen
shillings and sixpence when Brian died. Lew's final offer
was thirty-five shillings a share, so the financial gain to
everyone, including John and Paul, was very considerable.'
James put Grade's offer to the board of Northern Songs,
who represented more than three thousand outside share-
holders. The decision was unanimous: accept the offer,
which would bring in £10 million in cash.

Dick James's theory was that he was doing the Beatles,
and John and Paul as the major songwriters, a favour.
Northern Songs was, he believed, very vulnerable to all
kinds of financial corporation takeovers, and with the
Beatles at loggerheads they would suffer badly if different
factions in the City pulled it to pieces. Better, he thought,
to sell to ATV, where at least it would be under the roof
of a serious, stable music publishing house. 'The protection
the Beatles' songs could have within the framework of a
much larger company like ATV, as has been proven, was
much safer. When ATV took it over the wolves stopped
baying. It would have been wrong to sell Northern Songs
to John or Paul individually and with Allen Klein and Lee
Eastman representing them each, they could hardly buy it
jointly at that stage,' James told me at the time.

John was furious at what he considered a betrayal of
his interests without giving him any options. At a meeting
at Paul's house, Lennon tore into James. 'I tried to point
out to John that his capital gain was at the lowest rate of
tax paid anywhere in the world, as opposed to his tax from
record sales which were subject to ordinary income tax,'
says James. But John was inconsolable. Paul was annoyed,
but John, said Dick James, was 'hurt and I was very sorry,
and Yoko was annoyed.'

During this tense meeting, James tried to win John
over. He told Lennon about the huge lump sum coming

his way from the sale: 'Well, John, at least this means you can put some money by for your children.'

John's cynical retort ended any cosiness: 'I have no desire to create another fucking aristocracy,' he said bitterly.

Relations between John and Paul began to decline swiftly after John left the group. And although it had been John who made the break, it was a public relations tactic by Paul that broke the news to the world. With his first solo album, called *McCartney*, he issued a press release with forty-one questions and answers which left the world's media in no doubt that Paul was out of the group. It contained barbed references to his non-association with the Beatles. Issued in question-and-answer form, part of the text ran:

Did you enjoy working as a solo?

Very much. I only had me to ask for a decision and I agreed with me.

Is this album a rest away from the Beatles or the start of a solo career?

Time will tell . . .

Is your break with the Beatles, temporary or permanent, due to personal differences or musical ones?

Personal differences. Business differences. Musical differences. But most of all because I have a better time with my family. Temporary or permanent? I don't know.

Is it true that neither Allen Klein nor ABCKO (his company) have been or will be in any way involved in the production, manufacturing, distribution or promotion of this new album?

Not if I can help it.

Lennon was furious at what appeared a pre-emptive strike by McCartney to gain the momentum and wrest the decision-making role from him. Paul's dislike of Yoko was one thing; to upstage him by causing the world to surmise that Paul was the one taking the initiative was another. John reacted with a beautifully laconic piece of venom: by telephone he told me for an article I wrote: 'I received a phone call from Paul last Thursday afternoon. He said: "I'm going to leave the Beatles as well." I was happy to hear from Paul. It was nice to find that he was still alive.

'Anyway, Paul hasn't left. I sacked him.'

The sour relationship with Paul continued right up until John and Yoko left to settle in America in 1971. John and Yoko and their newly named Plastic Ono Band had taken flight in a surge of activity that camouflaged the McCartney situation, from the public at least. But when Paul usurped him by releasing the press statement, John was livid. The two men had little contact, but newspaper conjecture carried on. McCartney again ended the world's speculation with a letter to the *Melody Maker* on 29 August 1970:

> In order to put out of its misery the limping dog of a news story which has been dragging itself across your pages for the past year, my answer to the question: 'Will the Beatles get together again?' is no.
>
> *Paul McCartney*

By the end of 1970 Paul McCartney began proceedings in the High Court to wind up the Beatles' partnership. Even against the background of bickering it was a difficult decision: he made it during a sojourn with Linda at his farm in Campbeltown, Argyllshire. 'It's not easy being in a top job one second and the next someone says: "Well, we're breaking the group up." And you haven't got a job. It screwed my head for years,' he says. As for the questions that persisted about a reunion: 'It's like asking a divorced couple: Are you getting back together? . . . when you can't stand to look at each other.' It was agony, 'suing my best mates and being *seen* to sue my best mates. That was the worst.' The Beatles were formally ended as a performing group in the High Court on 12 March 1971 and a receiver appointed to look after their business interests. The Beatles continued only as a business name.

On a personal level, the wrangles continued and began to manifest themselves in Paul and John's music. Four months before John left for America in September 1971 Paul released a solo album made with Linda McCartney, *Ram*. Two songs in particular, 'Too Many People (Going Underground)' and 'Back Seat Of My Car' (ending with the chant, 'We believe we can't be wrong'), were unsubtle jibes at John and Yoko. Quite why Paul chose to pick a fight on record, and in public, with such a master of invective as John, will always be a mystery. Lennon's reply was the vitriolic 'How Do You Sleep?', on his classic *Imagine* album. Unlike Paul's songs, John's tactics were not cloak-and-dagger but a full frontal assault:

> So Sgt Pepper took you by surprise
> You better see right through that mother's eyes
> Those freaks was right when they said you was dead
> The one mistake you made was in your head . . .
> You live with straights who tell you you was king
> Jump when your mama tell you anything
> The only thing you done was Yesterday
> And since you've gone you're just Another Day

How do you sleep? . . .
A pretty face may last a year or two
But pretty soon they'll see what you can do
The sound you make is Muzak to my ears
You must have learned something in all those years

The rancour over Yoko, over Klein and Eastman, and how best to end the Beatles had now turned bitterly personal. At the root of it lay the fundamental truth which millions of Beatles fans still find unpalatable: Paul, with his gift for melody and musicianship, and love of popularity, headed securely for the world of entertainment where he will always be a giant figure. John was on a perpetual adventure, picking up and adopting, then quickly rejecting ideas and causes, writing poetry, and writing from within himself. He was an artist with a distinct anti-Establishment backbone. McCartney greatly admired John's mercurial, often whimsical, style, his originality, his arrogance, his wit. To a lesser extent Lennon acknowledged Paul's strengths as a songwriter. But John had little time for craftsmen, dismissing them as 'people who could write little ditties to order'. He sweated over his own work. His post-Beatles writing was inspired by personal relationships, observations, and events. John could recognize Paul's commercial power, but it was sentimental in contrast with Lennon's reluctance to show feelings. They were right for each other at a certain period of their lives. By 1971 they had irrevocably parted company, both personally and artistically, and John's feelings were further inflamed by Paul's digs at Yoko, whom John regarded as part of him.

The fight continued in public. Paul gave an interview to *Melody Maker* in November 1971, emphasizing that although the music had ended, business problems still faced

them: 'I just want the four of us to get together somewhere
and sign a piece of paper saying it's all over and we want
to divide the money four ways.

'No one else would be there, not even Linda or Yoko
or Allen Klein. We'd just sign the paper and hand it to
the business people and let them sort it all out. That's
all I want now. But John won't do it. Everybody thinks
I am the aggressor. But I'm not, you know. I just want
out.

'John and Yoko are not cool in what they are doing. I
saw them on television the other night and thought that
what they are saying about what they wanted to do together
was basically the same as what Linda and I want to do.

'John's whole image now is very honest and open. He's
all right, is John. I like his *Imagine* album but I didn't like
the others. *Imagine* is what John is really like but there was
too much political stuff on the other albums. You know, I
only really listen to them to see if there is something I can
pinch.' (He laughed.)

What did Paul think of 'How Do You Sleep?'? 'I think
it's silly. So what if I live with straights? I like straights. I
have straight babies. It doesn't affect *him*. He says the only
thing I did was "Yesterday". He knows that's wrong. He
knows and I know it's not true.'

Referring to the Beatles album, *Let It Be*, Paul said:
'There was a little bit of hype on the back of the sleeve for
the first time ever on a Beatles album. At the time the
Beatles were very strained with each other and it wasn't a
happy time. It said it was a new-phase Beatles album and
there was nothing further from the truth. That was the last
Beatles album and everybody knew it . . . Klein had it
re-produced because he said it didn't sound commercial
enough.'

Talking of John's Toronto concert with Eric Clapton,

Yoko, and Klaus Voormann, Paul said: 'John wanted to do
a big thing in Toronto but I didn't dig that at all. I hear
that before he went on stage he was sick and that's just
what I didn't want. Like anybody else I have been nervous
because of the Beatles thing.

'I wanted to get in a van and do an unadvertised concert
at a Saturday night hop at Slough Town Hall or somewhere
like that. We'd call ourselves Rikki and the Red Streaks or
something and just get up and play. There'd be no press
and we'd tell nobody about it. John thought it was a daft
idea.

'Before John said he was leaving the Beatles I was lying
in bed at home one night and I thought I would like to
get a band together like his Plastic Ono Band. I felt the
urge because we had never played live for four years. We
all wanted to appear on a stage but not with the Beatles.
We couldn't do it as the Beatles because it would be so
big. We'd have to find a million-seater hall or something.'
And in a remark which made John smile, Paul said what
he thought of New York: 'I went for a walk in Central
Park and there was a layer of dirt on the grass everywhere.'
The grass on his farm in Scotland, where he had one
hundred sheep on sixty acres of land, was so much better
than American grass.

John's letter of reply, which was published in the *Melody
Maker* two weeks later, was accompanied by a request that
it be published in full to give 'equal time' to his side of
the story. Part of the letter referred to McCartney's claim
that if he (Paul) had appeared at George Harrison's summer
1971 Bangladesh concert in New York, Allen Klein would
have taken the credit for pulling the Beatles back together
again. John's letter, positively dripping with anger, ran as
follows:

Dear Paul, Linda *et all* the wee McCartneys,
Thanks for your letter.
1. We give *you money* for your bits of Apple.
2. We give *you more money* in the form of royalties which legally belong to Apple (I know we're Apple, but on the other hand we're *not*).
Maybe there's an answer there somewhere ... but for the millionth time in these past few years I repeat, *What about the TAX?* It's all very well, playing 'simple, honest ole Paul' in the *Melody Maker* but you know damn well we can't just sign a bit of paper.

You say, 'John won't do it.' I will if you'll *indemnify* us against the tax man! Anyway, you know that after we have *our* meeting, the fucking lawyers will have to implement whatever we agree on — right?

If they have some form of agreement between *them* before *we* met, it might make it even easier. It's up to you; as we've said many times, we'll meet you whenever you like. Just make up your mind! E.g. two weeks ago I asked you on the phone, 'Please let's meet without advisers, etc. and decide what we want', and I emphasized especially Maclen [John and Paul's songwriting partnership company within Northern Songs] which is mainly our concern, but you refused — right?

You said under *no condition* would you sell to us and if we didn't do what you wanted, you'd sue us again and that Ringo and George are going to break you John, etc. etc.

Now I was quite straight with you that day, and you tried to shoot me down with your emotional 'logic'. If *you're not* the aggressor (as you claim) who the hell took us to court and shat all over us in public?

As I've said before — have you ever thought that you might *possibly* be wrong about something? Your conceit about us and Klein is incredible – you say you 'made the mistake of trying to advise them against him [Klein] and that pissed them off' and we secretly feel that you're right! Good God! You must *know we're right about Eastman* . . .

One other little lie in your 'It's only Paulie' *MM* bit: *Let It Be* was not the 'first bit of hype' on a Beatle album. Remember Tony Barrow? And his wonderful writing on 'Please Please Me' etc. etc. the early Beatle Xmas records!

And you gotta admit it was a 'new-phase Beatle album', incidentally written in the style of the great Barrow himself! By the way what happened to my idea of putting the parody of our first album cover on the *Let It Be* cover?

Also, we were intending to parody Barrow originally, so it was hype. But what was your *Life* article? Tony Barrow couldn't have done it better. (And your writing inside of the *Wings* album isn't exactly the realist is it?) Anyway, enough of this petty bourgeois fun.

You were right about New York! I do love it; it's the ONLY PLACE TO BE. (Apart from anything else, they leave you alone too!) I see you prefer Scotland . . . I'll bet you YOUR piece of Apple you'll be living in New York by 1974 (two years is the usual time it takes you – right?).

Another thing, whadya mean *big thing* in Toronto? It was completely spontaneous, they rang on the *Friday* – we flew there and we played on the *Saturday*. I was sick because I was stone pissed. Listen to the album, with no rehearsal too. Come on Macka! Own up! (We'd never played together before!) Half a dozen live shows – with no big fuss – in fact we've been *doing* what you've said the Beatles should do, Yoko and I have been doing it for three years! (I said it was daft for the Beatles to do it. I still think it's daft.) So go on and do it! Do it! Do it! E.g. *Cambridge*, 1969, completely unadvertised! (A *very* small hall.) *Lyceum* Ballroom, (1969, no fuss, great show – thirty-piece rock band! 'Live Jam' out soon!) *Fillmore East* (1971) unannounced. Another good time had by all – out soon!!) We even played in the streets here in the Village (our spiritual home!?) with the great David Peel!! We were moved on by the cops even!! It's best just to DO IT.

I know you'll dig it, and they don't even expect the Beatles now anyway!

So *you* think *Imagine* ain't political, it's 'Working Class Hero' with sugar on it for conservatives like yourself!! You obviously didn't *dig the words*. Imagine! You took 'How Do You Sleep?' so literally (read my own review of the album in *Crawdaddy*). *Your* politics are very similar to Mary Whitehouse's – saying *nothing* is as loud as saying *something*.

Listen, my obsessive old pal, it was George's press conference not dat old debbil Klein! *He* said what *you* said – 'I'd love to come but . . .' Anyway, we did it for basically the same reasons – the Beatles bit. They still called it a Beatle show – with just two of them! [Ringo played drums in the superstar band George Harrison formed for the spectacular Bangladesh concert in New York.]

Join the Rock Liberation Front before it gets *you*.

Wanna put your photo on the label like uncool John and Yoko do ya? (Ain't ya got no shame!) If we're *not* cool, WHAT DOES THAT MAKE YOU?

No hard feelings to you either. I know basically we want the same, and as I said on the phone and in this letter, whenever you want to meet, all you have to do is call.

All you need is love
Power to the people
Free all prisoners
Jail the judges
Love and peace
Get it on and rip 'em off

John Lennon

P.S. The bit that really puzzled us was asking to meet
WITHOUT LINDA AND YOKO. I thought you'd have understood BY NOW that I'm JOHNANDYOKO.
P.P.S. Even *your own* lawyers know you can't 'just sign a
bit of paper' (or don't they tell you?).

The wounds were deep and lasting. Relations between
John and Paul were badly damaged by the encounter.
When John wrote that letter, two months after arriving in
New York, he scarcely realized that he would never visit
Britain again. And it would be four years before Paul finally
visited him in New York, the Beatles dead and the business
hatchet still not properly buried. At the time of their
friction George Martin said: 'I don't think Linda is a substitute for John Lennon any more than Yoko is a substitute
for Paul McCartney.' The producer of the Beatles' records
was judging each artist's new direction in music. He was
also, unknowingly, echoing their desires. John had shed the
Beatles, Paul, and Britain. And he was opening his mind.
    The Beatles phenomenon, he said, was so enormous that
he had had to be a Beatle and nothing else. 'It was not a
monster at the beginning. We communicated with people,
in clubs and ballrooms; we spoke to people and it was really
great. But then it became a kind of machine. It's like a guy
who makes millions, say Rockefeller or Getty. They become
totally obsessed by money, how to make more. That's how

the Beatles became, and that's what I could not accept. There wasn't a moment to think about anything else, so the Beatles was just a period in my life.' Before the Beatles, he had known nothing about world politics, but he had been aware of his position within Liverpool society – 'trying to get into university and all the silly things that go with that.'

But he accepted that the Beatles had a vital social influence. He always seized on anyone who denied the importance of the Beatles to the world. *He* was allowed to denigrate the group, but woe betide anyone else who did, particularly musicians. 'The Beatles had a social impact then became sterile like a government that has stayed in power too long. When that situation arises, you abdicate. So we abdicated.'

EIGHTEEN

PEACE

'We are willing to be clowns if it helps spread the word'

JUST BEFORE going to America in 1971, John told me: 'We'd like to be remembered as the Romeo and Juliet of the 1970s.'

Yoko continued: 'When people get cynical about love, they should look at us and see that it *is* possible.' They were holding hands, smiling, and obviously meant every word. I had asked them what their real aims were, in the heat of the great controversy surrounding their union and demonstrations for peace.

'I'd like everyone to remember us with a smile,' said John. 'But, if possible, just as John and Yoko who created world peace forever. The whole of life is a preparation for death. I'm not worried about dying. When we go, we'd like to leave behind a better place.'

In the wake of the limping Beatles and the *Two Virgins* album furore, three other major landmarks had just re-shaped John's life. The speed of events was breathtaking.

In February 1969 Yoko was divorced from her second husband, Anthony Cox. Seven weeks after that, John and Yoko had married. Five days after that they staged the renowned bed-in demonstration for peace in Amsterdam. And a month after their wedding John formally changed his middle name by deed poll from Winston to Ono. He was following his maxim to Paul, 'Do it!' with a speed that was not to let up for the next six years.

John's formal change of name from Winston to Ono was a mark of togetherness, but it had a diplomatic motive too. Yoko had said to John, light-heartedly but with meaning: 'I don't like being known as Mrs Lennon. How would *you* like it if you had to change your name upon marriage to Mr John Ono? Why should that not be?' (Ono is Yoko's given surname which she does not drop upon marriage.) She was intent on asserting her independence and even wrote a song, 'Mrs Lennon', which, she says now, summed up her cynicism at the irony of the situation.

'My God, it really is unfair,' admitted John as they joked about it.

Then, Yoko recalls, John 'showed what an incredible politician he was.' He had repeatedly told Yoko that he disliked his middle name, Winston, with its wartime connotation and implication that he was somehow a subscriber to the spirit of the upper-class 'British empire and all that'. It made him feel hypocritical. 'I don't want that name. It's always following me around,' John told Yoko.

'He hated being compared in any way with Winston Churchill,' she says. 'His incredible idea of having his middle name changed to Ono, to accommodate my request, made me feel good and amazed me at the same time. He said I could carry on being known as Yoko Ono, and why not, and he had made a step towards me without dropping Lennon, which nobody wanted him to do, anyway.'

John decided to have the ceremony performed by the Commissioner of Oaths on the roof at Apple. But there was a technical problem: he was told that day that, while he could adopt the name Ono, he could not renounce the given name of Winston. What he decided to call himself was totally up to him and he was re-registered as John Winston Ono Lennon that day. John grumbled: 'Why am I paying all these lawyers if I'm not getting rid of Winston?'

The legalities of whether John still owned the name Winston dragged on for months. 'I don't feel patriotic enough to keep the name,' he said. 'I am John Ono Lennon.' In all the oaths that he swore during his statements on the winding-up of the Beatles in 1970 John was written down as John Ono Lennon, and all his personal documents were named accordingly. He often signed himself with just his new initials: J.O.L. But when it came to his American immigration battle between 1972 and 1976, he diplomatically added back the name Winston and the Green Card was eventually made out to him in the name of John Winston Ono Lennon. 'Although he may never have technically lost the Winston, he disliked it and never used it,' says Yoko. Her own situation is exactly the same: the world knows her as Yoko Ono, the name she prefers, but technically she is Yoko Ono Lennon. John particularly liked to add extra 'o's to his name because he and Yoko said the letter was a sign of intuitiveness and was good on psychic grounds, too. 'Between us,' Yoko says, 'we were very psychic. We knew all the time what the other was thinking, what was going to be said by the other, our responses, everything. It was sometimes unnerving.'

Their wedding was unconventional but romantic. Based in Paris for a couple of weeks in March 1969, they decided to charter a plane and marry in Gibraltar. The bride and groom wore white tennis shoes and their clothes were also white. Yoko wore a white linen mini-dress and coat, a huge-brimmed white hat that contrasted vividly with her flowing black hair and white socks. John had a white jacket and off-white corduroy trousers. The man who had been cast as the waspish Beatle, hard and cynical, was old-fashioned about his marriage. 'We are two love birds,' he said. 'Intellectually we didn't believe in getting married. But one doesn't love someone just intellectually. For two people, marriage still has the edge over just living together.' At the ceremony he stood before the registrar in the British Consulate office with one hand in his pocket and the other holding a cigarette. 'Oh, that wasn't important at all,' he answered when asked if it was irreverent. 'The event was *ours*. If I can't stand and do what I like at my own wedding . . .'

They had their honeymoon, he explained, before the wedding. 'Just eating, shopping, and looking round Paris. In love in Paris in the spring was beautiful. We're both tremendous romantics!' They would have liked to have been married in church by the Archbishop of Canterbury, but that was impossible because divorced people could not be married in church.

The scorn that had been directed at Yoko vanished immediately. People suddenly realized that she was human after all. 'I got so emotional at the wedding I broke down and John nearly did, too,' she said. 'This man, rabbiting on about "Do you take this woman for your wife?" – it was a tremendous experience.' Back in Paris after only a seventy-minute stay in Gibraltar, John and Yoko went to the Plaza Athénée Hotel. Yes, Yoko reflected, marriage was old-fashioned, but both of them definitely respected it as an institution. John said that from then on they would do everything together, as artists and as husband and wife. Yoko said she would certainly not be the traditional wife, if that meant bringing him his slippers. She added that their marriage was one of their happenings, very important and indicative of the future. 'We're planning another one in the next seven days. You'll know soon enough when it is.'

*

The next stop, Amsterdam, a few days later, was to be the pivotal event of their peace campaign. Since they had already appeared on stage at London's Royal Albert Hall in a large white bag in December 1968 and as Yoko had fast gained a reputation for leading John into the realms of fantasy, it should not have been so surprising. But John and Yoko were in a hurry to ram home some principles. The mid-1960s had educated the world into accepting that rock stars could have brains; some saw their role as messianic. John, encouraged by Yoko, sensed the power that being a Beatle had given him and believed it could be used intelligently to advocate peace. He had first been encouraged to launch a peace campaign in a letter from Peter Watkins, producer of the film *The War Game*. Watkins spoke of the obscenity of war and the power of artists like John; reflecting on his appearance in the anti-war film *How I Won The War*, John became totally committed to the idea.

For seven days in the presidential suite of the Amsterdam Hilton John and Yoko lay in bed together in white pyjamas. They were surrounded by flowers, and two notices adorned their bedhead: 'Bed Peace' and 'Hair Peace'. They invited the press, and during that week nearly one hundred reporters from all around the world came to watch the event that became known as the Amsterdam bed-in for peace. What was *this*? Mad John and crazy Yoko having a public honeymoon? In the eyes of the conventional world they had now cooked up the most outrageous happening of all.

'Ha! They all thought John and Yoko were going to fuck in front of the world's press for peace,' John laughed. 'That was never on, and anyway we're far too shy to do anything, *anything*, like that.' The idea was to stage a genuine demonstration when they knew that publicity

would be guaranteed: 'The press would have found us whatever we'd done for a honeymoon, so we decided to invite
the press along and get some publicity for something we
both believe in,' John said later. Sporting a beard and with
his hair at its longest, John urged others to grow their hair
as a symbol of their peace campaign; strangely, John also
seemed calmer during the week in Amsterdam. Fans
besieged the hotel, listening patiently to the messages of
peace that John and Yoko propounded. They kept the windows of their room open so they could hear the fans in the
street outside. And the press, at once bemused and amused
by the whole episode, was cynically grateful. Good old John
and Yoko had given them a decent story, at least. John saw
it more profoundly: he believed the peace message had got
across. Hundreds of newspapers and radio and television
programmes had sent out their message. It was better
propaganda than any prime minister had yet achieved. As
for the fans: well, he was old now (twenty-eight at the
time), and Yoko was thirty-six; he felt that his days as a
pop idol had run out and that it was time to concentrate
on more serious work.

    At the time the Amsterdam bed-in was regarded by
many as a stunt or a joke. A cynical British police chief
described it as disgusting, adding: 'If wealth does this to
people then I do not want it. Power corrupts.' But John
and Yoko had optimism firmly on their side: if there was
a wave of cynicism in 1969, then in the years since John and
Yoko's palpable sincerity and the importance and urgency of
their message and motive have rung true throughout the
world.

    There was never any let-up, either, in their proclamation
of love for each other: signs proclaiming 'John loves Yoko'
and 'Yoko loves John' hung next to them in bed for seven
days. And when Yoko told John her £3 10s. wedding ring

was too large and was slipping off her finger, John drew a temporary one in ink on Yoko's finger while the real one went for shrinking. A solid streak of conformity, convention, tradition, and romanticism bound them together while the world had exactly the opposite impression of them. They were much more demonstrative in their affection for each other than many 'normal' husbands and wives; and with John and Yoko, every facet of their partnership was played out in public. They quickly damped down any speculation that Yoko, because of her far-out stand in art, was an aggressive fighter for women's liberation who had hammered her views into a chauvinistic Beatle. 'John is a very aggressive, masculine man and I enjoy being submissive,' said Yoko. But three years of observing Yoko had changed John's outlook. By the time they married he was re-thinking his whole attitude to women. Yoko's strength convinced him that to go on looking for merely physical attributes would never satisfy him. As he commented: 'I guess I was looking for a woman who would give me everything I got from a man, intellectually, as well as the fact that she was female.' He took a keen interest in women's emancipation partly because Yoko had demonstrated her equality and often superiority. John resented very strongly the middle-class snubs that Yoko had suffered: after she had appeared nude with him on the *Two Virgins* album cover, she was called an 'ugly old cow', and he felt she should fight back. 'How dare they? I think she's beautiful,' he said. More important, he knew something that was going to be much harder to get across: mentally, intellectually, and conceptually Yoko not only suffered racial prejudice and opposition from all women and, naturally, Lennon's girl fans from the Beatles days, but as an artist she was years ahead of her time and her work was constantly misunderstood. What Amsterdam convinced him of was that she should strike out even more, together with him, for feminism, and articulate it, while he should also shed the mental restrictions of being labelled a Beatle.

The fecundity of their partnership was nourished more in Amsterdam than anywhere. 'We are willing,' said John, 'to become the world's clowns if it helps spread the word for peace. Too many people talk about it but not enough do anything.' With his famous name and Yoko's ideas, they would continue doing things for years that would force people to react, he said. After the previous year's acorns in Coventry Cathedral and the 'bagism' on a London stage, Bag Productions, John and Yoko's film and production company, was formed, based at the Apple headquarters. John Lennon, man of peace, had been launched. As with everything he ever did, he was serious, intense, simple, hurried, and infectious. As he admitted in song, it wasn't easy, 'the way things are going, they're gonna crucify me.' The world had become used to the abrasive, opinionated Beatle. It had slowly realized he meant Yoko to be more than a passerby in his life when they married. For the next eleven years John Lennon was gradually to jump the biggest hurdle of all, the foundations of which had been set up in Amsterdam: the pop star idolized by millions was to become known as a spokesman and campaigner for goodwill and humanitarianism.

There was a double edge to John's adoption of the peace cause. It came at a perfect time in his life, with the Beatles at a crossroads. And he had reflected that, for six years as a pop star, he had reluctantly been conscious of his image, not getting too involved in politics or philosophy. It had always been against his nature: after he had tripped up over his remarks on Jesus Christ in 1966, Brian Epstein's rule that the Beatles should be non-controversial seemed to make sense. Lennon wanted to condemn publicly American aggression in Vietnam at the height of the Beatles' fame. Epstein warned him against it, and John, who for a time did not want the roller-coaster of Beatlemania to wane, went along with the 'party line'. It was a bitter pill to swallow.

Now, with fame and wealth, he would pretend no more. He told the Amsterdam press conference: 'All I'm saying is peace. We're not pointing a finger at anybody. There are good guys and bad guys. The struggle is in the mind. We must bury our own monsters and stop condemning people. We're all Christ and we are all Hitler. We are trying to make Christ's message contemporary. We want Christ to win. What would He have done if He had advertise-ments, records, films, TV, and newspapers? Well, the miracle today is communications. So let's use it!'

John and Yoko's method was expensive. Hotel suites and travelling expenses ran into thousands of pounds a week as they continued their European trip that spring. The critics tried another pin-prick: wouldn't it be better if John gave some money to the starving rather than indulging himself and his ego? He was ahead of them on that one: he regularly sent money to needy refugees, particularly in Biafra, that era's crisis point. All his life John was to give away thousands of pounds to charities and good causes. He did it quietly, not wanting the publicity of the rich, demonstrative pop star displaying his wealth.

Amsterdam was only the start. As a continuation of the Coventry Cathedral acorn plantation, John and Yoko sent a pair of acorns to prime ministers throughout the world, urging them to plant them symbolically for peace, as they had done.

Films had always intrigued John, and he and Yoko decided they would make them another aspect of their work together. Their first two, shot at Weybridge, were *Smile* and

Two Virgins. Smile was Yoko's idea and was typically spare in its conception: simply a shot of John's face, smiling, in different expressions which were multiplied by the camera to complete a film lasting nearly an hour. *Two Virgins* was similar in theme, using John's face superimposed on Yoko's. Made early in their relationship, they were not so important as films as in sealing the chemistry between John and Yoko. Yoko was John's launching pad, and it was she who showed him the true dimensions of his talent as a communicator.

He loved, too, the sense of humour in her work. Their third film, *Rape*, virtually parodied the story of the Beatles' escalator to success. A girl's reaction during her pursuit by journalists reaches a desperate finale in which she struggles violently and attacks a television camera. The film's première on Austrian TV followed the Amsterdam bed-in in March 1969. John and Yoko flew to Vienna and petrified the staid community by announcing that their press conference would be held where they were staying – the dignified and historic Hotel Sacher. The press conference rocked the august foundations of the grand old hotel. John and Yoko, by now christened 'Joko' by some cynics, appeared sitting on a trestle table covered totally by a white sheet. 'Bagism', they explained, was part of their peace drive.

John desperately wanted his propaganda machine for peace to have a big launch in America, then heavily involved in the Vietnam war. Asked why he had not had a bed-in there, he had answered: 'Because I don't want to get shot.' His honesty usually got him through. The real reason, however, why they could not stage a bed-in in New York, as they wanted, was because John was refused a visa in May 1969: the London drugs conviction had blocked his freedom of movement. Montreal proved a happy alternative, and John, by now an enthusiast of the telephone that he used to hate, used the proximity with North America to do literally hundreds of phone interviews with radio, television, and newspaper people anxious to learn what lay behind the Amsterdam idea.

'One problem with what we're doing,' he said, 'is that we'll never know how successful we are. With the Beatles, you put out a record and either it's a hit or it's a miss. I don't expect the prime ministers or kings and queens of the world to suddenly change their policies just because John and Yoko have said "Peace, brother". It would be nice! But it's *youth* we're addressing. Youth is the future. If we can get inside their minds and tell them to think in favour of non-violence, we'll be satisfied. What's the point of getting fame as a Beatle and not using it?!' John's urgency, his enthusiasm, and the still-glowing embers of Beatlemania in Canada and North America made for enormous press coverage. Since John never made any bones about his hunger for publicity for the peace cause, he viewed the seven-day Montreal bed-in as a winner.

He clinched it by making one of his strongest pieces of music. For months he had been using the phrase 'Give it a *chance*' when pleading with reporters to listen to the peace campaign fairly. Amid the huge spread of carnations in his hotel room, he was inspired to write the snappy little chant, 'Give Peace A Chance'. It quickly became popular with the entourage, and John decided to order a portable eight-track tape recorder so that it could be recorded. Among the people singing along on the chorus were Timothy Leary, high priest of the drug culture, Montreal rabbi Abraham Feinberg, and comedian Tommy Smothers. The spontaneity of the song and John's unmistakable conviction gave it a sharp edge. The peace campaign now had an international anthem.

Just as with 'Give Peace A Chance', so many of John's phrases, inextricably linked with his humour and masterful

word-play, serve as soundtracks for his life. Once his world
was rolling with Yoko, John's one-liners and his song lyrics
became even more memorable. 'The sixties were all about
learning to swim,' he said once. 'So when you've learned to
swim – swim!' Another classic summing up of the Beatles
was: 'The dream is over . . . nothing's changed. Just a few
of us are walking around with longer hair.' And, with his
1975 album of rock 'n' roll songs, John coined the phrase:
'You shoulda been there (signed) Dr Winston O'Boogie.'
'Imagine', his best-loved song, has a wealth of allegorical
lines destined to enchant people for ever.

One of John's proudest word collaborations with Yoko
came as the finale of their peace campaign in 1969. It had
been a spine-tingling year. The simplicity of the slogan
they invented gave it its power: 'WAR IS OVER! If you
want it. Happy Christmas from John and Yoko.' Huge
billboards went up in eleven cities around the world to
display the poster, and thousands of posters were distributed
internationally. A full two years later, at Christmas 1971,
John and Yoko joined together with the black children of
the Harlem Community Choir in New York to make their
classic Christmas song, 'Happy Xmas (War Is Over)'. The
chorus, 'War Is Over, if you want it,' lived on, which
pleased John. 'And so this is Christmas,' he sang. 'And
what have you done?/Another year over, a new one just
begun.' By the end of 1969, though, John realized that the
energy he had poured into the peace campaign needed one
final boost. The answer, of course, lay in music.

To aid the United Nations Children's Emergency Fund
he got together the Plastic Ono Band for a show at London's
Lyceum ballroom. With the backdrop of the 'War Is Over!'
billboard John assembled George Harrison, Eric Clapton,
Klaus Voormann, the Who's Keith Moon, singer-pianist
Billy Preston, and the Delaney and Bonnie Band. Yoko sat

at John's feet on the stage, covered for much of the time by a white bag. Nobody was in any doubt, after a full year of propaganda, that they meant what they preached. On Christmas Eve they went to Rochester Cathedral, Kent, to join a sit-in and fast to spotlight world poverty. The cynics could not resist the temptation to take a negative view: Lennon was talking about poverty, they sneered, while arriving at the steps of the cathedral in a Rolls-Royce. John's retort was: 'Would they want me to walk here? The people who criticize us have cars. If they give up theirs, first, for peace, I'll give up my Rolls.'

It took Britain time to get used to John's antics. He was prepared for total rejection by Beatles fans because in his mind he had ceased to be a pop star. 'I've left all that to the Monkees,' he told me. But that summer, a heart-warming example of teenagers' support gave John and Yoko the feeling that the peace campaign, and their partnership, had succeeded.

   In an opinion poll among readers of *Disc and Music Echo* John was voted the most popular Beatle, and, the paper reported, his extrovert behaviour had 'made him a figure of respect rather than ridicule.' The paper asked: 'Some people think John Lennon's behaviour since he met his wife Yoko has been eccentric. What do you think?' The majority of young readers felt he was 'eccentric, but harmless and sincere.' A fifteen-year-old girl said: 'I thought he was very eccentric when he married Yoko but my opinions towards him are now changing because I can see some sense in what he's aiming at.' A nineteen-year-old Scotsman said: 'That John Lennon's behaviour pattern is tending towards the unorthodox cannot be denied, but Lennon is no orthodox character. He is an honest, sincere, Christ figure of a man in whom the passions of peace flow strongly and there are too many out to crucify him.' A Midlands teenager replied: 'I never used to take very much notice of the Beatles as individuals before but I do now. John isn't just a guitar stomper any more. He is . . . well, I suppose you could call him a saint.' And another said: 'He's doing more good than most politicians. At least he's taking action to try to get peace, which is better than sitting discussing it.' It was not all honey, however. One critical fan said: 'The Beatles would be better off without John Lennon. He's going downhill and unfortunately he has enough influence over the rest of the group that, unless he leaves, the Beatles could go down with him.'

John also emerged as the Beatle people would most like to meet. 'I'd like to talk to him about peace,' wrote a sixteen-year-old girl. 'I also admire the way he stands up in front of the public even though they treat him disgustingly.' And: 'I'd like to try to assess whether his endeavours on behalf of world peace are sincere or just the self-indulgent whims of a very rich, egotistical young man.' Among pop fans the news that John had overtaken Paul as Britain's favourite Beatle was big news. And the fact that John achieved it for his ideas, rather than his music or his good looks, made an even greater impact. Crucially, too, John and Yoko's peace efforts, while scoring a direct hit for them, had not, in the main, affected public love of the Beatles, even though traditional British bluntness put a sting in the tail of a poll that boosted John's morale: 'Going off with the Maharishi to do this meditating lark ruined them,' said one boy. 'They should have retired after *Sgt Pepper*,' said another. But John was ecstatic at the results. He sent me, as the paper's editor, an enigmatic drawing 'as my way of saying thanks to all your readers who are with us.' He threw in a typical aside before the end of our phone conversation: 'Hey, why don't you ask the readers what they make of the drawing? We could have another poll on that!'

So we did. The response was enormous, the interpretations deep, patient, and understanding. 'The drawing is about peace, present and past,' said one reader. 'The two faces are reflected images of themselves, with John as a modern-day saviour. The scene is tranquillity – a pleasant day, sunshine, an animal in the foreground. . . . Peace. It could also represent the Nativity, with a stable on the horizon and an animal waiting for the birth.' And another went further: 'The Lennon cartoon is a visionary work showing John and Yoko after deification. The playing card symbolism in the representation of John and Yoko suggests that in the process they have lost their personal identity (as in the case of Henry VIII in a pack of cards) to be known only as "God" or "The Gods". This interpretation is supported by the fact that Lennon has no eyes. The title ("ART") suggests John and Yoko have attained divine status on artistic merit rather than through their efforts for peace.'

At last John felt vindicated. So many readers of *Disc and Music Echo*, a large proportion of them teenagers, felt a rapport with his cause for peace that he plunged headlong into a long and exhausting schedule of press interviews. The paper had also canvassed opinion on John and Yoko's new music, asking for reactions to their *Life With The Lions* album. (The title was a wry piece of word-play by John, invoking the radio series of his childhood, *Life With The Lyons*.) Many young people sympathized with the new, avant-garde direction in which the chief Beatle was going with this far-out Japanese artist. 'They are sending out feelers to explore new areas of experimental music,' wrote one enthusiast. 'Instead of taking tentative steps, like many groups, John and Yoko have gone in head first and are courageous to have done this. Although we cannot yet understand much of their music, I am sure it will be accepted in ten years' time.' Others wrote of how much they enjoyed its sound, simplicity, and emotion. Long-time Lennon observer David Stark wrote: '*Life With The Lions* is a haunting, intriguing experience. Its pure concept is so refreshing and the sadness of the music – it *is* music – just makes me happy.' As always, one fan put the knife in but with humour: 'This new music by John and Yoko certainly has something to offer. It makes me appreciate my other albums much more than I did before!' John loved that. 'Tell him avant-garde is French for bullshit,' he said, laughing.

Despite his involvement in the cause for peace, John decided he had to find time, in mid-1969, to find a new home for him and Yoko and also to take her on a short holiday. Weybridge held too many memories of his old life as a trapped Beatle. So Kenwood was sold, and he settled on Tittenhurst Park. The vast, thirty-roomed Georgian mansion just outside Sunningdale, Berkshire, cost John £150,000. When he went for a look at the 300-year-old house, John floored the estate agent by describing its sprawling grandeur as 'functional'. Included in the estate were seventy-two acres of parkland, featuring formal gardens, a farm, cottages, outhouses, and a lodge at the entrance gates. The two-storey house had seven main bedrooms, three reception rooms, three bathrooms, a large kitchen area, and extensive staff quarters. The striking feature of Tittenhurst, which attracted John and Yoko, was its tranquillity. Only twenty-six miles from London, it offered an oasis of peace and space in which John could plan his recording studio so that no neighbours would be affected.

Just before moving in, John and Yoko set off on a trip north. John had spent a year consistently telling Yoko about Aunt Mimi, his roots in Liverpool, and his childhood holidays in Scotland with 'Mater', his Aunt Elizabeth.

The perfect holiday for them both would be by car. 'I took Yoko round the streets of my youth in Liverpool and to meet all my relatives,' John said later. He also mentioned to me a vague plan to return one day to Liverpool and stage an event with Yoko at his old art college.

John kept up occasional contact with Cynthia because he felt guilt at the loss of his son, Julian, from his regular company. When he moved into his new Ascot home, John asked for Julian to be a regular weekend visitor. One weekend Yoko's daughter, Kyoko, was visiting her too, and the four of them set off for Liverpool and Aunt Mimi, and Durness, where Aunt Mater and Uncle Bert ran the croft where John had holidayed as a lad.

Mater gave him a cool reception. She had loved her nephew as a child, was proud of him as a Beatle with his wife and son, but the new-look John, complete with bushy, unkempt beard, biblical-length hair, a strange reputation for displaying himself in bed, and the new wife he introduced, was not so acceptable. John told her that he wanted to secure custody of Julian, then six years old. 'You've ruined all chances of that,' said Mater curtly. 'You've made your bed, now lie on it.' An angry John left, with Yoko, Julian, and Kyoko, with John driving a hired Austin Maxi saloon for the Highlands.

He was an erratic driver, and his attention tended to wander. On a narrow country road not far from Mater's house at Golspie, Sutherland, he missed a bend, and the car rolled over, ending up in a ditch. John was the most badly hurt, and blood poured from his face. Yoko, too, had facial injuries. A passer-by called an ambulance, and they were taken, with Kyoko and Julian, to hospital. John's face had seventeen stitches and Yoko's fourteen. Kyoko needed four stitches, while Julian, the least affected, suffered shock.

Cynthia was astonished to hear the news of the car accident on the television news. She had no idea that John and Yoko were taking Julian on a long car journey. She phoned Peter Brown, the Beatles' assistant, and asked to be taken to the hospital so that she could bring Julian home. Unfortunately they got on a plane going to Belfast, not Scotland. Eventually, another flight from Belfast and a four-hour taxi ride later, Cynthia arrived at the cottage hospital to be told that Julian had just been sent to stay with Mater. John and Yoko did not want to see her. She set off immediately to collect Julian from Mater's, and they returned to London next day.

The whole strategy behind the 'peace offensive' called for constant action. Headline hunting was, by John's admission, a key part of his philosophy. He had always felt uneasy about the Beatles' acceptance of the MBE in 1965, which he thought symbolized the Beatles selling-out to the Establishment. Four years later, with the Beatles in ruins, John felt it was a good time to have the courage of his earlier convictions. He would send his medal back to the Queen and do it as a gesture for peace.

John's chauffeur, Les Anthony, was despatched from Tittenhurst to Poole, Dorset, and Aunt Mimi. She proudly kept the medal on top of her television set. 'Mr Lennon said would you lend him the MBE medal for a while,' said Les Anthony when he arrived.

Said Mimi: 'I said, "Yes, but tell him, don't forget it's mine and I want it back." ' The next day she was as aghast as the rest of Britain to read that John had returned it to

the Queen at Buckingham Palace, accompanied by the
following letter:

Your Majesty,
I am returning this MBE in protest against Britain's
involvement in the Nigeria-Biafra thing, against our
support of America in Vietnam, and against 'Cold
Turkey' slipping down the charts.

> *With Love,*
> *John Lennon of*
> *Bag*

A copy was also sent to Prime Minister Harold Wilson.
Reaction was immediate: it was a rare event for anyone,
particularly a Beatle, to return an honour bestowed by the
Queen. Cranky old Lennon hit the headlines again and
achieved his purpose. He explained that he had always felt
uncomfortable at receiving it; he believed the Beatles were
part of the Establishment, and he had accepted it because
he was a Beatle. Now he was rejecting it as his right. The
reason behind its return was to draw attention to his peace
campaign. The mention of 'Cold Turkey', his latest record,
was 'humour to stop it from sounding like it was another
stupid letter to the Queen from some boring colonel.'

Aunt Mimi, furious, was on the phone immediately.
'Over my dead body would I have given you the medal
back to insult the Queen with. She's just a figurehead. Why
did you go and embarrass her?' John told her he meant to
keep up his long protest for peace and that this was a good
way. 'John, you can't worry about the whole world,' she
sighed. 'It's good that you do contribute and give money
but this way was so ridiculous.' John was used to Mimi's
condemnations, but this time she left him in no doubt: 'He

broke my heart over that. And also, he didn't tell me first why that medal was being taken away.'

Predictably irate lords and ladies, not to mention retired colonels, bellowed that what they feared all along had now been amply demonstrated by that young lout Lennon. He was a bad egg, a disgrace to the country, a mere pop idol, totally unworthy of receiving the honour in the first instance. (Although John had rejected the medal, the honour itself remained; he was still technically an MBE. Recipients can send back their medals, but they cannot renounce an honour once it has been bestowed.)

Lord Wilson, who as prime minister had originally recommended the award to the Queen, remembers John fondly and now believes he was 'naïve' in sending his medal back. 'John Lennon lived his life from day to day,' Lord Wilson told me. 'He didn't have to look two, three, five years ahead and people in showbiz don't have to have a relationship with fifty to a hundred countries, all of whom have different ideas. The prime minister has got to think in terms of long-term relationships.'

Lord Wilson had no regrets over having recommended the award. 'John's rejection of it was his personal right. The award at the time shocked a great many people because the press was mainly hostile to me. They'd spent all their time trying to keep Labour out of government. Many of them had not come to realize what the role of the Beatles in young people's lives had come to be. The award was well earned.' Many of John's critics at this time felt that he was setting a bad example to youth by his drug-taking. Lord Wilson took a more understanding view: 'It's easy to condemn. He was living a very, very strange existence when on the platform, broadcasting, or doing music for a bit of fun. As a superb performer, he was under great strain and he would not at any cost want to fall below the performance standard he had set himself.

'It was tragic that he had to take something. I don't suppose it was necessary but a lot of people his age had a shot of it. But if he was going to do it, it was a pity he didn't keep it to himself. People who worshipped the ground on which he walked would say that if he does it, it's all right, never mind what Dad and Mum say.' Resentment of John by the media, said Lord Wilson, stemmed partly from the fact that most journalists were of an older generation and 'resented the kids making all that money.' He told me: 'John Lennon used to put his hands very deep into his pockets if he heard of a good cause, and despite the lack of publicity, on which his trade sort of depends, most gifts were anonymous.'

Another aspect of John's past which reappeared in his life in that summer of 1969 was his father. Much as he often tried, John found it impossible to shake off his roots. He had never properly forgiven his father for deserting him in childhood. But his conscience and sentimentality won the day occasionally: he had, for example, invited Freddy Lennon to the party to launch the *Magical Mystery Tour* back in December 1967. The event, at London's Royal Lancaster Hotel, had ended with John and his father getting very drunk and dancing happily together. (John spent a lot of time chatting up women other than his wife. Singer Lulu was furious and remonstrated angrily with John for his bad behaviour.)

John told friends that he would have preferred to have totally resolved his relationship with his father but that obviously it was not possible. He always looked two ways at their division and his father's abdication of his responsibilities by going to sea when John was a toddler. 'Some parents,' said John, 'just can't take the responsibility of kids. I realize that now. I would like to have had a better relationship with him, but we didn't and that was OK, too. It's the way it was meant to be.' The loss of his ebullient mother, killed in a road accident, was different. He rarely spoke of her, but when he thought of her, tears were never far away.

The early 1970s found John and Yoko in complicated situations over Julian and Kyoko. Both their former partners were looking after their respective children, but John and Yoko wanted regular contact. It proved harder to achieve than either expected.

Cynthia, with her second husband-to-be, Roberto Bassanini, was so anxious to keep good relations with John and Yoko that she invited them to her housewarming party in Kensington, London. John and Yoko, Paul, George, Ringo and his wife, Maureen, and Neil Aspinall all went. John had a good chat with Roberto, and Cynthia hoped she had staged a successful event. But suddenly tension developed as the Beatles recalled the factors that separated them, both professionally and as husband-and-wife teams. 'It wasn't successful,' agrees Cynthia. 'It taught me that you can't step back into the past. Too many dramatic things had happened to all of them and the break-up of the very first Beatle marriage came home to them. They were all shell-shocked after they'd been there a while. Tight, nervous, everybody watching everyone else.'

Shortly afterwards, John phoned Cynthia: 'I want to come round and see Julian.' Their son had started at a new school, and John wanted to check on his progress. He spent two hours alone with Julian in his bedroom, talking and drawing with him on the six-year-old boy's blackboard. 'He was really bright, cheerful, and friendly,' says Cynthia. He gave her a book to read by an American psychologist, Dr Arthur Janov, saying it was proving a great eye-opener to him. 'Oh no,' said Cynthia to herself. 'Not another! Either it's Janov or the Maharishi or drugs and vegetarianism!' But John said he had been feeling guilty about his absence from Julian and that Janov had convinced him that he should see his son more often, alone.

Yoko's contact with Kyoko was much more complex. In December 1969 John and Yoko holidayed in Denmark with Anthony Cox, Yoko's second husband, together with his new wife, Melinda, and Kyoko. Anthony Cox pronounced John 'a great guy'. Everything looked set fair for harmonious access. But it was not to be so easy.

The issue of custody of Kyoko was never properly resolved when Yoko and Tony Cox were divorced, and Yoko expected free access to her daughter. But after an ugly experience in Majorca in 1971, when John and Yoko were detained by police for a day on suspicion of kidnapping her, Anthony Cox vanished with Kyoko. The search in Majorca had appalled John and Yoko. 'How can you kidnap your own daughter?' said Yoko. Anthony Cox's evasiveness with the eight-year-old girl was what decided John and Yoko to move to New York. They first visited there in June 1971, believing that Cox had taken the girl into the city. Courtroom appearances and visits to the Virgin Islands, plus private detectives and international publicity, never properly resolved Yoko's and John's desire for a peaceful relationship with Kyoko and Anthony Cox. But in September 1971, while they were living temporarily in Manhattan's St Regis Hotel in the hope of finding Kyoko, they decided to live permanently in America. Yoko, who knew every corner of the city in which she had grown up in the

1950s, took John walking round it, and he needed little urging to convince him that it was the right environment for an artist. John applied the same logic, and description, as he had when first seeing Tittenhurst Park. 'Yoko and I seemed to be forever coming to New York,' he explained later. 'It seemed more *functional* to come and live here.'

Two critical events preceded the emigration. In early 1970, while workmen were still re-structuring Tittenhurst to John and Yoko's specifications, Mr and Mrs Lennon began bickering. It was not surprising. For three intense years since their first meeting they had not been out of each other's sight. There was no danger of a split, but every conversation was edgy. Yoko was very weary of the Apple battle and the resentful atmosphere towards her. She missed her daughter. John was tense too, but he could see no way out of the forest. He was desperate to solve the Beatles' business wrangle. He buried himself in endless television, concentrating on very little except the commercials, which had always fascinated him and given him occasional lines for songs. John in a foul mood was bad news for anyone near him: he would bark or scream at the slightest intrusion into his self-imposed silence. But both he and Yoko realized the reason for their tension: 'We were close friends, twenty-four hours a day, as well as artists,' recalls Yoko. 'No relationship survives without highs and lows. It's realization of the situation that's vital.'

Luck had been a main ingredient in John's life. His childhood was marred, but once he was in his teens his music and lucky breaks had been his salvation. The greatest break in helping him through this particular psychological barrier came from the book by Janov that he had tried to persuade Cynthia to read. It was called *The Primal Scream (Primal Therapy: The Cure for Neurosis)*. John was hooked as quickly as he had been on drugs and meditation. Janov's cool logic regarding the treatment of neurosis made total sense to John. Like everything he touched, he had to plunge into it at full tilt — and he could never go into something like this alone. Yoko was a quick believer too. They phoned Janov in California and invited him to Ascot. Primal therapy might well have been designed exactly for John in his state of mind at that time.

Its theory was simple. It worked on the assumption that the patient had layers of defences which needed stripping down to reveal the real person. By owning up to fallibilities and frailties and confessing to oneself the struggle of childhood, particularly one's relationship with parents, the person who underwent therapy willingly would come face to face with his real self again, literally screaming away the pain. It was simple, but in John's case, effective. Janov had his first sessions with John and Yoko over three weeks at Tittenhurst Park. Then he told them they would have to go to the Primal Institute in California to continue the course. There was no choice for John: he was deriving an enormous amount of personal strength from talking himself through the agony of his childhood and his inhibitions about his lost parents. He and Yoko stayed in California for four months, renting a house in Bel Air and plunging into what he later described to me as something 'much more important to my life than the Beatles.' He went on: 'Janov showed me how to feel my own fear and pain, therefore I can handle it better than I could before, that's all. I'm the same, only there's a channel. It doesn't just remain in me, it goes round and out.'

One of John's most endearing characteristics, honesty, was to pour out of him as a result of primal therapy. The new John sang of his childhood in heart-rending songs: in 'Mother', 'Mother you had me/But I never had you . . . Father, you left me/But I never left you.' In 'Working Class

Hero' he sang of the pressures of his school years, which partly explained his outlandish behaviour; in 'Isolation', he pinpointed the dilemma of being John and Yoko: 'Just a boy and a little girl/Trying to change the whole wide world.' And in 'God' he therapeutically listed all the points of reference which his mind wanted to offload: 'I don't believe in magic . . . I don't believe in Jesus . . . I don't believe in Elvis . . . I don't believe in Zimmerman [Bob Dylan] . . . I don't believe in Beatles/I just believe in me/ Yoko and me/And that's reality.' The starkness of his confessional was searing, simple, and it made a staggering impact on those who had written off the post-Beatle Lennon as a freaky sideshow. A straight song, 'Love', demonstrated that he could even compete with McCartney in this route of romance; the poetic beauty of the song attracted Barbra Streisand, who recorded her own version, as did many other artists. *John Lennon/Plastic Ono Band*, with John often accompanying himself on the piano, featured Yoko, with Klaus Voormann on bass and Ringo on drums. It stands as an album many of John's contemporaries feel is one of rock's greatest works. Only Bob Dylan, with less introspective genius, can have his work compared with *Plastic Ono Band* and its successor, *Imagine*, for soul-baring intensity and such a forceful projection of intense emotions. And even Dylan never wrote so personally. The two albums, appearing in 1970 and 1971 in the wake of Dr Janov's primal therapy, were vital signposts for John's future psyche. He often described himself as a chameleon. With these two albums, he stepped outside the traditional rock 'n' roll formula to show his inner self and to prove that at least two of his old images were inadequate. Hard old Lennon, the Liverpool rocker, would no longer do. Nor would the image of the lunatic peacenik. John came of age in 1970 and 1971. A change of country, to accommodate his philosophy, seemed the natural next step.

On the eve of their final departure from British soil, John and Yoko appeared on BBC television's Michael Parkinson chat show. Yoko read some excerpts from *Grapefruit*, which John praised; Parkinson described the book as incomprehensible. John retorted: 'It's so simple, it eludes you. A lot of people over here don't understand it but a lot of people in America understand it because there's a lot of avant-garde there, especially in New York, which is where she lived for ten years. A lot of people who read the book when it was published ten years ago in limited form are now professors in American universities and *Grapefruit* is part of the curriculum in film schools.'

Parkinson persisted: 'I think the creative phase that you're going through at present . . . you've got to accept, that it's alienated you, particularly John, from the people that originally loved you in this country.'

John replied, 'When I left Liverpool with the group, a lot of Liverpool people dropped us and said: "Now you've let us down." When we left England with the group to go to America, we lost a lot of fans who had begun to feel as if they owned us. Well, the Liverpool people did and they did until we decided to leave. The same in England, a lot of people dropped us because we went to America. But of course we got a whole pile more, a different audience. And it's the same now. I'm not going to sort of gear my life just to attract an audience. I started off playing music because that's what I wanted to do. And in front of an audience is how you do it. And now it's not very different. I mean, then I sang "All You Need Is Love", and now I might sing "Power To The People". And the message is basically the same. It's just sort of slogans. The alienation started when I met Yoko; people do not seem to like people getting a divorce, you know. It's all right to do it quietly but we can't do it quietly. So we fell in love and it's unfortunate! We fell in love and we married. A lot of people think that to be odd, but it happens all the time. Yoko just happened to be Japanese which didn't help much. And so everybody had this impression that John's gone crazy. All I did was fall in love like a lot of people do who are already married, who married somebody very young. And that's all we did. I know we did *Two Virgins* which didn't help much!'

Yoko added, 'I'd be a masochist if I loved this country, where I'm constantly abused. It's a bit tough on me, you know.'

Parkinson responded: 'Another reason for people taking a dislike of you is because you've become known, again through the newspapers in this country, as the woman who broke up the Beatles. But that's not true?'

'That's not true,' John answered. 'Listen, I'll tell you. People on the street and kids do not dislike us. It's the media. We go on the street and lorry drivers wave and say, "Hello, Yoko, hello, John," and all that jazz. I judge it by that. . . . Nobody could break the Beatles up. We broke ourselves up. When Brian [Epstein] died we got a bit lost because we needed a manager, all of us are artists and we're nothing else. We can't manage ourselves or look after ourselves in that way. But it's a lot for four big heads like the Beatles to stay together for such a long time. In the early days there was the thing of "making it" big, or breaking into America and we had that goal together . . . but when we reached twenty-eight or twenty-nine . . . our personalities developed and they were a bit stifled with the Beatles. And between us now we sell ten times more records than the Beatles did.' This was not true, and, typically, John said it to demonstrate a point rather than accept the facts. By the end of 1970 sales of Beatles records totalled approximately 500 million units worldwide. The *Guinness Book of Records* states that between February 1963 and January 1972 the Beatles sold 545 million records. In the period January 1963 to August 1966 when they ceased to tour, the estimated international attendance at Beatles concerts was 2,676,000. The four Beatles as soloists (taken either separately or together) did not fill anything like that number of seats or sell anything like that number of records.

Michael Parkinson asked John how deep the hurt was between him and Paul McCartney. 'It's fairly deep,' John replied. 'We're playing Monopoly now with real money and so it's pretty serious. But I can't see it lasting and I think it'll probably cool off. It'll take a year after the whole thing is settled, moneywise, probably for us to relax a bit.'

Getting immersed in the spirit of things, Parkinson got inside a bag in the studio while he questioned John and Yoko. 'Hey,' said John, 'imagine if a black guy went for a job at the BBC and he had to wear a bag. They wouldn't know what coloured people were and there'd be no prejudice, for a kick-off!'

Staying on the theme of the bag and relating it to the Beatles, John continued: 'There's no conceivable reason why the Beatles should come back together again because we're all individuals and in the Beatles we grew out of it. The bag was too small. I can't impose far-out music and far-out films on George and Paul if they don't want to do it. We have to live our lives separately. We've grown up now. We've left school. We never *left* school. We went straight into showbiz.'

Yoko interjected: 'Michael, this is a typical example. We are so nostalgic and we're talking about the past. But we have to live in the present. You can burn the past. That's why even in this book, *Grapefruit*, I'd like people to burn it after they've read it.'

John said finally: 'There's a beautiful story Yoko told me about a Japanese monk, which happened within the last ten years. He loved this fantastic golden temple so much that he didn't want to see it disintegrate. So he burned it . . . that is what I did with the Beatles. I never wanted them to slide down, making comebacks. I said when I was twenty in the Beatles: "I'm not going to be singing 'She Loves You' when I'm thirty." ' (John had a fine memory for generalization but a poor recollection of details. The interview he was referring to was with me for the *Melody Maker* on 24 October 1964. He had actually said: 'I don't want to be fiddling round the world singing "It's Been A Hard Day's Night" when I'm thirty, do I? I said during a conversation with Mick Jagger that I'd be out of it in a few years. I enjoy playing really but in America it was spoiled for me because of the crap there . . . meeting people we don't want to meet. I suppose I'm a bit intolerant.') 'Well, I was thirty this year [*sic*]. I didn't force it to happen this year. It just happened naturally.

'I guessed that by the time I was thirty I would have grown out of it. And I have, you know. And the guy burned the temple. And most people still like the Beatles and have a pleasant memory of them . . . let's remember them like that and remember their music like we remember people from the past. That's fine.'

British singer George Melly, whose clash with John over his musical roots is discussed in the first part of this biography, met a very different ex-Beatle in the television show. (Melly was on the same Parkinson programme.) 'We had a very nice talk this time,' says Melly. 'Not very productive because it was difficult to understand what they were getting at, exactly, except for peace and love. But their gentleness and affection for each other was very, very powerful. I really felt warm to them because I didn't expect

to. They irritated me with their bagism and the fact that
they were very rich and constantly making humble gestures.
If only the acorns had done some good or the bagism had
persuaded people to be peaceful. But it just irritated most
people and I felt it wasn't very useful. Together, though,
she with her dreamy beads and long hair, he with long hair
and granny glasses, and both holding hands constantly, they
were charming, childlike.' Contrasting vividly with the
drunken John who had seven years earlier berated Melly at
a publisher's party, he was warm and polite.

'There you are, you see, Yoko,' John said, when they
came to leave Melly. 'There *are* nice people in England.'

NINETEEN

CHANGE

'My function in society is to be an artist'

JOHN FIRMLY believed in the adage that the best method of defence is attack. In the late 1960s, when he had married Yoko and taken a battering from both the press and public opinion about their liaison and 'stunts for peace', John countered with some of his most forceful interviews. He still loved talking, particularly about himself: one of his strongest themes on his publicly declared love for Yoko was that they were doing the Establishment a favour by making marriage fashionable against all the odds.

Talking to the new, post-Beatle Lennon, one encountered the man as he had originally been in Liverpool: in a hurry, warm and generous, full of invective, incurably idealistic. Between his marriage to Yoko in 1969 and their move to New York in 1971, I had many interviews with him, covering a wide range of topics. He said to me in 1969: 'Go on – ask me some questions that will get on the front page of the dailies. I'm not a moptop any more. I can say what I like!'

His ego was always big, but he said that he would rather have a following that did not seek his autograph. 'If kids want my signature and I'm in the right mood and it's the right person, they can have it. But it depends on the

person who asks.' Living with Yoko had changed his outlook: there was nothing he had, materially, that he could
not do without, now that he had found inner peace. 'I'm
glad to have got the pop star thing out of the way. It was
good and it gave me this freedom. But we grew up, grew
apart.' He always firmly declared that the Beatles did not
set any trends. 'We never did start anything. We were just
part of the whole sixties thing, the movement, the fashion,
the change in attitude among a load of people. The Beatles
were just in the middle of it.'

Because of his nudity on the *Two Virgins* album cover,
John said people thought of him as 'a perverted crank. They
think Yoko and I are ravers, only interested in sex and
causing a stir. But really, we're the quietest pair of spinsters
around.' He was a vegetarian, and Yoko usually baked their
bread. He wanted a farm so that they could grow their own
macrobiotic food. 'It works like Zen Buddhism or meditation – you eat what you think's best for you and it's
commonsense to me that you shouldn't eat most of the
chemically treated rubbish most people seem to stuff themselves with. The trouble is most vegetarians don't get
enough protein. My diet's based on meal, bread which Yoko
makes, rice, and no sugar. We have honey if anything needs
sweetening.' But he wore leather shoes, I pointed out. 'I
still wear the shoes I had before I changed my views. I don't
see the point of not using them. I won't buy any more
leather ones, though. I'm always wearing sneakers. I don't
think animals were meant to be eaten and worn. We have
enough resources to do without them. But it's big business
again, you see.' Did he feel better, I asked him, since giving
up meat? 'Yeah, but a car can last a long time on the wrong
petrol. One day it packs up. I feel better mentally but
maybe my diet's not right for everyone.'

He told me the best thing to come out of the Beatles

was the power it gave him to do other things from a platform people would notice. 'I'm using my power all the time by doing things like releasing an album called *Two Virgins*. There are generation gaps and other gaps, plenty of them, in this world and they all need closing. I'm trying to open people's minds. There's nothing horrible about nudity. People said the Rolling Stones, and Elvis, and long hair were all obscene but they accepted them in the end. I hope it's the same with my scene. A lot of narrow minds need expanding. People say I offend "normal" people. . . . Society's full of people who think of themselves as normal, who aren't. It's as wrong as judging me as a hippy because I happen to have long hair. It's more what a man's scene is in his mind than how he looks or what he wears. You can be a pretty cool bin man.'

He believed in religion and had not regarded the Maharishi as a substitute for it. 'The Maharishi was good for me, like anybody who has something to tell you that you don't know enough about. He was no substitute for anything, though. There's a lot of good in Christianity but you've got to learn the basics of it, and the basics from the Eastern beliefs, and work them together for yourself. . . . Yoko and I are fighting a bit of a fight to spread understanding and a kind of freedom. I don't expect everybody to understand us but I just wish they'd try to be a bit more open-minded, that's all. Beatles wives always had a hard time, probably because the fans resented us marrying. I got more stick because I was the loud-mouth – and then I went and got meself a new wife without asking permission. And a Japanese one at that! It's "How dare Lennon go off with this woman who's not a housewife?" ' They were hurt by a lot of anti-Japanese mail.

He pointed out that he wanted to use power constructively. 'When we say, "War is over, if you want it", we mean that if everybody demanded peace instead of another television set, there'd be peace. If you like, we're the Tolpuddle Martyrs of our day. People said the first trade union leaders were fighting a losing battle, but when people realized what they could achieve by banding together and demanding their rights, they got it. It's a communal thing. Everybody has power, not just John and Yoko. We want to spread awareness.' In himself he was striving for perfection but doubted if he would achieve it. 'I'd like to be like Christ.' He described himself as a Christian communist, 'in a pure sense, not in the way Russia or Italy think of Christianity or communism.'

He consistently denied that he wanted to be seen as a leader. 'I'm not falling for that one. Like Pete Seeger said, we don't have a leader, but we have a song, "Give Peace A Chance". I refuse to be a leader. . . . Our whole mistake is having leaders and people we can rely on or point a finger at.'

Yoko often took up a point during the interviews. 'For instance,' she said, 'many people say . . . don't do anything that is misleading, like showing your genitals. Always keep a clean image so that people can believe in your peace movement.

'But that's exactly what the Establishment is doing ['And that's what the Beatles did, too,' said John], taking their children to church on Sundays. This is showing that "I'm the President of the United States and I'm all right and I'm healthy and very moral et cetera." You don't get anywhere that way. You just become another hypocrite and you're playing the Establishment game. We don't want to do that. We try to be honest and the point is, if we are really honest, just to make it between us is really a lifetime thing. And if we can't make it together and endure each other the world is nowhere.

'If ordinary couples can make it together and make it

with their children and so forth, love-wise ['She doesn't mean "make-it" as in "lay",' interjected John], then you can look after the world.'

John said: 'One thing we've found out is that love is a great gift, like a precious flower or something.' He often harkened back to romantic analogies. 'You have to feed it and look after it and it has storms to go through, and snow, but you have to protect it. . . . It's like a pet cat. You know, people get a cat and they don't want to feed it, or they get a dog and they won't want to walk it. But love has to be nurtured like a very sensitive animal because that's what it is. And you have to work at love. You don't just sit round with it and it doesn't just do it for you. You've got to be very careful with it. It's the most delicate thing you can be given.'

'People hide from each other all the time,' he continued. 'Everybody's frightened of saying something nice about somebody in case they don't say something nice back or in case they get hurt. . . . Everybody's uptight and they're always building these walls around themselves. All you can do is try and break down the walls and show that there's nothing there but *people*. It's just like looking in the mirror. . . . Of course we mustn't take ourselves too seriously. What we try and do is be non-serious about things but we are very serious about being not serious!'

Yoko said: 'We may be too serious, even. We try to have a sense of humour and to smile at everyone, a really genuine smile from the bottom of our hearts.'

John's laconic humour always permeated his work, even at a peak of his peace campaign with Yoko. To a circle of friends at Christmas in 1969, he sent a dry, hilarious item called 'The John Lennon London Diary 1969'. He had handwritten an entry for each day. Most were a very slight variation on the same words: 'Got up, went to work, came home, watched telly, went to bed.' It was a beautiful parody of the routine of life. But, like John, it was unpredictable: forgetfulness and boredom set in as he continued and one or two entries read: 'Got up, went to work, came home, watched telly, went to bed, fucked the wife,' for example. It was reassuring for some to know that Lennon's wit was still intact, come drugs, bagism, or peace.

Demonstrative humour was more difficult for Yoko. Critics constantly jibed at her expressionless demeanour. In truth she has a cool, subterranean sense of humour. Her smiles are few because, as a child, her mother warned her against too much smiling lest it be construed by people as a sign of weakness.

The theory that Yoko's inscrutability had vanquished John's sense of fun was knocked firmly aside when they released a 1970 calendar which, month-by-month, captured in photographs their lives together. The calendar featured excerpts from his songs, his writings in *A Spaniard In The Works* and *In His Own Write*, plus quotations from *Grapefruit*. John set off the calendar with this original piece, demonstrating that his gobbledegook type of wit was still intact:

> wonsaapoatime therewas two Balloons called Jock and Yono. They were strictly in love-bound to happen in a million years. They werer together man. Unfortunatime-table they both seemed to have previous experience — which kept calling them one way oranother. (you know howitis). But they battled on against overwhelming odd-ities, includo some of there beast friends. . . . Being in love they cloong even the more together man — but some of the poisoness-monster of outrated buslodedshi-throwers did stick slightly and they occasionally had to resort to the drycleaners. Luckily this did not kill them

and they werent banned from the olympic games. They lived hopefully ever after, and who could blame them.

Paradoxically, it was John, rather than Yoko, who wholeheartedly publicly championed the cause of women's liberation once he had met her in the early 1970s. Len Wood of EMI Records recalls a visit to the Apple office at Broadway, New York, which had to be cut short. 'Yoko was going to a rally for women's rights, but she was most insistent that John should be the only male there,' says Wood. She was on the phone impressing on women that if they banned her husband from attending the rally, that would be a kind of reverse bigotry; she won her case and John attended. And on her striking double album, called *Approximately Infinite Universe*, she satirized the women's liberation movement with a song called 'What A Bastard The World Is'. 'So they would scream and kick out all the men? *Then* what are they going to do?' asked Yoko. 'I told John, and he agreed, that feminism involves men too. John helped the movement towards equality more by *doing* something, like househusbandry, than a million people demonstrating for it. . . . Initially, feminists thought that the fact that I was married was a betrayal of the whole idea. As for the idea of really *loving* John, and saying so – *loving a man*, what was *this?* I wrote a song called "I Want My Man To Rest Tonight", which was addressed to my feminist sisters and said: let's not blame our men too much. They are doing their best. That was sniggered at. But I think in a male chauvinist society it was just as difficult for men too. They had to adjust. The reason I did not become an extreme feminist was a lot to do with living with John. He was a good influence.'

Reflecting on her early years in London, Yoko says: 'I was getting sick and tired of the pseudo-intellectual, elitist atmosphere of the circle I was in in London. I was thinking: Am I going to end up as the Queen Mother of the avant-garde world, always meeting these snobs talking about elitist kicks? I was starting to feel frightened.

'When I started to make the bottoms film I became very known in England in a strange sort of way – like to taxi drivers, that sort of thing – and my elite friends were so very upset about that. They were saying: "Well, she copped out, she went commercial."

'I said: "It's great to communicate your art with the working class. What *is* this?" But all the same they stopped inviting me to their tea party; just sort of inverted snobbery.

'Around this time I met John. The first song we recorded on *Approximately Infinite Universe* was "Song For John". It was a song I made actually before I met him. I was hoping to find somebody who'd fly with me, or whatever, and I made a demo record. It's the first demo of mine that John listened to when he visited me and that's why, for sentimental reasons, I called it "Song For John". It's the same tune, same lyrics.'

The Lennons at home were much more traditional as husband and wife than their public face indicated. 'There's nothing I like more,' John told the *Melody Maker*, 'than to get home at the end of the day and sit next to Yoko and say, "Well, we're together at last." Although we may have been holding hands all day, it's not the same when we're working or talking to the press. We feel a hundred miles apart by comparison.'

Yoko confessed that she was lonely before she met John. 'Most people in the world are very lonely. That's the biggest problem,' she said. 'Because of their loneliness, they become suspicious. When I met John I started to open up a little, through love, you know, and that's the greatest thing that happened to me yet. . . . I never met anybody else who could understand me. We understand each other so well and I'm not lonely any more. Through loneliness, I was starting to become a very firm and strong ego. That's melting away and that's nice.'

John described his pre-Yoko loneliness this way: 'I didn't have full communication with anybody and it took a bit of adjusting. She re-discovered or cultivated the thing that existed in me before I left Liverpool, maybe, and re-cultivated the natural John Lennon that had been lost in the Beatles thing and the world-wide thing. She encouraged me to be myself because it was me she fell in love with, not the Beatles or whatever I was.

'When you get sidetracked you believe it, and when you're in the dark you believe it. She came and reminded me that there was light and when you remember there's light you don't want to get back in the dark again.'

Yoko continued: 'It's the falling in love bit. You start to see all sorts of things that you don't see if you're not in love. I found that he has all these qualities that he was hiding away. Music-wise, he was doing all sorts of freaky things at home, just recording it on a cassette, but not really showing it publicly.

'Publicly he was doing the Beatles things. But he showed me all these cassettes and things and I said: "Why don't you produce these as records?" I performed the role of a mirror in a way. He was doing all those things anyway. I didn't suggest them. It was there and that goes for his drawing, paintings, and poetry too, especially his drawings. I think he's better than Picasso.'

John stopped her. 'She's biased!'

On another visit to Ascot, John particularly wanted to talk to me about his rationale behind the peace crusade. How exactly did they seek to make the world more peaceful? I wanted to know. What would John do, for instance, if he was elected prime minister?

'I'd stop selling arms to Nigeria and all that. I'd get rid of the army and the air force and become a Sweden. I'm not a practical guy, I only know peace can exist, and the first thing is for the world to disarm.

'But would I have enough power, as a prime minister, to do this? How much control does Wilson have? What chance would a peacenik prime minister have? I don't know. I just know things are not very good now and it must be worth a try.'

Life with the Lennons down at Ascot was a communal affair: members of the Krishna Consciousness Society hung around, and John and Yoko would join them in their chanting. The Lennons liked this scene: it appealed to John's ideas of 'mixing with the people'. He was philosophical and decisive in his attitude to his wealth.

'You don't have to be poor to be a communist,' he said, laughing. 'My money that was earned as a Beatle, it's almost a by-product. I'm not just going to give it all away to some people, just so that I can starve like a lot of others. What's *that* going to achieve?

'But the money doesn't give me any hang-ups. . . . Both Yoko and I have this dream of living in a small cottage in the country, eventually. But we ended up with this big Georgian house. Now we're going through this big house scene before moving on.'

'But for the moment we enjoy it,' said Yoko passively.

John said that he got more pleasure from old 78 records than from revelling in the size and glory of his home. 'It means nothing to me,' he declared. 'A little bit of ivory I bought in Japan, that's my grossest material possession which I like as much as anything.'

'Material pleasures are all right as long as they don't clog your mind,' observed Yoko.

'I wouldn't worry,' John said, 'if I never had a thing. If it took too much to carry on living in this big house I wouldn't want to stay and live here . . . but I'm hoping to farm some of the land. The Krishna people are helping me to do this. . . . We're hoping to grow non-chemical food — maybe we can sell it to Harrods.'

He reflected on the Beatles' touring days like this: 'Those old tours were OK at the time but once we had taken over from Helen Shapiro, there was nothing else to do, except for us to go around and other people to see us standing there, doing the same songs and not hearing a note.

'The Stones seemed to get a good thing in Hyde Park but it's different for us. We're not that type. Jagger is the Charlie Chaplin of rock and roll — it's OK for Mick because he's dancing around like a puppet and putting on a show. We don't. We couldn't stand the shell of unreality, standing there like four dolls in the middle of Shea Stadium. It killed our music.

'But when I see a group like The Band playing, I think we should have got going again before now.'

Did he, I asked, think the Plastic Ono Band would survive as long as or longer than the Beatles? He dodged the answer with some facts: 'I think it will survive — you know my records with Yoko and the Plastic Ono have sold well. We sold twenty-five thousand copies of *Two Virgins* in the States and sixty thousand of *Life With The Lions*. That's good going in the States.

'Our new album, *John and Yoko's Wedding Album* is going to sell as well. But in Britain we only sold about five thousand of each of those albums. I can understand that though.'

'See, Americans like our albums because if you land in New York, it's like *Life With The Lions* anyway. If you play it in Britain, it doesn't have the same urgency, because of the environment. It'll be a few years before they turn on to that sort of thing properly here.'

'But we are patient,' said Yoko, 'because we are doing something worthwhile.'

John summarized the division between himself and the Beatles: 'I am an artist and my art is peace and I happen to be a musician. My music is done with the Beatles — that's where I get my wages from. The peace thing isn't a gimmick. Other people make it a gimmick. Yoko and I are serious.'

He clearly believed passionately in the peace campaign. 'It's the goodies and the baddies, the Blue Meanies, and the rest. I think I'll win because I believe in what Jesus said.'

Drawing on his Gitanes cigarettes in the Apple office, John devoured newspapers with an intensity that floored those who worked with him. He surprised the Apple team by his contradiction of his own image. The tough-talking Beatle was replaced, with Yoko at his side, by a man who was funny, gentle, and kind but nobody's fool. He strutted down the corridors, hands on hips. Gradually it was conceded that their partnership was impregnable, their message pure and sincere. It took time, though, and probably only sank in when Apple turned sour, the Beatles were officially pronounced dead, and John and Yoko had moved on to the next phase of their lives.

But for three years, for every success John counted there were people with trip wires, testing him. John enjoyed the challenge; some of his finest eloquence came during self-justification.

The 'Smile' box was a favourite way of getting the conversation going. It was a box that you had to open, and inside it was a mirror that told the truth about your expression. The box, concocted by John and Yoko, kept many baffled and bemused because it had no message other than how the 'viewer' reacted. This, John would repeat to anyone, was Art with a capital A. Yoko described it as 'con art', which was short for conceptual art; meaning that the idea behind the piece was more important than the exhibit. John described Yoko as 'straight from Duchamp and Dada, but she's Now.' As a book, he said, *Grapefruit* stood alongside the Bible.

As a film maker, he was definitely interested in the avant-garde and art. Two films took up his time in 1970: *Apotheosis* followed on from *Self Portrait*, and *Erection* followed on from *Rape*. *Apotheosis* featured a balloon taking off from a snowy field in an English village and climbing into the clouds. The soundtrack is the fading noise of barking dogs, a hunting horn, and a gun being fired. When the balloon reaches the clouds, silence reigns for five minutes. The onus is on the viewer to interpret. The same is true of *Erection*: this film, made over nine months, depicts a hotel being erected in London's West Cromwell Road. The bizarre touch is the inactivity and slow progress made by the builders.

Art possessed John by the time he and Yoko made plans to go to live in America. He reflected on what they had achieved since 'going public'. The Amsterdam bed-in, he considered, was one of the greatest happenings of the century. Not because of what they had done but because of people's reactions: it was illogical, *marvellous*, that they hit the headlines just by getting married and going to bed to ask for peace. It was an Event. Communication, he intoned, was everything. 'The English are eccentrics. I'm just another one from a long line of eccentrics.'

He thought advertising their art was not reprehensible, rather a clear duty. People who believed they were stunts were naïve. 'Andy Warhol – the biggest publicity man in the world! Salvador Dali! Or Duchamp!' All artists struggled for publicity if they knew what they had to do, he said.

He was a revolutionary artist, and he'd been consistent, right from 'All You Need Is Love' to 'Power To The People'. He was dedicated to change and to revolution in forcing people to think and react positively. Art for art's sake was decadent; he was writing songs for people to express themselves with. For example, at concerts in America, thirty thousand people had sung 'Give Peace A Chance', and twenty thousand were singing 'Power To The People' on the streets. Use of art for propaganda was totally right. To deny that was 'like saying, don't make knives in case you kill with them.'

He wrote songs for himself, primarily. 'You can't blame me or the song. I'm not here to provide power to the people: I'm *singin'* about it. I'm the songwriter who sang the song about it that the people sang at the meetings they held. That's all. That's my job. Like, if we're a community on an island, I'd be the singer. Somebody would be the carpenter, somebody else would be the cook. My function in society is to be an artist.

'You see,' he went on, 'society is under the delusion that art is something you have extra, like crème de menthe or something. But societies don't exist with no artist. Art is a functional part of society: if you don't have artists you don't have society. We're not some kind of decadent strip show that appears on the side. We're as important as prime ministers or policemen. So "Power To The People" isn't expected to make a revolution. It's for the people to sing, like the Christians sing hymns.'

He liked slogans, he continued. 'I like advertising. I love the telly.' He hated classical music; it was too slow. 'It's "then" music. It really is a load of crap. I think I write much more relevant music for today than the classical composers. . . . And where's today's classical music? There isn't any.'

His song 'Instant Karma!' was much more important than most of the classical music he had heard. 'It's about human beings, which is more than can be said for the classics. "Instant Karma!" is about action and reaction. Whenever you do something, whatever it is, there's a reaction to it. Even if you cough, you cough germs out all over the place. If you cough love out, out goes love. That's what "Instant Karma!" is – it's a great step forward. The greatest artists always come round to simplicity. It took Picasso sixty years to go through the whole bit and learn to paint like a child. I hope to record and write songs like an adult child.'

He was always at his most vociferous on the subject of peace. 'I'm not under any illusion. My contribution will be small in the light of the universe. Compared with the size of the earth, what John and Yoko achieve will be small, but it's the best we can manage. It takes time to be taken seriously. It took the Beatles time and then they were taken too seriously sometimes.' Yes, he agreed, the peace campaign was costing him a fortune, 'but you reap what you sow. Whatever you do, you get something back for it.'

I asked him why he equated himself with Christ so frequently during this period of self-revelation. 'I was brought up a Christian, Sunday School and all that. It's OK, I have nothing against it except that it organizes itself as a business, the Church. What I do like about it is that

Christians talk about being perfect; so was Christ and I was taught that as a child. Christ is the one who most people in the West refer to when they speak of good people. . . . If I could do what Christ did, be as Christ was, that's what being a Christian is all about. I try to live as Christ lived. It's tough, I can tell you.'

Did he believe in God? 'I don't know that anyone like me, who questions everything down to the colour of his socks, can believe in an old man in the sky.' He was very thoughtful and silent for several minutes. 'I believe in something, definitely. I believe there is a force at work that you can't physically account for.'

During talks like these John would often stop himself from getting carried away or sounding portentous. 'Hey,' he would say. 'My Auntie Mimi says I sound too serious when I go on like this. She also reckons that having my hair cut short like this has turned me into a skinhead. Mimi — I'm happier now than I've ever been!'

John and Yoko's unique partnership derived partly from the great difference in their backgrounds. 'She had hardly heard of the music that turned me on, like Elvis and "Heartbreak Hotel". I had all that to get through to her,' he explained. She gave John new insights into art. What constantly surprised them both was how, almost five years after first meeting, on the eve of their departure from London to New York, they could not get enough of each other's company. 'Her and Elvis, they both turned me on most in my life. They're the greatest influences. It's a miracle. We're more in love than ever,' he said. By then Yoko had suffered three miscarriages. John worried that they were his fault, that his heavy use of drugs had made him infertile or had a bad effect on Yoko's body. 'John needs to rest,' said Yoko just before they left for America.

'No drugs except tobacco, and I've been off that for a year too.'

Their togetherness was precisely what alienated many people who considered them 'over the top' in mawkish sentimentality. 'People say that if we're together twenty-four hours a day, we must get sick and tired of each other but it's the contrary,' said Yoko. 'We got so addicted to that situation that we miss each other more. It's a very strange scene.'

John weighed in: 'Somebody said: "Won't you get so reliant on each other that you can't manage without each other?" and we said yes! The only thing that could split us is death and we have to face that . . . and we don't even believe we'll be split then, if we work on it.

'Our only worry in the world is that we die together, otherwise even if it's three minutes later it's going to be hell. . . . Most marriages have a little pretence going on and we thought: are we going to have to pretend that we're happy together because we daren't say that we want to be apart? But that doesn't happen. When two of you are together, man and wife, there's nothing that can touch you. You have the power of two people, the power of two minds, which is a pretty powerful thing.'

TWENTY

THE MUSIC:
1966–1971

'Let me take you down 'cos I'm going to . . .'

FROM 'STRAWBERRY Fields Forever' through to 'Imagine', John Lennon's work, in and out of the Beatles, was distinct and highly personalized. While Paul McCartney's gift lay in composing love songs, John was incapable of songwriting as a craftsman, 'for other people'. Nonetheless, he admired McCartney compositions, particularly 'Here There And Everywhere' and 'For No One'. Conversely, the extrovert McCartney found it hard to write about himself. In that, John Lennon excelled. For although he loved the speed of rock 'n' roll, he thought the golden oldies of that genre were unbeatable; his own writing would have to act as a mirror of his personality, particularly as he grew older and more observant, and wanted more from life than teenagers screaming his name. At twenty-six, John wanted his music to express the important things in his life: his childhood memories; his assiduous reading of newspapers and magazines; his love of words and sharp observation of the unexpected phrase; his own frailties and rejection of the tough-guy Beatle image; and an increasing interest in humanitarianism.

During his life Lennon had demystified rock 'n' roll,

which he believed was conceptually the best form of communication through music. As an artist, he had been vulnerable, idealistic, and a worrier, lapsing into a frequent insecure dissection of who-wrote-what in the Lennon-McCartney songs. He was never totally able to stand back sufficiently from his own songs and accept their social impact. What he did, inside the Beatles, long after they split, and even when he was dead, was to inject his unique personal experiences into popular music.

Often described as the best-ever pop single, 'Strawberry Fields Forever', released in 1967, marked the start of the vital change in John's music. It was attributable to several factors: his meeting with Yoko at the end of 1966; his disillusionment with the Beatles myth; his use of drugs; and the important influence of Bob Dylan who led the way in putting *himself* into his songs.

Strawberry Field was a real place, a Salvation Army home just down the road from Aunt Mimi's in Woolton. It was a special place where she sometimes took him for ice-cream cornets and garden fêtes. John enjoyed his childhood memories: 'Nothing is real/And nothing to get hungabout. . . .' It was Lennon in wonderland, re-creating the era of childhood simplicity when he knew he was happy.

Musically it invoked the very spirit of psychedelia raging that year. To get the required dreamy effect of trees, fields, and escapism, Lennon and producer George Martin spliced together two quite different versions of the song. It was a superb piece of technical editing by Martin and conjured up perfectly the ethereal feeling of the lyrics. From 'Strawberry Fields' onwards it was a one-way ticket for John: his music would be more incisive, more personal, more reflective, and more adventurous.

John's public persona became more intimidating from 1967. His droopy moustache gave him a sombre, almost

sinister look, and sometimes, when he was under the influence of drugs, he wore a manic leer. With his hair cut
short, his confidence was now apparent: so much so that he
now wore his glasses in public.

The genius of John's writing was first captured on *Sgt
Pepper's Lonely Hearts Club Band* with the songs 'A Day In
The Life' and 'Lucy In The Sky With Diamonds'. *Sgt Pepper*
marked rock music's coming of age, its scope and intention
resulting in critical respectability. John's input on it showed
that rock 'n' roll had come a long way since Elvis Presley's
first recording sessions thirteen years before. It was prime
'pop art', seminal psychedelia. It also marked the apogee of
studio technology at the time: four-track machines, Mello-
trons, and forty-one-piece orchestras. Six months in the
making, the cost was enormous – £25,000. Just to have
the album was to be part of a special world, with the jokes
on the run-out grooves, the note for the family dog, the
badges and cut-outs, the coloured inner sleeve, the pretty
pictures, and lyrics printed for the first time on a rock
album.

The original idea behind the album was that it should
be a concept LP: a memory of a day in the life of Liverpool
children (which was to have included both 'Penny Lane'
and 'Strawberry Fields'). A double album, evoking lost
innocence, adolescence, and maturity. But *Sgt Pepper* grew
and grew, and the original plan disappeared (although ves-
tiges were retained with 'A Day In The Life' and 'When
I'm Sixty-Four'). In its place came an album that broke
new ground with the segueing of tracks, the lyrical obtuseness, the rich production, and lavish instrumentation.

The material on the album was culled from various
sources: 'When I'm Sixty-Four' even went back to Liverpool
in the late 1950s. Lennon collaborated with McCartney on
this song, adding the memorable names 'Vera, Chuck and

Dave'. He also threw in the caustic: 'What do you see when you turn out the light/I can't tell you but I know it's mine,' to Paul's 'With A Little Help From My Friends'.

In 'Lucy In The Sky With Diamonds' Lennon immersed himself in the fantasy world of Lewis Carroll. It is a vivid, colourful world. Just 'Climb in the back with your head in the clouds/And you're gone!' The girl 'with kaleidoscope eyes' represents some sort of salvation, but it is transitory and you're back, forever caught in that marshmallow world of dreams and fantasy. Paul helped with the lyrics and music.

'Getting Better' was John continuing to obviate his guilt about the women in his life, coming to terms with it directly, following on from the oblique inferences in 'Norwegian Wood'. Although 'Getting Better' is generally considered a McCartney song, and Paul certainly had the germ of the idea in the studio, John contributed some crucial, highly personal words. It was a classic example of how they helped each other in their writing.

> *I used to be cruel to my woman*
> *I beat her and kept her apart from the things she loved*
> *Man I was mean but I'm changing my scene*
> *And I'm doing the best that I can*

It was an indication of how he had mellowed; the guilt was apparent and made public. 'I was a hitter,' John explained later. 'I couldn't express myself and I hit. I fought men and I hit women. That is why I am always on about peace. It is the most violent people who go for love and peace. I am a violent man who has learned not to be violent and regret his violence. I will have to be a lot older before I can face in public how I treated women as a youngster,' he told David Sheff in *Playboy* magazine in 1980.

'Being For The Benefit Of Mr Kite!' was taken straight
from an antique circus poster, which John transposed – in
conjunction with George Martin's imaginative tape loops
and cut-ups – into a beguiling cameo. 'Good Morning
Good Morning' was a throwaway, inspired by a Kellogg's
cornflakes television advertisement, which was on in the
background while Lennon was in a vaguely 'writing' mood.
John's songs for *Sgt Pepper*, while technically superior to
anything he had yet attempted, were pillaged from the
usual random sources: circus posters, advertisements, and
newspaper cuttings.

The album's supreme achievement is still the massive
'A Day In The Life'. Again Lennon culled the song from
disparate sources – newspaper headlines, his filming of *How
I Won The War* in Spain in 1966, and snatches of conversation. Paul's middle eight slotted neatly into the scenario.
After hearing the words 'went upstairs and had a smoke',
the BBC screamed 'drugs' and promptly banned the song.
Lennon's jaundiced vocal is perfectly suited to the distanced
picture of a man seated, 'read[ing] the news today,' and
from that preface the song unfolds. The seemingly random
flow ends with the enigmatic line which was inspired by a
news item John read in London's *Daily Mail*: 'Now they
know how many holes it takes to fill the Albert Hall.' 'A
Day In The Life' marked the pinnacle of the Beatles'
recorded output. It tested George Martin's abilities to the
breaking-point, in his having to encourage a classical
orchestra to 'freak out', and to come up with an arrangement
that sounded like 'the end of the world', sustaining the
final note for forty-two seconds.

George Martin translated the impossible into sensational reality. The cumulative effect of the album was
devastating. After playing it for the first time, there was no
choice but go right back to the beginning again, rather

than — as had been the way with previous Beatle records —
searching out individual tracks. The depth and variety of
the album led to acts as diverse as Joe Brown and Joe
Cocker covering songs from it.

At the time the scope and flair of *Sgt Pepper* ensured
that it stood alone, the very zenith of rock 'n' roll. It
ushered in the prime era of English psychedelia.

The scope and triumph of the album gave John even
greater impetus. Barely had the dust settled than the Beatles
were back within a month with a new single. John's composition 'All You Need Is Love' was premièred on the global
Our World TV show. (It was a mark of the Beatles' position
by then that they were chosen as Britain's representatives
for this prestigious satellite link-up.) Four hundred million
people saw the group première the anthem of the Love
Generation; it took the Beatles to set the seal of
acceptability on the hippy movement — although in truth
it had already begun to burn itself out in Haight Ashbury,
San Francisco, by the time the single was released. Hearing
it now is like activating a museum piece, but then, all
those years ago, there were enough people who believed
that all you needed *was* love and that entry into Shangri-la
was gained simply by wearing flowers in your hair.

On the finished single, just as it is fading, Lennon can
be heard singing a cheerfully distorted 'She Loves You', as
though publicly burying the Beatles legacy. The single's B-
side was 'Baby, You're A Rich Man', a question-and-answer
song, which Lennon originally viciously 'dedicated' to Brian
Epstein as 'Baby, You're A Rich Fag Jew'. 'How does it feel
to be one of the beautiful people?' asked Lennon, a question
millions asked of him. Like many other songs of the period,
it was a combination of two quite different songs: McCartney had the title and some odd lines in his head while
Lennon supplied the questions.

And there was still more to come. 'Hello, Goodbye' was the final Beatles single of 1967. It was Paul's all the way through, another question-and-answer song, which perfectly captured the querulous atmosphere of the time. The B-side was 'I Am The Walrus', a Lennon *tour de force*, a psychedelic maelstrom. Here was John tripping into wonderland again, with the lyrics inspired by Lewis Carroll's poem 'The Walrus and the Carpenter' from *Alice in Wonderland*: 'To me, it was a beautiful poem. It never occurred to me that Lewis Carroll was commenting on the capitalist and social system. I never went into that bit about what it really meant, like people are doing with Beatles work. Later I went back and looked at it and realized that the walrus was the bad guy in the story and the carpenter was the good guy. I thought, Oh shit, I picked the wrong guy!'

The riff came about when John was going through one of his 'Nowhere Man' periods, and was actually 'Sitting in an English garden waiting for the sun.' He heard a police siren in the distance, and the first three lines of the song flashed through his head. The lyrical obscurity left the song wide open to interpretation, and to the end even Lennon admitted that *he* never really knew what the song was actually *about*. Much of it was obviously devious Lennon word-play. He was absorbing acid like milk, which must be where lines like 'Semolina pilchards climbing up the Eiffel Tower' come from. 'I am he as you are he as you are me and we are all together' was very much the feeling of the period. The song was also Lennon's sole contribution to the *Magical Mystery Tour* film, which the BBC premièred on Boxing Day 1967 (he also had a co-writing credit on the throwaway instrumental 'Flying'). *Magical Mystery Tour* was a scrappy project, conceived in the wake of Brian Epstein's death. But there were occasional highlights, including the surreal walrus sequence, with eggmen and walruses floating dreamily past the camera.

The Beatles' psychedelia persisted. At one time the group's extraordinary and still unreleased 'What's The New Maryjane' was scheduled by John as an official Plastic Ono Band single. 'Maryjane' is a euphemism for marijuana, and the song features Lennon dreamily intoning such lyrics as: 'She likes to be married to Yeti/Be grooving such cooky spaghetti!'

The Beatles' first single of 1968, 'Lady Madonna', was another solo McCartney effort, which saw the group return to their rock 'n' roll roots, a decisive move away from the lyrical and musical complexities of *Sgt Pepper*. In August they inaugurated the Apple label, which was launched with the marathon 'Hey Jude' single, another solo McCartney work. The B-side, though, was pure Lennon: 'Revolution' was his explicit comment on the student riots which had split Europe and America in the summer of 1968. In France radical students came close to overthrowing the government, and in America there were massive protests at the country's growing involvement in Southeast Asia.

With Bob Dylan in seclusion, the demonstrators looked to the Beatles and the Rolling Stones for guidance and leadership. The Stones offered the swaggering *Beggar's Banquet* album which included the call-to-the-barricades rock of 'Street Fighting Man'. John was much more cautious, and when the Beatles' 'message' came through him it was almost pessimistic. 'Revolution' acknowledged that 'we all want to change the world' but sagely counselled: 'But when you talk about destruction/Don't you know that you can count me out?' For the first time the Beatles sounded like another generation advising their young: 'You say you got a real solution/Well, you know, we'd all love to see the plan.' John sat firmly on the fence. He recorded two versions of the song, one in which he asked to be included 'in', and another in which he asks to be left out. It was to be a further three years before he would advocate 'Power To The People'. The radical element in him would take some years to develop, but, typically, when it did Lennon opted for it whole-heartedly. In 1968 'Revolution' still showed the Beatles adhering to 'flower-power' values, 'love is all you need'. There was never any justification for violence, said John in his music. The ends could not justify the means.

Yoko's growing influence on John began to manifest itself in his music. The first real evidence of this came in November 1968 with the release of the controversial *Two Virgins* album. It was the third album issued on Apple (George Harrison's *Wonderwall* can claim the distinction of being the first Beatle solo album). *Two Virgins* was recorded at Weybridge, utilizing tape loops and splices. Most Beatles fans found it completely unacceptable, consisting as it did of random electronic gurglings and burps.

The Beatles' first real musical punch of the year, in addition to the 'Hey Jude' single, came with *The Beatles* (or 'White Album'), their first double album, released exactly five years after *With The Beatles* on 22 November 1968. Here was the first real proof that the Fab Four weren't the happy beat quartet of fond memory, and there was a clear distinction between Lennon and McCartney songs. It took them away from the production complexities of *Sgt Pepper*, and even allowed for the inclusion of outside musicians (Eric Clapton, Nicky Hopkins, Dave Mason, and, of course, Yoko Ono). It was, again, very much an album of its period. 'Jamming' was a recent development in rock; Jimi Hendrix's *Electric Ladyland* of the same year included star guests; and 'supergroups' were developing as musicians broke away from the strictures that they felt record companies imposed on them.

Even the more orthodox rock 'n' roll of the 'White Album' showed Yoko's influence. John's prolificness is reflected in his total of thirteen songs on the album. The only real concession to the avant-garde was 'Revolution 9'; Lennon's other songs reflect his love for good, old-fashioned rock 'n' roll. Even from a visual angle the album is a reflection of the Beatles' desire to shake off their past – the plain white cover is a deliberate reaction against the colourful layers of *Sgt Pepper*.

The variety of Lennon's styles on the finished album is encouraging, from the beguiling 'Dear Prudence' to the nursery-rhyme charms of 'Cry Baby Cry'. Lennon's writing focused almost exclusively on Yoko: even 'Julia', his heartfelt tribute to his mother, was as much about Yoko. He told *Playboy*: 'She inspired *all* this creation in me. It wasn't that she inspired the songs, she inspired *me!*' The fans were not alone in thinking that Yoko was the one person responsible for John's barely veiled hostility towards the group. Paul, George, and Ringo saw her influence on John and their music as pernicious. Yoko herself commented in 1980: 'I went to bed with this guy I liked and suddenly the next morning I see these three in-laws standing there!'

Of the songs on the 'White Album', 'Dear Prudence' was conceived during meditation in India and was written to coax Mia Farrow's sister Prudence out into the sun. 'Glass Onion' was a song designed to bemuse Beatle freaks ('The Walrus was Paul' was Lennon's concession to McCartney in the light of his obsession with his new partner). Lennon later described the song as 'just a throwaway', but his reference to former glories – 'Strawberry Fields', 'Lady Madonna', 'The Fool On The Hill' – gave fans a field day in exercising their own interpretations.

The most tragic case of misinterpretation of Beatle lyrics came when Charles Manson convinced himself that on the 'White Album' the Beatles were exhorting him and his 'family' to rise and destroy. It was, according to Manson's warped mind, the Beatles giving him the go-ahead for a bloody revolution. He tragically misinterpreted Paul's 'Helter Skelter' as a prelude to Armageddon, unaware that it was simply an English expression for a fairground slide. Manson also convinced himself that Harrison's 'Piggies' was a licence to kill pigs and that somewhere in the electronic mayhem of John's 'Revolution 9' there was a call to arms; this subsequently resulted in his bloody murder of Sharon Tate in California.

'The Continuing Story Of Bungalow Bill' was 'a sort of teenage social comment song' and marked the first orthodox Lennon-Ono collaboration. (She can be clearly heard singing the line 'Not when he looked so fierce.') It is populated by characters from comic books. 'So Captain Marvel zapped in right between the eyes' is straight from the territory of Stan 'The Man' Lee. It is a fragmentary, haunting song with echoes of Lennon's 'On Safairy With Whide Hunter' from his first book.

'Happiness Is A Warm Gun' was inspired by a caption in an American magazine, which George Martin showed John in the studio. The cruel irony of the phrase inspired the song and provided its title. The acid fragments are still there in sections such as 'Like a lizard on a window pane . . . the man in the crowd with the multicoloured mirrors on his hobnail boots.' But a line like 'A soap impression of his wife which he ate and donated to the National Trust' is pure Spike Milligan, whose Goonish word-play John loved so much.

'I'm So Tired' is both Lennon's greatest song on the album and one of his finest ever. Recorded very late one night at Abbey Road, it perfectly captures that weary resignation, that three o'clock in the morning feeling, with the bizarre couplet: 'Although I'm so tired, I'll have another cigarette/And curse Sir Walter Raleigh, he was such a stupid get!' Still at the centre of the song is that plea for calm, 'a little peace of mind', which was John's cry for help – except that now there was someone to answer that cry.

'Julia' is a haunting, wistful fragment, for the mother Lennon never had enough time to know and for the companion he so desperately needed. The song managed to reconcile past and present and found Lennon recognizing his own frailty in the first line: 'Half of what I say is meaningless.' The impression of all the songs on the album is that they are fragments which developed into finished songs at the last moment. One feels Lennon pouring his heart out, for the past, the present, the future. The songs are scraps of paper, riddled with ambiguity and tragedy, dry and lacerating humour, sometimes touching and affecting, sometimes throwaway and disposable.

'Yer Blues' was a tongue-in-cheek dig at the British blues boom of the late 1960s, which boasted groups like Fleetwood Mac, Ten Years After, and Chicken Shack. It is nonetheless still a bleak and bitter song, which took shape in India – 'trying to reach God and feeling suicidal.' 'Yer Blues' conjures up an iconoclastic, nihilistic world: 'Blue mist around my soul/feel so suicidal/even hate my rock 'n' roll.'

'Everybody's Got Something To Hide Except Me And My Monkey' prefaces later songs like 'I Want You' and 'Come Together', repetitive lyrics written in gratitude to Yoko. 'Your inside is out when your outside is in,' Lennon sang. And who knew it better than he?

'Sexy Sadie' was directed at the Maharishi, who 'made a fool of everyone,' promising the Beatles peace on earth and spiritual enlightenment but ending up as someone they distrusted. Lennon admitted that he 'copped out' by not naming the Maharishi in the song, but everyone knew who the bitter put-down was aimed at. The whimsy of 'Cry Baby Cry' took Lennon back to Alice's magic garden: for the King and Queen of Hearts read 'The King of Marigold' and 'The Duchess of Kirkcaldy'. The song is cruel and spiteful – 'Make your mother cry, she's old enough to know better' – as only children can be.

Following the cacophony of 'Revolution 9' comes the syrupy 'Good Night'. It is hard to believe that Lennon was responsible for two such different songs. 'Good Night' was written for Julian Lennon and given to Ringo to croon. It was a George Martin *tour de force*, Busby Berkeley colliding head on with a radio favourite of John's childhood, Uncle Mac: 'Good night, children . . . everywhere.' As Lennon later laconically admitted: 'It was possibly overlush!'

The *Yellow Submarine* soundtrack surfaced in January 1969. The film was a contractual obligation for the group and United Artists. For the finished animated film only four new songs were required, which duly appeared on the album (an example of the Beatles giving less than full value for money). It bore all the hallmarks of having been hastily finished, with John's 'Hey Bulldog' and George Harrison's 'Only A Northern Song' knocked off as fillers. 'Hey Bulldog' was an unusually bitter Lennon song of the period – 'What makes you think you're something special when you smile? . . . You think you know me, but you haven't got a clue!'

At the beginning of 1969 the Beatles were beginning to crumble. The making of the film *Let It Be*, which began in January, was, in the main, not a happy affair, and tensions soon re-surfaced. On 2 March John and Yoko appeared at an avant-garde jazz concert in Cambridge (part of their set would appear on the *Life With The Lions* album a few months later). Significantly, it marked the first time a Beatle had ever appeared solo on stage. 'Get Back' was the first Beatles single of 1969, a McCartney rocker. The other side was Lennon pouring his heart out to Yoko in 'Don't Let Me Down', a strong and persuasive riff with a stirring Lennon vocal.

As the *Let It Be* project sprawled on into an indefinite future and moved further and further away from its intended naturalism, the Beatles began recording what ended up as the *Abbey Road* album. John, meanwhile, launched his Plastic Ono Band project. Plastic Ono was never intended as a full-time group. The nucleus was always to be John and Yoko, and it involved whoever happened to be around. In the case of Lennon's anthem 'Give Peace A Chance' it was a cast of hundreds! While the flippancy of the verses recalled Lennon's *In His Own Write* and his love of word-association, the message of the chorus was imperative and sincere.

The Lennons' paranoia about the public's scorn was apparent on the next 'Beatles' single, 'The Ballad of John and Yoko' (only Paul and John actually appear on it). It was markedly autobiographical, a narrative account of John and Yoko's recent activities: 'Christ you know it ain't easy, you know how hard it can be/The way things are going, they're gonna crucify me.' Set to an infectious, shuffling, old-time rock 'n' roll rhythm, it was naïvely effective.

Plastic Ono gave Lennon the opportunity to escape from the Beatles' mantle; the band's product could be recorded and released as quickly as possible and need not have the same care and attention lavished on it that the world had come to expect from the Beatles. It was a safety valve and one of which Lennon grew increasingly fond. Lennon talked about its inception to BBC Radio's Andy Peebles: 'Plastic

Ono Band was a concept of Yoko's, which is an imaginary band. The first advert was a photograph . . . of some pieces of plastic with a tape recorder and a TV in it. . . . And her idea was a completely robot pop group . . . There was supposed to be a party for the release of the "Give Peace A Chance" record but we'd had a car crash or something so we couldn't come; so at the dance hall where they had the party for the Plastic Ono Band, all the press came to meet the band, and the band was onstage, which was just a machine with a camera pointing at them, showing them onstage themselves. So the Plastic Ono Band is a conceptual band that never was. There never had been any members of it, and the advert said "You are the Plastic Ono Band". So I just want to clear that, it wasn't the re-forming of a new band like Wings or a Hollies, or whatever, where you have a name and you belong to it. There's never been anybody in that band. There are no members.'

The album *Live Peace In Toronto 1969*, which resulted from Plastic Ono's appearance at the rock 'n' roll festival in September, is something of a potted history of John Lennon's life at the end of the 1960s. Songs drawn from the early Hamburg days ('Blue Suede Shoes' and 'Money') nestled next to current Beatles hits like 'Yer Blues', which was included as Lennon had enjoyed performing it on the never completed TV show *Rolling Stones' Rock and Roll Circus*. Lennon's dependence on drugs ('Cold Turkey') jostled with his desire for peace ('Give Peace A Chance'). The other side of the album comprised potent songs by Yoko with 'Don't Worry Kyoko' and 'John John (Let's Hope For Peace)'.

Meanwhile the Beatles limped on. Chronologically the set that ended up as *Abbey Road* was recorded *after* their final album, *Let It Be*, but because of the concomitant problems surrounding that album, *Abbey Road* was released first in September 1969. There was no need for a title or a name on the album cover, despite the fact that the four figures diligently trooping over the zebra crossing were virtually unrecognizable as the quartet the world knew as the Beatles. Side one of *Abbey Road* consisted of separate songs – almost like the old days. Lennon's syncopated 'Come Together', which opened the album, was based around a line from Chuck Berry's 'You Can't Catch Me'. Lennon cited it as one of his favourite Beatle tracks, describing it as 'funky . . . bluesy'. The competition was strong on that album. George Harrison's two best-remembered Beatle songs were there ('Something' and 'Here Comes The Sun') as well as a clutch of McCartney classics. 'I Want You (She's So Heavy)' could well be John's definitive song of the period. Lennon pours out remorseless lyrics, pleading with Yoko: 'I want you so bad/It's driving me mad.' 'Because' came about from some Beethoven chords Yoko was playing on the piano, which were re-shaped by John, who then added some touchingly devoted lyrics: 'Love is old, love is new/Love is all, love is you.'

The second side of the album was made up of fragments from India and from Weybridge. Songs that were started, alone and together, but never finished. Somehow they produce a seamless suite. After 'Because', Lennon's contributions were characters who flickered across his imagination, 'Mean Mr Mustard', 'Polythene Pam', and 'Sun King' sung in cod Spanish. All were rooted in reality but distorted by drugs and his tendency to leave projects incomplete. Following on the heels of the 'White Album', *Abbey Road* displayed the Beatles as four individuals, who were nonetheless somehow bound together by some strange, tenacious loyalty.

Before the end of 1969 Lennon released the second Plastic Ono Band single, the harrowing 'Cold Turkey', which came out at the end of October just before the Beatles' 'new' single, 'Something'. The single was pulled off *Abbey Road* at the insistence of Allen Klein to bring in some immediate cash. It was the first time a Beatles single had been released *solely* to make money.

'Cold Turkey' seemed only to emphasize the disparate musical directions in which the Beatles were going. It was raw and powerful with the terse message 'Play Loud' printed on the label. It was strong rock 'n' roll, with thunderous drumming from Alan White, and the lyrics drew on Lennon's harrowing experiences with heroin, graphically depicting the pain and suffering of addiction and withdrawal symptoms. It performed comparatively weakly in the world charts, possibly because the subject was too spine-chilling for public taste. 'When I wrote it, I went to the other three Beatles and said, "Hey kids I think I've just written a new single!" But they all said, "Umm . . . aeee . . . well", because it was going to be my project and so I thought, bugger it, I'll put it out myself!'

Let It Be had by this time, in contrast to the free-and-easy Plastic Ono releases, developed into a monster with three separate producers – George Martin, Glyn Johns, and Phil Spector – all trying to salvage something from the sessions at Twickenham and Apple studios.

By November 1969 the Lennons issued *The Wedding Album*, a verbal collage of their lives together during the year. Along with *Two Virgins* and *Life With The Lions*, it stands on the shelf of those collectors determined to possess everything of the Beatles.

At the beginning of a new decade the Beatles were still together as a group, but the ties that bound them were thin and close to snapping. The last rites had to be administered, and the *Let It Be* album and film effectively did just that. Before the album's release a profusion of Beatle solo projects helped to fuel rumours of the eventual split – Ringo's *Sentimental Journey* and Paul's *McCartney* albums were released. John chipped in with another Plastic Ono single, the breezy 'Instant Karma!'. It was produced by Phil Spector because Lennon was one of the few people involved with *Let It Be* who felt that Spector had earned his salary for his work on the finished album. 'Instant Karma!' was written and recorded in one day, emphasizing Lennon's belief that records (particularly singles) should have the immediacy of newspapers. Lyrically, it marked Lennon's 'We all shine on' mood and his belief that togetherness and love could still save the world. 'It just came to me. Everybody was going on about karma, especially in the sixties. But it occurred to me that karma is instant as well as it influences your past life or your future life. . . . Also, I'm fascinated by commercials and promotions as an art form. I enjoy them. So the idea of instant karma was like the idea of instant coffee, presenting something in a new form.'

Prior to the release of the *Let It Be* album, the eponymous single was released in March 1970. It was a Paul McCartney epic, although he publicly voiced his dissatisfaction with Spector's doctoring of the finished tapes. The B-side was a rarity – 'You Know My Name (Look Up The Number)'. A throwaway number, written and recorded by Lennon in 1967, it features McCartney, the Beatles' road manager, Mal Evans, and saxophonist Brian Jones – the late member of the Rolling Stones, who was friendly with the Beatles. It is an enchanting, sleazy cabaret number, set in a mythical night-club – 'Slaggers' – with Lennon acting as MC and showman and McCartney crooning in his best put-on Vic Damone style.

The *Let It Be* album was finally released in May 1970. What had originally been intended as spontaneous proof of the Beatles' very existence and vitality comes across as a doctored valediction. 'It was hell,' recalled Lennon bitterly. 'Even the biggest Beatles fan couldn't have sat through those six weeks of misery.' The whole saga surrounding the 'finished' album was a sad reflection of how disillusioned the Beatles had become about their recording, their future, themselves, and, tragically, their music. The original intention was to show the group 'warts and all', deliberately stripping away all the lavish production of their albums of the previous four years, to capture their spontaneity in the studio. The world was to eavesdrop on the Beatles in rehearsal and see them shape their songs for their next album. Over thirty hours of music are on tape somewhere; much has surfaced on sporadic bootlegs. You can listen to the undoctored versions of 'The Long And Winding Road', 'Let It Be', 'Across The Universe', the full version of 'Dig It', and great original material like the rockabilly 'Suzy Parker'. You can also hear the Beatles work out on songs of their youth, Hank Williams's 'You Win Again', Cliff Richard's 'Move It', Elvis's 'Good Rockin' Tonight', Chuck Berry's 'Memphis, Tennessee', Lennon's ripe parody of 'House Of The Rising Sun', and workouts on Dylan's 'Blowin' In The Wind', and 'All Along The Watchtower'. Ironically, John Lennon began collecting Beatles bootleg albums in 1974 when he could begin to enjoy re-living his past.

By the end of the film and recording sessions of January 1969 neither the Beatles nor George Martin could face wading through the miles of tapes. Given the original 'natural' idea of the project, Phil Spector was called in to edit and polish up the material and give the world the Beatles album it expected. Spector was a legend. He had virtually invented the idea of the record producer with his mini teen epics of the mid-1960s: 'Then He Kissed Me', 'River Deep, Mountain High', and 'You've Lost That Lovin'

Feeling'. All were conceived and executed on a Wagnerian scale with Spector inventing the 'wall of sound', utilizing multi-tracking, massed instrumentation, and laborious overdubbing. He was a genius, but like all geniuses, he could be difficult and unpredictable. Lennon recalled the *Let It Be* debacle: 'It just was a dreadful, dreadful feeling . . . We were going to let it out in really shitty condition. I didn't care. I had thought it would be good to let the shitty version out because it would break the Beatles myth. It would just be us, with no trousers on and no glossy paint over the cover, and no hype. "This is what we are like with our trousers off – would you please end the game now?" '

But the old magic did surface, even during those acrimonious final days. The album's opening track, 'Two Of Us', was a McCartney song for Linda, but (in context) it becomes a moving requiem to two Liverpool kids, burning with ambition and talent: 'Two of us sending postcards, writing letters on my wall/You and me burning matches, lifting latches, on our way back home.' It is a memory of Liverpool as it was, when the world was open and bright for conquest, not shrouded in the acid connotations of 'Strawberry Fields'. At the dismal end, 'Two Of Us' serves as a moving reminder of that bright beginning.

'Dig A Pony' celebrated Lennon's omniscience – 'You can celebrate anything you want . . . You can penetrate any place you go . . . You can radiate everything you are.' But as the refrain runs, 'I told you so, all I want is you.' That was definitely meant for Yoko. 'Across The Universe' was a song that infuriated Lennon at the time. He woke up one morning with the line 'Pools of sorrow, waves of joy' running through his head and proceeded to construct the song from it. The version on the album was 'subconscious sabotage' on his part, in the name of experimentation. One version ended up on a World Wildlife Fund charity album with two Beatles fans singing the 'Nothing's gonna change my world' chorus. 'The original track was a real piece of shit,' he recalled with some bitterness, 'I was singing out of tune and instead of getting a decent choir, we got fans from outside . . . Apple Scruffs or whatever you call them. They came in and were singing all off-key. Nobody was interested in doing the tune originally . . . Phil slowed the tape down, added the strings . . . He did a really special job.' The 'Jai Guru Deva OM' refrain harkens back to the days of gurus and avatars who could save the world. The song caught Lennon at a time when all his creativity and sexuality were being devoted to Yoko but when: 'Words are flowing out like endless rain into a paper cup . . . Thoughts meander like a restless wind.' Restless, the artist in him was beset by relentless images and a burning desire to create, while he wilfully stripped everything down for Yoko. 'Nothing's gonna change my world,' he sang. But it had.

'Dig It' was an example of the 'new-phase Beatles album' which the *Let It Be* album sleeve boasted. Distilled from a five-minute stream of consciousness rap, the existing forty-eight-second track finds Lennon invoking Manchester United boss Matt Busby, Doris Day, and a series of acronyms, ending with the emphatic 'Whatever it is, whoever you are – just dig it!' Lennon's sardonic comments pepper the finished album – opening the album with 'I dig a pygmy by Charles Hawtrey,' prefacing the beautiful 'Let It Be' with the iconoclastic 'Now we'd like to do 'ark the Angels come,' digging up the traditional 'Maggie Mae', disembowelling 'Danny Boy', and pre-empting 'Get Back' with an improvised chorus of 'Sweet Loretta Fart/Thought she was a cleaner, but she was a frying pan.' It is only the tip of the iceberg, though, and unfortunately it is the poor-quality bootlegs which give a greater indication of the album's original concept.

'I've Got A Feeling' was a Lennon-McCartney collaboration of sorts. The first half of the song is all Paul, while the 'Everybody had a hard year' section onwards is John. 'One After 909' was a genuine collaboration, written in 1959 in those dim and distant Liverpool days and disinterred for their last album together. Here was a joyous slice of Eddie Cochran-style rock, written by two teenagers with no real idea of that so-distant America, culled instead from images of contemporary rock 'n' roll songs, with John and Paul singing enthusiastically together on the chorus. Sharply evocative of those earlier, sunnier, and simpler days, it seems now a glorious finale to the partnership of Lennon and McCartney; as the years passed and the acrimony between the two men subsided, their preferred memory was, indeed, of 'sagging off school' as Liverpool boys and writing songs in the back of the Beatles' van.

All of John Lennon's subsequent musical activities would, inevitably, be measured alongside his achievement in creating the Beatles. They were the single most influential pop group ever. Their sounds and personalities had irrevocably altered not only the music but the social fabric of the Western world. They were synonymous with youth culture and pop art. At the onset of a new decade, Lennon – perhaps more than anyone – was aware of his responsibilities and of the legacy he was condemned to carry.

The public had been warned of the 'new' Lennon by 'Cold Turkey'. Released in October 1969, it was John's harrowing confession of withdrawal from heroin. As the third single from the Plastic Ono Band, it went into the charts both in Britain and America, although not high enough to please John, who cited its poor performance in his letter to the Queen when returning his MBE.

To Beatles fans, the record was astonishing, even from John. Yet it was perhaps his most honest moment in making his music a catalogue of his life. He sang:

> *Temperature's rising, fever is high*
> *Can't see no future, can't see no sky*
> *My feet are so heavy, so is my head*
> *I wish I was a baby, I wish I was dead.*

The urgency of his voice, the nature of the record as a clear reference to his drug habits, the strength of Eric Clapton's guitar work on it, and the dramatic departure from anything previously heard from John and the Beatles mark it as a milestone in his life. 'Cold Turkey', uncomfortable at the time, now defines precisely the open heart of Lennon.

The Plastic Ono Band helped John to expunge the Beatles myth, and the catharsis engendered by Janov's primal therapy manifested itself on the *John Lennon/Plastic Ono Band* album, which reached the shops a fortnight before Christmas 1970. It still stands as one of the bleakest, most compellingly honest albums ever released by a major rock artist. On it Lennon exorcized his past and offered precious little hope for his future. Its bleakness took root in his childhood, particularly on 'Mother' and 'My Mummy's Dead', a plaintive cry from a spiritual orphan. 'Mother' was harrowing; Lennon's hair-raising vocal, the sparse instrumentation, and chilling lyrics were a public mourning of his dead mother and castigation of his absent father. There was no cosiness, no imagery, nothing to hide behind here. 'Working Class Hero' was bitterly dismissive of the system that bred Lennon, that 'gave you no time instead of it all.' It is a twentieth-century folk song, for Everyman; a withering, scornful attack on a society that 'Keeps you doped with religion and sex and TV/But you're still fucking peasants as far as I can see.'

For many, the album's most despairing track is 'God', Lennon's litany of rejection of his past which concludes with the withering 'I don't believe in Beatles.' The dream was finally over. As he commented: ' "God" was put together from three songs. I had the idea that God is the concept by which we measure pain, so that when you have a word like that, you just sit down and sing the first tune that comes into your head . . . I don't know when I realized that I was putting down all these things I didn't believe in. So I could have gone on, it was like a Christmas card list: where do I end: Churchill? Hoover? I thought I had to stop. I was going to leave a gap and just fill in your own words; whoever you don't believe in. It had just got out of hand. And Beatles was the final thing because I no longer believe in myth and Beatles is another myth.'

Lennon's writing was as sparse as the instrumentation. The album, in fact, must be the sparsest Phil Spector has ever given his name to. Lennon admitted later: 'I started from "Mother" onwards, trying to shave off all imagery, pretensions of poetry, illusions of grandeur, what I call à la Dylan, Dylanesque . . . As they say, Northern people are blunt, right, so I was trying to write like I am.'

That very bluntness shook many people on what amounted to Lennon's first solo album. There were no walruses or glass onions, no more masks to hide behind – here was the soul of John Ono Lennon. That 'Northern bluntness' was apparent on 'Working Class Hero', with its two 'fucks' that EMI cut out on the inner sleeve. (The censorship was applied only in Britain; Capitol, which released the album in America, printed the words.) By then Lennon didn't care. He'd been performing to order for too long. If the public wanted John Lennon, they would have to take him on his own terms. He wasn't John Beatle any more.

There *were* moments of softness on the album: the beautiful ballad 'Love' which spoke of 'needing to be loved'; 'Hold On' was Yoko's plea: 'Hold on John, it's gonna be alright.' But the overwhelming feeling of the album is one of sadness, sadness for a past he never had, for the mother he missed, for the growing up in public. For all the fake gurus. For Yoko. For himself. It was from the heart.

Lennon's deliberate denunciation of his past was a brutal beginning to a new decade. With the Beatles gone, there seemed nothing to replace them musically or as a full-time occupation. Coupled with the long, confessional interview he did with *Rolling Stone* editor Jann Wenner in 1970, *Plastic Ono Band* renounced the past with all the accumulated bitterness and rancour of John's thirty years.

By early 1971 John and Yoko had thrown their hats firmly into the political arena. 'Power To The People' was a slogan echoing round the world at the time. The civil disturbances in Northern Ireland were erupting into civil war. The Nixon administration had taken the gloves off when they murdered four students at Kent State University during a demonstration in 1970. The Lennons became more and more active in radical politics. They donated money to Michael X's Black House, recorded a single, 'Do The Oz', for the defendants in the infamous 'Schoolkids Oz' trial, and Lennon gave an interview to Tariq Ali's left-wing paper, *Red Mole*: 'I think we must make the workers aware of the really unhappy position they are in, break the dream they are surrounded by. They think they are in a wonderful, free-speaking country, they've all got cars and tellies and they don't want to think there's anything more to life. They are prepared to let the bosses run them, to see their children fucked up in school. They're dreaming someone else's dream, it's not even their own.' Lennon was expanding the resentment that had fuelled 'Working Class Hero'. Many found Lennon's avowed socialism at odds with his personal wealth, but John was quick to counter his critics and always managed to equate it with his rapidly changing beliefs.

'Power To The People' was the most obvious musical indication of the Lennons' growing political involvement, even if it was only a type of catchy sloganeering which was to manifest itself more fully on the album *Some Time In New York City*. It recalled an earlier Lennon statement – 'Revolution' – but this time he committed himself: 'Say we want a revolution/We better get it on right away/Well you get on your feet/And out on the street.' Now he was advocating direct involvement and action. His fence-sitting days were over.

He could not have produced a greater contrast with his next album, and in no way did he see it as ironic that he was following his most politically motivated single with his lushest and most romantic album to date.

Imagine was released in October 1971 and is probably the album most associated with John Lennon, with the haunting title track, the poignant 'Oh My Love', the vitri-olic 'How Do You Sleep?', and the resonant 'Jealous Guy'. *Imagine* revealed a mellower Lennon. Although the basic themes of pain and suffering were still there, its lavish instrumentation was light years away from the primal stark-ness of *Plastic Ono Band*. Virtually all the songs speak of his devotion to Yoko. Only 'I Don't Want To Be A Soldier' and the resounding 'Give Me Some Truth' strayed from the theme . . . as of course did 'How Do You Sleep?', his attack on Paul McCartney. In case any listener missed the object of his scorn, a postcard was included with *Imagine* that showed Lennon in a delicious parody of McCartney's *Ram* album cover. 'Those freaks was right when they said you was dead' sang Lennon in a vicious put-down. He was referring to bizarre rumours, particularly in America, that McCartney was, in fact, dead.

Imagine was classic Lennon. The album's title track was a beautifully melodic song which he had written in a plane, on a hotel bill. He always took trouble to tell people that Yoko had helped him with it, particularly its original inspiration on the theme of Utopia. Such was the intrinsic beauty of the song and the sincerity with which Lennon sang it that it will stand forever as an international anthem. All Lennon was asking was that we should *imagine* a world without possessions or religion.

The world was by now so used to an abrasive, hard-faced Lennon, that a song like 'Jealous Guy', which actually apologized for causing hurt and pain and recognized his emotional vulnerability, seemed uncharacteristic. On 'Crippled Inside' he sang once again of pain but without sounding self-pitying. 'One thing you can't hide/Is when you're crippled inside' – that was something John Lennon never did, and he was respected for his honesty in conveying that pain by a world he viewed with an artist's eye.

Lennon recognized the difficulties of sustaining a relationship, of shedding his hard-man image and becoming a fully rounded person. On *Imagine* he finally reconciled his efforts with his craft. The album makes comfortable listening, thanks in no small part to Spector's co-production and the lavish arrangements, although lyrically Lennon was still speaking as directly as ever.

The reason, of course, was Yoko, who had helped round John off as a person and had given him a perspective on his life. She had taken him into whole new areas, which initially proved to be dead ends (the avant-garde of *Two Virgins* and Side Two of *Live Peace In Toronto*). Latterly, however, she had steered him in the more fruitful directions signposted by *Imagine*. John's devotion to her manifested itself particularly on the beautiful 'Oh My Love' and the ebullient 'Oh Yoko!'. It was hard to reconcile the man who could write such sensitive love songs with the juvenile tough guy who could also sharpen his knife for the malice of 'How Do You Sleep?'. But then, John Lennon always was paradoxical.

The cumbersome 'I Don't Want To Be A Soldier' was a clumsy intrusion, a laborious protest song, railing against the 'straights' who let themselves be hoodwinked into the army or other Establishment professions. 'Give Me Some Truth', though, was a blisteringly effective and sustained attack on the falsity of Nixon's America.

Musically, *Imagine* packed real punch with legendary saxophonist King Curtis, Nicky Hopkins, Badfinger's Tom Evans and Joey Molland, George Harrison, and Phil Spector all contributing. Lennon spoke fondly of the finished album and pinpointed its strengths: ' "Imagine", both the song itself and the album, is the same thing as "Working Class Hero" and "Mother" and "God" on the first disc. But the first record was too real for people, so nobody bought it . . . You see "Imagine" was exactly the same message but sugar-coated. Now "Imagine" is a big hit almost everywhere – anti-religious, anti-nationalistic, anti-conventional, anti-capitalistic but because it is sugar-coated it is accepted. Now I understand what you have to do. Put your political message across with a little honey.'

But the honey was to stay in the jar during 1972. By the time *Imagine* was in the shops, John and Yoko had left England and settled in New York.

TWENTY-ONE

AMERICA

'New York is the Rome of today'

WITH THE Beatles written out of his mind and the thrust of the peace campaign over, John by 1971 was a curious amalgam of superstar, artist, and mercenary. He reiterated that he could no longer be a 'slave to gold records', but he was too much of a realist to be dragged too deeply into the esoteric world of art. He imposed his own limits on everything.

He had lived his thirty-one years on a cliff, consistently pushing himself and his abilities to the edge. He often remarked on the 'nearly' situations which punctuated his life: how he nearly got kicked out of school; how he nearly got expelled from art college but escaped to Hamburg just in time; how he was nearly lulled into a safe, rich, bourgeois existence at Weybridge when Yoko entered his life; how the Beatles broke up at exactly the right time for him. What had anchored him to the wide world, whatever was happening in his life, was his obsession with looking outside, rather than inside, himself.

Yoko's battle for custody of her daughter, Kyoko, took her and John to New York in 1971. John's attraction for the country had already been whetted by a visit that summer. He and Yoko had staggered fans by playing at a jam session with Frank Zappa and his Mothers of Invention at Fillmore East; in a show that ended at dawn, John had surprised even himself by announcing: 'This is a song I used to sing when I was in the Cavern in Liverpool.' It was called 'Well (Baby Please Don't Go)'. He had a neat line in self-deprecation: 'I did rhythm and booze, and Yoko sang on stage with what she calls voice modulation, which to the layman is screaming!'

In Britain John had explained why he felt so drawn to America, both on a personal and on an artistic level. 'It's Yoko's old stamping ground,' he explained, 'and she felt the country would be more receptive to what we're up to . . . in the States we're treated like artists. Which we are! Or anywhere else for that matter. But here [in Britain] I'm like the lad who knew Paul, got a lucky break, won the pools, and married the actress.

'It's like 1940 here,' he said, warming to the theme. 'It's like coming back to Denmark or somewhere. It's really the sticks, you know. While in New York there's these fantastic twenty or thirty artists who all understand what I'm doing and have the same kind of mind as me. It's just like heaven after being here. Oh, it's terrible. You've seen how they treat me in the press. There is an avant-garde here, but it's small.'

Political and other events had also depressed him in London: he was unhappy with the persecution of the editors of *Oz*, the Northern Ireland crisis infuriated him, and when internment without trial began there, he declared that Britain should pull out and let Northern Ireland sort out its own problems; he didn't like the adoption by Britain of the decimal currency system that year. The only thing that made him smile was a record by Dave Edmunds, 'I Hear You Knocking', which Lennon rated as one of the finest sounds he'd heard in years. He played it endlessly, together with a single by B. B. King, 'The Thrill Is Gone'.

On 3 September 1971 John and Yoko left London to settle in New York. For nine years it was to prove an artistic and spiritual haven for him. 'It's the Rome of today, a bit like a together Liverpool,' he said to me shortly after the move. 'I'd always like to be where the action is. In olden times I'd like to have lived in Rome or Paris or the East. The seventies are gonna be America's.'

When they arrived, John and Yoko made for Greenwich Village, which Yoko knew well from her days as a loft artist. They took a two-room apartment there at 105 Bank Street. A piano was quickly moved in, but mostly they shunned possessions. The apartment was spartan; the bed was a mattress covered with an American flag as a bedspread. They lived and dressed frugally, John in jeans, denim jacket, and T-shirt and Yoko in jeans, black turtleneck sweater, and boots.

An early visitor was Bob Dylan, re-acquainting himself with his musical roots. He took John on a sightseeing tour of the Village, pointing out all the clubs and explaining the diversity of artistic activities that went on. John was immediately captivated by the freewheeling atmosphere.

As well as renting the Bank Street apartment, they rented another nearby from ex-Lovin' Spoonful drummer, Joe Butler. They also bought bicycles, 'the best way to get around the Village,' Dylan advised them. John's was a conservative, English, sit-up-and-beg handlebar model, Yoko's Japanese – pure coincidence, she said.

Yet even in those heady first few months John kept in touch with what was happening at home. He phoned Apple in New York and London regularly; he telephoned Aunt Mimi in Dorset to be warned against living in bad old

America for too long; and he often went with Yoko to the
Apple office at 1700 Broadway.

One day, amid the mountain of mail awaiting him, was
a copy of the *Melody Maker* containing a reader's letter.
Headlined 'Dear JohnandYoko', it read:

> We love you very much and if all rock stars save one
> were to be lined up against a wall tomorrow and shot,
> you would be the one we'd save.
>
> But we're finding it more and more difficult to under-
> stand your simultaneous espousal of Rock Liberation and
> Mr Pete 'the President's friend' Bennett, promo man
> extraordinary (do you like being a 'product'?).
>
> Allen Klein may be a beautiful person but as far as
> we simple record buyers are concerned he's just another
> shrewd capitalist taking his cut wherever he can. Apple
> may be a wonderful company but all we notice is that
> its records get steadily more expensive and shorter (*vide*
> the new Mary Hopkin album with five short songs a
> side. Once upon a time *With the Beatles* had fourteen
> solid tracks on it.). If we want some Yoko music we
> have to fork out over four quid. Can you remember the
> time when you were lucky to afford an album a month?
> That's our upper limit.
>
> Power to the people, yeah – but which people? We
> were the Beatles' people all right but we still don't know
> if we're yours. We're T. Rex's, and Slade's – there they
> are on *Top of the Pops* (it might be rubbish but it's all
> we've got) and at St George's Hall, Bradford (at sixty
> pence a bit cheaper than a super album of your Fillmore
> gig). Are you one of us?
>
> So please, dear JohnandYoko, give us a break from
> your public nasties on Paul (we're not very interested
> in your tax situation) and start explaining what rock

liberation can mean when art and money are so mixed up. There aren't many people who can explain it. Peter Townshend has had a go; now it's your turn. Happy Christmas. Love,

Simon and Gill Frith,
Keighley, Yorkshire

Lennon's reply was instantaneous and revealing. On Apple-headed notepaper he personally typed his lengthy, rational reply which the *Melody Maker* published.

John's postscript about John Sinclair indicated his affinities during those early months in New York. As Lennon comments, Sinclair, a left-wing writer, had been jailed for possessing two joints of marijuana, and John and Yoko attended a benefit rally at Ann Arbor, Michigan, which resulted in Sinclair being freed within three days after serving two years of his sentence. The breakthrough thrilled John.

Left-wing personalities and political activists who began to infiltrate his life saw John as their Pied Piper. An early cohort in the Village was David Peel, an underground personality who amused John with his songs 'The Pope Smokes Dope' and 'Have A Marijuana'. Recalling that period, John said: 'I'd just arrived in New York and all these people, Jerry Rubin, Abbie Hoffman, David Peel, they were right on the corner when I was going out for a walk in the Village. It was that kind of community. I loved it. As usual, Lennon falls in the deep end, goes overboard, no half measures. At the time, though, it was a good scene and they meant no harm.'

Yoko felt safe in the Village; she was particularly keen on Jerry Rubin's philosophical book *Do It*, which had been on the Japanese bestseller list. John's first confrontation with the Village scene came when he dropped in, alone, to a clothes shop, the Limbo Shop, on St Mark's Place, only two weeks after arriving in New York. The best-known hippie in the village ran up to him to shake hands and say: 'Hello, my name is David Peel, I work for Elektra Records.' They chatted for some time, and a couple of nights later Peel was astonished when John and Yoko turned up at his concert in Washington Square Park. They enjoyed the irreverence of it all and left the show chanting 'The Pope Smokes Dope'. It was the first of several encounters with Peel, who could scarcely believe that a Beatle was drawn to his scene, for whatever reason.

Shortly afterwards, Rubin told Lennon that Peel was going to do a 'walkabout', singing on the streets. John, with guitar, called on Peel and with Yoko went along Second Avenue singing 'The Pope Smokes Dope'. Fifty people joined the sidewalk minstrels. 'It was totally natural, spontaneous, and great.' Unfortunately, the police thought a wandering Beatle was a security risk and broke it up.

Lennon loved street people as long as they were not phonies. What irritated him was when hangers-on bothered him, asking for money, drugs, or started to talk of the Beatles. He wanted to communicate with people on an ordinary level. New York, and particularly the crowd he was introduced to by Jerry Rubin, seemed to offer that; coupled with the radical politics preached by Rubin and his friends, it was John's automatic haven for the early months in the Village. Rubin effectively screened most of the people who wanted to get near John.

Peel's memory of those days with John is of a superstar who intuitively grasped the Village vibrations but could not become totally involved because he was a 'millionaire trendy'. Says Peel: 'John and Yoko were brilliant. They knew how to ad lib quicker than anybody I've ever met. What they liked doing best was getting things done

LENNON

quickly. They hated wasting time. John was open-minded, learned a lot, he had access to a lot of people, and he always *listened*. He wasn't as committed to the radical thing as a lot of us but because he was a Beatle he could make a call and get things done.'

Life for John and Yoko in the Village was a series of moments. John was so high on his freedom there that he even produced an album by Peel and his band, the Lower East Side. 'John was an excellent producer,' says Peel. 'He had that Phil Spector Wall of Sound down pat, with every-thing exaggerated. He was heavily into *action* in the studio. . . . We had six guitars and ten congas and Yoko even played congas a little. "All right, let's go, *next*," he'd shout. . . . He was deadly serious but knew how to have fun. I never saw Lennon so happy as he was doing my album. John said: "Go in and play like you play on the street" – but how could I with that fantastic sound behind me?' The album, out on the Apple label, was instantly banned all over the world because it included 'The Pope Smokes Dope'.

Peel and his band played several times with John and Yoko. He was at the benefit rally for John Sinclair and on David Frost's TV show, and he jammed many times in their Bank Street apartment with John often playing washboard. Peel also played during their appearance on Dick Cavett's TV show and at a Madison Square Garden charity concert for retarded children and adults. Peel was moved to write a song, 'Lennon For President'.

'I used to go over to Bank Street a lot to jam, especially to eat dinner,' he says. 'I knew a good free meal when I saw one. Yoko was a terrific cook of macrobiotic food.' Only one thing irritated Peel: that John maintained his bodyguards while he was in the Village. 'Nobody would bother him when he was with us. Allen Klein said to

Lennon that the reason he liked hanging around me was because Peel does everything Lennon was afraid to do himself: that's what I did. I brought out the side of John that just wanted to go crazy, party all night. But the bodyguards . . . he was cynical and mistrustful. A lot of people wanted handouts. He was paranoid about it.

'When you are close to John Lennon, the guy's so powerful and aware of the world events that you start losing your own identity. Being so close to him for a year or so was good and bad, you know. Look . . . as soon as the carriage turned back to a pumpkin, Cinderella was a housemaid. When you're with John Lennon you're a prince. When his trendy thing is over, you go home a pumpkin. Twelve midnight, you're back in your rags doing what you did before. Like me.'

Life among the Greenwich Village hippies was a natural diversion of fun and freedom for John. But President Nixon's American government viewed it as something almost sinister. From the start of 1972, only a few months after setting foot on American soil, John was faced with an immigration battle that proved almost stranger than fiction.

John was in America on a temporary visa which expired on 29 February 1972. As early as January he and Yoko realized that staying in America permanently might not be easy and that the government could use John's 1968 drugs conviction to refuse them a visa, known as a Green Card. Lawyer Leon Wildes was among those interviewed by them that month in their Bank Street apartment before the real problems began. 'John was quieter than Yoko,' recalls the urbane Wildes. 'While she asked us questions, he was making us tea.' At that time there was no interest expressed in permanent residence in the USA. 'The interest was only in staying a couple of months so they could continue their efforts to find Kyoko; they were in the middle of some complicated custody proceedings.'

Wildes told them that if all they wanted was an extension of another month or even three, 'You don't really need my help. The Apple solicitor can handle it as the custody problem is one of the strongest reasons you can give for the extension of a temporary stay.'

But Yoko answered: 'Yes, we really *do* need your help.' A puzzled Wildes was appointed as their immigration lawyer; he was, frankly, too much of a heavyweight lawyer to be dealing with a simple extension of John's visa. He had no idea, initially, that John was being harassed.

One of the Beatles' classic songs, 'We Can Work It Out', had been written by Paul. But John had injected the middle lines which made the song special: 'Life is very short and there's no time/For fussing and fighting my friend.' But as his initial foray into the relaxed New York lifestyle gave way to tension and worry, he began to realize that fussing and fighting was precisely what he would have to do to clear his sullied name and stay in the country he wanted to adopt.

The source of the government's hounding lay in the little-known Senate Internal Security Sub-Committee. Many politicians were surprised that the committee still existed; it had originated in the 1950s during the scares of communist infiltration. Even in 1972 it apparently operated on the same philosophy: anyone with a view different from the government's was subject to investigation.

The committee received a memorandum suggesting that Lennon might be bankrolling or otherwise supporting the group that had disturbed the 1968 Democratic Convention and, it was feared, might do the same at the Republican Convention due to be held in 1972. Says Leon Wildes:

'Lennon, of course, always denied that he had anything to do with, or had any knowledge of, this plan, if it existed. Nor was he really interested, he said. I always believed this, because he was a principled kind of guy and he wasn't interested in disturbing, rather in stating his piece, explaining his position.' (John's denials were underlined by David Peel's opinion that Lennon was never a believing radical and by John's statements throughout his life that his true role was to write songs and make music. His liaison with Jerry Rubin and others had, however, left him exposed to the charge. When he deviated from the role of writer-musician, he always ran into problems.)

The committee chairman sent the memorandum to John Mitchell, who was attorney general, with jurisdiction over the entire immigration process and also chairman of CREEP, the 'Committee to Re-elect the President'. A note at the foot of a covering letter said that a copy had been sent to the White House. 'There was obviously an interest by the Nixon administration, at the highest levels, in what John was doing,' says Wildes.

Evidence of a government campaign mounted. The *New York Times* summed it up:

According to the government documents which Mr Lennon's lawyer Leon Wildes obtained from the government under court orders, Senator Strom Thurmond, Republican, of South Carolina, wrote a personal and confidential letter to the then Attorney General, John N. Mitchell, on 4 February 1972 suggesting that action against Mr Lennon could avoid 'many headaches'. Attached to the Thurmond letter was a memorandum from the files of the Senate Internal Security Sub-Committee, asserting that a commune group was preparing to go to California to disrupt the 1972 Republican National Convention, and that a confidential source had learned 'that the activities of this group are being financed by John Lennon.' A second memo from the same files contended that 'radical New Left leaders plan to use Mr Lennon as a drawing card to promote the success of rock festivals, to obtain funds for a "dump Nixon" program.'

The Thurmond letter discovered by Wildes had a handwritten footnote: 'Can we keep him [Lennon] out?' And the New York district director of immigration acknowledged that he had been specifically told from 'on high' what action to take on Lennon and exactly when to start deportation proceedings.

Initially, in March 1972, John was ordered to leave America within two months, which allowed some breathing space. John became extremely tense. Winning the right to stay in America was a matter of principle, and other worries were adding to his jitters. There was the complex lawsuit with Northern Songs and Maclen Music in London dating back to the rights to his songs written since 1965, with Yoko. There was a simmering battle with Allen Klein. John was a confused, angry man during the early days in America. He drank too much and smoked too many Kool cigarettes.

He suspected that his immigration problem might have been part of a wider plan to split the unity of youth which, in the early 1970s, was such a potent force. With Paul McCartney marooned in Britain because of his own drugs bust, John afraid to leave the US because he wouldn't get back in, Jimi Hendrix and Jim Morrison, two catalysts of the youth culture, dead, and the Rolling Stones being carefully watched, Lennon thought that it was perhaps a plot. 'They're chopping off the "revolution" at its source,' he said. 'So there'll be no more mass gatherings like the Woodstock peace festival. These things inspire change. Politicians don't want change, so it's in their interests to split us all up.

'I'm not the only rock star who's harassed, but nobody else tried to stay here in America. And nobody else hung out with the baddies like I did. Maybe I'm dumb but I'm interested in people. I wanted to find out what they had to say about everything. I didn't want to read a book on them, so I met them all to find out where it's at, y'know. Now in 1968, the cops beat up some people at a Chicago convention. I'm discussing with Jerry Rubin, Allen Ginsberg, and everybody what they're talking about – and they're saying, "Shall we go to San Francisco to have an anti-war rally?" Next thing it's in the papers that John and Yoko are going to lead a vast rally in San Diego with all these people!'

In April 1972, John and Yoko addressed a crowd in New York which was protesting against America's bombing of North Vietnam. Clearly John would not be hounded or compromised by any threat of deportation. At the same time he wanted the freedom to stay in New York. The pulse of the city was right for him.

Once the machine was rolling on checking Lennon out, it was unstoppable. Agents from the FBI (Federal Bureau of Investigation) attended his concerts, studied his song lyrics – particularly those on the heavily political *Some Time In New York City* album – and CIA (Central Intelligence Agency) men shadowed him in his private life. John's phone conversations were tapped so much that he rarely bothered to use it; instead Yoko did most of the talking. The FBI strongly suggested at one point that John 'be arrested, if at all possible, on possession of narcotics charges' so that he might be 'immediately deportable'. Why this was not followed through is unknown; John was smoking marijuana in Bank Street quite often, and it would have been easy for police to arrest him.

Leon Wildes now set to work with a counter-plan of meticulous detail and careful strategy. 'The government wanted to be able to prove that Lennon was an undesirable because of his 1968 marijuana conviction,' he says. 'They planned to ease him out by bringing proceedings against him as an "overstay" on his temporary visa, telling him that unless he accepted this deal and got out voluntarily, they could always charge him with being deportable as a person with a drugs conviction. That way, he would be seen to be not leaving voluntarily but forcibly. They thought he would not want that and they believed that with a carrot-and-stick routine they could force him out within a month or two in mid-1972.'

While accumulating his proof of the government vendetta, Wildes managed to secure a 'waiver', a six-month extension for John and Yoko, which changed their status from Non-Immigrant Visa to that of Visitor of Distinguished Merit and Ability. John Lindsay, mayor of New York and one of Lennon's main protagonists, had in former years helped to write and reform America's immigration laws: 'There's a thing called Suspension of Deportation by which, if a good character is proved, and there are sound and equitable reasons not to execute a technical deportation, the attorney general can suspend it. John Lennon was not the first by any means to be the beneficiary of a waiver of the technicality,' he told me.

This enabled John to appear on TV on the influential *Dick Cavett Show*. Typically, he didn't shrink from confronting the situation head-on, telling millions of viewers that he was being followed by government detectives and that his phones and Wildes's were being tapped.

Although he was nervous about it, John's friend, the black comedian Dick Gregory, who had also been the victim of phone tapping, had convinced him he should tell the world about it.

John described his feelings at the time: 'I'm not saying they had plans other than just keeping tabs on me, to see what I was up to, who I was seeing. But I felt followed everywhere by government agents. Every time I picked up my phone there was a lot of noise. Somebody gave me a number that if you call it, you get this feedback sound that confirms your phone is being tapped. And I did it and it did. Suddenly I realized this was serious, they were coming for me, one way or another. They were harassing me. I'd open the door and there'd be guys standing on the other side of the street. I'd get in the car and they'd be following me and not hiding. That's what got me paranoid. They wanted me to see I was being followed. Anyway, after I said it out on the air, on TV, the next day there was nobody there. Was I dreaming? No, I wasn't. Look, my lawyer, who's as square as the next one, started to agree. He found his phones were being tapped and he didn't know how to prove it either.'

What the Nixon government had not considered was the enormous groundswell of public opinion in John's favour. During several lawsuits, which included Leon Wildes suing the government at one stage over a technicality in the irregularity of a temporary visa, he pleaded humanitarianism under the Freedom of Information Act. 'There were people in the United States completely deportable, who nevertheless were allowed to remain here; I claimed that Lennon would probably fit within those standards, but since the standards had never been published we were entitled to the benefit of any doubt.' Further, Wildes claimed that Lennon was suffering selective prosecution for political rather than legal reasons.

The battle to get a Green Card took four agonizing,

exhausting years. It was a long, dark tunnel, but during nerve-wracking days when Leon Wildes would call once or twice daily with news of an advance or a setback, John received heartening support from some of the most influential people in the USA.

Mayor John Lindsay was one. 'This town,' he told me, 'always had a very important history of welcoming contributing talent. I could see no over-compelling reason to get rid of this kind of artist. John Lennon was a major force as we saw it, far more good than bad. Some people just didn't understand the nature of the beast. They didn't really know what Lennon stood for, didn't understand his world, his music, his behaviour, his whole theory of life. A lot of middle-aged politicians, and people who didn't want to stick their neck out, sometimes through fear, took the "pull up the drawbridge" attitude. I was interested in the cause and in this city, and anxious that this country demonstrated to John Lennon that he was welcome here. It seemed unthinkable that a major artist should be shown the door. This city has good Philharmonic, and good opera, and good Carnegie Hall, but it also has the John Lennons.

'Unless there's vigilance, civil liberties suffer. Governments start poking about and letting you know they're using police tactics. My colleagues in city government could sense that this was no hula-hoop thing, here today and gone tomorrow. We sensed that John Lennon's threatened deportation was affecting young people very deeply. It was in the tradition of New York that there remained a mixture of talent in the city.' He also stressed that his role in the Lennon battle, writing to the commissioner of immigration in Washington pleading for the deportation order to be dropped, was not to condone John's use of drugs. He did not consider that Lennon was damaging the community by his drug-taking.

John was particularly grateful also for the interest and campaign of Jack Anderson, the highly rated writer with the *Washington Post*. Anderson, who has a reputation for tenacity and exposé reporting, had written about the 'Watergate' tactics, being used to hound Lennon. 'When Jack Anderson started writing about what was happening,' Lennon told me, 'I knew I had to go on fighting until I won.' When John was murdered, Anderson recalled the immigration battle in a column in the *New York Daily News*:

> The immigration service reserves a special bureaucratic hell for aliens who have the slightest taint of narcotics in their past. Thieves, rapists, and even murderers have less trouble gaining admission to the United States than someone convicted of even the most minor drug charge. Six years ago, John Lennon . . . came close to being deported because of a 1968 marijuana charge in England. I took up his case in 1974. I reported that the deportation move was really a political vendetta against Lennon who had been outspoken in his opposition to the Vietnam war. Lennon was able to beat the trumped-up deportation order partly because of official embarrassment over my columns and partly because of the superb legal work of his attorney, Leon Wildes. Since that time the public attitude has changed towards both the Vietnam war and the drug habits it spawned. Most Americans now agree with Lennon that the war was a tragic mistake and his arrest for possessing a small amount of marijuana for personal use is no longer considered a horrendous crime.

Another ally was Washington lawyer Steve Martindale. Visiting New York, he met the Lennons at a party also attended by Mayor Lindsay and his wife, Mary. 'John and Yoko were extremely shy,' says Martindale. 'Yoko took the lead in explaining the problems they were having with the US government. I suggested they come and spend some time in Washington and we would get to the bottom of it.

'When they came I had a dinner for them. Henry Kissinger was there, so was Senator Alan Cranston. John and Yoko were awed by it all. . . . As I remember it, Henry [Kissinger] put in a call to John Mitchell [the attorney general] and we succeeded in softening the government up somewhat.'

The political and diplomatic ramifications of the case were lost on John. He reacted strongly, though, to one twist to Leon Wildes's reports to him. When Yoko was granted permission to remain a permanent resident, he erupted. Wildes told him to cool it; the government was playing into their hands, he argued, by putting itself in a position of attempting to split up a married couple. 'That was why I applied separately for Yoko's permit,' says Wildes. 'I got her acknowledged to be an outstanding artist.'

Wildes's ace lay, ironically, in tracing with Yoko the circumstances of John's 1968 drugs bust. John had told Wildes that at the time he had been forced to plead guilty because of Yoko. That was the only action he could take: 'If I pleaded innocent, I would still have been convicted. Yoko at that time in England was an alien, and unless I took the rap they would have charged her and she would have been deported.' Wildes surmised that, since John had been advised by the best legal counsellors in London, what he said could be true. After all, the police pounced on him in a flat that he didn't own, where John had been tipped off by a *Daily Mirror* reporter in advance about their coming and had even cleaned up the flat. He *could* have been framed. And pleading guilty might well have been the best way

A new dawn for John with Yoko by his side. They are photographed outside their new home, Tittenhurst Park, Ascot, Berkshire, in September 1969, a month after moving in (Tom Blau/Camera Press)

Seated at the white piano, on which he wrote his anthem 'Imagine', at Tittenhurst Park. Yoko now has the piano in her New York home (Tom Hanley)

Moving to New York in 1971, John and Yoko enjoyed the simple life in their new home in Greenwich Village (Ben Ross/Camera Press)

Above: In July 1973, John attended the Watergate hearings in New York, in which the government of President Richard Nixon was indicted. He and Yoko followed the events closely (Associated Press)

Right: After a four-year battle, John won his vital Green Card in July 1976 from the US Immigration Department. This gave him the freedom to leave and re-enter the country (Bob Gruen/Star File)

Above: John and Yoko during rehearsals for the 'One To One' concert at Madison Square Garden, New York, in August 1972 (Bob Gruen/Star File)

Left: John, Yoko and their friend Elliot Mintz during their five-month holiday in Japan in the summer of 1977; they are photographed outside the sushi bar in Karuizawa where they usually ate lunch (Nishi F. Saimaru)

A Japanese-style family, pictured in the Dakota apartment when Sean was just one month old. This was the start of John's time as a self-styled house-husband and doting father (Bob Gruen/Star File)

John at the control desk during the recording of his final album,
Double Fantasy, at the Record Plant, New York, in 1980
(David Spindel)

Above: A few days before he was killed: John and Yoko in the garden of their favourite local coffee shop, La Fortuna, near their Dakota home (Lilo Raymond)

Below: In New York's Central Park, across the road from his home, John is immortalized in an area designated Strawberry Fields. Yoko stands with Sean at the 'Imagine' point which forms a permanent memorial to him (Bob Gruen/Star File)

Above: A rare photograph of family unity: John's widow and his first wife, with their respective sons by John, are at Julian Lennon's concert at the Beacon Theater, New York, in 1988. Later, the family gathered at the Hard Rock Café (Bob Gruen/Star File)

Below: After all the bickering, Paul and Yoko came together in January 1994 when Paul made an emotional speech to induct John posthumously into the Rock and Roll Hall Of Fame. Sean is at Yoko's right at the moving ceremony at Manhattan's Waldorf-Astoria Hotel (Bob Gruen/Star File)

out. Wildes decided to pursue this and hoped to win the point in the US Court of Appeals.

Chief Judge Kaufman, with two other judges, provided a positive answer. By a two-to-one vote, they ruled that John's conviction could not be recognized as a conviction for the '*illicit*' possession of marijuana. He had been convicted purely on the discovery of the marijuana on his premises – under British law at the time guilty *knowledge* was not something that needed proving before a conviction could be made. 'In the US,' says Wildes, emphasizing the legal difference, 'there's no such thing as a crime where the government doesn't have the burden of proving that the man had a guilty intent.' The Court of Appeals remanded Lennon's case until the immigration service could re-consider the discretionary aspects of the case. They also admonished the government.

News of this triumph, a major hurdle in the case which virtually broke the government's back, came to Leon Wildes unofficially. A clerk at the Court of Appeals phoned: 'Mr Wildes, I shouldn't be doing this because it's still not in final form, but I'm a long-time Lennon fan . . . there is a decision here which will be in final form in an hour or two, and if you want to send someone down I'll give them a copy of it, in which you win the case two to one.'

Under the headline 'Deportation of Lennon Barred by Court of Appeals', the *New York Times* reported the case on 8 October 1975:

In the twenty-four-page decision Judge Irving R. Kaufman issued a strong warning that the courts will not condone selective deportation based upon secret political grounds. This alluded to government documents that were submitted to the court, indications that the Nixon administration started deportation proceedings against

Lennon in 1972 for fear that the former Beatle would make appearances in the United States promoting opposition to the then President.

In his summing-up and ruling in John's favor, Judge Kaufman said the court did not take lightly Lennon's claim that he was the victim of a move to oust him on political grounds. 'If in our two hundred years of independence we have in some measure realized our ideals, it is in large part because we have always found a place for those committed to the spirit of liberty, and willing to help implement it. Lennon's four-year battle to remain in our country is testimony to his faith in the American dream.'

Says Wildes: 'I can't describe how my feelings were after four years of courtroom appearances, with and without John.' He called Lennon immediately.

'What do you *mean*? We've won?' John asked.

The cautious Wildes said he must remember they agreed they would never claim victory. 'But John, what I thought couldn't happen has happened. The court is remanding the case back to the Immigration Service, saying they may not consider your conviction. I think the government is now wiped out and they're not going to get into all the other political things they've been threatening, your writing and your songs and all the nonsense they were going to scrape together.'

The following morning John had double cause for jubilation. His son Sean Ono Lennon had been born safely at 2:00 A.M. and the precious Green Card was on the horizon.

It was nearly a year before John actually received the Green Card (which is actually blue). On the appointed day John, dressed in suit and black tie, went to court. Paradoxically, the effect of the immigration battle had been to transform lawyer Wildes's dress style from suits into jeans and long hair, while John began veering towards the formal every time there was immigration business to discuss. In court John ritualistically answered the questions put to him by Wildes:

Have you ever been convicted of any crime anywhere in the US?

No.

Have you ever been a member of the Communist Party or any other organization that may seek to overthrow the US government by force?

No.

Do you intend to make the US your home?

I do.

Will you continue your work here?

Yes. I wish to continue to live here with my family and continue making music.

The speeches in John's favour were eloquent and forceful. Sam Trust, president of ATV Music which owned the rights to John's compositions, told the court: 'There are two very positive reasons why Mr Lennon should be allowed to remain in the US. The music scene in the US is in the doldrums right now and the current resurgence of interest in the Beatles and their material proves that they are the most powerful source of music in the last thirty years. I believe we can look forward to many new innovations in music if Mr Lennon is allowed to remain in this country.'

Trust's second point was that Lennon was a tremendous revenue generator. 'The US will be the scene for the reception of that revenue if he is allowed to remain here,' he said.

Writer Norman Mailer was next to take the stand. He described John as 'a great artist who has made an enormous contribution to popular culture. He is one of the great artists of the Western world. We lost T. S. Eliot to England and only got Auden back.'

Wildes read out a letter from the bishop of New York, the Rt Revd Paul Moore. Emphasizing John's contribution to the culture of New York, the bishop praised him as a 'gentleman of integrity'.

Gloria Swanson told the court that for years she had been actively interested in the physical fitness of New York's youth. 'My husband met John Lennon in a health food store in this city and we found we had feelings in common on this subject. Good food is essential to physical well-being and we are anti-junk-food. I hope very much that he will help us in this sphere. We must educate the country and the Lennons will help do something about it.'

Among the other witnesses who had given evidence to support John's claim to stay in the US were the noted sculptor Noguchi and TV personality Geraldo Rivera. Also in the courtroom were composer John Cage and actor Peter Boyle, both close friends of John and Yoko.

As Judge Ira Fieldsteel announced his verdict, John embraced Yoko, dressed radiantly in white, and the packed courtroom burst into spontaneous cheering.

Outside the courtroom John was buoyant, but he spoke quietly. 'The Immigration Service has finally seen the light of day. It's been a long and slow road but I am not bitter. On the contrary, I can now go and see my relations in Japan and elsewhere. I can travel now! Until today my attorney wouldn't even let me go to Hawaii for a vacation in case I couldn't get back. Whenever I flew to Los Angeles I was paranoid in case the plane was diverted to Tokyo on the way!'

Wildes's celebratory gift to John to mark the success was a leather passport case, bearing the bald eagle and the seal of the United States.

The emotional stress on John during the four-year campaign had been enormous. 'I didn't know him before it, but he'd obviously been a light, airy, *up* person,' says Leon Wildes. 'The psychological strain showed. It had a big effect on him, putting him down.'

John's dry humour did, however, surface on a television show discussion about the case. He went with Leon Wildes. John said to his announcer: 'I want you to interview *Leon*.' The announcer diplomatically said he wanted more time with John. Lennon pleaded for his lawyer: 'Look, let Leon go on. His mother's watching!'

John always remained both puzzled and angry at the immigration hassle. He summed up his feelings in a typically incisive sentence: 'I can't understand it. I always thought the Statue of Liberty said "*Come*". . . . Now I'm going home to crack open a tea-bag and start looking at some travel catalogues.'

John felt completely at home in New York where he had battled for so long to stay. 'My life here is not dissimilar to what it was in England, actually. One's life revolves around family or friends or the work you do. My life for the past ten years since I became "famous" has changed, but basically it's a bedroom, a studio, a TV, a night out, back home! And they talk an American version of English on TV and it goes on a bit longer, all night. But beyond that there's not much difference.

'I imagine New York is like London must have been in

the Victorian days when Britain was at the height of its power or on the decline. The American Empire is now what the British Empire *used* to be. The French had their empire – Paris was cooking. And America now has the empire of the world even though they're losing bits of it. It has that quality about it. And although Washington's the capital, a lot of the action is in New York because that's where the monied people are and it's an old place that's been built up, so that although it's not physically big it's big in the amount of power and the number of people here. I reckon it must have been like this in Queen Victoria's day in London, when everybody wanted to be there. Or even when that Bloomsbury group, Virginia Woolf and all those people, were writing their books and poetry. This is like that: it's where a lot of people come to and I became enamoured of it.'

He also liked the fact that there was no language problem. 'Fortunately or unfortunately they speak English so I just fitted in. It's pretty hard to pinpoint what an American is: they're all Italian-Americans or Irish-Americans or African-Americans or Afro-Americans. It's *nice* here.'

During the period of worry over the Green Card, his mind had travelled back to his English roots. He particularly enjoyed an invitation from the *New York Times* to review scripts of *The Goon Show* which he and his Uncle George had chortled over back in Liverpool when John was fourteen. The Goons, especially Spike Milligan, inspired the Beatles, he often said, as much as Elvis Presley and Chuck Berry had. They were to the Beatles' generation what the Beatles were to the next.

When Princess Anne married Captain Mark Phillips, John stayed up all night in Los Angeles to watch the royal wedding on television. 'It was the right and proper thing for an Englishman abroad to do such a thing,' he explained, tongue in cheek. 'It was a good excuse to have a few drinks to toast the royal family.'

He took special pleasure in teasing the public about a Beatles reunion, rumours of which continued to simmer in the early 1970s.

'Beatles to re-form?' screamed the writers excitedly in 1973 when John, George, and Ringo got together in Los Angeles for a Ringo Starr solo album session. In a parody of the Paul McCartney press release which still irritated him, John released this statement under the headline of 'Newswecanalldowithout':

> Although John and Yoko and George, and George and Ringo, had played together often, it was the first time the three ex-Beauties had played together since – well, since they last played together. As usual, an awful lot of rumours, if not downright lies, were going on, including the possibility of impresario Allen De Klein of grABCKO playing bass for the other three in an as-yet-untitled album called *I Was A Teenage Fat Cat*. Producer Richard Perry, who planned to take the tapes along to sell them to Paul McCartney, told a friend: 'I'll take the tapes to Paul McCartney.'
>
> The extreme humility that existed between John and Paul seems to have evaporated. 'They've spoken to each other on the telephone – and in English, that's a change,' said a McCartney associate. 'If only everything were as simple and unaffected as McCartney's new single "My Love", then maybe Dean Martin and Jerry Lewis would be reunited with the Marx Bros and *Newsweak* could get a job,' said an East African official. – Yours Up To The Teeth, John Lennon and Yoko Ono.

The two years preceding Sean's birth while the immi-

gration battle continued were packed with dramatic events
for John. As a musician, he encountered many peaks and
troughs. His rock 'n' roll album produced by the legendary
Phil Spector, one of his all-time heroes, was fraught with
personal clashes. As a man, he descended into the worst
period of his life, lurching in a drunken haze around California. The reason for that appalling episode was traceable to
his marriage. In the autumn of 1973 he and Yoko split up.

'Yoko and I had a breakdown, one way or another,' John
told me during their separation. 'We'd been together seven
years, y'know, and it wasn't like a normal marriage where
the man goes off to work all day, or even the accepted
showbiz marriage where one of the partners gets involved
in something that splits them up for months through work.
We were together *just about twenty-four hours of every day!*
So it was bound to happen that we'd snap.' Their private
problem was exacerbated by the pressure of the immigration
issue.

John and Yoko's split took everyone by surprise. They
had been together as friends and artists, as well as man and
wife, in one of the most publicly demonstrated love matches
of the century. But John was a notoriously difficult, volatile,
moody man to live with; during a creative lull, such as he
experienced around this time, his insecurities manifested
themselves in immature behaviour. He smoked too much,
becoming edgy, and spent days on end in his bedroom in
solitude. His hands went clammy with nervousness and
worry at meeting even his closest friends. And, given the
chance, he drank too much. Yoko knew only too well of
the danger signs when booze was readily available, and kept
a tight grip on its visibility in the Dakota.

She decided that a temporary split was essential. 'There
was never any need for a divorce,' she says coolly. 'I knew
we would be back together again, eventually.' But John

needed time to straighten himself out and, perhaps, they should learn for a while to live without each other. If drinking and having a wild time was something he was missing, she reasoned, it was best that he got it out of his system and played out his fantasies while retaining contact with her by phone.

John was not happy about the decision. 'She kicked me out, pure and simple,' he said later. 'I was behaving stupidly and I'd lost whatever it was about me that she found good in the first place. It was grow-up time and I'm glad she made me do it.'

Yoko says: 'John and I were artists together and husband and wife together. We were competitive, also, to a point: he would write something and I'd say something like, "Well, that's nice, I've got something now *I've* just written," and we would try to stretch each other as writers. It wasn't so surprising, really that we should separate for a while. It turned out to be the best thing that could happen.'

By then, they had moved into an apartment in the Dakota building at 1 West 72nd Street in Manhattan, from where they also ran their company, Lenono. Working as their secretary at the Dakota was a twenty-two-year-old woman born in New York of Chinese parents. May Pang was trusted. She was loyal, efficient, and hardworking for two very demanding people, and she loved John's music. When John and Yoko agreed on the split, Yoko suggested John should head for California; to go outside America was impossible at the time because of the Green Card problem, and anyway, Yoko said, he should experience Los Angeles.

Elliot Mintz, John's closest male friend in America since 1971, says it was Yoko who said May should accompany John. 'Obviously,' says Mintz, 'for John Lennon to go alone to Los Angeles, where he'd never been before except with the Beatles, was out of the question. Here was a man who had not driven a car in America, could not walk into a supermarket and purchase food, who couldn't take his laundry to the corner, who didn't make phone calls, didn't know how to compute a tip on a bill, didn't know where to locate restaurants, and who knew hardly anyone in Los Angeles except me. He would have been totally helpless. It was practical to send his secretary, May Pang, with him to look after him. I suppose Yoko knew it was likely there would be intimacy between the two of them. She took a mature view, knowing John: "Better with May than galloping around with the golden groupies."

'And Yoko believed May could handle it. May did not smoke, drink, or take drugs, she was not part of any weird Los Angeles orgy scene.' But it was never a love match, says Mintz, who saw them together often. 'To think that John ran off with May to leave Yoko Ono would require a remarkable suspension in logic. John could not sustain May's company for more than a matter of hours without incredible fatigue setting in. It was not a love affair. It was a relationship born out of the convenience of the moment. I do not wish to publicly embarrass the lady. She did a fairly effective job of doing just that in her own book. It is one thing to merchandise the memories but her contention that she was the other woman in John's life is nonsense. May contrived a quasi-fictional scenario in an attempt to give form to a relationship that was not there. From the moment John met Yoko to the last hour of his life, she was the only woman who shared his love.'

Elliot Mintz's closeness to John developed, curiously, from his first association with Yoko. In 1972 Mintz was working as a disc jockey and star television interviewer, well on the road to becoming a Dick Cavett-style commentator; in Los Angeles he reported for *Eye-Witness News* and had a growing reputation as a penetrating interviewer of statesmen, politicians, and celebrities. When John and Yoko's controversial album *Some Time In New York City* was released in June of that year, Mintz conducted a one-hour interview/profile for the radio station KLOS with Yoko, tracing the background to her meeting with John. He asked her unusual questions: whether the people in her dreams spoke English or Japanese, what quotes from her book *Grapefruit* meant to her, and how she wanted to be remembered when she died. Her answer was, 'Just say that John and I loved, lived, and died.' Next day she called to ask for a correction to be taped to that sentence: it was re-recorded to say: 'John and I lived, loved, and died.' Mintz had never really understood her music or avant-garde stance, but he sensed a 'wonderful quality' in the lady over the telephone. Still, it was one of two thousand radio interviews he had conducted over a decade, and he thought it would probably go no further. 'It was really quite a beautiful interview,' said Yoko, 'and we loved the tone of it.'

A few days later about three hundred letters had arrived at Mintz's office enthusiastically enquiring about the Yoko interview. Hesitantly, Mintz phoned Yoko to tell her about the letters. To his surprise, she was fascinated to hear about every one. And that conversation began a unique telephone friendship between Yoko and Mintz that went on nightly for many months. Yoko believes it is sometimes possible to tell more of a person on the phone than in person, when appearances can sometimes distract or inhibit both parties. With Mintz in California and Yoko in New York, they spoke every night on 'everything – religion, films, politics, love, death, books, romance. And every time I spoke to Yoko her perceptions on anything we talked about, even something innocuous, brought a perspective on the subject that had never occurred to me,' says Mintz. 'I was beginning to understand why John, who had seen it all, done it all, knew it all, been around the block four million times, had to stop when he met Yoko. All her thoughts were original.'

Finally, after months of these nightly conversations, John could stand the curiosity no longer. Who was this disc jockey his wife was always talking to? Typically, he decided to get in on the act and did a radio interview with Mintz.

Within months of striking up the telephone friendship, John and Yoko decided to take a car journey across America in their old station wagon, with a driver. John often remarked on how little he had seen of the country: 'We only went to America to buy records unavailable back home and give concerts in the old days. I needed to go in some of the coffee shops at four in the morning and get a chocolate milk shake, that kind of thing, just do it normally like the rest of the people do. Yoko and I wanted to experience the heartland of this country.'

A meeting with the mysterious Mintz was part of the programme. When they met him at the house they had rented in Santa Barbara, they presented him with the demonstration record of *Some Time In New York City*, the highly charged political album containing 'Woman Is Nigger Of The World' and a song about Attica State Prison. After spending the day with John and Yoko, Mintz returned to Los Angeles and broadcast the entire album, freezing all commercials and inviting listeners' reactions. Next day John and Yoko phoned him to ask how it went.

'I have the good news and the bad news,' replied Mintz. 'The good news is that it went great, the bad news is that I was fired.' The lyrical content of the album had offended the sponsors. John and Yoko thought it was hilarious.

'My radio career had just collapsed,' says Mintz, 'and they just sat there laughing.'

John said: 'Oh well, now you don't have a job, you might as well come with us. We're going up to San Francisco.' Mintz did just that, spending a month with them at the Miyako Hotel in San Francisco, and from that first meeting he became John and Yoko's close friend and confidant. Lennon trusted him completely.

Born on 16 February 1945, Mintz is, crucially, an Aquarian like Yoko. A man who speaks and moves with total precision, he shared with Lennon a similarly dry sense of humour and an interest in literature. During the fifteen-month period Lennon was away from Yoko, Mintz saw him and also spoke to Yoko on the phone nearly every day. 'Don't ever ask me to keep a secret from the other,' he told both of them. 'You are both my friends.'

When John and May Pang stepped from the plane at Loss Angeles airport in October 1973 Mintz was there to meet them in his 1956 Jaguar. John wanted to cash some traveller's cheques, but they reached the bank – Lloyds on Sunset Boulevard – just after it had closed. 'I knocked on the window and the teller shook his head,' says Mintz. 'I took John and moved him in front of the window and suddenly the doors swung open, security guards came out and the vault opened and the president of the bank appeared.

' "Would you care for some coffee, Mr Lennon?"

'John said: "I just want to turn this into some money." '

The amount turned out to be $10,000, so John sat down and signed his name on the back of one hundred cheques, each valued at $100.

'John,' said Mintz, 'maybe I should take that cash and put it in my cheque account for you. It's a lot to carry around.'

The bank manager said: 'Maybe we can interest you in a long-term checking account?'

John said: 'No, no. I'll keep the money in me pocket.' He'd never handled so much cash in his life and wanted the 'feel' of it. He took $10,000 and stuffed it in his jacket. It was the very first time in his life, he said, he had been inside a bank.

Mintz joked: 'If things go well next week, I'll take you to the supermarket.' John laughed. 'How did it feel, being in a bank, then, John?'

Lennon answered: 'It felt exactly the same as anywhere else. All I did was autograph bits of paper.'

The famous record producer Lou Adler had loaned John and May Pang a house on Stone Canyon Road, Bel Air. 'He was incredibly unhappy because of his estrangement from Yoko during the entire "lost weekend",' says Mintz. 'It was the low point of his life. Three days after arriving, at 10 o'clock in the morning, he arrived outside my house shouting: "Wake up, wake up. I've been trying to get you on the phone." I was astonished to see him up so early. I asked: "How long have you been up?" He said: "I haven't been to sleep yet. Can you get Yoko on the phone for me?" He was having trouble with the phones and with the time difference between California and New York. I later asked him why he appeared so low, during that period, and he said that he felt alienated, lost, and consistently unhappy, especially when he was drunk. It was a vicious circle: the more morose John became, the more he drank and the more depressed he became. And the worst thing I can say about my old friend John Lennon,' says Mintz, 'is that he was a lousy drinker. He just couldn't handle booze.

'The Los Angeles months marked the end of an era for John. The wild streak that showed itself in the Lennon of the Liverpool back streets and, later, of Hamburg ended on the Sunset Strip in Hollywood. Later he told me that he just wanted to show the boys that he could get as low as any of them. He could drink more, stay awake longer, play more rock 'n' roll music, and be just as outrageous as the rest of them. It was a restless farewell to a persona he had already outgrown. That crazy recording session with Phil Spector, whom he loved and admired; the bar hopping with Keith Moon, Harry Nilsson, and Ringo; the Hollywood parties and the nights that knew no end; all of it was an exercise in letting go. If most people did any of those things it would mean nothing. When John Lennon did it, the effect became larger than the reality of the actual events.'

Lennon's behaviour in Los Angeles filled him with remorse and regret; it was infinitely worse than his days in Hamburg. There at least he had the excuse that he was a young man on the prowl. Now, in California with the woman he loved back in New York, monitoring his every move and telling him he was in no state to return to her, John plunged down and down. His wild behaviour included a drunken audience with Jerry Lee Lewis and a ridiculous exhibition of foul-mouthed drunkenness, interrupting the Smothers Brothers show at the Troubadour Club on Sunset Boulevard. Worst of all was when he went on the rampage in the house at Bel Air. With musicians who had been drinking at Phil Spector's record session, John had returned to the house drunk on vodka. He became violent and went round smashing the gold records hanging on the wall (one for Carole King's multi-million-selling *Tapestry* album), throwing vases against stained glass windows, wrecking furniture, tables, and chairs. For his own safety, Spector and his bodyguard put Lennon – who had smashed his spectacles – into bed, tying his wrists and ankles to prevent him doing any more damage. A horrified Mintz got an alarm call from May Pang and was at the house within minutes. May was concerned for John's safety. A drunken Lennon

screamed at May: 'Keep that bastard Jew away from me.'
Mintz left.

By next morning John had forgotten nearly everything.
He told May Pang to assure Lou Adler that he would meet
the cost of all the repairs to his house and contents. His
first call of apology was to Mintz. 'In all the time I've
known you,' he said contritely, 'the very worst thing I could
think of to say to you was that you were a bastard Jew. I
guess I really must love you.' Then he phoned everybody
else.

John's drunkenness in California probably extended to
about a dozen times in the whole fifteen months; unfortunately on too many occasions he got drunk in public. And
he drank anything that had the right effect. 'Give me a
Remy Martin, a B&B, a Courvoisier, an Amaretto, a Tia
Maria, anything of that sort,' he'd tell the waitress or
bartender. He ate chocolate and candies and junk food.

When John was sober, Mintz would try to tell him he
was making a fool of himself. Lennon's rejoinders were as
caustic as they had been during his Hamburg and Beatle
days: 'Don't get real on me. If you don't like being around
me when I'm that way, why don't you just fuck off?' Next
day, full of regret, he would apologize – in his fashion:
'Why did you stay with me last night? God, if you were
that way, I'd not stay with *you!*'

Tough, cynical, angry, bitter, and confused, John leaned
on drink for the same reason he always had: he was insecure.
He desperately wanted to return to Yoko after only a week,
but the sober lady, busy pursuing her career in New York
as an avant-garde artist and poet, was not listening to his
pleas. They talked frequently by telephone, sometimes for
minutes, sometimes for hours. John explained that one of
the reasons why he was getting drunk so easily was because
his body's resistance to alcohol had been reduced by the

drugs he had taken at the height of his days as a Beatle. 'All of his thoughts, all of his longing, had to do with his desperation to get back to Yoko, and to his frustration with her telling him he didn't sound ready,' says Mintz. 'Although he said he was ready to return it was clear he was not.' While he fretted, however, Yoko told her friends that she was certain she and John would re-unite one day. It was only a matter of time.

Confirming Lennon's inability to handle liquor, Mintz says: 'If he had one glass of wine, I'd have to cancel all plans for the next three days. And he was so argumentative! He would start an argument and keep it going just for the sake of having a row and winning it. The basis of the argument was not so important as the row itself. But he was never evil or terrible – just drunk. I saw him that way twice in Las Vegas, once in Japan, twice in New York, and perhaps a dozen times in Los Angeles.'

But John crossed certain personal frontiers in California. Elliot Mintz took him to see one of his favourite artists, Jerry Lee Lewis, at the Roxy in Los Angeles. 'I had only three childhood idols,' he told Mintz. 'Elvis, Carl Perkins, and Jerry Lee, and I haven't seen any live. Let's go!' John was totally immersed in the driving rock 'n' roll that had first inspired him, classics like 'Whole Lotta Shakin'' and 'Great Balls of Fire'. Jerry Lee did his wildest show, playing the piano with his toes. Lennon led the applause at the end of each song. After the show Elliot took John backstage and introduced him to Lewis. John just sank to the floor, and kissed Jerry Lee's shoes. 'That's all right, son,' drawled Jerry Lee. 'You just get up now.'

The encounter had a strange parallel with the occasion on which he had met Elvis. There was, he decided, no future in talking to artists. 'I'm a record man,' he told me.

'I don't like live work or going to concerts. They usually
let you down.'

Ten years earlier, living at Weybridge with Cynthia, John
had a sign hanging in his kitchen. It said simply: 'The
drunk and the glutton shall come to poverty.' It would be
easy to view the California debacle as a worthless alcoholic
escapade, but in many ways it was essential because John
had never had a chance to grow up. It had all been done
in public as a musician. This gave him the opportunity.
One of his biggest dreams was to experience Las Vegas.
'What's it like, what's it like, Elliot?' he kept asking Mintz.
'Take me there. Fix me a drink and we'll go.' One drizzly
day Mintz agreed to take him. 'But John, take it easy. If
we're going to Las Vegas, let's at least get there sober.'
    As they drove down La Cienega, not far from Mintz's
home, John's eye was caught by a flashing sign: 'The Losers'
Topless Club'. 'Feels right,' he said to Mintz. 'Let's pull in.'
Mintz was incredulous: it was two o'clock in the afternoon.
Once in the bar, with the topless barmaid filling up his
glass as quickly as he drank and Motown records
accompanying the two topless dancers, John became more
and more uneasy. He quickly realized the futility and sleaz-
iness of it all. Even in California he was able to diagnose
bad taste through his alcoholic hazes. After a few minutes
John had seen enough. 'As we left The Losers,' recalls
Mintz, 'John started singing softly in my ear: "We make
them paint their face and dance – Woman is Nigger of
the world." He could be the observer and the observed
simultaneously.'
    In Las Vegas John acted out all his fantasies. At Caesar's
Palace John 'was enchanted by the casino atmosphere for a
while, but it was the longest weekend of my life,' says

Elliot Mintz. 'The house kept us supplied with drinks and we sat in the chairs by the roulette wheel for hours. He devised the John Lennon Las Vegas system; taking a ten-dollar chip and placing it on every number on the table. John became convinced he had a system that would guarantee him a 35–1 win with each turn of the wheel. The plan was less than successful. The gambling over, we went for a walk around the casino until the spotlight fell on him and four hundred people besieged him. Cocktail hostesses began fawning over him, saying things like: "Hey, I grew up listening to the Beatles." And John was off. The plastic, crazy, neon city of Las Vegas was even more empty to him than Los Angeles. And even LA he had christened as "the place you stop off to buy a hamburger".'

John consoled his sorrows over drinking sessions with friends Harry Nilsson, Keith Moon, Klaus Voormann, Ringo Starr, Jim Keltner, and Mal Evans, 'Big Mal', the faithful friend from Liverpool days who had been the Beatles' road manager. Evans, whose giant frame belied his soft, warm personality, was a former telephone engineer who drifted into the Beatles camp by doing part-time work as a bouncer at the Cavern. As road manager alongside Neil Aspinall on all the Beatles' world tours, he had a particularly strong relationship – gruff but intuitive – with the moody Lennon during Beatlemania. When the Beatles split, Mal felt lost. He moved to Los Angeles, fell victim to drink and drugs, and allegedly pulled a gun on a girl in his Hollywood flat on 5 January 1976. The police were called, but Mal barricaded himself in. They smashed the door down to be confronted by Mal holding a gun; they shot him dead. The news of yet another fatality in the Beatles family saddened John, but he coped with it as he had with all other tragedies: by not dwelling on it for long.

George Melly, whose meetings with John seemed to

punctuate key events in Lennon's life – the Beatles, meeting Yoko, and estrangement from her – was in a bungalow at Hollywood's Chateau Marmont Hotel when an aggressive John arrived at dawn with Harry Nilsson and Derek Taylor. 'I wouldn't guarantee what substances were involved in creating his condition,' says Melly, 'but certainly drink was a contributory one. They were all high on an all-night raid. Suddenly one of us mentioned Jackie Pye, the Liverpool wrestler. He was famous in Liverpool as the baddie of the wrestling circuit. Although John was much younger than me, Jackie Pye, it turned out, had spanned our youth. We had both seen him. His favourite trick was blowing his nose between his thumb and forefinger and flicking the snot at the referee. He was known as Dirty Jackie Pye. Once we hit this area of shared knowledge we were in hysterics.' Amid the palm trees of Hollywood, two lapsed Liverpudlians recalled an eccentric slice of their youth.

Four months later a similarly wild John arrived in New York and headed for Derek Taylor's suite at the Algonquin Hotel. With Harry Nilsson again, John was drunk and began trying to smash the chandeliers in Derek's suite. The next thing that happened was a 2:00 am phone call in the hotel to George Melly's female publicity agent. 'He demanded sex with her,' says Melly. 'She replied: "I'm asleep. Go away." I couldn't help reflecting, when I heard about it next morning, on the number of girls around the world who would have received that phone call from John Lennon with a certain enthusiasm.'

As John described his songs as 'personalized diaries', it was not surprising that the music he made during the separation period comprised messages to Yoko and elements of self-pity. *Walls And Bridges*, an album made during the California period, included such songs as 'Nobody Loves You (When You're Down And Out)'. I asked him what he meant by the enigmatic album title. He answered: 'Walls you walk into and bridges you cross over. Deep stuff!'

The biggest psychological bridge John had to cross during his absence from Yoko was a meeting with Julian, who was then ten and living with Cynthia. They had spoken on the phone, on Cynthia's insistence, regularly since John had gone to America. But for nearly three years they had not met. Cynthia believed that as John was isolated in California, he should see Julian. This caused John anguish and torment right up until Julian's visit. He believed that he had been a neglectful father, and he could not summon up the inner strength to pick up the pieces.

When Cynthia and Julian flew into Los Angeles Airport just after Christmas 1974, John was nervous. He had no idea of how his reunion with his son would go and whether the boy would warm to him. And he dreaded seeing Cynthia again. Once a link had been broken, especially such a strong one, John felt that it should be severed for ever. Mentally he was a million miles away from life with Cynthia in Liverpool and Weybridge. There was the extra complication of her meeting May Pang.

At the airport and in the limousine that took Cynthia and Julian to their hotel, John was jittery. He was cool with Cynthia; a 'hello' and a peck on the cheek was all he could manage. But Julian's excited chatter about the flight on a jumbo jet and arrival in America broke the ice on the car ride. John realized how thrilled he felt to see Julian and kissed him affectionately.

Next day, the plan was for John to take Julian, alone, to Disneyland. Says Cynthia: 'John wanted to whip into the hotel, take Julian away, and not communicate with me which was fine by me. Unfortunately, Julian flew into a tantrum in his bedroom, screaming on the floor, hysterical.'

Julian dug his heels in, insisting he wanted his mother *and* father on the outing.

'Look, John,' said Cynthia, 'I'm sorry but he won't go anywhere with you without me. You can hear him in the other room.' Reluctantly John gave in.

A tense day for John, Cynthia, and May and Mal Evans followed. 'I felt miserable trailing round Disneyland with them, but Julian had a great time and that's what mattered.' Still John would not face Cynthia, who stayed several stages behind the party for most of the time. 'John could not look me in the eyes,' says Cynthia. 'He seemed in a total panic that we might start talking and he avoided looking near me as much as he could for the whole day.' They were forced together for a lunch of bacon and flapjacks and syrup, with John talking in a stilted fashion about the virtues of American junk-food, but the atmosphere was awful.

As well as being 'deeply upset' by John's aloofness, the ever-practical Cynthia was worried about Julian. 'I wanted a proper conversation with John about Julian's education, his future, and what he thought should be done for our son. I pushed once or twice but John looked the other way. After two or three rebuffs I gave up. I just hoped that the relationship between John and Julian would gain strength.'

And it did. The boy went off with a handful of balloons and many hugs and kisses from his dad. Their friendship developed warmly in later years, as Julian confirms. One of the reasons for this was Julian's own musical talent, which showed itself even at this age.

By the late 1970s Julian as a teenager was establishing a friendship with John. 'It was more of one man to another than the usual father and son relationship,' says Julian, 'because he had been away from me a lot, and he said he realized that. I was just getting through to him and growing up myself and growing out of the silly giggling I did as a young teenager that really annoyed him, when Dad was killed.' He sorely regrets being robbed of the time to develop the bond that was growing between them.

As Julian moved inexorably towards a life in music, he developed a particularly strong rapport with Sean. 'I feel a terrific blood closeness with Sean,' says Julian. 'We're going to get on well.' His relationship with his stepmother, on the other hand, will always require diplomacy. Yoko and Cynthia have kept a wary distance from each other since the divorce. 'I'll feel better with both my mother and Yoko when I'm older and more established on my own ground as a musician,' said Julian in 1984. 'I like to keep an open line with everyone and not hurt anybody's feelings.' Both personally and professionally as a singer-songwriter, being the son of John Lennon will never be easy.

By 1983, at the age of twenty, Julian had dropped his teenage plans to launch a group with the name of the Lennon Drops, and arrived in London, alone, to set up a flat and tackle, head-on, the job of becoming a singer-songwriter-bandleader. Tony Stratton Smith, boss of Charisma Records, was highly impressed with Julian's songwriting and sent him for six weeks to an obscure château in France where Julian's confidence, as well as his musicianship, improved enormously. He was initially signed to Charisma and secured the support of the outstanding American producer Phil Ramone, who has worked with major artists of the calibre of Paul Simon, Billy Joel, Frank Sinatra, and Bob Dylan.

Julian was totally aware of the pitfalls and expected to be accused of cashing in on his father's name. Clearly he was in a 'no-win' situation. However, 'I just have to do it,' he told me. 'Partly, I feel that with my father dead someone should keep the tradition alive. He was a major, successful singer and writer and it's up to me to try to carry on to keep the name Lennon going in the field of music.

'I feel music in my blood. It would be asking for trouble to do it my father's way and style.' Vocal similarities with John are obvious: 'I can tell the sound is similar when I hear myself, but I don't do it consciously. I did love the way Dad sang, and there's nothing wrong with taking a bit of inspiration from him, surely? Others do, so I don't see why I shouldn't. His work has influenced me, but I'm very self-conscious about the criticism that is bound to come. It's both an advantage and a disadvantage being the son of John Lennon. I'm determined to live it down and live it up! I feel confident I can handle it and grow as a songwriter and singer. Dad told me the Beatles thing was something he enjoyed breaking away from and in a sense I'm trying to break away from him while remaining Julian Lennon all my life. He would understand. Dad's best work came when the Beatles finished. . . . He told me the Beatles were fun while they lasted but he would never do it again.'

Cynthia's last, bitter experience of John occurred on a flight from New York to Los Angeles. Again, John was with May Pang, and Julian, who had been with him in New York during the making of the *Walls And Bridges* album; Julian had even played the drums on one track called 'Ya Ya'. While Cynthia had stayed at the Pierre Hotel in New York, Julian had stayed with John and May. After a few days a cheery John had phoned his former wife and asked her to go with them to Los Angeles. Cynthia thought that perhaps the breakthrough had come and they could have a decent relationship. She looked forward to the five-hour flight.

But when they boarded the plane, John's mental barricade went up again. He was with May and Julian in the first-class section, completely ignoring Cynthia, who was sitting behind them, for the entire journey. 'It was total and utter rejection,' she remembers. 'I couldn't get through. I'd fought hard to get John and Julian together, in ways John would never know about. But whenever we looked at each other, it was like utter panic by John. He couldn't cope with me. He must have felt threatened by me, that I was after him and wanted him and me to get back together. But I wasn't. All I wanted was mental communication for the sake of the one thing in life John and I still had in common: a son. I shall never understand why two people who had a child could not talk normally without threats or worries or fear.' Finally Cynthia broke down on the plane and wept. It was the last time she saw him.

Such was John's state during his separation from Yoko that it is amazing that he reached out to his son, establishing the basis for their future mental rapport, as well as making some superb music with lyrics sharply evocative of his mental condition. To cope with his former wife, in addition, and all the memories she evoked, was impossible for him that year. At the time the estrangement from Yoko was enough of a problem.

In New York in mid-1974 I spent two days and nights with John while he was making *Walls And Bridges*. He talked openly about his depression, how he was missing Yoko, but that he expected they would re-unite. He was living with May Pang in a modest, one-room apartment at 434 East 52nd Street, overlooking the East River. He loved cities with rivers, he said; New York's affinity with Liverpool made him nostalgic. In the Record Plant studios John was at his mercurial best, changing lyrics and putting the gloss on some of his new songs. One evening over a Chinese meal he talked at length to me, both about his life as a

New Yorker and how he was gradually coming to terms with realizing what went on in the Beatles years.

That year George Harrison played a solo tour of America, and John was rumoured to be planning to play at his New York concert. In the end he didn't because he had a row with George over what John called 'The Famous Beatles Agreement', the final dissolution of the group that required all four signatures. John was the last to sign. 'I was supposed to sign this on the day of the concert but I wouldn't. My astrologer told me it was the wrong day for business. [John finally signed the same day he visited Disneyland with Julian.] George was furious at the time because I hadn't signed it when I was supposed to and I was informed that I needn't bother to go to George's show. I was relieved because there wasn't any time for rehearsal and I didn't want it to be a case of John jumping up and playing a few chords. I went to see George at Nassau and it was a good, tight show. George's voice was shot but the atmosphere was good and George's performance was great. I saw George after the Madison Square Garden show and we were friends again.' Harrison had resolutely refused to sing major Beatles hits on the tour – 'a basic mistake,' said John, 'easy to spot when you're not making one. But people definitely wanted to hear the old stuff.' The songs George did perform included John's 'In My Life', though with slightly altered lyrics; 'Something'; 'While My Guitar Gently Weeps'; and 'For You Blue'.

In the past two years, John said, he had changed his attitude towards the Beatles. 'The period when I rejected the Beatles years in my mind was when I was just out of the Janov therapy treatment,' he explained. 'I'd been mentally stripped bare and I wanted to shoot my mouth off to clear it all away. Now it's different.

'When I slagged off the Beatles thing, it was like

divorce pangs and, me being me, it was blast this, fuck the past. Remember all those articles we did together in the old *Melody Maker* – "Lennon Blasts Hollies" all over the back page? And the *Daily Mirror* piece: "Lennon Beats Up Local DJ At Paul's 21st Birthday Party!" I've always had a bit of a mouth and when a thing begins that way, you have to live up to it. Then Paul and me had that fight in the pages of the *MM*. It was a period I had to go through. I sort of enjoy the fight at the time, that's the funny thing.

'Now we've all got it out and it's cool. I can see the Beatles from a new point of view. Can't remember much of what happened but I've started taking an interest in what went on while I was in that fish tank. It must have been incredible.'

Part of John's therapy in growing out of the Beatles was to recognize their importance to his life. On a long car journey across America he took a pile of Beatles cassettes to re-acquaint himself with the work which nobody would forget. And when, in 1974, America's devoted Beatles fans made it possible to stage a Beatlefest, John wanted to be counted in as a fan of his old group. Beatles films, guitars from John and Paul, Ringo's old drumsticks, and other memorabilia were gathered by John when he met Mark Lapidos, who was then launching the Beatlefest at New York's Commodore Hotel, and who still runs the conventions several times a year all around America. 'John nearly even came to the first one to pick the winner of the charity raffle and see who won his old guitar,' says Lapidos. 'But he chickened out at the last minute.' John did, however, enthuse to Lapidos about the whole idea of Beatlefests which have since become established throughout America.

Four years later a Beatlefest assistant, Roger Berkley, bumped into John in the street and told him that the 1978 convention was coming soon. Had John any message? 'Yeah, just tell them the music was the thing,' replied John. It had taken a long time, but John Lennon had come to terms with being an ex-Beatle. He even enjoyed it.

'I'm into collecting memorabilia as well,' he told me in our interviews. 'Elton John came in with these gifts for me, stills from the *Yellow Submarine* film. Great! He gave me these four dolls of John, Paul, George, and Ringo. I thought: Christ, what's *this?* A Beatle collecting Beatle dolls? But why not? It's history, man, history. I went through a phase of hating all those years and having to smile when I didn't want to, but now I'm out of it, it's great to look back on it, man. Great! Why haven't I ever considered the good times instead of moaning about what we had to go through?'

He had even gone some way towards mending his relationship with McCartney. 'He was here in New York recently. We spent two or three nights together talking about the old days. It was cool, seeing what each other remembered from Hamburg and Liverpool. So y'see, all that happened when I blew my mouth off was that it was like an abscess bursting, except that mine, as usual, burst in public.

'Look, when the Beatles did a tour, we hated it and loved it. There were great nights and lousy ones. . . . It wasn't all pie and cookies being a Beatle but in 1970 people just wanted big-mouth Lennon to shout about the lows. So I made a quick trip [his therapy with Janov] to uncover the hidden stones of my mind and a lot of the bats flew and some of them are going to have to stay. I've got a perspective now, that's a fact.' He must have exorcized the ghosts because he even went to the Broadway production of the successful theatrical production *Sgt Pepper*; watching it would have been like looking into the mirror of his own mind as well as his body.

John loved buttons. On the nights I saw him his badge was half an apple between bread slices. 'Work that one out,' he said. 'It doesn't mean that I own half of Apple. Elton gave me the badge. It means I'm schizophrenic!'

John was alive, crackling with good humour and his old rapier-like observation. Leaving the recording studio, he walked with me for five minutes before hailing a cab. I mentioned that it was a strange contrast with the police-protected limousine rides he had been used to. Ah, he said, that was precisely what he loved about New York. 'I get 'em all the time. Not in California – they're looking for stars there and it's unsafe. But here in New York, I found all the paranoia was inside my own head. It's so safe here. I feel free, walking the streets. Nobody hassles you. I reckon most of the cab drivers in New York know me, I've taken so many, and I *love* seeing the city from the inside of a cab.'

At the end of the journey, John, always an enormously generous tipper, gave the cabbie $10 for a trip that cost less than half that amount.

'Excuse me, sir,' said the cab driver, 'but aren't you John Lennon?'

'Nah,' said John. 'I wish I was. I wish I had his money.'

Inside his apartment John regaled me and photographer Bob Gruen with the bizarre story that he had seen flying saucers from his window. He was serious. 'Look,' he said, 'it's true. I was standing, naked, by this window leading on to that roof when an oval-shaped object started flying from left to right. It had a red light on the top. After about twenty minutes it disappeared over the East River and behind the United Nations Building. I wonder if it might have been carrying out some research there.

'They all think I'm potty, but it's true. I shouted after it, "Wait for me, wait for me!" But I'm not kidding, May and I saw it. I didn't believe it either.' He had phoned the police, who said there had been other reports of the sighting of a flying saucer. 'But I didn't tell them who it was on the phone. I didn't want newspaper headlines saying: "Beatle Sees Flying Saucer". I've got enough trouble with the immigration people already.'

'And you'd not been smoking or drinking?' I said.

'No, God's honest truth. I only do that at weekends or when I see Harry Nilsson.'

We watched television for hours. John watched himself on a news bulletin coming out of court earlier that day where he had been to listen to yet another round in his immigration battle. Reporters, surprised to see John formally dressed in dark suit and tie, asked him if he was confident of winning his case.

'Yes, I'm confident,' said John.

'Why?' asked a reporter.

'Because I'm big-headed, as usual,' said John. 'I like it here. I want to stay. Amnesty! Amnesty!

'It's absolutely alive, that's why I have got to live in New York and got sick of Los Angeles,' John told me. 'There's a buzz here. I like the way you can get or do anything you like at any time of the day or night. . . . If I couldn't live here, I'd live in Paris. I love the French. They're so bloody rude.

'Look here, New York gives you television all night. It's better than the BBC Light Orchestra.'

John had been consumed by the Watergate scandal. 'Any country,' he said, 'that produces the Watergate affair has got to be number one with me. I sat watching every bit of it on TV and couldn't believe it. They kept asking the witnesses questions and the guy replied: "That is inoperative." Everything they were asked that was meant to make 'em tell the truth, they said: "That is inoperative." I'm

gonna try it when they start asking me hard questions.
"Inoperative. All questions about the Beatles inoperative." '

Part of John's fascination for Watergate can be traced
to his love of causes: he loved wearing buttons that championed people or attitudes and during 1975 wore one saying
simply 'Elvis'. Other badges, or 'buttons' as he grew to call
them when his language became peppered with American-
isms, included 'Indict Rockefeller for murder', 'Listen to
this button', and 'Not Insane', a phrase coined by the parody
group Firesign Theatre.

Throughout 1974 John made a determined, conscious effort
to pull himself back from the precipice of emotional and
intellectual disaster which threatened him during his Cali-
fornian exile. He drank less. He made music. He immersed
himself in serious subjects like Watergate during his own
immigration battle. He even demonstrated to Britain that
the appalling international publicity he had received in Los
Angeles did not reflect a numbing of his sense or his
memory. When singer-songwriter Todd Rundgren criticized
his activities in the *Melody Maker*, John tore into him with
the same ruthlessness he had used against Paul McCartney.
In a style that combined his old satire with vitriol, John
wrote Todd (whom he called Sodd Runtlestuntle) an hilarious letter he called 'Opened Lettuce'.

One of the highlights of the year and a turning point
in his life came when he went to Caribou recording
studios in Colorado to record with Elton John. The two
men were warm friends. Elton, a total fan of 1960s music,
loved the mixture of hard man and soft romantic in John
which all who knew him recognized under that sometimes
manic exterior. Lennon, for his part, thought Elton's music
and his industry were magnificent. He loved the nature of

the man, his stage act, and his songs. Elton had worked in Dick James's music publishing office in London when the Beatles had sent in their demonstration tapes, so the link with John went back a long way. (Lennon was always attracted to extroverts; he sought only one autograph in his life, and that was Mae West's, secured for him by Elliot Mintz. 'Now, what's this fella's last name?' Mae West asked as she signed.)

    John's song 'Whatever Gets You Thru The Night', on which Elton played keyboards, was his first chart-topper in America as a soloist. When they made the record, Elton told John that it was a number one; John laughed at him. 'No, I'm out of favour here. It would be nice but it's not a number one.' Elton made John promise that if it did reach the top, he would appear in concert with him. John was so certain it would not that he readily agreed. And so the stage was set for John to appear at Elton's Madison Square Garden concert on Thanksgiving Day, 28 November 1974.

    Before he was committed to the New York show, John went to see Elton's concert in Boston and he remembered thinking, Thank God it's not me, as he watched Elton dressing to go on. 'I got stage fright just looking at him!' said John. 'By the time I got on to the stage at Madison Square Garden with all the screaming and shouting [twenty thousand people gave Lennon a conquering hero's welcome], I thought what is *this!* I hadn't heard it since the Beatles. The place was really rocking.'

    Elton wanted John to sing 'Imagine', but Lennon flatly refused. 'I didn't want to come on like Dean Martin, doing my classic hits. I wanted to have some fun and play some rock 'n' roll. And I didn't want to do more than three because it was Elton's show.' As well as the number one hit, John sang 'I Saw Her Standing There' and 'Lucy In The Sky With Diamonds'.

The significance of the show lay in much more than John's appearance. Elton had remained very friendly with Yoko during John's separation. Backstage before they went on, John received a gardenia with the message: 'Good luck, love, Yoko'. 'Hey,' John said to Elton. 'Look what Yoko sent me. I'm glad she's not here tonight. I'd never be able to go on.'

But Yoko was in the audience, shedding tears of joy at John's triumphant performance. Elton, in on the secret, had told her he wouldn't 'let on' to John, or neither Lennon nor he would have been able to perform. Backstage, John was floored when she walked into the dressing-room. Although they had spoken literally thousands of times on the phone, they had not seen each other for a year.

'You were great, John,' she said simply. She looked poised and attractive; John was palpably emotional at seeing her. It was one of the best moments of his life.

Before the show John had talked about their separation to me: 'Yoko and I, well we had this little falling out. We're two artists and we found it hard living together. We'll see what happens. I still speak to her on the phone most days. She phoned me from London the other day and said: "Hey, it's nice here. Remember the autumn with all the leaves?" And I said: "What are you trying to say, Yoko? I know it's nice, but are you trying to unsettle me in New York? It's nice *here* − remember the noise?"'

January 1975 proved the watershed month. John had been for several talks with Yoko to maintain contact. Finally he phoned and told her he was fit and ready, in every way, to return. And he did, after a reunion afternoon tea at the Plaza Hotel. Symbolically, that same month the Beatles as a business enterprise were finally dissolved in the High Court in London.

'I'm as happy as Larry to be back with her,' said John. 'It was a tough year for me. It's all right wondering whether the grass is greener on the other side but once you get there all you find is more grass. I don't know whether I'll ever learn that lesson about life. We had a mutual separation and a mutual getting back together. Look, she ain't no chick that you say: "OK, I'll see you Friday," or, "I'm coming back Monday." You're dealing with a fully aware human being. There's no treating her like your chick, you know . . .

'It fell in place again. It was like I never left. I realized this was where I belonged. I think we both knew we'd get back together again sooner or later, even if it was five years, and that's why we never bothered with divorce. I'm just glad she let me back in again. I was allowed back! It was like going out for a drink but it took me a year to get it.'

In talking about his love for Yoko, John was able to look at their period of separation with a new perspective. 'I'm the one who's supposed to know everything, but she's my teacher. She's taught me everything I know. The lessons are hard and I can't take it sometimes and *that's* why I freaked out. When we were separate, it was *me* making an asshole of myself in the clubs and in the newspapers. It wasn't her. She missed me as a human being and she loved me but *her* life was ordered. *I* went back to *her* life. It wasn't the other way round.' Drily, he added: 'Yoko and I are proud to say that our separation was a failure.'

The period of estrangement and the terms of the reunion were an exceptional example of one woman's love of her man. Yoko's surveillance of John's activities, particularly with May Pang in Los Angeles when she monitored their every move from the Dakota – much to their chagrin and astonishment – reached epic proportions. Yoko's telephone calls to John were often less than five minutes apart; as soon as he put the phone down she would ring again, or *he* would ring back with something that was on his mind in connection with business, or to pass the time of day by recounting his activities. She knew every twist and turn of his drunken extravaganzas. And it said much for John's desire to rehabilitate himself that not once, given the freedom and three-thousand-mile distance from New York to Los Angeles, did he move anywhere without Yoko knowing his phone number.

The fifteen-month 'lost weekend' ended after many pleas by John to be allowed back. 'I'm ready to come home,' he said, so often.

'No you're not, not yet,' she replied.

Yoko kept him totally informed about the business machinery which she was keeping well oiled, increasing their prosperity. Finally, when she eventually told him by telephone to come home, her conditions were, like her own personality, simple but serious and demanding: he would have to act with more maturity; not drink; travel alone frequently to keep their relationship fresh and assert his individuality; and not relapse into the self-pitying attitude that had caused their rift. In brief, she demanded that he return to the positive thinking and firm discipline that had marked the John Lennon she once knew. John reacted well to the unpalatable truth that he had been impossible to live with.

This reunion and John's house-husband period made Yoko seem to many people a manipulating, psychic, power-wielding egotist who would stop at nothing to get her way. This judgement hid the truth from people who didn't want to face it: Yoko's appeal, to John and the people close to her, was that she was such a strong-minded, artistic individualist. She combined all this with a fearsome practicality. Above all, she would not tolerate weakness in people. Many people who were aware of their own frailties winced at Yoko's intuitive recognition of their failure to do anything about them. John did not; he wanted his woman forceful, intelligent, powerful, domineering, and one step ahead of the game.

He loved Yoko and knew he needed her to reassert himself both creatively and as a man. 'He was a simple, but complex man,' reflects Yoko. 'I mean, when we got back together after that separation, John said he had gone out for a walk for the morning paper and a cup of coffee and hadn't bothered to return. In a way, it *was* like that. At that time, we couldn't live together and we couldn't live apart properly either. But we did know it was just a matter of time straightening things out.'

Not for nothing did John call Yoko 'Mother' – to her face, and to their friends, and in little notes he left on the kitchen table. As well as being his lover, she was a distinctly maternal figure to him and, as Yoko herself says, a substitute for his Aunt Mimi.

TWENTY-TWO

SECLUSION

'Sean may not have come from my belly but I'm gonna make his bones'

BY HIS early thirties John Ono Lennon had travelled mental and physical journeys that most people cannot hope for in a lifetime. Not all of his breadth of vision had stemmed from his millionaire status; if the money had given him freedom, it had also imprisoned him. Material possessions, anyway, had never been his first priority on becoming successful. As he had demonstrated when he embraced Yoko Ono in 1966, the star trip of being a Beatle was not enough to satisfy him. He always needed intellectual stimulation, and New York provided it.

Back at the Dakota, he was a totally transformed man. He talked about the major change of direction in his life. 'The idea of being a rock 'n' roll musician and artist sort of suited my talents and mentality and the freedom was great,' said John. 'But then I felt boxed in. I found out I wasn't free, and it wasn't because of a contract. The contract was a physical manifestation of being in prison. I might as well have gone to a nine-to-five job, as carry on the way I was carrying on. And there's two ways to go. You either go to Las Vegas and sing your great hits, *if you're lucky*, or you go to hell, you know, actually literally *dying*,' he told David Sheff.

John was always a restless man, in constant need of new challenges. It took him a long time to throw off his rock 'n' roll restrictions, but America was the melting pot in which he finally outgrew pop stardom and impressed himself on the world as a great man. The peace campaign had taken a long time to sink into the world's consciousness as something real and genuine. People had been slow to realize that even a young Beatle could have important qualities of leadership, however much he rejected the role. It took even longer for them to accept that the tough, loud-mouthed Lennon was, underneath, exactly the opposite. His ability to project that difference and articulate a warm humanitarianism, both in his music and by example, made him a model for generations of libertarians.

One of the popular myths about Lennon has been that he was tough, hard-hearted, vicious, and unsentimental. One of the great myths about Yoko Ono is that she is a manipulative witch, power-hungry, and cold. The reverse is true in both cases. Lennon was incurably romantic all his life, and that quality manifested itself with great intensity after his reunion with Yoko. Yoko too has often been emotional, tearful, and compassionate.

What gave her a reputation for toughness and what John loved was her industriousness, tenacity, and her enjoyment of business. Her concentration on detail and her memory are legendary. Her energy level floors everyone around her; she is not an orthodox sleeper by night, but during the day takes five or six fifteen-minute 'catnaps'. Most mornings she is behind her office desk before nine.

'She's an original,' John told me. 'And she can come on as strong as any man. She's usually ahead of all of us. And at the same time, she's a woman. And when you meet someone like that, you drop everything. It's goodbye to the gang you used to drink with. Or, in my case, the guys in the band. You don't go and play football any more. Once I found *the* woman, the boys became of no interest whatsoever, other than that they were like old schoolfriends: "Hi, how are you, nice to see you. How's your wife?" That old gang of mine was over the moment I met Yoko – that was the end of the boys. It just so happened the boys were well known and weren't just the local guys at the bar. Coming face to face with anyone like her was something I never expected to do.' He was besotted with this woman who often gave him a hard time, rebuked him for his deficiencies, and advised him to stop drinking and become a fanatical health enthusiast. Yoko, a non-drinker, eventually banned alcohol in the Dakota.

A few weeks after their reunion, John had good reason to heed her words. Yoko was pregnant. By spring 1975, a happy John was sending postcards to half a dozen of their closest friends: 'Here's a hard one for you to take: not only are John and Yoko back together. They're pregnant.'

Like so many major events surrounding the couple, the pregnancy was not an accident. And there had been problems leading up to it. In 1972, a year before their separation, they had visited San Francisco. There, through a journalist friend, they were introduced to a ninety-five-year-old Chinese herbalist and acupuncturist, Dr Hong. John was worried about his health. For about twelve years, since the Hamburg days and throughout Beatlemania and his early relationship with Yoko, he had abused his body. Pep pills in Hamburg had led to marijuana and LSD in the Beatles years; he had tried heroin but, being in favour of living, had quickly rejected it.

He continued to smoke marijuana occasionally in his early days in New York. By 1972, however, John was found to have a low sperm count. It was thought it might be a result of the punishment he had meted out to his body. Dr

Hong, he was advised, might be able to help. The doctor's advice was given to both: John had to renounce all drugs except cigarettes and go easy on alcohol. For Yoko, the doctor prescribed a 'magic potion' which would increase the chance of her fertility. Her age, thirty-nine then, was not a problem, said the doctor. They would eventually have a child, he said, if they lived cleanly and ate healthily. As it turned out John's 'lost weekend' got in the way of the doctor's advice, but by the time he returned to Yoko he was in good shape. The Lennon I saw frequently during the last six months of 1974 was sober, lean, fit, and clearly determined to stay that way.

So when Yoko announced her pregnancy, John was thrilled but not completely surprised. The child was not merely a hope on the horizon. It had been desperately wanted and planned for – something of which they were both proud. It was, says Yoko, as if their getting back together was blessed.

John made one of the most crucial decisions of his life on learning of Yoko's pregnancy. For twelve years he had been involved in music-making and being a public figure, and a break would be timely. He decided to retire from the business voluntarily. He would concentrate on being a father-to-be and then a dad. Like a mother hen, he began fussing over Yoko in a way that amazed their friends. They perhaps did not realize that seven years earlier he had camped at Yoko's bedside during a miscarriage. True to his character John became totally immersed in every aspect of Yoko's pregnancy, reading baby books, going to health classes with her, cushioning her from stress, even to the point of being bossy. 'Stay right where you are. Don't move. If there's any rushing around to do, I'm gonna go.' He treated Yoko as if she were ill rather than pregnant. He was worried about her age – forty-two: she was very healthy, but she was slight and had already suffered three miscarriages while with John. He was not taking any chances.

Many parents, according to John, conceived their children as 'Saturday night specials'. In America, the phrase he chose was unfortunate: it means handguns that have not sold well during the week and are offered as bargains on Saturdays. What John meant was that most parents conceived their babies 'after a couple of glasses of Scotch, when restraint was cast to the wind.' He was fascinated by the fact that about a hundred million people in America, half the population, were under the age of forty, and were born as a result of the 1945 post-war baby boom. John and Yoko were particularly proud that their child was sought after with love.

One of Yoko's favourite indulgences was chocolate cake. John insisted she stayed in bed every morning while he ordered it from the Silver Palette store for her, together with any other food or drink she fancied. One day Elliot Mintz arrived from Los Angeles. 'Let's go and buy Mother some clothes,' said John. John and Yoko felt strongly that the politics of pregnancy in America were bizarre: the country worshipped perfect bodies, youth, and skinniness, and pregnancy seemed to be hidden. 'I think Yoko looks exquisite, beautiful,' John said as Yoko grew larger. He walked along Madison Avenue with Elliot until they saw a shop with beautiful silk and satin lingerie, and expensive dressing-gowns. Inside, he was characteristically generous, buying everything he thought Yoko might like. When it came to pay, John took out his gold American Express card, embossed with the name John Ono Lennon. Then the name of the store on the bill hit him straight between the eyes – it was called Lady Madonna. John burst our laughing.

The irony was that 'Lady Madonna' had been written by Paul. 'Another bloody McCartney song!' said John, laughing. In hotel lifts and restaurants everywhere he had been plagued for ten years by another McCartney gem, 'Yesterday'. In the Palm Court of New York's Plaza Hotel, where John liked to take afternoon tea, the violins would strike up 'Yesterday' in his honour, oblivious of the fact that he would have preferred 'Imagine'. Now 'Lady Madonna' was playing the same trick.

The usual crowd of about three hundred gapers pressed against the windows of Lady Madonna. John Lennon shopping for maternity wear was special. As John sprinted away for a taxi, a chauffeur chased him and said: 'Hey, Elton's in a limousine over there. He just came in from London and wants to give you a ride.' John ran across, and the two men embraced and went to Elton's hotel, the Pierre, where John told Elton of his 'retirement' plans.

Back at the Dakota Yoko looked appreciatively through the clothes that John had chosen. A woman who favoured simple and stark designs and colours, she was not particularly enamoured, particularly by the 'I love babies so much I'm having one' T-shirt which so amused John. She was touched, though, by his romantic shopping spree.

John and Yoko studied natural childbirth: 'It's not just Yoko giving birth to a child,' said John. 'It's both of us.' They attended classes for months and had very few visitors or doctors at the Dakota. The natural childbirth method, whereby the woman gives birth in a dark room and the father is present to see the baby placed immediately after birth against the mother's breast, excited both of them. 'Imagine, Elliot,' he said to Mintz, 'not having the baby touched by rubber gloves on its arrival in the world, but by skin straight away!'

John expected the child to be a boy, and he and Yoko went through books of names to check their meanings. When John went shopping for toys, he was incredulous at the amount of junk on sale in various shops. At Macy's department store, he looked at beds and finally decided there would be no cribs, which he described as 'wooden cages for kids'. Their child would sleep between him and Yoko for as long as possible; and he did.

At the peak of Yoko's pregnancy she looked in superb health thanks to John's nursing. He, too, was sharp, aware, and enjoying life. Just as Yoko went into hospital, John's long immigration battle was nearing its end. On 8 October 1975 a triumphant Leon Wildes phoned John to explain that he thought his Green Card application would be successful. 'Do me a favour, Leon,' John replied. 'I don't quite get this. I'm not following you. Look, Yoko's at the hospital, she's going to be induced in a couple of hours . . . stay right by your phone and I'll call you as soon as I'm there – you can explain it to Yoko.'

Yoko fully understood. Lying in bed in the New York Hospital private room in which Jacqueline Kennedy Onassis gave birth to Caroline Kennedy, she said on the phone: 'Come over with Ruth [Mrs Wildes] and let's all read the report together.' The four spent the night by Yoko's side. The Wildeses left the hospital at midnight. Two hours later, at 2:00 am, on John's thirty-fifth birthday, Yoko gave birth to a baby boy. It was a hazardous delivery. John was at the hospital throughout the period of the birth, but when things became tense he was not allowed in. The baby was born by Caesarean section, and Yoko, who had to be given a blood transfusion, nearly died.

John was well aware of the danger Yoko was in, and the Lennon temper flared when Yoko was just coming round from sedation. John was jittery and wanted to get inside to see her immediately. A doctor walked up to John at a critical moment, saying: 'I love Beatle music. I just want to shake your hand.'

'Fuck off. Save my wife's life,' rasped an angry John. He was fuming with rage.

Nurses, too, had asked for his autograph. He was furious that the doctors and nurses were talking to him instead of attending to Yoko and the baby. It was an anger from which he would never recover. 'They were totally indifferent to Yoko's pain and to Sean — they wanted my *autograph* at a time like that!' Sean proved a healthy, happy baby, but both John and Yoko were sad that he had not been born by the active method, 'flesh touching flesh'.

Back home, John's 'first phone call was to his Aunt Mimi in her seaside bungalow in Poole, Dorset. 'It's a boy, it's a boy, Mimi,' he said excitedly. 'And we've named him Sean.'

'Oh, John, you've *branded* him,' she said.

'It's Irish for John, Mimi,' John went on, 'but don't worry, Mimi, he'll be raised internationally and he'll be a citizen of the world.' At 6:00 am a jubilant John phoned Leon Wildes. 'It's John. I'm a father!' There was no controlling him, says Wildes. 'He was ecstatic, bouncing around his room as he spoke.' A Polaroid snapshot of the baby was sent, triumphantly, to Dr Hong, who had been such a psychological boost to John and Yoko.

In the months following the birth John allowed very few visitors to the Dakota. He was afraid they might spread germs. Nobody except John or Yoko was allowed to touch Sean. It was the single most important thing in his life. Elliot Mintz, visiting the family a month after the birth, was asked to take the first picture of mother, father, and baby. Mintz's first view of Sean, sleeping with Yoko, was shadowed by John 'shushing' him to be quiet and not risk waking up the child. Telegrams of congratulation had poured in from all over the world, many remarking on the fact that Sean was born on John's birthday. 'It figures,' some

joked, 'that the two of you would make this another one
of your events!' But John took even that seriously: 'The
baby decides the time and place and which family to have.
Yoko did not give birth to Sean; Sean came through Yoko
as a miracle and a gift to us.'

'Well,' said Yoko shortly after the birth, with characteristic
incisiveness, 'I've carried the baby for nine months and
brought him into the world. Now it's your turn to look
after him.' John was in full agreement. It was a good time
for a total change in emphasis in his life. Yoko went into
the office downstairs full-time to manage the family business, while he raised Sean in their seventh-floor apartment.
John being John, it turned into a consuming passion of
incredible intensity. Both he and Yoko fulfilled their new
roles with distinction. Four months after Sean's birth John's
recording contract with EMI/Capitol expired, and he
decided not to renew it, the first time in fifteen years that
he had not been tied to a recording deal.

During the next five years John became, as he described
himself, a house-husband. His attention to Sean was total.
The baby was fed, washed, bathed, dressed, and taught to
read by him. He hated changing his nappies, but he did it
all the same. No babysitters were needed. When Sean was
about six months old John saw a pimple on him. Agitated,
he went round to twenty members of the office and domestic
staff forbidding them to give Sean sugar of any kind in his
diet: 'Sean may not have come out of my belly but I'm
gonna make his bones.'

During the years of seclusion, Elliot Mintz visited John
and Yoko dozens of times. 'We shared the special moments,'
he recalls, 'Thanksgivings, Christmas Eves, Christmas Days,

New Year's Eves, Sean's birthdays. They were the most glorious of times.

'I have never seen two people so much in love. They lived their lives with such conscious awareness. John would frequently walk over to Yoko, who might be sitting on the edge of the bed with Sean. He would hold her small hand in his and look deeply into her eyes and smile then whisper "Hello" very softly, as if he was making direct contact with her very essence. They would embrace and I would disappear. I remember reading that Brian Epstein once said he was happiest when the four Beatles and he were in a room together without anyone else, before a concert. For me, during those five years, John and Yoko and little Sean together as a family in the Dakota embodied everything that was special between lovers.'

Sean's full name is Sean Taro Ono Lennon. Says Yoko: 'John insisted that he should have one Japanese name. Taro is like Sean or John in Japanese, that kind of name. John loved it.

'In Japanese law a child belongs to the father's family. As a result of that mothers who have babies by accident sometimes have a terrible time . . . if they don't know who the father is and the mother cannot claim the child as hers. John and I wanted Sean to be as international as possible.' As well as having British and Japanese names and being born in New York, Sean Taro Ono Lennon has dual American and British nationality and his birth was registered in both New York and London.

There are already signs that Sean will emerge as formidable, strong-minded, and witty as his father. At the age of eight, he told me he was 'a real computer whizz'. At school, where the ever-present bodyguard accompanied him, standing within sight of him all day, every day, Sean said he was 'better at languages than adding up, but most of all I'm a real expert at using my free time.' He had a typical eight-year-old's contempt for the girls in his class, who outnumbered the boys: 'They're just not so nice as us so we beat them at dodge ball.' Although he agreed he was rather young to be considering his future, Sean said: 'I have been thinking about what to do but I haven't yet answered myself. I might be a singer or a crazy scientist or a geologist or an archaeologist.' As for his father's music: 'Sometimes it's good, sometimes not so good.' John would grudgingly have agreed with that one.

Elton John, whose concert was so instrumental in re-uniting John and Yoko, is Sean's godfather.

John scarcely needed the news of his father's death in April 1976 to persuade him to pour even more zeal into raising Sean. His own lack of parental stability as a child had nagged away at him over the years, and he was deter-mined that Sean would have a father he knew and grew up alongside. Although he could not claim to be a struggling 'mother figure', with the everyday physical pressures of millions of parents (he had a domestic staff to cushion him), John supervised everything that went into the boy's early years: food, drink, toys, books, sleep. After a year he helped Sean to toddle and walk. Television was banned. 'He's not gonna see people shooting each other,' said John. He even wheeled him in a carriage around Central Park.

John was so immersed in baby-rearing that when Paul McCartney arrived, unscheduled, with a guitar at the Dakota one day and had the doorman announce him, John did not believe it could be him. Hoax phone calls were a regular problem. Paul had to be put on the phone by the doorman in the Dakota reception area to convince John that it was really him. When he went upstairs John gave him a frosty reception. 'Do you mind calling before you come round next time? This is not Liverpool, y'know. In

New York, you don't just drop in on people like this without warning.' He went on to explain that he was tired from a hard day's work with Sean. Paul left in a huff. John's opinion of Paul's work at this time was very low. He described him to friends as 'like Engelbert Humperdinck'. John was contemptuous of the fact that his old partner apparently wanted merely to continue as before; he referred to Mick Jagger and Paul jointly – and contemptuously – as the 'Rolling Wings'. There was more to life, implied John, than rock 'n' rolling into your forties. 'I've diarrhea'd on rock 'n' roll,' he said.

As he walked around New York's Central Park during his 'house-husband' years, one of the friendly faces John occasionally encountered was that of Sid Bernstein. The man who had promoted the Beatles' American tours from their first shows in 1964 had tried several times to re-unite them for massive charity concerts. Each time there had been no official response; John said he 'didn't go for all that Al Jolson, down-on-one-knee' pleading that became Bernstein's style in expensive appeals to the Beatles in the *New York Times*. But when John saw Bernstein walking around the park or on the Upper East Side, they embraced and did not mention the Beatles. 'It was always casual talk about my family and Sean, who was sometimes with him,' says Bernstein. 'I knew not to mention the Beatles. He only ever mentioned the past to me once, describing Shea Stadium as the top of the mountain.' John's forgetfulness made an impression on Bernstein: 'I saw him several times with Yoko and he introduced me to her every time as if we'd never met. Finally Yoko had to say to him: "John, I *know* Sid now." '

Their paths crossed twice. In 1974, John phoned Bernstein and asked him for the name of a really fine Italian restaurant in New York. After he had a good dinner at

Palucci's, behaving perfectly with Harry Nilsson throughout the night, John sent a huge spray of flowers to Bernstein
with a note of thanks for a good recommendation. And in
1975, John phoned to ask for tickets for a concert Bernstein
was promoting at Carnegie Hall. The performer was Jimmy
Cliff, a star of reggae, a music style which particularly
captured John's affection in the cosmopolitan atmosphere
of New York. Sid Bernstein had no tickets left, but his
daughters gave up theirs when they heard John Lennon
wanted to go.

Bernstein later presented the New York production of
a play called *Lennon*, first shown at Liverpool's Everyman
theatre in 1981. It was artistically mediocre, concentrating
heavily on John's 'tough guy' image and failing to capture
his multi-faceted personality and sensitivity. Nevertheless,
the play was notable for establishing the huge range in ages
of John's appeal: children and teenagers who were not born
when John formed the Beatles attended alongside their
parents whose memories of Lennon were powerful. When
shots rang out at the end of the play to simulate the murder,
the audience sobbed. In New York, the play failed and
came off at the Entermedia Theatre, off Broadway, after
only nine weeks.

While John was busy nursing Sean, Yoko revelled in
her role as businesswoman. By the evening, after a long
programme of meetings in her office, she would say: 'It's
been a hard day. I'm tired.'

John's house-husband wit was quick: 'Well, what do
you think *I've* been doing? Bringing up a baby is work, as
well! Don't give me that "hard day at the office, dear" bit.'

He pointed out that he had even begun reading cookery
books to improve his performance.

Yoko set about demonstrating her business acumen with
typical determination. 'It was a two-year plan,' she says,

'which quickly ran to five years when John told me how much money he wanted and I realized I couldn't achieve *that* amount within two years.'

Hitherto Yoko had been totally unmaterialistic. 'I survived throughout my earlier years,' she says, 'by not accumulating money, partly because my mother enjoyed luxury and was always showing me diamonds. Part of me rebelled against that and despised it. I felt I never wanted to lead a life like that, thinking so much about gold and diamonds and beautiful clothes.

'So until 1975 I was the opposite of a money person. But when John and I decided that I would be a businesswoman, I told myself that in order to attract money and do the new job well I'd have to reconstruct my psyche. My old attitude of not wanting to get into money just wasn't going to do.

'I meditated on it. I visualized all the materially good things in the world — diamonds, silk, velvets, art — and tried to see those things in my mind with love, which I never did before. I just opened my mind to all those things instead of rejecting them. And John immediately bought me this diamond, heart-shaped necklace, almost as a signal that I was changing. The usual me would have said, out of snobbery: "Oh, what do I want that for?" But instead I looked at its beauty and thanked him. I tried to see the beauty in the good properties we have. And we said: "If we are going to have it, we have to *act* as if we have it already, not as if we are just starting with money."

'So I went and bought great clothes most weeks and John would really enjoy seeing what I'd bought. It wasn't a question of getting these things in order to *own* them, more like reversing all my attitudes towards possessions. I really trained my mind to enjoy the things that were positive about money.'

With no head for statistics and without making any mathematical calculations, Yoko began presiding over the Lenono business with a clear mind and intuitive powers that devastated all those who dealt with her. John and Yoko's first decision was that their cash would be invested in things that were ecologically inoffensive: 'We wanted nothing to do with energy or oil or big chemical corporations or any of the other things we could have invested in,' says Yoko. 'We wanted things that were peaceful to control and caused us, and the world, no problem.'

Yoko's first business venture was the gradual acquisition of five apartments in their beloved Dakota building on West 72nd Street. The setting for the film *Rosemary's Baby*, the intimidating Dakota was not easy to gain access to: major stars before John and Yoko had been refused permission by the committee which decides who may be granted residence there. John and Yoko had to attend a screening meeting to establish that they would be peaceful, respectable residents, particularly when Yoko set about buying each apartment that fell vacant. They so loved its decorous atmosphere that there was never any danger they would abuse it. John sat watching the sun rise across Central Park. The all-white room (including the furniture and the white piano on which John wrote 'Imagine', which now has Yoko's photographs of her family on it) was their *pièce de résistance*. The piano, John's gift to Yoko on her birthday in 1971, when they were living in Ascot, bears his inscription, 'This morning, a white piano for Yoko.' It remains in position. Asked why she needed all the apartments, Yoko replied quixotically: 'It's just that John and I always wanted to live in a house.'

After the Dakota had been established as a major investment, Yoko turned to agriculture. Four farms were purchased, in the Catskill mountains, Virginia, Vermont, and upstate New York. Covering some sixteen hundred acres, the farms were reckoned to be worth nearly $1 million. Yoko's particular talent was her timing: her notoriety as a businesswoman went up several notches when one of her investments, a prize Holstein cow, one of 250 head of cattle they owned, fetched $265,000 – a world record – at the New York State Fair at Syracuse. The exceptional Lenono cow was expected to produce over six thousand gallons of milk a year. 'Only Yoko Ono,' said an amused John, reading about the sale in a newspaper while holidaying alone in Bermuda, 'could sell a cow for a quarter of a million dollars!'

A vital advantage of owning the farms was that their produce – eggs, milk, and vegetables, all produced without chemicals – was shipped down to New York at least once a week, ensuring that John, Yoko, and Sean had a healthy diet, which was as free of additives as possible.

Yoko's astute purchase of properties and the hiring of staff to run them became another time-consuming but profitable operation. For $450,000 the Lennons acquired a stunning weekend retreat, a house at Cold Spring Harbor, Long Island, overlooking the Atlantic. Yoko, particularly, loved this home, which was close to Manhattan but also in the fresh air of the countryside – important for Sean. They also bought a sixty-three-foot ocean-going yacht called *Isis* and a sloop which John named *Strawberry Fields*.

Then there was West Palm Beach, Florida, where $700,000 bought the Lennons a beachfront mansion, El Salano, built in 1919 and once owned by the Vanderbilt family. With seven bedrooms, five servants' rooms, indoor and outdoor pools, and its own fifty yards of sand by the ocean, the house proved the most expensive of all their properties: most of the year it stood empty, except for a small staff; John and Yoko managed only one month's visit a year. Art, a big collection of carpets, and Eastern artifacts were other assets.

Naturally their critics had an easy target. Here was the man who had sung 'Imagine no possessions' accumulating more, at the behest of his shrewd wife, than he would ever need. But a changed John had decided, as always, that if he was going to retire and be a non-musician for a few years and father Sean, then with the Beatles, Apple, and Allen Klein out of his system, he would have no better manager than Yoko. And, following the dictum of his life, 'Don't do things by halves,' Yoko quickly enhanced their fortune. By the late 1970s, John's estate was conservatively valued at $150 million, with millions more coming in every year in royalties from record sales and songwriting.

Yoko talked to me about how she reconciled her business and her art. 'I think that most artists have this complex: they think they should suffer and struggle and always be miserable or else they can't be creative. John and I had that for a while. We were very aware of that side of being artists. But we tried to reverse the trap that artists fall into – because we didn't want to be miserable when we obviously had money and possessions. After all, being miserable is a pretty high price to pay for being an artist!' As to her business methods: 'Money, and making it, is fundamentally a state of mind. I often used to wonder why some people were rich and naturally talented at multiplying their money and others not. It sometimes comes down to attitude. A great many very intelligent people have no money and as a Greenwich Village artist wanting only recognition, I used to be one of them. But then I also had an inverted snobbery towards money. I thought it was silly to go on looking for it. I've changed.' In business deals, however, men were chauvinistically distrustful of her judgment – 'or, rather, they became upset by the fact that my judgment was right and it came from a woman. There *have* been some struggles with men in business because I am a woman.' Conversely, she had also benefited: 'Sometimes the men underestimate a woman so much that they reveal their tactics too soon. Then they find out how resilient I am.'

For John, walking away from music for a few years was much harder than carrying on: 'I know because I've done both. It was very hard because shouldn't I be going, like "to the office" or "producing something"? I don't exist if my name isn't in the charts or I'm not seen at the right club. It's like the guys aged sixty-five who've said: "Your life's over. Time for God." It's self-imposed, yes, but still the feeling was there, this whole big space that seems to be unfillable. And of course, it's naturally got to be filled because that's the law of the universe. . . . And it was filled by a fulfilling experience, to put it in a little cute phrase.'

John and Yoko did not venture out much in 1976. John's commitment to rearing Sean, supervising his every moment, was total. He explained: 'People asked me: "What are you doing now?"

'And I'd say: "Looking after the baby and baking the bread."

'And they'd say: "Ha ha. No, no, what else do you do?"

'And I'd say: "Are you *kidding?* It's a full-time job, as every housewife knows." There were no secret projects in the basement.'

Making music was low on his agenda, but a passion for discovery was high. John's determination that Sean should be healthy was stimulated by his own splendid health. As part of a self-imposed diet, he and Yoko had a forty-day fast when they drank only fruit and vegetable juices. When they came off the diet, they were convinced of the importance of health foods and vitamins.

Baking bread was a passion that lasted for a few months and, while he enthused about it, everybody had to know. 'Elliot,' he told Mintz by phone one afternoon, 'an extraordinary thing has happened. I've just baked my first loaf of bread. I saw it rise in the oven, I did it from start to finish.' John took a Polaroid photo of the loaf and sent it by air courier to his bemused pal three thousand miles away. John was overjoyed and proud of his achievement. 'I feel I've conquered something,' he said to Yoko, and he didn't mean merely by baking bread. The thrill wore off somewhat when the entire staff of the Dakota enjoyed his bread so much that 'drivers, and office boys, and accountants, and everyone came for one and I'd make loaves on Friday that'd be gone by Saturday afternoon.' He decided: 'Screw this for a lark. It was becoming routine. And I don't get a gold record or a knighthood . . . nothing!'

John's cooking was enthusiastic but limited. He would chop up a huge amount of vegetables, put them, occasionally with fish, into a big crockpot, which simmered for days on the cooker. Permanently beside it, loving the warmth, were the three cats, Michu, Sasha, and Charo. The longer the crockpot simmered, he reasoned – quite fallaciously – the better the food would taste. That, with perfectly cooked rice, and sometimes boiled eggs – rather watery and rarely cooked properly – was his culinary height, together with the bread.

He insisted that people followed the eating method that he had adopted from a macrobiotic guru: the practice of constant chewing. Drinking anything with meals was disallowed in the Dakota, as was alcohol. Every bite had to be chewed twenty times because John had been told that if he ate and washed it down with any liquid, he would be taking away the work of the digestive enzymes, particularly ptyalin, the enzyme in saliva that begins the digestion of food. Anybody eating a Lennon crockpot combination was ordered to chew until the ptyalin naturally dissolved it. Elliot Mintz recalls a visit by John and Yoko to Manhattan's East-West macrobiotic restaurant in which about one hundred people sat facing each other, chewing, with no conversation. Mintz began: 'Well, it's great to see you two, how's it been going?' John rebuked him, placing fingers across his mouth to indicate that there should be no talking.

When Sean was two John decided to try to learn Japanese. For two hours a day, three days a week, he went to a language school in Manhattan. The technique was similar to that employed in many language classes: the complete immersion method with no English spoken. John also bought a series of cassettes. Much to Yoko's chagrin, he would attempt to practise on her. But his combination of Liverpudlian and American made it hard for him: after two months of battling to absorb the intonation, he could manage only about forty words. He gave up after a brave try, much to Yoko's relief.

The more successful his wife became 'downstairs', the more he trusted her vision. Yoko's business moves were supported by advice from a retinue of astrologers, numerologists, and tarot card readers. Every member of the Lenono staff, and most people who came into close proximity to them, were 'checked out' through their astrological sign in infinite detail. Thus Yoko arrived at the conclusion that there were good days for business and also days when she should sign nothing and just listen, days on which neither of them should travel, and days on which it would be bad to be in contact with someone who had the wrong 'sign rising'. Yoko had always been heavily into 'vibrations', good and bad. Her application of her hunches into a science began to shape their movements and those of their closest friends: 'If Yoko said it would be advisable for John or for me to fly six thousand miles in an easterly direction and stay at that point for exactly four and a half days,' says Elliot Mintz, 'John would say: "Go with it. Trust her. She's always right." '

In June 1977 John, Yoko, and Sean went to Japan for an extended visit of several months. They had been there for nearly eight weeks when a phone call from Elliot Mintz in Los Angeles broke the news: Elvis Presley was dead. There was a pause on the line before John said of his teenage idol: 'Elvis died in the army.' Another pause. 'How? What happened?' The information was sketchy; Mintz had just heard the news on the radio. The impact on John was minimal, his reaction almost callous. He reserved his emotion for the living. Between pauses, John said to Mintz: 'Well, the difference between the Beatles and Elvis was that with Elvis the king died and the manager lived and with the Beatles the manager died and we lived. I never wanted to be a forty-year-old who virtually died singing his golden hits in a jump-suit in Las Vegas. Oh, please send two white gardenias to Elvis's grave, saying: "Rest In Peace, Love John and Yoko." '

Next day Mintz flew out to join the Lennons for a long Japanese holiday. Mintz, clearly affected by the death of a rock legend, was chastised by John. 'Don't talk to me about Elvis. He's dead. Don't try to sell me on the dreams and myths of these people. Elvis is dead. It's all over. It's unhealthy to live *through* anybody.'

Mintz flew to Tokyo and then took a train two hundred miles north to the small town of Karuizawa. The Lennon he found there was a dramatically refreshed man. In two years, he had renounced rock 'n' roll for fatherhood and house-husbandry. It was now time to concentrate on the restoration of his own mind and body. For five months John enjoyed the cleanest, wisest, physically fittest period in his life, with no alcohol, no drugs, exercises of every kind from cycling and swimming to yoga every day, and none of the foods he had leaned on so much in New York: chocolate, honey, English muffins. He cut down drastically on his beloved French cigarettes. He had a constant diet of *sushi* and rice and joked that 'Yoko likes to feed me dead fish.'

'In Karuizawa, we all did a lot of cycling and stayed at a very old, beautiful hotel, the Mampei,' says Mintz. 'Yoko's family has a home in this town; there were no Westerners or tourists and we did not have a car. John enjoyed having Sean sit on a seat across his crossbar in front of him.'

The Japanese experience proved idyllic for John. In their constant search for strong, black coffee, which both John and Yoko loved, they would drag Mintz on five-mile mountain road expeditions, Yoko's long hair flying behind her in the wind as she led the other two, John in T-shirt and shorts, with hair almost shoulder length, keeping up with her, and Mintz trailing 'and fully expecting a cardiac arrest' behind them. The coffee café, Mintz avers, was worth it. Yoko also took them to exclusive and exotic restaurants. Often the fish for their dinner would be pulled from a stream next to the restaurant. Their search for authenticity was not always felicitous. John was a little squeamish when he was asked to drink 'the best turtle soup in Japan' from the shell of the turtle he had seen alive only a few minutes earlier.

The fifteen-course traditional Japanese dinners, during which the three of them hardly spoke, were often preceded by the mineral baths which left John's skin glowing, his hair with a brilliant sheen, and Yoko's longer hair at its best. On one occasion when the two men were taken to a bathing area and Yoko went off to a women's area, two hostesses began to undress John and Elliot. John reacted incredulously: 'What's going on? Where's Mother?' As fast as the waitresses unbuttoned his shirt buttons, he would do them up again; finally, when he entered the water, he started swimming strongly.

'It's not for swimming,' Yoko rebuked him from the other side of the partition that separated men from women. 'It's for bathing, to refresh yourself before dinner.' But John was always a powerful, enthusiastic swimmer, and enjoyed teaching Sean.

In Karuizawa, John told Elliot how wonderful it was not to be recognized, not to have to be on guard or be attentive to strangers. A few Japanese smiled at him in recognition, but he felt no pressure. At Yoko's mother's house, often wearing a suit and his old Quarry Bank school tie, he enjoyed many afternoons sitting on the porch, something similar to an old southern plantation verandah, drinking coffee, eating cakes, and cycling back to the hotel later, singing songs and whistling.

In the ancient capital town of Kyoto John became immersed in the Buddhist temples. 'When we went into these and stood before the statues of Buddha, there were small areas where we wrote our prayers down,' says Mintz. 'John was genuinely into it. He clasped his hands, closed his eyes, bowed his head and prayed. . . . Yoko took us to a monastery in Kyoto where there was a religious order of very elderly women. It was irrelevant that John couldn't understand a word of the conversation. He was deeply moved. The religiosity of Japan definitely made an impression on him.'

En route home the family moved to the Okura Hotel in Tokyo, where they occupied the gigantic presidential suite.

Here the throb of city life made John eager to get back to New York. 'He got out his acoustic guitar in the living-room of the suite and sang some old songs,' says Mintz. 'And he said he was getting a bit homesick.' The suite was so large that John even played football with Sean in it.

It was here that John quixotically played his last 'public' performance, which happened quite by accident. The gigantic hotel suite had elevators that arrived straight into the Lennon lounge. John was sitting quietly playing 'Jealous Guy' to himself and Elliot Mintz one evening when the elevator doors opened and a Japanese couple – who had evidently arrived on the wrong floor – walked out to find a singer-guitarist whom they did not recognize. All the same they sat and listened as John continued the song. 'John was in a wonderful mood, playing gently and beautifully,' recalls Mintz. 'The people simply applauded and went back down the elevator.' They were the last two strangers who ever watched and listened as John performed.

When the time came to finish the Japanese holiday Yoko consulted her numerology. She decided that the 'signs' were all wrong for the two men to fly direct from Tokyo to New York. She would return straight home to the US while John, Sean, and Elliot were to fly Tokyo–Hong Kong–Dubai–Frankfurt–New York. Their twenty-six-hour flight would mean changing planes at Dubai and Frankfurt. It sounded arduous, but John believed implicitly in Yoko's prescience and totally trusted her ability to 'read the cards' which charted their movements.

On the long night flight from Dubai to Germany John became homesick, recalling the Beatles' early days in a conversation that Mintz will always remember as Lennon at his frankest. In the Lufthansa 747 jet Sean played with his car race track in the upper level of the plane with a nanny, while Mintz sat with Lennon with the seats on either side of them, as usual, empty. When flying he and Yoko always bought two seats on either side and in front of them to leave free. That way, John said, 'I make sure I don't sit next to somebody asking me when the Beatles will get back together again.'

Mintz had by that time known Lennon for six years, but he had never seen him so sentimental, pensive, reflective, and talkative. Even his old Liverpool accent had partly returned. It was the side of John Lennon that the public had never seen. He spoke of his childhood, his sexual fantasies, how he felt when the Beatles first came to America, and the feeling he had when the plane first touched down on the soil of the country that had first inspired his music. He talked of his relationship with his mother, and the tears welled up as he recalled her premature death; he was in the reminiscent and confessional mood which often overcomes long-distance fliers; he repeatedly spoke of his love of Yoko, and his chattiness reassured Mintz, who was a nervous flier. John was particularly proud of the fact that he had his luggage down to a fine art: a large briefcase with one change of clothing and pyjamas.

The overnight stop in Frankfurt was John's one visit to Europe in nine years. It was marked by a bizarre encounter with a hotel receptionist, aghast at unexpectedly checking in a former Beatle. Rooms were not readily available, so John introduced Mintz as Paul McCartney. Rooms were suddenly found. 'I guess,' Mintz said to an unamused John, 'the clerk liked the fact that I wrote "Yesterday".'

Next day, John, Sean, and Elliot continued their journey to New York. At Kennedy Airport John got a special thrill from the passport controller's greeting. As John handed him his British passport and remembered the four-year immigration battle he had endured, the immigration man said to him: 'Welcome home, Mr Lennon.' John turned and

smiled to Elliot, then caught sight of Yoko, standing alone
to welcome him with an embrace. Back at the Dakota a
revitalized Lennon rediscovered with pleasure the forty
hours of *Goon Show* tapes which Yoko had given him as a
birthday gift.

John made other foreign trips. He went alone to Cape Town
for a few days, staying at the Mount Nelson Hotel. He
went to Hong Kong and Singapore and enjoyed walking
incognito among the local population. His wit never
deserted him. To Bob Gruen, his New York photographer
friend, he sent a card from Hong Kong saying simply: 'Far
East, man!' accompanied by the little doodle which told
any recipient of a card that it was a genuine Lennon
message. John and Yoko flew to spend one night in Cairo
at the pyramids, where Yoko developed a fascination for
Egyptian artifacts and bought the mummy that lies in her
white room at the Dakota. John's solo journeys were a real
education for a man who had been cushioned by company
since his first travels out of Liverpool to Hamburg in 1960.
Even dialling room service in a hotel was an adventure for
him. Most of the time, he enjoyed simply sitting watching
foreign television in blissful isolation in his room.

Few people recognized him on his foreign trips, and in
Hong Kong he enjoyed walking around the harbour among
the local workers, 'just watching'. He had not enjoyed such
freedom since his days in Hamburg before the lunacy of
Beatlemania. The only occasions on which John was forced
to admit his identity were when he handed his gold American Express card to the hotel desk clerks. From each city
he telephoned Yoko in the Dakota and Aunt Mimi in
Dorset to give his hotel number, and to enthuse about the
hum of a city, a skyline, a sunset, or even to crow over

the fact that he was walking around shops and hotel lobbies without being hunted.

John was fortunate that he was not hounded, for in view of his name and his fame, he was astonishingly vulnerable. All public figures risk harassment by the public as soon as they step outside their front doors; for a lapsed Beatle and solo star of stature, who had a reputation as a recluse, to be travelling alone to the far-flung corners of the world, totally alone, was a brave adventure. In the case of John Lennon, it had an extra hazard: one of his most surprising flaws was an inability to detect hangers-on, phoneys, parasites, or even dangerous people who sought his company, his approval, his warmth, or his encouragement. There were two sides to his attitudes towards people and handling of them: the tough, abrasive, no-nonsense, street-wise Liverpudlian who believed everyone should battle their own way through life, as he had; and then there was John the sucker, the 'easy tap' for most causes that reached his ears, particularly if they were tinged with radicalism and sounded sincere. An incurable sentimentalist and fundamentally kind, John leaned this way, preferring to give any dubious characters the benefit of the doubt. It made him a poor judge of people who walked up to him. He did *not* possess a sound sixth sense of those who were around him to exploit him, because he tended to take people at face value. This became dangerous as he chose to confront his stardom and fly around the world alone, or walk the streets of New York and give his autograph to anybody who appeared, to him, to be innocuous. It was a trait that enabled him to break free of the strictures of stardom. It might also have cost him his life.

Nearly twelve years after their first meeting, John and Yoko had achieved a serenity in their partnership that anyone might envy. 'We would argue, of course,' says Yoko.

'We were two very temperamental, very emotional, people. Friends and lovers, musicians and artists, man and woman, husband and wife.' Even when they fought, John had a unique method of breaking the deadlock. He would write a song or poem and either play the song to Yoko or strategically place the written poem where she would see it privately. 'That was part of our communication,' she says. 'We were both shy, we didn't go out often, certainly not to parties or anything like that. So we were literally together for fourteen years with very few breaks. John and I stood for peace and love but standing for peace doesn't make either of us holier than thou. John and I together were human beings, and by no means were both of us totally peaceful. Anger, hurt, vulnerability, were all a part of John. When we met, we were like two *driven* people and it was like a fantastic meeting of two crazy souls. John was more hurt than me by the public reaction to my early work. I was the "laugh". People said: "Oh, we can't listen to *her*." And John would be choked by that. But it's like John would say, everything takes its time and in a favourite phrase of his, *it will all work out in the end*.

'What people *did* take a long time realizing was that John might not have been a great, technically proficient guitarist, but listen now to "Why" on the *Plastic Ono Band* album and his playing is fantastic, far-out. Our fusion, with my singing and his playing, was something he realized was special much later. He said he could not have played like that with anybody, it was more than a duet of artists, but a coming together of the two of us.'

Yoko likens their partnership with that of Robert Browning and Elizabeth Barrett-Browning. John thought of them more like Scott and Zelda Fitzgerald. Whichever analogy one uses, their marriage and mutual love was a quite triumphant and justly celebrated public romance. It survived many hurdles: the ridicule of the public; the taunts of John's old 'friends', in and out of the Beatles' circle, and those of millions of Beatle fans in the early days; and a lengthy separation. As Yoko comments, 'We found that the love thing was bigger than both of us.'

During the first two years of his seclusion John was so immersed in being a father and taking an interest in Yoko's business transactions that the outside world virtually passed him by. He hardly ever went out shopping after that trip for Yoko's maternity wear. He rarely answered the flashing light of the telephone. He left the staff to order the food, and on the occasions when he did phone a shop, he became irritated by shop assistants' refusal to believe that he really was John Lennon.

By the time of his Japanese visit, however, John had changed. Galvanized by Yoko's exceptional success in buying property, farms, and *objets d'art*, John began an excursion into acquisition. Like all his other enthusiasms, he went all the way while it lasted; this particular passion had its roots in planning Sean's life.

John decided to shower Sean with toys, games, and books, practising a 'reverse materialism' on him. Lennon's theory was that he, and millions like him, were raised in the belief that he would grow up and be able to afford the first car, the first house, the first good suit, and the first guitar . . . and it was always 'tomorrow'. He wanted to try to wipe out this aspiration early in Sean's life: 'I don't want him hooked on being a consumer throughout his teenage years.' So Sean was given anything he fancied. A walk around the famous New York toy store, F.A.O. Schwarz, would cost John thousands of dollars. He spent vast sums on robot games at a store called Forbidden Planet in Greenwich Village; John also dabbled in computer games and bought Sean the most progressive ones. 'I'm giving him all the crap while he's young so that by the time he's ten, this kind of stuff won't mean anything to him. He'll have had his fix.'

It was a theory that only a rich man could apply. But it worked. By the time he was eight, Sean Lennon's proudest possession was a valueless collection of rocks. He had developed a great interest in the formation of stones, stalactites, minerals, and anything geological. His great hobby, besides computers, was hunting by the seashore for rare seashells. No expensive toys or brilliant pieces of engineering impressed him: beautiful electric train sets and gadgets by the crateload lay, forgotten, in a warehouse when I visited him in 1983.

When it came to spending and collecting for himself, however, John had immatured with age. In Japan a typical spending spree in Tokyo's 'electronic village' would find John walking down the aisles pointing out and ordering literally dozens of sophisticated amplifiers, turntables, and speakers, which were shipped back to the Dakota and set up in each room. 'You know how Mother feels about wires,' he said to Elliot Mintz, who had accompanied him on the expedition, 'well, with this little lot, there'll be no need for any wires to trail around the house.'

Airline mail order catalogues fascinated him. He loved to be surprised by items he ordered on a plane, simply by filling in his American Express number; these arrived at the Dakota weeks or months afterwards, long after he had forgotten about them. A 'stereo pillow', a pillow with built-in speakers, amused him; there was a portable desk with foam-rubber backing; breakfast trays on which he would take Yoko her favourite extra strong, black coffee; and he developed a fetish for collecting attaché-cases. He had dozens in leather and other materials in all shapes and sizes, and carefully fixed the combination lock of each to include the figure nine which marked important events in his life. He was similarly attracted to manicure sets and collected dozens. If he walked into a store and found a pair of jeans that fitted him properly, he would ask for ten pairs in different colours to be sent to his home.

If that was the 'little child inside the man', there was plenty of seriousness in John to balance it out. An avid reader all his life, he spent the years of seclusion establishing a superb library of leatherbound, antiquarian books. He studied the history of the early slaves who were sent from Africa to his native Liverpool and were used, he said, to build the huge houses in the port alongside which he had grown up. He loved philosophy books and sent Elliot Mintz *The Lazy Man's Guide to Enlightenment*.

When John and Yoko went out, it was as if to re-live their early, simpler lives as student and artist. Away from the grandeur of the Dakota, light years away from rock 'n' roll, totally removed from Eastern influence, their choice was usually a small yet elegant coffee shop run by an Italian husband and wife. It was decidedly European in its atmosphere and sold only pastries and superb coffee and chocolate. For John and Yoko, for four years from the day it opened in 1976, Café La Fortuna at 69 West 71st Street, one block from their home, was a refuge.

Vincent Urwand, the owner, developed a bond with them. Only once did he have to chase away a gaggle of fans who gathered with cameras to disturb their peace. About four afternoons a week John would wander in, with or without Yoko, and sit down for his *cappuccino* and Gitanes and to read any newspaper that had been lying around his home. In summer they sat in the garden at the back of the café.

When Sean was a toddler, John would bring him in

with a rope around him. 'You got him like a dog, strapped
up round his chest!' said Vincent.

'I've gotta have him tied up or else he runs wild. I can't
keep up with him when he runs off,' explained John. Special
ice-cream, without sugar and containing honey, was made
for Sean at John's request.

John often struck up conversations with other people
in La Fortuna. One, a German religious fanatic, tried unsuccessfully to stir John up about his ambivalent attitude to
organized religion. For the most part, though, it was a
haven, a grass roots contact with an unpretentious café.
Vincent Urwand comments, 'John told me how they used
to go round second-hand shops in this neighbourhood and
buy old-fashioned hats and dresses. One day John phoned
me and said that he and Yoko would provide me with the
picture of themselves I'd asked for, for the wall. And when
it came it was John wearing a derby hat with a paper
moustache, Sean with the American flag draped around
him, and Yoko in a big hat and an old-fashioned dress that
you'd never see her in. They loved surprising people.'

Despite banning sugar for Sean, John's craving for chocolate remained undimmed: Vincent often sold him bars of
imported dark, bittersweet Italian-made Luisa chocolate:
with American Hershey bars they were his favourite. Years
earlier John's sweet tooth had got the better of him in a
phone conversation from New York to me in London: he
asked me to bring him some of his childhood favourites,
chocolate-covered Bath Oliver biscuits. He often asked British visitors to bring him foods that were unobtainable in
New York.

At the café, the Urwands had little interest in modern
popular music. Coincidentally, John was opening out in his
music tastes at the time, and Vincent successfully introduced him to his own favourites, jazz and the popular music

of the veteran performers. 'I gave John some 78 rpm records and he asked me to make up a tape for him. Next time he came in, he said how much he'd enjoyed it.' The music consisted of songs by Al Jolson, Benny Goodman, Mae West, Duke Ellington, and the jazz of Fats Waller and Louis Armstrong. 'I had a long discussion with John on opera and classical music but as it turned out he developed a real liking for stuff which I played and he really thought they were special: Bing Crosby, the jazz violinist Stephane Grappelli, and Gracie Fields singing "Now Is The Hour". John told me he loved her singing.' The visits, each week for four years when he was in New York, made John 'one of the family' inside that little café. Yoko even took her mother there, when she visited from Japan, to demonstrate a little how she and John lived.

John ignored rock music completely during the mid-1970s. It was as if the consolidation of his love for Yoko and the birth of Sean had brought out the true romantic in him. Although he hated overt, gushing, lovey-dovey sentimentality, John was a 'pushover' when it came to romantic music. John and Yoko's favourite song and movie at this time was Barbra Streisand's 'The Way We Were'. It was some distance from 'A Hard Day's Night' and Chuck Berry.

Yoko's gift to John for his thirty-eighth birthday was a very special antique: a 'bubble-top' Wurlitzer jukebox of the style popular in American soda fountain shops in the 1950s. It took only 78 rpm records, and its arrival coincided with John's increasing interest in nostalgic music. The first batch of records ordered for the Wurlitzer were mostly 1950s hits like 'Dream Lover' by Bobby Darin; Frankie Laine; Johnnie Ray's 'Little White Cloud That Cried'; and as many Bing Crosby records as he could get. Here was real irony: Crosby's 'Please', which John had heard just as the Beatles were getting started eighteen years earlier in Liverpool, had inspired John to write their first big hit, 'Please Please Me'. Another favourite was 'As Time Goes By', by Dooley Wilson.

The Wurlitzer jukebox was the centrepoint of a creation by John on New Year's Eve 1979. He decided, with Elliot Mintz, to establish a private club called the Club Dakota, one small room which would be his equivalent of an Englishman's private club. With the Yamaha electric piano bought for his birthday by Elton John, he would give private recitals to a favoured few.

The Club Dakota's only members were John Lennon and Elliot Mintz. When Yoko attended, just once on that New Year's Eve, John was dressed in tails and his old Quarry Bank brown-and-yellow school tie. The appeal of the 'club' for John was its exclusivity. He even broke the hallowed 'no alcohol' rule there, agreed between himself and Yoko, allowing himself a bottle of old cognac.

Breakfasts in the Edwardian room of the Plaza Hotel were another regular pleasure. John had a special affinity with the hotel. The Beatles had stayed there when they first visited America in 1964. In the mornings the Lennons would have a late breakfast of black coffee (John ate eggs Benedict, Yoko split pea soup), before moving across to the tea-room where the violinist greeted them playing 'The Way We Were' and 'As Time Goes By' while they held hands. On Sean's seventh birthday the same violinist visited the Dakota to play 'Happy Birthday' for him. When they were out together, John and Yoko frequently held hands. 'When their kind of 1940s music struck up,' says Elliot Mintz, 'they behaved like high school sweethearts. They were *finished*, gazing at each other. . . .'

Memories of Liverpool permeated much of John's thinking from that day in 1976 when he secured his Green Card.

Most nights he would telephone Aunt Mimi. Often he would reassure her that he had triumphed magnificently over the monster that was the Beatles. Several times he tried to persuade his aunt to go and live with him and take one of their Dakota apartments: 'No fear, John. You'll never catch me over there. I never have liked Americans. And *you* shouldn't be there, either. It's no good for you. Come back and live in England.' John told her he preferred New York, but he now knew better than to argue with her.

Around the world Beatles fans had regarded John as a recluse since he had got his Green Card. His world travels to Japan, Hong Kong, Singapore, and South Africa had gone unnoticed. He and Yoko travelled incognito as the Revd Fred and Ada Ghurkin. Outside the Dakota the one person who knew precisely where he was on all his trips was Aunt Mimi. When he was in New York, he would phone her at 9:30 pm precisely British time, 4:30 pm New York time. 'I knew it was him; every night it rang almost on the dot,' she says. 'And it was, "Mimi, I'm in Bermuda, Cairo, Tokyo . . ." or wherever. Always gave me his phone number and said I could reverse the charges and call him back but I never wanted to do that.'

For Sean's fourth birthday and John's thirty-ninth, on 9 October 1979, the Lennons threw a party at the Tavern on the Green, an elegant, glittering restaurant in Central Park. John was dressed soberly but wore his Quarry Bank tie to which he had grown attached. A Beatles fan sent a picture of John to a surprised Aunt Mimi, who challenged him about it. 'Who are your spies?' John said. 'Look, I've carried it around with me everywhere these past few years. I just like it.' It confirmed Mimi's lifelong suspicions about her nephew's sentimentality: 'He was a great big baby. He was no tough nut, never. I think he sometimes wanted people to think he was, but deep down, he was as soft as butter.'

Proof of this theory, which Mimi held all her life, sometimes against the odds, came at the start of 1980. In one of his daily phone conversations, John said: 'Right, Mimi, now I want you to put your affairs in order.'

'What affairs?'

'Now look, Mimi, everything belonging to you, I want it.'

'What do you mean, John? If it's that important to you, you can have anything you like now. But what have you on your mind?'

The next part of John's request shattered her. The degree of his memory of all her possessions, particularly the items he had grown up with back at 251 Menlove Avenue, was almost overpowering. 'Mimi, you remember that painting that Uncle George did when he was at Liverpool Institute in Form 4A? It was a watercolour of a kind of Chinese vase. I'd like that.' It was the picture at the far end of the hall that had faced John as he had walked in from school or college every day. Mimi found it in her loft.

'John wanted every single photograph of me that I could lay my hands on,' said Mimi. And he gave her a vivid description of the china that had been on a plate rack high on the wall of the entrance hall and dining-room at Mendips. 'It's gold, Mimi, and it's got blue in it and a sort of rusty red. Coalport, Spode, and Crown Derby. And don't forget to send me the teapot.' Mimi always had a weakness for collecting china; it formed a central part of the decoration of the house in which John grew up. 'He asked for the really heavy cut-glass claret jugs, an enlargement of a photograph of my mother when she was a beautiful twenty-one-year-old. John wanted all my silver, all the cutlery I was not using that he'd seen at Mendips, any old cup and saucer, salt and pepperpots, anything. He said: "There's no need to do anything with it. Just leave it for collection." And John had a removal firm ship it all to him in crates.' John was developing an increasing fascination for his roots; he told friends he intended to write a *Forsyte Saga*-type story based on his family.

His final request was for Mimi to send something that had been passed down in her late husband's family of Smiths for generations: an antique grandfather clock, inscribed 'George Toogood, Woolton Tavern'. Uncle George, whose full name was George Toogood Smith, had taught John the time on it. The Toogoods were John's ancestors, a fact he had discovered, said Mimi, in his teenage years when he walked his Woolton girlfriends around the graveyard of St Peter's Church. Mimi had the handsome wooden clock serviced, and John arranged for it to be shipped over to New York. It ticks away loudly still in the Dakota kitchen, framed symbolically by pictures carefully chosen and positioned by John: one black-and-white picture of John and Yoko above it, and a Polaroid snapshot of John and Yoko on a boat looking at each other, next to it.

John's emotional side came over loudly and clearly during 1980. 'Remember,' he would say to Mimi, 'those holidays you sent me on in Scotland with Mater [his Aunt Elizabeth]? And the postcard I sent you: "Dear Mimi and Uncle George, I caught my first trout today. . . ." Have you still got those cards, Mimi?' And the aunt who had lectured him so sternly about getting on with his studies would find it hard to keep the tears back.

Although Mimi had never seen Sean, whom she regarded as her grandson, she must have known everything there was to know about him. John regaled her most nights with a blow-by-blow account of what Sean was doing and how he was.

'John,' she said, 'don't make the same mistake that I did and wrap your life around a little boy. That's what *I* did, and what did I get?'

'Was I that bad? A worry to you?' And they would both laugh about the years when his conscientious aunt told him he was wasting his time playing the guitar at the Cavern club instead of getting a proper career.

Throughout 1980 John sent out clear signs to his aunt that he loved and respected her for her strictness and her care of him. 'You were right,' he told her. 'But I knew I could paint and draw . . . and *write*. I'm forty this year. I'm going to make one more record, Mimi, then I'm going to do some writing.'

TWENTY-THREE

THE MUSIC:
1972–1980

*'No longer riding on the merry-go-round, I just had to
let it go'*

NOBODY TOLD me there'd be days like *these!*' chanted
John, alone and simply, in a record Yoko released four
years after his death.

In 1984, four years after John's murder, it was a simple,
stark reminder of the powerful, allegorical word-play with
which he had mesmerized millions for twenty years. There
had been diversions, of course: back-to-the-roots rock 'n'
roll; the tender, loving ballads on *Double Fantasy*. But here,
now, in a song that was at once danceable to and which
lyrically outclassed any contemporary rock 'n' roll, the
words of 'Nobody Told Me' were as relevant to the 1980s
as the psychedelic anthems he created earlier were for the
1960s. Lennon's posthumously released album was a far
more articulate, concerned, symbolic, and creative piece of
work than that produced by many living artists in popular
music. Together with the searing, chilling song he wrote
for Yoko, 'Grow Old With Me', the album *Milk And Honey*
demonstrated to all his friends – and those who had branded
Double Fantasy as maudlin – that Lennon was a master who
had not lost his muse.

Double Fantasy and *Milk And Honey* have provided the most moving love songs from Lennon, because they feature lyrics written and sung around the time of his happiness as a husband and father in America. They were albums that accurately reflected his mood in 1980. But the man who had arrived in New York some nine years earlier, mentally high on his fixation for Yoko and the vibrancy of the country, with his eyes wide open seeking new mental horizons, provided some astonishingly provocative music and writing that demonstrated how he loved championing causes.

All the vitality Lennon felt he was getting from his new home poured into the *Some Time In New York City* album, which was released in 1972. Jerry Rubin, the political activist with whom John had become friendly, had put him in touch with a hard-rocking New York band, Elephant's Memory (three of whose songs were included on the soundtrack of the film *Midnight Cowboy*). Rejuvenated politically and musically, Lennon spontaneously plunged into the recording, finishing the album in nineteen days. It was a hasty decision and one which he later came to regret. *Some Time In New York City* does have moments of energy, particularly the driving 'New York City' which conveys Lennon's enthusiasm for his new home. You can even overlook such trite lines as 'His name is David Peel/ And we found that he was real', such is the vitality of the song. Yoko's songs on the record have a charm of their own. 'Sisters, O Sisters' and 'We're All Water' are lyrically invigorating. The haunting quality of her singing and the pile-driving Elephant's Memory meant that the songs stood up on their own.

'Sunday Bloody Sunday' and 'The Luck Of The Irish' were drawn from Lennon's first-hand knowledge of the Irish community in Liverpool, and they convey Lennon's rage at the British troops' occupation of Northern Ireland. 'The Luck Of The Irish' managed, however, to retain some of Lennon's charm.

Where the album falls down is in Lennon's trite and repetitious sloganeering. After being a leader for so long, Lennon was now being led. His direction was dominated by Rubin and Hoffman, who were hardly objective, and while the causes they championed were noble, 'John Sinclair', 'Attica State', 'Angela', and 'Woman Is The Nigger Of The World', for example, are almost offensively single-minded. The victimization of 'subversive elements' by the Nixon administration (which considered Lennon as one) was reprehensible, and it was important that someone of Lennon's stature should speak out against such iniquities. Dylan's 1971 single 'George Jackson' was fired by that same sense of outrage, but Dylan wisely confined his sentiments to a single. Lennon had proved throughout his career that he was one of rock's most articulate spokesmen, able to clarify and delineate problems with a perception and wry humour that few of his contemporaries could match. To hear him endlessly repeat other people's slogans was dispiriting.

Lennon resented the criticism that the album attracted – that he was writing simple lyrics – even though he had always claimed to dislike his songs 'being digested and analysed like the Mona Lisa.' 'I Want To Hold Your Hand' was simple, he said; if he constantly sought praise, he could write more surrealistic material like 'I Am The Walrus'. What motivated him on his arrival in New York was the ease of writing political songs and rushing them out on a record, just as he had always wanted. 'Most other people express themselves by playing football at weekends or shouting. But here am I in New York and I hear about thirteen people shot dead in Ireland and I react immediately. And being what I am I react in four-to-the-bar with a guitar break in the middle,' he told Roy Carr in the *New Musical Express.* 'I don't say, "My God, what's happening, we should do something." I go: "It was Sunday Bloody Sunday/And they shot the people down . . ." It's not like the Bible. It's all over now. It's gone. It's finished.' Music, as a form of communication, was his main concern.

To its credit, the album did possess immediacy, as Lennon remembered: 'When we made that album, we weren't setting out to make the Brandenburg Concerto or the masterpiece everybody always tries to write, paint, draw, or film. . . . The point now is that I want to say whatever it is I've got to say, as simple as the music I like. And that's rock 'n' roll, and to match the lyrics to the music. So now it's . . . AWOPBOPALOOBOP Get Outta Ireland. I suppose it looks more preachy than it really is.'

Some Time In New York City was a realization of Lennon's ideal record at that time: it should have the immediacy of a newspaper and reflect current affairs (the album packaging was based on the *New York Times*). But *Some Time In New York City* did little to enhance Lennon's reputation. Side Three was recorded at the UNICEF Lyceum Benefit in 1969. It includes a workmanlike version of 'Cold Turkey' and continues with Yoko screeching that 'Britain killed Hanratty' (the British murderer who was hanged amidst great controversy in 1961). Side Four included the Zappa jam, with a competent version of the old Olympics hit 'Well (Baby Please Don't Go)' dredged up from the Cavern days.

Lennon swiftly realized he had gone too far. He had lost objectivity, and his craft had suffered. He told New York writer Peter Hamill in 1975: 'It almost *ruined* [my work]. It became journalism and not poetry. And I basically feel that I'm a poet. Then I began to take it seriously on another level, saying, "Well, I am reflecting what is going on, right?" '

Lennon had laid himself wide open for criticism, and the reviews that the album received were a chastening experience for him. At the beginning of 1973 he and Yoko had moved into the Dakota building, and he kept a low profile. Just before Christmas 1972 John and Yoko's 'Happy Xmas (War Is Over)' single was belatedly released in the UK. The Christmas novelty single is a great tradition in Britain. The Lennons' single took up their 'War Is Over, If You Want It' slogan and turned it into a memorable Christmas hit. The message is simply that we should work together and shed a little love, a suitably apposite message for Christmas, and one which echoes round the world every year when it is re-released. The choir on the record is the children's Harlem Community Choir.

Not until the end of 1973 did Lennon feel confident enough to release a new album. *Mind Games* marked a return to the melodicism of *Imagine* and was a distinct departure from the polemics of his previous album. As an indication of his commitment to the project, it was the first album he had produced by himself. He gathered the best session musicians New York could offer. Names like Jim Keltner, David Spinozza, Michael Brecker, and Sneaky Pete Kleinow, regularly featured on albums by Bob Dylan, Ry Cooder, the Rolling Stones, Bruce Springsteen, and the Flying Burrito Brothers. The inherent lushness and attempt to return to former glories could be found on the album's title track, which announced: 'Love is the answer, and you know that for sure.'

John was always one of the great rock 'n' roll vocalists, although he was reticent about his own vocal abilities. He had always allowed his voice to be buried on record, but on 'Tight A$', the album's second track, there is a freewheeling return to rock 'n' roll with Lennon's voice well to the fore. It is not as hard as it could have been (the backing is far too polite), but Lennon is still in great voice and the song rolls along. 'Bring On The Lucie (Freda People)' is another of those cautious rockers – 'OK boys, let's go over the hill,' he announces as the song plunges into its riff. But he doesn't go far enough and lapses back into vacuous slogan-eering. The song is redeemed by some tasty dobro playing.

'Out The Blue' is a beautifully restrained love song, haunting and poignant. John's devotion to Yoko was aching: 'All my life's been a long slow knife/I was born just to get to you.' That feeling persisted on 'I Know (I Know)'. And there was the first indication of Lennon's efforts to bridge the gap between East and West with the schoolboy Japanese of 'Aisumasen (I'm Sorry)' and 'You Are Here', which over-turned Kipling's maxim that 'East is East and West is West and never the twain shall meet.' Lennon maintains that the twain *shall* meet: 'From distant lands, one woman, one man.'

Mind Games has several pleasant tracks – notably the title song – but it suffers from too many mid-paced rockers and lacks his usual lyrical inventiveness. The old radical Lennon had gone (as solace he offered a silent 'Nutopian International Anthem'). The love poet of *Imagine* had gone. The confessional troubador of *Plastic Ono Band* had gone. By the end of 1973 Lennon sounded listless and uninspired. After its release he went on his 'long weekend'.

Walls And Bridges, released in October 1974, was an open letter to the absent Yoko. Many of the songs were pleading, an uncharacteristic role for Lennon. The album was cockier than *Mind Games*, mainly because of Bobby Keys's raunchy sax playing and some generally fine instru-mental back-up. The album was conceived and recorded while Lennon was just coming out of a bender of Dylan

Thomas proportions. His old friend Harry Nilsson was closely involved. As far back as 1968 Lennon had congratulated him on his imaginative Beatle medley on his *Pandemonium Shadow Show* album, and the two had collaborated on Nilsson's *Pussy Cats* LP in California earlier in the year.

Walls And Bridges was a beautifully packaged album, with drawings courtesy of the twelve-year-old John Winston Lennon, an imaginative cut-out sleeve, a lyric book, and plenty of Dr Winston O'Boogie's (a jokey pseudonym John sometimes used) aphorisms. Elton John, an ardent Lennon fan (and at the time himself the most successful British act since the Beatles) guested on the hit single 'Whatever Gets You Thru The Night', which turned out to be the album's best track. A cocky rocker, it had suitably irreverent lyrics: 'Whatever gets you thru the night, s'alright, s'alright.'

On the slower songs like 'Old Dirt Road' and 'Nobody Loves You (When You're Down And Out)' – which he always saw Sinatra as singing – Lennon sounded maudlin. On 'Bless You' he even comes over as sluggish. '#9 Dream' was a barely marked progression from 'Aisumasen'. It had the requisite dreamy atmosphere to match the lyrics and was as much about the number nine, which Lennon always considered lucky, as it was about his state of mind.

'Scared' could lyrically have come from his first album, Lennon laying himself open to the world at large: 'I'm scared . . . No bell, book or candle/Can get you out of this . . . I'm tired of being so alone/No place to call my own/Like a rollin' stone.' 'Going Down On Love' was a plea to Yoko: 'Your love has gone . . . And you shoot out the light/Ain't coming home for the night.' The finished album was a definite improvement on the listless *Mind Games*, but it was hardly vintage Lennon. He recalled the circumstances at the time: 'This last year has been an extraordinary one for me personally. And I'm almost amazed that I could get *anything* out. Musically, my mind was a clutter. It was apparent on *Walls And Bridges*, which was the work of a semi-sick craftsman. There was no inspiration and it gave an aura of misery.'

Significantly, two of the biggest stars of the 1970s, Elton John and David Bowie, played a substantial role in getting Lennon back on the tracks: Elton because he coerced Lennon into appearing with him at his Madison Square Garden concert on Thanksgiving Night 1974 and Bowie because he asked Lennon along to help out on the sessions that made up his 1975 *Young Americans* album. In the studio Lennon backed vocals on what he said was always one of his favourite songs, Bowie's histrionic reading of 'Across The Universe'; John also co-wrote 'Fame' with Bowie and guitarist Carlos Alomar. The song gave Bowie his first American number one hit, while Elton also helped Lennon there with 'Whatever Gets You Thru The Night'.

Lennon's next album to be released was *Rock 'n' Roll* in February 1975. It was a project that had fascinated him for years, and the story behind the album went back to when Chuck Berry's publisher, Morris Levy, had threatened to sue John for alleged plagiarism; Levy claimed that 'Come Together' from *Abbey Road* ripped off Berry's 1956 'You Can't Catch Me'. (Both songs do include the line: 'Here comes old flat top.') In an out of court settlement, Lennon agreed to record a number of Chuck Berry songs for a forthcoming album, which laid the seeds for *Rock 'n' Roll*.

At an artistic and emotional crossroads in 1973, Lennon felt that he needed a producer to dictate how he sang, to help recreate the feel of those rock classics, to advise, and to inspire him. Having dropped Phil Spector after *Some Time In New York City*, and having produced *Mind Games* himself, Lennon now approached Spector again and asked him to work on the new album, originally called *Oldies But Mouldies*. (This was a neat parody on the sub-title of the first Beatles' hits collection released in 1966, *Oldies But Goldies*.) Although a virtual recluse, Spector agreed, and they subsequently recorded many tracks together. But a growing estrangement developed between them, and the sessions grew more and more protracted. (Studio costs alone for the four tracks John considered to be rescuable were $90,000.) Finally Spector disappeared completely, taking the master tapes with him. There was talk of a car crash, rumour piled upon rumour, and not even John could get past the armed guards around the Spector mansion. Eventually Lennon retrieved the tapes, but Spector (once again living the life of a recluse) was no longer interested in pursuing the project. In a burst of energy Lennon tore into the Record Plant in New York at the end of October 1974 and in a mere four days laid down ten new tracks to complete the album. Because of his enthusiasm for the project, and because of Levy's *Roots* album suddenly being made available, *Rock 'n' Roll* was issued only four months after *Walls And Bridges*.

The cover picture alone, by Jürgen Vollmer, was worth the price of the album: John, sneering in a Hamburg doorway in 1961, fresh-faced, every inch a rocker. Blurred figures rush by hurrying to the future, while Lennon stands, as if waiting for the past to catch up with him. Lennon cherished the very *idea* of the album, and effortlessly pitched himself back in time: 'All the words to "Stand By Me" and "Be-Bop-A-Lula", I knew them all from being fifteen, they all just came back to me, just like that.'

In many ways *Rock 'n' Roll* is the definitive John Lennon album. Even when he had toyed with the avant-garde and radical politics, John had remained a rocker at heart. He saw rock 'n' roll as 'the great motivator' and always paid homage to the greats who inspired him. He was genuinely modest about his own songwriting abilities and felt he had never written anything to equal 'Whole Lotta Shakin' Goin' On'. Now stripped of the peace and primals, he stands supreme as the cocky rocker who took on the world and almost beat it. *Rock 'n' Roll* is a human jukebox, with Lennon pouring his heart into his roots. It's far more than simply a rehash of twenty-year-old Chuck Berry and Little Richard songs. Each song on the album is stamped with his personality, infused with Lennon dynamism. The rockers are harder than anything Lennon had done in years, the ballads softer. While rock 'n' roll itself was looking for a direction in 1975, John Lennon was looking imaginatively back at its history.

The album spans the glory years of rock 'n' roll, from Little Richard's 1956 'Rip It Up' to Sam Cooke's 1962 'Bring It On Home To Me'. It covers John's adolescence, picking up the flickering signals of Radio Luxembourg, through art school and teenage groups, right up to the birth of the Beatles. Those songs were the soundtrack to his life, before the world went mad – the shuffle beat of Buddy Holly's 'Peggy Sue', the chilling 'Be-Bop-A-Lula', the raucous 'Ready Teddy' and 'Bony Moronie', the rolling 'Ain't That A Shame', the poignant 'Stand By Me' – Lennon hadn't sung better since *Plastic Ono Band*. His act of homage gave him the shot in the arm he needed.

The most touching aspect of the album comes right at the end of Side Two. He finishes a tender version of Lloyd Price's 'Just Because', treating it affectionately, delivering almost a parody of 1950s recording clichés. The spoken bridge and slow fade culminate with him saying: 'This is Dr Winston O'Boogie saying goodnight from the Record Plant East. We've had a swell time. Everybody here says Hi. Goodbye.' It was as if John knew the album was a watershed. He told Andy Peebles: 'Something flashed through my mind as I said it. Am I really saying farewell to the business? I looked at the cover I'd chosen, which was a picture of me in Hamburg the first time we got there [*sic*]. I thought, this is some sort of cosmic thing. Here I am with this old picture of me in Hamburg in sixty-one and I'm saying farewell from Record Plant, and I'm ending as I started, singing this straight rock 'n' roll stuff.'

With Yoko pregnant, Lennon channelled all his energies into caring for his wife. Nothing more was heard of him on record for five long years. A fortnight after Sean was born in October 1975, *Shaved Fish* was released. It was a timely, well-assembled collection, embracing the range of his work since 1969. Opening with a snatch of 'Give Peace A Chance', and finishing with 'Happy Xmas', the album ran through the facets of his career: Lennon as junkie ('Cold Turkey'), as political activist ('Power To The People'), as idealist ('Imagine', '#9 Dream'). It was an impressive roster. Perhaps more convincingly than any of the four Beatles, Lennon proved with this LP that he had achieved the impossible – he had forged his own identity. He had reconciled his art with his life and proved himself able to cope with his past.

During Lennon's years of silence the English music scene became convulsed with the iconoclasm of punk. 'No more Elvis, Beatles or Stones in 1977' screamed the Clash. The young punks were bored and angry with the remote rock élite. They wanted their own heroes and were not content with second-hand idols, whose lives and music bore no relation to their own.

It marked the first generation gap in music since the broadside delivered by the Beatles and Bob Dylan all those years before. The anarchic approach of the Sex Pistols and the Clash to rock 'n' roll left many of the old guard

684   LENNON

marooned. Lennon remained one of the few rock Establishment figures who was not ridiculed. Perhaps they remembered his struggles and the ridicule *he* had faced, which bore comparison with their own vendetta. For his own private reasons Lennon, wisely, did not opt for punk. He had other things on his mind during the punk upheaval – being a father and a husband, and becoming a human being instead of adopting roles and causes.

During those years of silence he listened to Hank Williams, Carl Perkins, Jerry Lee Lewis, the B52s, Lene Lovitch, Bruce Springsteen, Madness, John Gielgud reading Shakespeare, and 'everything Bing Crosby had ever done'. He listened but did not comment. As the punks created their own idols, he breathed a sigh of relief as he watched the mantle pass on: 'God help Bruce Springsteen when they decide he's no longer God . . . when he gets down to facing his own success and growing older and having to produce it again and again, they'll turn on him and I hope he survives it.' John watched his idols and contemporaries fall, succumbing to the sort of pressures he had wisely managed to avoid.

During those five private years the anger seeped out of John Lennon. There is a school of rock theory that says the only *great* music comes out of anger and frustration, from the energy of youth. It has its point; that *is* where much of rock's motivation has come from. It follows that comfort and contentment see the original intentions vanish and disappear (McCartney's domesticity, Dylan's pulpit-bashing). And yet we have no right to expect our idols to suffer for the sake of their music. If they are enjoying security and happiness, then, inevitably, that is what will be reflected in their music. It is that feeling of contentment and domesticity which permeates *Double Fantasy*.

'(Just Like) Starting Over' was released on 24 October

1980, the first single from John Lennon in five years. Despite the convulsions in pop music during his silence, despite the contempt with which most icons of the 1960s were held, a tremor ran through the music industry – Lennon was back! John now had something fresh to say musically. Sean was five, and he wanted to give his son a birthday present. And he chose the method he knew best.

The songs for the album were mostly written in a three-week burst in Bermuda. But then Lennon was never one to labour over a song. He once told David Bowie: 'Look, it's *very* simple: Say what you mean, make it rhyme, and put a backbeat to it!' John and Yoko had a ball in the studio – Lennon was exultant at being back. 'We cut twenty-two tracks in two weeks!'

Double Fantasy was released in mid-November 1980 on the newly inaugurated Geffen label. With its release some ardent Lennon fans felt twinges of disappointment. They thought it simply showed John and Yoko washing their clean linen in public. Gone was the old *Angst*-ridden Lennon, the poet who carried the world's troubles on his shoulders. With the tracks evenly split between them, the Lennons now offered domestic bliss as the solution. It should have been obvious to everyone what public face the inscrutable Lennon would present. His wife and child were now his whole world. What else could he (or did he want to) write about? *Double Fantasy* was the most honest Lennon album since *Plastic Ono Band* in that it perfectly reflected his state of mind. The demons were vanquished. The past was firmly put in its place. With Yoko and Sean, and after forty years of trial and torment, John Lennon had found peace.

In all truth, and ridding ourselves of the poignancy that irrevocably surrounds *Double Fantasy*, it is not a great album. In retrospect it is, of course, John Lennon's final vinyl statement in which the tracks were produced, mixed, and sequenced exactly as he intended. A song like 'Beautiful Boy (Darling Boy)' takes on a terrible beauty in the aftermath of Lennon's murder, as he sings to his son: 'Close your eyes and have no fear/The monster's gone and your Daddy's here.' The morning he promised Sean at the end of the song never came.

'Starting Over' was the album opener, ushered in by the ringing of Yoko's personal 'wishing bell' – it was a deliberate ploy: 'I put it on *Double Fantasy* to show the likeness and difference from "Mother" to "Starting Over",' said John. Before, tolling bells had emphasized doom. Now there was a chirpy cheerful bell, indicating a willingness to start again. What was appealing was the diehard rock 'n' roll voice he chose (à la Elvis): 'It was the fifties-ish sound because I had never really written a song that sounded like that period, although that was my period, the music I identified with. So I just thought, why the hell not? In the Beatle days, that would have been taken as a joke. One avoided clichés. But now those clichés are not clichés any more,' he told *Playboy*.

'Woman' was a beautifully sustained Lennon ballad, written in fifteen minutes; it is already a classic. It recalls the fragility of 'Imagine' and touchingly recognizes that Yoko understands 'the little child inside the man'. 'Dear Yoko' finds Lennon again in fine 1950s voice, pleading his love. It is a rockier version of 'Oh Yoko!' from 1971 and perfectly summarizes the intensity of their relationship: 'Without you I'm a one-track mind, dear Yoko/After all is really said and done/The two of us are really one.' (Yoko's seven songs on the album were her most accessible to date and proved she had an even more contemporary edge than her husband.)

'Watching The Wheels' is Lennon's answer to all those who speculated on his state of mind during his five-year silence: 'People have been saying I'm lazy, dreaming my life away, all my life,' John commented. 'Pop stars were getting indignant in the press that I wasn't making records. I couldn't believe it, they were acting like mothers-in-law.' To counter that speculation, Lennon wrote of what he actually was doing: 'watching shadows on the wall . . . No longer riding on the merry-go-round/I just had to let it go.' Finally, after years of pressure, Lennon could slide off the helter skelter and leave the fairground. The song was powerfully autobiographical.

It could come as no surprise to him, though, that people were fascinated by his silence. Rock 'n' roll is a notoriously short-lived profession. The only comparable absences were when Elvis entered the army in 1958 and Dylan's enforced seclusion following his motorcycle crash of 1966. Rumours spread. The remote rock star becomes a mythical figure. People couldn't believe that John Lennon, probably the most talented rocker of his generation, could be *happy* simply making bread! He realized people still looked to him for answers, but by 1980 the only answer he could offer was: 'Just sitting here watching the wheels go round/ I really love to watch them roll.' He told *Rolling Stone* in 1980: 'They're my own wheels, mainly. But you know, watching myself is like watching everybody else. The hardest thing is facing yourself. It's easier to shout "Revolution" and "Power To The People" than it is to look at yourself and try to find out what's real inside you and what isn't, when you're pulling the wool over your own eyes.' Lennon was well aware of the disappointment that his new-found peace would cause his fans but had no wish to compromise his own feelings to satisfy them: 'I cannot be a punk in Hamburg and Liverpool any more. I'm older now, I see the world through different eyes . . . As Elvis Costello said— "What's so funny 'bout peace, love and understanding?" '

In the terrible aftermath of John's death in December 1980, 'Starting Over', 'Imagine', and 'Woman' all reached number one on the British charts. The three songs he performed with Elton John in 1974 appeared on a single, and *The John Lennon Collection* was the number one album for Christmas 1982.

When the shock of Lennon's murder eventually subsided, the *Milk And Honey* album was released in January 1984. Recorded at the *Double Fantasy* sessions in August 1980, the album follows the format of its predecessor, the tracks evenly divided between John and Yoko. The single, 'Nobody Told Me', was among John's best since 'Imagine', a jerky compelling rocker (with Lennon again favouring that 1950s vocal style) which raced into the British charts. It stands as a tribute to his innate musical ability that 'Nobody Told Me' sounds as ebullient and infectious as anything Lennon had ever done.

Milk And Honey has a harder feel to it than *Double Fantasy* because of the obvious rawness of the Lennon tracks. As Yoko told Andy Peebles, the temptation for any outside producer would have been to over-produce the whole album (as Norman Petty did with Buddy Holly's posthumous recordings). So the resultant album retains its charm and spontaneity, notably on the lovely 'Grow Old With Me', with Lennon on piano, accompanied by a rhythm box. There is a grittiness on the album's rockier tracks, showing that, right to the end, Lennon was a rocker. Rock was both his heritage and his legacy.

There are moments of mawkishness, as in '(Forgive Me)

My Little Flower Princess', but on the whole it is the moments of touching greatness we remember. 'I Don't Wanna Face It' carries on the theme developed in 'Watching The Wheels' with Lennon advocating that people find another hero, he has had enough: 'Say you're looking for a place to go/Where nobody knows your name/You're looking for oblivion, with one eye on the Hall of Fame/I don't wanna face it . . . Well I can dish it out/But I just can't take it,' 'I'm Stepping Out' opens the album with Lennon taking on the character of Lonnie Donegan of 'Rock Island Line' vintage, before stepping into traditional blues territory, with John revelling in his role as house-husband.

The perfect marriage occurs at the end of Side One, as Lennon's 'Three, four . . .' ushers in 'Nobody Told Me', with his ruminating on Nazis in the bathroom and little yellow idols, punctuated by wistful cries of 'Strange days indeed Momma.' Next to it, Yoko's poignant, brief ' "O" Sanity', probably her most incisive recorded song, ends with the terse: 'Let it go, cut it out!'

'Borrowed Time' has Lennon facing the uncertainties of middle age in a world no longer conveniently divided into black and white: 'The more I see, the less I know for sure,' he sings, although maintaining that 'It's good to be older.' For John, 'Grow Old With Me' had become a pleasant vision of his and Yoko's future. He wanted to include it on *Double Fantasy* but couldn't decide on the song's arrangement. As the album's deadline drew closer, it was held over for the follow-up and appears here in this charming, uncluttered version.

The album is peppered with Lennon's on-mike asides, his count-ins, and snatches of studio conversation, which add to the casual eavesdropping atmosphere for the listener. *Milk And Honey* is full of charm and tragedy. The tragedy lies in the fact that as a musician and poet John Lennon was back finding his musical feet. On the sleeve of his 1975 *Rock 'n' Roll* album, Dr Winston O'Boogie simply wrote: 'You should have been there.' Thanks to the music of John Lennon, we were and always will be.

TWENTY-FOUR

THE COMEBACK

'Life begins at forty'

THE WORD spread like a forest fire at the beginning of August 1980: John Lennon, the hermit, the Howard Hughes of rock, the man who had freaked out to become a house-husband and led a mysterious, reclusive life for five years, was back. At a New York recording studio he was recording a new album. With Yoko Ono. Amid US election fever (Carter was to lose to Reagan in November), and as fifty-four Americans were held hostage in Iran, the news from the Lennon camp was like a beacon of light.

John's decision to return to recording had been made in Bermuda a month earlier. Bermuda proved yet another watershed for John. He had gone there because he felt that until then he had done so few things alone in his life. He decided to go by sea with a five-man crew on his yacht *Isis*. The crossing from Newport, Rhode Island, is notoriously rough at certain times of the year, and the yacht was tossed around in heavy seas. With the crew falling sick one by one, it fell to John to take the controls, which he did successfully. 'There was crockery falling all over the place and it was really rough with the waves coming up over the boat,' John recalled later. 'I thought I was supposed to be the passenger but I had a go.' He told Aunt Mimi of it by

phone when he reached Bermuda; he had felt like an old
sea captain, the sort that sailed into Liverpool. John said
he had sung himself songs as he steered the yacht to keep
us his morale: mostly Beatles oldies, 'Strawberry Fields
Forever', 'Getting Better', 'Please Please Me'. Mentally he
was slowly turning full circle.

In Bermuda, in a rented house, the idea was for John
to relax totally and go swimming and sailing. But he could
hardly stay off the phone each day, trying to reach Yoko.
Incredibly he sometimes found his busy wife in business
meetings, unable to be interrupted. It was then that he
wrote the evocative song 'I'm Losing You', which he played
to her over the telephone.

At the Forty Thieves discothèque and also on the radio
John heard the music he was listening to being described
as 'new wave'. It struck him that there was nothing new
about it. Yoko had been writing and performing much
more imaginative material, in the same genre, ten years
earlier. At the time she was rejected as a freak. Perhaps, he
mused, the world was ready for her now. It inspired him
to write songs furiously. One of his first was 'Woman', that
paean not only to Yoko but to women everywhere, which
laid bare his deepest affections for them. Over the next
week or two, during his daily phone conversations with
Yoko, he sang and played her his latest compositions and
she reciprocated with her new work. The stage was set. On
his return to Manhattan, he and Yoko had around twenty
songs between them, some finished, some unfinished.

'(Just Like) Starting Over' epitomized precisely what
John felt about his return to recording. His earliest influences in rock 'n' roll – Elvis Presley and Roy Orbison –
were recalled on the sound and atmosphere of the song.
The album's concept, a combination of songs by both husband and wife, was poetically captured by the title, *Double*

Fantasy. John had been enraptured by a flower of this name while out walking in the summer in botanical gardens in Bermuda. It suited the tone of the album perfectly.

Back in New York, John was in superb mental and physical shape for the recording sessions. Seen outside the Hit Factory studios on West 54th Street, Manhattan, he looked sprightly and smiling. For the first time in eighteen years he was free of a contract: he had written the songs and was making the record purely for himself. No record deal was in the offing – the plan was to find a label when they had completed the work. The working pattern and atmosphere at the recording studios was both civilized and organized. Potted plants and flowers were ordered; there was a waiting room with comfortable chairs for everyone to relax; the musicians chosen to accompany John and Yoko were kindred spirits whom they admired as players: Andy Newmark (drums), Hugh McCracken (bass guitar), Earl Slick (guitar), Tony Levin (bass guitar). The competition among New York musicians to be on John Lennon's comeback album was enormous.

Yoko knew John was hungry for a successful return to work. He was particularly anxious for success in Britain. Phone calls to Aunt Mimi, imported tapes of British television shows like *Fawlty Towers* and *Monty Python*, and anything that gave him a sighting of the green British countryside, had made John almost misty-eyed when he thought of his native land. 'But England's not gonna go away,' he told anyone near him who asked when he was planning to return. 'It's still going to be there when I want to go and have a look at it.'

He was in majestic form in the recording studios. His voice had achieved a resonance that was still the quintessential John Lennon but with a wordliness brilliantly mirrored in the lyrics of his songs.

Elliot Mintz had attended a number of *Double Fantasy* recording sessions. They were unlike any recording session for a John and Yoko album, he remembers. 'Yoko made it very clear to everyone that there was to be no alcohol or drugs of any kind during the making of that album. When it was time to break for dinner she had exquisite servings of fresh *sushi* delivered to the studio for the musicians and crew. A large colour photograph of Sean was taped over the television screen that faced the mixing console. There were dishes of raisins and sesame seeds placed around the control room. An assistant set up a small room with an interior look that resembled one of the rooms in the Dakota. Some pieces of furniture and art were placed in there so they would both feel comfortable and at home during the breaks.'

In November 1980 Elliot again flew in from Los Angeles to hear the final tape of *Double Fantasy*. John and Yoko had received the first complete master cassette on the night he arrived. 'John escorted me into the old bedroom and asked me to sit at the foot of the bed, while John and Yoko lay down with their heads propped up on the pillows – the stereo speakers were on the mantelpiece behind them. It was about ten at night and John dimmed the lights as he pushed the play button on the cassette. He played it loudly.'

As Mintz listened to the music, he was reminded of another time. 'We had met for the first time almost ten years before. I thought about that first experience in California when we listened to the acetate of *Some Time In New York City*. John once told me he remembered points in his life recalling the songs he was writing at the time. That night I was consciously reviewing the decade of adventure I had shared with John and Yoko: the birthdays, Christmases, trips around the world, months in Japan, John's Lost Weekend in California, the first time I saw Sean.'

The cassette ended, and the three of them chatted excitedly into the night. When Elliot finally left, John walked him to the front door of the apartment. He was wearing pyjamas under an antique Japanese robe. Elliot thought he had never looked better or seemed more optimistic. 'His enthusiasm was contagious – it was the best time of his life.'

'If you wake up before noon,' John said to his best male pal, 'we can meet for breakfast in the old hotel.' As he turned the brass doorknob, Mintz recalls hearing the sound of bells.

'They used to have a string of chimes draped around the doorknob. Whenever anyone came or went, the bells would make a delicate sound as they rubbed against the door. We used to joke about it being a subtle, Zen-like alarm system.'

As the elevator door closed, Mintz heard the bells chime again as John closed the door. They spoke by phone in the weeks ahead, but Mintz never saw John again.

With enough songs to make an album and plans for two more beyond that, John became apprehensive about signing a contract with the right record company. Free of both EMI/Capitol and Apple, John was anxious not to sign with a major corporation. The album was sought by many companies, but too many wanted to hear the music before talking about a deal. John regarded that as an insult to his integrity after eighteen years of making records. The album eventually went to David Geffen, whose empathy with major artists for more than a decade was matched by his acceptance of the record 'on trust', with not a note played to him before the deal was done. Geffen had been instrumental in discovering Joni Mitchell, Jackson Browne, and the Eagles. His Asylum label had also boasted Tom Waits and Linda Ronstadt. Before signing the Lennons, his biggest coup had been to persuade Bob Dylan away from CBS for two albums in the mid-1970s. *Double Fantasy* helped establish his label, which would later also attract Elton John, Asia, and Peter Gabriel.

For the fans, the five-year wait had been a long one during pop music's darkest and least creative decade since its birth in 1955. John's return was a timely marker of rock's silver anniversary. He wanted to start a new decade and one which pointed up not down. As far as he was concerned the 1960s were hip and the 1970s appalling. Only the birth of Sean had redeemed the previous decade for him. Family relationships, love, and personal communication were now the foundation of his music, and he applied all the passion and articulacy to his mature love songs that he had to his Beatles hits. John had too much sense to wade back with all the sounds of yesteryear, and he avoided the trap of becoming an embarrassing forty-year-old rocker. For her part, Yoko responded to John telling her that her music of a decade before was now fashionable with the remark: 'I'm not going to do all that *old* stuff.' Fittingly sub-titled 'A Heart Play', *Double Fantasy* traced the path for family relationships which John had found so enriching and now wanted others to share.

It was a natural evolution for a man who had come full circle. When John had returned from seclusion and Bermuda, he was heavily in favour of survival. He had seen too many of his rock 'n' roll contemporaries die prematurely, martyrs to their own myths: Elvis Presley, Jimi Hendrix, Brian Jones, Buddy Holly, Eddie Cochran, and also James Dean and Marilyn Monroe. John did not believe in any 'live fast die young' philosophy. He did not want to be a hero. He wanted to carry on making his marriage better, making music, raising his son. And in the year 1981 he would sail to Britain as part of a short concert tour, also taking in New York, Los Angeles, San Francisco, and Hamburg. 'Yes, we'll have real fun on this tour,' John said. To mark the new album Yoko gave John a gold watch inscribed on the back: 'To John. Just Like Starting Over. Love Yoko.'

At the age of thirty-nine, when he re-entered the recording studios, Lennon was at a mental peak. No other major rock star had achieved such intellectual and physical maturity yet maintained an aura of rugged warmth. As John put it succinctly but with his customary edge, when he spoke of people who wanted to carry on in rock bands into their forties: 'So the Stones have been going for a hundred and twelve years. Yippee!' That, he implied, was no achievement. *His* success could be measured by the fact that he had grown up, not grown old, in the same field. Many middle-aged pop stars from the 1960s invited the question: 'What are you going to do when you grow up?' John was determined it would never be addressed to him. He confounded the cynics by returning with his own highly personal stance, that somehow reached out to old and new music fans. In defeating all the odds, John had also beaten the system that chewed artists up before spitting them out as tired and worn.

John crystallized his outlook and his life as a family man on his new song 'Cleanup Time'.

'I'm not interested in being a sex symbol,' John said. He reiterated his pride and the unity with his wife and family: 'It was an enlightening experience for me, as the house-husband . . . because it was a complete reversal of my upbringing . . . I did it to experience what it was like being the women who've done it for me. And it's the way of the future. I'm glad to be in on the forefront of that.'

He felt that for a period he had lost the initial freedom of the artist by 'becoming enslaved to the image of the artist.' Many artists killed themselves because of that, John said. Yoko had been his mental liberation, salvation, inspiration.

'Life begins at forty, so they promised. I believe it, too. I feel fine. I'm . . . excited. It's like twenty-one, and saying: "Wow, what's gonna happen?" '

TWENTY-FIVE

THE END

'What does it mean that when you're such a pacifist you get shot?'

ON THE afternoon of Saturday 6 December 1980 John went alone to Café La Fortuna for his customary *cappuccino* and reading of the newspapers. Vincent Urwand playfully teased him about his comeback album.

'Look, you've had all those years of wildness and success in the Beatles. You don't need the money. What are you doing all this for? You're enjoying being a husband and a father!'

John laughed. 'I swore I'd look after that boy until he was five, and he's five and I feel like getting back to my music,' he replied. 'The urge is there. It's been a long time since I wrote a song, but they're coming thick and fast now.' John sent Vincent a demonstration copy of *Double Fantasy*, autographed by him and Yoko.

That same evening John phoned Aunt Mimi. Enthusing about his record, he told her about its success, how pleased he was with it, and how he was thinking about a world tour. Mimi, used to his capriciousness and visions of Utopia, was unconvinced by his *bonhomie*. 'John,' she said, in the peremptory voice he knew and secretly loved, 'John, you're an idealist looking for a lost horizon. You would make a saint cry!' For thirty-five years she had listened to him articulating his dreams. They both enjoyed banter.

'Oh, Mimi don't be like that . . . You see, I'll *see you soon* and we'll bring Sean. Goodnight, God bless, Mimi.'

Two nights later John was dead.

At the Dakota John and Yoko were among the most popular residents. The exclusive apartment block's vetting committee, which had allowed them to buy up five apartments comprising thirty-four rooms in nine years, had been vindicated. The surest test of their acceptance came from the doormen and desk staff. While some celebrated Dakota residents treated the staff dismissively and bossily, John and Yoko always treated them as equals, with, in the words of several, perfect manners. John was so popular and such a generous tipper that the staff almost fought to deliver his packages to the seventh floor. Throughout his life John trusted everyone. A fatal flaw in him was a lack of perception in judging which people were 'on the level' with him. He was honest and expected the same of everyone.

Jay Hastings was a twenty-seven-year-old front desk clerk in the oak-panelled entrance hall of the Dakota. He checked every arrival and every package and phoned through to any apartment for permission to release the door lock and allow a visitor access. With the constant stream of artists, businessmen, and delivery people arriving at the Dakota's forbidding Gothic entrance, 'You get to be a pretty shrewd judge of character,' he says.

Growing a beard in midsummer 1980, John quizzed Jay Hastings about how he kept his facial hair looking so trim. Hastings told him he must buy a pair of plastic, snap-on guides for his razor. 'You mean as if I'm cutting grass?' said John. 'That's amazing. They make *that* kind of thing for people with beards?' But within a few weeks Lennon was in the lobby with neither beard nor spectacles, carrying a guitar case and *en route* for Bermuda. Jay asked him where the beard had gone. 'Oh, there was a picture of me with it in the paper and people recognized me everywhere after that,' replied John. 'I just wanna roam *free*! Nobody will expect me to look like this.'

On so many nights Jay Hastings had awaited John's cheery whistle as his five-foot-eleven frame strode distinctively the thirty-second walk from West 72nd Street up the steps into the hallway. '*Bonsoir*, Jay!' John would often say.

At the beginning of December 1980 John was particularly 'up', Hastings recalls. 'He had the album out, *Double Fantasy*. He was going back and forth two miles to the studio most days, leaving late afternoon and returning between ten-thirty and eleven-thirty, with Yoko. I'd listen out for the slam of their black limousine door. I could always tell his walk. And I waited for that whistle.'

The night of 8 December was particularly balmy. After spending five hours in the studio John and Yoko returned, their car pulling up at 10:49 pm. José, the doorman, left his sentry box to open their car door. John walked ahead of Yoko into the archway. A man's voice called out: 'Mr Lennon?' As John turned round, his murderer shot five bullets from a .38 revolver into his back. Contrary to popular belief, John was not shot in the chest. The bullets caught his arm and, mostly, his back as he turned his head to face his murderer.

Horrifying, chaotic scenes followed. Yoko, hysterical, screamed for an ambulance. John staggered up the six steps to Jay Hastings' office, eventually falling on his left side onto the floor, moaning, 'I'm shot, I'm shot.' Hastings ripped his own jacket off and covered John with it; then he immediately pressed an alarm button connected directly to the police precinct. Within two minutes a police car had arrived. They decided there was no time to wait for an ambulance. Jay Hastings helped the police carry John to their car which sped to Roosevelt Hospital. There doctors tried instant heart massage but to no avail. John died from a massive loss of blood.

At the Dakota the cassette recorder and tape that John was carrying when he fell were slowly picked up. Yoko later took possession of his spectacles. The music in his hand, destined for their next album, was Yoko's 'Walking On Thin Ice'. Back home from the hospital, Yoko composed herself enough to issue a simple statement to a shattered world: 'John loved and prayed for the human race. Please do the same for him.'

As the news of his murder broke, the world's airwaves were filled with his music. Tragically, incredibly, the moment of his death was also the time he came alive in the minds of millions. He was guaranteed immortality on a scale that neither he, nor the world's ageing Beatles fans, would ever comprehend. Not since the murder of President John F. Kennedy in 1963 had the world been so enraged, stunned, and simply hurt by an assassination. Lennon's murder transcended that of even a major statesman because John was so much closer to his public. For one awful moment, a world that didn't care was brought together, and in its grief remembered *how* to care. As shock turned to anger, as statesmen paid their tributes to his talent and human qualities, as the Dakota flag hung at half mast in his honour, the bitter irony sank in: the rebel who had finally found tranquillity in his life and who had preached peace and love, offered hope, inspired millions with his imagination, self-deprecating wit, compassion, and new example of family commitment, had died by the gun.

John was cremated at Hartsdale Crematorium, New York State. Millions mourned him, often with celebrations of his music which eclipsed the desire for revenge. Tributes poured in from around the world as people went on pilgrimages: to Menlove Avenue; to Liverpool College of Art; to Mathew Street, once the home of the Cavern; to New York's Central Park, where Yoko's request for a world-wide ten-minute silence was marked by 400,000 people assembling opposite John's home, heads bowed; and to Hamburg, where Astrid Kirchherr still remembers the terrible depression. 'The city seemed to close for days,' she says. Millions mourned the loss of their adolescence, for John had supplied the soundtrack to it. At a time when we could expect no more from rock 'n' roll, its voice as a form of youthful rebellion long gone and the battle for teenage assertiveness won, John had survived with a rare dignity. He had made the transition so few manage, from young rocker to artist, and in forty years he had always refused to be bought. When he outgrew the Beatles, he stayed true to himself. The world mourned the loss of his arrogance, his humour, his warmth, his frailties, and, above all, his humanity.

John was acutely aware of the fact that the number nine had dominated his life.

He was born at 6:30 pm (six plus three making nine) on 9 October 1940. Sean was born on 9 October 1975. Brian Epstein first saw John and the Beatles at Liverpool's Cavern on 9 November 1961, and he secured their record contract with EMI in London on 9 May 1962. The debut record, 'Love Me Do', was on Parlophone R4949.

John met Yoko Ono on 9 November 1966. John and Yoko's apartment was located on West 72nd Street, New York City (seven plus two making nine), and their main

Dakota apartment number was also, at first, 72. The bus he had travelled on as a student each morning from his home to Liverpool Art College had been the 72.

The registration number of the car that knocked down and killed his mother was LKF 630 (nine). It was driven by Police Constable number 126 (nine).

'Penny Lane' (nine letters) is in postal district 18 (nine) in Liverpool (nine). *Sgt Pepper* has nine letters, as do the names of some key people who touched John's life: Mimi Smith: Jim Gretty who sold John his first real guitar at Frank Hessy's shop; Mr Stevenson, his art college principal; Bob Wooler at the Cavern; the Maharishi; and Bill Harry of *Mersey Beat* newspaper.

Early Liverpool venues for the Beatles included Jacaranda (nine), Blue Angel (nine), and Cassanova (nine).

Julian Lennon was born at Sefton General Hospital, 126 (nine) Smithdown Road, Liverpool. Both John's mother and his stepfather were pronounced dead there.

At school he sat nine General Certificate of Education exams, and failed them all.

John's first group was called the Quarry Men (nine letters).

When John first met Cynthia she was living at 18 (nine) Trinity Road, Hoylake.

The cover of John's album *Walls And Bridges* features a painting he did at age eleven. This shows a football player with a large nine on his shirt.

John's songs included 'Revolution 9', '#9 Dream', and 'One After 909', which he had written at his mother's home at 9 Newcastle Road, Wavertree, Liverpool. When he moved his Aunt Mimi from Liverpool to Sandbanks in Dorset, her new address was 126 Panorama Road, the combination of figures striking John as his special number.

He even joked to me that one of his most important

songs had nine key words: 'All we are saying is Give Peace A Chance.'

When John went gambling in Las Vegas, the number he repeatedly chose on the roulette wheel was nine . . . and he usually lost with it.

In Paris in 1964 during the Beatles' tour he received a death threat letter which made him nervous: 'I am going to shoot you at nine tonight.' John sold Tittenhurst Park to Ringo on 9 September 1973. He believed the sign of a marriage 'written in the stars' was that the names of John Ono Lennon and Yoko Ono Lennon together featured the letter 'o' nine times.

When John was killed, at 10:50 pm in New York on 8 December 1980, the five-hour time difference meant that it was 9 December in Britain. His body was taken to Roosevelt Hospital. It was situated on Ninth Avenue, Manhattan. John was pronounced dead at 11:07 pm (nine).

Within two hours of the shooting Elliot Mintz was on American Airlines Flight 10 from Los Angeles to New York. His mother had phoned from there to say she had heard a radio bulletin that John had been shot. Mintz's car radio was not working; as he drove to Los Angeles airport he hoped and believed that Lennon had survived. 'Just after take-off, I was sitting alone when the cockpit door opened. A stewardess appeared with tears streaming down her face. A lady asked her what was the matter. "John Lennon is dead," I overheard her say.' For the five-hour flight, Elliot remained in his seat in the darkened cabin in a state of shock. He went directly to the Dakota to be with Yoko.

'It was about six in the morning when I arrived. The police had not disturbed the spot where it happened.

The image of the broken glass and the chalk marks and
John's blood on the cement will haunt me for ever.

'I stood by the door to the old bedroom. For a long
time I just listened to Yoko crying before I knocked.'

'It's me,' Mintz whispered. 'I'll be right here if you
need me.' He stayed for the next two months, answering
phones, sorting mail, meeting reporters, co-ordinating
security, following up calls from psychics and psychotics,
and generally supporting Yoko and Sean. Later he was asked
to inventory all John's precious possessions, noting the
many photographs that Aunt Mimi had posted to her surrogate son months before.

'No one ever gets over a tragedy of this magnitude,'
says Mintz. 'You just learn to readjust, to cope, to deal with
a different reality. Yoko and Sean have been an inspiration to
me. They are now the keepers of the wishing well. Her
optimism and sense of dignity prevail. John and Yoko
represent a prototype for couples of the future. Their love
and honesty and conviction are now part of everyone whom
they touched. He was very special.'

On 10 December 1980 Yoko, who had the appalling
job of breaking the news to five-year-old Sean, issued the
following statement from the Dakota:

> I told Sean what happened. I showed him the picture of
> his father on the cover of the paper and explained the
> situation. I took Sean to the spot where John lay after
> he was shot. Sean wanted to know why the person shot
> John if he liked John. I explained that he was probably
> a confused person. Sean said we should find out if he
> was confused or if he really had meant to kill John. I
> said that was up to the court. He asked what court — a
> tennis court or a basketball court? That's how Sean used
> to talk with his father. They were buddies. John would

have been proud of Sean if he had heard this. Sean cried later. He also said, 'Now Daddy is part of God. I guess when you die you become much more bigger because you're part of everything.'

I don't have much more to add to Sean's statement. The silent vigil will take place December 14th at 2 pm for ten minutes.

Our thoughts will be with you.
Love, Yoko and Sean

None of the public responses were as simple and eloquent as those of the hundreds of fans who stood vigil for days outside the Dakota, with banners bearing quickly scrawled slogans like: 'Strawberry Fields Forever, John', 'We'll Never Forget Him', and, movingly, 'Christmas In Heaven'.

Upstairs in her bedroom as the fans stayed there playing transistors with a non-stop, twenty-four-hour soundtrack of John's music, Yoko could scarcely stand the pressure. 'It began,' she recalls, 'on the night of the murder. As it wore on, throughout the week, it nearly drove me crazy. All day and all night, the music . . . after what had just happened, it was unbearable.' She valued the fans' touching letters, which still arrive every day.

Such spontaneous, heartfelt emotion came through a love of a man, his music, and what he represented. For, although John shunned the role of leader, he was, despite his reluctance, the inspiration for a generation's ideals. He never wanted to be a god, certainly not a dead martyr. 'Make your own dreams and do things for yourself. I can't wake you up. You wake *you* up,' he said. All he had done, he implied, was leave a few signposts; but he positively rejected any theory that he was saying 'Follow me, this is how it is.' Gandhi and Martin Luther King were great examples, he pointed out, of non-violent people who had died violently. He never understood that, he said. Unnervingly, one of the last sentences he said to a friend, David Sheff, for *Playboy* magazine, was: 'What does it mean that when you're such a pacifist you get shot?'

In the weeks that followed, as the world's media were flooded with discussions of John's life and music, Yoko went into seclusion in the Dakota. She decided to cut off all her hair as a mark of respect for her husband. She closed off the bedroom they used to sleep in. Out of all the hundreds of gifts John had showered on her in the red velvet boxes he knew she loved, she took only two items to keep by her side – ironically they were *her* final gifts to *him*: the inscribed gold watch she had given him a month before he died, and a tiny American flag pin made up of red rubies, white diamonds, and blue sapphires. Yoko is rarely seen without the diamond necklace which John bought at Tiffany's and which she wears in the picture on the sleeve of *Double Fantasy*.

Inside the apartment Yoko instructed staff that every picture and painting on all the walls was to be left, for ever, precisely as John had wanted. There were, interestingly, no Beatles pictures or gold records hanging there. Significantly, the only one of John as a musician was the original picture of the twenty-year-old Lennon standing in a Hamburg doorway, every inch a rock 'n' roller.

'I think,' said Yoko when I met her a few months after the murder, 'that in many ways he was a simple Liverpool man right to the end. He was a chameleon, a bit of a chauvinist, but so human. In our fourteen years together he never stopped trying to improve himself *from within*. We were best friends but also competitive artists. To me, he is still alive. Death alone doesn't extinguish a flame and a spirit like John.'

John and Yoko probably saw more of each other in

fourteen years than most married couples see of each other in a lifetime. It was hardly surprising that, in the wake of his assassination, Yoko became severely depressed alone in her bedroom. Staring out of the window, she ate only mushrooms and chocolate cake for nearly three months and smoked her Nat Sherman brown cigarettes until she felt that there was a clear choice facing her: she could either return to work, managing the family business as before, or she could go back to making a record. She finally decided on both: John would have liked that.

Her first decision astonished those who did not know her. She wanted to stay at the Dakota. John was part of the place. She felt him over her shoulder. And when she finally emerged, walking every day past the very spot where John was shot, she felt the inner strength of his invisible presence.

'I have strong emotions of sorrow, and hate, and resentment, but where do you put them?' she said to me. Gaunt, nervous of her first newspaper interview since the murder, she chainsmoked throughout and had carefully checked all the signs, astrologically, beforehand to ensure that we should talk. (The interviews, which took place at the Dakota, appeared in London's *Daily Mirror* on 12 and 13 August and subsequently in dozens of international publications.)

Scorned and vilified no more, Yoko Ono as a widow ironically gained a respect she would have preferred not to have earned. The world which had once jeered suddenly applauded her dignity. 'Do you know how that feels? For ten years I was the devil,' she said to me. 'Now suddenly I am an angel. Did the world have to lose John for people to change their opinion of me? It's unreal. If it brought John back, I'd rather remain hated.'

To regain her sanity and to make some statements, Yoko went back to the recording studio. When she went into the Hit Factory to record *Season of Glass* with many of the musicians who had worked on *Double Fantasy*, she conquered a voice choking with emotion and sang her compositions charged with grief and anger. 'Making the record was definitely a therapy, the only way I could survive,' she says. 'I felt John was with me all the time in the studio.' Her songs 'Goodbye Sadness' with the sound of four gunshots and the ambulance siren on 'No, No, No' are stunningly evocative of the murder. And at one point she shouted on the record, 'You *bastards*. We had *everything!*' Yoko ran into a major controversy on her choice of photograph for the sleeve which showed John's blood-covered spectacles, which she had retrieved on the night of the murder. 'Tasteless,' said her critics.

Yoko disagreed: 'John would have approved and I will explain why. I wanted the whole world to be reminded of what happened. People are offended by the glasses and the blood? The glasses are a tiny part of what happened. If people can't stomach the glasses, I'm sorry. There was a dead body. There was blood. His whole body was bloody. There was a load of blood all over the floor. That's the reality. I want people to face up to what happened. He did not commit suicide. He was *killed*. People are offended by the glasses and the blood? John had to stomach a lot more.'

John's assassin, Mark David Chapman, was twenty-five. He came originally from Decatur, Georgia, but had been living in Honolulu with his wife, Gloria. He had worked as a hospital security guard and a printer but had left, alone, for New York several days before 8 December 1980. He stayed at the Olcott Hotel on West 72nd Street, just two hundred yards from the scene of the murder. That day, clutching a copy of John and Yoko's *Double Fantasy* album, he loitered outside the Dakota building and succeeded in getting John's autograph. Nobody had any reason to regard the fans who often stood outside the Dakota as a threat.

In a fifteen-minute hearing on 9 December in a packed Manhattan Criminal Court, the district attorney said: 'This man came to New York with a specific purpose. He has done it. Chapman deliberately premeditated the execution of John Lennon in a cool, calm, rational, and intelligent manner.' Chapman's lawyer said the murderer had told him he had always been a great fan of Lennon: 'He told me he had admired him very much ever since he was ten years old. My impression was of a very confused character.'

Chapman was subsequently sentenced to between twenty years and life imprisonment, first going to Rikers jail and later to the top-security Attica State Prison, New York, as convict number 81A3860. There, he became arguably the most closely guarded man in the world, because of the distinct possibility of reprisals from other prisoners irate about having Lennon's murderer near them. John's friend, the singer-songwriter Harry Nilsson, involved himself in a campaign to ban handguns in America.

Yoko, warily opening John's drawers and books in the months after his death, found notes from him to her which she had never seen. 'Mother, don't forget the clocks are one hour fast . . . Daddy.' Others, more affectionate, brought her to tears. 'Don't forget the kettle's on.' 'Mother, I'll be back in an hour.' She cried often and speaks of John in the present tense: 'His spirit is in the world for ever,' she declares.

It was three years before she could bear to listen to the songs he planned for their follow-up album to *Double Fantasy*. Finally, weeping openly when she re-discovered his aching love songs to her, 'Grow Old With Me', she had a cassette recording of it encased in sweet-smelling, rare

Bermudan cedarwood, a favourite aroma of John's. The music box, engraved 'Milk and Honey, Love Yoko and Sean, Xmas, '83, NYC,' was sent to her friends one month before the final album, *Milk and Honey*, was released.

Back in England Aunt Mimi, suffering from a respiratory illness, sold Sandbanks in Dorset and went to live with her sister Anne near Liverpool. Heartbroken, she turned off the radio whenever John's voice came on. 'I shall never recover,' she told me.

On a visit to Liverpool in 1984 with Sean, Yoko gave £10,000 for educational aid to students at Liverpool Polytechnic, once called the College of Art. She took Sean to the Pier Head, to all John's old haunts, to look at Menlove Avenue, and to meet an Aunt Mimi tearful with joy. 'Just like John,' said Mimi when she saw Sean.

John's will left half his wealth, calculated at the time of his death at more than $150 million and growing by more than $50,000 a day from songwriting and record royalties, to Yoko, with the other half held on trust for undisclosed beneficiaries. The will contained a provision that if any named beneficiary objected or took court action, they were to receive nothing. Many of the beneficiaries would have been charities.

John and Yoko had launched the Spirit Foundation, a charitable organization which distributes money to all kinds of causes ranging from old people's homes to handicapped children. Their income was 'tithed' – 10 per cent of it was automatically deducted and covenanted to the foundation. In what turned out to be an appalling irony, a year before he was shot dead John had donated $1,000 to a campaign to help provide New York policemen with bullet-proof vests.

Yoko continues to be heavily involved, anonymously, with a great deal of charity work. In 1983, she decided to simplify her life. After selling the house in West Palm Beach and their farms, she planned to give approximately £3 million to charities and orphanages around the world. These included the Salvation Army hostel in Liverpool's Strawberry Field, John's childhood inspiration.

In New York's Central Park a triangular-shaped piece of land was designated Strawberry Fields in John's honour. At the opening ceremony, performed by long-time John Lennon admirer Mayor Ed Koch on 21 March 1984, Yoko broke down. It was a project she had begun shortly after John died. Sixteen years earlier John and Yoko had planted acorns in the precincts of Coventry Cathedral. That acorn was now symbolically a tree, she said. As a mark of world love and sharing, which John cared about, she had written to heads of state throughout the world asking for a plant, rock, or stone of their nation to be sent for Strawberry Fields in Central Park. 'This is the nicest tribute we could give to John,' says Yoko. It was, fittingly, the place they had sat down and talked after their last walk together. Julian Lennon, in New York recording his debut album, attended the ceremony. On 20 March, the date of John and Yoko's wedding anniversary, Yoko presented Sean with a full collection of his parents' recorded work.

In a bittersweet evening, Sean chose 'Instant Karma!' as his first favourite. Yoko broke down again when 'Imagine' came on. They played record after record through the night, totally absorbed in the music of the man they loved.

John Lennon was not only a genius. He was also a man of profound commitment, total integrity, and intensive activity: a glance at the sheer volume and pattern of his life's work confirms that. His honesty and wit, his vulnerability, his lack of pomposity, his unique artistry, spirit, and roman-

ticism endeared him to millions. The grief that followed
his murder, and the celebrations of his life and work, spanned the world.

As a twentieth-century philosopher, he set an example
of imagination and humanitarianism. Although he would
hate to be deified, a light went out on 8 December 1980.
But his music and his spirit shine on.

CHRONOLOGY

1933

18 FEB.   Yoko Ono born in Tokyo.

1938

3 DEC.   John's future mother, Julia Stanley, a cinema attendant, weds seaman Alfred (Fred) Lennon at Mount
Pleasant Register Office, Liverpool.

1939

10 SEPT.   Cynthia Powell born in Blackpool.

1940

9 OCT.   John Winston Lennon born at 6:30 pm at Oxford
Street Maternity Hospital, Liverpool.

1941

SPRING   John left in the care of his aunt, Mary Smith (Aunt
Mimi), and Uncle George at 251 Menlove Avenue,
Woolton.

1942

APRIL   Fred Lennon, having been away at sea for long periods since his son's birth, leaves home for good while Julia Lennon moves in with her new man, John Dykins.

1945
SEPT.   John starts at Dovedale Primary School, Liverpool.

1946
JULY   Fred Lennon suddenly returns and takes John to Blackpool, intending never to return. John's mother, Julia, tracks them down and gives her five-year-old son the choice of staying with his father or mother. He eventually chooses Julia, who returns him to Liverpool to stay with Aunt Mimi.

1952
JULY   John leaves Dovedale Primary School.
SEPT.   John starts at Quarry Bank High School.

1955
5 JUNE   George Smith, John's uncle, dies at age fifty-two.

1957
MAY   John forms the Quarry Men skiffle group with some school friends.
24 MAY   First-ever Quarry Men public performance at a street carnival in Rosebery Street, Liverpool.
6 JULY   Paul McCartney attends a Quarry Men performance at Woolton Parish Church Fête and meets John Lennon for the first time. He later joins the group.
JULY   John leaves Quarry Bank High School.
SEPT.   John starts at Liverpool College of Art where he soon meets Cynthia Powell, his future wife, and Stuart Sutcliffe, to become his closest friend and a future Beatle.

1958

6 FEB.   After seeing them perform at Wilson Hall, Garston, Liverpool, George Harrison joins the Quarry Men.

15 JULY   Julia Lennon dies after a road accident outside Mimi's Menlove Avenue house.

1959

29 AUG.   The Quarry Men (John, Paul, George and Ken Brown) play at the opening night of the Casbah coffee club, run by Mona Best, mother of the Beatles' future drummer, Pete.

15 NOV.   The group, now renamed Johnny and the Moondogs, fail an audition for 'star-maker' Carroll Levis at Manchester Hippodrome.

1960

5 MAY   The group, now renamed the Silver Beetles, fail an audition to back Billy Fury but are chosen to back another young singer, Johnny Gentle, on a Scottish tour.

20 MAY   That tour – the group's first – begins.

2 JUNE   The group change their name to the Beatles for their first local 'professional' engagement at Neston Institute.

JULY   John leaves Liverpool College of Art.

16 AUG.   The Beatles travel to Hamburg and open at the Indra night-club two days later.

5 DEC.   John arrives back in Liverpool penniless, after four months in Hamburg and a dispute with their employer there. George had been deported for being under-age; Paul and Pete Best had been ordered to leave after allegedly causing a fire in their digs.

1961

21 MAR. The Beatles make their debut at the Cavern club, a jazz/beat cellar in Liverpool city centre.

JUNE   A single, 'My Bonnie', by Tony Sheridan, with backing by the Beatles, is released in Germany.

6 JULY   The first edition of *Mersey Beat*, the Liverpool music paper, appears. John contributes a front-page article entitled 'Being a Short Diversion on the Dubious Origins of Beatles' and, over the next two years, contributes many other poems and articles to the paper.

1 OCT.   John and Paul take a fourteen-day holiday in Paris.

28 OCT. Brian Epstein, a local record shop owner, learns of the Beatles' existence.

9 NOV.   Epstein attends a lunchtime performance of the Beatles at the Cavern.

3 DEC.   Epstein invites the Beatles to his shop and offers to manage them.

1962

1 JAN.   The Beatles travel to London for an audition at Decca. They do not learn of their failure until March and are subsequently rejected by several other top record companies.

24 JAN. Brian and the Beatles enter into an official management contract.

1 FEB.   The first Epstein-organized engagement, at a small café in West Kirby, Cheshire for £18.

2 FEB.   The Beatles' first official out-of-town date, in Manchester.

8 MAR.   The group appear on BBC radio for the first time, on the Light Programme's *Teenager's Turn*.

10 APRIL Stuart Sutcliffe dies of a brain haemorrhage in Hamburg at age twenty-one.

9 MAY	Brian Epstein secures a recording contract for the Beatles with Parlophone, a small label within EMI.
4 JUNE	Epstein and the Beatles sign with EMI.
6 JUNE	The Beatles' first recording session, at the Abbey Road studios, London, NW8.
16 AUG.	Pete Best, the Beatles' drummer, is sacked.
18 AUG.	Ringo Starr leaves Rory Storm and the Hurricanes and fills the vacant drummer's seat with the Beatles.
22 AUG.	A Granada television film crew capture a few minutes of a lunchtime Beatles performance at the Cavern.
23 AUG.	John Lennon marries Cynthia Powell at Mount Pleasant Register Office, Liverpool. That same evening the Beatles, with John, fulfil an engagement in Chester.
4 SEPT.	'Love Me Do', the group's first single, is recorded.
1 OCT.	Epstein and the Beatles sign a five-year management contract.
5 OCT.	'Love Me Do' is released.
17 OCT.	The Beatles make their television debut on Granada's north-west regional programme *People and Places*, singing 'Love Me Do'.
27 OCT.	'Love Me Do' enters the *Melody Maker* singles chart at number forty-eight.
17 DEC.	The Beatles make their fifth and final club trip to Hamburg.

1963

19 JAN.	The Beatles make their nationwide television debut, on *Thank Your Lucky Stars*.
2 FEB.	First UK tour, with Helen Shapiro, begins.
11 FEB.	In one eleven-hour session, the Beatles record their first LP.
22 FEB.	Northern Songs, publishers of all future Lennon-McCartney compositions, is formed.

2 MAR.   'Please Please Me', the groups second single, hits number one on the *Melody Maker* chart.

8 APRIL   A son, John Charles Julian, is born to Cynthia and John Lennon at 6:50 am at Sefton General Hospital, Liverpool; he weighs six pounds, eleven ounces.

28 APRIL   John and Brian Epstein fly to Spain for a twelve-day holiday.

4 MAY   The Beatles' first LP, *Please Please Me*, tops the *Melody Maker* chart.

18 JUNE   John physically assaults Cavern master of ceremonies Bob Wooler at Paul's twenty-first birthday party in Huyton, Liverpool.

21 JUNE   The John/Bob Wooler incident is big news in the *Daily Mirror*.

29 JUNE   John's first solo appearance on television, on BBC's *Juke Box Jury*. (The programme was recorded on 22 June.)

3 AUG.   The Beatles' 292nd, and last, appearance at the Cavern.

8 AUG.   A daughter, Kyoko, is born to Yoko Ono and her husband, Anthony Cox.

13 OCT.   First signs of Beatlemania as the Beatles appear on *Sunday Night at the London Palladium*.

31 OCT.   Hysteria at Heathrow Airport as the Beatles return from Sweden after a series of concerts.

4 NOV.   The Beatles appear in the Royal Variety Performance at the Prince of Wales Theatre, London. John utters his famous witticism.

27 DEC.   In *The Times*, John and Paul are described as 'the outstanding English composers of 1963'.

1964

1 FEB.   'I Want To Hold Your Hand' tops the singles chart in *Billboard*, the USA's premier music trade magazine.

7 FEB.   Mass hysteria greets the Beatles' arrival at Kennedy Airport at the start of their American tour.

9 FEB.   An estimated seventy-three million people watch the Beatles perform on television on the *Ed Sullivan Show*.

11 FEB. The Beatles' first American concert, at the Coliseum, Washington, DC.

2 MAR.   Back in England, the Beatles begin shooting their first feature film, *A Hard Day's Night*.

23 MAR. Jonathan Cape publishes Lennon's first book, *In His Own Write*. It is an instant critical and commercial success.

4 APRIL The Beatles occupy the top five places on the *Billboard* American singles chart.

23 APRIL Foyle's holds a literary luncheon in John's honour at the Dorchester Hotel, London. John's speech, supposed to be the highlight of the occasion, lasts just five seconds.

19 JUNE Charles Curran, a Conservative MP, states in Parliament that John's book highlights the poor education in Liverpool and that Lennon himself is illiterate.

6 JULY   The film *A Hard Day's Night* receives its world première in London.

10 JULY Liverpool honours its four famous sons with a civic reception. Estimated crowds of 100,000 line the route of their procession from Speke airport to the city centre.

15 JULY John and Cynthia buy their first mansion, Kenwood, in the 'stockbroker belt' at Weybridge, Surrey.

19 SEPT. Oxfam prints 500,000 Christmas cards using a specially donated Lennon drawing.

1965

9 JAN.   John appears on Peter Cook and Dudley Moore's *Not Only . . . But Also* BBC television programme reading

his poetry, accompanied by Moore and Norman Rossington.

15 FEB.   John passes his driving test.

18 FEB.   Northern Songs becomes a public company, quoted on the London Stock Exchange.

22 FEB.   Shooting of the Beatles' second feature film, *Help!* begins in the Bahamas (for tax reasons).

18 MAR.   John gives his former schoolfriend and one-time Quarry Man Pete Shotton £20,000 and together they form Hayling Supermarkets Ltd and open up for business on Hayling Island, off the Hampshire coast.

12 JUNE   Buckingham Palace announces that the four Beatles are to be made Members of the Order of the British Empire (MBE).

13 JUNE   Several MBE holders return their medals, furious over the Beatles' award.

24 JUNE   *A Spaniard In The Works*, John's second book of poetry and nonsense prose, is published by Jonathan Cape.

29 JULY   *Help!* receives its world première in London.

3 AUG.   John buys Aunt Mimi a bungalow in Poole, Dorset, and she moves down from Liverpool in October.

15 AUG.   56,000 fans attend a Beatles concert at Shea Stadium in New York. The proceedings are filmed for a future television special.

26 OCT.   Hysteria at Buckingham Palace as the Beatles attend their MBE investiture ceremony.

31 DEC.   Fred Lennon, John's father, releases his first and only single on Pye Records entitled 'That's My Life (My Love And My Home'): it is an artistic and commercial disaster.

1966

1 MAR.   *The Beatles at Shea Stadium* receives its world première on BBC television.

4 MAR.   London's *Evening Standard* publishes an interview with
           John by reporter Maureen Cleave. Tucked innocently
           in the middle of the article, John expresses an opinion
           that the Beatles are more popular than Jesus and that
           Christianity will vanish and shrink. There is no reac-
           tion from the British public.

1 MAY   The Beatles give what later turns out to be their last
           live performance in Britain, in the *New Musical Express*
           pollwinners' concert at the Empire Pool, Wembley.

26 JUNE   The Beatles' emotional return to Hamburg to play a
           concert.

5 JULY   Riots rage in Manila, capital of the Philippines, after
           the Beatles supposedly snub the president's wife.

29 JULY   *Datebook* magazine re-publishes in the USA – out of
           context – John's interview with Maureen Cleave.

31 JULY   Radio stations in Birmingham, Alabama, ban all
           Beatles music after learning of John's comments about
           Jesus. Other towns in the 'Bible Belt' soon follow,
           and huge bonfires of Beatles records and memorabilia
           are organized.

6 AUG.   In the midst of the American uproar over John's
           comments, Brian Epstein hurriedly flies to New York
           to defend him publicly.

8 AUG.   After learning of John's Jesus comments, the South
           African Broadcasting Corporation (SABC) announces
           a ban on the playing of all records composed or played
           by the Beatles.

12 AUG.   At the start of the Beatles' third official American tour
           in Chicago, John, under severe pressure, reluctantly
           apologizes to the world for his statement on Jesus.

29 AUG.   Thoroughly fed-up after three years of constant tour-
           ing, the Beatles give their last live performance ever,
           at Candlestick Park in San Francisco.

6 SEPT.   In a bar near Hanover, near the set of the film *How I*

Won The War, John's Beatle locks are cut in preparation for his first solo acting role. He is given a pair
of 'granny glasses' to wear.

19 SEPT. Shooting of *How I Won The War* switches to Almeria,
Spain.

9 NOV. John visits the Indica Gallery in Masons Yard, Duke
Street, London SW1, for a preview of a nine-day
exhibition by a Japanese artist, Yoko Ono, entitled
Unfinished Paintings and Objects. He is introduced to
Yoko by the gallery owner, John Dunbar.

26 DEC. John appears in Peter Cook and Dudley Moore's *Not
Only . . . But Also* TV programme in a comedy sketch,
telerecorded on 27 November. The 'granny glasses'
from the *How I Won The War* film are still there and
they stay with John, forming part of his new image.

1967

17 FEB. EMI releases a revolutionary new Beatles single –
John's 'Strawberry Fields Forever' backed with Paul's
'Penny Lane'. Ironically it becomes their first record
to fail to reach the coveted number one spot on some
charts since 'Please Please Me', released four years
earlier.

20 MAY The BBC bans John's 'A Day In The Life' from the
forthcoming Beatles LP, because its lyrics might
encourage drug-taking.

1 JUNE *Sgt Pepper's Lonely Hearts Club Band*, the Beatles' most
ambitious LP yet, is released.

25 JUNE The Beatles appear before an estimated audience of
400 million people from twenty-four countries, singing 'All You Need Is Love' on the world-wide TV
link-up show *Our World*.

24 AUG. Various Beatles with wives and relations, including
John and Cynthia, attend a lecture on transcendental

meditation by the Maharishi Mahesh Yogi at the Hilton Hotel, London.

25 AUG. The Beatles and their wives travel by train from London's Euston Station to Bangor, North Wales, to attend a weekend seminar on meditation by the Maharishi. John's wife Cynthia, after a frantic dash, misses the train by seconds. John's disappearance down the platform without her seems symbolic of the future of their unsteady marriage.

27 AUG. While the Beatles are away in Bangor, Brian Epstein is found dead in his flat at 24 Chapel Street, Belgravia, London, SW1. The Beatles hurriedly return to London.

11 SEPT. Shooting of the ill-fated *Magical Mystery Tour* TV film starts in Cornwall.

30 SEPT. John and George appear with the Maharishi on *The Frost Programme* on ITV with presenter David Frost.

11 OCT. John anonymously sponsors an exhibition at the Lisson Art Gallery, London, NW8 entitled *Yoko Plus Me*. It runs until 14 November.

17 OCT. John, Paul, George, and Ringo attend a memorial service for Brian Epstein at the New London Synagogue, Abbey Road, London NW8.

18 OCT. The world première of *How I Won The War* in London.

20 NOV. The BBC ensures that John's composition 'I Am The Walrus' receives no radio or TV exposure, although it officially denies actually banning the song.

4 DEC. A new Beatles venture, the Apple Boutique, opens in Baker Street, London NW1.

16 DEC. John, George, and the Maharishi attend a UNICEF gala in Paris.

26 DEC. The world première of *Magical Mystery Tour* on BBC television. A critical disaster, it is the Beatles' first public failure.

1968

5 JAN.   John and his father, Fred, meet at John's Weybridge
            home. John gives his blessing to his father's impend-
            ing marriage to nineteen-year-old former Exeter Uni-
            versity student Pauline Jones. The couple announce
            that the wedding may have to wait until the bride is
            twenty-one years old as her mother refuses to give
            her consent. Instead they travel to Scotland, outside
            the English court jurisdiction, and marry there.

16 FEB.   John and Cynthia, with George and his wife Pattie,
            fly to Rishikesh, India, for an extensive course of
            meditation under the Maharishi. Paul, with fiancée
            Jane Asher, and Ringo and his wife, Maureen, follow
            on four days later.

12 APRIL   John and George with their wives hurriedly leave
            Rishikesh two weeks earlier than expected. They feel
            that the Maharishi is not such a holy man after all.
            Paul, Jane, Ringo, and Maureen have already left.

15 MAY   John and Paul appear on the *Tonight Show* on Ameri-
            can television to announce the formation of Apple
            Corps. John also takes the opportunity to denounce
            the Maharishi publicly.

15 JUNE   John and Yoko Ono plant two acorns outside Coven-
            try Cathedral as part of the National Sculpture Exhi-
            bition. It is the couple's first 'event'.

18 JUNE   John and Yoko attend the opening night of *In His
            Own Write* at London's National Theatre, a play
            adapted from John's two books by his friend, actor
            Victor Spinetti.

21 JUNE   Apple Corps buys grandiose premises at 3 Savile Row,
            London W1.

1 JULY   The opening of John's first art exhibition, *You Are
            Here*, dedicated to Yoko, at the Robert Fraser Gallery
            in Duke Street, London W1. Prior to the opening

John and Yoko release 365 helium-filled balloons over London.

17 JULY World première of the Beatles' *Yellow Submarine* cartoon film in London.

31 JULY The Apple Boutique closes after two days of stock clearing free of charge to the general public.

22 AUG. Cynthia sues John for divorce on the grounds of adultery with Yoko Ono Cox.

18 OCT. Police raid the flat at 34 Montagu Square, London W1, owned by Ringo but the temporary home of John and Yoko. They discover 219 grains of cannabis resin. The couple are also charged with obstructing police in the execution of a search warrant.

19 OCT. At Marylebone Magistrates' Court John and Yoko are remanded on bail until 28 November.

25 OCT. John and Yoko announce they are expecting a baby in February 1969.

8 NOV. Cynthia is granted a decree nisi in the Divorce Court because of John's adultery with Yoko. The petition is uncontested, but it is announced that John has made 'generous and proper provision' for his wife and child.

21 NOV. Yoko has a miscarriage. John stays with her at Queen Charlotte's Maternity Hospital in Hammersmith, London W6, in a spare bed. When that is no longer available, he sleeps on the floor beside her.

28 NOV. John pleads guilty to unauthorized possession of cannabis at Marylebone Magistrates' Court. He is fined £150 plus 20 guineas costs. Both John and Yoko are found not guilty of obstructing the police.

29 NOV. *Unfinished Music No. 1: Two Virgins*, John and Yoko's first avant-garde album together, is released. Its content is completely overshadowed by the furore over the album cover, which shows the couple stark naked

in full-frontal pose on the front cover with a rear view on the back cover.

10 DEC.   Kenwood, John's Weybridge home, is put up for sale.

11 DEC.   John and Yoko participate in the never-completed Rolling Stones TV special *Rock and Roll Circus* at Wembley TV studios.

18 DEC.   John and Yoko appear onstage in a large white bag at the Royal Albert Hall during *Alchemical Wedding*, the underground art movement's Christmas party.

23 DEC.   John and Yoko dress up as Father and Mother Christmas, handing out presents, at the Apple Christmas party at Savile Row.

1969

2 JAN.   Shooting of the disastrous *Let It Be* film commences at the cold Twickenham Film Studios.

3 JAN.   30,000 copies of John and Yoko's *Two Virgins* are confiscated in New Jersey on the grounds that the sleeve is pornographic.

18 JAN.   John tells Ray Coleman in an interview for *Disc and Music Echo*: 'Apple's losing money every week . . . if it carries on like this, all of us will be broke in the next six months.'

30 JAN.   The Beatles perform live on the roof of the Apple building in Savile Row. The event is captured on film for the *Let It Be* project.

2 FEB.   Yoko Ono is divorced from Anthony Cox in the Virgin Islands.

3 FEB.   An American, Allen Klein, is appointed to look after the Beatles' financial affairs at the insistence of John, George, and Ringo. Paul opposes Klein's involvement.

2 MAR.   John and Yoko appear in an avant-garde jazz concert at the Lady Mitchell Hall in Cambridge.

20 MAR. John and Yoko fly from Paris to Gibraltar where they stay for just seventy minutes. During that time they are married by Registrar Cecil Wheeler in the British Consulate building. They then return to Paris. John comments: 'It was all very quick, quiet, and British.'

24 MAR. John and Yoko lunch with Salvador Dali in Paris.

25–31 MAR. John and Yoko's first big 'event' – the Amsterdam bed-in for peace. For seven days the couple hold court in Room 902 of the Amsterdam Hilton and give literally hundreds of interviews and messages about peace.

31 MAR. John and Yoko fly from Amsterdam straight to Vienna for the world TV première of their film *Rape*, shown later that evening. The couple also hold a quick press conference at the Hotel Sacher to launch the film and appear completely encased in a white bag, their voices being the only clue to their identity.

1 APRIL Back in London, John and Yoko appear on Thames Television's *Today* programme, inviting host Eamonn Andrews to join them in bed before the cameras.

21 APRIL Bag Productions, John and Yoko's film and production company, is formed.

22 APRIL In a formal ceremony before Señor Bueno de Mesquita, the commissioner of oaths, John changes his middle name from Winston to Ono. The ceremony is on the roof of the Apple building at 3 Savile Row, London W1.

4 MAY John and Yoko buy Tittenhurst Park, a mansion in Sunningdale, Ascot, Berkshire. They move in during August.

8 MAY John, George, and Ringo sign a business management contract with Allen Klein. Paul refuses.

9 MAY *Unfinished Music No. 2: Life With The Lions*, John and Yoko's second 'experimental' album, is released on the

Zapple label, Apple's newly formed avant-garde record label.

16 MAY   John's application for a United States visa is rejected because of his drug conviction in November 1968. He planned to stage a New York bed-in.

24 MAY   John and Yoko with Kyoko, Yoko's daughter from her marriage to Anthony Cox, fly to the Bahamas to stage their bed-in for peace at the Sheraton Oceanus Hotel. They leave the island within twenty-four hours because it is further from the United States than John had believed and because the humid 86° temperature is not conducive to seven days in bed.

25 MAY   The Lennons arrive in Toronto but are detained at the airport for two and a half hours by the Canadian Immigration authorities. They are eventually released on their own recognizance. It is nearly midnight before they are able to check into a downtown motel.

26 MAY   The Lennons and their entourage fly to Montreal and announce their intention to hold a bed-in at the Queen Elizabeth Hotel. John invites the Canadian prime minister, Pierre Trudeau, to join him and also to plant acorns for peace. Says Trudeau: 'I don't know about his acorns, but I'd like to see him if he's around. He's a good poet.'

26 MAY– John and Yoko hold another seven-day bed-in in
2 JUNE   Room 1742 of the Queen Elizabeth Hotel.

30 MAY   The Australian Broadcasting Commission (ABC) bans the new Beatles single, 'The Ballad Of John And Yoko' on the grounds that it is blasphemous.

1 JUNE   From their bed John and Yoko record 'Give Peace A Chance'. They are assisted by a roomful of people including the Smothers Brothers, Timmy Leary, the Canadian Radha Krishna Temple, Derek Taylor, Murray The K, and the local rabbi.

2 JUNE   John and Yoko leave the hotel early in the afternoon
          and quickly move on to Ottawa for a university con-
          ference on peace. Later that evening they fly back to
          London.

1 JULY   After visiting John's aunt in Durness, Sutherland,
          Scotland, John, Yoko, Kyoko, and Julian, John's first
          child, have a car accident in Golspie. No other vehicle
          is involved. They are taken to the Lawson Memorial
          Hospital where John receives seventeen stitches in a
          facial wound, Yoko fourteen stitches, and Kyoko four.
          Julian suffers shock.

2 JULY   Cynthia travels to Scotland to see and retrieve Julian.

3 JULY   Still hospitalized after their car crash, John and Yoko
          are unable to attend the press launch of the Plastic
          Ono Band at Chelsea Town Hall, London SW1. In
          their place stand perspex tubes with fitted micro-
          phones, tape recorders, and amplifiers.

4 JULY   'Give Peace A Chance', John's first solo single,
          credited to the Plastic Ono Band, is released.

6 JULY   John, Yoko, and Kyoko fly back to London from the
          Golspie Hospital in a specially chartered helicopter.
          John tells the delighted Golspie local newspaper: 'If
          you're going to have a car crash try to arrange for it
          to happen in the Highlands. The hospital there was
          just great.'

10 SEPT. An evening of John and Yoko films at the New
          Cinema Club in the Institute of Contemporary Arts
          (ICA) in London's Pall Mall. Those shown are *Self
          Portrait, Smile, Honeymoon, Two Virgins*, and *Rape*. An
          unidentified couple sit on stage throughout encased
          in a white sack, though nobody is quite sure whether
          it is John and Yoko themselves. The audience reaction
          to the evening is filmed by an infra-red camera hidden
          out of view.

12 SEPT.   At very short notice John and Yoko are asked to appear live at a Rock 'n' Roll Revival concert in Toronto, scheduled for the following day. John hurriedly gathers together Eric Clapton, Klaus Voormann, and Alan White to join him and Yoko in forming a makeshift Plastic Ono Band.

13 SEPT.   The Plastic Ono Band fly from Heathrow to Toronto, grabbing their only chance to rehearse on board the plane. Later that night they take the stage at the Varsity Stadium and perform 'Blue Suede Shoes', 'Money', 'Dizzy Miss Lizzy', 'Yer Blues', 'Give Peace A Chance', and a new Lennon composition, 'Cold Turkey', as well as two lengthy Yoko compositions, 'Don't Worry Kyoko' and 'John, John (Let's Hope For Peace)'.

25 SEPT.   After months of protracted dealings in the City (London's financial district), John and Paul lose control of Northern Songs and thereby the full rights to all of their past – and a good deal of their future – compositions, to Lew Grade's ATV Music.

OCT.   John invites his father to his house at Tittenhurst Park for what is to be their last meeting.

12 OCT.   Yoko loses a baby expected in December – her second miscarriage – at King's College Hospital, Denmark Hill, London SE5.

3 NOV.   An evening of John and Yoko films at Nash House, London SW1, under the collective title of *Something Else*. A second such evening is held a week later, on 10 November.

7 NOV.   Apple releases John and Yoko's *Wedding Album*. The luxurious package contains not only a record but a copy of their marriage certificate, various pictures, two booklets, a poster, and a photograph of a slice of wedding cake.

13 NOV.   A group of hippies travel to Ireland to inspect a tiny

uninhabited island, Dornish, off the coast of County Mayo. It is being offered to them rent-free by John Lennon who bought it in 1966 at a cost of £1,500.

25 Nov. (Announced 26 November) John returns his MBE medal to Buckingham Palace 'in protest against Britain's involvement in the Nigeria-Biafra thing, against our support of America in Vietnam, and against "Cold Turkey" slipping down the charts.' His letter is signed 'With Love, John Lennon of Bag.'

27 Nov. Buckingham Palace reports that Mr Barry Hearn, who returned his medal in 1965 when the Beatles were awarded the MBEs, has asked for its return following John's return of his medal. Unfortunately, Buckingham Palace cannot locate it.

1 Dec. John and Yoko offer to buy a thirty-two-foot caravan school for gipsy children to be situated on an unofficial site at Caddington, near Luton, Bedfordshire.

3 Dec. John is asked to play the part of Christ in the Tim Rice/Andrew Lloyd Webber musical *Jesus Christ Superstar*, to be staged in St Paul's Cathedral.

4 Dec. Rice and Lloyd Webber withdraw their offer, stating that the part would be better suited to an unknown actor.

9 Dec. Apple announces that John and Yoko are to make a film about James Hanratty, the convicted and executed British murderer. It would reveal facts never before disclosed, they claim.

11 Dec. John startles a crowd of two hundred people outside the Kensington Odeon, there for the première of *The Magic Christian*, which starred Ringo, by slowly carrying past a banner reading 'Britain Murdered Hanratty'.

12 Dec. *The Plastic Ono Band – Live Peace in Toronto 1969* is released by Apple.

14 Dec. A white sack labelled 'A Silent Protest For James

Hanratty', with two anonymous wriggling occupants (John and Yoko?), is taken to Speakers' Corner, Marble Arch, London W1, where Hanratty's father calls for a public inquiry into his son's hanging. A petition is later handed in to 10 Downing Street.

15 DEC. The Plastic Ono Supergroup – John augmented by Yoko, George Harrison, Eric Clapton, Billy Preston, Keith Moon, and many more – play at a *Peace for Christmas* concert at the Lyceum Ballroom in London in aid of UNICEF.

16 DEC. Huge posters and billboards go up in various locations in eleven cities world-wide reading: 'War Is Over! If You Want It. Happy Christmas from John and Yoko.'

23 DEC. Back in Canada for the third time in seven months, John and Yoko have a fifty-one-minute private conference with Prime Minister Pierre Trudeau in Ottawa. They later describe him as 'more beautiful than we expected' and add, 'If all politicians were like Trudeau there would be world peace.'

24 DEC. Back in England John and Yoko briefly join a sit-in and fast outside Rochester Cathedral in Kent to call for peace and spotlight world poverty.

29 DEC. John and Yoko fly to the small village of Aalborg in Denmark to holiday with Kyoko at the home of Anthony Cox and his new wife, Melinda.

30 DEC. ITV transmits *Man Of The Decade* – a sixty-minute television programme split into three twenty-minute segments featuring John F. Kennedy, Mao Tse-tung, and John Lennon. John's section includes a lengthy, newly recorded interview filmed at Tittenhurst Park.

1970

5 JAN. From Denmark John announces that all future pro-

ceeds from his songs and records will go towards promoting peace on earth.

15 JAN. An exhibition of fourteen John Lennon lithographs opens at the London Arts Gallery in New Bond Street, London W1.

16 JAN. Detectives from Scotland Yard raid the exhibition and confiscate eight of the lithographs, which are deemed to be erotic and indecent.

19 JAN. It is reported that sales of *Bag One*, the collection of John's lithographs, have rocketed since the police raid. Three hundred sets are for sale at £550 each.

20 JAN. Still in Denmark John and Yoko have their hair cropped in the barn of Anthony Cox's north-Jutland retreat.

22 JAN. All fourteen John Lennon lithographs go on show at the London Gallery in Detroit, USA – to no reaction.

27 JAN. Back in England John writes, records, and mixes his next single, 'Instant Karma!', all in one day. Phil Spector produces. It is released just ten days later.

28 JAN. The London exhibition of John's lithographs – with only six remaining on show – comes to its scheduled end at the London Arts Gallery.

4 FEB. John and Yoko swap their shorn hair, neatly tied up in plastic bags, for a pair of blood-stained Muhammad Ali boxing trunks in a ceremony with Michael X, the notorious Black Power leader, on the roof of X's 'Black House' in Holloway, north London. John and Yoko intend auctioning the trunks to raise money for peace.

11 FEB. John pays the outstanding fines, totalling £1,344, imposed on ninety-six people involved in protests against the South African rugby team who played a match in Scotland in December 1969.

12 FEB. The Plastic Ono Band appear live in the studio on

the BBC programme *Top Of The Pops* singing 'Instant Karma!' (The entire show was telerecorded on 11 February.)

25 FEB.   A summons is served on the London Arts Gallery for showing John's lithographs — 'an indecent exhibition contrary to the Metropolitan Police Act, 1839.'

22 MAR.   In an interview with the French magazine *L'Express*, John reveals that the Beatles smoked marijuana in the toilets at Buckingham Palace prior to their MBE investiture in 1965. A palace spokesman curtly replies: 'Obviously when people come along to an investiture toilet facilities are available.'

29 MAR.   John sends a telephone message, broadcast to eight thousand people at a Campaign for Nuclear Disarmament (CND) rally in Victoria Park, Bethnal Green, east London. During his message he reveals that Yoko is expecting a baby in October. Later in the year she miscarries again.

1 APRIL   Defence lawyers in the London Arts Gallery prosecution trial compare John Lennon's works with those of Picasso.

10 APRIL   Paul McCartney announces his resignation from the Beatles.

LATE   John and Yoko travel to Los Angeles to undergo four
APRIL   months of primal therapy under Dr Arthur Janov.

27 APRIL   The lithographs court case is dismissed in favour of the London Arts Gallery, and the exhibits are returned.

13 MAY   World première of the Beatles' *Let It Be* film in New York. None of the four attend.

1 AUG.   John's first wife, Cynthia, re-marries, to Italian hotelier Roberto Bassanini.

8 DEC.   John records a mammoth interview with *Rolling Stone* magazine.

11 DEC.   *Plastic Ono Band*, John's stark and brilliant first true 'solo' album, is released.

31 DEC.   Paul begins proceedings in the London High Court to end the Beatles' partnership.

1971

21 JAN.   *Rolling Stone* publishes Part One of its extensive John Lennon interview. Part Two follows on 4 February.

3 MAR.   South African Broadcasting Corporation (SABC) finally lifts its ban on Beatles music implemented on 8 August 1966, although John Lennon compositions, vocals, and solo work remain blacklisted.

12 MAR.   Paul wins Beatles court case in London. A receiver, James Douglas Spooner, is appointed to look after the group's business and financial affairs, superseding Allen Klein.

23 APRIL In Palma, Majorca, John and Yoko are escorted by Spanish police to the magistrates' court and questioned over the alleged abduction of Yoko's daughter, Kyoko. Anthony Cox complained to the police after her disappearance from a playground.

3 MAY   John and Yoko pass through Heathrow Airport on their way from Trinidad back to Majorca to see the justices there about the custody of Kyoko.

15 MAY   World première of two more Bag productions, *Apotheosis (Balloon)* and *Fly* at the Cannes Film Festival, attended by John and Yoko.

1 JUNE   John, in possession of a nine-month US visa issued on 31 May, jets to New York with Yoko in an attempt to locate and gain custody of Kyoko.

6 JUNE   John and Yoko make a surprise appearance on stage with Frank Zappa and the Mothers of Invention at the Fillmore East in New York City.

JULY   John records his *Imagine* album over seven days at

Tittenhurst Park and two days at the Record Plant in New York.

15 JULY   John and Yoko attend a promotion and book-signing session at Selfridges giant department store on Oxford Street, London, for the re-publication of Yoko's *Grapefruit*.

17 JULY   John and Yoko are interviewed on the BBC *Parkinson* TV show. It turns out to be their last public appearance before leaving the UK for good.

19 JULY   John and Yoko hold a press conference at the Apple HQ in Savile Row to talk about *Grapefruit*. John says: 'In England I'm regarded as the guy who won the pools. She's [Yoko] regarded as the lucky Jap who married the guy who won the pools. In America we are both treated as artists.'

11–31   A programme of five John and Yoko films is shown
AUG.   at *Art Spectrum*, a potpourri exhibition of modern art held in the Great Hall at London's Alexandra Palace.

11 AUG.   More than one thousand demonstrators, including John and Yoko, march past the Ulster Office in London. The demonstration is split between those supporting the *Oz* editors, who are being tried for publishing an obscene underground paper, and those against internment and the use of troops in Northern Ireland. John says: 'The two matters are integral and cannot be divided.'

12 AUG.   John and Yoko send £1,000 to the 'fighting fund' of the Upper Clyde [Scotland] Shipbuilding union who are refusing to stop work after being made redundant. The previous week they had sent roses.

3 SEPT.   John and Yoko leave English soil for the last time and fly to New York.

9 SEPT.   John, on the *Dick Cavett* US television show, says that the Beatles broke up 'because of Beatlemania and

screaming crowds that drowned out the music, not
because of Yoko Ono.'

8 OCT.   John's classic *Imagine* album is released.

9–27   Yoko's art exhibition, with John as a guest artist,
OCT.   entitled *This Is Not Here*, takes place at the Everson
            Museum of Art in Syracuse, New York. A television
            special about the show is transmitted on 11 May
            1972.

6 NOV.   After a day of large-scale demonstrations in New York
            City, a benefit concert for the casualties of the Attica
            prison riots at the Apollo Theatre includes a surprise
            stage appearance by John and Yoko. (On 13 Septem-
            ber, four days after prison camp guards had been
            taken hostage, one thousand New York State troopers
            had invaded the prison under a pall of tear gas, killing
            twenty-eight prisoners and nine hostages in the
            process.)

11 DEC.   John and Yoko perform live at a benefit rally held in
            the Crisler building, Ann Arbor, Michigan, for left-
            wing writer John Sinclair who had been jailed for
            ten years in 1969 for possession of two marijuana
            cigarettes. Fifty-five hours after the rally, on 13
            December, Sinclair is freed on bail.

15 DEC.   John and Yoko attend a reception in honour of U
            Thant, the retiring United Nations secretary-general.

18 DEC.   John and Yoko visit Houston, Texas, to try to gain
            access to Kyoko.

22 DEC.   Houston, Texas. Anthony Cox is jailed for five days
            after refusing to allow Yoko to visit Kyoko.

1972

13 JAN.   John and Yoko appear on US television on the *David
            Frost Show*.

5 FEB.   John and Yoko, in temperatures well below freezing,

are among four hundred demonstrators outside the New York building of British Overseas Airways Corporation (BOAC), supporting union leaders' boycott of British exports as a protest against British policy in Northern Ireland.

14–18 FEB. John and Yoko co-host the *Mike Douglas Show* on US television in the absence of Douglas. Every night they feature interviews and music, and on one show John plays live and jams with his teenage idol, Chuck Berry.

17 FEB. John and Yoko's forty-minute colour film of the campaign for an inquiry into the Hanratty execution of 1961 is shown in the crypt of St Martin in the Fields, London.

29 FEB. John and Yoko's US visas expire. They are granted a routine fifteen-day extension in order to make a fresh application.

3 MAR. Yoko is finally awarded custody of Kyoko, but Anthony Cox flees with the child and cannot be found.

6 MAR. The temporary extensions of John and Yoko's visas are cancelled at the instigation of the deputy attorney general, and the couple's four-year battle against deportation begins.

16 MAR. John and Yoko are served with deportation orders because of his 1968 London drugs conviction. Yoko says it will cause the couple to lose the custody of Kyoko, although both she and the child's father, Anthony Cox, are still in hiding.

22 APRIL John and Yoko address the crowd at the National Peace Rally in New York, protesting against the bombing of North Vietnam.

27 APRIL (Announced 29 April) John Lindsay, the mayor of New York City, appeals in a letter to the com-

missioner of immigration and naturalization in Washington, DC, for John and Yoko's deportation order to be dropped. He says that the proceedings are 'a grave injustice' and adds that the real reason behind the order is not John's 1968 London drugs-conviction but because the couple 'speak out with strong and critical voices on the major issues of the day.'

11 MAY   John appears on the *Dick Cavett Show* and claims he is being followed by government agents and that his telephone is being tapped.

17 MAY   At a deportation hearing before the immigration authorities in New York, John says, 'I don't know if there is any mercy to plead for, but if so, I would like it for both us and our child.'

12 JUNE   *Some Time In New York City*, John and Yoko's angry and heavily political album, is released in America. Its anti-British content, together with copyright problems, prevents simultaneous UK release, which does not happen until 15 September.

2 JULY   John and Yoko's lawyers prepare a final brief, outlining the reasons why the couple want to stay in the USA.

4 JULY   On American Independence Day, Lord Harlech, former British ambassador to the USA, writes to the Immigration and Naturalization Service in John's defence.

30 AUG.   The Madison Square Garden arena in New York City hosts two *One To One* concerts in aid of retarded children and adults. John and Yoko with the Elephant's Memory band appear on the bill with Stevie Wonder, Roberta Flack, and Sha Na Na. A total of $1.5 million is raised including $60,000 donated by the Lennons. A TV special recorded at the concerts is aired on 14 December.

6 SEPT.   John and Yoko with Elephant's Memory appear live
on Jerry Lewis's Muscular Dystrophy telethon.

23 DEC.   *Imagine*, a film made to accompany the album of the
same name, receives its belated world première on US
television.

1973

22 JAN.   Northern Songs and Maclen Music of London and
New York sue John for over $1 million claiming that
he, with Allen Klein's encouragement, intentionally
and unlawfully violated a 1965 agreement that the
companies would have exclusive rights to his compositions, whether written solo or in collaboration with
someone else. Five songs are in dispute, all written
with Yoko and with half-copyright claimed by Ono
Music Ltd. Ironically, Paul McCartney had recently
gone through a similar ordeal when he tried to write
with *his* wife, Linda.

23 MAR.   John is ordered to leave the US within sixty days, but
Yoko is granted permission to remain as a permanent
resident. The couple are not present at the hearing
but issue a statement from the West Coast: 'Having
just celebrated our fourth wedding anniversary, we
are not prepared to sleep in separate beds. Peace and
Love, John and Yoko.'

24 MAR.   John formally appeals against the sixty-day deportation order.

31 MAR.   John, George, and Ringo's management contract with
Allen Klein and his company ABCKO expires and is
not renewed.

28 JUNE   Allen Klein and ABCKO Industries sue John for a
total of $508,000 over allegedly unrepaid loans.

9 SEPT.   Tittenhurst Park, John and Yoko's Ascot home, is put
up for sale.

18 SEPT. Ringo Starr buys Tittenhurst Park.

OCT. John and Yoko separate after four and a half years of marriage. John flees to Los Angeles.

OCT.– John records a prospective album of rock 'n' roll
DEC. standards with Phil Spector producing. The sessions eventually disintegrate into a drunken nightmare, and Spector runs off with the tapes. After much wrangling, John finally retrieves them in June 1974.

24 OCT. John sues the US government, demanding it admit or deny whether he and/or his lawyer, Leon Wildes, have been the subject of illegal wiretapping or surveillance by the FBI.

2 NOV. John, George, and Ringo bring legal action in the High Court against Allen Klein and ABCKO (nicknamed grABCKO by John), claiming damages for alleged misrepresentation. Klein responds with a counteraction, suing for lost fees, commissions, and expenses.

16 NOV. John's *Mind Games* album is released.

11 DEC. John sends £1,000 to the ailing British underground paper *IT* (formerly *International Times*). It eventually folds eight months later.

1974

1 FEB. It is reported that the costs of all three appeals to stop the hanging of Michael X (real name Michael Abdul Malik) have been met by John. X was found guilty of murder in Trinidad. (After many further appeals and much deliberation, Malik was eventually executed on 16 May 1975.)

MAR.– Mayhem and drunkenness abound during the record-
MAY ing of *Pussy Cats*, a Harry Nilsson album, produced by John at the Record Plant in Los Angeles. Similar scenes are rife at the Santa Monica home they share with Keith Moon and Ringo Starr.

13 MAR. John is ejected from the Troubadour night-club in West Hollywood after hurling insults and foul language at the Smothers Brothers during their act. Encouraged by his drinking pal Harry Nilsson, John tries to assault the Smothers' manager Ken Fritz, and Brenda Mary Perkins, a waitress-cum-'photographer' who tries to take a Polaroid snapshot of John while he is being thrown out of the club.

27 MAR. The Los Angeles district attorney dismisses a citizen's complaint filed against John by Brenda Mary Perkins who claims to have been slapped during the fracas at the Troubadour.

17 JULY John is again ordered to leave the US within sixty days, and again he lodges an appeal.

31 AUG. John claims in court what people have come to realize over the previous few months: that the Nixon administration tried to have him deported not because of his 1968 London drugs conviction but because they mistakenly believed that he was one of the organizers of a possible anti-war demonstration to be held at the Republican Convention in 1972.

4 OCT.   John's *Walls And Bridges* album is released.

8 OCT.   John meets music publishing and record company executive Morris Levy to discuss an out-of-court settlement over his copyright infringement of the Levy-owned Chuck Berry composition 'You Can't Catch Me' on 'Come Together', recorded for the Beatles' *Abbey Road* album in 1969.

1 NOV.   John requests a federal judge to allow him the right to question immigration officials in connection with an alleged police vendetta, led by former Attorney General John N. Mitchell, which arose after John began supporting the Democrats in 1972.

16 NOV. John's first 'solo' US number one as 'Whatever Gets

You Thru The Night' tops the *Billboard* singles chart. Elton John, who had played keyboards on the recording, had made John vow that if it reached number one he would have to join him on stage some time in the future.

28 Nov. John keeps his promise and makes a surprise appearance onstage during Elton's Thanksgiving Day concert at Madison Square Garden, New York, singing three songs.

27 Dec. John, accompanied by his son Julian, and May Pang, spends the New Year holidays at Disneyland, Los Angeles.

1975

Jan. John returns to New York and is re-united with Yoko at the Dakota. Yoko is soon pregnant.

9 Jan. The partnership of The Beatles and Co is finally dissolved in the London High Court.

Mid-Jan. David Bowie, in New York to record his *Young Americans* album, invites John to play guitar on his version of the Lennon song 'Across The Universe'. While together, they also write and record 'Fame'.

8 Feb. American TV advertisements appear for the semi-legal Lennon album *Roots*, available by mail order from Morris Levy's Adam VIII label.

21 Feb. EMI/Capitol rush-releases John's *Rock 'n' Roll* album to counteract *Roots*. Litigation looms large again as Morris Levy sues for $42 million.

1 Mar. John and Yoko make their first public appearance together since their reunion at the annual Grammy Awards ceremony in Los Angeles.

6 Mar. John issues a statement that his eighteen-month separation from Yoko 'was not a success' and that he has returned to live with her in New York.

18 APRIL BBC television transmits its famous *Old Grey Whistle Test* interview with John.

13 JUNE US television airs a *Salute to Lew Grade* TV special in which John appears live, singing 'Imagine' and 'Slippin' and Slidin'' backed by a 'two-faced' band – John's none too subtle dig at Grade. It was his last live appearance before an audience.

19 JUNE John sues former Attorney General John N Mitchell, and other US law officers, for 'improper selective prosecution' arising from the deportation attempt.

13 JULY John is awarded a total of $144,700 by a New York court for lost royalties and damaged reputation over the *Roots* album.

23 SEPT. John's deportation order is temporarily halted on humanitarian grounds because of Yoko's pregnancy which has reached a critical stage.

7 OCT. The New York State Supreme Court votes by a two-to-one decision to reverse the deportation order, instructing the Immigration Service to re-consider John's request for resident status. The chief judge adds: 'The court cannot condone selective deportation based upon secret political grounds.'

9 OCT. At the age of forty-two and on John's thirty-fifth birthday, after three previous miscarriages, Yoko gives birth at the New York Hospital to their first child – a son – named Sean Taro Ono Lennon. 'I feel higher than the Empire State Building,' says John.

1976

5 JAN. Mal Evans, the Beatles' former road manager, aide, gofer, and confidant, is shot dead by police in Los Angeles.

6 FEB. John's recording contract with EMI/Capitol expires and is not renewed. For the first time in nearly fifteen years, John is not tied to a contract.

1 APRIL   Freddy Lennon, John's father, dies in Brighton General Hospital, England, at age sixty-three.

APRIL   During the Los Angeles recording of Ringo Starr's *Rotogravure* album, John makes his last commercial studio appearance for four years, playing piano on his own composition 'Cookin' (In The Kitchen Of Love)'.

27 JULY   John's battle to remain in the US is finally over when his application to become a permanent resident is formally approved at a special hearing in New York. He is awarded his precious Green Card, number A17–597–321, and proclaims: 'It's great to be legal again.' The judge, Ira Fieldsteel, informs John that he can apply for US citizenship in 1981.

20 SEPT.   New York promoter Sid Bernstein, the man behind the Beatles' American tours in the 1960s, places a page advertisement in the *International Herald Tribune* asking the Beatles to perform a reunion concert for charity – possible revenue $230 million.

OCT.   John begins his 'retirement' and house-husband period, bringing up Sean at the Dakota.

1977

10 JAN.   All outstanding litigation between the Beatles/Apple Corps and Allen Klein/ABCKO is dropped after a settlement costing Apple $5 million and ABCKO $800,000.

20 JAN.   John and Yoko attend Jimmy Carter's presidential inauguration gala in Washington, DC.

JUNE   The Lennon family travel to Japan for five months.

1978

4 FEB.   John and Yoko pay more than $178,000 for several plots of land in Delaware County, New York, for use

as a vacation retreat and to raise Holstein cows. It is also revealed that the couple are buying every apartment that becomes available at the Dakota building.

16 JUNE   John unsuccessfully tries to prevent the London *News of the World* newspaper publishing extracts from *A Twist of Lennon*, the book written by his first wife, Cynthia.

1979

27 MAY   John and Yoko place whole-page advertisements in the *New York Times*, the London *Sunday Times*, and a Tokyo newspaper, entitled: 'A Love Letter From John And Yoko. To People Who Ask Us What, When and Why.'

9 SEPT.   Sid Bernstein makes a public plea for three Beatles reunion concerts – to be held in Cairo, Jerusalem, and New York, in aid of the Vietnamese 'boat people'. Possible revenue, $500 million.

21 SEPT.   Kurt Waldheim, secretary-general of the United Nations, gets in on the act and also asks the Beatles to perform a reunion concert in aid of the 'boat people'.

15 OCT.   John and Yoko contribute $1,000 to a campaign to provide New York City policemen with bullet-proof vests.

31 DEC.   Bag Productions, John and Yoko's film and production company formed in 1969, is dissolved, along with several other ventures from the late 1960s.

1980

28 JAN.   John and Yoko buy a beachside mansion in Palm Beach, Florida, to add to their ever-growing list of property investments.

20 MAR.   John and Yoko celebrate their eleventh wedding anni-

versary in West Palm Beach, Florida. John gives Yoko a diamond heart and five hundred fresh gardenias. Yoko gives John a vintage Rolls-Royce.

23 MAY   To gain independence and boost his confidence, John goes alone to Cape Town, South Africa, for a holiday.

JULY   John and a five-man crew sail to Bermuda on *Isis*, his sixty-three-foot yacht. While there, he begins to compose music again.

2 JULY   A Holstein cow owned by John and Yoko is sold for a world record $265,000 to buyer Steve Potter at an auction in New York State Fairgrounds, Syracuse, New York.

4 AUG.   John and Yoko enter the Hit Factory recording studios in Manhattan to record their first album in six years.

SEPT.   Over three weeks John and Yoko record a mammoth interview for *Playboy* magazine.

22 SEPT. David Geffen, former top executive with Warner Brothers and Asylum Records, signs John and Yoko to his newly formed independent record label, Geffen Records, and announces that their new album will be entitled *Double Fantasy*.

29 SEPT. The first publication of a 'comeback' interview – in *Newsweek*.

9 OCT.   Yoko celebrates John's fortieth birthday and Sean's fifth by having a message of love sky-written over Manhattan.

17 NOV.   *Double Fantasy* is released.

5 DEC.   John records an interview for *Rolling Stone*.

6 DEC.   BBC disc jockey Andy Peebles flies to New York to record a lengthy radio interview with John and Yoko.

8 DEC.   John gives an interview for RKO Radio.

8 DEC.   (9 December in the UK) John Ono Lennon is shot dead.

10 DEC.   John Lennon is cremated at Hartsdale Crematorium, New York State.

10 DEC.   Yoko Ono issues a statement in which she explains how she broke the news of his father's death to Sean.

14 DEC.   A ten-minute silent vigil in Lennon's honour is observed around the world at 2:00 pm EST.

14 DEC.   Extracts from John's final interview, with RKO Radio, are broadcast across the United States in *John Lennon: The Man. The Memory.*

20 DEC.   Having previously peaked at eight and slipped down to twenty-one, '(Just Like) Starting Over' vaults back to the top position on the UK singles chart.

24 DEC.   '(Just Like) Starting Over' is certified gold in the USA, having sold one million copies.

27 DEC.   As it did in Britain, '(Just Like) Starting Over' ascends the US singles chart, up from three to number one and staying there for five weeks, while *Double Fantasy* jumps from eleven to one.

1981

JAN.   John's psychedelically painted 1956 Bentley S-1, previously donated to the Smithsonian Institute in Washington, DC, is auctioned for $50,000 in the USA.

3 JAN.   Cavern Mecca, a privately run information centre for Beatles fans, opens in Mathew Street, Liverpool, the first permanent tribute to the group in the city.

10 JAN.   *Double Fantasy* is simultaneously certified gold and platinum in the USA, signifying the sale of more than one million copies. In Britain, 'Imagine' hits number one on the singles chart – it stays for four weeks, to be dislodged only by another Lennon single, 'Woman'.

16 JAN.   Acceding to John's wish that 'Woman' follow first single '(Just Like) Starting Over', this track is issued

as the second single from *Double Fantasy*. It climbs to number two in the USA and one in the UK.

18 JAN.   At a cost of more than $200,000, Yoko places whole-page advertisements in several Sunday newspapers in six countries around the world, a letter dated 11 January and headed 'In Gratitude', responding to the good wishes and messages she has received since 8 December.

18 JAN.   BBC Radio One begins the first broadcast of Andy Peebles's 6 December 1980 interview with John and Yoko, a five-part series of Sunday afternoon programmes titled *The Lennon Tapes*. The BBC also publishes a transcript of the interview as a book.

1 FEB.   EMI announces that it has sold more than two million Lennon records in the UK since his death.

7 FEB.   The single 'Woman' climbs to number one in the UK staying for two weeks. And *Double Fantasy* climbs to number one on the UK album chart, also staying for two weeks.

20 FEB.   Yoko's 'Walking On Thin Ice' is issued as a single, later peaking at thirty-five on the UK chart, her only British chart single in her own right.

20 FEB.   Yoko gives her first radio talk since John's murder, with BBC New York interviewer Chrissie Smith, for broadcast on Radio Four's *The World This Weekend* current affairs programme on the twenty-second.

MAR.   It is announced that a John Lennon Peace Forest is to be planted in Galilee, Israel.

MAR.   Paul McCartney's own quarterly fan publication, *Club Sandwich*, publishes a high-quality tribute issue to John, utilizing never-before published photographs by Linda.

13 MAR.   With permission from EMI, DJM Records issues, for the first time, three recordings from John's 28

November 1974 stage appearance with Elton John, at Madison Square Garden, New York City. Only one of the three, 'I Saw Her Standing There', had been previously available.

14 MAR.   A version of Lennon's 'Jealous Guy' by Roxy Music, described as a 'tribute', reaches number one in the UK, where it stays for two weeks.

27 MAR.   'Watching The Wheels' is issued as the follow-up single to 'Woman', climbing to number thirty in the UK and ten in the USA. UK sales of the single 'Imagine' pass a million.

29 MAR.   Two thousand locals attend a memorial service for Lennon held at the Anglican Cathedral in Liverpool.

30 MAR.   Philip Norman's biography *Shout! The True Story of The Beatles* is published.

1 APRIL   The single 'Woman' is certified gold in the USA.

16 APRIL New York City Mayor Ed Koch sets aside a section of Central Park to be re-named Strawberry Fields.

3 MAY   The *Sunday Times* publishes an extensive interview with Yoko, given to Philip Norman at the Dakota on 22 April.

15 MAY   George Harrison issues a new single, 'All Those Years Ago', a tribute to John. It gives him his biggest hit in eight years, reaching number two in the USA and thirteen in the UK.

22 MAY   Yoko makes her first official public appearance since John's death, accepting New York City's highest cultural award, the Handel Medallion, at City Hall.

12 JUNE   Yoko issues her first solo album since 1973: *Seasons Of Glass*, recorded after John's death and co-produced by Phil Spector. The cover arouses controversy, showing John's blood-spattered and smashed spectacles, as they were found after his assassination.

15 JUNE   EMI issues boxed set of its already-available Lennon

albums, with a booklet comprising facsimile articles from the *Liverpool Echo* newspaper.

15 JUNE   Yoko Ono, Geffen Records, and Warner Bros records are jointly named in a copyright infringement lawsuit alleging that in her *Double Fantasy* track 'I'm Your Angel' Yoko plagiarized the 1928 standard 'Makin' Whoopee'.

24 AUG.   Lennon's murderer, Mark Chapman, is jailed for a minimum of twenty years and a maximum of life, for his crime.

SEPT.   *Double Fantasy* co-producer Jack Douglas files suit against Yoko Ono and Geffen Records alleging non-payment of his royalties. Ono countersues. Douglas also reveals that he surreptitiously recorded all of John and Yoko's 1980 sessions at the Hit Factory, capturing not only music but control room conversations and everything else that occurred.

SEPT.   Fresh from his all-out attack biography of Elvis Presley, author Albert Goldman announces that his next project will be a biography of John Lennon.

5 SEPT.   Cynthia Lennon Twist, as she calls herself, launches the first ever exhibition of her drawings in Long Island, New York, mostly featuring impressions of her involvement with the Beatles illustrated in her 1978 biography, *A Twist of Lennon*.

9 OCT.   Yoko pronounces this date, John's birthday, International World Peace Day.

9 OCT.   A seven-foot-tall marble statue of John Lennon is unveiled in Los Angeles.

28 OCT.   *Lennon*, a musical play, opens in Liverpool, running until 12 December and touring Britain thereafter.

16 NOV.   Not for the first time, EMI re-releases John and Yoko's 1971 seasonal single 'Happy Xmas (War Is Over)' in the UK. It reaches number twenty-eight.

DEC.   Liverpool City Council relents to public pressure and
            names four streets on a new housing estate after the
            Beatles: John Lennon Drive, Paul McCartney Way,
            George Harrison Close, and Ringo Starr Drive.
            The street signs are formally unveiled on 16 August
            1982.

22 DEC.   A tiny, inscribed Lennon self-portrait sells for £8000
            at Sotheby's in London at the first major rock memor-
            abilia auction.

1982
JAN.   After discussions spanning several months, Liverpool
            City Council and Yoko Ono agree to the opening of
            a new health centre in John's name on Merseyside.

JAN.   *The Playboy Interviews with John Lennon & Yoko Ono*,
            the complete transcript of the marathon autumn 1980
            interviews conducted by David Sheff, is published in
            book form for the first time.

24 FEB.   A weeping Yoko, accompanied by Sean, receives the
            'Album Of The Year' award for *Double Fantasy* at the
            twenty-fourth annual Grammys, in Los Angeles. In
            her speech, Yoko says, 'I think John is with us today.'

7 MAR.   BBC Radio One broadcasts a two-hour special, *The
            Beatles At The Beeb*, which captures the imagination
            of the world, featuring recordings made by the group
            in BBC studios between 1962 and 1965.

9 APRIL   Elton John – Sean's godfather – issues his new album
            Jump Up!, which includes the John Lennon tribute
            song 'Empty Garden (Hey Hey Johnny)' written with
            Bernie Taupin.

20 APRIL   In an official ceremony at the chosen site, Yoko for-
            mally announces the planning of a three-and-a-half-
            acre area in Central Park, New York, visible from the

Dakota building, set aside in John's memory and to be called Strawberry Fields.

26 APRIL Paul McCartney issues his first new album since John's murder, *Tug Of War*. Its closing track is 'Here Today', a loving tribute to Lennon.

10 MAY Queen include the tribute song 'Life Is Real (Song For Lennon)' on their new album *Hot Space*.

5 AUG. At the conclusion of Elton John's performance of 'Empty Garden (Hey Hey Johnny)', Yoko and Sean, who is wearing a 'Working Class Hero' T-shirt, join him on stage at Madison Square Garden, New York City, receiving a five-minute standing ovation.

5 OCT. The British stage musical *Lennon* opens off-Broadway in New York, but poor box-office business soon leads to cancellation.

11 OCT. A new book, *The Ballad Of John And Yoko*, written by the editors of *Rolling Stone*, is published in the UK.

13 NOV. George Martin awards the first annual 'John Lennon Scholarship' prize, organized and sponsored by the Performing Right Society.

15 NOV. A 'best of' compilation album, *The John Lennon Collection*, is issued in the UK by EMI and in the USA by Geffen, the result of a deal that sees the two companies pool their material. The 1970 *John Lennon/Plastic Ono Band* album track 'Love' is issued as a UK single to promote the new collection, which is also the subject of a TV advertising campaign. In the USA, the trailer single is 'Happy Xmas (War Is Over)'. The album reaches number one in Britain, staying there for six weeks, and thirty-three in the USA.

29 NOV. Yoko issues her second solo album since the death of John, *It's Alright*, this time with a new label, Polydor.

1983

JAN.   *John Lennon: A Family Album*, a book of rare photographs from John's 'house-husband' period, especially
featuring the 1976 visit to Japan that he made with
Yoko and Sean, is published exclusively in that
country by the photographer Nishi F. Saimaru.
Reportedly, Yoko later has the book stopped, and it
does not see more widespread publication until 1990.

MAR.   Peter Brown, with co-writer Steven Gaines, authors
The Love You Make: An Insider's Story Of The Beatles,
the first scurrilous biography of the group.

21 MAR. Pink Floyd issue new album *The Final Cut*, including
a tribute to John Lennon, 'Not Now John'.

23 MAY Mike Oldfield releases his new album *Crises*, including
a tribute to Lennon, 'Moonlight Shadow', also a
number four single in the UK.

JUNE   Three projects for 1984 move a step closer towards
fruition: a US television 'docudrama' about John and
Yoko's relationship, sanctioned by Yoko; the first permanent Beatles exhibition in Liverpool, Beatle City;
and the excavation, also in Liverpool, of the original
Cavern club, to re-open as part of a shopping development on the Mathew Street site.

18 JULY May Pang, John's former mistress, publishes *Loving
John*, her account of their time together, co-written
with Henry Edwards.

18 JULY During a refit of the control room, number two studio
at EMI's famous Abbey Road Studios in St John's
Wood, London, opens its doors to the public for
the first time, to show three times daily the special
presentation *The Beatles At Abbey Road*. It closes on
11 September.

1 SEPT. John's handwritten lyrics for 'Imagine' sell for £6500
at Sotheby's in London.

11 SEPT.   Yoko loans several of John's original artefacts to the Peace Museum in Chicago, staging a special exhibition from this date.

OCT.   Yoko announces a sale of John Lennon property and memorabilia, with money raised to be given to various causes. Yoko states, 'My donations are made in apology as a member of the human race and in memory of the war casualties.'

9 OCT.   *John Lennon: Summer Of 1980*, a photographic portfolio showing the collected works of eight photographers from that period, is published.

13 OCT.   Liverpool City Council unanimously passes a proposal that all four Beatles, John posthumously, be awarded the Freedom of the City.

17 OCT.   Following the signing of a long-term recording contract with Atlantic in North America and Charisma in the UK, Julian Lennon flies to France to write and record his debut album, with Phil Ramone as producer.

4 NOV.   Paul Simon releases his new album *Hearts And Bones*, containing a tribute track to John Lennon, 'The Late Great Johnny Ace'.

29 NOV.   Yoko visits the UK, taking Sean to his father's homeland for the first time. After a few days they fly on to Japan, staying there until mid-January.

1 DEC.   Yoko participates in an Apple business meeting with Paul McCartney, George Harrison, and Ringo Starr at the Dorchester Hotel in London.

16 DEC.   Polydor releases the first posthumous Lennon record release to feature previously unissued material – the interview album *Heartplay – An Unfinished Dialogue*. It contains extracts from John and Yoko's lengthy autumn 1980 conversations with David Sheff of *Playboy* magazine.

1984

9 JAN.   To trail the forthcoming release of *Milk And Honey*, Polydor issues the Lennon single 'Nobody Told Me', which makes the Top Ten in both the UK and USA.

20 JAN.   Yoko and Sean fly from Japan back to England, including a much-publicized visit to Liverpool on their itinerary, visiting the Cavern club, John's former home on Menlove Avenue, and Aunt Mimi.

27 JAN.   Polydor issues *Milk And Honey*, the long-awaited Lennon/Ono follow-up to *Double Fantasy*, which the couple were working on up to the time of his death. It climbs to number three in the UK and eleven in the USA.

13 FEB.   John's schoolboy friend Pete Shotton, with whom he maintained contact until his death, publishes *John Lennon: In My Life*, his account of their friendship.

MAR.   *Playboy* magazine contains a chilling feature exposing the ruthless 'lying, thieving and back-biting' suffered since his death by Yoko at the hands of her and John's former friends.

9 MAR.   Polydor issues another John Lennon single, 'Borrowed Time', again taken from *Milk And Honey*.

21 MAR.   Flanked by Sean, Julian, and Mayor Ed Koch, Yoko officially opens the Strawberry Fields site in Central Park.

2 APRIL   After a trial spanning several days, Yoko is ordered to pay *Double Fantasy* co-producer Jack Douglas $2.5 million in back royalties plus more than $600,000 interest.

9 APRIL   Beatle City, the world's first permanent exhibition centre devoted to the group, opens in Liverpool.

13 APRIL   *Milk And Honey* is certified gold in the USA.

25 APRIL   Liverpool's first official statue of the Beatles, sculpted

by John Doubleday, is unveiled at the new Cavern Walks shopping complex.

26 APRIL The Cavern Walks complex, including the excavated Cavern club, is officially opened.

24 MAY Former Ono tarot card reader John Green publishes his scandalous *Dakota Days* memoir.

JUNE Random House publishes *Come Together: John Lennon In His Time*, an important biography written by Jon Wiener based upon his in-depth research into Lennon's political and counter-culture activities and his analysis of the hitherto secret FBI Lennon files.

3 JUNE A thirty-minute *Milk And Honey* special is broadcast on MTV in the USA, comprising promotional videos and other Lennon footage.

23 JUNE Sotheby's auctions 123 John Lennon lots in New York, supplied by Yoko, raising $433,345 for the Spirit Foundation.

28 JUNE *John Winston Lennon, 1940–1966*, the first volume of Ray Coleman's exhaustive two-part biography of John Lennon, is published in the UK.

15 JULY Polydor issues another Lennon single from *Milk And Honey*, 'I'm Stepping Out'.

30 AUG. 'The Treasury Of Art And Poetry,' a sixteen-page unpublished John Lennon manuscript dating from circa 1960, sells for £16,000 at a Sotheby's auction in London.

21 SEPT. Polydor issues *Every Man Has A Woman*, a twelve-track compilation of Yoko Ono compositions covered by other artists, including the previously unreleased John Lennon recording of 'Every Man Has A Woman Who Loves Him' and young Sean Lennon singing 'It's Alright'.

24 SEPT. To trailer his forthcoming album, Charisma Records in the UK issues the debut single by Julian Lennon,

'Too Late For Goodbyes'. A promising debut, it reaches number six.

9 OCT. Yoko donates $90,000 to the Salvation Army's Strawberry Field children's home in Liverpool, bringing her total donations to date to $100,000.

15 OCT. Charisma Records issues *Valotte*, the debut album by Julian Lennon, named after the town in France where it was recorded. It reaches number twenty in the UK and seventeen in the USA.

22 OCT. *Double Fantasy* is certified triple-platinum in the USA, signifying sales of three million copies.

30 OCT. *John Ono Lennon, 1967–1980*, the second volume of Ray Coleman's exhaustive two-part biography of John Lennon, is published in the UK.

16 NOV. Polydor issues John's recording of Yoko's 'Every Man Has A Woman Who Loves Him' as a UK single.

26 NOV. Charisma Records issues a second Julian Lennon single in the UK, the title track from his album *Valotte*.

DEC. The Liverpool museum and information centre Cavern Mecca, run by fans for the fans, closes owing to lack of funds.

8 DEC. The fourth anniversary of John's death is marked in the UK by the television broadcast of *Yoko Ono: Then And Now*, a self-produced documentary. It is issued on home-video a few days later.

9 DEC. Having raised more than £300, a small band of dedicated Lennon fans based in Edinburgh, Scotland, unveil a memorial bench in his name in a city park.

1985

9 JAN. Julian Lennon's *Valotte* is certified gold in the USA.

18 FEB. With worldwide sales of *Valotte* having reached 1.5

million, Charisma Records issues a third UK single from the album, 'Say You're Wrong'.

13 MAR. *Valotte* is certified platinum in the USA.

23 MAR. Julian embarks upon his first concert tour, opening a US jaunt with a two-night stint at the Majestic Theater in San Antonio.

APRIL *Listen To These Pictures: Photographs Of John Lennon*, the collected Lennon prints of New York photographer Bob Gruen, is published.

MAY Yoko appoints a New York company, Marigold Enterprises, to market official John Lennon merchandise in the USA.

13 MAY In Liverpool, Charles Lennon, John's uncle, unveils 'John Lennon', a new, luxurious British Rail 'Pullman' engine to serve the London–Liverpool route.

29 JUNE A psychedelically painted Rolls-Royce Phantom V car once owned by Lennon is auctioned by Sotheby's New York for $2.2 million, eclipsing the $200,000–300,000 estimate.

10 AUG. Beating off earlier bids by Paul McCartney and Yoko Ono, Michael Jackson buys ATV Music for a reported $47.5 million; the star item in the collection is the Northern Songs publishing catalogue of Lennon/McCartney music.

3 OCT. Photographer Dezo Hoffman publishes *John Lennon*, a collection of shots spanning 1962 to 1970. A tie-in London exhibition opens on 7 October.

4 OCT. The B-side of Elton John's new single 'Nikita' is his second tribute to John Lennon, an instrumental entitled 'The Man Who Never Died', recorded at approximately the same time as his first, 'Empty Garden (Hey Hey Johnny)', issued in 1982.

9 OCT. Marking what would have been John's forty-fifth birthday, Yoko, accompanied by Sean, formally opens

the three-and-a-half-acre garden at the Strawberry Fields site in New York's Central Park, planted with trees, shrubs, and flowers gathered from across the world and with $1 million backing from Yoko.

2 NOV.   The *Lennon* play, which first opened in Liverpool but subsequently flopped in New York, opens in London for the first time.

11 NOV.   EMI releases as a home-video *Imagine*, the documentary made by the Lennons to promote John's 1971 album.

18 NOV.   EMI issues John's 'Jealous Guy' as a UK single for the first time.

22 NOV.   Amid rumours that she is planning a concert tour, Polydor in the UK issues *Starpeace*, a new album by Yoko Ono.

25 NOV.   'Because', a new Julian single, is issued in the UK, taken from the forthcoming album of the *Time* musical produced by Dave Clark.

28 NOV.   A one-hour production, *Stand By Me: A Portrait Of Julian Lennon*, is issued as a home-video. In the meantime, Julian is in the Bahamas, recording his second album with producer Phil Ramone.

DEC.   Poor attendance causes Radio City, owners of Beatle City, to put the Liverpool exhibition centre up for sale. It remains temporarily open, however, closing in 1986.

2 DEC.   Starring Mark McGann as John and Kim Miyori as Yoko, the 150-minute 'docudrama' *John And Yoko: A Love Story*, sanctioned by Yoko, receives its première on US television.

6 DEC.   The BBC television series *Everyman* transmits *John Lennon: A Journey In The Life*, mixing drama with documentary, and with acclaimed actor Bernard Hill cast in the Lennon role. It is immediately followed

by *Yoko Ono: A Life After John*, a fifteen-minute TV broadcast of an interview given recently by Yoko to Andy Peebles.

6 DEC.   Hunter Davies, writer of the only authorized biography of the Beatles, published in 1968, loans a number of original handwritten artefacts – letters and song lyrics – to the British Museum, where thcy are displayed in the Manuscripts Room along with Shakespeare, Dickens, Elgar, and the Magna Carta.

8 DEC.   BBC Radio One broadcasts a one-hour special celebration, *The Words And Music Of John Lennon*.

1986

23 JAN.   At the Waldorf-Astoria Hotel in New York City, Julian and Sean Lennon present awards at the inauguration launch of the Rock and Roll Hall of Fame.

24 FEB.   Under an agreement with Yoko Ono, EMI issues more first-time John Lennon product: an album and home-video of the Lennons' 30 August 1972 'One To One' charity concert appearance at Madison Square Garden, *John Lennon: Live In New York City*.

25 FEB.   Julian Lennon is among five nominees in the Best New Artist category at the twenty-eighth annual Grammy Awards presentations, won by Sade.

28 FEB.   In Brussels, Belgium, Yoko begins her first concert tour since John's death, and only her second ever. A string of European dates are booked to follow. Shows in North America are set to begin on 1 April, to be followed by shows in Japan and possibly in Australia.

10 MAR.   Charisma Records trailers an imminent Julian Lennon album by releasing the track 'Stick Around' as a UK single.

14 MAR.   The US TV cable channel Showtime broadcasts *The Lennon Legacy: Two Generations Of Music*, comprising

the world TV première of both *John Lennon: Live In New York City,* Julian Lennon's long-form video documentary *Stand By Me,* the Beatles' feature film *Let It Be,* and a new fifteen-minute interview with Yoko.

21 MAR.   Yoko's concert tour reaches Britain, and she plays at the Wembley Conference Centre, north London.

24 MAR.   Charisma Records, in association with new parent company Virgin Records, release in the UK Julian Lennon's second album, *The Secret Value of Daydreaming,* where it breaks into the Top 100 for just one week, at ninety-three. In the USA it climbs to thirty-two.

3 APRIL   Liverpool exhibition Beatle City is sold by parent company Radio City to Transworld Leisure, which announces its intention to keep the venture based in Merseyside. Later in the year, however, Transworld collapses, and it is revealed that it never paid Radio City for the purchase, so the station once again sets out to find a buyer.

MAY   Former New York bar band Elephant's Memory, with whom John and Yoko worked in 1971–72, sue Yoko Ono for $34 million over her release of the 1972 'One To One' concerts as the album and video *John Lennon: Live In New York City.* The band claim that it was a charitable event, but that if Ono is making capital out of the new releases then she should share the revenue.

6 MAY   EMI issues an album of Dave Clark's musical *Time,* with three Julian Lennon tracks included.

7 MAY   Julian is among the performers at the first International Music & Media Conference in Montreux, Switzerland. He soon moves to Switzerland for a year, and Yoko also sends Sean there for schooling.

12 MAY   Julian performs in concert in Britain for the first time with a show at the Royal Albert Hall in London. It's just one of two dates rescued from a full European tour itinerary, due to have begun on 27 April in Copenhagen, which has been cancelled owing to lack of public interest. Other summer dates, booked for the USA, Australia, and Japan, remain unchanged. Also, Charisma/Virgin issues a new Julian Lennon single in the UK, 'This Is My Day', another track from *The Secret Value Of Daydreaming*.

15 MAY   Her planned tour of the United States and Canada is cancelled owing to poor ticket sales, Yoko Ono performs the first of just four shows this date in San Francisco. The other concerts are held in Los Angeles, Montreal, and New York. Yoko abandons plans to play in Japan and Australia.

22 MAY   *The Secret Value Of Daydreaming* is certified gold in the USA.

28 MAY   In Miami, Julian embarks on a forty-city North American concert tour, his second.

8 JUNE   The *Lennon* play gives its last performance in London.

15 JUNE   Yoko makes a brief appearance on stage during a concert in the Amnesty International *A Conspiracy Of Hope* tour, at Giants Stadium in East Rutherford, New Jersey.

30 JUNE   Another Julian Lennon UK single from Dave Clark's *Time* project: 'Time Will Teach Us All', with backing vocals supplied by Stevie Wonder.

6 OCT.   Harper & Row publishes the first posthumous collection of previously unseen John Lennon poetry and prose: *Skywriting By Word Of Mouth*.

16 OCT.   Julian participates in filming for Chuck Berry's movie *Hail! Hail! Rock 'n' Roll*.

3 NOV.   EMI issues another collection of previously unreleased

John Lennon music, the album *Menlove Ave.*

17 NOV.   Julian makes a guest appearance on the album *The
          Hunting Of The Snark*, a rock interpretation of the
          Lewis Carroll poem, recorded in 1985.

30 NOV.   The London Weekend Television arts series *The South
          Bank Show* features *The Dream Is Over*, a ballet based
          upon John Lennon music, written by Christopher
          Bruce.

7 DEC.   Yoko's involvement in the Strawberry Field home in
          Liverpool is the subject of a British TV religious
          programme, *The Human Factor*.

8 DEC.   In Prague, Czechoslovakian police disperse the four
          hundred fans gathered at a public memorial service
          for John Lennon.

1987

JAN.   *Yoko Ono*, an unauthorized biography by Jerry Hop-
          kins, is published.

12 FEB.   Yoko Ono is among many prominent Westerners par-
          ticipating in a five-day conference in Moscow, 'Inter-
          national Forum For A Nuclear-Free World And The
          Survival Of Humanity'. The conference ends on 16
          February, and she returns to the USA via England,
          where on the eighteenth she visits anti-nuclear women
          protesters outside the Greenham Common airbase
          near London.

1 APRIL   Julian makes a guest appearance in a Royal Albert
          Hall concert performance of *The Hunting Of The Snark*.

4 APRIL   Yoko presents the first 'John Lennon New Age Award'
          to rock concert promoter Bill Graham during the
          1987 New York Music Awards, held at the Beacon
          Theatre. (A second such award has yet to materialize.)

24 APRIL Christopher Bruce's ballet *The Dream Is Over*, based
          upon the 1970 album *John Lennon/Plastic Ono Band*,

is premièred at the Sadler's Wells in London.

5 AUG.   An interview given to two students by John Lennon in December 1968 is sold with copyright for £21,500 ($38,500) at Sotheby's in London.

10 SEPT. *The Lennon Companion*, a collection of essays and critiques about John and his work, is published.

1988

18 JAN.   US radio syndication company Westwood One broadcasts a three-hour special as a curtain-raiser to a new weekly series of one-hour shows, *The Lost Lennon Tapes*, narrated by former Lennon confidant and Yoko's media representative, Elliot Mintz. Made in conjunction with the Lennon Estate, the year-long series promises to unveil all the lost treasures from John's personal tape archive, broadcasting demos, alternate mixes, and all manner of audio rarities never before heard by the public.

20 JAN.   Yoko, Sean, and Julian join George Harrison and Ringo Starr on stage at the Waldorf-Astoria Hotel in New York City for the third annual Rock and Roll Hall of Fame dinner, at which the Beatles are inducted.

JUNE   Yoko appears in Japanese television commercials for KDD, the country's international telecommunications monopoly.

9 AUG.   Paul McCartney issues a statement labelling as 'trash' Albert Goldman's forthcoming biography of John Lennon, presently being serialized in a British daily newspaper.

22 AUG.   Albert Goldman's biography *The Lives Of John Lennon* is published.

8 SEPT.   John's half-sister, Julia Baird, publishes her account of his life, *John Lennon, My Brother*.

14 SEPT.   Yoko Ono counters Albert Goldman's biography of John Lennon in a one-hour Westwood One radio special hosted by Elliot Mintz and broadcast across the USA.

16 SEPT.   Yoko is a surprise guest at the annual PRS 'John Lennon Scholarship' presentation, in London.

19 SEPT.   Yoko attends a preview of a new six-day John Lennon art exhibition – *Imagine* – which opens at the Business Design Centre in London on the twentieth. From London, the exhibition travels around the world.

30 SEPT.   A pavement star bearing John's name is unveiled by Yoko Ono outside Capitol Records' Tower building, along the Hollywood Walk of Fame.

3 OCT.   Three years in the making, Yoko's authorized documentary feature film about John's life, *Imagine: John Lennon*, opens in the USA. Just as she has given Westwood One direct access to the Lennon Archive for the radio series *The Lost Lennon Tapes*, so has she given the film's producers, Andrew Solt and David Wolper, unlimited access to the Estate's prodigious film and video collection, comprising considerable quantities of unseen footage. *Imagine: John Lennon* is also a coffee-table book, and EMI/Capitol issues a tie-in album and single 'Jealous Guy' (in USA) and 'Imagine'/'Jealous Guy' (UK).

9 OCT.   The rarely seen footage of the Plastic Ono Band's debut live performance, at the Rock 'n' Roll Revival Show in Toronto, Canada, on 13 September 1969, is shown on the US cable TV network Cinemax. An international video release follows.

25 OCT.   Yoko attends a special preview of *Imagine: John Lennon* in London. The British première is three days later, on the twenty-eighth.

DEC.   A new restaurant/night-club, Lennon's, opens in Central London, with Cynthia Lennon fronting the venture. Around this time, she also begins marketing her own brand of perfume, 'Cynthia Lennon's Woman'.

26 DEC.   The Michael Jackson film *Moonwalker*, on release in the UK from this date, features Sean Lennon in a cameo role. Yoko and Sean have established a friendship with Jackson over several years.

1989

JAN.   Sid Bernstein, who promoted Beatles concerts in New York, announces plans for a spectacular tribute to John Lennon, to be staged in Milwaukee on 9 October in conjunction with the Milwaukee Symphony Orchestra and the Milwaukee Ballet, although both organizations swiftly issue statements denying involvement.

5 JAN.   The movie album *Imagine: John Lennon* is certified gold in the USA.

18 JAN.   Contrary to earlier announcements that it would broadcast for one year only, the weekly series *The Lost Lennon Tapes* begins a second year on US radio.

30 JAN.   *Double Fantasy* switches from Geffen Records to Capitol Records.

20 FEB.   Julian trailers his forthcoming album by issuing a new single, 'Now You're In Heaven'.

27 MAR.   Julian releases his third album, *Mr Jordan*.

26 JUNE   Virgin issues another Julian Lennon single, 'You're The One'.

JULY   Practising barrister and British journalist Fenton Bresler publishes *The Murder Of John Lennon*, an investigation into the circumstances of John's assassination at the hands of Mark Chapman, asserting CIA involvement.

1 JULY   In Manchester, Julian plays the first of four UK concerts this week.

29 JULY   In Charlotte, North Carolina, Julian Lennon begins a
           full North American concert tour.
2 AUG.   During a concert at the Beacon Theatre, New York,
           Julian is joined on stage by half-brother Sean, and
           they duet together. After the show, during another
           rare moment of harmony, Cynthia and Yoko, and their
           respective Lennon sons, socialize together.
SEPT.   The panel of judges appointed by the PRS declines to
           award a winner for the 1989 John Lennon Scholarship,
           owing to the poor level of entries.
SEPT.   Cynthia pulls out of the Lennon's restaurant venture
           in London.
SEPT.   Yoko Ono opens the Bag One Gallery on West 79th
           Street, New York City, to sell high-quality high-price
           'official' Lennon merchandise.
9 OCT.   From Japan, Yoko announces a new scheme, 'Green-
           ing Of The World', to promote global awareness
           about environmental issues via records, books, films,
           exhibitions, and other events, with all proceeds to
           be channelled through the Spirit Foundation. Yoko
           announces that from 1990, his fiftieth birthday, 9
           October will be named after John as 'The Day Of
           Love'. One of the first GOW events is to be a major
           concert, to take place in Liverpool in May 1990, with
           top artists performing Lennon songs.
8 NOV.   The many outstanding lawsuits between the Beatles'
           Apple Corps and Capitol/EMI, as well as inter-group
           disputes, are settled via one broad agreement
           announced on this date.
11 DEC.   At a Los Angeles press conference, Sid Bernstein, with
           Cynthia Lennon, announces 'the show of the century',
           an ambitious John Lennon tribute set for Milwaukee
           on 12–13 March 1990. Glossing over the fact that
           their previously announced October 1989 event failed

to materialize, Bernstein and Cynthia promise a line-up that will include George Harrison, Paul McCartney, Ringo Starr, Phil Collins, Michael Jackson, Elton John, Eric Clapton, Rudolf Nureyev, Mikhail Baryshnikov, and Liza Minnelli.

1990

JAN.   For the second year in succession, Westwood One Radio announces the continuation – indefinite this time – of the weekly US radio series *The Lost Lennon Tapes*.

6 FEB.   Yoko wins a New York State Supreme Court ruling that forbids Marilyn Goldberg, formerly of Marigold Enterprises, from licensing reproductions of Lennon's art. Yoko and Marigold signed a merchandising agreement back in 1985. A full trial is expected to follow.

20 MAR.   Yoko attends a preview of a London exhibition of her art – the type of art that she exhibited in the 1960s – and a season of her films. It opens on the twenty-first, runs until 23 April, and then travels around Europe.

25 MAR.   On the twenty-first anniversary of their bed-in there, the Amsterdam Hilton re-opens Room 902 as 'The John and Yoko Honeymoon Suite', furnished with Lennon records, books, a guitar, and even a pair of 'granny glasses'.

APRIL   A restructured PRS John Lennon Award is granted to the Salford College of Technology, near Manchester, for a three-year period.

1 MAY   Following the closure of Beatle City, and before that Cavern Mecca, Liverpool is able to boast a permanent Beatles exhibition centre again with the opening of The Beatles Story.

5 MAY   After months of planning, the 'John Lennon Scholar-

ship Concert' takes place at a specially cleared area at the Pier Head in Liverpool, with many major artists each performing one or more Lennon compositions. Ringo Starr and Paul McCartney both supply videos; George Harrison does not participate at all; and the audience figure is disappointing – just fifteen thousand spectators when forty-five thousand had been expected. Yoko and Sean attend the concert, which is taped and broadcast on British television later the same evening, and preserved for future transmission in the USA. In the meantime, Cynthia Lennon and Sid Bernstein, whose March concert in Milwaukee again failed to materialize, announce a Lennon memorial concert at the Brandenburg Gate, Berlin, for 9 October. This event fails to take place, too.

9 JUNE   John's memory is honoured in the Soviet Union with a twenty-hour music festival in the Donetsk region.

10 AUG.   The Beatles Revolution, the first Beatles exhibition centre in London, opens, run by the buyers of Liverpool's Beatle City.

13 SEPT.   Another biography is published, Sandra Shevey's appalling *The Other Side Of Lennon*.

OCT.   A range of Lennon clothing goes on sale in France, authorized by the Lennon Estate.

1 OCT.   EMI releases *Lennon*, a definitive boxed-set collection of John's post-Beatles recordings, 1969–80. Issued in compact disc form only, the set encompasses seventy-three tracks.

6 OCT.   BBC Radio One launches *In My Life: Lennon Remembered*, a ten-programme documentary series with each of the one-hour programmes focusing on a particular aspect of his life or career. The series ends on 8 December, so it spans the two important anniversaries, what would have been his fiftieth birthday, and

the tenth anniversary of his murder. The BBC also
publishes a tie-in book of the series.

9 OCT.   To mark the fiftieth anniversary of John's birth, Yoko
participates in a ten-minute ceremony inside the
Trusteeship Council Chamber at the United Nations
building in New York, in which Madam Perez de
Cuellar – wife of the UN secretary-general – reads a
short introduction, an archive tape of John urging for
peace is aired, and Yoko delivers a four-minute speech,
followed by the playing of 'Imagine'. The event is
broadcast live around the world to any radio station
willing to take the feed, supplied free of charge by
Yoko: a reported one thousand stations in fifty countries do so. In the USA, it is followed on air by a
ninety-minute Westwood One radio special, *John
Lennon: They Say It's Your Birthday.*

12 NOV.   The BBC issues on cassette and compact disc the full
interview conducted with John and Yoko by Andy
Peebles on 6 December 1980.

22 NOV.   *John Lennon: A Family Album,* featuring the exclusive
photographic collection of Nishi F. Saimaru, is published in the UK and USA for the first time. It
was previously available only in Japan and had been
withdrawn from sale there following pressure from
Yoko.

3 DEC.   Sanctioned by Yoko and out for the first time on
home-video, EMI UK releases *John And Yoko: The
Bed-In,* the Lennons' film of their May 1969 Montreal
event.

6 DEC.   Pauline Lennon, the young second wife of John's
father Freddy, publishes a book, *Daddy Come Home:
The True Story Of John Lennon And His Father.*

7 DEC.   Combining highlights from the 5 May Liverpool concert with videos of other top acts performing Lennon

songs, and Lennon archive footage, the TV special *A Tribute To John Lennon* is transmitted on US television.

7 DEC. The Lord Mayor of Liverpool commemorates the tenth anniversary of John Lennon's death, and his fiftieth birthday, by unveiling the city's first official plaque in his honour, at the permanent exhibition centre The Beatles Story.

21 DEC. Undaunted by the Liverpool concert in May, widely considered to have been a failure, Yoko stages a second such event in John's memory – a 'Greening Of The World Concert' – at the Tokyo Dome venue in Japan's capital. This event spans two days, ending on 22 December, and features a blend of local and international acts, again performing Lennon songs, with Yoko and Sean participating. A combined audience of seventy-eight thousand attends.

1991

4 JAN. With the United Nations' war deadline against Iraq eleven days away, singer Lenny Kravitz joins forces with Sean and Yoko to write an updated version of 'Give Peace A Chance'. Recording takes place over the next few days at various studios in the USA and England.

15 JAN. On the expiry date of the UN's deadline for Iraq to leave Kuwait, Virgin Records in the USA rush-releases the new 'Peace Choir' version of 'Give Peace A Chance'. It is issued in the UK on 28 January but meets a blanket BBC ban against the broadcasting of strong war/peace records effective while the Gulf war is being waged. There is no such ban in the USA, but the record nonetheless meets resistance by US radio programmers and the listening public.

18 FEB. A long-form video documentary showing the making

of the Peace Choir's 'Give Peace A Chance' is issued.

20 FEB. Yoko Ono attends the thirty-third annual Grammy Awards, in New York City, to receive a 'Lifetime Achievement Award' granted posthumously to John Lennon.

26 MAR. Sean Lennon makes a guest appearance on *Mama Said*, the new album by Lenny Kravitz, issued this day.

15 APRIL The 7 December 1990 US television special *A Tribute To John Lennon* is issued on home-video as *Lennon: A Tribute*.

3 MAY Yoko mounts another season of her films, at the Public Theater in New York, closing on 16 May.

12 JULY In a court victory described as a US constitutional landmark, the US 9th Circuit Court of Appeals finds in favour of Jon Wiener, author of *Come Together*, the account of John Lennon's counter-culture activities, and instructs the FBI to release sixty-nine documents it withheld on grounds of national interest when, earlier, Wiener won access to the FBI's burgeoning files. The FBI contests the action.

5 AUG. Virgin Records in the UK issue 'Saltwater', a new single to promote Julian Lennon's forthcoming fourth album.

27 AUG. Virgin issues Julian Lennon's new album, *Help Yourself*.

29 AUG. Declaring 'All my memories are intact but the past is over now . . . it's time for a change,' Cynthia Lennon sells off most of her remaining items of John Lennon memorabilia, including his most intimate love letters, in auction at Christie's in London. The sale realizes in the region of £60,000.

8 OCT. On the eve of what would have been John's fifty-first birthday, three students from Salford College of Technology, near Manchester, England, are the latest

recipients of the John Lennon Award instigated by the Performing Right Society, the British music royalties collection organization of which Lennon was a lifelong member.

9 OCT.   Frederic (Fred) Seaman publishes an account of his years as an assistant to John Lennon, *Living On Borrowed Time – A Personal Memoir*. The book paints a particularly ugly portrait of Yoko Ono.

16 OCT.   Yoko and Sean attend a party in New York to launch the compilation album *Two Rooms: Celebrating The Songs Of Elton John And Bernie Taupin*.

11 NOV.   Following the outstanding success of 'Saltwater', which peaked at number six on the British chart, equalling the position of his 1984 début 'Too Late For Goodbyes', Julian Lennon issues the title track of the album *Help Yourself* as the follow-up single.

25 NOV.   Yoko attends a special event at the Hudson Theater in New York to commemorate the death on 25 October of the US concert promoter Bill Graham.

6 DEC.   Mary Smith – John's Aunt Mimi – dies at the age of eighty-eight at her home in Poole, Dorset, bought for her by John in 1965.

12 DEC.   Cynthia Lennon, Yoko Ono and Sean attend the cremation of John's Aunt Mimi. Paul McCartney, George Harrison and Ringo Starr send wreaths.

1992

MAR.   Described as a 'personal sketchbook' of Lennon drawings and captions, US publisher Cadence Books issues *ai: Japan Through John Lennon's Eyes*.

2 MAR.   Yoko Ono issues *Onobox*, an extraordinarily comprehensive 105-track compilation of her recorded work since 1968, spanning six CDs. A nineteen-track 'best of' compilation, *Walking On Thin Ice*, follows.

23 MAR. Intended to run for just fifty-two weeks, the US radio series *The Lost Lennon Tapes* concludes with its 218th edition, more than four years after it began.

APRIL *The Hours And The Times*, a sensitively portrayed fiction-based-on-fact movie focusing on John Lennon and Brian Epstein's April–May 1963 holiday in Spain, and the pair's alleged homosexual liaison, is screened in New York.

6 APRIL Julian Lennon issues another single in the UK, 'Get A Life', again taken from the *Help Yourself* album.

1 MAY British TV commercials for the sports-shoe manufacturer Nike feature John Lennon's recording of 'Instant Karma!', its use sanctioned by Yoko Ono. To coincide with the campaign EMI reissues 'Instant Karma!' as a single in certain European countries.

15 JULY A new Lennon musical, *Imagine*, opens at the Playhouse Theatre in Liverpool.

OCT. Previously presented in Australia, the stage-play *Looking Through A Glass Onion – John Lennon In Words And Music* opens in London. It closes after just a few days.

5 OCT. Picture Music International, a division of EMI, issues *The John Lennon Video Collection*, a compilation of promotional clips and TV appearances made by John for his post-Beatles music.

16 NOV. Containing slightly different footage from the 1986 release *John Lennon: Live In New York City*, Yoko Ono sanctions the British release on video of *John Lennon: One To One*, also filmed at the 30 August 1972 concert in New York.

1993

17 APRIL An exhibition of Yoko's art opens in Los Angeles. Among the exhibits, reproduction copies of which are on sale to the public, is a bronze replica of John's

smashed and blood-stained spectacles from the night
of his murder, available for $25,000.

NOV.   Yoko launches another exhibition, *Family Album
           (Blood Objects)*, in Los Angeles. In addition to the
           bronze replica of John's bloody spectacles, visitors also
           have the chance to purchase a bronze sculpture of
           the bullet-riddled shirt worn by John when he was
           murdered (selling at $35,000).

1994

JAN.   Yoko contributes to *A Chance Operation – The John
           Cage Tribute*, a double-CD.

15 JAN.   John Lennon's friend and sometime musical partner
           Harry Nilsson dies, aged fifty-two. He had suffered a
           heart attack in February 1993.

19 JAN.   Paul McCartney flies to New York to induct John
           Lennon (this time as a solo artist; the Beatles' induc-
           tion as a group occurred in 1988) into the Rock 'n'
           Roll Hall of Fame, reading a 1,200-word speech writ-
           ten in the form of an open letter to his former partner.
           Afterwards, Paul and Yoko, with Sean, publicly patch
           up their former differences and hold a joint press
           conference. It is during this visit that Yoko gives Paul
           a cassette recording of John's unfinished and unissued
           composition 'Free As A Bird', in order that he may
           return to England and, together with George Harri-
           son and Ringo Starr, complete the recording, thus
           reuniting all four Beatles, through the miracle of
           technology, for the first time in twenty-four years.
           The song is intended for use in what is tentatively
           being called *The Beatles' Anthology*, Apple's official 'the
           Beatles' story as told by the Beatles' TV series set for
           screening in 1995.

MAR.   The movie *Backbeat* opens to critical acclaim, telling the story of the love affair between Stuart Sutcliffe and Astrid Kirchherr, set amid the backdrop of the Beatles' first visit to Hamburg in 1960.

30 MAR. *New York Rock*, a rock opera – 'an urban story of love, loss and hope' – loosely based on the lives of John and Yoko, opens at the WPA Theater in New York, off-Broadway. With script and music written by Yoko, the show includes gunshots. Press notices are critical and its limited season ends on 17 April.

SEPT. Bag One Arts, Inc. – the commercial wing of the John Lennon Estate, administered by Yoko – licenses a range of men's apparel based on John Lennon's artwork. By 1995, however, the two parties have fallen out, a lawsuit ensuing.

15 SEPT. A two-song audio tape recording of John Lennon performing with the Quarry Men skiffle group at the evening dance which followed the Woolton parish church fête on 6 July 1957, the occasion when John met Paul McCartney for the first time, is sold at auction at Sotheby's, London, for £78,500 (including commission). The buyer is EMI Records. The chance recording was made by Bob Molyneux, who kept the existence of his tape a secret for thirty-seven years.

OCT. A brief clip of John's American TV appearance on 9 September 1971 on *The Dick Cavett Show* is included in the new Tom Hanks movie *Forrest Gump*, which, in 1995, goes on to win a clutch of Academy Awards.

30 NOV. Amid a wave of media hysteria, EMI Records issues *Live At The BBC*, a double-CD collection of the Beatles' BBC Radio music recordings, taped 1963–5. It goes on to sell 6 million copies worldwide within the first six months of release.

30 DEC. Ringo Starr's first wife, Maureen, dies at the age of forty-seven following a long battle against leukaemia.

1995

FEB.   Following their work on 'Free As A Bird' in the spring of 1994, Paul, George and Ringo complete, with new contributions, a second unfinished John Lennon work-in-progress, 'Real Love', for *The Beatles Anthology*. Once again, the tape is supplied to them by Yoko. (In this instance, however, the song is previously known to record buyers: one of John's several demonstration versions was included in the soundtrack to the 1988 movie *Imagine: John Lennon*.) Work by Paul, George and Ringo on a third unfinished John Lennon piece, 'Now And Then', is never completed, however.

22 FEB.   Cynthia Lennon makes her début as a recording artist in her own right, releasing as a single a version of 'Those Were The Days', as sung by Apple's Mary Hopkin in 1968. (The record is promoted by a video in which Cynthia is seen visiting Beatles sites in Liverpool on a tourist bus.) With this, the tally of John Lennon's relations appearing on record reaches five: his father Freddy, his two sons Sean and Julian and his two wives Cynthia and Yoko. A sixth, John's Uncle Charlie, can also be heard singing 'Where Are The Ships Of The Mersey?' on a publicly available tape. Despite some media interest, Cynthia's disc sells poorly.

MAR.   Bag One Arts launches another product line: two limited-edition portfolios of lithographs of John's facsimile handwritten lyrics, the first covering compositions written in what is called *The Beatles Years*, the other covering *The Solo Years*. The selling price is $2,000 per set.

11 MAR.   The increasingly positive relationship between Yoko

and Paul McCartney is underlined when, during a visit to England, Yoko and Sean join Paul, Linda and the McCartneys' children at a spontaneously arranged recording session at Paul's private studio. The resulting tape, featuring a jam entitled 'Hiroshima, It's Always A Beautiful Blue Sky', with Yoko taking the lead vocal, is taken away by Ono when the session ends and eventually broadcast on Japanese TV. In due course, former enmities resurface and the friendship cools once more.

APRIL   Yoko adds her signature to 2,500 copies of a luxuriously produced limited-edition book, *Sometime in New York City*, featuring photographs of John and Yoko taken by Bob Gruen. The book sells at £276 per copy.

4 APRIL John's friend Kenny Everett, the irreverent British radio disc-jockey and TV personality, dies of an Aids-related illness, aged fifty.

7 SEPT. Following her August 1991 sale, Cynthia Lennon again asserts that it is time to leave her past behind, auctioning at Christie's further items from her decade with John.

7 NOV.   Reprising the more experimental style of music-making she embraced in her early work for Apple Records, Yoko's first new album in nine years, *Rising*, is issued by Capitol. (The release is supplemented on 5 March 1996 by *Rising Mixes*, an album of variant remixes.)

12 NOV. Yoko makes a guest appearance in the US TV sitcom *Mad About You*.

19 NOV. *The Beatles Anthology* is premièred on US television by the ABC network, and the first new 'Beatles' song in twenty-five years, 'Free As A Bird', is dramatically unveiled. American viewers see *Anthology* as three

two-hour programmes, the other editions airing on 22 and 23 November, whereas, in most countries, it is broadcast as six one-hour programmes.

20 NOV. 'Free As A Bird' is released for airplay.

21 NOV. 'Free As A Bird' is available for purchase in record stores worldwide as the opening track on *The Beatles Anthology 1*. This is the first of three double CDs (triple-vinyl), released over the next eleven months, compiling previously unreleased outtakes and remixes from the period 1958–70, assembled at Abbey Road Studios by George Martin. This first collection spans 1958–64.

23 NOV. The second 'new' Beatles song, 'Real Love', is unveiled on British and American television. It will not be issued on disc until March 1996 as the opening track on *The Beatles Anthology 2*.

26 NOV. The first of the six-part TV series *The Beatles Anthology* is shown in the UK by the ITV network. Screened weekly, the series ends on 31 December.

4 DEC. 'Free As A Bird' is issued as a single. Hopes that it will attain the UK number one spot at Christmas are forlorn, however – it peaks at 2.

11 DEC. It is revealed that Linda McCartney has breast cancer.

1996

29 FEB. Yoko commences a short concert tour of the USA in support of *Rising*, playing seven dates inside four weeks, concluding on 25 March. Sean Lennon's band IMA provide her backing.

4 MAR. The Beatles' 'Real Love' is issued as a single.

18 MAR. *The Beatles Anthology 2*, the second collection of previously unreleased Beatles outtakes and rare mixes, this one spanning 1965–68, is issued worldwide.

8 JUNE Backed again by Sean's band IMA, Yoko performs in

concert in London, one of several European dates at this time.

22 JUNE   Yoko and IMA perform the first of four concerts in Japan, concluding on 1 July.

6 JULY   Wearing an eyepatch and sporting bright orange hair, Yoko performs at a free show in Central Park, New York, supported once again by IMA.

5 SEPT.   Cynthia Lennon again features heavily in the annual rock memorabilia auction at Christie's, London, selling such items as the garden furniture from Kenwood, her Weybridge home with John, 1964–68. Some items – including a four-poster bed – fail to reach their reserve, however, and are unsold.

10 SEPT.   Ray Coleman, journalistic companion of the Beatles and John Lennon, and the author of this book, dies after a long battle with cancer.

7 OCT.   Twice the length of the original TV series, the full ten-hour version of *The Beatles Anthology* appears for the first time, as eight 75-minute video-tapes.

28 OCT.   *The Beatles Anthology 3*, the final collection of previously unreleased Beatles outtakes and rare mixes, this one spanning 1968–70, is issued worldwide.

1997

1 JAN.   Paul McCartney is knighted in the Queen's New Year's honours list. (The investiture takes place at Buckingham Palace on 11 March.)

20 MAY   The US record label Rykodisc issues on CD the albums *Unfinished Music No. 1 – Two Virgins, Unfinished Music No. 2 – Life With The Lions, The Wedding Album* and *Yoko Ono/Plastic Ono Band*.

20 JUNE   Yoko and Sean attend a music industry luncheon in London to accept a posthumous award recognizing John Lennon's outstanding contribution to British

music. In an English newspaper interview at this time, Yoko confirms that she has been reconciled with her daughter Kyoko, now thirty-three.

22 JULY Rykodisc continues its programme of Yoko Ono music re-releases with *Fly, Approximately Infinite Universe, Feeling The Space* and, for the first time in the West, her 1974 Japanese album, *A Story*.

AUG. George Harrison undergoes a successful operation to remove a throat tumour – it proves to be benign.

7 SEPT. Beatles' friend and press officer Derek Taylor – who served the group in 1964, 1968–70 and again from the mid-1980s, including during the *Anthology* period – dies at his Suffolk home after a long battle with cancer.

8 SEPT. Rykodisc concludes its reissue programme of Yoko Ono music with *Seasons Of Glass, It's Alright (I See Rainbows)* and *Starpeace*.

25 SEPT. The American Civil Liberties Union, representing writer and historian Jon Wiener, finally secures victory over the FBI, the US government organization surrendering eighty previously censored pages from its files on John Lennon. Supplementing *Come Together: John Lennon In His Time*, his outstanding 1984 work on Lennon's political activism, Wiener incorporates the discoveries in a new book, *Gimme Some Truth: The John Lennon FBI Files*, published in the USA in January 2000. (At which time, the UK press momentarily theorizes on whether Lennon funded the IRA in the early 1970s, quickly proven untrue.)

27 OCT. EMI reactivates the John Lennon catalogue with a new twenty-track compilation album, *Lennon Legend*, which replaces the 1982 issue *The John Lennon Collection*.

1998

6 JAN. A new interview with Yoko is screened in the UK by BBC2 as *The Ballad of Yoko and John* – the title reflecting the current repositioning of her artistic credentials in the UK (and USA). She takes the opportunity to swipe at Paul McCartney, especially rebutting some comments published in his recent authorized biography *Many Years from Now*.

16 FEB. Yoko gives a major, in-depth interview to Sir Jeremy Isaacs in the BBC2 series *Face to Face*.

17 APRIL Linda McCartney dies at the McCartneys' hideaway home near Tucson, Arizona, after a long battle with cancer.

20 APRIL Interviewed in *New Yorker*, Sean makes clear his belief that the US government was responsible for his father's murder and that Mark Chapman, far from acting alone, was in some way their agent.

7 MAY Sean performs in concert at a London pub.

18 MAY By a remarkable coincidence, both of John Lennon's sons release albums this day in the UK – Sean issues his first, the eclectic *Into The Sun*, on the Beastie Boys' label Grand Royal, Julian releases the more melodic *Photographic Smile*.

19 MAY John and Yoko's five-day residence on *The Mike Douglas Show*, aired on US TV 14–18 February 1972, is released in its entirety as a video boxed set in the USA.

22 JUNE Yoko is conspicuously absent from a New York memorial service for Linda McCartney, organized and hosted by Paul. He did not invite her.

5 JULY Julian performs in Hyde Park, London, as part of a Prince's Trust rock gala.

20 JULY Julian vociferously attacks Yoko's integrity during an appearance on the BBC2 dinner-table chat show *Ruby*.

24 AUG.   A third half-sister to John Lennon, long believed to exist, surfaces for the first time when Ingrid Pedersen, fifty-three, reveals her story to the British newspaper *The Sun*. Certificates in her possession prove that she was born to Julia Lennon in a Salvation Army hostel in Liverpool on 19 June 1945; the father was believed to be a Welsh soldier. Named Victoria Elizabeth Lennon at birth, she was quickly adopted by a Norwegian man and his Liverpool wife. Though she discovered the truth of her background in 1966, she never contacted John Lennon.

3 NOV.   EMI issues *John Lennon Anthology*, a lavish four-CD boxed set assembled under Yoko's supervision, featuring previously unreleased music and speech tracks from his post-Beatles career, including home demos as featured in the 1988–92 US radio series *The Lost Lennon Tapes*, and studio outtake recordings, 1969–80, never before heard in any sphere. Highlights from the set are compiled on to a single disc, *Wonsaponatime*.

1 DEC.   Yoko unveils a 'War Is Over!' poster in Times Square, New York, temporarily reviving the campaign she and John first mounted in December 1969.

1999

9 JAN.   Yoko is back in England, attending the opening of an exhibition of her art in Colchester, Essex. From here it travels around Europe.

APRIL   John Lennon is voted the greatest rock singer of all time in a readers' poll conducted by the British music magazine *Mojo*.

3 JUNE   Cynthia Lennon displays drawings from her 1978 book about John, *A Twist of Lennon*, in a new exhibition in London.

13 SEPT. Apple's continued marketing of the Beatles leads to

the release of new album *Yellow Submarine Songtrack*, featuring remixed songs from the original 1968 film. The movie itself, dynamically improved in both sound and visual quality, is reissued at this time.

5 DEC. Yoko's artistic renaissance in the UK is confirmed when her career is the subject of ITV's arts programme *The South Bank Show*.

30 DEC. George and Olivia Harrison are attacked with a knife by a crazed intruder, intent on murder, at their home in Henley-upon-Thames, England, and are fortunate to survive with only minor injuries.

2000

1 FEB. American TV music channel VH1 screens a new drama, *Two of Us*, dramatizing (with much artistic licence) a 1976 visit by Paul McCartney to John Lennon at the Dakota building in New York.

13 FEB. BBC2 transmits *Gimme Some Truth*, a documentary about the recording of John's 1971 album *Imagine*, made with footage provided by Yoko, a little of it previously unseen but most having been included in the 1988 movie *Imagine: John Lennon*.

14 FEB. Featuring newly prepared remixes overseen by Yoko, EMI reissues the *Imagine* album in best-yet audio quality.

20 FEB. *The Sunday Times* resurrects allegations concerning John's relationship with the IRA, prompted by the publication in the USA of Jon Wiener's book, *Gimme Some Truth: The John Lennon FBI Files*.

22 FEB. Yoko denies allegations that John gave money to the IRA.

11 MAY With her work on display there, Yoko attends the opening of the Tate Modern Gallery in London.

DISCOGRAPHY

THE BEATLES – UK DISCOGRAPHY

Original singles

Oct. 1962	'Love Me Do'/'PS I Love You'
Jan. 1963	'Please Please Me'/'Ask Me Why'
April 1963	'From Me To You'/'Thank You Girl'
Aug. 1963	'She Loves You'/'I'll Get You'
Nov. 1963	'I Want To Hold Your Hand'/'This Boy'
March 1964	'Can't Buy Me Love'/'You Can't Do That'
July 1964	'A Hard Day's Night'/'Things We Said Today'
Nov. 1964	'I Feel Fine'/'She's A Woman'
April 1965	'Ticket To Ride'/'Yes It Is'
July 1965	'Help!'/'I'm Down'
Dec. 1965	'We Can Work It Out'/'Day Tripper'
June 1966	'Paperback Writer'/'Rain'
Aug. 1966	'Eleanor Rigby'/'Yellow Submarine'
Feb. 1967	'Strawberry Fields Forever'/'Penny Lane'
July 1967	'All You Need Is Love'/'Baby, You're A Rich Man'
Nov. 1967	'Hello, Goodbye'/'I Am The Walrus'

March 1968	'Lady Madonna'/'The Inner Light'
Aug. 1968	'Hey Jude'/'Revolution'
April 1969	'Get Back'/'Don't Let Me Down'
May 1969	'The Ballad Of John And Yoko'/'Old Brown Shoe'
Oct. 1969	'Something'/'Come Together'
March 1970	'Let It Be'/'You Know My Name (Look Up The Number)'

Original EPs

July 1963   Twist And Shout
'Twist And Shout'; 'A Taste Of Honey'; 'Do You Want To Know A Secret'; 'There's A Place'

Sept. 1963   The Beatles Hits
'From Me To You'; 'Thank You Girl'; 'Please Please Me'; 'Love Me Do'

Nov. 1963   The Beatles (No 1)
'I Saw Her Standing There'; 'Misery'; 'Anna (Go To Him)'; 'Chains'

Feb. 1964   All My Loving
'All My Loving'; 'Ask Me Why'; 'Money (That's What I Want)'; 'PS I Love You'

June 1964   Long Tall Sally
'Long Tall Sally'; 'I Call Your Name'; 'Slow Down'; 'Matchbox'

Nov. 1964   Extracts From The Film *A Hard Day's Night*
'I Should Have Known Better'; 'If I Fell'; 'Tell Me Why'; 'And I Love Her'

Nov. 1964   Extracts From The Album *A Hard Day's Night*
'Any Time At All'; 'I'll Cry Instead'; 'Things We Said Today';
'When I Get Home'

April 1965   Beatles For Sale
'No Reply'; 'I'm A Loser'; 'Rock And Roll Music'; 'Eight Days
A Week'

June 1965   Beatles For Sale (No 2)
'I'll Follow The Sun'; 'Baby's In Black'; 'Words Of Love'; 'I Don't
Want To Spoil The Party'

Dec. 1965   The Beatles Million Sellers
'She Loves You'; 'I Want To Hold Your Hand'; 'Can't Buy Me
Love'; 'I Feel Fine'

March 1966   Yesterday
'Yesterday'; 'Act Naturally'; 'You Like Me Too Much'; 'It's Only
Love'

July 1966   Nowhere Man
'Nowhere Man'; 'Drive My Car'; 'Michelle'; 'You Won't See Me'

Dec. 1967   Magical Mystery Tour
'Magical Mystery Tour'; 'Your Mother Should Know'; 'I Am The
Walrus'; 'The Fool On The Hill'; 'Flying'; 'Blue Jay Way'

Original albums

March 1963   Please Please Me
'I Saw Her Standing There'; 'Misery'; 'Anna (Go To Him)';
'Chains'; 'Boys'; 'Ask Me Why'; 'Please Please Me'; 'Love Me
Do'; 'PS I Love You'; 'Baby It's You'; 'Do You Want To Know

A Secret'; 'A Taste Of Honey'; 'There's A Place'; 'Twist And Shout'

Nov. 1963 **With The Beatles**
'It Won't Be Long'; 'All I've Got To Do'; 'All My Loving'; 'Don't Bother Me'; 'Little Child'; 'Till There Was You'; 'Please Mister Postman'; 'Roll Over Beethoven'; 'Hold Me Tight'; 'You Really Got A Hold On Me'; 'I Wanna Be Your Man'; '(There's A) Devil In Her Heart'; 'Not A Second Time'; 'Money (That's What I Want)'

July 1964 **A Hard Day's Night**
'A Hard Day's Night'; 'I Should Have Known Better'; 'If I Fell'; 'I'm Happy Just To Dance With You'; 'And I Love Her'; 'Tell Me Why'; 'Can't Buy Me Love'; 'Any Time At All'; 'I'll Cry Instead'; 'Things We Said Today'; 'When I Get Home'; 'You Can't Do That'; 'I'll Be Back'

Dec. 1964 **Beatles For Sale**
'No Reply'; 'I'm A Loser'; 'Baby's In Black'; 'Rock And Roll Music'; 'I'll Follow The Sun'; 'Mr Moonlight'; 'Kansas City'/ 'Hey-Hey-Hey-Hey!'; 'Eight Days A Week'; 'Words Of Love'; 'Honey Don't'; 'Every Little Thing'; 'I Don't Want To Spoil The Party'; 'What You're Doing'; 'Everybody's Trying To Be My Baby'

Aug. 1965 **Help!**
'Help!'; 'The Night Before'; 'You've Got To Hide Your Love Away'; 'I Need You'; 'Another Girl'; 'You're Going To Lose That Girl'; 'Ticket To Ride'; 'Act Naturally'; 'It's Only Love'; 'You Like Me Too Much'; 'Tell Me What You See'; 'I've Just Seen A Face'; 'Yesterday'; 'Dizzy Miss Lizzy'

Dec. 1965 **Rubber Soul**

'Drive My Car'; 'Norwegian Wood (This Bird Has Flown)'; 'You Won't See Me'; 'Nowhere Man'; 'Think For Yourself'; 'The Word'; 'Michelle'; 'What Goes On'; 'Girl'; 'I'm Looking Through You'; 'In My Life'; 'Wait'; 'If I Needed Someone'; 'Run For Your Life'

Aug. 1966 **Revolver**

'Taxman'; 'Eleanor Rigby'; 'I'm Only Sleeping'; 'Love You To'; 'Here, There And Everywhere'; 'Yellow Submarine'; 'She Said She Said'; 'Good Day Sunshine'; 'And Your Bird Can Sing'; 'For No One'; 'Doctor Robert'; 'I Want To Tell You'; 'Got To Get You Into My Life'; 'Tomorrow Never Knows'

June 1967 **Sgt Pepper's Lonely Hearts Club Band**

'Sgt Pepper's Lonely Hearts Club Band'; 'With A Little Help From My Friends'; 'Lucy In The Sky With Diamonds'; 'Getting Better'; 'Fixing A Hole'; 'She's Leaving Home'; 'Being For The Benefit Of Mr Kite!'; 'Within You Without You'; 'When I'm Sixty-Four'; 'Lovely Rita'; 'Good Morning Good Morning'; 'Sgt Pepper's Lonely Hearts Club Band (Reprise)'; 'A Day In The Life'

Nov. 1968 **The Beatles**

'Back In The USSR'; 'Dear Prudence'; 'Glass Onion'; 'Ob-La-Di, Ob-La-Da'; 'Wild Honey Pie'; 'The Continuing Story Of Bungalow Bill'; 'While My Guitar Gently Weeps'; 'Happiness Is A Warm Gun'; 'Martha My Dear'; 'I'm So Tired'; 'Blackbird'; 'Piggies'; 'Rocky Raccoon'; 'Don't Pass Me By'; 'Why Don't We Do It In The Road'; 'I Will'; 'Julia'; 'Birthday'; 'Yer Blues'; 'Mother Nature's Son'; 'Everybody's Got Something To Hide Except Me And My Monkey'; 'Sexy Sadie'; 'Helter Skelter'; 'Long Long Long'; 'Revolution 1'; 'Honey Pie'; 'Savoy Truffle'; 'Cry Baby Cry'; 'Revolution 9'; 'Good Night

Jan. 1969 **Yellow Submarine**
'Yellow Submarine'; 'Only A Northern Song'; 'All Together Now'; 'Hey Bulldog'; 'It's All Too Much'; 'All You Need Is Love' (*and seven soundtrack instrumental cuts by the George Martin Orchestra*)

Sept. 1969 **Abbey Road**
'Come Together'; 'Something'; 'Maxwell's Silver Hammer'; 'Oh! Darling'; 'Octopus's Garden'; 'I Want You (She's So Heavy)'; 'Here Comes The Sun'; 'Because'; 'You Never Give Me Your Money'; 'Sun King'/'Mean Mr Mustard'; 'Polythene Pam'/'She Came In Through The Bathroom Window'; 'Golden Slumbers'/ 'Carry That Weight'; 'The End'; 'Her Majesty'

May 1970 **Let It Be**
'Two Of Us'; 'Dig A Pony'; 'Across The Universe'; 'I Me Mine'; 'Dig It'; 'Let It Be'; 'Maggie Mae'; 'I've Got A Feeling'; 'The One After 909'; 'The Long And Winding Road'; 'For You Blue'; 'Get Back'

Important Post-1970 Beatles Albums

May 1977 **The Beatles At The Hollywood Bowl**
'Twist And Shout'; 'She's A Woman'; 'Dizzy Miss Lizzy'; 'Ticket To Ride'; 'Can't Buy Me Love'; 'Things We Said Today'; 'Roll Over Beethoven'; 'Boys'; 'A Hard Day's Night'; 'Help!'; 'All My Loving'; 'She Loves You'; 'Long Tall Sally'

Nov. 1994 **Live At The BBC**
'Beatle Greetings' (speech); 'From Us To You'; 'Riding On A Bus' (speech); 'I Got A Woman'; 'Too Much Money Business'; 'Keep Your Hands Off My Baby'; 'I'll Be On My Way'; 'Youngblood'; 'A Shot Of Rhythm And Blues'; 'Sure To Fall (In Love With You)'; 'Some Other Guy'; 'Thank You Girl'; 'Sha La La La

La!' (speech); 'Baby It's You'; 'That's All Right (Mama)'; 'Carol';
'Soldier Of Love'; 'A Little Rhyme' (speech); 'Clarabella'; 'I'm
Gonna Sit Right Down And Cry (Over You)'; 'Crying, Waiting,
Hoping'; 'Dear Wack! (speech)'; 'You Really Got A Hold On
Me'; 'To Know Her Is To Love Her'; 'A Taste Of Honey'; 'Long
Tall Sally'; 'I Saw Her Standing There'; 'The Honeymoon Song';
'Johnny B Goode'; 'Memphis, Tennessee'; 'Lucille'; 'Can't Buy
Me Love'; 'From Fluff To You' (speech); 'Till There Was You';
'Crinsk Dee Night' (speech); 'A Hard Day's Night'; 'Have A
Banana!' (speech); 'I Wanna Be Your Man'; 'Just A Rumour'
(speech); 'Roll Over Beethoven'; 'All My Loving'; 'Things We
Said Today'; 'She's A Woman'; 'Sweet Little Sixteen'; '1822!'
(speech); 'Lonesome Tears In My Eyes'; 'Nothin' Shakin' (But
The Leaves On The Trees)'; 'The Hippy Hippy Shake'; 'Glad All
Over'; 'I Just Don't Understand'; 'So How Come (No One Loves
Me)'; 'I Feel Fine'; 'I'm A Loser'; 'Everybody's Trying To Be My
Baby'; 'Rock And Roll Music'; 'Ticket To Ride'; 'Dizzy Miss
Lizzy'; 'Kansas City'/'Hey-Hey-Hey-Hey!'; 'Set Fire To That Lot!'
(speech); 'Matchbox'; 'I Forgot To Remember To Forget'; 'Love
These Goon Shows!' (speech); 'I Got To Find My Baby'; 'Ooh!
My Soul'; 'Ooh! My Arms' (speech); 'Don't Ever Change'; 'Slow
Down'; 'Honey Don't'; 'Love Me Do

Nov. 1995   The Beatles Anthology 1
'Free As A Bird' (speech); 'That'll Be The Day'; 'In Spite Of All
The Danger' (speech); 'Hallelujah, I Love Her So'; 'You'll Be
Mine'; 'Cayenne' (speech); 'My Bonnie'; 'Ain't She Sweet'; 'Cry
For A Shadow' (speech); 'Searchin''; 'Three Cool Cats'; 'The Sheik
Of Araby'; 'Like Dreamers Do'; 'Hello Little Girl' (speech);
'Besame Mucho'; 'Love Me Do'; 'How Do You Do It'; 'Please
Please Me'; 'One After 909' (sequence); 'One After 909'; 'Lend
Me Your Comb'; 'I'll Get You' (speech); 'I Saw Her Standing
There'; 'From Me To You'; 'Money (That's What I Want)'; 'You
Really Got A Hold On Me'; 'Roll Over Beethoven'; 'She Loves

You'; 'Till There Was You'; 'Twist And Shout'; 'This Boy'; 'I Want To Hold Your Hand' (speech); 'Moonlight Bay'; 'Can't Buy Me Love'; 'All My Loving'; 'You Can't Do That'; 'And I Love Her'; 'A Hard Day's Night'; 'I Wanna Be Your Man'; 'Long Tall Sally'; 'Boys'; 'Shout'; 'I'll Be Back' (take 2); 'I'll Be Back' (take 3); 'You Know What To Do'; 'No Reply' (demo); 'Mr Moonlight'; 'Leave My Kitten Alone'; 'No Reply'; 'Eight Days A Week' (sequence); 'Eight Days A Week' (complete); 'Kansas City'/'Hey-Hey-Hey-Hey!'

March 1996   **The Beatles Anthology 2**
'Real Love'; 'Yes It Is'; 'I'm Down'; 'You've Got To Hide Your Love Away'; 'If You've Got Trouble'; 'That Means A Lot'; 'Yesterday'; 'It's Only Love'; 'I Feel Fine'; 'Ticket To Ride'; 'Yesterday'; 'Help!'; 'Everybody's Trying To Be My Baby'; 'Norwegian Wood (This Bird Has Flown)'; 'I'm Looking Through You'; '12-Bar Original'; 'Tomorrow Never Knows'; 'Got To Get You Into My Life'; 'And Your Bird Can Sing'; 'Taxman'; 'Eleanor Rigby' (strings only); 'I'm Only Sleeping' (rehearsal); 'I'm Only Sleeping' (take 1); 'Rock And Roll Music'; 'She's A Woman'; 'Strawberry Fields Forever' (demo sequence); 'Strawberry Fields Forever' (take 1); 'Strawberry Fields Forever' (take 7 & edit piece); 'Penny Lane'; 'A Day In The Life'; 'Good Morning Good Morning'; 'Only A Northern Song'; 'Being For The Benefit Of Mr Kite!' (takes 1 and 2); 'Being For The Benefit Of Mr Kite!' (take 7); 'Lucy In The Sky With Diamonds'; 'Within You Without You' (instrumental); 'Sgt Pepper's Lonely Hearts Club Band' (Reprise); 'You Know My Name (Look Up The Number)'; 'I Am The Walrus'; 'The Fool On The Hill' (demo); 'Your Mother Should Know'; 'The Fool On The Hill' (take 4); 'Hello, Goodbye'; 'Lady Madonna'; 'Across The Universe'

Oct. 1996 **The Beatles Anthology 3**
'A Beginning'; 'Happiness Is A Warm Gun'; 'Helter Skelter';
'Mean Mr Mustard'; 'Polythene Pam'; 'Glass Onion'; 'Junk';
'Piggies'; 'Honey Pie'; 'Don't Pass Me By'; 'Ob-La-Di, Ob-La-
Da'; 'Good Night'; 'Cry Baby Cry'; 'Blackbird'; 'Sexy Sadie';
'While My Guitar Gently Weeps'; 'Hey Jude'; 'Not Guilty';
'Mother Nature's Son'; 'Glass Onion'; 'Rocky Raccoon'; 'What's
The New Mary Jane'; 'Step Inside Love'/'Los Paranoias'; 'I'm So
Tired'; 'I Will'; 'Why Don't We Do It In The Road'; 'Julia'; 'I've
Got A Feeling'; 'She Came In Through The Bathroom Window';
'Dig A Pony'; 'Two Of Us'; 'For You Blue'; 'Teddy Boy'; 'Rip It
Up'/'Shake, Rattle And Roll'/'Blue Suede Shoes'; 'The Long And
Winding Road'; 'Oh! Darling'; 'All Things Must Pass'; 'Mail-
man, Bring Me No More Blues'; 'Get Back'; 'Old Brown Shoe';
'Octopus's Garden'; 'Maxwell's Silver Hammer'; 'Something';
'Come Together'; 'Come And Get It'; 'Ain't She Sweet'; 'Because';
'Let It Be'; 'I Me Mine'; 'The End'

JOHN LENNON – UK DISCOGRAPHY

Original singles

July 1969	'Give Peace A Chance'/'Remember Love'
Oct. 1969	'Cold Turkey'/'Don't Worry Kyoko (Mummy's Only Looking For Her Hand In The Snow)'
Feb. 1970	'Instant Karma!'/'Who Has Seen The Wind?'
March 1971	'Power To The People'/'Open Your Box'
Nov. 1972	'Happy Xmas (War Is Over)'/'Listen, The Snow Is Falling'
Nov. 1973	'Mind Games'/'Meat City'

Oct. 1974   'Whatever Gets You Thru The Night'/'Beef
              Jerky'
Jan. 1975   '#9 Dream'/'What You Got'
April 1975   'Stand By Me'/'Move Over Ms L'
Oct. 1975   'Imagine'/'Working Class Hero'
Oct. 1980   '(Just Like) Starting Over'/'Kiss Kiss Kiss'

Original Albums

Nov. 1968 **Unfinished Music No 1: Two Virgins** – *John Lennon and Yoko Ono*
'Two Virgins No. 1'; 'Together'; 'Two Virgins No. 2'; 'Two Virgins No. 3'; 'Two Virgins No. 4'; 'Two Virgins No. 5'; 'Two Virgins No. 6'; 'Hushabye Hushabye'; 'Two Virgins No. 7'; 'Two Virgins No. 8'; 'Two Virgins No. 9'; 'Two Virgins No. 10'

May 1969 **Unfinished Music No 2: Life With The Lions** – *John Lennon and Yoko Ono*
'Cambridge 1969'; 'No Bed For Beatle John'; 'Baby's Heartbeat'; 'Two Minute's Silence'; 'Radio Play'

Nov. 1969 **Wedding Album** – *John and Yoko*
'John And Yoko'; 'Amsterdam'

Dec. 1969 **Live Peace In Toronto 1969** – *The Plastic Ono Band*
'Blue Suede Shoes'; 'Money (That's What I Want)'; 'Dizzy Miss Lizzy'; 'Yer Blues'; 'Cold Turkey'; 'Give Peace A Chance'; 'Don't Worry Kyoko (Mummy's Only Looking For Her Hand In The Snow)'; 'John John (Let's Hope For Peace)'

Dec. 1970   John Lennon/Plastic Ono Band – *John Lennon*
'Mother'; 'Hold On'; 'I Found Out'; 'Working Class Hero'; 'Isolation'; 'Remember'; 'Love'; 'Well Well Well'; 'Look At Me'; 'God'; 'My Mummy's Dead'

Oct. 1971   Imagine – *John Lennon/Plastic Ono Band (with the Flux Fiddlers)*
'Imagine'; 'Crippled Inside'; 'Jealous Guy'; 'It's So Hard'; 'I Don't Want To Be A Soldier'; 'Give Me Some Truth'; 'Oh My Love'; 'How Do You Sleep?'; 'How?'; 'Oh Yoko!'

Sept. 1972   Some Time In New York City
'Woman Is The Nigger Of The World'; 'Sisters, O Sisters'; 'Attica State'; 'Born In A Prison'; 'New York City'; 'Sunday Bloody Sunday'; 'The Luck Of The Irish'; 'John Sinclair'; 'Angela'; 'We're All Water' – *John and Yoko/Plastic Ono Band with a cast of thousands*
'Cold Turkey'; 'Don't Worry Kyoko (Mummy's Only Looking For Her Hand In The Snow)' – *John and Yoko/Plastic Ono Band with Frank Zappa and the Mothers Of Invention*
'Well (Baby Please Don't Go)'; 'Jamrag'; 'Scumbag'; 'Au' – *John and Yoko/Plastic Ono Band with Elephants Memory and The Invisible Strings*

Nov. 1973   Mind Games – *John Lennon*
'Mind Games'; 'Tight A$'; 'Aisumasen (I'm Sorry)'; 'One Day (At A Time)'; 'Bring On The Lucie (Freda People)'; 'Nutopian International Anthem'; 'Intuition'; 'Out The Blue'; 'Only People'; 'I Know (I Know)'; 'You Are Here'; 'Meat City'

Oct. 1974   Walls And Bridges – *John Lennon*
'Going Down On Love'; 'Whatever Gets You Thru The Night'; 'Old Dirt Road'; 'What You Got'; 'Bless You'; 'Scared'; '#9 Dream'; 'Surprise, Surprise (Sweet Bird Of Paradox)'; 'Steel And

Glass'; 'Beef Jerky'; 'Nobody Loves You (When You're Down And Out)'; 'Ya Ya'

Feb. 1975   Rock 'n' Roll – *John Lennon*
'Be-Bop-A-Lula'; 'Stand By Me'; 'Rip It Up'/'Ready Teddy'; 'You Can't Catch Me'; 'Ain't That A Shame'; 'Do You Want To Dance'; 'Sweet Little Sixteen'; 'Slippin' And Slidin''; 'Peggy Sue'; 'Bring It On Home To Me'/'Send Me Some Lovin''; 'Bony Moronie'; 'Ya Ya'; 'Just Because'

Oct. 1975   Shaved Fish – *John Lennon/Plastic Ono Band*
'Give Peace A Chance'; 'Cold Turkey'; 'Instant Karma!'; 'Power To The People'; 'Mother'; 'Woman Is The Nigger Of The World'; 'Imagine'; 'Whatever Gets You Thru The Night'; 'Mind Games'; '#9 Dream'; 'Happy Xmas (War Is Over)'; 'Give Peace A Chance' (live reprise)

Nov. 1980   Double Fantasy – *John Lennon and Yoko Ono*
'(Just Like) Starting Over'; 'Kiss Kiss Kiss'; 'Cleanup Time'; 'Give Me Something'; 'I'm Losing You'; 'I'm Moving On'; 'Beautiful Boy (Darling Boy)'; 'Watching The Wheels'; 'I'm Your Angel'; 'Woman'; 'Beautiful Boys'; 'Dear Yoko'; 'Every Man Has A Woman Who Loves Him'; 'Hard Times Are Over'

Posthumous albums

Nov. 1982   The John Lennon Collection – *John Lennon*
'Give Peace A Chance'; 'Instant Karma!'; 'Power To The People'; 'Whatever Gets You Thru The Night'; '#9 Dream'; 'Mind Games'; 'Love'; 'Happy Xmas (War Is Over)'; 'Imagine'; 'Jealous Guy'; 'Stand By Me'; '(Just Like) Starting Over'; 'Woman'; 'I'm Losing You'; 'Beautiful Boy (Darling Boy)'; 'Watching The Wheels'; 'Dear Yoko'

Dec. 1983   Heart Play – Unfinished Dialogue – *John Lennon and Yoko Ono*
(conversation)

Jan. 1984   Milk And Honey – *John Lennon and Yoko Ono*
'I'm Stepping Out'; 'Sleepless Night'; 'I Don't Wanna Face It'; 'Don't Be Scared'; 'Nobody Told Me'; ' "O" Sanity'; 'Borrowed Time'; 'Your Hands'; '(Forgive Me) My Little Flower Princess'; 'Let Me Count The Ways'; 'Grow Old With Me'; 'You're The One'

Feb. 1986   Live In New York City – *John Lennon*
'New York City'; 'It's So Hard'; 'Woman Is The Nigger Of The World'; 'Well Well Well'; 'Instant Karma!'; 'Mother'; 'Come Together'; 'Imagine'; 'Cold Turkey'; 'Hound Dog'; 'Give Peace A Chance'

Nov. 1986   Menlove Ave. – *John Lennon*
'Here We Go Again'; 'Rock And Roll People'; 'Angel Baby'; 'Since My Baby Left Me'; 'To Know Her Is To Love Her'; 'Steel And Glass'; 'Scared'; 'Old Dirt Road'; 'Nobody Loves You (When You're Down And Out)'; 'Bless You'

Oct. 1988   Imagine: John Lennon (music from the motion picture) – *John Lennon; *by the Beatles*
Real Love'; *'Twist And Shout'; *'Help!'; *'In My Life'; *'Strawberry Fields Forever'; *'A Day In The Life'; *'Revolution'; *'The Ballad Of John And Yoko'; *'Julia'; *'Don't Let Me Down'; 'Give Peace A Chance'; 'How?'; 'Imagine' (rehearsal); 'God'; 'Mother'; 'Stand By Me'; 'Jealous Guy'; 'Woman'; 'Beautiful Boy (Darling Boy)'; '(Just Like) Starting Over'; 'Imagine'

Oct. 1990   **Lennon** – *John Lennon*

'Give Peace A Chance'; 'Blue Suede Shoes'; 'Money (That's What I Want)'; 'Dizzy Miss Lizzy'; 'Yer Blues'; 'Cold Turkey'; 'Instant Karma!'; 'Mother'; 'Hold On'; 'I Found Out'; 'Working Class Hero'; 'Isolation'; 'Remember'; 'Love'; 'Well Well Well'; 'Look At Me'; 'God'; 'My Mummy's Dead'; 'Power To The People'; 'Well (Baby Please Don't Go)'; 'Imagine'; 'Crippled Inside'; 'Jealous Guy'; 'It's So Hard'; 'Give Me Some Truth'; 'Oh My Love'; 'How Do You Sleep?'; 'How?'; 'Oh Yoko!'; 'Happy Xmas (War Is Over)'; 'Woman Is The Nigger Of The World'; 'New York City'; 'John Sinclair'; 'Come Together'; 'Hound Dog'; 'Mind Games'; 'Aisumasen (I'm Sorry)'; 'One Day (At A Time)'; 'Intuition'; 'Out The Blue'; 'Whatever Gets You Thru The Night'; 'Going Down On Love'; 'Old Dirt Road'; 'Bless You'; 'Scared'; '#9 Dream'; 'Surprise, Surprise (Sweet Bird Of Paradox)'; 'Steel And Glass'; 'Nobody Loves You (When You're Down And Out)'; 'Stand By Me'; 'Ain't That A Shame'; 'Do You Want To Dance'; 'Sweet Little Sixteen'; 'Slippin' And Slidin''; 'Angel Baby'; 'Just Because'; 'Whatever Gets You Thru The Night'; 'Lucy In The Sky With Diamonds'; 'I Saw Her Standing There'; '(Just Like) Starting Over'; 'Cleanup Time'; 'I'm Losing You'; 'Beautiful Boy (Darling Boy)'; 'Watching The Wheels'; 'Woman'; 'Dear Yoko'; 'I'm Stepping Out'; 'I Don't Wanna Face It'; 'Nobody Told Me'; 'Borrowed Time'; '(Forgive Me) My Little Flower Princess'; 'Every Man Has A Woman Who Loves Him'; 'Grow Old With Me'

Oct. 1997   **Lennon Legend** – *John Lennon*

'Imagine'; 'Instant Karma!'; 'Mother'; 'Jealous Guy'; 'Power To The People'; 'Cold Turkey'; 'Love'; 'Mind Games'; 'Whatever Gets You Thru The Night'; '#9 Dream'; 'Stand By Me'; '(Just Like) Starting Over'; 'Woman'; 'Beautiful Boy (Darling Boy)'; 'Watching The Wheels'; 'Nobody Told Me'; 'Borrowed Time';

'Working Class Hero'; 'Happy Xmas (War Is Over)'; 'Give Peace A Chance'

Nov. 1998   **John Lennon Anthology** – *John Lennon*
'Working Class Hero'; 'God'; 'I Found Out'; 'Hold On'; 'Isolation'; 'Love'; 'Mother'; 'Remember'; 'Imagine (take 1)'; 'Fortunately' (speech); 'Well (Baby Please Don't Go)'; 'Oh My Love'; 'Jealous Guy'; 'Maggie Mae'; 'How Do You Sleep?'; 'God Save Oz'; 'Do The Oz'; 'I Don't Want To Be A Soldier'; 'Give Peace A Chance'; 'Look At Me'; 'Long Lost John'; 'New York City'; 'Attica State'; 'Imagine'; 'Bring On The Lucie (Freda People)'; 'Woman Is The Nigger Of The World'; 'Geraldo Rivera – One To One concert' (speech); 'Woman Is The Nigger Of The World'; 'It's So Hard'; 'Come Together'; 'Happy Xmas (War Is Over)'; 'The Luck Of The Irish'; 'John Sinclair'; 'The David Frost Show' (speech); 'Mind Games (I Promise)'; 'Mind Games (Make Love, Not War)'; 'One Day (At A Time)'; 'I Know (I Know)'; 'I'm The Greatest'; 'Goodnight Vienna'; 'Jerry Lewis Telethon' (speech); 'A Kiss Is Just A Kiss' (speech); 'Real Love'; 'You Are Here'; 'What You Got'; 'Nobody Loves You (When You're Down And Out)'; 'Whatever Gets You Thru The Night'; 'Yesterday' (parody); 'Be-Bop-A-Lula'; 'Rip It Up'/'Ready Teddy'; 'Scared'; 'Steel And Glass'; 'Surprise, Surprise (Sweet Bird Of Paradox)'; 'Bless You'; 'Going Down On Love'; 'Move Over Ms. L'; 'Ain't She Sweet'; 'Slippin' And Slidin''; 'Peggy Sue'; 'Bring It On Home To Me'/'Send Me Some Lovin''; 'Phil And John 1' (speech); 'Phil And John 2' (speech); 'Phil And John 3' (speech); 'When In Doubt, Fuck It' (speech); 'Be My Baby'; 'Stranger's Room'; 'Old Dirt Road'; 'I'm Losing You'; 'Sean's "Little Help" ' (speech); 'Serve Yourself'; 'My Life'; 'Nobody Told Me'; 'Life Begins At 40'; 'I Don't Wanna Face It'; 'Woman'; 'Dear Yoko'; 'Watching The Wheels'; 'I'm Stepping Out'; 'Borrowed Time'; 'The Rishikesh Song'; 'Sean's "Loud" ' (speech); 'Beautiful Boy (Darling Boy)'; 'Mr Hyde's Gone (Don't Be Afraid)'; 'Only You'; 'Grow

Old With Me'; 'Dear John'; 'The Great Wok' (speech); 'Mucho Mungo'; 'Satire 1'; 'Satire 2'; 'Satire 3'; Sean's 'In The Sky' speech; 'It's Real'

Nov. 1998 **Wonsaponatime** (selections from Lennon Anthology) — *John Lennon*
'I'm Losing You'; 'Working Class Hero'; 'God'; 'How Do You Sleep?'; 'Imagine' (take 1); 'Well (Baby Please Don't Go)'; 'Oh My Love'; 'God Save Oz'; 'I Found Out'; 'Woman Is The Nigger Of The World'; 'A Kiss Is Just A Kiss' (speech); 'Be-Bop-A-Lula'; 'Rip It Up'/'Ready Teddy'; 'What You Got'; 'Nobody Loves You (When You're Down And Out)'; 'I Don't Wanna Face It'; 'Real Love'; 'Only You'; 'Grow Old With Me'; Sean's 'In The Sky' (speech); 'Serve Yourself'

ACKNOWLEDGEMENTS

The author and publishers gratefully acknowledge the permission of David Sheff and G. Barry Golson at *Playboy* magazine for reproduction of parts of their 1980 interview with John Lennon and Yoko Ono; Bill Harry, editor and publisher of *Mersey Beat*, for access to John Lennon's first published writings; *Melody Maker* in London for permission to reproduce parts of several interviews conducted with the Lennons; Patrick Humphries, for his collaborative work with the author on the dissection of Lennon's music; Capital Radio, London, and interviewer Roger Scott for the statements by Paul McCartney on the break-up of the Beatles and on John's relationship with Brian Epstein; and Fenton Bresler for permission to reproduce part of his book *The Murder of John Lennon*.

INDEX